MUSIC AND
CIVILIZATION
ESSAYS IN HONOR OF
Paul Henry Lang

PAUL HENRY LANG

MUSIC AND CIVILIZATION

ESSAYS IN HONOR OF

Paul Henry Lang

EDITED BY

EDMOND STRAINCHAMPS

and MARIA RIKA MANIATES

IN COLLABORATION WITH

CHRISTOPHER HATCH

W · W · Norton & Company · New York · London

Copyright © 1984 by Edmond Strainchamps and Maria Rika Maniates

ALL RIGHTS RESERVED.

Published simultaneously in Canada by Stoddart,
a subsidiary of General Publishing Co. Ltd, Don Mills, Ontario.

PRINTED IN THE UNITED STATES OF AMERICA.

This book is composed in Garamond. Composition by NETS. Manufacturing
by The Murray Printing Company. Book design by Margaret Wagner.

FIRST EDITION

Library of Congress Cataloging in Publication Data
Main entry under title:
Music and civilization.

    Essays in honor of Paul Henry Lang: p.
    Includes index.
    1. Music essays. 2. Lang, Paul Henry, 1901–   . I. Lang, Paul Henry,
1901–   II. Strainchamps, Edmond, 1933–   . III. Maniates, Maria
Rika, 1937–   IV. Hatch, Christopher, 1926–   / ML55.L213   *1984*
1984   780   84-6114

ISBN 0-393-01677-3

W. W. Norton & Company, Inc.,
500 Fifth Avenue, New York, N. Y. 10110

W. W. Norton & Company Ltd.,
37 Great Russell Street, London WC1B 3NU

Contents

Contents

Foreword

THE ACTIVITIES of Paul Henry Lang—musician, teacher, scholar, editor, and critic—have affected so many individuals in such diverse fields of music and the humanities that when we set about devising a practicable list of contributors we faced an almost herculean assignment. Reluctantly we simplified the task by including on our list only his former students and colleagues in the department of music at Columbia University. Though the process of selection still proved difficult, we dare to believe that the completed book has achieved its primary goal; the contributors' essays, now gathered together and presented to Paul Lang, clearly reflect the extraordinary influence he has exerted on those who worked with him and learned from him during his thirty-eight years at Columbia.

The title we chose for this collection is not merely a reference to his magisterial first book, *Music in Western Civilization*. It hints at his philosophy of scholarship, which goes beyond the limitations of problem solving and reaches the broadest dimensions that measure the life of the mind. His hopes and fears for musicology are grounded in this philosophy:

> The greatest danger that threatens this burgeoning musicology is that its relationship to the humanities will become more and more tenuous if students eager to acquire scholarly status are taught nothing but specialized knowledge, independent of further connections; they will learn to master only the materials that make possible the acquisition of knowledge, not knowledge itself.

Members of the university community naturally represent considerable variety in individuality, beliefs, and principles; these differences are fruitful when they are related to, when they have reference to, a mutual center. And although the disciplines taught under the heading of the liberal arts do separate us, we can see, even within the framework of the different themes, the kindred nature of our research and the shaping of this research into communicable wisdom.*

Paul Henry Lang never forced upon his students or his fellow teachers any one goal or method of research. Instead he was content to encourage them to develop their particular gifts and skills, gently prodding them on occasion with Socratic comment. By precept and practice he set a standard both of excellence in scholarship and of mastery in literary style. Moreover, he never abandoned his conviction that musicological endeavors are worth little unless they illuminate our understanding of music as a humane subject.

For this reason we set out as liberal a framework as possible for the contributors, and when it came time to arrange their contributions by themes and methods, we found that they resisted easy classification. This was as it should have been, for the diverse and wide-ranging interests shown in these studies are an appropriate reflection of the very catholic interests of Paul Lang himself. Thus the essays have been grouped somewhat arbitrarily but with an eye on Paul Lang's chief concerns. As he has on innumerable occasions and with distinguished results, so several of the authors here deal with the great masters; the book begins with essays touching three of them—Mozart, Beethoven, and Wagner. The second section focuses on concert life and on the genesis and workings of music in the theater, matters with which Paul Lang has been closely involved over the years. Instruments and the transmission of music (for instance, notation, teaching, and publishing) provide the subjects of the third section, while in the fourth the topics pertain to biography, to style, or to the intersection of the two. Taking Paul Lang's work as a model, the studies in both these sections remain largely unconfined by rigid categories—organology, documentary biography, style criticism, and the like. So it is also with the fifth and last set of essays, which venture into the realms of aesthetics and theory. The volume closes with a selected list of P. H. L.'s writings.

However large or small the subject, each author has tried to link the solution of a specific problem with the meaning of music in a larger intellectual context. Paul Lang has seen this to be an essential purpose of musicology:

The musicologist should always remember that the true function of the scholar is the illumination of the particular in terms of the universal. And if he bogs down in his work and cannot seem to find his way out, he should be mindful of the paradox that, uniquely in the arts, ideas can transform facts.†

* Lang, "Musicology and Related Disciplines," in *Perspectives in Musicology*, ed. Barry S. Brook, Edward O. D. Downes, and Sherman Van Solkema (New York, 1977), 185.

† Ibid., 196.

Musicology, like every other humanistic and scientific discipline, justifies its existence by the discovery of ideas that can transform facts into communicable wisdom. But the boundary line between transformation and distortion must be constantly tested and probed, and Paul Lang has taught us that such exploration requires both rigor and insight. His influence has fostered a sense of how the imagination can be harnessed in a search for the truth.

With admiration, affection, and gratitude we offer this book to Paul Henry Lang. May he enjoy reading it as much as his friends have enjoyed preparing it for him.

EDMOND STRAINCHAMPS
MARIA RIKA MANIATES

MOZART'S *MESSIAH:*
"THE SPIRIT OF HANDEL"
FROM VAN SWIETEN'S
HANDS

CHRISTOPH WOLFF

THE VIENNESE performance of Handel's *Messiah* that took place in the spring of 1789 could well be called, *cum grano salis,* a performance of "Mozart's *Messiah*" or, perhaps even more appropriately, "van Swieten's *Messiah.*" For it was Baron Gottfried van Swieten (1733–1803), prefect of the Imperial Library, diplomat, and music patron, who had commissioned Mozart to prepare a performance of this oratorio.[1] It is indeed important to realize, with respect to the arrangement of both this and other Handel works, that "in the first place, the reorchestration of these scores was not Mozart's idea."[2] Van Swieten was responsible for revising and editing the German translation of *Messiah* by Friedrich Gottlieb Klopstock and Christoph Daniel Ebeling, and, considering his background as an active if amateurish composer, his musical input must have been quite substantial as well. It is the purpose of this essay to examine the cooperative efforts of van Swieten and Mozart, especially the significance of van Swieten's guiding hand, and to discuss some related aspects concerning the reception of Handel's music in Germany toward the end of the eighteenth and the beginning of the nineteenth centuries.

Mozart's initial encounter with the baron dates back to the spring of 1782, when he wrote to his father in Salzburg: "I go every Sunday at twelve

---

1. K. 572; the arrangement has appeared in a critical edition as vol. 2 of series X/28 of the *Neue Mozart-Ausgabe,* ed. Andreas Holschneider (Kassel, 1961 [Kritischer Bericht, 1962]). On van Swieten, see the article by Edward Olleson in *The New Grove* 18: 414f.; also Olleson, "Gottfried Baron van Swieten and His Influence on Haydn and Mozart," (Ph.D. diss., Oxford University, 1967).
2. Paul Henry Lang, *George Frideric Handel* (New York, 1966), 676.

noon to Baron van Swieten, and there we play nothing but Handel and Bach."[3] This experience at the beginning of Mozart's Vienna period turned out to have a crucial bearing on his subsequent orientation and development as a composer. One need hardly stress that the fugal studies in particular contributed decisively to a stylistic modification and differentiation in the musical language of a composer seriously striving for new horizons in his métier.

Any close affiliation with van Swieten and his circle ceased for a few years after 1784, but ties were resumed during 1787–88, when Mozart was asked to succeed Joseph Starzer as director of the baron's oratorio concerts. Starzer, a founding member of the Viennese Tonkünstler-Sozietät, had been instrumental in producing a series of oratorio performances under the sponsorship of van Swieten, beginning in December, 1779, with a very successful presentation of Handel's *Judas Maccabaeus*—the first performance of a Handel oratorio in Vienna. Besides oratorios by Handel, the concerts in subsequent years included works by C. P. E. Bach, Hasse, Graun, and others. They reached their peak with the premières of Haydn's *Creation* (1798) and his *Seasons* (1801); the librettos for both pieces were provided by van Swieten. Mozart, who had occasionally served as harpsichordist under Starzer, was put in charge of the concerts after the latter's death in 1787. This position also meant that Mozart was now responsible for arranging the scores, whenever necessary, and adapting them to specific prerequisites or restraints. Like operas, oratorios almost invariably needed adjustments to suit changing performance conditions. Mozart's first project in the spring of 1788 was the performance of C. P. E. Bach's *Auferstehung und Himmelfahrt Jesu,* and it was followed by Handel's *Acis and Galatea* in November of the same year, then by *Messiah* in 1789, and by *Alexander's Feast* and the *Ode for St. Cecilia's Day* in 1790.[4]

Mozart's encounter with these four large-scale choral works by Handel did not remain without repercussions in his own compositional output. Handelian influence appears most notably in the treatment of the choral sections of the late operas[5] and especially in the *Requiem*. With respect to the latter work, it need hardly be mentioned that in the Kyrie the first subject of the double fugue represents a direct borrowing from the *Messiah* chorus "And with His Stripes We Are Healed."

I

THERE were two performances of *Messiah* in 1789, one on March 6 and one on April 7, both at the residence of Count Johann Esterházy. Much of the original material used for these concerts has survived:[6] namely, the printed text book,

3. *Mozart: Briefe und Aufzeichnungen/Gesamtausgabe,* ed. Wilhelm A. Bauer and Otto Erich Deutsch, 3 (Kassel, 1963): 201 (letter of April 10, 1782).

4. K. 566, 591, and 592; for details see the entries in the Köchel catalogue, 6th ed. (1965).

5. Arias such as "O Isis und Osiris" from *The Magic Flute* are indebted to Handel with respect to their melodic shapes and phrases as well as their plain and chordal instrumental accompaniment.

6. See the discussion of the sources in *Neue Mozart-Ausgabe,* X/28, vol. 2, Kritischer Bericht.

the complete set of performance parts, and, most importantly, Mozart's working score.[7] Of the last, unfortunately, only the third part has come down to us; the entire score, however, was meticulously copied sometime in the 1790s, so that we are well informed about the contents of Mozart's original. Nevertheless, only the third part, which has Mozart's autograph entries, permits us to pursue specific compositional procedures. It seems reasonable, though, to view the procedures in the third part as representative of the nature of the arrangement in general. And it is this working score that helps to define Mozart's role in the *Messiah* arrangement in concrete terms and to modify the prevailing opinion of Mozart's Handel reorchestrations as a primarily, if not exclusively, Mozartean manipulation.

It is not known exactly when Mozart's work on Handel's *Messiah* began. The entry in his *Verzeichnüss* reads only, "Im Monath März für Baron Suiten Händels Messias bearbeitet."[8] This note actually belongs to another entry made in late April, 1789, and for this reason cannot accurately reflect the time span in question. The first performance had taken place on March 6, 1789. Nevertheless, there seems to be little doubt that Mozart's work began only after van Swieten had been concerned with *Messiah* for quite some time. And it is very likely that a number of crucial decisions regarding the scope and nature of the arrangement were made by the baron without consulting Mozart.

The working score for the arrangement was prepared by van Swieten, who had his copyists put together a skeleton score on twelve-stave music paper; Handel's original was copied in such a way that empty staves between the upper string systems and the lower vocal systems were left available for the addition of wind accompaniments. One of the purposes of the arrangement was to modernize the instrumentation according to the late eighteenth-century Viennese predilection for "Harmonie-Music"—"Harmonie" referring to a mixed ensemble of woodwind and brass instruments. "Auf die Harmonie setzen," in contemporary and Mozartean terminology,[9] means the scoring of a piece for such a mixed wind ensemble, which formed an increasingly significant section of the standard orchestra. The general format of the arrangement of the Handel oratorios, including the choice of "harmony instruments" and the overall composition and size of the performing ensemble, was predetermined by van Swieten. Thus Mozart worked within a given framework, and it is readily conceivable that van Swieten went even beyond setting up this framework and suggested certain concrete compositional effects.[10] We know, for instance, that van Swieten made very specific suggestions to Haydn concerning the musical interpretation of the

7. Prague, Czech National Museum, Lobkowitz Archive, *X.B.b.4.* I am indebted to the museum for providing a microfilm of the source and granting permission to reproduce Plates I–VI.

8. See Köchel catalogue, 6th ed., 645.

9. See *Mozart: Briefe und Aufzeichnungen*, 3: 213 (Mozart's letter of July 20, 1782) and also the numerous "Harmoniestücke," K. 361, 385, 388, etc. (list in Köchel catalogue, 6th ed., 998).

10. Regarding van Swieten's experience in compositional matters, see Ernst Fritz Schmid, "Gottfried van Swieten als Komponist," *Mozart-Jahrbuch, 1953*, 15–31.

text of *The Creation* and *The Seasons,* whose librettos he had written.[11] In keeping with van Swieten's taste and the prevailing aesthetic concept of the time, instrumentational effects were used to underscore and illustrate the words and the meaning of the text. And Mozart's *Messiah* arrangement, too, responds quite directly to pictorial elements as they occur in such movements as "All We like Sheep." Handel's original accompaniment already suggests in its motivic design the "going astray" of the sheep, but Mozart's added wind accompaniment intensifies the original motivic gestures in a very pointed manner:

EXAMPLE I

11. See Max Friedländer, "Van Swieten und das Textbuch zu Haydns 'Jahreszeiten,' " *Jahrbuch der Musik-bibliothek Peters* 16 (1910): 47–56.

It may well be that this, and similar treatments elsewhere in the score, were suggested to Mozart by van Swieten. But the working out of these ideas was left to Mozart, and it remains characteristic of his arrangements that he has never superimposed any ideas that dominate or substantially alter the Handelian original. This consistent restraint plays an important role in Mozart's *Messiah* arrangement, and it probably conformed to van Swieten's goal of keeping as closely as possible to the original work. This goal governed van Swieten's changes and adjustments in the Klopstock-Ebeling translation as well as his decisions concerning the alternative movements from the 1767 London edition. Moreover, in sharp contrast to the German performance tradition of *Messiah*,[12] very few cuts were made.

The following examples taken from Mozart's partially autograph working score demonstrate a few specific aspects of his Handel arrangement. Each example functions as a particular case in point, showing a varying degree of compositional involvement with the original.

1. The most extensive changes in Part III of the oratorio occur in the aria "The Trumpet Shall Sound," and these were made for two apparent reasons. First, there were evidently no capable clarino players available in Vienna at the time. Second, and of equal importance, the German Biblical terminology for "the last trumpet" is "die Posaunen [trombones] des jüngsten Gerichts." The decision to arrange the piece for a brass ensemble consisting of two horns plus clarino obviously reflects a twofold intention—to give the trumpet a less soloistic exposure and, at the same time, to reproduce a reasonable imitation of trombone sonority,[13] one that would make the proper illustrative effect on a German audience. It seems conceivable that these basic decisions were made by van Swieten and that Mozart simply realized the baron's ideas. In any event, Mozart was extremely careful in the execution of his task. The working score reveals that only after three attempts did he come up with a final resolution of the problems. He canceled two earlier versions in which he had experimented with the rather tricky balances that result from using a pair of horns and a single trumpet (see Plate I). The score also shows that Mozart must have felt obligated to respect the Handel original; without a doubt it would have been much easier for him had he decided to stay less close to what Handel had done. That van Swieten definitely intervened during the work on this aria can be shown by reference to the adjustments necessitated by the omission of its middle section. The decision to cut the B part of the original da capo structure was made only after the whole piece had been copied and, apparently, also after Mozart had already begun working on this movement (Plate II). The cut as such was made by van Swieten as a result of his work on the text; the accommodation of this idea remained Mozart's task.

---

12. A brief discussion of the early performances in Walther Siegmund-Schultze, "Über die ersten Messias-Aufführungen in Deutschland," *Händel-Jahrbuch*, 1960: 51–109.
13. Trombones are used elsewhere in Mozart's *Messiah* arrangement, primarily as vocal reinforcement; for reasons of compass trombones could not be used in this aria.

44

PLATE I. Prague, Czech National Museum, Lobkowitz Archive, X.B.b.4; fol. 44: No. 35, aria "Sie schallt, die Posaun," mm. 10–16 (staves 4–5 in Mozart's hand)

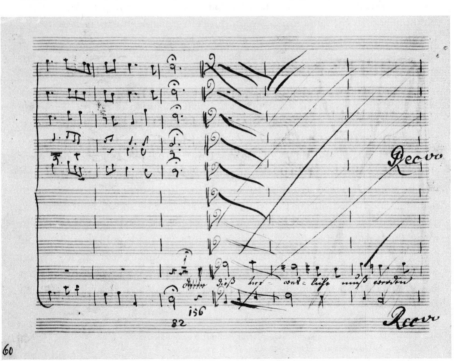

60

PLATE II. Fol. 60, aria "Sie schallt, die Posaun," m. 80ff.

2. The chorus "Since by Man Came Death" shows in Mozart's arrangement an equally noticeable departure from the original design in as much as the accompaniment and the choral presentation were reorganized for the entire movement. The original a cappella sections receive a somber instrumental accompaniment of two oboes, two clarinets, two bassoons, and three trombones, underscoring the retrospective expressivity of these sections, which end on a Phrygian cadence. For this piece the choral forces are divided into four groups in order to intensify the much milder structural contrast of Handel's original. Again it seems reasonable to assume that van Swieten provided the basic conception and that Mozart executed it. But surely both of them aimed at musically representing an aura of mystery in anticipation of the sounding of the last trumpet. The text of the connecting recitative reads, "Behold, I tell you a mystery; we shall not all sleep, but we shall all be changed in a moment, in the twinkling of an eye, at the last trumpet."

3. Only rarely are compositional decisions prompted by interpretative concerns. In most of the movements Mozart's instrumentation merely amplifies and supplements the original modest accompaniment by means of additional "Harmonie-Music." The opening of the aria "I Know That My Redeemer Liveth" presents an example of Mozart's working procedures, which are anything but mechanical in nature (see Plate III). He had originally planned to include

PLATE III. Fol. 2, aria "Ich weiss, dass mein Erlöser lebet," m. 1ff. (staves 3–7 in Mozart's hand)

two clarinets and two bassoons, but then restricted himself to using—in addition to the violas as supplements to the string section—only one flute, one clarinet, and one bassoon. The composition of the accompanying ensemble varies a great deal from movement to movement, and it is sometimes impossible to determine the reason for Mozart's choice. In this particular instance, however, his intention seems to have been to emphasize the predominant role of the principal melody of the aria. While the clarinet merely doubles the original violin line, the flute and bassoon join in by doubling in the upper and lower octaves respectively. The new viola line demonstrates Mozart's sense of balance; a counterweight is indeed needed to preserve the contrapuntal quality of the setting. Handel's two-part counterpoint has been subtly transformed into a three-part fabric.

4. A revealing change occurs in the duet "O Death, Where Is Thy Sting?" Handel's original contains the basso continuo as the sole instrumental accompaniment. Mozart adds two violas (Plate IV), which function as a quasi-continuo realization, but at the same time display considerable contrapuntal qualities whenever they play independently of the vocal parts. Apparently, Handel's accompaniment in this piece, restricted as it was to the thoroughbass, was unacceptable to late eighteenth-century ears. In this respect Mozart merely fulfilled the aesthetic demands of the day. On the other hand, he did not choose a full-scale instrumental ensemble for the added accompaniment and he did not in-

PLATE IV. Fol. 63, aria "O Tod, wo ist dein Pfeil," m. 1ff. (staves 1–2 in Mozart's hand)

clude any winds. He preserved the dominant vocal nature of the original duet by
a supportive string instrumentation. The two violas proceed mainly in unison
and they emphasize the "sempre legato" declamatory style of the piece by tying
over all repercussive notes.

   5. Sometimes, albeit rarely, Mozart changed the original declamatory
style of Handel. For instance, in the aria "I Know That My Redeemer Liveth"
he inserts an extra measure at the conclusion of the vocal part. The original is
marked "Adagio" at this point, but Mozart specifies exactly the *ritenuto* effect
for this passage by writing out the actual note values for the ritardation.

EXAMPLE 2

Handel

Mozart

   A change Mozart made in the basso continuo of the recitative "Then Shall
Be Brought to Pass" affects the original declamation in a different way. The
harmonic rhythm in Handel's recitatives is often paced without specific concern
for the text. This is not to say that Handel has disregarded the meaning of the
text. On the contrary, Handel has paid close attention to it in harmonizing expressive words and key phrases according to their meaning. The pacing of the
harmonic changes, however, is a rather different matter. Mozart's rewriting of
the basso continuo in measure 2 implies a subtle criticism of Handel's text
treatment with respect to chordal pacing:

EXAMPLE 3

Mozart delays the change of harmony so that the change coincides precisely with the point right after the colon, at the outset of the quintessential message "Death is swallowed up in victory."

6. The most drastic deviation, a truly conceptual departure, from Handel's original takes place between the two concluding choruses. The lengthy G-minor aria "If God Be for Us" is canceled. Whether Mozart or van Swieten was responsible for this decision cannot be determined. There exists an apocryphal letter from van Swieten to Mozart, in which the decision to replace "the cold aria" is attributed to Mozart.[14] The working score reveals that the aria had been included in the copy but was canceled before Mozart had even touched it. A note in van Swieten's hand on the last page of the aria actually suggests that it was his idea to replace the aria with a recitative (see Plate V). Be that as it may, the case indicates the congenial relationship between the two men, and surely both must have been in favor of leaving this aria out. The concept and design of the newly composed recitative could, of course, only be Mozart's. The function of the short piece was to provide a link between the E♭-major ending of the chorus "But Thanks" and the D-major opening of the chorus "Worthy Is the Lamb." Mozart's *accompagnato* recitative displays a highly dramatic force, modulating from G minor to A major and incorporating a modal shift, D major to D minor, in measure 9 to emphasize the central point of the text: "Christus ist's, der starb. . . ." This recitative, whose autograph score immediately follows the canceled aria in the working score (see Plate VI), creates a climactic emphasis toward the end of the oratorio. While Handel's aria of 178 measures did not really link the two framing choral movements but instead provided a point of repose and contrast, Mozart's fourteen-measure piece connects them in a most convincing manner. Both versions, Handel's original and Mozart's arrangement, reflect a strong sense of drama. But they differ in much the same way a Baroque opera differs from its later eighteenth-century counterpart. In addition, it is Mozart's very specific ideal of an operatic finale that contributes to the reshaping and reinterpretation of Handel's oratorio finale.

II

A N examination of Mozart's working score of *Messiah* indicates van Swieten's considerable input. Although it seems impossible to determine precisely how much he was involved in matters of the most immediate musical relevance, it goes without saying that he not only bore the main responsibility for the undertaking as a whole, but also provided many stimulating ideas and oversaw much of the operation. It is most certainly van Swieten who must be given credit for an approach that aimed at preserving the Handel original to an extent that was without precedent in Germany. There had been a number of *Messiah* perform-

---

14. *Mozart: Briefe und Aufzeichnungen*, 4: 77 (letter dated March 21 [*sic*], 1789). The earliest source for the text of the letter is Franz X. Niemetschek, *Leben des K. K. Kapellmeisters Wolfgang Gottlieb Mozart* (Prague 1798), 31.

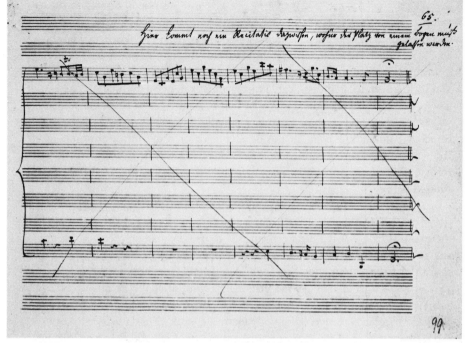

PLATE V. Fol. 99, canceled G-minor aria; note in van Swieten's hand, "Hier kommt noch ein Recitativ dazwischen,wofür der Platz von einem Bogen muss gelassen werden"

PLATE VI. Fol. 98, recitative "Wenn Gott ist für uns," m. 9ff. (in Mozart's hand)

ances, most notably those under the direction of C. P. E. Bach in Hamburg and J. A. Hiller in Berlin, Leipzig, and Breslau. But of all known early performances in Germany and Austria the Viennese *Messiah* of 1789 was the least abridged and mutilated one. Van Swieten must surely be counted among those few individuals whose seminal influence helped establish and shape the milieu in which the music of the past became gradually an integral part of the musical scene. A culminating point in the development of this fruitful atmosphere of Romantic historicism was reached only forty years later, in 1829, with the performance of Bach's *St. Matthew Passion* at the Berlin Singakademie under Mendelssohn.[15]

Despite the unquestionable importance of van Swieten's contribution to the *Messiah* performance, it is Mozart's artistic behavior that was responsible for the overall quality of the arrangement. Of course, in many respects Mozart appears to be following either the suggestions of his mentor or the technical and stylistic requirements of his time and generation. But there remain numerous smaller and larger details on the genuinely compositional side of the arrangement—as the examples discussed above have shown—which demonstrate a remarkable degree of congeniality with Handel's work. This is especially true of the restraint exercised by Mozart and the subtlety of his additions and changes. It is not suprising, therefore, that the arrangement soon became recognized as a major achievement. In fact, the performance tradition of *Messiah* in nineteenth-century Germany was virtually built on Mozart's arrangement. The publication of the score in 1803 by Breitkopf & Härtel of Leipzig[16] was the most significant milestone in the German Handel renaissance. A publication announcement was issued by Breitkopf in 1802 in the *Allgemeine musikalische Zeitung,* its text largely prepared by van Swieten.[17] But the aesthetic views expressed in the article can only be attributed to the journal's chief editor, Friedrich Rochlitz. He discusses the nature of the reworking of Handel's oratorio in considerable detail, mentioning specifically the "freer use of wind instruments" to set off the "uniformity and length" of Handel's original arias, which often used only voice, one treble (violin) part, and bass. In particular he praises the "progressive taste" of Mozart's arrangement and its unsurpassable new accompaniment, conceived "ganz im Geiste Händels" ("completely in Handel's spirit").

This reference to the spirit of Handel reminds us of Count Waldstein's prophetic remark in 1792 to the young Beethoven upon his leaving Bonn for

---

15. See the detailed account in Martin Geck, *Die Wiederentdeckung der Matthäuspassion im 19. Jahrhundert* (Regensburg, 1967). Symptomatic of the broadening scope of the performances of historical music and the changing social background of its audience is the fact that the *St. Matthew Passion* in 1829 drew well over a thousand listeners while the *Messiah* performance in 1789 took place in the private home of a nobleman.

16. Responsible for preparing the edition was August Eberhard Müller, later cantor at St. Thomas, Leipzig; regarding the changes he made in the Mozart arrangement, see R. Bernhardt, "W. A. Mozarts Messias-Bearbeitung und ihre Drucklegung in Leipzig 1802–03," *Zeitschrift für Musikwissenschaft* 12 (1929): 21ff.

17. Repr. in Köchel catalogue, 6th ed., 646.

Vienna: "you shall receive Mozart's spirit from Haydn's hands."[18] Waldstein and Rochlitz use the term *spirit* in very much the same way. The spirit of Handel, therefore, has not even the remotest connection with the modern notion of authenticity. Rochlitz certainly was aware of the fact that Mozart's and Handel's performance practices had very little in common, hence the need for "modernization." But of primary concern for Rochlitz and his contemporaries was the ideal value of a great and exemplary work of art, its aesthetic presence rather than its historical gestalt. Spirit of Handel, spirit of Mozart: the phrase attempts to capture aesthetic values too. It makes possible the linking of Mozart and Handel or Mozart and Beethoven on the level of abstract idealization; it establishes some common ground on which to build and common criteria for judgment.

The term *Geist* (*esprit*, "spirit") plays a key role in the aesthetic discourses of German idealist philosophy.[19] In Kant's *Kritik der Urteilskraft* (1790) an aesthetic definition of *Geist* is given: "Spirit, in an aesthetic sense, means the animating principle of the mind . . . the ability to represent aesthetic ideas" (sec. 49). The development of the meanings and connotations of the term *Geist,* however, cannot be separated from the concept of *Genie* ("genius") and *ingenium.*[20] The *Originalgeister* and the *Originalgenies* were understood to be the true leaders of mankind. In the basic concept of aesthetic art the original genius, i.e., the one who possesses *ingenium,* not only stands apart from the big crowd of his time, but also is admired for all time. This concept makes it possible to link past and present in a spiritual way; the original genius as personified in Handel or Bach, in Haydn, Mozart, or Beethoven becomes a timeless phenomenon that creates an entirely new situation and new perspectives on musical life and thought: the notion that a work of art can possess aesthetic autonomy is born. Handel's *Messiah* was not created as an autonomous work of art. Its reception in the course of history has rendered it autonomous, and Mozart's arrangement, its publication, and its subsequent performance tradition was the most decisive factor in this respect.

Mozart's *Messiah* in some sense also paved the way for Mendelssohn's *St. Matthew Passion.* While the reception of Bach as an instrumental composer had suffered virtually no interruption after 1750 (paralleling in this respect the reception of Handel as an oratorio composer), his reception as a vocal master certainly needed to be prepared for by Handel or, more specifically, by Mozart's *Messiah.*[21] It does not seem to be a mere coincidence that the significance and impact of both Mozart's *Messiah* and Mendelssohn's *St. Matthew Passion* rest largely on the aesthetic synchronization of past and present by means of a con-

18. *Thayer's Life of Beethoven,* rev. ed., ed. Elliot Forbes (Princeton, 1967), 115.
19. S. v. "Geist," *Historisches Wörterbuch der Philosophie,* ed. J. Ritter, 3 (Darmstadt, 1974): 174–99.
20. S. v. "Genie," *Historisches Wörterbuch der Philosophie,* 3: 279–303.
21. See Carl Friedrich Zelter's report "Händels Messias nach Mozarts Bearbeitung," *Berliner musicalische Zeitung* (1805), nos. 11 and 12.

temporary young genius who was spiritually linked with the great master. And there is one further and by no means marginal parallel: the performance of Bach's *St. Matthew Passion* in 1829 was no more Mendelssohn's idea than the performance of Handel's *Messiah* was Mozart's. In both cases there were guardian spirits—Carl Friedrich Zelter and Gottfried van Swieten—at the wheel of history.[22]

22. An earlier version of this essay has been read as a paper at the symposium on Handel's *Messiah* sponsored by the University of Michigan School of Music with the support of the National Endowment for the Humanities, Ann Arbor, Michigan, December, 1980.

THE "LAMBACH"
SYMPHONIES
OF WOLFGANG AND
LEOPOLD MOZART

NEAL ZASLAW

THE BENEDICTINE MONASTERY at Lambach, in Upper Austria near Wels, was a convenient way station for the Mozart family on their journeys between Salzburg and Vienna. Like many other Bavarian and Austrian monasteries of the time, Lambach provided rooms and meals for travelers, and maintained a musical establishment to ornament its liturgy and to provide entertainment. Amand Schickmayr, a friend of Leopold Mozart, was at Lambach from 1738 and had become abbot of the monastery in 1746.[1] At the beginning of January, 1769, the Mozart family, in returning to Salzburg from their second trip to Vienna, stopped at Lambach. We do not know how long they remained on this occasion, for the visit is not mentioned in the family's letters or diaries and in fact is known to us solely from inscriptions on two musical manuscripts.

The manuscripts in question are sets of parts for two symphonies in G major, one inscribed "Sinfonia / a 2 Violini / 2 Oboe / 2 Corni / Viola / e / Basso. / Del Sig:ʳᵉ Wolfgango / Mozart. / Dono Authoris / 4ᵗᵃ Jan. 769," and the other bearing an identical inscription except that in place of "Wolfgango" there appears "Leopoldo." For convenience of reference, the symphony at Lambach ascribed to Wolfgang will be referred to as "K. 45a," that ascribed to Leopold as "G16."[2] The two manuscripts, neither of which is an autograph,

---

1. Arno Eilenstein, "Die Beziehungen des Stiftes Lambach zu Salzburg," *Studien und Mitteilungen zur Geschichte des Benediktinerordens* 42 (1923–24): 196–232; Erwin Hainisch, *Die Kunstdenkmäler des Gerichtsbezirkes Lambach* (Vienna, 1959); *Mozart: Briefe und Aufzeichnungen/Gesamtausgabe,* ed. Wilhelm A. Bauer and Otto Erich Deutsch, (Kassel, 1962–75), 3: 291 and 6: 158.
2. The former number is a Köchel number, the latter is from the list of Leopold Mozart's works by Wolfgang Plath, *The New Grove* 12: 678.

were preserved in the monastery's archives, where they were discovered by Wilhelm Fischer, who published K. 45a in 1923.[3] Prior to that, however, K. 45a had been entered in the first and second editions of the Köchel catalogue as Anhang 221, one of ten symphonies known to Ludwig von Köchel solely from the incipits of their first movements, found in a manuscript catalogue belonging to the Leipzig firm of Breitkopf & Härtel.[4] Köchel's placement of these works in the portion of his appendix reserved for doubtful works should not be misconstrued: it reflected nothing more than his admirably cautious policy of tentatively regarding as suspicious any piece attributed to Mozart whose style and source situation he was not in a position to evaluate.[5]

In the third edition of the Köchel catalogue (published in 1937) the editor, Alfred Einstein, placed the rediscovered Symphony in G major, K. Anhang 221, in the chronology of authentic works according to the date on the Lambach manuscript. Speculating that the symphony had been written during the sojourn of more than a year in Vienna, he assigned it the number 45a appropriate to the beginning of 1768. The editors of the sixth edition of the Köchel catalogue accepted Einstein's and Fischer's opinion of the authenticity of Anhang 221/45a, as did Georges de Saint-Foix and many others who wrote about Wolfgang's early symphonies.[6] And Einstein's date of early 1768 for K. 45a was generally accepted too.[7]

In 1964, however, Anna Amalie Abert published a startling new hypothesis about the two G-major symphonies. She had come to believe that—like the accidental interchange of infants, which underlies the plots of a number of plays and operas—the two works had been mixed up, perhaps by a monkish librarian at Lambach. Abert founded her opinion on a close examination of the two symphonies and on comparisons between them and other symphonies thought to have been written at about the same time by Leopold and Wolfgang.

On the basis of stylistic analysis and aesthetic evaluation, Abert suggests that K. 45a was written in a more archaic style than G16 and that the former was less well written than the latter. She then reasons that, as Leopold was the older, the more conservative, and the less talented, of the two, he must have

3. Wilhelm Fischer, "Eine wiedergefundene Jugendsymphonie Mozarts," *Mozart-Jahrbuch* 1 (1923): 35–68.
4. *"Thematische Verzeichnis der sämtlichen Werke von W. A. Mozart,"* a manuscript formerly in the Breitkopf & Härtel archives in Leipzig but lost or destroyed during World War II. A copy of this manuscript from Köchel's *Nachlass*, with the title "Breitkopf-Härtel's/Alter handschriftlicher Catalog/W. A. Mozart's Original Compositionen/Abschrift," is in the archives of the Gesellschaft der Musikfreunde, Vienna, shelfmark 4057/38.
5. Köchel's Anhang was divided into five sections: I, Verloren gegangene Kompositionen; II, Angefangene Kompositionen; III, Übertragene Kompositionen; IV, Zweifelhafte Kompositionen; and V, Unterschobene Kompositionen. These important distinctions have unfortunately been suppressed in the most recent (sixth) edition of the Köchel catalogue, pp. 747–51.
6. Georges de Saint-Foix, *Les Symphonies de Mozart* (Paris, 1932); 27–28, English trans., *The Symphonies of Mozart* (London, 1947), 16–17; Jens Peter Larsen, "The Symphonies," *The Mozart Companion*, ed. H. C. Robbins Landon and Donald Mitchell (London, 1956), 159–61.
7. The only exception was H. C. Robbins Landon (*Mozart-Aspekte*, ed. Paul Schaller and Hans Kühner, [Olten, 1956], 43), who accepted Fischer's suggestion of Salzburg, 1767.

been the author of K. 45a and Wolfgang of G16. On comparing formal and stylistic characteristics of the first movements of the two symphonies with those of the first movements of other symphonies of that period by Leopold and Wolfgang, Abert finds that the first movement of K. 45a resembles Leopold's first movements while the first movement of G16 resembles those by Wolfgang. This formal comparison is supported by her reference to the (relative) monothematicism of the first movement of K. 45a, which is considered an archaic trait, and therefore likely to have come from the older composer. Certain aspects of K. 45a's construction—the adding together of many two-bar phrases and the excessive use of sequences—Abert believes to be characteristic of Leopold's works, while the more spun-forth and varied melodic ideas of G16 strikes her as akin to Wolfgang's technique. Her doubts about K. 45a have to do, "above all with the remarkable plainness and monotony of the second and third movements, which immediately catch the eye of the close observer of the symphonies K. 16 to 48." Accordingly, she edited the previously unpublished G16 as a work by Wolfgang, and it has since been performed, recorded, and discussed as such.[8]

There is, however, some documentary evidence that has long been known but never fully brought to bear on the question of the authorship of the two Lambach symphonies. It is found in the already mentioned Breitkopf & Härtel manuscript catalogue. A few words about this catalogue are in order. It constitutes a conscientious attempt from the early nineteenth century to list the incipits of all the known Mozart works, beginning with manuscripts in the Breitkopf archives and adding works that had been published or had survived elsewhere in manuscript. The source of each incipit is indicated next to it, in the right-hand margin. The catalogue is divided into twenty categories: wind music, dances, piano concertos, string quartets, symphonies, operas, and so on. At the end of many categories pages of empty staves reveal that further entries were anticipated. The first category, symphonies, contains seventy incipits followed by a few empty pages. Here as elsewhere the incipits were to have been noted on two staves. Many of the bass staves are blank, however, and this would seem to be the result of the cataloguer having in front of him a set of parts rather than a score—that is to say, when confronted with sets of parts, he copied only the incipits of the first movements of the first violin parts, perhaps intending to go back later to the basso parts but in the event never doing so. The symphonies appear in no apparent order, for they are arranged neither chronologically, nor by key, nor by number of movements, nor according to size of orchestra required. Their apparently random arrangement suggests that the cataloguer copied the incipits in whatever order the material happened to be found. Let us

---

8. Anna Amalie Abert, "Stilistischer Befund und Quellenlage zu Mozarts Lambacher Sinfonie KV Anh. 221/45a," *Festschrift Hans Engel zum siebzigsten Geburtstag* (Kassel, 1964), 43–56; *idem*, "Methoden der Mozartforschung," *Mozart-Jahrbuch, 1964*, 22–27; *idem*, Vorwort to W. A. Mozart, *Sinfonie in G ("Neue Lambacher Sinfonie")* (Kassel, 1965); *idem*, record liner notes for Archiv Produktion, Period XII, no. 409: *Leopold Mozart, Wolfgang Amadeus Mozart, 4 Sinfonien* (Hamburg, 1967).

therefore imagine for a moment a storeroom in which music has been piled over a period of many years without any filing system, and let us imagine further that we remove the music item by item in order to catalogue it by genre. We see that three principles might apply: (1) more recently acquired items would be catalogued first while earlier, more deeply buried acquisitions would be catalogued later; (2) items that came in at the same time might well have remained together and would therefore (if they were all of the same genre) be catalogued together; and (3) items discovered after the initial cataloguing was completed would be added at the ends of the appropriate categories. Looking over the list of seventy symphonies for some confirmation of this imagined scenario, our eye falls on nos. 16, 17, and 18, whose incipits reveal them to be Mozart's final trilogy of symphonies, K. 543, 550, and 551 respectively. These three works very likely formed some kind of unit in the Breitkopf archives.

The unit in question is the "opus." Title pages, catalogues, and advertisements of the second half of the eighteenth century customarily list symphonies as being either "périodique" or "en oeuvre," meaning, respectively, symphonies issued singly and those issued in groups as an "opus." Symphonies issued "en oeuvre" usually totaled six, but sometimes three, twelve, or another number. Wolfgang and Leopold were well aware of these conventions, which applied equally to prints and to manuscripts for presentation to patrons, and they sometimes assembled symphonies that way. For example, Leopold organized nine of his son's symphonies "en oeuvre" in the mid-1770s, possibly with an eye toward a presentation or a publication that never materialized.[9] Leopold also assembled three of Wolfgang's orchestral serenades "en oeuvre" with the interesting title "3 / Serenate cio e gran Synfonie."[10] In 1784 Wolfgang selected three recent symphonies which he planned to publish with a dedication to the Prince von Fürstenberg.[11] Other groups of six were undoubtedly assembled and circulated. When, for instance, in 1810 the Leipzig publisher Ambrosius Kühnel wrote to Wolfgang's Prague acquaintance and biographer Franz Xaver Niemetschek seeking unknown works of Mozart's to publish, Niemetschek replied that, in addition to certain familiar symphonies, he knew of "six small symphonies . . . a few of which are uncommonly beautiful."[12] And in 1777 Leopold exhorted Wolfgang (in a letter cited more fully below) to have "six good symphonies" copied at once, in order to have them ready for presentation to a patron. Furthermore, the set of nine of his son's symphonies that Leopold assembled in the mid-1700s was not the first such that he created. Early in the same trip to Vienna on the return from which occurred the visit to Lambach

9. K. 162, 162b/181, 173dA/182, 173dB/183, 161a/184, 161b/199, 189k/200, 186a/201, and 186b/202.

10. K. 189b/203, 213a/204, and 248b/250.

11. *Briefe*, 3: 319, and 6:704, but in the light of 7: 574. The symphonies were K. 319 and K. 385 (which did appear but without the dedication) and a third (which never appeared and may have been K. 338 or K. 425).

12. Rudolf Angermüller and Sibylle Dahms-Schneider, "Neue Brieffunde zu Mozart," *Mozart-Jahrbuch, 1968/70*, 235.

that concerns us here, Leopold wrote to his Salzburg friend Maria Theresa Hagenauer:

> I left Mr. Estlinger certain symphonies to copy, which I hope are now ready. These are the symphonies that I have to send to Donaueschingen. By the next post I shall send you a letter for the Prince, which should be enclosed with the symphonies and sent off by the mail coach.[13]

A now lost reply must have informed Leopold that the symphonies were ready, for less than a month later he wrote to Maria Theresa's husband, Lorenz:

> The six symphonies, which Estlinger has copied, should be rolled up well and given to the mail coach with the address: *A Son Altesse Sérénissime Le Prince de Fürstenberg etc, à Donaueschingen.* I shall write a letter to the Prince from here.[14]

In fact, Leopold (and later on Wolfgang) did correspond with the prince, and this connection was strengthened by the presence of the Mozart's former man-servant, Sebastian Winter, a native of Donaueschingen who served at the court from 1764. The Mozarts had visited Donaueschingen in October, 1766, and as Leopold reported to the Hagenauers,

> His Highness the Prince welcomed us with extraordinary graciousness. It was not necessary to announce our arrival, for we were already being eagerly awaited. . . . The Director of Music, Martelli, came at once to welcome us and to invite us to court. Well, we were there for twelve days. On nine days there was music in the evening from five to nine and each time we performed something different. If the season had not been so advanced, we should not have got away. The Prince gave me twenty-four louis d'or and to each of my children a diamond ring. Tears flowed from his eyes when we took leave of him, and truly we all wept at saying goodbye. He begged me to write to him often. Indeed our departure was as sad as our stay had been agreeable.[15]

On those nine evenings when music was performed at the Donaueschingen court, Wolfgang's earliest symphonies were almost certainly included, for the Mozarts had just produced them with success at concerts in London, the Hague, Amsterdam, Utrecht, Paris, Dijon, Lyons, and Zurich, between February 21, 1765, and October 9, 1766. Furthermore, a manuscript of Wolfgang's

---

13. *Briefe,* 1: 241 (letter of Oct. 14, 1767). The translations of the Mozart family's letters used in this article, taken from Emily Anderson, *The Letters of Mozart and His Family,* 2nd ed. (London, 1966), have occasionally been modified to render them more literal.

14. *Briefe,* 5 : 179 (letter of Nov. 10, 1767).

15. *Briefe,* 1: 231 (letter of Nov. 10, 1766).

Galimathias musicum, K. 32, in the Donaueschingen archives apparently dates from this visit, and the forces required to perform the *Galimathias* are the same as those required to perform Wolfgang's earliest symphonies.[16]

All this suggests that the copying of symphonies in October and November, 1767, was in compliance with the prince's desire to own some of Wolfgang's symphonies, works he had heard and enjoyed during the Mozarts' visit. It has been proposed, however, that the six symphonies copied in Salzburg in the autumn of 1767 were by Leopold himself rather than by his son.[17] This seems unlikely for two reasons: (1) the nature of the concerts the Mozarts gave while on tour virtually guarantees us that what the prince heard was music by Wolfgang (note, for instance, that when announcements for the concerts in question survive, they invariably include a statement to the effect that "all the symphonies will be of this little boy's own composition");[18] (2) Leopold had to a great extent given up the advancement of his own career in order to devote himself to promoting his son's. Emily Anderson surmised that the symphonies copied for Donaueschingen may have been six from among K. 16, 16a, 16b, 19, 19a, 19b, 22, and 42a/76,[19] which is a list of the earliest of Wolfgang's symphonies as entered in the third edition of the Köchel catalogue. Here the Breitkopf & Härtel manuscript catalogue offers us an important clue.

We have already noted that whoever copied the catalogue left space to add incipits at the end of many of the categories of works, and that this is true of the symphonies. Examining closely the list of symphony incipits, we see that after sixty incipits had been entered (all derived either from manuscripts in the Breitkopf archive or from published editions), two further groups of symphonies were added: a group of four whose source is given as "Westphal,"[20] and a group of six whose source is shown as "Gatti."[21] The contents of the "Gatti" group—all six apparently scores rather than parts—are as follows:

16. The personnel of the Donaueschingen court orchestra at a somewhat later date (1790) consisted of only two violinists, a violist, a cellist, a double-bass player, and pairs of flutists, oboists, clarinetists (who doubled on violin when not needed in the wind section), bassoonists, and horn players—a tiny ensemble just large enough to play symphonies. As happened in some other court orchestras of that time, however, the strings may have been reinforced by amateurs from the court. (Friedrich Schnapp, "Neue Mozart-Funde in Donaueschingen," *Neues Mozart-Jahrbuch* 2 [1942]: 211–23.)

17. *Briefe,* 5: 176.

18. Otto Erich Deutsch, *Mozart: A Documentary Biography,* 2nd ed. (London, 1966), 42, 44–45, 49–51, and 57–58.

19. *The Letters of Mozart and His Family,* 1: 74, n.5.

20. "Westphal" may perhaps be Johann Jakob Heinrich Westphal (b. Schwerin, 1756–d. Schwerin, 1825), whose famous collection of C. P. E. Bach manuscripts, acquired by François-Joseph Fétis, is now in Brussels. Ernst Gerber, Fétis, and Robert Eitner, as well as Albert vander Linden in *Die Musik in Geschichte und Gegenwart,* conflate his biography with that of the apparently unrelated Johann Christoph Westphal (b. Hamburg, 1773–d. Hamburg, 1828), son of the Hamburg music publisher of the same name, who also could have been the source of these symphonies.

21. "Gatti" must refer to Luigi Gatti (1740–1817), who was Hofkapellmeister in Salzburg from 1782 or '83 on. Between 1801 and 1804 he helped Nannerl Mozart to locate and have copied unknown pieces by her brother that were to be found in Salzburg. His aid enabled Nannerl to send music to Breitkopf & Härtel for the publication of their so-called *Oeuvres complettes* (see *Briefe,* 5: 223).

THE "GATTI" SYMPHONIES

B&H	KEY	K[1]	K[3]	K[6]	YEAR	SOURCE	COMMENT
65	D	38	38	38	1767	autograph	overture *Apollo et Hyacinthus*
66	E♭	16	16	16	1764	autograph	"first" symphony[22]
67	G	A221	45a	45a	?	Lambach copy[23]	"old" Lambach
68	C	A222	19b	19b	?	none	incipit only
69	D	19	19	19	1765	in Leopold's hand	——
70	F	A223	19a	19a	1765	in Leopold's hand	——

It is my hypothesis that the "Gatti" symphonies are a copy of the same set of six symphonies that Leopold Mozart sent to Donaueschingen at the end of 1767. If this hypothesis is correct, it has interesting implications—implications that will be explored in the rest of this article.

At the end of 1768, that is, shortly before K. 45a and G16 were given to the Lambach monastery, Leopold drew up a list of his son's compositions, which, he said, included "13 Synfonien a 2 Violini, 2 Haub: 2 Corni, Viola e Basso &c."[24] There has never been an entirely satisfactory identification of these thirteen symphonies, despite attempts to recreate the list. If we were to accept the six "Gatti" symphonies as dating from before September, 1767, then to make up the "13 Synfonien" we might add to them K. 16a, 22, 42a, 43, 45, 45b, and 48. This would appear to supply the necessary number of symphonies, but there are problems with accepting K. 16a and 38.

No one seems to have commented on how unlikely it is that the nine-year-old Wolfgang would have written a symphony in A minor at a time when so few minor-key symphonies were being composed—this point being a valid one despite the striking overture-sinfonia in D minor for *La Betulia liberata* of 1771 and an interesting adumbration of the stormy, minor-key orchestral style in a keyboard piece in G minor, K. 15p. Perhaps K. 16a was in fact composed by Mozart, not however, in 1765, but rather in the mid-1770s, when there was in Austria a brief surge of interest in writing minor-key symphonies.[25] Einstein's connection of the incipit of K. 16a with Mozart's earliest symphonies written in

---

22. K. 16 is probably not Mozart's first symphony, although it has always been so designated. There was most likely one earlier one, now lost. This missing work, which is alluded to in the article cited in n. 40 below, will be fully discussed in my forthcoming monograph *Mozart and the Symphony* (London: Oxford University Press, in press).

23. The Lambach manuscript of K. 45a remains there; the manuscript of G16 is now in the Stadtarchiv, Augsburg. Concerning the date and source of K. 45a, see the final paragraph of this article.

24. This important document is published, among other places, in *Briefe*, 1: 287–89, and fully explicated in Neal Zaslaw, "Leopold Mozart's List of His Son's Works," *Music of the Classic Period: Essays in Honor of Barry S. Brook*, ed. Allan Atlas (New York, 1984).

25. H. C. Robbins Landon, "La Crise romantique dans la musique autrichienne vers 1770; quelques précurseurs inconnus de la symphonie en sol mineur (KV. 183) de Mozart," *Les Influences étrangères dans l'oeuvre de W. A. Mozart* (Paris, 1956), 27–47.

London in 1764–65 was speculation and, in the absence of supporting evidence, should be treated as such.[26]

Furthermore, if we include in our tentative listing of the "13 Synfonien" the one-movement overture-sinfonia to *Apollo et Hyacinthus,* K. 38, because it appears among the "Gatti" six, logical consistency forces us to consider also the one-movement overture-sinfonia to *Die Schuldigkeit des ersten Gebots,* K. 35. There is a problem with including the sinfonias of K. 35 and 38, however, since those works (the whole works, not just the sinfonias) have separate listings of their own in Leopold's accounting of his son's output up to the end of 1768.

If the overture-sinfonias of K. 35 and 38 should therefore be omitted from the list of "13 Synfonien," what other possibilities present themselves? Curiously, two other candidates have been overlooked. These are the Symphony in D major, K. Anhang C11.07, and the Symphony in F major, K. Anhang C11.08. Both works are known only by their incipits in the Breitkopf & Härtel manuscript catalogue, where they bear the numbers 60 and 63 respectively. (Thus, like the "Gatti" symphonies, they are late entries on the list.) For unknown reasons but perhaps merely through accident, Köchel failed to list these two incipits in his catalogue, where by any consistent criteria they should have found a place with the ten other incipits of his Anhang 214–23. And in the third edition of the Köchel catalogue Einstein, in an attempt to remedy the inconsistency, perpetrated another, equally grave one. By 1936, when his labors on this edition of the Köchel catalogue were finished, Einstein considered the status of the ten lost symphonies, Anhang 214–23, to be as follows: one had been found and attributed to Leopold Mozart (K. Anhang 219/Anhang 219b/ [K⁶ = C11.06]), three had been found and accepted as genuine (K. Anhang 221/45a, Anhang 214/45b, Anhang 216/74g/[K⁶ = C11.03]), and one, though still lost, was known from a document in Leopold's hand to have been connected with the indisputably authentic K. 19 (K. Anhang 223/19a).[27] The remaining five symphony incipits (K. Anhang 220/16a, Anhang 222/19b, Anhang 215/66c, Anhang 217/66d, Anhang 218/66e) in no way differ in their source situation from the two that Köchel had overlooked (K. Anhang C11.07 and C11.08), yet Einstein inserted the former group into the main chronology while placing the two new incipits between items Anhang 223/19a and 223a/17 in the portion of the appendix reserved for doubtful works, remarking of the latter only that "nothing can be stated for want of further particulars."

One of these two inconsistently treated incipits belongs to the four "Westphal" symphonies in the Breitkopf & Härtel manuscript catalogue:

---

26. The only evidence that I am able to adduce in support of Einstein's assignment of such an early date for the incipit of K. 16a is its three-bar phrase structure, which is a prominent feature of Mozart's symphonies from the 1760s, but not those from the 1770s.

27. K. 19a was rediscovered in 1981. See Robert Münster, "Wiederauffindung und Erwerbung einer verschollenen Jugendsinfonie Wolfgang Amadeus Mozarts durch die Bayerische Staatsbibliothek," *Forum Musikbibliothek* (Feb., 1981): 32–36.

THE "WESTPHAL" SYMPHONIES

B&H	KEY	K¹	K³	K⁶	YEAR	SOURCE	COMMENT
61	D	A219	A291b	AC11.06	?	parts D-HR	Seiffert 13 = Theiss D11 = Grove D11[28]
62	a	A220	16a	16a	?	none[29]	only incipit known
63	F	———	A223a	AC11.08	?	none	only incipit known
64	G	318	318	318	1779	autograph	———

Even a superficial examination of this tabulation of the "Westphal" symphonies suggests that they comprise not a set of four, but rather a set of three earlier symphonies and a single symphony of later, separate origin. If the three symphonies B&H 61–63 do indeed form an opus, then one must assume either that all three are by Leopold or that No. 61, despite its previously unanimous acceptance as a work of Leopold's, should be attributed to Wolfgang. Until such time as the two lost symphonies of the "Westphal" group are found, however, this ambiguity is unlikely to be resolved (see note 29).

The source of the other "mistreated" symphony incipit, K. Anhang C11.07, was apparently a set of manuscript parts in the Breitkopf & Härtel archives, and inasmuch as the work seems not to have formed part of an opus with any of the works adjacent to it in the list, nothing further can be ventured about its provenance. One ought to raise the possibility, however, that it and K. Anhang C11.08 may have been among the "13 Synfonien" that, according to Leopold, Wolfgang wrote prior to his thirteenth birthday.[30]

For our present purposes the most important implication of the hypothesis that the "Gatti" symphonies are identical with the six symphonies sent to Donaueschingen in 1767 is, of course, that the "old" Lambach symphony, K. 45a, must be by Wolfgang and the "new" Lambach symphony, G16, by Leopold. And not only do these original attributions hold, but K. 45a—since it was left behind in Salzburg to be copied—must be assigned an earlier date. The earlier date is confirmed by the fact (known to Abert but not to Einstein) that the Lambach copies of both symphonies were the work of a Salzburg copyist.[31] From the Salzburg origin of the two Lambach manuscripts, we may deduce that they were completed before the Mozarts' departure from Salzburg in October,

28. The contents of the first and second of these catalogs of Leopold's works are incorporated into the third, which is cited in n. 2 above. For this symphony the source, *D-HR*, is Harburg über Donauwörth (West Germany), Fürstlich Oettingen-Wallerstein'sche Bibliothek.

29. While this article was in press, a source for K. 16a was discovered in Odense, Denmark. It is a nonauthentic set of parts with a watermark dated 1779. A preliminary evaluation on stylistic grounds by Jens Peter Larsen suggests that the piece may date from the early 1770s (personal communication).

30. For further discussion of these "13 Synfonien" see the articles cited in n. 24 above and in n. 40 below.

31. This copyist was in fact the selfsame Joseph Richard Estlinger mentioned above in Leopold's letter of Oct. 14, 1767 (see n. 14 above).

1767, for the correspondence between the Mozarts and the Hagenauers contains not the slightest hint of a request for the copying of any works other than the six symphonies left behind specifically for that purpose.

Correspondence from Leopold to Wolfgang of some years later, when the son was in Munich and the father at home in Salzburg, reveals important details of the Mozarts' manner of dealing with symphonies and with copyists while on tour, and it suggests how improbable it is that a symphony composed in Vienna would have been sent to Salzburg to be copied:

> . . . you should try to find a copyist, and . . . you should do this wherever you stay for any length of time. . . . Then . . . have in readiness copies of symphonies and divertimenti to present to a Prince or some other patron [*Liebhaber*]. The copying should be arranged so that *the copyist writes out at your lodgings in your presence at least the violino primo or some other principal part* [i.e., to prevent theft]. The rest he can copy out at home. It is absolutely essential that you should have something ready for *Prince Taxis,* and you should therefore quickly give the *oboe-, horn-,* and *viola-parts* of *six good symphonies* at once to one or (to speed up matters) to *several copyists.* You would thus be in a position to present the symphonies in fair copy to the Prince and still have the fair-copy *duplicated violin* and *bass* [parts] to be used on other such occasions . . . , to which you would only have to add the [parts for] *oboes, horns* and *viola.* . . . Basta! Wherever you are, you must look about immediately for a copyist, or else you will lose a great deal! Otherwise, of what use to you will be all the music which you have taken away? You really cannot wait until some patron [*Liebhaber*] has them copied; and, now that I come to think of it, *he would thank you for allowing him to do so* and would not pay you a farthing. It is far too laborious to have your compositions copied from the score, and a thousand mistakes will creep in unless the copyist works the whole time under your supervision. But he could come *for a few mornings,* when you happen to be in, copy out *the principal parts,* and then write out the remainder at his house. That is absolutely necessary.[32]

A few weeks later, when Wolfgang had reached Mannheim, his father again broached the subject of the symphonies Wolfgang had taken with him:

> I am not going to say anything more about having your works copied, which you ought to have arranged during your long visits to Munich and Augsburg, as the farther you travel the more expensive does copying become. You will remember, however, that I was very much against your taking so many symphonies with you. I just picked out a good number of them, but I naturally thought that you would leave some of them behind.

32. *Briefe,* 2: 58–59 (letter of Oct. 15, 1777).

Yet instead of putting several aside, you added to them others, and thus made such an enormous pile that you could not pack any of your church music. If I had been healthy and not so ill that I could hardly speak, I should have let you take with you not more than about four or six symphonies with the parts doubled for concert use, and all the others in single parts or scores.[33]

These two passages form part of the continual harangues that the nervous father addressed to his son, exhorting him to conduct his tour in the same way as the earlier tours, when Leopold himself was at the helm. From his remarks we may therefore infer that on the earlier tours it was Leopold's practice to bring along four to six symphonies in the form of scores with doubled parts, ready for use at short notice, and some others in score or single parts, which, with a couple of days notice, could be put into usable form by local copyists. Doubled parts (*Dubletten*) usually consisted of one additional part each for the first and second violins and the basso.

If we are right in hypothesizing that symphonies 65 to 70 in the Breitkopf manuscript catalogue are the same works as the six symphonies copied at the end of 1767, then K. 45a must once have existed in several copies: the one left behind in Salzburg for Estlinger to copy, the copy Estlinger made to send to Donaueschingen, and the set of parts taken to Vienna and then presented to the Lambach monastery. Leopold was able to make this gift precisely because he knew that, having reached the end of their tour, they no longer needed sets of parts of symphonies held in readiness for sudden performance opportunities. Furthermore, if (as I believe) K. 45a should indeed be dated prior to the departure for Vienna on September 11, 1767, then another apparent enigma vanishes. For in accepting Vienna as the place of K. 45a's creation, commentators have been made uneasy by the anomalous fact that the work is in the three-movement, Italian sinfonia format of the earliest symphonies written in London and Holland (K. 16, 19, 19a, and 22), rather than the four-movement, "concert" symphony format favored in Vienna and employed by Wolfgang in the symphonies (K.43, 45 and 48) that can confidently be assigned to the 1767–68 sojourn in Vienna.

To return to Abert's arguments: her stylistic observations are acute, and in the absence of documentary evidence we should be inclined to accept her conclusions. But are our analytical tools well enough honed to allow us to cut our decisions about attribution so finely? I fear not. Consider, for instance, that Abert found that the stringing together of two-bar phrases in K. 45a was atypical of Wolfgang, yet according to Ludwig Finscher, "the technique of many minor composers of the 1760s and 1770s—including Mozart—was to place two-bar, four-bar, and eight-bar sections in a row, sometimes adding a bar or

---

33. *Briefe*, 2: 182–83 (letter of Dec. 11, 1777).

changing the order of sections."[34] Besides, insofar as the more spun-forth style (*Fortspinnungstypus*) of G16 is a late Baroque trait and the more segmented style (*Liedtypus*) of K. 45a a *galant* trait, this distinction, far from supporting Abert's new attributions, contradicts them. To this we may add four additional points, which tend further to weaken Abert's attributions:

1. The earlier we think K. 45a was composed, the less surprised we should be at finding the apprentice-composer writing in an "archaic" style. In particular, Abert's comparisons of K. 45a and G16 with K. 43 and 48 are severely weakened by an earlier dating of K. 45a, for if the latter was composed in 1766 or the first part of 1767, then its "immaturity" of style in comparison with works from the end of 1767 and the end of 1768 is hardly unexpected. This was after all a period during which Wolfgang's musical knowledge and craft were growing by leaps and bounds. And if, as seems likely, K. 45a was written in Salzburg rather than Vienna, then it can have been written in a local tradition about which we are ill informed. Most of Michael Haydn's symphonies have now appeared in modern editions; however, he came to Salzburg only in 1763, after the period in question. Only a small, atypical sample of the symphonies of Leopold Mozart are available in modern editions; and none at all by other Salzburg symphonists such as Anton Adlgasser, Gasparo Cristelli, Luigi Gatti, and Ferdinand Seidel.[35]

2. Wolfgang himself immodestly claimed to be able to write in any style,[36] and his boast is in some measure borne out by the manner in which he assimilated musical styles and ideas during his tours.

3. Although Leopold was a generation older than his son and may not have had his son's originality, he was nonetheless an able, well-informed musician. Let us not forget that he too made the tours and heard the latest musical styles of western Europe. In the 1760s, he was a thoroughly up-to-date composer, while Wolfgang had yet to find his distinctive "voice." It is thus not difficult to believe that during that period father and son may have written symphonies in which the father's style was in some aspects more modern than the son's. And is it not reasonable to wonder whether some of Leopold's mature works may have been better made than some of his son's childhood works, in the genesis of which he so often took part as teacher, advisor, editor, and copyist?[37]

34. In *Haydn Studies: Proceedings of the International Haydn Conference, Washington, D. C., 1975*, ed. Jens Peter Larsen, Howard Serwer, and James Webster (New York, 1981), 103.

35. However, a volume of three symphonies by Anton Cajetan Adlgasser has recently appeared (*Denkmäler der Tonkunst in Österreich*, vol. 131 [Graz, 1980]), and volumes of the Garland Publishing series *The Symphonies, 1720–1840*, ed. Barry S. Brook, will contain symphonies by Adlgasser, Michael Haydn, and Leopold Mozart.

36. *Briefe*, 2: 265 (letter of Feb. 7, 1778).

37. Wolfgang Plath, "Zur Echtheitsfrage bei Mozart," *Mozart-Jahrbuch, 1971/72*, 19–36, esp. 24 (concerning K. 81/731). In this article Plath expresses skepticism about Abert's interchanging of Leopold and Wolfgang as authors of K. 45a and G16.

4. Finally, we must ask ourselves, how plausible is it that the manuscripts of the two symphonies were interchanged? After all, the titles and the inscriptions "Del Sig:ʳᵉ Wolfgango [or "Leopoldo"] Mozart" on the manuscripts of K. 45a and G16 were written by the Salzburg scribe. Only the final words on each manuscript, "Dono Authoris 4ᵗᵃ Jan. 769" are in a different hand, undoubtedly that of one of the Lambach monks. Are we then to believe that these two manuscripts were accepted from a copyist well known to the Mozarts, carried around by them for more than a year, used for performances, and presented to the Lambach monastery, without the usually punctilious Leopold having corrected these supposedly incorrect attributions?

The difficulties of assigning authorship to unauthenticated works written at about the same time and in similar styles are very great, although there have recently been some promising attempts at a new methodology in precisely the area that concerns us here—the mid-eighteenth-century symphony.[38] In the present instance, however, the objective reader may perhaps wonder whether the uncertainties of Abert's stylistic analyses are not, in the balance, canceled by the speculative nature of my proposed identity between the Breitkopf manuscript catalogue's symphonies 65–70 and the six symphonies copied in 1767 for Donaueschingen. But the Salzburg origins of the two Lambach symphony manuscripts and of their inscriptions constitute evidence of a different order. Several leading experts in music of the Classical period have laid down a precept in this matter which, while perhaps distressing for what it implies about the primitive state of our stylistic understanding, probably represents the better part of wisdom: when in matters of attribution stylistic and documentary evidence conflict, the documentary evidence must nearly always be given precedence.[39]

ALL OF THE ABOVE was written in the autumn of 1981. In April, 1982, there came into my hands an article by Robert Münster,[40] head of the music division of the Munich Staatsbibliothek, that contains new evidence confirming the correctness of my arguments in favor of Wolfgang's authorship of, and an earlier date for, K. 45a. The Munich Staatsbibliothek has recently acquired the

---

38. See Jan LaRue, "Mozart Authentication by Activity Analysis," *Mozart-Jahrbuch*, 1971/72, 40–49; Eugene K. Wolf, "Authenticity and Stylistic Evidence in the Early Symphony: A Conflict in Attribution between Richter and Stamitz," *A Musical Offering: Essays in Honor of Martin Bernstein*, ed. Edward H. Clinkscale and Claire Brook (New York, 1977), 275–94; and idem, *The Symphonies of Johann Stamitz: A Study in the Formation of the Classic Style* (Utrecht, 1981).

39. H. C. Robbins Landon, "Problems of Authenticity in 18th-Century Music," *Instrumental Music: A Conference at Isham Memorial Library, May 4, 1957*, ed. David G. Hughes (Cambridge, Mass., 1959), 31–56; *Haydn Studies*, 74ff.; and Jens Peter Larsen, "Über die Möglichkeiten einer musikalischen Echtheitsbestimmung für Werke aus der Zeit Mozarts und Haydns," *Mozart-Jahrbuch*, 1971/72, 7–18, repr. with the title "Über Echtheitsprobleme in der Musik der Klassik," *Die Musikforschung* 25 (1972): 4–16. Larsen, like Plath, expresses doubts about Abert's hypothesis.

40. Robert Münster, "Neue Funde zu Mozarts symphonischem Jugendwerk," *Mitteilungen der internationalen Stiftung Mozarteum* 30 (Feb., 1982): 2–11.

previously unknown, original set of parts for K. 45a. They comprise first and second violin parts apparently in the hand of a professional copyist, a basso part in the hand of Wolfgang's sister Nannerl, and the rest of the parts in Leopold's hand. (This distribution of copying duties supports my contention that Leopold's instructions to Wolfgang in his letters of October 15 and December 11, 1777, quoted above, accurately reflect their practices on earlier tours.) The title page of the rediscovered manuscript, also in Leopold's hand, reads: "Sinfonia/à 2 Violini/2 Hautbois/2 Corni/Viola/et/Basso/di Wolfgango/Mozart di Salisburgo/à la Haye 1766." K. 45a therefore forms a pendant to the Symphony in B♭ major, K. 22, also composed at the Hague, where the reception granted the Mozarts must have been enthusiastic, to judge by the number of concerts they gave: three appearances at the court between September 12 and 19, 1765 (for which a small orchestra may have been available); then two public concerts with the assistance of an orchestra on September 30, 1765, and January 22, 1766; and finally a gala appearance at court on March 11, 1766, on which occasion a good-sized orchestra was assembled as part of the festivities connected with the coming of age and investiture of William V, the prince of Orange.[41] K. 22, is dated December, 1765, and therefore was probably written for the concert of January 22, 1766. K. 45a may have been written for the investiture (along with the *Galimathias*), in which case it was part of what Leopold referred to in a letter to Hagenauer when he said that Wolfgang "had to compose something for the Prince's concert."[42]

---

41. The strings were approximately 6–6–3–3–2, with 4 oboists (2 of whom doubled on flute), 2 bassoonists, 4 hornists, 2 trumpet players, 1 timpanist, and a harpsichordist. See Monica de Smet, *La Musique à la cour de Guillaume V, Prince d'Orange (1748–1806) d'après les archives de la Maison Royale des Pays-Bas* (Utrecht, 1973), 33–34.

42. *Briefe*, 1: 219. When the present essay was already in press, an excellent article on the same subject by Gerhard Allroggen came to my attention. In his article ("Mozarts Lambacher Sinfonie," *Festschrift Georg von Dadelsen zum 60. Geburtstag,* ed. Thomas Kohlhase and Volker Scherliess [Neuhausen and Stuttgart, 1978], 7–19), also written before the rediscovery of the original manuscript of K. 45a, Gerhard argues along lines similar but by no means identical to those that I pursue and arrives at the same conclusion.

EVIDENCE OF
A CRITICAL WORLD VIEW
IN MOZART'S
LAST THREE SYMPHONIES
ROSE ROSENGARD SUBOTNIK

LET IT BE SAID at once that this essay is not an attempt to deduce logically or to prove in any scientific way the philosophical import of Mozart's last three symphonies. That is not possible. My attempt here simply is to point out signs of what I have come to understand as an important aspect of meaning in these works.

Nor is there room below for a detailed exposition of the methodological principles out of which this study has grown. Instead it will be taken as more or less axiomatic that formal conceptions and choices can be construed as powerful, though indirect and sometimes metaphorical, evidence of assumptions about the structure of reality. Likewise it will be assumed that from the formal relations perceived in an artwork, a critic can reconstruct plausibly in words some essential aspects of an attitude about what, if anything, is necessary or at least possible in reality as well as about the ways and respects in which man can impute intelligible meaning to it.

The methodological problems associated with what I call "particularity of identity" will for the most part be left for future studies. For example, I shall not consider the general bearing of stylistic typicality or atypicality on processes of interpretation, except in passing.[1] It must be acknowledged, however, that the significance and value I find in these symphonies—my reasons for choosing them as objects of analysis—inhere less in their presentation of a received cul-

---

1. In such a consideration, one would want to assess such suggestions as Walter Benjamin's that stylistic extremes yield more informative interpretations than do stylistic norms (see Charles Rosen, "The Origins of Walter Benjamin," *New York Review of Books* 24 [Nov 10, 1977]: 33).

tural style than in their structural particularity. I mean particularity here in the sense not so much of a distinctive individual identity as of a coherence among the diversified components in each work, a coherence much like that of a single complex organism.

Intrinsic to the very world view discerned here (and to the inherited view of our own culture) is the idea that the meaning or rationale of a structure can never be entirely separated from its particularity (the sensuous concreteness) of the form and techniques through which meaning is expressed, and that, consequently, such meaning yields no incontrovertible truth or justification on the basis of abstract universal principles. So in this respect it is important, indeed crucial, to distinguish between generalized and individualized aspects of these symphonies, and to note the relative emphasis given to each. This sort of distinction could be drawn from large-scale statistical surveys of conventional practice, using the methods developed, say, by Jan LaRue or, more recently, by David B. Greene.[2] Conversely, it could be drawn also from sketches and revisions if they provide enough evidence to indicate those elements the composer intended to endow with a refined (i.e., individualized) shape. In the present study, however, the notions of "general" and "particular" are defined mainly through analysis of the conceptual character of an element—the question to be decided being whether an element points toward broadly applicable principles, on the one hand, or toward an irreducible individuality of sensuous and expressive identity, on the other.

This study, like all interpretations of particular works, rests on some provisional assumptions about the significance of the original cultural and stylistic contexts of the works in question. Thus, my central hypothesis is as follows: the three symphonies give musical articulation to an incipient shift in philosophical outlook; this shift showed itself in a number of late eighteenth-century works of genius,[3] took on concrete implications with the success of the French Revolution, and marked a decisive turn in Western cultural beliefs toward what we, as postmodernists, can call a modern world view. In brief terms, this shift moved away from the "precritical" Enlightenment belief in abstract universal laws thought to govern the structure of reality and to give it intrinsically rational, even intelligible meaning insofar as the laws could explain this structure. From a precritical standpoint, it was still possible, among other things, to count on the existence of some supraindividual principle whereby all apparent irrationality (and by extension, all discord, suffering, and evil) could be justified as a rational necessity. The move toward a "critical stance" involved putting into question the universal status and metaphysical primacy of reason itself, for reason was gradually becoming recognized as a human construct or at least as a structure inextricably

2. Jan LaRue, *Guidelines to Style Analysis* (New York, 1970); David B. Greene, *Temporal Processes in Beethoven's Music* (New York, 1982), a methodologically fascinating book.

3. The categories of the present analysis as well as the terms *critical* and *precritical* stem from my comparative study of Immanuel Kant's *Critique of Judgment*.

embedded in concrete human expression, and was becoming human thought in turn became acknowledged explicitly as inseparable from the sensuousness and contingency, in a word, the particularity of individual and cultural experience. Not only was this shift eventually to engender in the West the spirit of what has been variously called relativism, pluralism, or, to use Arthur Lovejoy's phrase, diversitarianism,[4] a spirit which recognizes the diversity of values and rationales within human expression. It was also to foster the spirit of existentialism which, lacking Kant's confidence in the transcendental (abstract yet knowable) universality of reason, concedes the metaphysical uncertainty of any rational or meaningful foundation in the universe. From such a viewpoint, it becomes difficult to discover either the binding force of any principle transcending experience or any sort of rational or meaningful necessity for suffering. Not unnaturally, as such a world view develops, more and more attention is given to assessing the quality of actual, sensuous existence as well as to exploring the potential power of individual freedom and choice, at first within the strictures of general laws of reason, but eventually outside them. For whether such laws be those of Newtonian science, religious morality, standard artistic practice, or just plain common sense, both their universal validity and their metaphysical necessity are weakened by ever-deepening doubts as the laws themselves are broken with impunity or proven inapplicable or unpersuasive.

The origins of the shift can be traced, though with unavoidable simplification, to the sources of the enlightened world view itself, that is, to the emergence of Renaissance humanism, which could be called, plausibly but paradoxically, the beginning of the end of secure Western belief in God as the guarantor of a humane meaning in the universe (i.e., the beginning of the end of the noblest Christian vision). And Bertolt Brecht surely goes to the heart of Galileo's impact on thought in the seventeenth century, the century which, incidentally, created opera—the first secular musical structure in the West conceived on a scale sufficiently grand to rival that of religious music—when he identifies Galileo's vision of a universe as a blow to belief in the necessity of (actual, existential) suffering.[5] The idea of God as the ultimate governing force in the structure of the universe was gradually losing its character of absolute reality and immediacy and thereby much of its irrational terror—hence the eventual concept of "Enlightenment" and its capacity to unify a culture. Still, it retained considerable ideological power in Europe for several centuries after the emergence of humanism, as Galileo's own tragedy exemplifies. This power can be felt and even demonstrated metaphorically in numerous artistically significant musical structures as late as those of the last Baroque masters, above all Bach but also, for instance, Handel.[6]

4. *The Great Chain of Being* (Cambridge, Mass., 1936), 294.
5. See the speech of the Little Monk in Scene 7 of *Galileo*, in the English version by Charles Laughton (*Seven Plays by Bertolt Brecht*, ed. Eric Bentley [New York, 1961], 366–67).
6. Manfred Bukofzer, "Allegory in Baroque Music," *Journal of the Warburg and Courtauld Institutes* 3 (1939–40): 21; Edward E. Lowinsky, "Taste, Style, and Ideology in Eighteenth-Century Music," *Aspects of the Eighteenth Century*, ed. Earl R. Wasserman (Baltimore, 1965), 192.

Yet as elements of post-Baroque style gained prominence alongside eighteenth-century Baroque music, and to no small extent in the styles of Bach, Handel, and Vivaldi and, most strikingly, of such French composers as François Couperin and Rameau, European art music as a whole was taking an audible and historically decisive turn toward expressing secular beliefs and affirming their cultural dominance.[7] Though neither scientifically demonstrable nor identifiable without prior historical knowledge, this turn can be associated above all with a shift in aesthetic values that looked to the idealization of musical autonomy. This ideal, which would result eventually in attempts to liberate sound from meaning itself, is already evident in late Baroque music, not only in the increasing weight of music without words but also in the sheer physical enlargement of coherent musical structures generally. And the notion of autonomy can be even more readily linked with such aesthetic characteristics in post-Baroque styles as the collapse of referential or mimetic ideals (as exemplified in rhetorical affect or symbol) into ideals of expressiveness and purely sensuous pleasure. It seems no exaggeration to assert that one may discern in this new emphasis on musical (and artistic) autonomy a metaphor for the metaphysical autonomy of man himself—for his liberation from an older binding conception of God and for his conception of himself as a self-determining being and even as a creator rather than a creature. It is toward the end of this very century, after all, that the concept of creation, once associated exclusively with God, is decisively extended to the artist.

But again, though antirationalism and even elements of irrationalism could be cited in the literary writings of proto-Romantic figures such as Rousseau, post-Baroque Enlightenment culture did not immediately abandon all hope of an ultimate source of intelligible meaning in the world, a more or less posttheistic belief in universal reason. Largely stripped of Leibniz's metaphysics and operating (like Western science today) as a kind of successor to religious belief, this trust in universal reason dominated the more characteristically enlightened thought of Rousseau's French colleagues on the *Encyclopédie* and is equally evident in Rameau's theoretical writings on music. Even in Kant's critical philosophy itself, which exposed the intellectual vulnerability of rationalism by rallying so forcefully to its defense, the analysis of reality was shaped consciously by a vision of the universe as an ultimately rational (at least in the sense of a moral) structure. Indeed, Kant took great pains in the second part of the *Critique of Judgment* to affirm the pervasiveness throughout this structure of *Zweck* or "purpose." This notion not only allows the components of reality to be explained rationally in terms of their large-scale interrelationships of function, but

---

7. Paul Henry Lang's insistence on the secularity of Handel's religious music goes to the heart of the matter: the ability of music to project, through purely formal means, a significance that may be quite different from the meaning of an associated text (*George Frideric Handel* [New York, 1966], 215–18 and 383–93). Consider also the interpenetration of sacred and secular meaning so often remarked in Mozart's last opera and Mass.

also requires a continuing ascription of the laws of reason to a governing mind, that is, to God. At any rate, Kant's universe is fundamentally rational (though not fully comprehensible in a scientific sense) in that all its components are believed to have an underlying moral function or purpose, so that without exception they can be referred to universal laws of moral, or what Kant calls "practical," reason.

It is my conviction that belief in some sort of universal reason retained a governing, though no longer unchallenged, force in the construction of most European art music throughout the eighteenth century.[8] And although it is not possible to provide a systematic justification of method in this essay, I shall single out a few of the many interrelated formal characteristics in Mozart's last three symphonies as metaphorical signs of such a belief. All the characteristics are apparently normal in the sense that they constitute both common and unforced idioms within the style of these works, and all depend, ultimately, on a concept of tonality as a structural principle of general character and applicability. This concept had been clearly developed in European music as early as Corelli, and indeed there is a broad correlation between these intrinsically normative features in Mozart's last three symphonies and the common stylistic language of eighteenth-century European art music, a language which can be taken to signify a widespread cultural viewpoint. What distinguishes the classical formulation of this language, at least up to Beethoven, seems to be the conception of tonality not only as a principle of credibly general force or rationality but also as a means of shaping large-scale complex structures (metaphors for the universe itself?) which are fully and intrinsically intelligible, that is, intelligible in a self-evident as well as in an audible way.[9] That the realization of this conception required great individual powers of choice and purpose seems paradoxical. As will be seen, the essentially general character of this conception was undercut even as it was being realized. Before investigating this paradox, some of the more general traits themselves should be described briefly.

1. *The prevalence of complementary pairings of shape and an attendant effect of necessary connections.*

---

8. I would further argue that this belief became radically, indeed irreversibly problematic in Beethoven's music as well as irreconcilable with Romanticism.

9. In his article "The Mirror of Tonality," *19th Century Music* 4 (1981): 192, Lawrence Kramer misrepresents my theory of music history. My point is not that the Classicists are better composers than their successors but simply that the distinctiveness of the Classical style derives from the value placed by Classicism on the general intelligibility of an implicitly logical system, by virtue of the way Classicists formulated tonality. The Romantics and Schoenberg undoubtedly still wanted general intelligibility, but in using a syntax that became increasingly more individual than general, both in character and in formal significance, they traded the primacy of implicit intelligibility for that of precision of expression. In short, they faced the difficulty of achieving general intelligibility with basically individualized means. For them, persuading others of the rationality (or "logical necessity") of their system meant making explicit the rationality not of a conventionalized system but rather of individualized choice. They had to redefine rationality as an individual rather than as a general principle, much as Mozart began to do in his mature style.

In these works, as in Classicism in general, formal elements on all levels are organized normally into pairs of complementary structures, such as the antecedent–consequent or periodic phrase, a structure which invariably reasserts itself on the local level after disruption. On a broader level of, say, an entire composition, the I and V (or i and III) areas act as logical counterparts in that the V area normally (though in fact not always) emerges as a kind of necessity through preparation of its own dominant. With some notable exceptions, Mozart is likely to project the connection between I and V as a self-evident and therefore a universally binding necessity. He does not emphasize the actual arbitrariness, the cultural particularity, or conventionality of this connection by highlighting harmonic patterns so markedly disjunct or individualized (i.e., opposed to the very nature of convention in intricacy of inner relations or directions) as to disrupt the forward harmonic momentum and the establishment of a connection.

2. *Indicators of a functional conception of musical identity and difference, and an attendant effect of the general intelligibility of form.*

In these three symphonies the definition of formal elements as exemplified in periodic structure depends less on the effect of their particular sensuous configuration per se than on their functional relationship to other elements. Thus, alterations in a melodic configuration, which are routinely effected, for instance, to maintain a key, are less apt to call attention to their own literal construction than to act as transparent indicators of functional significance, much like the distortions of literal size and direction in perspective painting. Similarly, it is still normal for Mozart to ensure that a section of so-called "harmonic parentheses" is still understood primarily in terms of a larger structural function. The harmonically uncluttered sequential movement, rhythmic energy, and relative brevity of measures 50–64 in the finale of Symphony No. 39 provides an example of such parentheses, acting essentially as the affirmation of V. This procedure contrasts with the style of the Romantics, who liked to linger or expand on the atmospheric effects within such sections to the point of undermining the immediate audibility and relevance of their functional connections to a larger structure.

Such handling of formal elements projects an archetypal idea of structure that has great metaphorical power in the analysis and interpretation of man's reality, for it suggests that changes over time as well as surface physical differences are to be construed not literally (i.e., not as indicators of the existence or quality of individual identity, which is irreducible to general rational principles of explanation), but rather conceptually (i.e., as evidence of the underlying intelligibility of actual sensuous discrepancies, discords, and conflicts). Thus, both of the elements just mentioned can be adequately described with scarcely any reference to specific examples, and both can be ascribed to the general stylistic language of Mozart's culture. This is true of two other such characteristics discussed below.

3. *Suggestions of the necessity of rational resolution within form.*

One of the clearest examples of such a suggestion is provided in the second movement of the "Jupiter" Symphony by a technique common in Haydn's work: the return of material from the exposition (measure 7ff.) toward the end of the movement (measure 95ff.) after the omission of the material in its expected place in the recapitulation. It is as if with this return, the tonic proposition set forth at the opening were capable of being verified as valid in its entirety. Another suggestion of the same sort resides in Mozart's characteristic reduction of tension at the moment of recapitulation; for example, through lowered volume, linear descent, and sequence.[10] Typically absent is the rhetorical rise to a climax in the recapitulation, through which Beethoven seems to assert (in quasi-Kantian fashion?) the moral necessity of or at least moral need for a return to I. Rather, Mozart seems to accept uncritically the necessity of this return as self-evident. It is, of course, also possible, as will be seen below, to interpret some of his moments of recapitulation in other ways, for example, as expressions of resignation at the inability of individualized harmonic elements to break away from generalized tonal laws.

4. *The absence of explicit emphasis on the individual identity of each symphony as a whole.*

Compared to later composers, Mozart seems content to establish significance in these symphonies within a context of generally binding principles of function rather than through defining their unmistakable identity as individual structures. Thus, there is next to no interest either in explicit thematic links between movements or in a synthesizing close that links together the preceding movements.[11] Presumably, the listener is meant to make sense of these symphonies primarily by following internally intelligible relationships rather than, say, by giving each work a name.

The above four characteristics indicate that a precritical world view is normal in these three symphonies. Yet an erosion of that world view is also indicated by elements through which the symphonies, like other mature works by Mozart (consider the "Prague" Symphony), seem emphatically to counter that effect of the general stylistic homogeneity characteristic of his culture. This they do by forcing a response to themselves as particular sense objects. In a way, of course, the very success of Mozart relative, say, to J. C. Bach in projecting a vivid ideal of universality lies in the superior refinement and imagination—both qualities of individualization—of the elements projecting this ideal in Mozart's

---

10. On the sequence, see Charles Rosen, *The Classical Style* (New York, 1972), 48 and 58.
11. See Hermann Abert's remarks on finales in the Norton Critical Score of Mozart's *Symphony in G Minor, K. 550,* ed. Nathan Broder (New York, 1967), 83.

work. His last three symphonies, however, seem to move away somewhat from the ideal itself by means of an emphasis on elements with intrinsic individuality, that is, elements that impair the primacy of functional significance by calling attention to sensuous values.

One could say that Mozart the Classicist crystalized the general stylistic language of eighteenth-century music into a conception of an encompassing, yet particular, universal structure, only to dissolve that structure simultaneously into an expression of individual style. And just as a broad correlation seems possible between the intrinsically more general characteristics of these symphonies and the outlook of Mozart's culture, so too one is tempted to associate the intrinsically more individualized features of these works with Mozart's personal vision, and to assert, moreover, that the erosion of a cultural viewpoint inheres precisely in one person's deviation from the norms of that culture. Whether or not all changes in cultural outlook are effected in the first instance through individual deviation is a question of great complexity, given the great differences of values and concerns among various cultures, and one that cannot be answered here. Still, when the main content of a cultural viewpoint is that of confidence in general principles per se, and, likewise, when deviation from this viewpoint consists in the very opposition of individualistic principles to general ones, then the individual's impact on the state of cultural beliefs, if not unlimited in power, can be construed as having some special significance. Again, this is a question for consideration in some other place. In the present context, it is possible only to set forth some of the more intriguing individualistic aspects of these three symphonies.

A. Wholeness of Identity

UNQUESTIONABLY, Mozart's last three symphonies stop short of the self-conscious romantic stress on the single identity of a whole structure, yet all three, and especially the last two, contain numerous elements that give them a cohesiveness more explicitly defined than would be possible through the agency of nothing more than a cultural homogeneity of style. Whereas the second movement of Symphony No. 39, in its broadest formal outlines (though not in all of its particulars) and the third movement, in its fairly conventional simplicity and relative lack of propulsion, differ clearly from the norms of sonata structure set forth in the outer movements, the inner movements of Symphonies No. 40 and 41 seem fully integrated within the sonata conception that frames them, judging from their degree of structural, textural, and harmonic complexity or drive. Both the later symphonies are pervaded by the use of chromatic intervals or lines, often in a contrapuntal context; and it should be recalled that the sensuous value traditionally attributed by Western culture to chromaticism not only undermined tonality during the nineteenth century but also allowed chromaticism to signify some aspect of irrationality throughout Western musical history.[12] These symphonies also display small motivic resemblances among movements as well as larger patterns of similarity to be discussed shortly. But even Symphony No. 39 exhibits one striking element of wholeness in its pervasive and emphatic pitting of string color against wind in either antiphonal or contrapuntal contrasts. On one level, to be sure, this use of color reinforces a functional conception of identity and difference in that the technique in every movement is used either to clarify thematic significance, demarcate structural relations, or resolve preceding conflict.[13] Nonetheless, the very reliance on the sensuous element of color to reinforce and, in no small degree, to effect intelligibility tends to heighten the individual character of Symphony No. 39 as well as to weaken the primacy of functional (i.e., tonal) norms of rationality. From such a conception, it is not difficult to project an increasing emphasis on autonomy of pure sound such as has led to the divorce of sound from meaning in much twentieth-century music.

B. Disjunction

RELATIVE to norms of linear and rhythmic continuity found in later Baroque music, all subsequent music from the earliest post-Baroque styles through Beethoven's middle period is to some extent music of discontinuity. In the initial stages of this music, breaks between phrases and between sections create breaks in tension that Charles Rosen associates with a lack of "inner necessity."[14] Much of the interest of high Classical music arises indisputably from its ability to integrate such breaks into new conceptions of connectedness, mediation, and the temporal unity of concept and effect. And yet, certain aspects of the treatment of conventional discontinuities in Mozart's last three symphonies seem to call attention as much to the intractibility of disjunction as to the notion of transcending it. Why, for example, must music that has just affirmed a cadence in the dominant or relative major go on to dissolve harmonic certainty, as in the so-called development section? At the beginning of this section in the first movement of Symphony No. 39 (which features a melodic augmented fourth at measures 144–45) and even more strikingly at some point in the outer move-

---

12. See Max Weber, *The Rational and Social Function of Music*, trans. and ed. Don Martindale *et al.* (Carbondale, Ill., 1958), xxiv–xxx and 8–10.
13. For clarification of significance, see the first movement, mm. 26–40 (theme 1) and 98–101 (theme 2), and the fourth, m. 41ff. (theme 2). For demarcation, see the first movement, mm. 181–83 (announcement of the recapitulation), the second, mm. 27–29 and 53–64 (framing of a contrasting section), and the obvious contrast between minuet and trio themes. For reconciliation of earlier themes, see the second movement, m. 72, and the fourth, mm. 152–54 (union of expository variants in the recapitulation). Note also the prominent use of repeated-note motifs in all four movements and the pattern moving from pitch center G to C in the outer ones, a pattern that has a counterpart in the use of D minor in the outer developments of Symphony No. 40: first movement, mm. 134–38, and fourth, mm. 131–37.
14. Rosen, *Classical Style*, 44.

ments of No. 40, norms of logical harmonic movement are markedly abrogated. Hermann Abert concludes that, although the transition at this moment in the first movement of Symphony No. 40 "seems sudden," it is "inwardly entirely justified by what has gone before."[15] But Abert never explains this inward justification; and it may well be that in his introduction to Abert's analysis Nathan Broder is nearer the mark when he asserts that "the development sections of the first and last movements have baffled [all the theorists]."[16] Broder goes on to say, "There are many *descriptions* of what happens in these sections, but no analyst . . . has given a satisfactory explanation of the *function* of each occurrence there in terms of the whole organism." Furthermore, perhaps only some sense of the ultimate arbitrariness of structural discontinuities can explain Mozart's conspicuous use in Symphony No. 40, especially in its first movement, of chromatic lines as a kind of literal seal not only bridging anticonventional harmonic gaps but at times appearing even within apparently normal transitions—between V and I, or between principal structural subdivisions.[17] Conversely, scarcely any effort is made to conceal the tonal shifts occurring near the opening of the development sections in the outer movements of the "Jupiter" Symphony; they move with a conciseness that borders on the abrupt.

In the slow movement of each of the three symphonies—and to a greater degree the later the symphony—the transition out of the opening tonic section is marked by an increasing degree of ambiguity of structural significance. Rosen claims that when the change of key in the exposition is "startling and abrupt, and the new tonality is introduced without modulation . . . something in the opening section has made it possible."[18] Conceivably, the shift from tonic major to relative minor in Symphony No. 39 (measures 27–30) is "prepared" by an earlier momentary allusion to the tonic minor (measures 22–25). In the G-minor Symphony, however, the ostensibly slight disjunction between I and V that occurs at measures 19–20 has virtually no prior justification, and its effect seems to be actually heightened by the subsequent harmonic instability (measures 28–35) as well as by the clear reformulation of this passage in the recapitulation (measures 82–98, especially measures 86–93), both of which passages cast doubt on the precise structural function of the Bb gesture. The clear break at this point in the "Jupiter" Symphony will be discussed a little later.

15. Norton Critical Score of the *Symphony in G Minor*, 72.
16. Ibid., 69.
17. See the first movement, mm. 20–22 (restatement of theme 1), mm. 102–5 (opening of the development), mm. 160–65 (return to the recapitulation), and even mm. 281–86 (approach to the coda); also the third movement, mm. 36–38 (joining of the coda), and the fourth, mm. 133–35 (return to "convention" in the development); and compare with Symphony No. 39: first movement, mm. 22–25 (end of the slow introduction) and mm. 180–83 (return to the recapitulation).
18. Rosen, *Classical Style*, 68.

C. Analogy

ANALOGY, a technique that became common in Romantic music, refers to the presentation of elements (ranging from motifs to large-scale patterns) as parallel entities. By definition, then, analogy suggests the impossibility of bridging discontinuity through such rational principles of connection as function. And in contrast to complementary pairing, analogy admits of no completion, much less of necessary resolution, but instead can be extended indefinitely to encompass any number of members. Though large-scale patterns of coherence may emerge through analogy, they will be arbitrary, in the sense of freely chosen or individualistic patterns. Their tendency is to establish the particular identity of a work rather than the self-determining pattern of an implicitly logical structure. The effect of surface similarities and differences among elements likewise tends to be less the transparent indication of functional significance and more the purely sensuous experience of literal physical identities. The components of analogy frequently draw attention to their own self-contained coloristic qualities; in any case, where such components are not identical, the differences between them suggest arbitrary variance of surface rather than functionally rational development. Shifts between parallel major and minor modes are a good example of analogy. It is significant that this technique achieves some structural prominence in Mozart's last three symphonies: on a local level, for example, in the development section of the finale of No. 39 (measures 112–45); on a more extended structural level, again in No. 39, in the use of alternate triadic forms at the opening of the development sections in the outer movements (G minor in the first, measure 143; V of C in the last, measures 104–6); and in the "Jupiter" Symphony through the interpenetration of E major and minor triads or tonalities in the finale (compare measures 166–69, 207–19, and 241–44).[19] Abrupt, unmediated, and often stepwise transposition, commonly associated with Beethoven, is another analogical technique worthy of note in these works, especially in the "Jupiter" Symphony.[20]

In fact, the "Jupiter" Symphony could well be characterized as a study in analogy, beginning with the almost immediate shift of the opening C-major motif not to an altered, complementary consequent on V but rather to a literal transposition in G, complete with F♯ (measure 5). Mozart makes striking use,

---

19. Note also the prominent enharmonic shifts; for example, in Symphony No. 39, fourth movement, mm. 48–52 (beginning of the harmonic parenthesis) and mm. 112–14 (in conjunction with parallel major–minor shifts).

20. For sudden transpositions or abrupt stepwise movement, see Symphony No. 39, first movement, mm. 141–46 (which involves an augmented fourth), and fourth movement, mm. 104–9; No. 40, second movement, mm. 55–57 (opening of the development, with D♭ conceivably "prepared," though by no general rules of tonal logic, by m. 29); and No. 41, fourth movement, mm. 158–66 (opening of the development), and, in a sense, first movement, m. 123 (opening of the development as opposed to the G-major statement at m. 101).

for instance, of a locally analogical pattern of stepwise shift, from C to D to E, in the development of the first movement (measures 165–70) and in the "recapitulations" of the minuet[21] and the finale (measures 233–41) to create larger-scale analogical correspondences among all three C-major movements. At each of these moments, periodic complementarity unravels explicitly into parallel recurrence, and functional progression between unmistakable tonalities is momentarily threatened by elements of cross relation, even of polytonality, in the first and third movements, and by conflicts between harmonic and melodic "logic" in all three. Indeed, the effects are such as to suggest a conception of C not as the center of a functional tonality but as the mere identity of pitch which can be placed in any number of individually and perhaps arbitrarily chosen relationships. If the opening of the development in the finale of the G-minor Symphony may be likened plausibly to Schoenberg's row, then it does not seem altogether farfetched to compare the pervasive relationship between C and E in the "Jupiter" Symphony to Stravinsky's nonfunctional juxtaposition of polar pitch-centers or even to his fondness for the C–E relationship in particular.[22]

Moreover, in all the analogical instances just mentioned the parallelism is actually extended by the ensuing stepwise return from E to C (though this is not effected in the third movement until the "recapitulation" of the trio at measures 76–81, itself a moment of noteworthy internal analogical character).[23] Thus, the full large-scale pattern in each case is that of the palindrome, a pattern found elsewhere in the "Jupiter" as well, notably in the development section of the first movement, where it operates as the apparent means of closing the gap between G and E♭ that is opened up at the start of this section.[24] It seems worth mentioning here that similar patterns—that is, gap followed by closure—are cited by Charles Rosen in connection with various aspects of the Classical style, including the dynamics at the opening of the "Jupiter" Symphony itself. Rosen indeed seems to consider this pattern archetypal of the Classical power to mediate.[25] Is it not also conceivable, however, that in its order and its emphasis such a pattern signifies at least incipient recognition of real dichotomies or disjunctions that cannot be fully bridged by any general laws of reason? The palindrome, after all, is not a pattern of logical complementarity, and one cannot discount

---

21. Note the heavy doubling of C and D in mm. 30 and 34 in the minuet. Though the chain is broken harmonically at m. 34, E defines the melodic peak at m. 40.

22. On row, see Heinrich Jalowetz's comments in the Norton Critical Score of the *Symphony in G Minor,* 99–100. David Josephson, a fellow contributor to this volume, has pointed out to me another intriguing example of the C–E relationship in this symphony. The theme of the trio seems to be a retrograde variant of the minuet theme, starting with the leading tone to tonic cadence at m. 3 of the minuet. And in a sense the final cadence of the trio (ending in C–E–C, m .87) completes the thematic transformation by alluding to m. 4 of the minuet.

23. See Symphony No. 41, first movement, mm. 173–77 (here E, D, and C are supported by the harmony, but with parallel major–minor shifts), and fourth movement, mm. 245–49 (in a highly complex harmonic-contrapuntal context).

24. Hans T. David, "Mozartean Modulations," *The Creative World of Mozart,* ed. Paul Henry Lang (New York, 1963), 68 and 73.

25. Rosen, *Classical Style,* 82–83.

the significance of its association in structural terms with the music of another twentieth-century composer, namely, Bartók.

D. The Drive to an Unattainable Limit and Its Relation to Analogy

ALONGSIDE the undeniably connective force of functional principles, there are moments in these symphonies that suggest the unattainability of rational connections between disparate elements, elements which often involve a dissolution of momentum into the static condition of analogy. At the approach to the recapitulation, for example, the rhetorical diminution of force alluded to earlier could be construed as a resigned return to a pitch-center that cannot connect itself by logical necessity to something "other." For in all the sonata movements of these symphonies, except for the first movement of Symphony No. 41, the development section works its way toward an *unresolved* dominant in some key other than the tonic.[26] This pattern is most pronounced in the outer movements of Symphony No. 40: in the unresolved climax on V of D minor in the first movement (measures 138–39), and in the emphatically unresolved drive in the finale (measures 175–93) toward the tonal antipode C♯, a drive which stretches the unifying functional power of the tonic to the point of raising doubts as to the logical necessity (and invitable potency) of a resolution into I. This question may also be raised by Mozart's tendency (associated by Rosen to some extent with release of tension)[27] to reserve much of the harmonic instability for the recapitulation, not least because these very passages so often deviate sharply from unthinkingly conventional syntax (or transposition of the exposition) and thereby call sensuous attention to themselves.

Likewise, even the security of the arrival at V (or III) in the exposition, though normally eased by a dominant preparation, can be undermined in a striking way, and not just in the slow movements as already noted—for instance, in the sudden stalling on IV of III near the start of the third section in the first movement of the G-minor Symphony (measures 58–62). Such undermining is especially prominent in the first, second, and fourth movements of the "Jupiter" Symphony, in episodes within or near the dominant area that are centered on the pitches and sensuous quality of the C-minor triad.[28] In the second movement, this episode, ostensibly functioning as a bridge, undermines the very notion of "bridge" by rocking back and forth in a momentary stalemate be-

---

26. See Symphony No. 39, first movement, mm. 160–79 (V of C minor), and fourth movement, mm. 120–37 (V of C minor); No. 40, second movement, mm. 64–70 (V of C); and No. 41, second movement, mm. 56–58 (V of D minor), fourth, mm, 207–19 (V of E minor), and even the third movement, trio, mm, 68–75 (V of a minor).

27. Rosen, *Classical Style,* 79, though also 73 and 80.

28. First movement, mm. 81–85; second, mm. 19–27; and fourth, mm. 127–32.

tween i and v (now stripped, or dissolved, into F minor and C minor), as if to question whether and why V should ever be reached. The effect of a momentary, self-contained, sensuous digression—unconducive to logical tonal movement, much less required by it—is similar in all three movements. On the level of the entire symphony, the localized checking of forward drive establishes a remarkable pattern of analogy.

In fact, virtually all the so-called critical techniques adduced here are prominent in these three episodes. Together they help give the "Jupiter" Symphony a distinct, sensuous identity as a whole. Individually they help create a marked disjunction in conventional sorts of tonal patterns as well as in mood. All three play on the sensuous effect of analogical shifts between parallel major and minor. All three suggest the dissolution of C from a functional premise and goal into a conception of C as a pitch and an occasion for color. This suggestion gains particular vividness from the fact that C defines the center of the episode even in the F-major slow movement. (By a kind of reciprocity, F minor, which alternates with C minor and C major in the first episode of the F-major movement [measures 23–25], defines the color of the recapitulatory episodes in the two outer movements, both in C.) In the recapitulations of the outer movements,[29] moreover, the episodes are not transposed in a merely literal fashion, as they could be, but rather stretched physically, in length and range as if to force renewed active attention on their irreducibly sensuous reality and to suggest that an absolutely conclusive resolution, relying on the rational imperative of the tonic, is unattainable.

Rhetorical exaggeration of length and range is also evident in the second version of the slow-movement episode, which occurs in the development section (measures 47–55). Arguably, the absence of the episode in the recapitulation signifies the overcoming of the disturbance created by its presence in the earlier sections, where, though never exactly incomprehensible in structural terms, it nevertheless conjures up the powerfully contingent and irrational sides of actual sensuous existence, an existence such as cannot be totally reduced to prediction, explanation, or control by general laws. On the other hand, the episode's absence in the recapitulation may also be taken to mean that the recapitulation cannot provide anything closer to the degree of resolved tension than the one already presented in the earlier episodes themselves; the episodes can then be viewed as self-contained blocks lending themselves only to analogical variance, not to conclusive resolution even by means so powerful as the tonic (here F). Furthermore, the vestiges of the episodes that do show up in the recapitulation, centered on the notes C and Db (measures 73–75), can be read as signs of an unresolved drive that dissolves into an analogical statement and of the continuing possibility of conflict that cannot be wholly resolved by a generally rational conception of tonality; for these same two notes are prominent in the recapitula-

29. First movement, mm. 269–75; fourth, mm. 325–32.

tion episodes of the outer movements, notwithstanding the different key of the slow movement. And whereas the episode in the exposition of the slow movement broke away from the hold of C by way of D♭ (measures 23–24), the D♭ in the recapitulation (like the one in the corresponding section of the first movement, measures 271–75) cannot escape the pull of the pitch C and turns downward immediately toward an eventual, though not completely unchallenged, resolution in the tonic F. The resolution here does not dissipate totally the unsettling sensuous effect of the stalemate between D♭ and C.

To be sure, the last episode in the recapitulation of the finale does break through D♭ in a triumphant rise to the tonic (see the violin line, measures 328–32). Mozart has not, after all, relinquished his optimistic belief in Enlightenment rationality. But neither has he presented this belief in an untroubled or uncritical manner. Quite the contrary, in such music a path seems to be opened to a new world view, which challenges the ultimate rationality of reality, or at least alters radically the interpretation of rationality itself. What has been a conception of rationality as a universally unified and grounded structure seems to be changing in these works to the far more problematical notion of rationality as an individually or culturally particular vision.

BEETHOVEN'S PARODY
OF NATURE
RUTH HALLE ROWEN

Beethoven's inclusion of stereotyped bird calls at the end of the second movement of the "Pastoral" Symphony embarrassed even his friendly contemporaries and continues to perplex posterity. As if anticipating the reaction of Viennese society to the first performance at the royal Theater an der Wien on December 22, 1808, Beethoven wrote the phrase "mehr Ausdruck der Empfindung als Mahlerey" over the first violin part and had it placed on the initial program as well. Performer and audience alike might otherwise have thought that this parody of nature was merely superficial tone painting. Beethoven's notice that it was "more an expression of feeling than painting" was intended to counteract opposition to the obvious identification of the nightingale, the quail, and the cuckoo in the coda of a movement that otherwise conformed to the customary three-part construction of the time. Today we have a clearer idea of why Beethoven's use of the bird calls is an ingenious compositional jest, and something more than a direct imitation of nature.

Beethoven had been trying for years to get a good review in the *Allgemeine musikalische Zeitung,* a journal which had been edited since its inception in 1789 by Johann Friedrich Rochlitz. This periodical was published in Leipzig by Breitkopf & Härtel, the firm that would produce the parts for the "Pastoral" Symphony in 1809 and the full score in 1826. Between these dates there appeared a highly favorable article by Amadeus Wendt, entitled "Thoughts about the New Art of Musical Composition, and on Beethoven's Music, Particularly His *Fidelio.*"[1] The six installments of this article started with the issue of May

1. "Gedanken über die neuere Tonkunst, und van Beethovens Musik, namentlich dessen Fidelio." *Allgemeine musikalische Zeitung,* 17/21 (1815): 346–50. Portions of this installment also appear in Anton Felix

24, 1815, following the Leipzig performance of *Fidelio* by the Joseph Secondas Troupe. As soon as Beethoven heard about the glowing commentary, he wrote Tobias Haslinger, a young friend of his who managed a shop in Vienna for Breitkopf & Härtel, and asked him to send "Rochlitz's writing about B———'s writing," promising to return it posthaste.[2]

The section of Wendt's critique devoted to "Beethoven's musical character" may have provided the composer with more justification for composing descriptive or pictorial music than even he could have anticipated. After acknowledging that Beethoven's colossal genius was kindled by Mozart and Haydn, Wendt glorifies Beethoven for building a cathedral of romantic instrumental music up to the clouds. Wendt recognizes the boldness of fantasy in such works as the "ländliche Sinfonie" with its cheerful burst of nature and lively dances of merry shepherds, and he denies the need to defend the descriptive music, the tone painting for which Beethoven, like his teacher Haydn, seems to have an affinity. Discounting a few instances of jocularity, Beethoven remains what the musician can and must be: a painter of feeling. And inasmuch as feeling involves thinking, an ingenious composer's "tunings" of tonal fantasy may be also perceived by him objectively in pictures. Thus the composer, Wendt concludes, sees the scenes whose "tuning" he describes, and the visual perception that his vibrant tone pictures have for him may well reach the stage where he thinks he has portrayed something visible, something definite as to time and place.

Wendt uses the word *Stimmung* for a "tuning" either heard or seen, and he asserts that the aural excitement experienced during the generation of pitch through vibration is comparable to the pictorial excitement felt during the act of viewing a site.[3] Of course, the recognition of the sensory perception of music by seeing and feeling as well as by hearing was not a new concept. Boethius's triple classification of music in the sixth century enumerated universal music seen as the heavenly bodies moved, human music felt as the tempering of high and low tones into a single consonance, and instrumental music heard as sounds produced by tension, motion, and percussion. My reference to Boethius does not posit a direct influence by the latter on Wendt. All the same, it does not seem far-fetched to construe Wendt's "Stimmung" as a musical tuning of the world, both natural and human.

Moreover, Beethoven's strong reaction to seeing, feeling, and hearing na-

---

Schindler, *Biographie von Ludwig van Beethoven,* ed. Alfred Christian Kalischer (Berlin, 1909), 261–70. See also *Beethoven As I Knew Him: A Biography by Anton Felix Schindler,* ed. Donald W. MacArdle, trans. Constance S. Jolly (London, 1966), 182–86. For information on the possibility that this article was written by Michael Gotthard Fischer of Erfurt, see MacArdle, 195, n. 109.

2. *Beethovens sämtliche Briefe,* ed. Alfred Christian Kalischer (Berlin, 1906–8), 2: 291. The letter is also quoted in Alexander Wheelock Thayer, *Ludwig van Beethovens Leben,* ed. Hermann Deeters and Hugo Riemann (Leipzig, 1911), 3: 622 (Anhang IV). The English edition of Thayer's work (see n. 4) does not contain this letter.

3. In the English edition of Schindler's biography (p. 182), the words *Stimmungen* and *Stimmung* are translated as "moods" and "atmosphere" respectively.

ture concurrently has been affirmed by many an eyewitness. In the same month that he wrote to Haslinger for the Wendt article, Beethoven went to Baden, a resort near Vienna, to relax. Charles Neate, an English piano prodigy who had unsuccessfully sought formal instruction in composition from Beethoven, followed him there so that he could reach Beethoven as soon as the composer had finished working for the day. Neate later recalled how much Beethoven enjoyed nature as they walked along the valley and through the adjoining fields. He reported that nature was Beethoven's nourishment to such a degree that the composer seemed to exist on it. When Neate discussed the "Pastoral" Symphony with Beethoven and questioned him about his power of painting pictures in music, Beethoven is said to have replied that while composing he always had in mind a picture from which he worked.[4]

Anton Felix Schindler went so far as to designate the actual geographical location where Beethoven supposedly heard the nightingale, the quail, and the cuckoo, and he further substantiated Beethoven's interest in nature by adding a goldfinch to Beethoven's aviary. Schindler's walk with Beethoven took place in the environs of Heiligenstadt in the latter half of April, 1823, some fifteen years after Beethoven composed the "Pastoral" Symphony.[5] Schindler says that the sun shone as in summertime and the landscape sparkled in its most beautiful spring garb. While strolling through a pleasant valley threaded by a brook that murmured softly after its swift rush down a neighboring mountainside, Beethoven repeatedly stopped and let his contented gaze wander over the glorious landscape. Seating himself on the grass and leaning against an elm, Beethoven asked Schindler if any goldfinch could be heard in the top of that elm or in any other tree. But all was still. At that Beethoven is reported to have said, "Here I wrote the 'Scene by the Brook' and the goldfinches [*Goldammern*][6] up there, the quails [*Wachteln*], nightingales [*Nachtigallen*], and cuckoos [*Kukuke*] circling around

---

4. *Thayer's Life of Beethoven*, ed. Elliot Forbes (Princeton, 1964), 2: 619–20.

5. Schindler, *Biographie von Ludwig van Beethoven,* 3rd ed. (Münster, 1860), 1: 153–55.

6. The translator of Schindler's biography renders *Goldammer* as "yellow-hammer," as did George Grove (*Beethoven and His Nine Symphonies* [London, 1898]; see the Dover republication [New York, 1962], 211). In scientific terms, this is an accurate translation, one corroborated by standard German dictionaries (see *The New Cassell's German Dictionary* [New York, 1958], 203: "*Goldammer, f.* yellow-hammer [*Embiriza citrinella*]). The goldfinch, on the other hand, is called either *der Distelfink* or *der Stieglitz (Carduelis carduelis)* (pp. 106 and 451).

According to Roger Tory Peterson (*A Field Guide to the Birds of Britain and Europe,* 3rd ed. [London, 1958], 282 and 273), the yellow-hammer (*Goldammer; Embiriza citrinella*) has a metallic voice and its song is a rapid *chi-chi-chi-chi-chi . . . chwell,* usually written "little-bit-of-bread-and-no-cheese," whereas the goldfinch (*Stieglitz; Carduelis carduelis*) has an unmistakably liquid voice sounding like *switt-witt-witt-witt* and its song is a canarylike, liquid twitter, incorporating variations on call-notes. He also notes in *A Field Guide to the Birds* (2nd ed. [Boston, 1969], 224) that the European goldfinch has a more twittering song than its American counterpart.

If Schindler can be accredited as a reliable reporter, then one must ask which of the two birds Beethoven meant when he wrote down the arpeggiated song of the *Goldammer.* It seems improbable that he referred to the yellow-hammer proper, a bird whose metallic chirping has been interpreted in German as "Wie, wie, wie, hab ich dich so lieb" and "Es ist doch wirklich schööön" (Johannes Kneutgen, "Vogelgesang," *Die Musik in Geschichte und Gegenwart* 16: col. 1906). A more likely candidate is the European goldfinch with its canarylike song. Perhaps *Goldammer* was a colloquial German synonym for *Stieglitz/Distelfink,* just as the *Oxford*

composed along too." (We can understand the stillness of the scene all the more readily if we take into account the fact that Beethoven was physically deaf at the time.)

When Schindler asked him why he had not brought the goldfinch into the scene, Beethoven responded in writing by sketching a sixteenth-note rest followed by an ascending triadic arpeggio. This motive appears in various guises in the development section of the symphonic "Scene by the Brook," starting at measure 58. Beethoven elucidated the sketch by explaining: "That is the composer up there. Has she not a more important role to play than the others? With them it is only meant to be a joke." On further questioning by Schindler, Beethoven said he had chosen not to name this co-composer, since doing so would only have increased the great number of malicious interpretations of the movement. And these would hinder both the introduction and the appreciation of this symphony not only in Vienna, but elsewhere as well.

Schindler went on to remark that the symphony had been frequently called playful on account of the second movement. To refresh his memory, he cited a report in the *Allgemeine musikalische Zeitung* dated April 12, 1809. The reviewer, who was covering works performed at concerts in the Gewandhaus-Saale in Leipzig since the new year, concentrated on works known little, if at all, outside the city. He found the Andante con moto, identified by the composer as the "Scene by the Brook," gentle in feeling and execution, and very well unified. Although he thought it was too long, he said that the pictorial plan of the whole was ingenious. But he considered the individual, diminutive reproductions at the end to be incidental, and treated in a "scherzhaft" manner. In his words,

> No one—even if he did not like it at all, could hear it without a pleasant smile, since the subjects were portrayed so extremely effectively and were constructed motivically only as a joke.

The reviewer closed with the suggestion that an appropriate title might be "Phantasien eines Tonkünstlers."

In the parlance of the day, the noun *Phantasie* and its verb, *phantasieren,* had a variety of meanings. There was the fantasia—imaginative, fascinating, and magical—that cast its spell of enchantment on the unsuspecting listener. Such was the *Sonata quasi una fantasia,* Opus 27, No. 2, a work that Beethoven finally dedicated in 1802 to the seventeen-year-old Countess Giulietta Guicciardi. This gesture admitted Giulietta to the realm of the "zauberisches Mädchen," where amorous infatuation reigned. Beethoven's sonata-fantasy was dubbed subsequently the "Moonlight" Sonata by Ludwig Rellstab. This poet of imaginative lyrics set by Schubert and Liszt was not quite three years old when Beethoven's *Sonata quasi una fantasia* in C♯ minor was first published.

English Dictionary records that yellow-hammer is a dialect word for goldfinch, a bright-colored singing bird (see *The Compact Edition of the Oxford English Dictionary* [London, 1971], 281, 1.c.). One must bear in mind that, for all his love of nature, Beethoven was not an ornithologist.

Other species included the fantasia of an improvisatory nature on one or more given themes, and the potpourri fantasia, a medley of familiar melodies presented in the manner of quodlibet. The reviewer did not specify which of these connotations of *phantasieren* he had in mind with regard to the "Scene by the Brook." *Phantasie* also had an extempore implication that would not have appealed to Beethoven in connection with his symphony, so carefully organized down to the most minute detail. Aside from written composition in an improvisational mode, fantasia could designate improvised performance. Sometimes by public demand, a virtuoso pianist or organist was obliged to repeat on many different occasions an improvisation for which he was famous. The improviser might decide to brush up on techniques and powers of display beforehand, even to the extent of sketching a plan. Posterity remembers Beethoven's adversary, Georg Joseph Vogler, more for his skill at improvisation than for his compositions. Vogler had in his repertory a program number called *The Shepherd's Pleasant Life, Interrupted by a Thunder Storm, Which Subsides, and Is Then Followed by Naive and Sonorous Joy.* The program for this prepared improvisation parallels a composition for organ by Justin Heinrich Knecht, which had been published in Darmstadt in 1794.

Knecht had a penchant for composing music about nature. He was fortunate in having had the naturalist poet, Christoph Martin Wieland, as his mentor since the age of twelve, at which time the young Knecht's first attempt at composition—a Singspiel entitled *Abel und Kain*—was performed successfully at his school in Biberach. In 1784, Knecht wrote a "grand symphony" published as *Le Portrait musical de la nature.* Its descriptive captions concerning a beautiful country where the sun shines, the sweet zephyrs blow, the brooks cross the valley, and the birds warble, certainly suggest the pictorial aspects, if not the music, of Beethoven's "Pastoral" Symphony. Knecht dedicated his program symphony to his esteemed peer, the Abbé Vogler.

Beethoven and Vogler met in improvisational combat in 1803 at a musical soirée at the home of Joseph Sonnleithner, a founder of the Gesellschaft der Musikfreunde and later the librettist for Beethoven's *Fidelio.* Vogler was called upon first to improvise an Adagio and Fugue on a theme of four and a half measures proposed by Beethoven. Vogler in turn gave Beethoven the task of improvising on a theme of three measures consisting of the C-major scale in alla breve time. The encounter was described in a rather partisan way by Johann Gänsbacher, a clever young man who later became a pupil of Vogler:

> Beethoven's outstanding piano playing, imbued with an abundance of the most beautiful thoughts, indeed also excited me in an exceedingly uncommon manner, but still could not rouse my feeling to the enthusiasm with which Vogler's learned playing, instructed in harmonic and contrapuntal treatment, inspired me.[7]

7. Joseph Fröhlich, *Biographie des grossen Tonkünstlers Abt Georg Joseph Vogler* (Würzburg, 1845), 55.

Vogler had already tabulated his learning in harmony and counterpoint, and Knecht seconded his instruction in a number of theoretical treatises. For example, Vogler calculated that there were 528 possible modulations emanating from a triad built on a fundamental tone; Knecht amplified the count, reaching the grandiose total of 6336. Knecht further sifted and categorized the techniques for improvising such works as a prelude in chromatic style, a piece in gallant style with exchange of forte and piano, a fantasy with difficult leaps and arpeggios and with varied divisions of the beat, or a free fantasy with intermittent enharmonic progressions.[8]

With this kind of abundant information categorized in advance, the improviser could bring immediately the desired harmonic progressions to his fingertips. Such glib preparedness was foreign to Beethoven's mode of production. Beethoven observed nature, studied books, and created music at his own pace. He composed more willingly at a time and location of his own choosing than at audience command. He believed that one was truly improvising only when one gave oneself over, unconcerned, to whatever occurred to one while in the act of playing.[9] Those who championed Beethoven as an improviser appreciated his ability to develop a given theme on the spot and realized that usually he would relinquish to others the stunt of variation in the guise of motivic pyrotechnics.

The birds sang in poetry, they sang in their natural habitat, and in the composer's mind. They sang long before Beethoven was born, and they would sing ad infinitum. Artists painted pictures of birds. Poets and playwrights wrote about them. Composers celebrated them in music. For Beethoven, the bird calls, the motives with which he worked, were as natural to music as they were to the birds themselves. The quail scratched out a rigid monotone drone. The nightingale's pitch quivered gently into a trill, and the cuckoo's call leaped decisively downward. These natural, musical motives had been around since the dawn of time.

By day Beethoven composed and saturated himself with nature directly. By night he absorbed the poetic, philosophical, and scientific observations of others. His love of nature went beyond the enjoyment of beautiful scenery and the satisfaction of taking physical exercise outdoors. Among the books Beethoven kept by his bedside for evening reading was Christoph Christian Sturm's *Betrachtungen über die Werke Gottes im Reiche der Natur*. Schindler and, later, Ludwig Nohl mention the great influence Sturm's book had on Beethoven. Nohl singles out particular passages in Beethoven's copy that were marked by wax drippings and stains as indications of Beethoven's habit of sipping coffee and cogitating by candlelight.[10] Since Nohl limits himself to citing passages with ethical and religious connotations, he has skipped over some of Sturm's obser-

---

8. *Kleines alphabetisches Wörterbuch des vornehmsten und interessantesten Artikel aus der musikalischen Theorie* (Ulm, 1795), 16.

9. Joseph Schmidt-Görg, Hans Schmidt *et al., Ludwig van Beethoven* (New York, 1969), 158 (sketches, c. 1809 in the Beethovenhaus in Bonn).

10. *Beethovens Brevier* (Leipzig, 1870), 79.

vations that must have given Beethoven support as he parodied nature in his music.

Sturm's reflections are organized as an almanac, with "The Nightingale"[11] appearing on June 22. His popularized description of the bird's physical attributes and her musical prowess turns into a moral lesson only at the close. Sturm introduces the nightingale as the most harmonious minstrel in the entire feathered creation. After the choristers who sang during the day are hushed into repose, the nightingale begins her song, animating the woods and groves. Listening to her powerful notes, one might infer that she is a bird of large dimensions and that, being such an accomplished musician, she surpasses all other birds in beauty. On the contrary, she is a small bird whose color, figure, and appearance are far from the image of beauty and grandeur. To compensate, nature has conferred on the nightingale a voice that enchants all who hear it. Listen to her long quivering inflections—what richness, variety, sweetness, and strength! When she begins, it seems as though she were composing and rehearsing the air she intends to sing, and she then trills the prelude that announces her melody. The notes, as though repressed before, now burst forth with torrential force. A multitude of the most enchanting transitions and inflections succeed one another, and she pours forth notes, full, harsh, tender, quavering, abrupt, slow, in every possible variety of modulation. The ear of man eagerly absorbs these ravishing strains.[12]

On the next day, June 23, under the heading "Pleasures Which Summer Offers to the Senses," Sturm alerts his readers to the enchantment of daylight's feathered choristers, singing their cheerful notes in the fields. Even the murmuring of the brook and the roaring of the impetuous torrent delight the ear. How much closer could he have brought Beethoven to the "Scene by the Brook"!

One of Sturm's scientific predecessors in collecting and interpreting nature as part of universal knowledge was Athanasius Kircher, a German Jesuit. Kircher's travels took him from Würzburg to Rome, where his *Musurgia universalis or The Great Art of Consonance and Dissonance* was first published in 1650. In the first book, entitled "Anatomicus de natura soni et vocis," Kircher notates the calls of the nightingale, the quail, and the cuckoo both pictorially and musically.[13] A plate in his book illustrating the bird calls shows the tonal inflections of the nightingale *(luscinia)* on a five-line staff without clef or key signature. The syllabic voice of the cuckoo *(vox cuculi)*[14] and that of the quail *(vox*

---

11. *Luscinia megarhynchos (Nachtigall)*. Her song is loud and musical, each note rapidly repeated several times; the most characteristic notes are a deep bubbling *chook-chook-chook* and a slow *piu, piu, piu* rising to a brilliant crescendo (see Peterson, *A Field Guide to the Birds of Britain and Europe*, 232).

12. *Reflections on the Works of God in the Various Kingdoms of Nature and on the Ways of Providence, Displayed in the Government of the Universe*, trans. Frederic Shoberl (London), 1808, 2: 244–48.

13. *Musurgia universalis sive ars magna consoni et dissoni in X. libros digesta* (Rome, 1650); facs., ed. Ulf Scharlau (Hildesheim, 1970), 1: 28–32.

14. *Cuculus canorus (Kuckuck):* a mellow penetrating *cuc-coo*, sometimes with single or triple notes (see Peterson, 168).

PLATE I. Athanasius Kircher, *Musurgia universalis,* Iconismus III

coturnicis)[15] are notated on staves emerging from their pictorial images. The cuckoo's call is in the C clef with a key signature of B♭. There is no picture of the nightingale.

It is apparent that much of what Kircher has to say about the birds is an updating of Pliny's *Natural History,* first available in A.D. 77.[16] Pliny divides the birds into two categories: those with intellect for song and those that glory in the beauty of their plumage. The songbirds change color and voice according to the season. Cuckoos come out in the spring. Nightingales sing incessantly for fifteen days and nights while the buds are blooming. Quails migrate aloft over sea and land until they settle on the ground at their destination. The songs of all pigeons are similar in that they consist of a verse repeated three times. As for goldfinches (Pliny's *cardueles*),[17] they perform not only with their voices, but with their claws and beaks as well.

Pliny expresses astonishment that the nightingale's loud voice and constant flow of breath should come from such a tiny body. Her perfect knowledge of music is displayed as she modulates the tone, drawing it out into a long note on a continuous breath, varying it by inflection, dividing it minutely, binding it in twists and turns, and prolonging it by repetition. The tone can be suddenly reduced to a hum. At other times it is full, deep, high, throbbing, fluttering, or vibrating. Every art contrived by man, as exemplified by the exquisite techniques of the tibia, is produced in this little throat. Pliny cites as the omen of this sweetness the music sung by the nightingale who perched on the lips of Stesichorus, the Sicilian Greek poet, when he was an infant.

To substantiate the artfulness of the nightingale's song, Pliny points out that not all birds sing the same song. At first, younger birds are taught by having them imitate their elders. Then these birds develop so many skillful songs of their own that they command prices on the market equivalent to those paid for slaves. Pliny emphasizes the nightingale's diversity of song but makes no attempt to notate the melodic characteristics in tone or syllable. Although few poetic phrases from the lips of Stesichorus have come down to us, syllabic replicas of bird calls are preserved in Aristophanes's play *The Birds* (c. 414 B.C.). Aristophanes caricatures the power of the Greek gods by having the feathered creatures take over the governance of the world. Two Athenians urge the Hoopoe *(upupa epops)* to call the other birds together. When he summons his mate, the Nightingale, she responds offstage, imitated by an aulos. Aristophanes does not give any indication of the nightingale's melody as it is echoed by the wind instrument. He does, however, syllabize the onomatopoetic calls heard as the birds

15. *Coturnix coturnix (Wachtel):* a ventriloquist voice. The characteristic call of the male produces an accent on the first syllable, a repeated *quic, quic-ic.* The female has a wheezing double-note *queep . . . queep* (see Peterson, 100).

16. Pliny the Elder, *Natural History,* Latin with English trans., ed. Harris Rackham (Cambridge, Mass., 1947), 3: 309–67 (Bk. X).

17. Pliny, 10: 157, 116; Rackham, 3: 366–67.

congregate in flight. The recurrent refrain, *tiò tiò tiò tiotinx,* resounds thrice from the mountain top and through the woodland glade. This warbling melody gives way to a more accurate syllabic articulation when the fantasy turns to Pan's tonguing *totototototototototinx.* And the diphthongal refrain on the syllable *tiò* recurs when the sweet melodies of Phrynicus, the ancient lyricist, are recalled.

Other onomatopoetic bird calls written out by Aristophanes imitate the Hoopoe's *whoop-hoop-hoop-hoi* to attract the land birds, its trill, *triotò triotò totobrinx,* for the marsh birds as well as the rolling *r*'s and clipped *k*'s of its calls, *torotorotorotorotinx—kikkabau kikkabau—torotorotorotorolililinx,* to the sea birds. And of course, the call of the cuckoo inspired the central segment of the name of the town in the sky that the birds are building, Cloudcuckoobury.

The syllabic calls recorded in Kircher's book reveal French and German influences in their variance from the sounds of Aristophanes's birds. Kircher's hens shout *cu cu li cu.* They tongue *to to to to to* sharply when they lay eggs, and shake with a *glo glo glo* as they circle around the chicks. The cuckoo's *gucu,* sung to the interval of a descending minor third, bears an undeniable resemblance to the cuckoo call in the German folksong *Der Guckguck,* preserved in a sixteenth-century quodlibet by Wolfgang Schmeltzl.[18]

Beethoven too recognized the nightingale's diversity of song and followed the acoustic characteristics traditionally ascribed to the cuckoo and the quail in scientific, popular, and artistic sources. He placed the generalized bird calls in the coda of a movement whose underlying force had been on his mind for years before the symphony was first performed. As is well known, Beethoven worked and reworked his materials, and an idea he jotted down in a sketchbook frequently served as a motive for more than one composition. In a sketchbook from 1803, the brook murmurs in alla breve time with four dotted quarter-note beats to a measure.[19] The time value of the beat is shown by repetitive slashes and by the beaming of three eighth notes together. The beats are grouped in the traditional compound meter of the pastorale, with a duple division of the measure and a triple division of the beat. Surrounding this rhythmic sketch for the murmuring brook are plans for *Fidelio,* the "Eroica" Symphony, and the two four-hand piano marches Opus 45. By coincidence, one of the figures heard in these marches and in the second movement of the "Eroica" (a dotted-note rhythm followed by a longer note value), is also the call of the quail *(Wachtel)* at the close of the "Scene by the Brook." A similar motive had been sounded on a quail decoy whistle since the fourteenth century. French birdcatchers squeezed a *courcaillet,* a small skin bag filled with horsehair, to attract the quails. And in a print in a collection of engravings in the archives of the Kircher Museum in Rome, one finds an Italian hunter holding his *quagliere* as he looks at a flying quail.

18. *Der Guckguck* in *Guter seltzamer un kunstreicher teutscher Gesang* (Nuremberg, 1544). For a transcription, see Robert Eitner, "Das deutsche Lied des XV. und XVI. Jahrhunderts in Wort, Melodie und mehrstimmigem Tonsatz, Bd. I," *Beilage zu den Monatshefte für Musikgeschichte* 8 (1876): 59–65.
19. Gustav Nottebohm, *Ein Skizzenbuch von Beethoven aus dem Jahre 1803* (Leipzig, 1880), 55.

Beethoven composed a song on the call of the quail, and he offered to sell it to Breitkopf & Härtel in 1803 in a package with the marches of Opus 45. In his letter to the Leipzig firm, Beethoven pointed out proudly that his setting of the three verses of *Der Wachtelschlag* was entirely "durchkomponiert," a factor which seems not to have impressed the publisher. When Breitkopf declined Beethoven's offer, his friend, Sonnleithner, had the song published in 1804 by his firm, the Kunst- und Industrie-Comptoir.

The lyrics of *Der Wachtelschlag,* by Samuel Friedrich Sauter, were written in 1796 and published in 1799 in the *Taschenbuch für häusliche Freuden* by K. Lang. Sauter's poem was based on an anonymous lyric which later found its way into Arnim's and Brentano's *Des Knaben Wunderhorn.* Both the German folk poem and Sauter's paraphrase imitate the rhythm of the quail call by means of a poetic foot. Outcries such as "Fürchte Gott!" and "Bitte Gott!" fairly sing forth a dotted rhythm on the first two syllables followed by a combined accent of stress and duration on the third. The unity of thought in the three verses of Sauter's text may have prompted Beethoven to write a through-composed setting for the three stanzas. The quail calls to the listener from a concealed position among the stalks in the cornfields, telling the inhabitant of the earth to see the splendid crops in the field and to trust in God that the Lord of Nature, so terrifying in the storm, will not tarry long. In Beethoven's music for the second stanza, which features the repeated call "lobe Gott! lobe Gott!" the monotone melody and the flow of harmony in the triplet accompaniment are decidedly reminiscent of the first movement of the "Moonlight" Sonata. Later, when it was suggested to Beethoven that he set this movement to words, he may have felt he had already attempted this mission.

Beethoven was not the first composer to represent a quail call with a dotted three-note motive. Corona Schröter's *Die Wachtel,* which she herself published in Weimar in 1786, has a text closely resembling the folk poem *Wachtelwacht,* later published from a flyleaf in *Des Knaben Wunderhorn.* Demoiselle Schröter was a talented singer, a protégé of Johann Adam Hiller in Leipzig, and a performing collaborator of Goethe in his Singspiel productions in Weimar. Although the friendship between Corona and Goethe was waning by the time she published *Die Wachtel,* their rapport with regard to the Singspiel is evident in her song. The setting is strophic, in the folk style approved by Goethe, and the quail motive conforms to a poetic foot.

It is evident that such cries as "Wollte Gott! and "danke Gott!" replaced Kircher's *bikebik bikebik* with aplomb as the quail beat sounded in strophic and through-composed settings. When a condensed German translation of the *Musurgia* was published in Holland in 1662, the illustrative plate was omitted. The notated calls of the quail and the cuckoo, but not of the nightingale, were retained in an example in the text. Perhaps the variability of melody from one nightingale to another, as well as the intricacies of ornamentation and the futility of trying to reduce the flexible tone to a series of definite pitches in the diatonic-chromatic enharmonic genera, discouraged the translator, Pastor Andrea Hirsch, from including the nightingale's song.

Beethoven himself gives us another tune for the nightingale in addition to the flute melody of the "Pastoral" Symphony. In 1813 he devised a pianistic bird to introduce Johann Gottfried von Herder's poem in the song *Der Gesange der Nachtigall*. Both the flute and piano melodies start on a repeated note breaking into a trill, in the manner of the first "modulation of the throat" in Kircher's representation. The flute nightingale begins on a *Vorschlag*, trills to the beat of the *Pulsschlag*, and ends on a *Nachschlag*, just as Johann Joachim Quantz prescribed in the chapter on the trill in his *Versuch einer Anweisung die Flöte traversiere zu spielen* (Berlin, 1752). The piano nightingale ventures further into the coloraturas and chromatics of Kircher's "Glottismi modulationum" (see Plate I). When the voice enters, Beethoven allows the poet's words, rather than the diminutive ornamental graces of the melody, to dominate the expression.

The nightingale had been special ever since Aristophanes's *The Birds*. Goethe too has a nightingale sing offstage in his play *Die Vogel*, and leaves it to the songster to supply the music. According to Goethe's stage directions, the nightingale sings a long, delicate aria of her choice. And in the epilogue Goethe recalls that Aristophanes, the insolent favorite of the graces, was the first writer to bring this subject matter to the stage.

The nightingale, unseen, heralds the spring with her magnificent song. The less imaginative and more visible cuckoo sits on a fence or perches in a pear tree, persistently singing *guck-guck* through rain or shine. If he gets wet in the rain, the warm sun will dry him off. In German folksong, the cuckoo symbolizes nature's command in the power struggle between spring's warmth and winter's frost. And in Goethe's poem *Frühlingsorakel*, the prophetic call of the cuckoo reaches beyond the strophic cage toward infinity, for the mumber of *cou, cou, cou*'s increases in alternate stanzas until the parenthetical conclusion, "Mit Grazie ad infinitum." In Beethoven's "Scene by the Brook," the song of the nightingale and the call of the cuckoo are inextricably intertwined with the beat of the quail. The triadic goldfinch organizes the tonal proceedings as the nightingale warbles through her *pigolismi, teretismi,* and *glazismi,* the quail drones its *bikebik,* and the cuckoo calls out *gucu* down to the fundamental note. Surreptitiously the flute-nightingale slips in an extra beat on repetition, while the oboe-quail and clarinet-cuckoos continue to carry on undisturbed. Thus the ensemble sings on, ad infinitum, on the chord of nature.

Beethoven knew that his Viennese audience and the generations to come would understand his intent with or without labels. He knew where he was intellectually, if not geographically, when he parodied the world and the order of nature in music.

IDEAS IN COMMON:
THE *LIEDERKREIS*
AND OTHER WORKS BY
BEETHOVEN
CHRISTOPHER HATCH

OF BEETHOVEN'S METHODS of sketching, Paul Lang has written, "It seems as though the germ of every idea had been in his soul from the beginning, growing slowly as Beethoven returned again and again, attempting to prune it down or extend it to the shape he desired."[1] If Lang's subject here were Beethoven's whole output rather than the sketches, the comment would still apply. And when Lang goes on to state that "the sketchbooks disclose the triumph of the *ars combinatoria* of old," the reader would not be wrong in thinking that what the sketchbooks disclose, the works themselves also demonstrate. However formulaic the ideas that were his heritage, Beethoven shaped and fused them so that the listener hears the familiar and the trite as old friends transformed.

To the question "What constitutes a musical idea?" no commonly accepted answer suggests itself. Nor does the following study, which searches out recurrences in Beethoven's work, propose to address this question directly. Instead, pragmatism controls the procedures relied on below. Fairly short configurations and progressions of tones are recognized provisionally as minimal musical ideas. Such entities are likely to be not only less extensive than the phrase but also less clearly delineated than the usual "theme" or "motif."

Theorists and analysts are skilled at tracing recurring ideas within a work, while every knowledgeable listener has on occasion noted that a given piece contains distinct echoes of others. These differing aproaches both touch on the present topic, namely, on Beethoven's reformulation of everyday musical ideas.

---

1. Lang, "Introduction," *The Creative World of Beethoven*, ed. Lang (New York, 1971), 10.

If a single composition is chosen as a base of operations, its correlations with other pieces can be isolated and described—a project that has primacy in the discussion to come. (The cognate pieces or passages may in turn exhibit similarities among themselves.) Sometimes the correlated ideas reassert themselves later on in the first piece, and this, a customary situation for analysis, is handled as a secondary topic.

As the chosen work, Beethoven's song cycle *An die ferne Geliebte,* Opus 98 (1815–16), will do as well as any other—maybe better, since it has recently been closely and revealingly examined by Joseph Kerman.[2] The search for parallel passages must here, for the sake of manageability, confine itself to other works or parts of works in E♭ major, the key of the *Liederkreis* as a whole. The first song and the last—the only ones in E♭—contain a cache of the ideas that are to be tracked in Beethoven's works.

Targets of opportunity, in other words, the E♭ pieces in which musical parallels to the *Liederkreis* show themselves, cover a wide range in terms of both chronology and genre. Pieces written as early as the Bonn years and as late as the mid-1820s, vocal works and instrumental works for solo piano, chamber groups, and orchestra have consanguinity with the ideas of Opus 98, songs 1 and 6. The degree and nature of the relationship can only be discovered by assaying the instances of parallelism one at a time. Behind all the instances—and outside this study—lies a question of ultimate interest: what causes an already expressed idea to resurface? But first things first. A plain case-by-case account of how certain ideas recur can map one small area in the creative world of Beethoven.

AT THE BEGINNING of Opus 98 (see measures 1–3 in Example 7a below, p. 63)[3] two elements stand out—the harmonic move I–VI and, as regards the melody, the downward leap E♭–G. Both have cognates in other pieces by Beethoven. The I–VI progression, plus the descending parallel thirds from G–B♭ to E♭–G, shows some likeness to the beginnings of the song *An die Hoffnung,* Opus 32 (1805), and the piano sonata Opus 81a, "Das Lebewohl, Abwesenheit und Wiedersehen" (1809–10). (See Example 1a, measures 1–3, and Example 1b, measures 1–2.)

These two pieces themselves share a number of ideas, which are set out in Example 1. Sometimes the parallel passages are as differently expressed as the

2. Kerman, "*An die ferne Geliebte,*" *Beethoven Studies,* ed. Alan Tyson (New York, 1973), 123–57. See also Barbara Turchin, "The Song Cycles of Beethoven and Kreutzer," chap. 2 in her "Robert Schumann's Song Cycles in the Context of the Early Nineteenth-Century *Liederkreis*" (Ph.D. diss., Columbia University, 1981), 51–96.

3. The extracts given in some of the musical examples below have been simplified, condensed, and reduced in various ways. Their fairness as representations must be checked against the scores themselves. Beams in the vocal parts conform to the prevailing practice of today. The schematized "graphs" are given not in order to present the only or the best analytical interpretations but to highlight similarities between passages.

EXAMPLE I

(a.)

progressions in Example 1a, measures 17–19, and Example 1b, measures 5–7; these progressions are distanced from each other by transposition at the fifth. Sometimes the related ideas disagree in important respects; for instance, the progressions just cited proceed on into quite divergent deceptive cadences (compare Example 1a, measures 19–22, and Example 1b, measures 7–8). Yet the congruences between the several short passages come frequently enough to deserve passing mention at the very least, especially in light of their identical order and the correspondences in dynamic markings.

Little of what these examples share is to be found in *An die ferne Geliebte*. With regard to Opus 32 and Opus 98, perhaps there was once a chance for a closer correspondence between the two.[4] A sketch of the melody that came to open the cycle hints this. (See Example 2, in which the sketch and the first vocal phrase of Opus 32 are aligned so as to demonstrate an obvious similarity and again a much more far-fetched one.) Yet the works themselves testify against

EXAMPLE 2

a. Opus 98, sketch (Transcr. Nottebohm, *Zweite Beethoveniana,* 336)

b. Opus 32

c. Same as a

4. Kerman, 133–34, finds a likeness of musical form between the *Liederkreis* and Beethoven's second setting of the poem *An die Hoffnung,* Opus 94 (sketched 1813; composed 1815?; published 1816).

EXAMPLE 3

a. Opus 81a   b.

such a likeness. Between *An die ferne Geliebte* and the slow introduction of the piano sonata the kinship seems just as small. One situation, however, does provoke comment. By measures 12–16 of Opus 81a the material of measures 9–11 will have been condensed and the outer voices for the most part exchanged. (The arrows in Example 1b indicate the bass for the new progression, Example 3a.) Transposed and reinverted (Example 3b), these chords sound much like the underlying harmonies in Opus 98, song 1, measures 5–7 (see Example 7a). But this island of likeness floats in a sea of differences. (A longer, if more veiled parallelism referring to measures 5–9 of the cycle's first song is given in Example 4, which is taken from Beethoven's canzonetta *La tiranna*, WoO 125 [1798–99].)

EXAMPLE 4

a. Opus 98, No. 1

The tonal-modulatory circuits marked out in Opus 32 and the introduction of Opus 81a have special significance for *An die ferne Geliebte* only when the two earlier works are viewed as a pair. Opus 32 reaches from E♭ to its VI♮3 in the C-major moment in measures 12–17, while the song cycle contains a C-major song (no. 5), and one that modulates for a time from G to C (no. 2). The sonata introduction closes with a shift of focus from an A♭-minor triad (IV♭3) to an A♭-major one, while songs 3–4 of Opus 98 provide an A♭-major frame for a section (the second half of song 3) in A♭ minor. Thus, taken together, *An die Hoffnung* and the opening of Opus 81a attain the boundaries of the harmonic realm traversed in the *Liederkreis*.

As to the downward leap in the third measure of Opus 98, the E♭–G already mentioned, Joseph Kerman aptly calls this "the richest feature of tune

EXAMPLE 5

a. WoO 87

b. Opus 98, No. 1

number 1."[5] The beginnings of two Adagio movements from different concerted works for voices and orchestra will show this feature in conjunction with others that occur near the beginning of the *Liederkreis*. Example 5a, taken from an aria in the Cantata on the Death of the Emperor Joseph II, WoO 87 (1790), displays two elements of the cycle's first phrase. The aria opens with the melodic outline of Opus 98, measures 2–3, and goes on to a measure that closely resembles the very opening (see Example 5b). In Opus 116, the terzetto *Tremate, empi, tremate,* which dates mainly from 1801–2, the opening of one section (Example 6a) evidences strong rhythmic, melodic, and chordal similarities with the first nine measures of *An die ferne Geliebte*.[6] (Compare Example 7a' and Example 6b, and notice the closer similarity between the opening of an Opus 98 sketch, Example 6a', and the melody of Example 6a.) It must be remarked that in neither the cantata nor terzetto excerpt is the descending Eb–G especially noteworthy.[7]

5. Kerman, 145.

6. Later on in this section of Opus 116 the melodic move Bb–Ab–Ab–G is prominent, and the harmonic context of these notes is akin to that surrounding the chromatic descents shown in Ex. 3 above. A deceptive cadence to bVI is another feature of the harmony in this section.

7. In his dissertation Douglas Johnson has transcribed an initial idea that Beethoven set down when at work in 1797 or '98 on a violin sonata in Eb that was to become Opus 12, No. 3. This idea in ¾ starts with a three-note rise and fall of scale steps 5–8–3. (See Johnson, "Beethoven's Early Sketches in the 'Fischhof Miscellany': Berlin Autograph 28" [Ph.D. diss., University of California, Berkeley, 1978], 577–78 and 1108.) Also relevant here is another sketch in Eb—one not associated with any known completed work—found on p. 65 of a sketchbook used by Beethoven in 1799. It is an eight-measure melody that expresses something of the same opening thought in a more elaborate form and in 6/8 meter. (See *Ein Skizzenbuch zur Streichquarteten aus Op. 18: SV 46,* transcr. Wilhelm Virneisel, Skizzen und Entwürfe: eine kritische Gesamtausgabe, vol. 6 [Bonn: Beethovenhaus, facs., 1972; transcr., 1974].) Beethoven's concert aria *Ah perfido,* Opus 65 (1795–96), presents at the setting of the words "Per pietà, non dirmi addio" an Eb melody that resembles those shown in Exx. 5 and 6 above. It is supported by the harmonic progression I–V–VI. The vocal line in the next measures moves from 2 to 6 in terms of scale steps and is supported by II; thus it resembles the comparably placed measures of *An die ferne Geliebte*—song 1, m. 4, and song 6, mm. 3–4. In the aria the setting of the upcoming words, "Tu lo sai," uses a formula like the 6–5–6 pattern mentioned in connection with Ex. 19a below (p. 70).

EXAMPLE 6

a′. Opus 98, sketch (transcr. Nottebohm, *Zweite Beethoveniana*, 335)

a. Opus 116

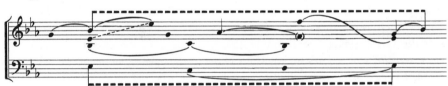

b.

One Beethoven work, namely, the Piano Trio Opus 1, No. 3 (1794–95), does cut out larger swathes of likeness to the opening song of the *Liederkreis* (Example 7).[8] Here the whole strophe of song 1 is mirrored in the earlier work, where the relevant passages of the theme-and-variations movement are the opening of variation 3 and the close of variation 2. In diverse ways the beginnings of all four phrases given in Example 7 embody the same idea, which is shown in Example 8. In it a top-voice motion of scale steps 5–6–(5)–4 proceeds concurrently with a progression from I to II ($\frac{6}{3}$ or $\frac{6}{5}$) or IV.[9] In the phrases from the trio, labeled 3 and 4, the excerpts up to the arrows (↓) are both variations of the same music. (This arises from the fact that the movement's "theme," that which is to be varied, rounds out its own small form by a return to its opening.)

8. The finale of Opus 1, No. 3, a movement not cited elsewhere in the present study, has momentary resemblances to Opus 98. Compare Opus 1, No. 3, finale, mm. 44–49, with Opus 98, e.g., song 1, mm. 9–10 and 39–41. Again, the échappée cadential figure singled out for mention by Kerman, 141, appears in another form in the trio finale, e.g., mm. 87–89. Lastly, the disposition of the alternating V and I chords in the finale, mm. 89–97, can perhaps be likened to the same in Opus 98, song 6, mm. 5–6, and in Beethoven's *Maigesang*, Opus 52, No. 4 (to be discussed below), e.g., mm. 38–42.

9. For a justification of recognizing an implied initial fifth degree such as Bb at the outset of Ex. 7b′, see William J. Mitchell, "The *Tristan* Prelude: Techniques and Structure," *The Music Forum* 1 (1967): 176–79.

Juxtaposing phrases 3 and 4 with phrases 1 and 2 may point up ways in which the two halves of the melody from the *Liederkreis* open as variants of one another.[10]

EXAMPLE 7

a'.

a. Opus 98, No. 1

b. Opus 1, No. 3, second movement

b'.

EXAMPLE 8

10. Other evidence for this is offered by Kerman, 145–46. As for the relations of phrases 3 and 4 in Ex. 7, the status of the melody and bass as foundations for variation procedures in Opus 1, No. 3, slow movement, is taken up by Rudolf Flotzinger, "Die barocke Doppelgerüst-Technik im Variationenschaffen Beethovens," *Beethoven-Studien*, Österreichische Akademie der Wissenschaften: philosophisch-historische Klasse, Sitzungs-berichte, vol. 270 (Vienna, 1970), 187.

Serving to ally phrases 1, 2, and 4 is the appearance, in either the melody or the bass, of the bracketed C–D–E♭, whose rise is coordinated with the top-voice neighbor C. (In phrase 3 alone are C and D, the encircled notes, left unlinked.) At the same time, not only does a complementary character for phrases 1 and 2 come out in the obviously balanced cadences on V and I (falling melodically on scale steps 2 and 1); it also appears in the matching use of descending thirds: phrase 1 fills in the intervals B♭–G and A♭–F, while phrase 2 does the same with the "intervening" C–A♭ and B♭–G (see Example 9). Furthermore,

EXAMPLE 9. Opus 98, No. 1

phrases 1 and 2 are paired by the presence of free inversion. Example 10 shows how the opening moves of phrase 1 are reversed in the first half of phrase 2. Simultaneously the bass of phrase 2 outlines the original melodic shape.

EXAMPLE 10. Opus 98, No. 1

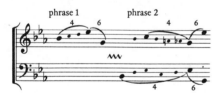

The status of the first C in the song cycle needs further investigation. Phrase 1 forms a memorable beginning for the work partly because of the mysterious role of this note as it displaces the initial B♭ in the melody. If it is a neighbor, as suggested in Example 7a′, it fails of any local completion, for it lacks the second B♭ shown in Example 8; rather it is enmeshed in an arpeggiation, C–E♭–G, in which the tonic note is given a prominence at odds with C's putative function as neighbor. Yet the alternative interpretation, taking this sixth step as one of a pair of rising passing tones, is undercut by the consonant support that it, but not its fellow, D, receives. Moreover, the C helps to express, albeit unassertively, the submediant chord that sounds out clearly on the eighth beat of the phrase. After this somewhat hazy beginning a prime pleasure to be gained from hearing or studying the whole of *An die ferne Geliebte* lies in a series of discoveries that will reveal the changed functions of the sixth step C.

In the rest of the opening strophe the vocal line invariably presents C as a note drawn strongly down. The whole strophe appears four more times in song 1, and in each the variation technique applied to the piano part alters the harmonic surroundings of the first C in the melody. The piano accompaniment comes to occupy what had been rests in measures 2 and 3. The note B♭, which was absent from measure 2, now sounds through the comparable measures and moves on the next downbeat to C functioning as the root of VI.[11] The changes make an unambiguous passing tone of the C in the vocal line.

In the cycle's interior songs, nos. 2–5, which are not cast in E♭, the sixth step continues to stand out. As a stressed detail, for instance, it appears in the opening strain of the second A♭-major song, no. 4 (see Example 11). There the submediant F, acting as a complete upper neighbor, is joined with a set of descending thirds that match those labeled "phrase 2" in Example 9 above. In song 5, in C major, the sixth step A appears as a temporary tonic; both the top voice and the bass attain an A to make the A-minor moment.[12] Example 12 gives a skeleton of the whole strophe, whose repetitions constitute the song overall. After the arrival in A minor the vocal line includes a structural ascent to the tonic C. This rise appears in Example 12 as an inner voice moving up by the scale degrees 5–6–7–8.

EXAMPLE 11. Opus 98, No. 4

EXAMPLE 12. Opus 98, No. 5, mm. 12–26

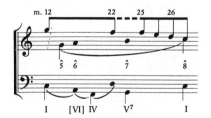

Since the beginning of the last song, no. 6, reintroduces in disguised form the opening of the whole cycle, the original pitches, the rising C–D–E♭, are reasserted (see Example 13a).[13] They come with a new bass line, descending

---

11. At the end of the whole cycle the same B♭–E♭–G melody is stated within the tonic triad. For the significance of this last appearance of the music that opens the cycle and for citations of other pieces using the device it represents, see Kerman, 138–40.

12. The harmonic move here in Opus 98, No. 5, from its tonic, C major, to the subdominant, A minor, can be compared to the same modulation in the two C-major settings by Beethoven of Goethe's *Neue Liebe, neues Leben*, WoO 127 (1798–99), and Opus 75, No. 2 (1809).

13. On the kinship between the opening strains of song 1 and song 6, see Kerman, 145–46.

stepwise and coupled with parallel thirds. Differing from the earlier music (see Examples 7a and 8 above, p. 63), this reformulation of the idea suppresses the initial Bb and, along with it, the tonic triad to which it belongs. Unlike the opening measures of song 1, Bb following the first C is almost immediately given prominence. The descending parallel motion shown in Examples 13a and b, which ultimately derives from measures 1–2 of the cycle, has been prepared by the close of the preceding song. Near the very end of song 5 the indicated parallel sixths in C minor fall on the same scale degrees—6–5–4–3 and 4–3–2–1—as the thirds expressed in measures 1–2 of song 6. Moreover, the emphasized figure Ab–G–F–Eb (♪♪♩) sets out once again the notes that act as the bass for the beginning of the next and last song.

EXAMPLE 13

a. Opus 98, Nos. 5–6

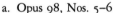

In Beethoven's Piano Trio Opus 1, No. 1 (1794–95), a passage from the finale, measures 173–208, shows a basic similarity to the parallel-thirds technique of Example 13a, as IV$^6_3$ proceeds in four even rhythmic paces to I$^6_3$. In both pieces the parallel thirds subsequently extend their march down to accomplish or suggest a move from an established key to a new one a third below (see Example 14, brackets x and x')—in the trio from C minor to Ab major, in the song from Eb major to C minor. In both, the standard downward motion is at one point reversed and replaced by rising parallelism (Example 14, brackets y and y′); the trio still moves in thirds, while the song covers the same ground using voice transfer and voice exchange. Finally, both passages close emphatically on the dominant, approached through a similarly prolonged chord; the extended I of the song (bracket z′) is comparable to the extended V of the trio (bracket z), through the chords marked ⊕ are not represented in the song. In the trio finale as in the song cycle the celebration of the dominant is followed by the most weighted moment of recapitulation, with the reappearing themes in both pieces starting on scale steps 3 and 5 only. Overall, thirty-six measures of the trio find themselves reborn in the new context of *An die ferne Geliebte*.

EXAMPLE 14

a. Opus 1, No. 1, finale, mm. 173–208

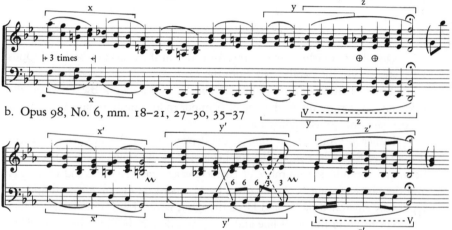

b. Opus 98, No. 6, mm. 18–21, 27–30, 35–37

Initial descending parallel thirds such as mark the beginnings of these passages appear elsewhere in Beethoven's E♭ works. They are found, for instance, in the snippet that is Example 7b, above, from variation 3 of the Piano Trio Opus 1, No. 3, second movement. More akin to the opening of song 6 of the *Liederkreis*, however, is the outset of the Allegro in the first movement of the E♭ String Quartet, Opus 127 (1823–24).[14] The song and the quartet alike (Examples 13a–c) embark on the descending parallelism from the subdominant at the joining of one section to another. With this use of the subdominant area they

---

14. Otto Zickenheiner recognizes the framework of descending thirds in the theme of Opus 127, first movement, Allegro, and traces its evolution through the movement. (See Zickenheiner, "Zur kontrapunktischen Satztechnik in späten Werken Beethovens," *Beethoven-Jahrbuch* 9 [Jahrgang 1973/77]: 563–65, esp. Ex. 8.)

   Deserving of notice here is a passage from Beethoven's "Pathétique" Sonata, Opus 13 (1797–98?), finale, mm. 79–94. The likeness of these measures (at the transposition of a fifth) to the music that opens Ex. 7b, above, from the trio of Opus 1, No. 3, second movement, was called to my attention by Glenn Stanley of Columbia University. These measures in the piano sonata, which come right after a full close in C minor, are controlled by the same descent of thirds (namely, A♭–C to F–A♭) as is present in Exx. 7b and 13a–c, above, and Exx. 16a and 23a–b, below. In addition, their top part begins with a melodic contour also found in Opus 127 in the passage schematized in Ex. 13c. Like the music of Ex. 16a, each phrase of the Opus 13 citation constitutes an address to the dominant of A♭ major.

define a method of enjambment between sections or movements that appear in
other E♭ works. The procedure shows itself, for example, at the boundary of the
slow introduction and the Allegro in the first movement of Opus 81a and at the
beginning of the scherzo in the Piano Trio Opus 1, No. 1 (the preceding movement is in A♭; see Example 15). A related, if more radical procedure launches a
whole work from the subdominant area. The E♭ Piano Sonata, Opus 31, No. 3,
sets out in this way, from II$_5^6$ chord.

EXAMPLE 15. Opus 1, No. 1, Scherzo, mm. 1–15

One detail attaches itself to the A♭ chord in the course of both the Opus
127 passage and the parallel one from the *Liederkreis*. In each the top voice ac-
quires ornamentation in the form of B♮ and D. In the song a B♮ serving as the
lower note of a turn allows the key of C minor momentarily to linger as it hints
for one last time at its leading tone.

Earlier in Opus 98, in song 3, the dependence of B♮ on C is a recurrent
feature (see Example 16). In fact the beginning of this song, which turns out to
be in A♭, reproduces a number of characteristics that mark the end of song 5
and the onset of song 6. Approached by V^7 chord on G, an A♭ triad appears
repeatedly environed by B♮ and D, as though it were VI in C minor; then comes
an ascent to E♭ in the vocal line and a stepwise descent of thirds from A♭–C to
E♭–G, as though moving from IV to I in E♭.

EXAMPLE 16. Opus 98, No. 3

In linking the several songs that make up the whole cycle, B♮ (or C♭) in the vocal line plays a primary role. The opening of no. 2, a song in G major, has displaced the preceding song's fifth degree, B♭, with B♮; now the new note acts as the initiator of a stepwise climb (measures 5–31) up a sixth to G. (Rising and falling thirds support this ascent, as shown in Example 17.) Near each boundary that ends songs 2, 3, 4, and 5 the B♮ or C♭ is followed by a half-step rise, either stated directly or implied. From song 2 to song 3 the B♮ settles on the third of the A♭ major chord (see Example 16a, and notice the voice part, *sein!* to *Leich-*), from song 3 to song 4 the C♭ as mediant of A♭ minor yields to C♮ as mediant of A♭ major (see Example 18a), and from song 4 to song 5 B♮ functions as the leading tone of C major (see Example 18b). The way Examples 18a and 18b are aligned may help indicate other melodic and harmonic components shared by songs 3 and 4 at their closes. (These passages, like the boundary between songs 1 and 2, introduce the B♮ or C♭ following music in which B♭ has a clear identity as a normal scale degree.) Finally, in joining song 5 to song 6, the B♮–C move arises purely in the piano part at the end of song 5 (see Example 13a above, p. 66).[15]

EXAMPLE 17. Opus 98, No. 2

EXAMPLE 18

a. Opus 98, Nos. 3–4

b. Opus 98, Nos. 4–5

15. See Kerman, 141–43, for a different view on half-step links between the several songs of the cycle.

Since song 6 is in E♭, C returns to its original place as submediant. The piano prelude of this song toys again with its mixed potentialities as a neighbor or passing tone. Beginning with the music given in Example 13a above, and closing with that given in Example 19, this prelude everywhere reworks the phrases of song 1.[16] Where the balanced character of the first song's repeated strophe springs in part from the melodic inversion mentioned above (see Example 10 above, p. 64), a like balance takes place between the two halves of the piano prelude in song 6; that is, an answer is given to the opening four falling parallel thirds by the later four rising parallel sixths (see Examples 19b and 20). The first two measures of Example 19a enlarge on the intervallic pattern 6–5–6 occurring in measure 5 of song 1 (see Example 7a above). As in the simpler statement in the earlier song, the C's throughout Example 19 are upper neighbors, though the ascending sixths tentatively evoke the submediant step's ability to rise.

EXAMPLE 19. Opus 98, No. 6

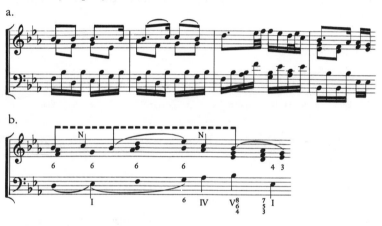

EXAMPLE 20. Opus 98, No. 6

In the so-called da capo of song 1 with which song 6 closes, the end of phrase 2 (see Example 7a above) is redone in a way that drives C upward (Example 21). An emphasized leading tone having been attained, the line continues to ascend. What had been in the first song a C drawn strongly down is now captured in a mounting motion—B♭–B♮–C–D–E♭. This removes all directional ambiguity like that which colors the first C in song 1.

16. Ibid., 146.

EXAMPLE 21. Opus 98, No. 6

b.

Of all Beethoven's works the song *Maigesang,* Opus 52, No. 4,[17] offers perhaps the most striking parallels to moments in Opus 98, No. 6. Before assaying this, a glance at another noteworthy kinship may be in order. There is much in common between this early song *Maigesang* and the piece that evinces the greatest likeness to the opening song of the *Liederkreis,* namely, the slow movement of the Piano Trio Opus 1, No. 3. Example 22b outlines the music that opens each strophe in the song; above this, Example 22a shows the first

EXAMPLE 22

a. Opus 1, No. 3, second movement

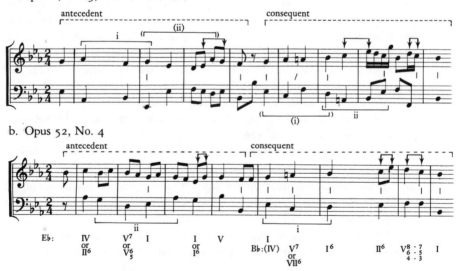

b. Opus 52, No. 4

17. This setting of Goethe's *Mailied* ("Wie herrlich leuchtet mir die Natur") is one of eight songs, dating from as early as Beethoven's Bonn years, that were published in 1805 as Opus 52. Earlier *Maigesang* had been reworked as an F-major aria for tenor and orchestra (WoO 91, No. 1) for use in 1796 as an insertion in Ignaz Umlauf's Singspiel *Die schöne Schusterin.* There its text is "O welch ein Leben! ein ganzes Meer." Some portions of the orchestral introduction in the aria differ substantially from the song's prelude, given as Ex. 23a below.

part of the theme for the trio movement. The harmonic, intervallic, melodic, and motivic parallels between the two are patent. In fact, so similar are the two excerpts that if one were to reverse the positions of their consequent phrases—to follow the trio's antecedent with the song's consequent and vice versa—one would create unwonted repetitions in establishing the two keys (E♭ and B♭) of the two phrases. In short, between the two passages the likeness is extensive and all-pervasive.

What a curious thread between initiatory ideas in several works is implied here. The path runs from *Maigesang* to the theme of the variations movement of Opus 1, No. 3, thence to its variations, specifically nos. 2 and 3, and finally to the first song of the *Liederkreis*. No one would claim that Opus 52, No. 4, and Opus 98, No. 1, use the same music, yet they are linked in a way the slow movement of the trio demonstrates better than any description or analysis could.

As to the sixth song of the cycle, its descent of thirds from an opening subdominant finds an echo at the beginning of *Maigesang*, whose piano prelude is given in Example 23a—a prelude that has been called "a little master-piece."[18] The role played by the 4–3 figures in the early song reminds one not only of the sixth song in Opus 98 but of its first as well (see Example 7a above). A further kinship with song 6 reveals itself in measures 6–8 of *Maigesang*. Here the music matches what is perhaps the most telling stroke in Opus 98 (Example 23d).[19] Despite the discrepancy in expressive force, the two passages occupy similar places in that both are approached by a cadence on the dominant and both are implicated in an elision of phrases. Now for the first time in *An die ferne Geliebte* since song 3 (see Example 16b above, p. 68) does the vocal line ascend by step from B♭ to E♭. Not since the first song, moreover, has the move been made as scale degrees 5 to 8 in the key of E♭. At the same time, the excerpt makes a range of references to other ascents involving B♮ (or C♭) to C♮ (see Examples 12, 13a, 14b, 16a–b, 17, 18a–b, and 21 above)—ascents that are in several instances preceded by B♭.

As for further similarities to *Maigesang*, the slow movement of the Fourth Symphony, Opus 60 (1806), manifests a momentary agreement with measures 4–7 of the song, as Ex. 23a′ suggests. On the other hand, its bass B♭–G–A♭ points up a transient likeness also to the quoted measures of Opus 98, No. 6. The melody in the symphony, however, does not continue to rise after the C♮. Later in the slow movement, in measures 8–9, the note C acts as an upper neighbor to B♭ in a fashion faintly akin to the C near the beginning of Example 19a above (p. 70).

The symphonic movement and the last song in the *Liederkreis* show one congruence of a mainly harmonic-modulatory sort. The excerpt given from the

18. Hans Joachim Moser, *Das deutsche Lied seit Mozart*, 2nd ed. (Tutzing, 1968), 299. In comparing this prelude to Opus 98, No. 6, one may want to take note of the indicated intervals—the thirds and sixths—in Ex. 23a and to liken this "invertible counterpoint" to the technique from the *Liederkreis* summarized in Ex. 20.

19. Of the measure that is the first half of Ex. 23d, Kerman (p. 148) says, "This bar seems to hold the entire tonal dynamic of the composition in a nutshell."

EXAMPLE 23

a′. Symphony No. 4, second movement

a. Opus 52, No. 4

b.

c.

d. Opus 98, No. 6

e. "Non so più"

a. (continued)

song, Example 23d, is preceded by a march of chords that attain the first "clear dominant in the total key scheme of the cycle."[20] The root progression is G–C–F–B♭, with the G and F chords acting as applied dominants. Measures 20–26 in the slow movement of the symphony progress through the same chords with a like unobstructed yet deliberate tread. For the symphonic movement as for *An die ferne Geliebte* this is the first strong move to the dominant.

A potentially distracting excursion from Beethoven's works to one of Mozart's may nevertheless prove profitable at this point. A look at "Non so più" in *Le nozze di Figaro* (1786), Act I, is appropriate here, since this aria offers a similarly weighty moment (Example 23e) to set beside the "Und du singst" passage in Beethoven's *Liederkreis*. In Cherubino's "Parlo d'amor con me" the rise to E♭ is again—and now twice over—strongly impelled by the use of the rising suspension. (Indeed these measures contain a striking instance of the victory of tonality over local consonance as at the close a "G-minor root-position triad" yields and resolves itself into I^6.)

"Non so più" presents other parallels to the ideas of *An die ferne Geliebte*. Both pieces signal at the earliest possible moment the importance of the sixth degree by having it as the note through which the vocal line first disturbs the tonic triad. In measures 1–6 of the Mozart aria the ascent B♭–C–D–E♭ takes on an extensive significance. It provides the top voice in a I–II$^6_5$–V^7–I progression in which C acts as a passing tone, a function achieved by a registral transfer and facilitated by an F-to-F upward leap in the vocal line (Examples 24a–c). Subsequently measures 6–9 set about confirming B♭ as the principal note of the top voice (Example 25a). They do so in a way that condenses elements from the earlier phrases (Examples 25b and c) and that resembles a fragment from the last song in *An die ferne Geliebte* (see the opening of Example 19a above, p. 70).

EXAMPLE 24. "Non so più"

EXAMPLE 25. "Non so più," mm. 6–7

A final glance at this song might call to mind further passages from two Beethoven pieces that have been cited above—*An die Hoffnung,* Opus 32, and *La tiranna,* WoO 125. Example 26b gives a reduction of music from Opus 98, No. 6, measures 24–27 (see Example 23d plus the two chords that precede it). Aligned with this scheme are Example 26a, showing the harmony in measures 24–28 of *An die Hoffnung,* and Example 26c, showing the harmony in measures 21–26 of *La tiranna.* A musical montage of Examples 26a and c might distantly echo the idea expressed in the Opus 98 citation, especially since the top

EXAMPLE 26

a. Opus 32 (See Ex. 1b, m. 25ff.)

b. Opus 98, No. 6

c. WoO 125

voice of each includes a descending arc from one E♭ to another. Yet overall neither excerpt bears more than a dim resemblance to the passage from the song
cycle.

Such would-be kinships as these shade off into what is entirely fortuitous
or trivial. Without a clearer definition of musical idea, an atomistic jumble of
observations threatens. Surely Paul Lang, in speaking of Beethoven's recurrent
ideas, meant something less rudimentary than most of the fragments referred to
or exemplified above. Maybe such bits of music should be denied the designation *idea*. The word is probably better used in a larger sense, reserved, say, for
an original conception by which the artist's will totally governs all facets of a
work.[21]

Still, the resemblances pointed out do exist. If many of them are perhaps
of no great moment, some—for instance, the match between Opus 32 and the
slow introduction of Opus 81a, and the congruence of parts of Opus 98 with
Opus 1, Nos. 1 and 3, and with *Maigesang*—seem to provoke questions. First,
the most necessary query: given the number of works by Beethoven and the
limits of his style, are such parallels inescapable and revelatory of nothing other
than their own existence? Or, quite the contrary, are particular likenesses clues to
a web of subtler interconnections which link a family of kindred pieces in E♭?[22]
(And, with "Non so più" in mind, is it a family that includes more than just

---

21. For instance, in comments on Beethoven's Opus 98 itself, Paul Mies relies on such a thought, making use
of the term *Grundidee*. (See Mies, "Der Titel von Ludwig van Beethovens Op. 98," *Beethoven-Jahrbuch* 9
[Jahrgang 1973/77]: 346.) Concerning the philosophical underpinnings of concepts like this one, see Patricia
Carpenter's contribution to the present volume, pp. 394–427, and Charlotte M. Cross, "Three Levels of
'Idea' in Schoenberg's Thought and Writings," *Current Musicology* 30 (1980): 24–36.

22. The following list may be relevant to this question. It enumerates the tempo indications and the meters of
the interlinked pieces and passages by Beethoven mentioned in the present article and thus provides possible
clues as to at least tentative groupings. An additional movement has been entered at the end of the list, since it
too shows a number of specific likenesses with pieces cited in this article.

An die ferne Geliebte, Opus 98, first song	
Ziemlich langsam und mit Ausdruck	¾
An die Hoffnung, Opus 32	
Poco adagio	¾
Piano Sonata Opus 81a, first movement	
Adagio	¾
(Allegro	₵)
La tiranna, WoO 125	
Andante	¾
Cantata on the Death of Joseph II, WoO 87, "Hier schlummert"	
Adagio con affetto	¾
Tremate, empi, tremate, Opus 116, "Son queste, amato bene"	
Adagio	¾
Ah perfido, Opus 65, "Per pietà, non dirmi addio"	
Adagio	¾
Piano Trio Opus 1, No. 3, second movement	
Andante cantabile con Variazioni	¾
An die ferne Geliebte, Opus 98, last song	
Andante con moto, cantabile	¾
Piano Trio Opus 1, No. 1, finale	
Presto	¾

Beethoven's music?) With respect to the vocal and programmatic works especially, a related topic might arise: to what extent do these pieces express certain discernible emotions—more specifically, a feeling of deprivation or loss mingled with yearning and hope? Finally, one might want to consider the unlikely chance that among these similarities there exist intentional self-references, conscious or subconscious, on Beethoven's part. Without more evidence at hand, however, the resolution to none of these problems is within reach.

Despite this, parallels and recurrences may be usefully pondered for the divergent testimony they offer. As configurations of tones they have the kind of particularity and objectivity beloved of the analytical theorist. They are each part of a finished product. At the same time, the implications of parallel passages point outside the single work per se toward individual fixations and historical conventions—that is, toward repositories from which music is drawn. So a study of recurrences like those singled out above straddles the dividing line between what has been shaped and what awaits shaping.[23] Perhaps this duality can be of help when the so-called creative process comes under scrutiny.

In the past the devising of music has often been taken to be the manipulation of notes or the solving of compositional problems, as one might view the creating of an oil painting as a matter of brushstrokes or of geometrical arrangements. Yet, indisputably, painting also shapes and controls image, symbol, and motif; might music be said to work in somewhat the same way with "ideas"? If so, an opportunity unfolds, a chance to reinterpret the meaning of the "compositional process" as this is currently understood. Of course, over the years the examination of sketches and autographs has yielded invaluable results. But distinct from the subject matter in this field, a composition in the making also shows itself to be a fresh emergence of ideas already embodied in other works. Taking this as a premise, sustained and systematic investigation of moments that recur from piece to piece might serve to define those things the composer's mind most consistently adheres to and effectively commands as he puts his music in place.

String Quartet Opus 127, first movement	
(Maestoso	¾)
Allegro	¾
Maigesang, Opus 52, No. 4	
Allegro	¾
Symphony No. 4, Opus 60, second movement	
Adagio	¾
String Quartet Opus 74, finale	
Allegretto con Variazioni	¾

23. Studies of the morphology of themes implicitly cover the same divided ground. See, e.g., Flotzinger, 159–94; Herbert Seifert, "Einige Thementypen des Barock bei Beethoven," *Beethoven-Studien,* Österreichische Akademie der Wissenschaften: philosophisch-historische Klasse, Sitzungsberichte, vol. 270 (Vienna, 1970), 143–57; and Bence Szabolcsi, "Maqam und Modell bei Mozart und Beethoven," *Beethoven-Symposium: Wien 1970,* in the same series, vol. 271 (Vienna, 1971), 167–75. Also see, concerning Wagner, Edward A. Lippman's contribution to the present volume, pp. 102–16. Of course, for a multitude of purposes and over many years countless musicological publications and other writings on music have discussed all sorts of recurrences and resemblances between pieces, but the absence of an accepted methodology has left this one of the least "scientific" areas in music scholarship.

DWIGHT AND PERKINS
ON WAGNER:
A CONTROVERSY
WITHIN THE AMERICAN
CULTIVATED TRADITION,
1852–1854

ORA FRISHBERG SALOMAN

"FROM ABOUT 1830, a small vanguard of private citizens . . . set themselves with almost religious zeal to 'make America musical' in the exact image of contemporary Europe as they saw it."[1] Who were these individuals, to what extent did they share similar values and ideals, how did they view European music and its role, and how can the answers to these questions clarify distinctions within the cultivated tradition around the middle of the nineteenth century?[2] At the outset it can be suggested that considerable diversity existed among those who tried to support the development of art music in America. In this connection, to examine the writings and music of this group in relation to the surrounding intellectual currents may be illuminating. Today the cultivated tradition receives comparatively little scholarly attention for several reasons: art music in America in this period is judged to be almost wholly derivative, the tradition was so tied to Europe that it virtually excluded the characteristic American vernacular and folk idioms, and there persists a tendency to equate "high" culture with an elitism that seems to be opposed to the avowed democratic ideals of American society.

1. Charles Seeger, "Music and Class Structure in the United States," in his *Studies in Musicology, 1935–1975* (Berkeley and London, 1977), 225.
2. See the discussion of the term *cultivated tradition* by H. Wiley Hitchcock, *Music in the United States: A Historical Introduction,* 2nd ed., Prentice-Hall History of Music Series (Englewood Cliffs, N. J., 1974), 51–60.

All these topics can be explored by studying a controversy that developed between John Sullivan Dwight (1813–93), American editor and music critic, and Charles Callahan Perkins (1823–86), American composer, writer on the arts, and generous patron. The subject matter of their dispute was the music and theories of Richard Wagner, and the exchange took place between Dwight as the influential owner-editor of *Dwight's Journal of Music: A Paper of Art and Literature* (1852–81)[3] and Perkins as an American composer abroad and the "Leipsic Correspondent" for the journal from 1852 to 1854. Although both men were leaders in the cause of art music and had in common the heritage of Boston and an education at Harvard College, their critical divergence on Wagner reveals what is more interesting—a number of differences in philosophical, religious, and aesthetic ideals.

The disagreement occurred at a time of cultural, theological, and social ferment in America. Boston, the birthplace of Dwight and Perkins and the home of the journal, was in this period atypical in its zealous cultivation of intellectual pursuits and its commitment to interconnecting personal and community ideals.[4] The intense and exhilarating interest in natural beauty and in spiritual expression that was awakening in New England literary and musical circles during the 1830s and 1840s forms a "counterpart to the ebullient Romanticism"[5] of Europe and Britain; the result was an American adaptation of Romanticism somewhat at odds with the prevailing culture, which had its own pragmatic concerns. The small group of writers, ministers, and teachers that included Dwight was powerfully affected by German philosophical thought, particularly Kantian idealism, and its varied interpretations in English and French sources.

Enriching this matrix of ideas was a liberalization of religious tenets that had gradually transformed parts of the Boston-Cambridge area from strongholds of Calvinistic doctrine to less severe and radical domains of Unitarian, Transcendental, and Utopian beliefs, thus marking a shift from "a God-centered theology to a man-centered society."[6] The new concept of man that emerged from these humanistic and ethical concerns paralleled American Romantic literary ideas and democratic ideals of personal freedom and intellectual diversity. In this setting, notions of human worth and perfectibility fostered social service aiming at justice in life on earth.

In the matter of social responsibilities and related values, individuals who upheld divergent ideals could share commitments with respect to the larger society. Dwight, Perkins, and other Bostonians of the new urban middle class or wealthy capitalist group, whose interests overlapped to a great extent at this

---

3. The complete run of *Dwight's Journal* has been put out in arepr. ed. (New York, 1968). Hereafter in the text reference to it will give information in the following order: vol. no./issue no. (date), page no.
4. Martin Green, ed., *The Problem of Boston: Some Readings in Cultural History* (London, 1966), 13, 21, and 23.
5. Perry Miller, ed., *The American Transcendentalists: Their Prose and Poetry* (Garden City, N. Y., 1957), x.
6. Milton Rugoff, *The Beechers: An American Family in the Nineteenth Century* (New York, 1981), xiii and 184.

time,[7] expressed themselves in essentially moral terms and believed it to be their proud civic duty to establish, or to participate in, cultural and philanthropic organizations in order to improve the life of the community. The mission to instill values and provide access to institutions for the broad community is one aspect of American Victorianism, which can be defined as a set of standards intended for the general benefit of all citizens and propagated didactically by a communications system that used the English language, particularly the printed word, as its medium.[8]

John Sullivan Dwight, as a Transcendentalist concerned with the inner, spiritual forces of music, communicated his personal ideals through the outer, social institution of his periodical, which for thirty years gave him a chance strongly to advocate his philosophical views in print. *Dwight's Journal* is a uniquely Transcendentalist document functioning in a larger American Victorian framework; it took a didactic approach to the education and aesthetic cultivation of its readers and in this way tried to elevate musical taste. Different ideals but similar cultural values motivated Charles Callahan Perkins. Scion of a prominent family and grandson of a founding patron of the Boston Athenaeum, Perkins throughout his life would devote his wealth and energy to "doing artistic good"[9] by encouraging the arts in America. Both men ultimately influenced a broad community beyond the one thousand or so subscribers supporting the journal during its first year; they did so through their active organizational affiliations with the Handel and Haydn Society, the Harvard Musical Association, the Committee to Build the Boston Music Hall, the Musical Fund Society, the Massachusetts Historical Society, the Boston School Committee, and many other groups.

Just as Ralph Waldo Emerson and other New England writers assigned a guiding instructive function to the poet in society, so Dwight and Perkins envisaged an edifying role for the composer and the public concert. At midcentury, Boston was one of the two American cities with an urban middle class capable of sustaining an active musical life. According to Victorian standards, this included the enshrinement of the "great masterpieces" in public concerts as equivalents to "the Lyceum or the good book"; as Dwight explained it, "we New Englanders are a people who go also to learn, where we go to be amused . . ." (I/18 [Aug. 7, 1852], 142).

The general development of aesthetic enjoyment in the nineteenth century has been recognized as an important phase in the history of civilization—one in which the response to art was "all the more fervent for having to act as a substitute for religion."[10] Dwight made his contribution to this process by applying Transcendentalist thought to music. His radical revolt against Calvinistic dogma and, later, Unitarianism was manifested in the writings he published when he

7. Daniel Walker Howe, ed., "Victorian Culture in America," *Victorian America* (Philadelphia, 1976), 12.
8. Ibid., 16–17 and 23.
9. Samuel Eliot, *Memoir of Charles Callahan Perkins* (Cambridge, Mass., 1887), 7.
10. Johan Huizinga, *Homo Ludens: A Study of the Play-Element in Culture* (Boston, 1955), 202.

was a contributor to the *Dial* in 1840–44 as one of the West Street group, when he was a member of the associationist community that established the Utopian Brook Farm experiment and put out the *Harbinger,* for which he wrote in the later 1840s, and, finally, when he was the editor of his own long-lasting journal. His musical convictions had had their origin in religious and philosophical thought current in what were primarily literary circles of the 1830s and 1840s. Despite the enormous changes in American society and culture, he continued to expound these convictions through all the years of existence of *Dwight's Journal's.*

When he was young, Dwight read widely in German philosophy and Romantic literature. Through his book of translations, published (with notes) under the title *Select Minor Poems from Goethe and Schiller* (1839), he made a contribution to George Ripley's series *Specimens of Foreign Standard Literature.* Dwight also revered the works of Coleridge and Carlyle. The latter has been called the "perfect middleman" for the movement of new ideas,[11] and it was to Carlyle that Dwight dedicated his volume of translations. In their correspondence on the subject Dwight and Carlyle agreed that the Germans were "chief of the family at present" in the speaking and singing department, though they acknowledged the kinship and mutual admiration of Englanders New and Old.[12]

Throughout this period, which includes his years at Harvard College and Harvard Divinity School, as well as the time he spent as a Unitarian minister before joining the Transcendentalist circle, Dwight worked conscientiously to become ever more proficient as a musician. He practiced the piano and flute, studied available scores, read and performed chamber music with friends, and, finally, taught music at Brook Farm from 1841 to 1846. Apparently more knowledgeable musically than the mere "literary amateur of music"[13] he has been called, Dwight during his Brook Farm years instituted his New England "Mass Clubs" made up of farmers, workers, teachers, and others who gathered to study the choral literature.[14] In this communal endeavor Dwight applied his conviction that to enable human beings to become familiar with "the beautiful and the infinite" was to improve society by bringing people into contact with greatness.

His perspective was complicated by conflicting tendencies that acknowledged the existence of the "intelligent few" among the multitude, on whose be-

11. Van Wyck Brooks, *The Flowering of New England* (New York and London, 1952), 200.

12. George Willis Cooke, *John Sullivan Dwight: Brook-Farmer, Editor, and Critic of Music,* new ed. by Kenneth Walter Cameron (Hartford, Conn., 1973), 11.

13. Walter L. Fertig, "John Sullivan Dwight," *The New Grove* 5:792; based in large part on his "John Sullivan Dwight, Transcendentalist and Literary Amateur of Music" (Ph.D. diss., University of Maryland, 1952). For a more sympathetic approach, see Marcia Wilson Lebow, "A Systematic Examination of the *Journal of Music and Art* Edited by John Sullivan Dwight: 1852–1881, Boston, Massachusetts" (Ph.D. diss., University of California, Los Angeles, 1969). In setting the limits of her fine study, Lebow omitted the category of foreign correspondence and thus did not treat the Dwight-Perkins interaction.

14. Cooke, 22; Brooks, 252–54.

half he strove to assure full access to cultural institutions. To locate the source of this dilemma, it should be recalled that Transcendentalism was a way of thinking that concerned itself not only with a new emphasis on individual self-worth but also with epistemological theory. Transcendentalism rejected all dogma and any rituals and creeds associated with organized religion. It replaced the Calvinistic doctrine of human sin with a positive faith in individual will. Belief in revelation by intuition increased the value of self-reliance. Every person could gain knowledge both of the perceived physical world by rational analysis through the power of "Understanding" and of the unseen world of pure ideas by intuition through the realm of "Reason." Despite its name, "Reason" was seen as the "highest power of the soul,"[15] in Emerson's phrase, and one which could grasp truth and beauty directly by "transcending" the barriers of sense and time. Having a capacity to acquire knowledge through intuition, all people were spiritually equal and could be held responsible for their individual thoughts and actions.

Dwight early gave voice to a clear statement of his ideas in an address delivered before the Harvard Musical Association in 1841;[16] these ideas were later to be frequently repeated in *Dwight's Journal*. The core of his musical philosophy was a plea for the universal acceptance of music as a "language of natural religion" intuitively available to everyone. Believing that music was one of the "noblest creations of the mind" and the "highest outward symbol of what is most deep and holy," Dwight asserted that it acts to make man conscious of new worlds within him. Rejecting all traditional religious associations in music, Dwight, in marked contrast to Perkins, declared that music had a meaning in itself independent of its occasion or function. He called for a reconciliation of sacred and secular in music instead of the usual separation; he mentioned Beethoven's instrumental adagios as an example, for he considered them to be sublime prayers regardless of their nominal designation as secular music.

Similarly, Dwight contended that music is greater than anything it undertakes to illustrate or adorn. To emphasize his reaction against all creeds, he explained that Mass movements by Beethoven, Haydn, or Mozart chosen for study with his Mass Clubs were not to be viewed as Catholic sacred music but as universal spiritual statements. Dwight believed that music was an autonomous and supreme language totally independent of words. It followed from this fundamental premise that instrumental music was superior to vocal; "music compromises something of its own peculiar eloquence to even the most judicious union with poetry."[17] His aesthetic preference for symphonies and chamber music can be regarded as the natural outcome of his philosophical outlook. A concern for the spiritual essence of the musical experience was the central force governing Dwight's critical perspective.

15. Russel Blaine Nye, *Society and Culture in America, 1830–1860*, New American Nation Series, vol. 3 (New York, 1974), 329–30.
16. Dwight, *Address Delivered before the Harvard Musical Association* (n. p., 1841), 5–13.
17. Ibid.. 12–13.

If the German model in music, philosophy, and literature was strong for Dwight, it directly influenced the early career of Charles Callahan Perkins. Before his departure to study music at the Leipzig Conservatory, Perkins had already produced several compositions and served as president of the Handel and Haydn Society in 1850–51. (He would again serve as its president from 1875 to 1886 and become an author of its *History*, at which job he was succeeded on his death by Dwight.) The society was then, and had been since its inception, a middle-class group made up mostly of tradesmen and musical amateurs; as a grandson of a prominent merchant and as an aspiring composer, Perkins was in a dual sense the principal exception.[18] A devout Episcopalian, Perkins held views markedly different from Dwight's regarding religion and its connection to music. He fervently revered oratorios as sacred music bearing a divine message. *The Creation* and *Elijah* were performed by the society in public concerts during his first year in office.[19] In 1852 and 1853, having heard Handel oratorios sung in London and Düsseldorf, he sent excited letters to *Dwight's Journal* in which he set down his awed impressions of the performances along with comments about tempo and other practical concerns intended to assist his colleagues in the society (I/14 [July 10, 1852], 108).

As a student and occasional foreign correspondent for the journal Perkins found himself in an intensely musical environment. Leipzig, which had a distinguished tradition, was in the nineteenth century the location of the conservatory organized by Felix Mendelssohn as well as of the historical concerts introduced and directed by him with the Gewandhaus orchestra. There also Schumann had founded and contributed to the respected journal for new music, the *Neue Zeitschrift für Musik,* and there Richard Wagner had been born. The prestige and curriculum of the Leipzig Conservatory were known in America through reports sent by young Americans and through Lowell Mason's favorable descriptions, published in *Dwight's Journal* as well as in book form.[20] In 1851 the conservatory was still a center of Mendelssohn's influence, and the faculty colleagues whom he had selected—Ignaz Moscheles for piano, Moritz Hauptmann for harmony and counterpoint, Ferdinand David for violin—became Perkins's teachers and advisors.

Perkins sent enthusiastic accounts of his musical activities to *Dwight's Journal.* At least nine communications appearing between May 29, 1852, and January 21, 1854, can be identified as having been written by Perkins; most bear a single initial, P, below informative reports on musical life in Leipzig, Düsseldorf, Berlin, Dresden, Paris, and London. The young composer abroad praised Moscheles's pianism and Hauptmann's knowledge, expressed his preference for the Gewandhaus orchestra over all others, and offered his judgment of

---

18. H. Earle Johnson, *Hallelujah, Amen! The Story of the Handel and Haydn Society of Boston* (Boston, 1965), 33–34.
19. Perkins and Dwight, *History of the Handel and Haydn Society,* repr. ed., 2 vols. (New York, 1977), 1: 144–6 and xi.
20. Lowell Mason, *Musical Letters from Abroad,* repr. ed. (New York, 1967), esp. Letter XV, 71–78.

Mendelssohn as successor to Beethoven. Beyond the Leipzig circle he admired operas such as *Alceste, Die Zauberflöte,* and *Fidelio,* but scorned Halévy's excessive brass instrumentation. He praised symphonies of Haydn and Beethoven, but professed an inability to understand the last movement of Beethoven's Ninth (I/14 [July 10, 1852], 109). Personal observation confirmed a view shared from afar by Dwight—that excellence in orchestral performance standards currently existed in Germany because through education the people had acquired an aesthetic taste that enabled them to expect it:

> . . . in Germany alone can such enjoyment be found—in Germany alone does music form an essential part of the people's existence; and therefore only in Germany will the demand create the perfect performance of the *chef d'oeuvres* of the great masters. (III/11 [June 18, 1853], 87)

Chamber music by Beethoven, Mozart, Haydn, Schubert, and Mendelssohn was also very important to Perkins both as a composer and as a pianist. In the regular Sunday musicales in Leipzig at which he played, new works of his were performed along with new pieces by such Boston friends as James C. D. Parker and William Mason, who were then studying in Leipzig or Weimar. On his return to Boston his devotion to chamber music continued; there he participated in public concerts with members of the Mendelssohn Quintette Club.

If Perkins praised the works of others for their "pleasing melody" and "purity of style" while disapproving of excessive dissonance or virtuosity, his own compositions of this period reflect these standards.[21] Clarity of design marks his chamber music, which is written in an idiom characteristic of the earlier nineteenth century. These works employ sonata designs in their first and last movements, with slow song forms and scherzos as inner movements. They are competently constructed and show attention to the details of instrumental balance; a gentle lyricism pervades the melodic writing. The music demands technical proficiency but is not especially flamboyant. The works that include piano demonstrate Perkins's personal knowledge of the keyboard by incorporating idiomatic figurations and coloristic devices.

Dwight's critical reviews of music by Perkins expressed both approval of good musical ideas carefully developed, of which he found evidence, and a desire for overall unity (described as spontaneous organic connection deriving from a single "germinal inspiration"), which he thought was lacking (VI/10 [Dec. 9, 1854], 78, and VI/22 [Mar. 3, 1855], "157" [recte 175]). When the London critic Henry F. Chorley praised Perkins for "eschewing the modern defects calling themselves romanticisms," Dwight countered with the wry comment that

---

21. *Eight Melodies/Huit Mélodies* (Paris: Brandus et Cie., 1849); *Quatuor,* Opus 8 (Leipzig: Breitkopf & Härtel, [1853]); *Troisième Quatuor,* Opus 9 (Leipzig: Breitkopf & Härtel, [1853]); *Trio,* Opus 10 (Leipzig: Breitkopf & Härtel, [1854]); *Pensées musicales pour piano et violon,* Opus 11 (Leipzig: Breitkopf & Härtel, [1855]).

Perkins's "good sense" in following older models in his chamber music was not consciously intended to divert his countrymen from "good *new* things" (IV/6 [Nov. 12, 1853], 46). Dwight favored the inner movements over the outer ones in Perkins's chamber works. On one occasion he advised his young fellow townsman that his Third String Quartet was not necessarily imbued with greater clarity and effectiveness than had been his Second Quartet, despite the later work's ambitious scope and elaborate themes and "even if it have more in it, both of musical ideas and learning" (V/8 [May 27, 1854], 62). Dwight sought for the emergence of a characteristic personal style, and although certain that no "slavish copying of models" was present, he acknowledged the general stylistic and structural influence of Mendelssohn on Perkins's music (IV/10 [Dec. 10, 1853], 78, and VI/22 [Mar. 3, 1855], "157" [recte 175]).

Dwight's stern yet kindly reviews underscore his active interest in the compositions of Perkins and other young Americans studying abroad. William Henry Fry's "Declaration of Independence in Art," announced in his New York lectures and reported by Dwight (II/23 [Mar. 12, 1853], 180–82, and II/26 [Apr. 2, 1853], 201–2) from accounts in the *New York Musical World and Times,* had opened a round of battles over an Americanism that decried the dependence of American concert life on foreign composers and demanded public support for American compositions.[22] Although Dwight could not find most American vernacular music acceptable, he did foster the composition and performance of new works by Perkins, Parker, and, later, John Knowles Paine among others. He never doubted the importance of encouraging original music by "native classical composers" as a means of stimulating the growth of an American art music.

Rarely did Dwight differentiate between "classical" and "romantic" as terms by which to designate styles in European music. Generally he included music from Haydn to Wagner within the broad category "classical," which he distinguished from music of a "light" variety (IV/18 [Feb. 4, 1854], 141). He believed that for American composers of his time a period of foreign study, particularly in Germany, was desirable as a link to the compositions of the European "masters." Upon his recommendation original works by Perkins and others were performed in the United States first at informal public readings (IV/6 [Nov. 12, 1853], 46) and subsequently at public concerts of chamber music.

In avowing a personal preference for German instrumental music while at the same time soliciting and publishing in his journal a wide range of opinion from at home and abroad, Dwight showed that he recognized the distinction between critical and editorial responsibilities. Paul Henry Lang, from his own broad knowledge and vast experience in both areas, has described the varied professional expectations for each:

22. See also Barbara A. Zuck, *A History of Musical Americanism,* Studies in Musicology, 19 (Ann Arbor, 1980), 18–19 and 26.

Editorship of a great scholarly journal is a difficult thing and is entirely different from the activity of the creative writer or critic. A critic can be subjective and can with fighting spirit represent a powerful individual tendency or taste in the musical world. The editor must deny himself, he must see with the eyes of many people at the same time, and, like the good *concierge,* must watch every door.[23]

Between the first issue of *Dwight's Journal* in April, 1852, and the exchange between Dwight and Perkins on Wagner occurring in January, 1854, there appeared a remarkable group of major articles, translations, program notes, and commentaries relating to Wagner. Sought out and printed for an openly didactic purpose by Dwight in his capacity as editor, they introduced Wagner to a segment of the interested American musical public at a time when the Germania Musical Society was performing instrumental pieces from *Rienzi, Tannhäuser,* and *Lohengrin.* During this period the journal carried a four-part discussion by Dwight of Wagner's life and aesthetic theories, three translations of excerpts from *Oper und Drama* that give Wagner's views of traditional opera by Mozart, Rossini, Weber, and Auber, translations of two commentaries by Wagner on Beethoven's Symphony No. 9 and on his own *Tannhäuser* Overture, Dwight's front-page translations (in five issues) of Liszt's discussion of *Tannhäuser,* three consequential reviews by Dwight of performances of the *Tannhäuser* Overture and of a special "Wagner Night," as well as another, related essay on orchestral music, and communications for or against Wagner by Robert Franz, Chorley, and Perkins.

In the midst of these efforts, Dwight was gratified to receive a congratulatory letter from what he regarded as musical "head-quarters," the Leipzig *Neue Zeitschrift für Musik,* praising his "musical catholicity" in the cause of new as well as traditional art music (III/17 [July 30, 1853], 132–34). In his own journal Dwight replied that he as yet knew very little of the new music, but he announced that he stood ready to receive the newest and the oldest alike provided it possessed "the true vitality of Art." Dwight treated the controversial theories of the "composer of genius" respectfully and tried to mediate between adherents of "Young Germany" and the "oracles of the old school," who regarded Wagner's music "as a vain attempt to overthrow the very foundations of musical art" (II/10 [Dec. 11, 1852], 78).

When discussing Wagner's life, Dwight culled data from Fétis's *Revue et gazette musicale,* though he recognized Fétis's anti-Wagner stance. When considering Wagner's aesthetic theory, he extracted material mostly from *Oper und Drama,* published in Leipzig in 1852, and from some German critical sources. Having access solely to the poems of *Der fliegende Holländer, Tannhäuser,* and *Lohengrin,* and lacking precise information about other poems and sketches then

---

23. Lang, Introduction to Alfred Einstein, *Essays on Music* (New York, 1956), xi.

in progress, Dwight regarded Wagner's theories of music and drama as directly pertinent to those works already heard in full by the European public. Specifically, he believed that *Lohengrin* most fully illustrated Wagner's principles as explained in *Oper und Drama* (II/10 [Dec. 11, 1852], 77).

At this time Dwight was fascinated and awed by Wagner the man; his radical artistic and political views appeared heroic, original, and appropriate for a person of venturesome spirit. Dwight was intrigued by the artist who could create both music and poetry in addition to innovative aesthetic theory. Wagner's early independence, his passion for Beethoven's symphonies, and what he called his cultivation of "poetry only from the musical point of view" were attractive to Dwight (II/9 [Dec. 4, 1852], 69–70). Wagner's disappointments in Paris, his initial lack of wide public acceptance, and his proposal to reorganize the royal theater at Dresden were recounted with admiration for the composer as a strongly "self-reliant" and practical man of the theater.

On the basis of the music and writings known to him, Dwight believed that Wagner's practice, then gradually being revealed in America, would surpass his aesthetic theory, with which he was in fundamental disagreement. If the artwork of the future could arise only from a marriage of poetry and music, with poetry interpreted as the masculine and music as the feminine expressive element, as Wagner's governing simile would have it, then absolute instrumental music could not exist as a self-generating power. According to Dwight's understanding of this central element in Wagner's aesthetic theory as expressed at this time, orchestral music could find its fulfillment only through multiple functions in a composite work of art destined for the stage, an idea diametrically opposed to Dwight's basic convictions from their earliest formulation.

Wagner's view of Beethoven's Ninth Symphony as a critical point of transition between music of the past and music of the future caused Dwight to respond by acknowledging the work to be a milestone in a long musical tradition. He was convinced that neither Coleridge nor Goethe nor Shakespeare stood as fully revealed to mankind as did Beethoven through the corpus of his work, which consisted primarily of instrumental music. Dwight's readers in Boston had recently had an opportunity to hear a complete performance of Symphony No. 9, for which Dwight in his accustomed fashion had provided information by publishing Wagner's "Programme to the Ninth Symphony of Beethoven" (II/18 [Feb. 5, 1853], 137–39). In contrast to Wagner's vision of the essential connection of tones to the "word-verse," Dwight reiterated his position that tones, as a spiritual language capable of imparting a sense of the Infinite and of binding human beings at the most profound level to each other and to a universal source, would continue, through the power of instrumental music, to have "more to utter than words and voices can convey" with their definiteness of meaning (II/21 [Feb. 26, 1853], 166). His Transcendental convictions placed instrumental music at the head of a musical hierarchy, above anything with which it might be joined, and he viewed with misgivings what he took to be its sacrifice in a union with words. Although his reasons were not Wagner's, Dwight could agree with Wagner's criticism of singers' abuses such as had occurred in the history of traditional opera, but he did not share the evolutionary thinking that led Wagner to reject conventional number opera (an affirmation of the separation of the arts, so the composer thought) in favor of his own music dramas. Wagner's dynamic sense of history contrasted with Dwight's essentially suprahistorical approach.

Among the musical ideas in Wagner's writings that he considered problematic, Dwight cited, as one instance, the proclaimed revolution in modulation that might in the end destroy the tonal basis of harmonic unity and, as another, the apparently intrinsic connection of the melodic principle to the "word-verse." Regarding the former, Dwight readily conceded that music of his time—by Chopin and Schumann, among others—had fruitfully extended the limits of traditional tonality, but he asserted that Wagner was the first to make the expansion of the tonal vocabulary a major compositional principle.

More troublesome for Dwight, in view of Wagner's aesthetic theory and musical practice, was the degree to which music could achieve independence. Dwight was, after all, particularly interested in how the composer alone, without the poet's words, could convey the inexpressible. He described Wagner's use of orchestral gesture and instrumental representation of hidden motivation for actions, reminiscences designed to assist the audience, and expression of "justified presentiments." He questioned whether these practices were inconsistent with Wagner's original premise regarding the capacity of instrumental music, but concluded that Wagner had considered it from an entirely significative point of view in a dramatic work for the stage (II/22 [Mar. 5, 1853], 173–74).

With respect to Wagner's music, Dwight's essays and reviews of this period make clear his palpable admiration for the way Wagner uses the "modern" orchestra in *Tannhäuser* and *Lohengrin*. Dwight bolstered his own evaluations in this area with criteria adapted from the writings of Wagner's advocates. Robert Franz's romantic descriptions praised the pure instrumental sonority achieved by Wagner through "unheard of combinations of sound" (II/22 [Mar. 5, 1853], 170). Dwight, who was also favorably impressed by the new sonority, recognized that there was a connection between Wagner's instrumentation and his harmony. Another factor stressed by Franz and acknowledged by Dwight was the integral unity of Wagner's musico-dramatic conceptions requiring that judgment be postponed until music and poetry could be heard together in a full performance. Liszt's detailed literary and musical discussion of *Tannhäuser*, which Dwight translated from a German volume of 1853 taken from the original French articles in the *Journal des débats* of 1849, provided Dwight with an attractive defense of the *Tannhäuser* Overture; in Liszt's view it was a complete and independent symphonic poem on the same subject as the opera—a symphonic poem written according to inherent musical logic and symmetry consistent with the "rules of classical form" yet richer than the "best models in this" (IV/9 [Dec. 3, 1853], 65).

In the translated program by Wagner to the *Tannhäuser* Overture (IV/3 [Oct. 22, 1853], 17) as in Liszt's essay, Dwight found confirmation for his moral interpretation of the overture's final section as one in which reason and the senses, the spiritual and the material, are reconciled through the power of redemption. For Liszt, the return of the radiant theme of the pilgrims emerging from the unrestrained delirium of the Venusberg, with its magical instrumentation and novel effects, signaled the victory of spirituality over the "allurements" of the "tempting illusions" that had preceded it (IV/8 [Nov. 26, 1853], 58). Dwight told his readers how important it was to recognize the connections between each concert excerpt and the drama from which it was taken. In his review of the important "Wagner Night" given by the Germanians as well as in the Liszt essay, he conscientiously annotated brief orchestral titles and carefully explained the dramatic position of orchestral pieces from *Tannhäuser* and *Lohengrin*. Although Dwight virtually dismissed the "noisy" *Rienzi* pieces as having an early style, he consistently and enthusiastically praised the *Tannhäuser* Overture as "so admirable a whole in itself, . . . strikingly imaginative and beautiful"; he also lauded the *Lohengrin* excerpts for their "unique and spiritual beauty" (IV/10 [Dec. 10, 1853], 78).

With his knowledge of Wagner's music limited to these few orchestral pieces, Dwight incorporated them within a longstanding classical instrumental tradition, of which they were modern manifestations. At this point in his life he was ready to accept new instrumental music that did not challenge his vision of contemporary music as a natural extension of the past: "Are not the warmest worshippers of Handel, Bach, Beethoven, just the very men who hail with most enthusiasm a Schumann and a Wagner" (IV/18 [Feb. 4, 1854], 141)? Thus it was that he endorsed a new subscription series proposed by the Germanians and arranged to fit a historical plan beginning with Haydn and ending with Wagner, the composers who were, in Dwight's view, "the first and the last word of all that can fairly be called great orchestral music" (IV/10 [Dec. 10, 1853], 77).

A year before the public exchange between Dwight and Perkins concerning Wagner, Perkins sent a report to *Dwight's Journal* that appeared under the heading "Our Leipsic Correspondence" (II/14 [Jan. 8, 1853], 110–11). Perkins had recently heard Gluck's *Alceste* in Berlin and Wagner's *Tannhäuser* in Dresden; they had made almost totally opposite impressions, which led Perkins to state that Wagner believed "himself to be the creator of what Gluck really did create, and of which his attempt is nothing but a most incomplete and pale copy—namely, Dramatic Recitative." Comparison of this extended letter with a diatribe by Chorley entitled "Schumann and Wagner," which appeared shortly thereafter (II/16 [Jan. 22, 1853], 121–22; taken from the London *Athenaeum*), reveals a close similarity in the anti-Wagner arguments. Dwight offers an editorial note stating that Chorley had recently spent time in Leipzig, and he prefaces the article with the observation that Chorley's opinions, "smacking of strong prejudice," represent only "*one* side" of a question then dividing the musical world abroad.

The controversial letter by Perkins and Dwight's reply, printed together under the title "Our Wagnerism" (IV/16 [Jan. 21, 1854], 125–26), set out their opinions against this background, following the appearance of the many articles on Wagner. The communication by Perkins, dated November 11, 1853, and bearing his full signature, referred to Dwight as a "lover of modern German music" in recognition of the number of substantial articles that had been appearing throughout the year. Perkins acknowledged at the outset that in concert the Overture to *Tannhäuser* was novel and brilliant, but he contended that Dwight would modify his views had he an opportunity to be in Germany to hear the new works and see the full productions.

As his aesthetic premise Perkins chose a conflict between truth and beauty, about which he agreed with Fétis. In their opinion beauty was the primary object of musical works and truth unattainable in an opera. Accepting without difficulty the operatic combination of music and poetic text, Perkins attacked Wagner for three main reasons: the "falsity" of Wagnerian recitative; the related "destruction" of melody, equated by Perkins with beauty but allegedly denied by Wagner for the sake of verisimilitude; and his own conceptual discomfort with a hybrid work of art which, to Perkins, constituted neither opera nor drama. Perkins inveighed against "the modern school of music," notably omitting Mendelssohn from a very diverse group that included Wagner, Liszt, Berlioz, Schumann, and Brahms. Perkins wrote that the modern school had gained the support of "the young musicians who are brought up to believe that their first compositions must be modelled upon the Ninth Symphony and that the First is a puerility." His own position emerged clearly in his defense of those who "still make German Art estimable," namely, the conservative professors at the Leipzig Conservatory (Moscheles, Hauptmann, Ernst Friedrich Richter) and the "best musical critics of France and England" (Fétis and Chorley).

Despite the educational background and the many cultural values held in common by the two Bostonians, Dwight's published reply expressed views diverging from those of Perkins. Dwight appears to have considered Perkins's letter a challenge to the integrity of his editorial practices. He recalled his devotion to printing fair and impartial accounts of the world's musical events, particularly when new and controversial matters were at issue, and he contended that the publication of descriptive essays by admirers or detractors of a composer did not imply his own agreement. Dwight cautioned that in Leipzig Perkins might be subject to the influence of "prejudice and party," whereas he himself could view the situation dispassionately from a distance.

Dwight further stated that he was neither for nor against Wagner and the German "New School." In this connection he affectionately described certain works by Schumann, thereby setting up a contrast to some less favorable opinions of Perkins. With respect to Wagner, Dwight reiterated his central objection to Wagner's aesthetic theory (as he then understood it) concerning the inseparability of music and poetry. As to Wagner's music, Dwight again expressed his unqualified admiration for the *Tannhäuser* Overture as the only complete piece by Wagner that he knew. The orchestral excerpts by Wagner that he had heard stimulated his interest in the other music, about which he said he was reserving judgment.

Having defended the high professional and ethical standards of *Dwight's Journal* as well as having stated his own critical preferences, Dwight reminded Perkins of their shared admiration for such major composers as Beethoven, their hero, and Mendelssohn. Asserting that the world should not condemn Wagner before giving his works a disinterested hearing, Dwight offered this most explicit summary of his views:

> Should we become enamored, therefore, of the new tone-prophets, it could not be by their converting us from our old lovers. So far as we find aught to advocate in Schumann or in Wagner, it is not *against,* but *with,* their noble predecessors. For catholic in Art we do wish and intend to be, and must accept that which affects us with a sense of the divine and beautiful, whether it be new or old. . . . (IV/16 [Jan. 21, 1854], 126)

To Perkins the threat posed by the "new school" to the cause of "true Music and high Art" was self-evident. To Dwight cultivated music was music in a broad European Classic-Romantic tradition. New and American works could be supported insofar as they evinced a continuity with that tradition. The means he recommended through which Americans might be made "a musical people" were musical education, frequent opportunities to hear the great masterpieces, and the encouragement of original composition (VI/22 [Mar. 3, 1855], 173–75).

Perkins's musical tendencies, his veneration of Mendelssohn, and his direct relations with the Leipzig Conservatory circle increased his susceptibility to anti-Wagner bias. These factors led Perkins, like Chorley, to condemn Wagner's use of the musical language. By contrast, Dwight acclaimed the orchestral Wagner and helped to introduce his music and ideas to Americans in the 1850s. Dwight's capacity to support Wagner in this period was limited less by specific musical objections than by a fundamental inability to accommodate Wagner's aesthetic ideas (or what he understood them to be)—in this he resembles Hanslick.[24] Dwight fully recognized Wagner's greatness, but he questioned the autonomy available to music when it was joined to a text. His Transcendental convictions regarding instrumental music as being the highest kind of spiritual expression came increasingly to dominate his absolutist aesthetic position.

The opposing views of Dwight and Perkins on Wagner show how philosophical, religious, social, aesthetic, and musical differences can reveal them-

---

24. See Lucy Beckett, "Wagner and His Critics," *The Wagner Companion,* ed. Peter Burbidge and Richard Sutton (New York, 1979), 376–79.

selves in the musical thinking even of those who represent generally similar backgrounds, attitudes, and values. Distinctions of this sort indicate how important it is to examine documents in relation to their surrounding intellectual context. *Dwight's Journal,* with its conflicting tendencies arising from Transcendentalism and from American Victorianism, is a case in point. The participation of various socio-economic groups in the developing cultivated tradition (Dwight's Mass Clubs and the Handel and Haydn Society are examples) suggests another avenue for inquiry. Just as diversity of approach was a considerable asset in the shaping of American society, so again it may be an important tool today in the evaluation of all the traditions that contribute to the history of music in America.

"ONE DOES NOT DEFEND THE SUN": SOME NOTES ON PÉLADAN AND WAGNER

ISABELLE CAZEAUX

IN THE DAYS OF *la belle époque* and the preceding generation, one could find two kinds of reasonably educated Frenchmen: those who treated Wagner like a quasi-deity, and those who deemed much of his work sacrilegious, nerve-racking, or ludicrous. Hardly anyone from this milieu could afford to profess utter indifference to Wagner or to pretend that he had not existed. And so, particularly after his death, Wagner became a significant force in French culture of the time.

It was probably not in French music, however, that his influence was most strongly felt. Wagner had relatively few emulators among French composers aside from César Franck, some of his direct disciples such as Vincent d'Indy, and, to a much lesser extent, Ernest Reyer and Alfred Bruneau. Some of Fauré's last works contain passages which modulate almost constantly, and Debussy's *Pelléas et Mélisande* shares certain superficial traits with *Tristan und Isolde*. Early in their careers Fauré and especially Debussy had recognized many admirable features in Wagner's music dramas, but their youthful enthusiasm eventually waned.[1] Unlike German composers, Gallic musicians were masters of the understatement, and in their music as a whole as well as in many of their critical writings they assumed a gentle but unequivocal stand against Wagner's heroic and grandiose concepts and his thick orchestration. A number of French music

---

1. Another composer who had little in common with Wagner but could be moved to tears by his music was Ravel. His friend Ricardo Viñes reports that on All Saints' Day, 1896, when the Prelude to *Tristan* was played at the Concerts Lamoureux, the supposedly cold and cynical Ravel trembled and sobbed. He explained unashamedly that he had the same reaction every time he heard the piece. (See Nina Gubitsch, "Le Journal inédit de Ricardo Viñes," *Revue internationale de musique française* 1 [1980]: 190–91.)

critics, whose delicate ears had been accustomed to music in the style of Auber and Ambroise Thomas, occasionally described less traditional works—Bizet's *Carmen,* for example—as "Wagnerian." Needless to say, the adjective was hardly regarded as flattering.[2]

Among French writers, Wagner's influence (or presence) was quite another matter, as Léon Guichard has pointed out in his masterly study of the subject. Théophile Gautier, his daughter Judith and her sometime husband, Catulle Mendès, as well as Baudelaire, Verlaine, Henry Céard, and Elémir Bourges were a few of Wagner's admirers. Léon Bloy and Gide considered Wagner's effect pernicious; Barrès and Claudel were at first fascinated and later repelled by his forceful music dramas.[3]

For Joséphin Péladan (1858–1918)—poet, playwright, novelist, theologian and occultist—Wagner could do no wrong and belonged in the same category as Leonardo da Vinci and Balzac, "the Wagner of the novel."[4] An ardent Catholic in spite of a distant Calvinist ancestry, Péladan pitied Protestants because they had no Blessed Mother in Heaven.[5] It was no doubt in a similar spirit that he took some water from the stream one day and ran after a little Jewish classmate in order to "christen" him.[6] Péladan's deep faith in Roman Catholicism did not prevent him from criticizing the actions of some churchmen past and present, and from drafting a sixty-page open petition to Pope Pius X, respectfully suggesting that he be more liberal in matters of divorce.[7] Neither did it stop him from practicing occultism, which he did not consider dichotomous with religion, or from becoming—along with Stanislas de Guaïta—a founder of the Ordre Kabbalistique de la Rose+Croix Orthodoxe in 1888.[8] Two years later, he seceded from the orthodox order and established another organization

2. See Danièle Pistone, "Wagner et Paris (1839–1900)," *Revue internationale de musique française* 1 (1980): 7–84.

3. Léon Guichard, *La Musique et les lettres en France au temps du Wagnérisme* (Paris, 1963).

4. "Balzac a été le Wagner du roman; il a tout épuisé. Après lui on redit, et mal" (*Pérégrine et Pérégrin,* quoted in Edouard Bertholet, *La Pensée et les secrets du Sâr Joséphin Péladan* [Lausanne and Paris, 1952–58], 4: 223 and 499).

5. "Ah! la Vierge, la Sainte Vierge, comme je la sens, et que je plains ces malheureux protestants qui n'ont pas de mère dans le ciel" (*La Terre du sphinx,* quoted in Bertholet, 2: 275).

6. Emile Dantinne, *L'Oeuvre et la pensée de Péladan* (Brussels, 1948), 15.

7. "Supplique à S. S. le Pape Pie X pour la réforme des canons en matière de divorce," *Mercure de France,* Jan., 1904 (Bertholet, 2: 102–18). It was Péladan's opinion that it would be to the Church's interest to raise the intellectual level of its sermons as well as its artistic standards. An awareness of Wagner and his works might be a first step in achieving this goal (*Réponse à Tolstoï* [Paris, 1898], 175).

8. "Pour Péladan, l'étude de l'occulte ne s'oppose nullement à la religion, comme le vulgaire se l'imagine trop souvent; bien au contraire, ce sont deux disciplines qui se complètent parfaitement. . . . Occultistes vrais et religieux sincères . . . recherchent, par des moyens différents, un même but: l'union avec le divin" (Bertholet, 1:17). Péladan's interest in magic was by no means an anomaly in his day. Several Parisian bookshops specialized in the subject. Gounod frequented the occultist Paul Lacuria (Bertholet, 1: 265), and Debussy wrote music for Jules Bois's esoteric play *Les Noces de Sathan* (Guichard, 308). Judith Gautier, who translated *Parsifal* into French, had studied occultism with the celebrated Eliphas Lévi. Her friend Péladan dedicated his *Théâtre complet de Wagner* to her, and she in turn nominated him for election to the Académie Goncourt, but without success. (See M. Dita Camacho, *Judith Gautier: sa vie et son oeuvre* [Paris, 1939], 185. See also Elaine Brody, "La Famille Mendès: A Literary Link between Wagner and Debussy," *The Music Review* 33

more to his Catholic taste: the Ordre de la Rose+Croix, du Temple, et du Graal. In fact, Péladan, perhaps more than anyone else in his time, was able to link occultism closely to literature and the arts and thus to make it an important part of a *Gesamtkunstwerk*. He attempted to promote lofty moral and aesthetic ideals, with tradition as a basis and beauty as a means; and he therefore organized, in the last decades of the nineteenth century, a series of Salons de la Rose+Croix at which exhibits were held. Rigid rules governed the choice of subjects acceptable for inclusion. Naturalistic, patriotic, and humorous themes were automatically rejected.[9] The Sâr (or master), as Péladan came to be called, obviously had little use for laughter in any context.[10] Refined women, in particular, should remember that "boisterous laughter is a sign of vulgarity and of lack of decorum, and that it is particularly distasteful to superior people; a smile is sufficient."[11] Péladan's attraction to Wagner's art, in which traces of humor are rare, is understandable in view of his serious attitude. Aside from that, the Sâr was harmless. Indeed, many of his notions—e.g., that art and education should not be debased for the pleasure of mediocrities—are by no means absurd. He took Tolstoy to task for asserting that art should be immediately understood by everyone. Péladan did not believe in art for art's sake, but in art for God's sake. Art should be neither realistic nor impressionistic. Rather than represent contemporary mores, one should depict the opposite of life and thus raise the spiritual and aesthetic level of the beholder. In his mind, "the work of art should be a corner of heaven descended to earth."[12]

[1972]: 177–89.) Péladan was grateful to Mme. Gautier for showing him her personal relics of Wagner: a lock of the composer's white hair, some dried bread he had once touched, and the letters in French he had written her (*Le Théâtre complet de Wagner* [Paris; 1894], vi).

9. Robert Pincus-Witten, *Occult Symbolism in France: Joséphin Péladan and the Salons de la Rose-Croix* (New York and London, 1976), 207–17.

10. In his novel *L'Androgyne* ([Paris, 1891], 153–54), Péladan says:

représenter les moeurs actuelles sera toujours malsain et d'un art bas; le théâtre comme la statuaire n'a d'autre destination que l'héroïque; à l'instant où un acteur a mis les mains dans les poches et parle comme à la rue, la canaille a envahi cet art, né comme tous, dans le sanctuaire. . . . Le rire est le propre du bourgeois et de l'enfant, c'est-à-dire d'une bête et d'un inconscient.

For obvious reasons, the Sâr loathed Zola and compared him unfavorably with Wagner in *La Guerre des idées* ([Paris 1916], 311): "Wagner nous a purifié du Réalisme. De Nana à Elizabeth, de l'Assommoir à Montsalvat, mesurez si vous pouvez, la distance." Guichard points out, however, that Zola's conception and use of myth and repetition may have brought him closer than Péladan to Wagner's genius (pp. 145–46).

11. "Elle se rappellera que le rire bruyant est un signe de vulgarité et de manque de tenue et qu'il déplait particulièrement aux gens supérieurs; le sourire suffit" (*Comment on devient fée,* quoted in Bertholet, 1: 107). That Péladan appeared ridiculous to some of his contemporaries because of his unusual garb—velvet doublet with lace jabot, suede shoes, medieval robe with Spanish cape—does not seem to have bothered him unduly. (See Guichard, 146.) As he stated in *Comment on devient artiste ou ariste,* "Pardonne ce qui t'est fait à toi-même en tant que personne; ne pardonne jamais ce qui t'est fait comme intellectuel" (Bertholet, 1: 185). Judging from his portraits, he wore these clothes with elegance. It is therefore difficult to understand why Parisians attached so much importance to his appearance, considering that they have traditionally been tolerant of sartorial eccentricities.

12. "L'oeuvre d'art doit être un coin du ciel descendu sur terre" (See *Origines et esthétique de la tragédie* [Paris, 1905]; see also Dantinne, 21; Bertholet, 3: 257, and 4: 14, 107, 396, and 493, in connection with Péladan's *Réponse à Tolstoï*).

Concurrently with his artistic salons, Péladan organized musical and literary soirées or Gestes de la Rose+Croix, where similar principles were observed. Noble masterpieces (by men only) were presented at these gatherings.[13] They included works by Palestrina, Bach, Tartini, Mozart, Beethoven, Franck and his students, and, of course, Wagner. The Sâr paid tribute to Wagner and Franck in lectures he gave after performances of their music. Several contemporary composers were represented, notably Erik Satie, Louis Benedictus, and Bihn Grallon. Satie wrote incidental music for Péladan's plays Le Fils des étoiles and Le Prince de Byzance, as well as three Sonneries for the order. He soon made a public disavowal of the Sâr's influence on his own aesthetics, however, and thus put a swift end to their collaboration.[14] Benedictus, companion of Judith Gautier, who was herself a Rosicrucian, wrote music for Péladan's unpublished play Le Mystère du Graal. He dutifully played an uncut piano transcription of Parsifal on the same program, during which the Sâr spoke on "The Myth of the Grail and Its Magical Significance." Selections from Benedictus's one-act opera about Beethoven, La Sonate du clair de lune, were performed at the first Soirée de la Rose+Croix.[15]

Péladan advised worthy initiates to spend their spare time (assuming they had any) in churches in the morning, in museums and libraries in the afternoon, and at the theater in the evening, especially whenever works by Corneille, Racine, Shakespeare, or Wagner were being presented.[16] A product of Jesuit education, Péladan wrote on subjects as varied as Joan of Arc, Rabelais, and Wagner. Any questions raised about the authenticity of the saint's visions he considered exceedingly insolent, and comparable to asking where Wagner had seen the miracle of the flowers on Good Friday. Genius, like sainthood, lay beyond our comprehension. Since a masterpiece was an artistic mystery, one should not try to understand or explain the reasons for its existence.[17] It was perhaps as much because of this conviction as because of his superficial musical knowledge that Péladan did not subject Wagner to minute musical dissection. He was more in his element when he discussed effects of music than music per

13. "Constitution de la Rose+Croix, du Temple et du Graal," art. XVII, quoted in Bertholet, 3: 171.

14. The Missa Papae Marcelli was performed with forty voices at the opening concert, according to René-Georges Aubrun (Péladan [Paris, 1904], 17; see also Bertholet, 3: 160, 171–72, and 175; Pincus-Witten, 207–17; Guichard, 143; Patrick Gowers, "Satie's Rose-Croix Music [1891–1895]," Royal Musical Association Proceedings 92 [1965–66]: 1–25; Rollo Myers, Erik Satie [New York, 1968], 23–25). Péladan's L'Androgyne contains a "stele" to César Franck, "the greatest master of French music since Berlioz."

15. Bertholet, 3: 160 and 172; Guichard, 143; Camacho, 155, 185, and 195. Mme. Gautier had the literary version of La Sonate du clair de lune published in 1894. Benedictus wrote incidental music for her play on a Japanese theme, La Marchande de sourires, and also collaborated with her on a study of Eastern music, Les Musiques bizarres à l'Exposition de 1900. He died in 1923 and was buried near the grave of his talented and delightful friend, who had been so faithful to Wagner's memory that she used to have her manservant announce dinner by playing the theme of the Ride of the Valkyries on his cornet. (See Camacho, 172 and 189.)

16. Bertholet, 1: 42.

17. Le Secret de Jeanne d'Arc, quoted in Bertholet, 2: 214–15.

se.[18] His definition of aesthetics was "a superior vibration"; to him music was essentially inspirational, a force to be felt rather than expounded in theoretical terms. So sure was he of the validity of his contention that he ascribed the same conviction to his idol:

> Wagner was hardly concerned with the endorsement of his colleagues and the approbation of competent people; he preferred the blanching or weeping of the guileless to the laudatory nod of the learned masters of counterpoint.[19]

The Sâr, with perhaps a touch of regret about the lacunae in his own formal training, asked whether the French universities realized that music was an integral part of education.[20] He advocated the study and comprehension of chamber music and drawing, but not by everyone, since "all vulgarization of art is a crime; one should be taught to be sensitive to the arts, not to ape them."[21] Spending the summer at Bayreuth and Munich might be a step in the right direction, he suggests. After all, one could not expect to derive much edification from the Paris Opéra, where an audience of imbeciles had failed to appreciate Wagner.

In order to further improve one's general culture, one ought to learn Latin, Greek, Hebrew, and Sanskrit, but not modern languages, for they take up time unnecessarily. One could always read foreign masterpieces in translation. Péla-

---

18. Much has been made of the Sâr's dilettantism in relation to music. As Ernest Lasserre pointed out in "Péladan et Wagner," *Nouvelle Revue du Midi*, special issue (1924), quoted in Bertholet, 4: 460–61:

> Péladan, poète et esthète, manque . . . de connaissances techniques. . . . On ne peut pas affirmer . . . que Péladan, un poète, sente profondément cette poésie de la musique wagnérienne.

Another contemporary, the composer-conductor Delbruyère, agrees with this assessment. (See Bertholet, 4: 462.)

> Péladan, malgré son ouvrage sur les opéras de Wagner, n'était à tout prendre qu'un amateur—passionné, il est vrai, mais qui subissait plutôt la musique qu'il n'en pénétrait le sens à la façon des professionnels. Il avouait pourtant que dans l'élaboration de son oeuvre littéraire, il lui arrivait de s'asseoir devant le piano et d'évoquer grâce aux sons de l'instrument, pendant que ses doigts malhabiles erraient sur le clavier, des phrases et des pensées qu'il n'aurait pas su trouver autrement.

Indeed, Péladan's *Théâtre complet de Wagner* is essentially a detailed scene-by-scene plot description, with a biographical introduction. The Sâr himself freely admitted his lack of formal musical knowledge: "Je ne fais de la musique qu'avec un doigt sur le clavier. . . . J'avoue mon incompétence musicale" (*La Guerre des idées*, 329). Still, he took musicologists to task for dwelling on this deficiency while ignoring the flawless taste he had manifested in the composition of his musical programmes (ibid.):

> Les musicographes prétendront que je n'entends rien à la musique, quoique j'aie donné quelques preuves de goût, en montant la messe du Pape Marcel, la première fois que j'ai composé un programme; en célébrant Franck avant le public; en donnant à Vittoria la palme de la polyphonie vocale.

19. "Wagner s'inquiétait peu du suffrage de ses confrères et des approbations compétentes; il préférait l'ingénu pâlissant ou pleurant, au hochement laudatif des doctes du contre-point. Etre senti, pour lui, c'était la bonne façon d'être compris" (*Introduction à l'esthétique*, quoted in Bertholet, 3: 279 and 284).

20. Ibid., quoted in Bertholet, 3: 279.

21. "Toute vulgarisation d'art est un crime; il faut enseigner à sentir les arts, non pas à les singer. . . . L'ariste conçoit l'art sacerdotalement et l'approche des chefs-d'oeuvre comme une dévotion de l'esprit" (*Comment on devient artiste ou ariste*, quoted in Bertholet, 1: 146 and 163; see also *L'Androgyne*, 23).

dan regretted that Wagner's music dramas were sung in "the horrible German language, this nightmare invented for the ear, this bear's growling, which spoils even Wagnerian opera."[22] Elsewhere he states that "the only German language worthy of study is instrumental polyphony, with its four grandiose stages: Handel, Haydn, Beethoven, Wagner."[23]

The Sâr believed that since "one remains faithful to the first poets one has read,"[24] it was important to be exposed at an early age to the best in literature and the arts. In a lecture on German art, he stated:

> Art has no fatherland; it is itself the ideal fatherland of the human elite. . . . *Tannhäuser* and *Lohengrin* . . . are masterpieces, gifts of God to the whole world. Indeed, anyone who does not admire Wagner is not civilized.[25]

In a similarly enthusiastic vein the Sâr wrote that "the gods have no fatherland on this earth and Wagner is a god."[26]

Hand in hand with Péladan's internationalism went his aversion to colonialism, militarism, and any simplistic music associated with it. He abhorred the *Marseillaise,* "this bellow [that] signifies the reign of the rabble."[27] And he once addressed an open letter to the archbishop of Paris complaining that a diocesan priest had allowed the *Marseillaise* to be played in his church during Mass.[28] At the same time, he did not consider it incongruous to have excerpts from Wagnerian stage works performed in church. Anticipating that a French triumph would end the First World War, he expressed the pious wish that "on the day of victory, under the vaults of Notre-Dame, it be granted to us to hear the fulgurating trumpets of *Lohengrin.*"[29] As for *Parsifal,* he held it to be the equivalent of a Mass because the Eucharist is represented on the stage.[30]

---

22. "L'horrible langue allemande, ce cauchemar inventé pour l'oreille, ce grognement d'ours qui gâte jusqu'à l'opéra wagnérien" (*La Victoire du mari,* quoted in Bertholet, 4: 81). This comparison of German to the sound of an animal is somewhat reminiscent of Rousseau's equation of sung French with barking, because of the peculiarities of the language. Péladan at least had the excuse that he did not know German, which is more than Rousseau could claim about French, his native tongue.

23. *La Guerre des idées,* 304.

24. "On demeure l'homme des premiers poètes qu'on a lus" (*Réponse à Tolstoï,* 106).

25. "L'art n'a pas de patrie; il est lui-même patrie idéale de l'élite humaine. . . . *Tannhäuser* et *Lohengrin* . . . furent des chefs-d'oeuvre, ces dons de Dieu à toute la terre. Oui, l'homme qui n'admire pas Wagner n'est pas un civilisé" (Bertholet, 4: 336; see also *La Guerre des idées,* 75–76).

26. "Les dieux n'ont pas de patrie sur la terre et Wagner est un dieu" (*La Guerre des idées,* 311).

27. "Cette gueulerie signifie la canaille devenue reine" (*Réponse à Tolstoï,* 229).

28. Bertholet, 4: 123. Rossini's *Stabat Mater* he found equally unsuitable (*L'Art idéaliste et mystique,* 2nd ed. [Paris, 1909], 218).

29. "Au jour de la victoire, sous les voûtes de Notre-Dame, qu'il nous soit donné d'entendre les fulgurantes trompettes de *Lohengrin*" (*La Guerre des idées,* 311).

30. Ibid. It was precisely for that reason that Léon Bloy considered Wagner to have made a sacrilegious abuse of liturgy. (See Guichard, 103–32.)

> L'énorme abus des formes liturgiques est de faire manger le Corps . . . et faire boire le Sang de Jésus, sur une scène de théâtre, aux chevaliers du Graal, lesquels sont nécessairement des cabotins.

In *La Vertu suprême* (Bertholet, 4: 186–88), Péladan décrit the inauguration of a Rosicrucian chapel dur-

Péladan expressed admiration for some purely instrumental music, provided that it was not too literally descriptive. Beethoven's late quartets and the prelude to *Tristan* were among his favorites. Yet he believed that music with words was a higher form of art. It had been suggested that he believed this because he knew more about literature than he did about music.[31] Or perhaps the Sâr, a Frenchman to his fingertips, was simply echoing Fontenelle's remark, which was to represent the majority opinion in France for some two hundred years: "Sonate, que me veux-tu?" When Péladan touched the sword of Geoffroy de Bouillon in Bethlehem, the first music that came to his mind was, naturally enough, the sword motif.[32] And yet he often betrayed a predilection for choral music. He intended to form a singing society for the purpose of reviving forgotten "vocal sublimities," including works by Victoria, Comes, Guerrero, and Morales, "which are more lofty than Bach's cantatas."[33] On another occasion, he imagined comments that a Greek-style chorus might have sung, had Wagner chosen to introduce one in *Tristan*.[34]

Péladan fought for the memory of his favorite composers. He reproved Tolstoy for not appreciating Beethoven's late works or those of Wagner, and did not hesitate to call the Russian a barbarian.[35] Max Nordau claimed that "music is the least intellectual of the arts," that Wagner, who wrote leitmotifs because he was incapable of inventing "real" melodies, was a degenerate, and that Péladan the mystic was another. The Sâr paid little attention to the personal attack, but he firmly refuted Nordau's position on Wagner.[36]

Péladan was convinced that music could elevate the soul and lead to devotion. As he said, "To admire is to pray."[37] He found analogies between music

---

ing which excerpts from *Parsifal* were played on the organ. At one point in the ceremony, Communion was taken to the sound of the Good Friday Spell.

31. Bertholet, 4: 461. And yet, the Sâr had kind words for some instrumental works: "Ces murmures de la forêt qui éveillent l'âme de Siegfried sont les voix cosmiques enseignant à l'homme le prodigieux mystère de sa conscience" (*L'Art idéaliste et mystique*, 40).

32. *La Terre du Christ* (see Bertholet, 2: 277). In another context, Izel—the heroine of *La Victoire du mari*—takes herself for Sieglinde and spontaneously sings the sword motif when she first meets her future husband.

33. *L'Allemagne devant l'humanité* (Paris, 1916), 197.

34. *Origines et esthétique de la tragédie*, 77–78.

35. *Réponse à Tolstoï*, 75 and 254.

36. *Comment on devient artiste ou ariste*, quoted in Bertholet, 1: 167–69. See also Thomas C. Day, "The Downfall of Western Music, As Described by Nordau, Spengler and Toynbee," *The Music Review* 37 (1976): 53–58.

37. *Comment on devient artiste ou ariste*, quoted in Bertholet, 1: 179. Similar comments are found in other of Péladan's works. For instance, in *L'Art idéaliste et mystique* (pp. 329–30) one reads: "L'humanité . . . ira toujours à la messe, quand le prêtre sera Bach, Beethoven, Palestrina." His *Réponse à Tolstoï* has the following statements (pp. 66, 130, and 260):

La fugue de Bach ou le motet de Palestrina éveille en moi la plus vive dévotion. . . . Je connais des convertis de *Parsifal* [qui] eussent résisté . . . aux catéchistes. . . . La beauté est reconnue par l'élévation qu'elle procure au spectateur. *Parsifal* est pout moi *l'oeuvre* parce que nulle autre ne m'a élevé si haut.

Péladan could not help but associate *Parsifal* with the exaltation experienced by a character after his first Communion in the novel *L'Androgyne* (p. 109):

L'hostie lui parut si lumineuse . . . qu'il ferma les yeux, physiquement ébloui. . . . Il aurait fait la question de Parsifal à Gurnemanz: "Pourquoi la nature me semble-t-elle transfigurée et telle que je ne l'avais jamais sentie? . . . La communion avec le Créateur l'avait rendu communiant avec la création."

and love, and asserted that Greek modes could express various emotions. One poem of his compares a woman to a lyre; another to an amorous symphony.[38] Péladan classified people according to planetary types; he found that the benefic Venus-Moon woman was very musical, sang well, and liked the music of Schumann and Schubert.[39] Music had its place in the Rosicrucian initiates' procreation rite, which required twenty-one days of spiritual preparation and artistic contemplation. It was recommended that works by Bach should be heard during the second week. By the fifteenth day less serene compositions by Beethoven might be substituted.[40] Perhaps because of an oversight, Wagner's music does not appear on the list.

Several characters in Péladan's novels are musicians or music lovers. In order to make ends meet, an unfortunate composer in *Le Panthée* is reduced to playing the piano at a fashionable seaside resort. There he treats the vacationers to his renditions of the Prelude to *Tristan* and Siegfried's Funeral Music, so as to raise their cultural standards. Predictably, his honorable endeavors meet with resistance. The immediate effects of the music include arguments between two guests, the shattering of a plate, and the shooting of a revolver in the direction of a rose.[41] Simone, the heroine in *Les Amants de Pise,* compares herself to the Flying Dutchman in her quest for absolute fidelity. The couple in *La Victoire du mari* almost have their marriage destroyed as a result of the husband's audition of the ethereal *Parsifal* and his subsequent reaction against the more passionate *Tristan und Isolde,* a work with which his wife so readily identifies.[42]

A number of writers are said to have used the leitmotif technique whenever a recurring phrase or idea is found in the course of their works. Whether they were inspired by Wagner or by earlier composers, or whether it was the composers who derived their reappearing themes from literary devices is uncertain. At any rate, the procedure appears in Péladan's novel *Coeur en peine,* as well as in his dramas *Sémiramis, Babylon* ("tragédie wagnérienne"), *Le Prince de Byzance* ("drame wagnérien"), and *Le Fils des étoiles* ("pastorale, or wagnérie kaldéenne"). And, unlike some authors who may have used the leitmotif technique without realizing it, the Sâr knew perfectly well what he was doing, for he openly declared himself a follower of Wagner, and he consciously tried to incorporate the German master's musical style in his own literary writings. The term *wagnérie,* therefore, represented an acknowledgment of vassalage and discipleship.

---

38. *Le Livre secret* (Paris, 1920), 33, 93, and 127. Péladan's modes include the Ionian, which expresses grace and wit, as well as the Lesbian, which symbolizes magnificence. Consequently, he labels Mozart's works as Ionian and Handel's as Lesbian (*L'Art idéaliste et mystique,* 153–55). The novel *Coeur en peine* contains chapters with musical titles, such as *Larghetto, Andantino, Motif du Graal,* and *Wagnérisme.* (See Bertholet, 4: 91–93; Guichard, 135.) Péladan's love poem *Symphonie,* with its musical vocabulary, is slightly reminiscent of Théophile Gautier's *Symphonie en blanc majeur,* written to honor a fair-skinned beauty. A dialogue in *Le Panthée* is entitled *Nocturne à deux voix.* (See Bertholet, 4: 117.)

39. *L'Art de choisir sa femme d'après la physiognomie,* quoted in Bertholet, 2: 332.

40. *Le Livre du Sceptre,* quoted in Bertholet, 1: 203.

41. Bertholet, 4: 18, 116–20, and 240.

42. Ibid., 4: 298; Guichard, 136–40.

Hail and glory to thee, Richard Wagner, thaumaturge and discoverer of the third world, conqueror and emperor of western theater![43]

So said Péladan on his return from a pilgrimage to Bayreuth: "Thou art my master and my author."[44]

According to Judith Gautier, Wagner was so far superior to the rest of mankind that human laws could not very well be applied to him.[45] The Sâr surely echoed her sentiments when, in his defense of Wagner against Nordau, he stated that "one does not defend the sun, accused of obscurity, or the sea, characterized as petty."[46]

43. *Le Théâtre complet de Wagner*, xii–xiii. See also Guichard, 136, 144–45, and 239; Bertholet, 3: 391 and 4: 461–62.

44. "Salut et gloire à toi, Richard Wagner, thaumaturge et découvreur du troisième monde, conquérant et empereur du théâtre occidental! Tu es, avec Balzac et d'Aurevilly, selon la parole de Dante à Virgile, mon maître et mon auteur" (*La Victoire du mari,* quoted in Bertholet, 4: 79).

45. *Le Troisième Rang du collier* (Paris, 1909), 151–52. Thus did the lady speak to Liszt about the man who was to become his son-in-law: "Quand il s'agit d'un être tellement au dessus de l'humanité que Richard Wagner, les préjugés et même les lois des hommes n'ont pas de valeur."

46. "On ne défend pas le soleil, accusé d'obscurité, ni la mer, qualifiée de mesquine" (*Comment on devient artiste ou ariste,* quoted in Bertholet, 4: 169). And because of Wagner's influence, Péladan believed that "le XIXe siècle s'appellera le siècle de Wagner" (*L'Art idéaliste et mystique,* 215).

THE FORMATION OF
WAGNER'S STYLE

EDWARD A. LIPPMAN

Personal individuality of style in Western music seems to have run its course from Josquin to Stravinsky, and to have achieved its most striking expression during the nineteenth century, when music was released more and more from the constraint of public styles grounded in social function. Ideas of progress, evolution, and original genius, which had come to occupy a dominant position in thought and culture in general, were accordingly able to exert their full influence on artistic creativity.

The church and the aristocracy, which had provided traditional stylistic definition, were no longer vital forces, and the middle classes, while furnishing a new market for routine and facilely attractive music, were also ideologically committed to personal liberty and individuality—beliefs that combined readily, as it turned out, with the most various political programs.

In Wagner's case, the dynamic potential of this state of affairs was realized with remarkable success, since Wagner combined creative genius with extraordinary executive ability and ruthless political opportunism. The works he composed as a student and fledgling in music testify more to his effectiveness and his will to succeed than to his originality. Unlike Schumann, whose individuality of style was manifest quite early in his career, Wagner continued to reveal his dependence upon imitation and models for a considerable time. But while Schumann's innovative brilliance was gradually succeeded by styles closer to convention, Wagner's individuality began to bring forth an apparently endless series of radical innovations with a creative power that has rarely been equaled. Indeed the stylistic individuality of each succeeding work is so pronounced that it obscures the personal features of style common to all of them, just as in a

larger framework the personal styles of the individual composers of the nineteenth century obscure the epochal features common to them all.

Except for the *Seven Compositions for Goethe's "Faust"* (1831) and the operatic fragment *Die Hochzeit* (1832), Wagner's early works, dating from 1830
to 1832, are almost all piano sonatas, overtures, and symphonies. They quickly
graduate from the status of student exercises, and achieve both performance and
publication. Since Wagner set out to combine the arts of Shakespeare and Beethoven, it is not surprising to find that the most important model for his early
music is Beethoven, who is imitated in the thematic invention, the motivic
workmanship, the more general structural layout, and the emotional content.
There are other influences, to be sure; we can hear the buoyancy of Rossini or
Schubert in the Sonata in B♭ major, Opus 1 (in the second theme of the first
movement), and Wagner said that the Symphony in C major (1832) sought to
fuse the styles of Beethoven and Mozart. But the voice of Beethoven is generally
uncontested by any other, particularly in the large Fantasia in F♯ minor, Opus
3, and in the concert overtures. The theme of the *König Enzio* Overture bears an
unmistakable resemblance to that of the *Leonore* overtures, a resemblance that
may have a particular explanation in the drama for which it was composed, for
the action involves the underground imprisonment of the hero, who is joined in
his fate by his beloved. We can also observe the influence, both in *Die Hochzeit*
and in the overtures, of Beethoven's powerful concluding sections of jubilation
and triumph. And in the last section of the fantasia, earlier themes are summa-
rily dismissed, one after another, by indignant recitative passages—a scheme
that was certainly suggested by the last movement of Beethoven's Ninth Symphony.

In the C-major Symphony, Wagner employs a rising major third (C–E)
without accompaniment at the opening of the slow movement, just as Beethoven had done in the "Hammerklavier" Sonata. The tonality of the movement
(A minor) is thus initially indecisive, the relative major is suggested (particularly
in the symphony, for this is the key of the preceding movement), and there is an
effect of anticipation or questioning. Beethoven prefixed the motif to the slow
movement as an afterthought. In its brevity, its indefinite quality, and its rising
inflection, it does not simply provide an introduction to the theme and the
movement, but becomes an entranceway into an expressive world and also sets
this world off, removes it to a distance. To Wagner this motif had a mystical
quality. It recurs in the movement as a kind of motto, its questioning unsatis-
fied. The Beethovenian background of the motif is reinforced by the passage
that follows it, which is reminiscent of the Allegretto—again the slow movement—of Beethoven's Seventh Symphony, a movement that must have fascinated composers of the Romantic period, opening as it does with a suspended
minor chord that unveils a distant realm. Here we come upon an evocative
"mute" accompaniment to which only subsequently a haunting melody is
added. The slow movement of Wagner's symphony clearly compounds elements
that had a certain modern appeal at the time. It does not yet transform these ele-

ments appreciably, but it does select them from a particular point of view; it regards them in a new way. The materials are essentially unchanged; they are transformed only in the act of perception and use.

Wagner's symphonic works of 1830–32, which lack individuality and are hardly more than competent, are distinguished structurally by a consistent use of motivic manipulation. This is the central feature, as we might expect, of a Beethovenian and generally Classic style. But the motivic technique is in no way individualized, nor has it been made part of the newer stylistic trends of 1830.

In addition to motivic technique but also incorporating it, another Beethovenian characteristic of great importance in the formation of Wagner's style is the crescendo, especially in the large sequential form that distinguishes Beethoven's development sections. The prominence of the crescendo in the early symphonic works increases in the later overtures of the thirties, developing into an intrinsic and decisive constituent of Wagner's later style. We find particularly in the overtures what may be called an obsession with the crescendo—a circumstance of particular interest when we recall that the crescendo was an original and essential factor of the Classical symphonic style as well as a characteristic device of the opera buffa overture, in which it enjoyed a vogue in Rossini's hands that even exceeded its enthusiastic reception as part of the Mannheim style. The Beethoven crescendo presents dramatic and portentous power; that of Rossini a fever pitch of excitement. Wagner adopts both (there is an example in the *Liebesverbot* Overture of the Rossini style), but that of Beethoven becomes crucial to Wagner's style and to its large mural effect. The overtures, most notably the *Columbus* Overture, reveal this feature in the process of adoption and transformation; it becomes the substance of the music and takes over much of the duration of the work. The crescendos in the later national overtures, on the other hand *(Polonia* and *Rule, Brittania),* are frankly there for audience impact only. But it is Beethoven, in any event, who is the major musical source of Wagner's large style and overwhelming power. The two men are connected by a common rebelliousness of spirit, which in Wagner continually threatens to become fanaticism.

In the operas of the 1830s—*Die Feen, Das Liebesverbot,* and *Rienzi*— Wagner continues to be dependent on outside styles and techniques, many of them now fashionable ones, in subservience to particular changing goals of success. The operas contain a highly diversified succession of selected stylistic features and devices, all directed to the end of dramatic effect; Wagner's mastery of operatic technique can rarely be called into question. But what characterizes these works above all else is the impressionability of their composer. The songs Wagner wrote in these years tell the same story. In all the works of the 1830s, to be sure, there are isolated passages that can be found relatively unchanged in Wagner's mature works, but they do not alter the derivative character that prevails; unsupported by their context, they do not become effective constituents of style. Wagner remains strangely slow to develop his individuality, in part perhaps because of the range of his musical sensitivity, but also because of the complexity of the stylistic world surrounding him as well as the intrinsic complexity of opera in particular (in Germany, it was still a descendant of the "mixed style"). On the other hand, his many journeyman years as a dramatic conductor obviously provided the best possible foundation for his type of synthetic mentality and for his career as a whole.

In *Die Feen* (1833–34), Wagner looks to German Romantic opera as a guide to subject matter, form, and style. The sustained triads of the opening, which provide an entrance into the supernatural realm, remind us at once of the opening of the *Midsummer Night's Dream* Overture. The melodies at times have a chordal construction, with an enthusiasm that derives unmistakably from Weber; or again they become affective and chromatic, in the fashion of Spohr. There is a ballade also, which in spite of its unusual satiric character, displays all the conventional features of the genre, including a foreboding trill and a shift to the major mode. Even in the colorful sequence of events, the inclusion of comic scenes, and the role of magic in the action, Wagner created a characteristic Romantic opera, one that was typically inattentive to the unity of the action and to the logic of the succession of events.

With the unexpected progression of the opening triads (which constitute one of the recurrent motifs of the opera), and with other such fundamental motifs of Wagner, we reach a type of stylistic feature in which it is often not possible to distinguish imitation or borrowing from the characteristics of the style of the period. To be sure, the features of public style must come from somewhere; there can be little question that they originate in the invention of individual composers. But this invention may in fact be a series of inventions, each in itself inconspicuous and unimportant, but all contributing to a significant stylistic innovation that will thus be a joint and impersonal accomplishment. Furthermore, anonymity will have a counterpart in the dissemination of such a characteristic. A composer may not know how he comes by it, whether he has adopted it from the public domain or from a particular use in the work of a particular composer; and—still more important—it will not really matter which path he followed. The triadic succession in question was a natural part of a generally increasing interest in nonfunctional chordal connections, and consequently ubiquitous—even spontaneously arising in different places or through different and simultaneous chains of influence. Among such public features of style, some centuries old but now securing a new currency, are the undulating patterns that refer to water or waves, or those connected with the rustling of leaves, or those inevitable cadential patterns (either designating the cadence or revealing its immanence), hardly programmatic at all, which seem always to be more definitely formulated than others. It is at the cadence that the expressive accented appoggiaturas of Romanticism are usually encountered, although they are also, like the expressive turn, more widely distributed.

It is characteristic of Wagner in all his works that he is extraordinarily sensitive to the existence and to the incipient formulation, however vague and ill defined, of such public motifs; that he displays them and insists on them relentlessly; and that he succeeds in giving them a definitive form—really, *the* definitive form. This is the more general aspect of the formation of his personal style, as contrasted with the specific borrowings, whether literal or transformed. What we are gradually coming to see, however—although it is clearly a logical requirement of any intelligible style and thus does not need any empirical demonstration—is that the variegated and individual styles of nineteenth-century composers, while they indeed obscure public features of style, can not replace these entirely.

Wagner's power in the formulation of public motifs can be seen readily in the case of a chromatic cadential pattern that occurs in the music of many composers during the first half of the nineteenth century, typically in a form such as we find in the last movement of Wagner's Piano Sonata in A major:

EXAMPLE 1. Wagner, Piano Sonata in A major, mm. 70–71

There is a prominent example in Marschner's *Vampyr* (in the terzett "Wie, mein Vater," Act I, No. 8), which may well have been a particular influence on Wagner:

EXAMPLE 2. Marschner, *Vampyr:* Terzett, mm. 35–37

In any event, the same extension of the initial tone of the cadence reappears in the Overture to *Rienzi,* where the cadence is used in conjunction with a number of related patterns (known particularly through their use in Beethoven), from which it seems to extricate itself finally as a climactic conclusion. And one finds another example in the terzett at the end of Act II of *Der fliegende Holländer.*

EXAMPLE 3

Rienzi, Overture, mm. 185–87   *Holländer,* Act II; Terzett, mm. 35–36

There is something of a festive and courtly character in this chromatic cadence, a quality that Wagner discerns and develops, and which he finally displays brilliantly on trombones in the Introduction to Act III of *Lohengrin:*

EXAMPLE 4. *Lohengrin,* Prelude to Act III, mm. 45–49

This form of the cadence had appeared a number of times many years earlier, in the last act of *Die Feen,* but without a clearly defined significance. Its use in *Lohengrin* represents a fulfillment. Wagner has taken a pattern relatively undefined in a "programmatic" sense, grasped its potential for expression, so shaped it and so deployed it in an appropriate context that it sums up the entire history of its own use. As a consequence, every earlier instance of the pattern tends to be heard in terms of Wagner's final conception, taking on something of its specific character and appearing as an incompletely realized and not fully formulated predecessor.

Das Liebesverbot (1835–36) derives much of its astonishing variety of style from opéra comique and opera buffa, but adds to such elements, as Mozart had done, serious features both of style and of action. The combination, of course, is a characteristic feature of Shakespeare's *Measure for Measure,* which is the souce of the plot. Indeed the serious side of the opera is by far the predominant one. *Fidelio* is its stylistic model. The heroism and idealism of Isabella are quite like those of Beethoven's heroine, while the perfidy of Ferdinand in the central intrigue is the counterpart of Pizarro's villainy. The general effect of the opera, however, is one of a colorful juxtaposition of styles, the sources of which range from *Fidelio* to the buffa ensemble, and include the Rossinian crescendo mentioned above as well as that sustained triadic progression by thirds which plays such a prominent role in the nineteenth century (and in *Tannhäuser, Lohengrin,* and *Parsifal*) as a symbol of religiosity. The overture is strikingly similar to the Overture of Hérold's *Zampa,* which also vividly projects the diametrical opposites of frivolity and severity that constitute the core of the action—and the central musical contrast—of *Das Liebesverbot.* The scene in which Isabella pleads for her brother's life is cast in a mold of Beethovenian nobility of feeling; the burning passion of the melody that conveys Ferdinand's lust produces a tour de force in the use of melodic turns and appoggiaturas, the symbols then current for intensity of feeling.

Rienzi (1838–40) is influenced mostly by Spontini and Meyerbeer. It makes consummate use of the outstanding features of French grand opera. There are incisive dotted rhythms, massive choruses, and a large display of forces. The libretto again features the selfless fidelity of sister to brother, here to the total exclusion of amorous relationships. Of the first three operas, *Rienzi* stands nearest to Wagner's personal nature, dealing as it does with political forces and with an impressive male figure moved by idealism. But it is a Wagner conquering Paris and in a sense Rome also; German national sentiment is sacrificed to foreign success and foreign style. In the 1840s there was to be a return to German models, which increasingly control and subordinate the French elements that remain.

In *Dors, mon enfant,* one of the songs Wagner wrote in Paris in 1839–40, conspicuous use is made of an upper grace-note ornament of a semitone or a whole tone:

EXAMPLE 5. Wagner, *Dors, mon enfant*

Dors __ en-tre mes bras, en fant plein de char-mes! Tu __ ne con-nais pas les sou-cis, les lar-mes;

Since Wagner wrote his French songs at least partly to make himself known in Paris by having a French singer present his music, he was doubtless making use of a vocal embellishment that was fashionable as well as effective. The embellishment enters *Der fliegende Holländer* (1841) by way of the spinning song, which was one of the first sections of the opera to be composed, but in various forms it penetrates this most German of operas. At the same time, the melody of the spinning song bears a certain resemblance to that of *Dors, mon enfant* in a more general way. Whatever other factors may underlie the connection of rocking a cradle and spinning, cyclical repetition is clearly a basic factor in their resemblance. Also relevant to the influence of French style on the opera is the existence of a later autograph version of Senta's ballade in French (to say nothing of a German version, *Schlaf', mein Kind,* of the cradle song).[1] But if the grace-note device is originally French, it is used in a most characteristically German fashion, as a ubiquitous unifying motif that appears throughout the opera in the most astonishingly varied forms and contexts.

The semitone and the whole-tone version each has its own significance, both in general and in the opera; their connection with minor and major respectively is obviously fundamental. The alternation of major and minor in itself has played a prominent part in music; the most well known example in Wagner's time was probably that of Schubert. But another Germanic model for the alternation can be found in Beethoven's Ninth Symphony, a much more influential stylistic source for Wagner, than was Schubert.

1. The French manuscript of the ballade (New York Public Library) was called to my attention some time ago by Richard Koprowski. The German version of the cradle song can be found in *Richard Wagners Werke,* ed. Michael Balling (Leipzig, 1912–c. 1929), vol. 15, *Lieder und Gesänge.*

EXAMPLE 6. Beethoven, Symphony No. 9: first movement, mm. 120–23

Here the lowered and natural forms of the sixth degree, which become the two versions of Wagner's embellishment, are strongly emphasized factors in the alternation, although it is hardly likely that this passage had any direct influence either on *Dors, mon enfant* or on the embellishments of *Der fliegende Holländer*. There is, nevertheless, in the spinning song espcially, a conscious use of the relationship between the ornamentation and the appoggiatura; Wagner so connects the two intrinsically that they come to comprise jointly a fundamental feature of Romantic melody, persisting in particular through all the changes in his own melodic style.

There are other ways in which the Ninth Symphony seems to have influenced *Holländer*. Indeed the relationship between the two can be taken as a touchstone of Wagner's stylistic maturity, for it involves a typically Romantic transformation of material rather than the more or less literal reproduction that characterizes his earlier works. The mysterious sustained fifths of the opening of the symphony become fortissimo in the opening of *Holländer;* the quiet descending fifths of the violins become the fortissimo ascending fifths of the horns; and Beethoven's crashing and forbidding theme itself is transformed into the opening motif of Senta's ballade. Quiet mystery and cosmic cataclysm become demonic presence and its fearful legend.[2]

Behind this Romantic use of given material there exists a whole frame of mind concerning the musical past; rather than being objectivized and retained, history is creatively transformed by the new perspective of the composer and put to use as an integral part of a novel stylistic complex. Very much of a piece with this use of the Ninth Symphony is Schumann's "poetic" view and transformation of Bach's polyphony and Bach's motifs. And Beethoven's feeling that it would no longer do simply to write a fugue, but rather that one must make a poetic use of the fugue, indicates the same attitude.

In the case of Wagner's *Holländer,* there is in the background not only Beethoven's Ninth Symphony but also the vivid and fantastic imagination of a child acutely sensitive by nature to tonal impressions. Wagner recounts a childhood experience in his autobiography:

---

2. It is also possible that the "redemption" section of the ballade melody derives from the slow movement of the Ninth Symphony, in which case Wagner would have converted the contrast between two movements of a symphony into a contrast between the two themes of a single "programmatic" movement (the ballade strophe or the *Holländer* Overture). A dramatic juxtaposition of this kind, of course, was not possible within one movement of a Classical symphony, for in Classical style, even thematic contrast was controlled by a governing principle of coherence.

Even the tuning up of the instruments set me into a mystical excitement; I remember specifically that the bowing of the fifths on the violin seemed to me like a greeting from the world of spirits—which I must mention in passing had a completely literal sense in my case. Even when I was a little child, the sound of fifths coincided exactly with the ghostlike, which had always excited me. I remember still in later times never walking past the little palace of Prince Anton at the end of the Ostallee in Dresden without terror; for in this neighborhood I had once and then repeatedly heard the tuning of a violin close at hand, that seemd to me to come from the stone figures with which this palace is fitted out. As I now also saw the well known picture in which a skeleton plays the violin to a dying man, the ghostlike quality of precisely these sounds impressed itself with particular force of my childhood phantasy.[3]

Thus the Ninth Symphony and even the tuning of an orchestra had already become fraught with the supernatural well before the creation of *Holländer*. The central place of the Ninth Symphony in the formation of Wagner's style is also heralded by his youthful piano arrangement of the score (1830). Ten years later, a performance of the symphony conducted by Habeneck in Paris made a powerful impression on him; it seemed to focus all the varied ideas and feelings that impinged upon him during his visit. At the furthest remove from his native environment, Wagner experienced a momentous change in orientation. The restless journeyman's period had finally culminated in the act of carrying a French grand opera to Paris in search of success at all costs. But the bitter disappointment of the pilgrimage, the poverty and distress, the crisis of imprisonment for debt—all these factors conspired to pave the way for an oppositely directed course back to Germanic material, Germanic style, and to Germany itself. Wagner's despair found expression in a number of vivid and autobiographical stories, and it also released his independence and originality of style, grounded now in the radical transformation of given material. The composition of the *Faust* Overture and *Holländer* signals a new creative intensity, rooted in Wagner's innermost nature; he began to consider subsequently a number of dramatic projects based on German history and legend—namely, *Die Sarazenin, Tannhäuser, Lohengrin,* and *Die Bergwerke zu Falun.*

The figure of Faust was an eminently appropriate part of this complex of associations. The *Faust* Overture, the only remaining movement of a projected *Faust* Symphony, shares the satanic mood and the key and the intensity of *Holländer;* it is no longer the routine prolongation of the Classical symphonic tradition, but the expression of a thoroughly modern transformation of the symphony as it is found at about the same time in Mendelssohn and Schumann. Indeed, Wagner produced in his *Faust* a work that is fully entitled to a status

3. *Mein Leben* (Munich, 1976), 36.

equivalent to that of Schumann's powerful *Manfred* and *Genoveva* overtures, and he did so some years earlier.

There remain, nevertheless, many traces of French style in *Tannhäuser,* in particular the jaunty processionals, the large mass scene of the second-act finale, and the saccharine "Song to the Evening Star." The stylistic diversity is further increased by the adoption of a popular Männerchor flavor in the hymns, which is evident at the very opening of the overture. Yet a comparison with *Rienzi* shows how far Wagner had removed himself from the world of grand opera. The influx of German feeling and German elements of style that was initiated in Paris is carried out in the 1840s by a progressive elimination of foreign influence. Wagner abandons the path of Gluck, Mayr, and Meyerbeer, which had its point of departure in the mixed style of the eighteenth century, for this route would no longer suffice. The creation of a truly national opera demanded a different and more distinctively German basis. Foreign models, however, are succeeded by German ones. And it is doubtless this general change in the mode of formulation of Wagner's style that produces the new stylistic homogeneity of *Lohengrin.* But just as *Holländer* was based to some extent on Marschner's *Vampyr, Lohengrin,* that masterwork of breathtaking perfection and stylistic consistency, is derived to a certain extent from Weber's *Euryanthe;* the dramatic structure is quite similar, and so is the buoyant, courtly air that is typically captured in dotted rhythm. Some influence seems to have been exerted by Auber's *Muette de Portici* as well, with respect to the formal layout of Elsa's bridal procession.[4] Indeed multiple influence must be kept in mind as an ever-present possibility, perhaps more the rule than the exception, and this is true of specifically musical properties as well as of external motivation and suggestion.[5] A great composer's mind is an incredibly rich, essentially inexhaustible storehouse of musical experience; ideas of every kind are always summoned up, consciously and unconsciously, in response to whatever musical project is undertaken. Simultaneous influences are even more a matter of course if we consider the vast variety of components that enter into a work under construction: dramatic action, complement of voices, orchestration, recitative style, orchestral and vocal melody, rhythmic patterns and types of harmonic progression, formal plans of numbers and scenes and acts, expressive and emotional character, and so on. What is more natural than that some familiar opera should act as a model with respect to dramatic plan, while a melody or an orchestral effect of entirely different origin is taken up at the same time—or at some time during the process of composition?

The three Romantic operas of the forties are the culmination of the genre;

4. See Hans Redlich, "Wagnerian Elements in Pre-Wagnerian Opera," *Essays Presented to Egon Wellesz,* ed. Jack Westrup (Oxford, 1966), 145–56. See also John Warrack, "The Musical Background," *The Wagner Companion,* ed. Peter Burbidge and Richard Sutton (New York, 1979), 85–112.

5. I have examined some examples of such multiple factors, largely extramusical ones, in "Theory and Practice in Schumann's Aesthetics," *Journal of the American Musicological Society* 17 (1964): 310–45.

and they prepare the way for the still more impressive stylistic development of the second half of Wagner's career. In this final formative process, all the earlier elements of novelty, originally without particular significance, were able to find their predestined place in a congenial context. What was called for by the intrinsic tendencies of music in general and of Wagner's style and aesthetic thought in particular was a transition from symmetrical melody and balanced melodic phrases to a freely constructed continuity in which symmetry was simply one possibility among others. This freer style operated with vivid and varied motifs rather than with melody, and these were assembled at first successively and then, with increasing frequency, simultaneously. The logic of continuity could be achieved in limitless juxtapositions, parallelisms, and antitheses. Coherence often required considerable repetition and sequence, but this apparent lapse into elementalism, like the balance of melodic phrases, was now part of an inexhaustible complexity that could support every shift of feeling and every turn of events in the external action. Motifs could even be extracted from a larger melodic whole, as they are from the theme with which *Parsifal* opens. This is, in a sense, a return to a Classical symphonic technique of fractionation, which is understandably evident in *Die Feen,* but unimportant in succeeding operas. Characteristically, though, the opposite takes place, and Wagner weaves wholes of varying extent from motifs as units, through a variety of types of repetition and juxtaposition. An entirely new mentality is necessary in the composer, a new type of imagination that is more realistic and less a manifestation of formal musical schemata. In Wagner's melodic phase, however, and especially in the three operas of the forties, his typical method of construction was not entirely foreign to the style that developed after 1850, for he worked by ringing melodic changes on an unvarying rhythmic pattern, so that the melody itself—although clearly articulated into phrases—was yet granted a certain freedom of indefinite extension.

The consistency of Wagner's later style was such, however, that it could bind together the most diverse elements. In its complex and changing relationships between orchestra and voice, it encompasses and unites an astonishing variety of material. The formation of this diversified vocabulary of motifs and melodic phrases, which varies in its nature according to the needs of the conception of each successive opera, is easily abetted by the adoption, often unchanged, of earlier original phrases and motifs that are amenable to Wagner's later purpose. There is an unerring sense of what is conformable to the musical world of each later work, and at the same time, of course, an equally unerring sense of what must be rejected as too subservient to older melodic formalities, too neutral to become part of the new programmatic character of the motivic invention. It is a change, in a word, from Romanticism to realism, whether the vividness or specificity in question is external, psychological, or as Wagner finally conceived it in accord with Schopenhauer, metaphysical. The consistency of a mature style is apparently due in part to borrowing from oneself, which is the closest approximation to an inventiveness that cannot be traced to its source at all. There follow two examples of earlier motifs which in their original occurrence have a merely incidental status, but which, essentially without transformation, Wagner turned to excellent programmatic account in *Der Ring des Nibelungen*. The first is from the Fantasia in F♯ minor (1832), and the second from an extended version of an aria from Marschner's *Vampyr* that Wagner had written for his brother in 1833.

EXAMPLE 7. Wagner, Fantasia,   EXAMPLE 8. Marschner, *Vampyr:* aria, mm.21–23
       m. 213

In the remarkable transformations of musical character that result from the operation of Wagner's imagination on the music that is his starting point, a new aspect of the use of borrowed material comes to light—an aspect that has as little to do with plagiarism as it does with the adoption of public musical configurations or with the duplication of style for purposes of compositional training. For a level of novelty is achieved in the products of Wagner's maturity that reduces the musical source of the creative process to unimportance, even to irrelevance. The original material, which is no longer really the origin of the end product but rather a musical constituent fused to a programmatic one and drawn up into a new imaginative or "poetic" complex, becomes part of a private workshop method. Just as this is true of the Ninth Symphony with respect to *Holländer,* it remains true of *Hans Heiling* with respect to *Der Ring des Nibelungen,* or of *Jessonda* with respect to *Tristan und Isolde.* As in the use of the Tarnhelm, we see only the transformed object, which is the effective one, and the magic resides in the transforming power. By comparing the point of departure with the result, however, we can gain some insight into the *modus operandi* of this power. There follows an illustrative passage from *Tristan,* which appears to derive, perhaps through a process of transformation of which Wagner was not conscious, from Spohr's *Jessonda:*

EXAMPLE 9
Jessonda (1823), Act I, finale

Tristan (1857–59), Act I, scene 5

To this let us add two passages of the *Ring* that similarly seem to have been prompted by Marschner's *Hans Heiling:*

EXAMPLE 10

Hans Heiling (1833), Act II, No. 9

Die Walküre (1854–56), Act II, scene 4

EXAMPLE 11

Hans Heiling, Act II, No. 12

Das Rheingold (1853–54), scene 4

In connection with a possible psychology of musical influence, it is of interest that the passages of *Jessonda* and *Tristan* are both concerned with death, the one in *Tristan* in a double sense, while the scene of *Hans Heiling* in which the

Queen of the Earth Spirits warns Anna that Heiling must be returned to his realm corresponds to the scene in which Brünhilde tells Siegmund that he must follow her to Valhalla, and the motif of Marschner that is compared with Wagner's musical description of the Nibelungen is initially sung by a chorus of gnomes rising out of the earth (the text is "Aus der Klüfte Schlund, durch der Erde Grund drängt hinauf, empor an das Licht hervor").[6]

But we are concerned primarily with the *difference* between Wagner and his predecessors. Wagner deepens the supernatural by making it elemental and metaphysical, and he makes it a logical part of an encompassing system of relationships. This is seen at once in a comparison of *Holländer* with *Vampyr*, or of course of *The Ring* with *Hans Heiling*. There is an equally obvious difference between the chromaticism of *Jessonda* and that of *Tristan*. While Spohr's chromaticism is ubiquitous in *Jessonda*, permeating inner lines, characterizing many approaches to cadences, and giving rise to passages almost literally the same as those of *Tristan*, it is not developed systematically into a language in its own right; it does not create a world alternative to that of tonality; nor is it charged with symbolic significance. Even in this sense, however, Wagner's achievements have predecessors. There is a passage in Schumann's *Genoveva* that glows with the guilt of passion when Golo, unable to control his desire, kisses the sleeping Genoveva; both the music and its meaning could easily come from *Tristan*. Indeed the roots of symbols often reach back into the past. But just as Spohr's chromaticism lacks the systematic elaboration and logical coherence of Wagner's, so do the individual instances of chromatic symbolism in the first half of the nineteenth century lack that concrete integration into an articulated sphere of meaning that Wagner created with each work. Only Liszt appears to have been working along the same lines.

More specifically, turning now to the three examples we have cited, when we compare the earlier passage with the later one in each case, what comes most forcefully to our attention is the intensification Wagner has effected, the compelling consequentiality of his formulation. The passage from *Tristan*, to be sure, incorporates a powerful rise and fall of feeling in place of the more static comparisons of *Jessonda;* but this too, of course, is part of Wagner's forcible logic of expression. And in the passage from *Die Walküre*, it is striking how Marschner's weak terminal descent is replaced by an insistent and logical upward sequence. Wagner accomplishes this change by introducing the additional motif of questioning at this point, as the text suggests. He closely integrates the motif into the melodic line of the initial phrase, extracting it, as it were, from the neutrality of its form in Marschner's melody. This procedure serves to increase further the convincing and definitive character of his melodic structure. At the same time, it is also an adaptation of symphonic technique: the question motif is really a part of the opening theme, and it overlaps itself in its sequential repetition. Toward

6. In the relationship between Schubert's *Erlkönig* and the Prelude of *Die Walküre*, the musical similarity would again seem to be grounded in a common subject matter.

the end of this scene, the motivic manipulation appears in the modern guise of transformation,which is connected characteristically with programmatic significance, in this instance with Brünhilde's decision to allow Siegmund to live.

It becomes evident here how Wagner both adopts and extends Classical symphonic methods of construction, with the enhancement of the drama as his goal. He opens up new horizons of melodic formulation by means of economical and incisive interrelationships that are impelled by sheer strength and directness of feeling. And the larger form that controls the motivic workmanship is given by the course of the dramatic action.

These same factors enter also into the passage from *Rheingold*. Again there is a logical progression from one motif to another, from accumulation to the subjugation it is based on, and there is an elemental simplicity and portentous significance which remain inaccessible to the music of *Hans Heiling*. But the essential features of Wagner's style that produce this result are seen more clearly in the process of formation of the style than they are in the style considered only in its finished form. This may indeed be true more generally in nineteenth-century music, as opposed to the sphere of public material that is characteristic of Baroque and Classic music, so that the method of the present investigation might profitably be applied more widely—to a comparison, for example, of Marschner or Weber with Beethoven, or of other nineteenth-century composers to their predecessors, taking care in each instance, of course, that the earlier composer was well known to the later one. For a transformational mentality, as opposed to a reliance on public themes and motifs and progressions, is nothing less than a corollary of the notion of originality and creative genius. There must indeed exist a community of style, but if originality is a dominant value, then disguise and metamorphosis will prevail. It is this rationale, then, rather than the mysterious action of some evolutionary Zeitgeist, that explains why the formation of Wagner's style is largely a *trans*formation.[7]

---

7. But transformation also characterized Wagner's treatment of the musical material within any one of his own works. Borrowing and internal technique involved the same basic process—a conclusion that seems merely to confirm common sense. A moment's thought suggests, however, that the relationship may be quite different in other stylistic periods. The use or adaptation of public material in the eighteenth century, for example, both in Baroque style and in Classic, bears no such simple relationship of identity to the compositional technique of the time. This type of relationship, therefore, which apparently has never been considered previously, doubtless represents another new investigative tool for the student of style.

BAROQUE OPERA
AND THE
TWO VERISIMILITUDES
PIERO WEISS

My TITLE derives from a formulation made by Lodovico Castelvetro in his commentary on Aristotle's *Poetics,* published in 1570:

> There are two kinds of verisimilitude: one is the kind that portrays realities that occur for the most part in a predictable way, and the other is the kind that portrays realities that sometimes stray from the wonted course. . . . So that one verisimilitude concerns the more frequent realities, and the other the infrequent realities; now both of these are verisimilar, but the second, because of its rarity, is more marvelous.[1]

Castelvetro's formulation found an echo in a memorable document. In 1637 the Académie Française issued its celebrated judgment on *Le Cid.* There Jean Chapelain, its chief author, wrote:

> From what we are able to gather of Aristotle's sentiments concerning verisimilitude, he recognizes only two kinds, the common and the extraordinary. The common comprehends those things which occur to people ordinarily, according to their condition, age, manners, and passions. . . . The extraordinary embraces things which occur rarely and beyond ordinary

---

1. *Poetica d' Aristotele vulgarizzata e sposta,* ed. Werther Romani, Scrittori d'Italia, vol. 264 (Rome and Bari, 1978), 520. His comment refers to *Poetics* 18, 1456ª24–25: "As Agathon says, it is verisimilar that many things should happen contrary to verisimilitude." Further on the subject in n. 6 below. For the original texts of the passages cited in the present article, see the Appendix, p. 125 below. All translations are my own.

verisimilitude. . . . In which are included all unexpected accidents which we attribute to Fortune, provided they are produced by a concatenation of those things that occur ordinarily.[2]

There could hardly have been a more symbolic moment and place for Castelvetro's two verisimilitudes to reemerge in print. French drama, having sown its wild oats in irregular tragedies, comedies, tragicomedies, and pastoral dramas, was just then entering its "classical" phase, one of extreme restraint and sobriety. The "rules" had gained ascendancy, and when the Académie Française had been asked to mediate between the detractors and defenders of *Le Cid,* its verdict had carried the added weight of political authority. Increasingly, French drama moved within the narrow confines prescribed by neoclassical doctrine. *Le Cid* had sinned not only against common verisimilitude, but against the extraordinary kind as well: had not the King, acting as a *deus ex machina* in Act V, commanded that Chimène marry Don Rodrigue? A marvelous denouement, if you will, but totally unbelievable, and disgusting besides. Corneille retired from the stage. And when he returned three years later, it was to produce *Horace,* the first of his great tragedies based on Roman history. Soon the three unities were enthroned, the setting of dramas became immutable, and the scenery remained frozen in place onstage.

But this was only one side of the coin. "Drive the baroque out of the door," says a distinguished French scholar, "and it climbs in through the window."[3] While tragedy, comedy, tragicomedy, and pastoral drama were on their good behavior, the *ballets de cour* went their unreconstructed way as before, flaunting fantasies and metamorphoses amid music and changing scenery. And now Mazarin imported the Italian opera, and Torelli's wizardry was enlisted by comedians and playwrights on behalf of the French theater. Thus was born the *tragédie à machines.* And where, now, were the rules? The encomiastic special number of the *Gazette* invoked them as it reported on all the scenic wonders of Corneille's and Torelli's *Andromède:* "The laws of the theater, when properly observed, find a place for the most irregular events under one or the other of the two verisimilitudes."[4] The Abbé d'Aubignac put the matter somewhat differently seven years later, in his influential *Pratique du théâtre:*

I shall not expatiate here on ordinary and extraordinary Verisimilitude, . . . since everyone knows that things which are naturally impossible become possible and verisimilar through divine power or magic; and that theatrical verisimilitude does not oblige us to represent only the things that occur in

2. Colbert Searles, ed., *Les Sentiments de l'Académie Française sur le Cid,* The University of Minnesota Studies in Language and Literature, 3 (Minneapolis, 1916), 27.
3. Jean Rousset, *La Littérature de l'age baroque en France: Circé et le paon* (Paris, 1954), 214. Apropos of "l'ostentation."
4. *Oeuvres de P. Corneille,* ed. Ch. Marty-Laveaux (Paris, 1862–68), 5: 279–80.

the everyday life of men; but that it contains within itself the *Marvelous,* which renders events so much the nobler in that they are unforeseen, though still verisimilar.[5]

The key words here are "divine power" and "magic." Indeed, extraordinary verisimilitude, like its cognate the marvelous, had never been far removed from the realm of the supernatural. And if one were to trace them back through Castelvetro to their sources in Aristotle (a labyrinthine journey, as I can testify), one would discover curious connections between the verisimilar and the irrational, and between the irrational and the supernatural.[6] Suffice it to say that miraculous fables could rightfully claim legitimacy as subjects for tragedy.

Corneille, who (like Lessing a hundred years later) made a careful study of Aristotle's *Poetics,* was well aware of this:

> The fables and the histories of antiquity [he wrote] are so intertwined that, to avoid drawing the wrong conclusions, we lend them equal authority upon our stage. It will suffice if we ourselves invent nothing which itself is unlikely, for they, having been invented long ago, are by now so familiar to the spectator that he will not be shocked to see them on the stage. All of Ovid's *Metamorphoses* is manifestly an invention;[7] we may draw subjects for tragedy from it, but not invent after that model, unless it be episodes of the same kind: the reason being, that, though we must invent nothing that is not verisimilar, and that these fabulous subjects, such as Andromeda and Phaëthon, are nothing of the kind, to invent episodes is but to add to a thing that was itself invented; and these episodes find a sort of verisimilitude in their relationship to the principal action; so that we might say that, supposing this could have happened, why then it could have happened as the poet describes it.
>
> Such episodes, however, would not be appropriate to a historical subject or to a purely invented one, for they would bear no relationship to the principal action, and would be less verisimilar than it. The appearance of Venus and that of Aeolus in *Andromède* were favorably received; but if I had made Jupiter descend to reconcile Nicomedes with his father, or Mercury to reveal Cinna's conspiracy to Augustus, I should have revolted my

5. 1: 67 (Amsterdam, 1715); facs., ed. H.-J. Neuschäfer, Theorie und Geschichte der Literatur und der schönen Künste: Texte und Adhandlungen, vol. 13 (Munich, 1971).

6. Castelvetro himself introduces the "marvelous" into the sphere of extraordinary verisimilitude by postulating a corrupt reading of the Greek text (p. 519); this may have influenced d'Aubignac. As for Aristotle, he cites Agathon's bon mot twice in the *Poetics:* once (see n. 1) with reference to unlikely twists of plot; later (25, 1461^{b}15) with reference to irrational elements in a poem. These irrationalities (τάλογα [táloga]) are to be defended either by appeal to common opinion ("so they say") or else by observing that sometimes such things do occur. The connection between the irrational and the supernatural is made in the passage cited in n. 10.

7. See L. P. Wilkinson, *Ovid Recalled* (Cambridge, 1955), 190, for Ovid's own disbelief in the fables of mythology: "These are the lying marvels of ancient bards I tell:/No day ever did or shall produce such things" (from the *Amores*).

audience, and the marvel would have destroyed all the credence which the rest of the action had obtained.[8]

I have quoted this passage in full because it contains all the theoretical premises of French operatic dramaturgy. Let me proceed to an *explication de texte*.

"The fables and the histories of antiquity are . . . intertwined." Are they? For all practical purposes, yes. There were skeptics and unbelievers in antiquity as there are and have been in the Judeo-Christian world, but that is neither here nor there. The tragedians made no distinction between history and fable, and neither did Aristotle. The distinction, then, is a modern one, in fact a Christian one: the omnipresence of classical mythology in Western art and poetry required it.

"We lend them equal authority upon our stage." "Authority," here, is a curious amalgam of credence (a word Corneille uses later) and legitimation. That is, we believe both fable and history when we see them enacted on the stage. And they are equally legitimate as dramatic subjects—legitimate, that is, under the "rules." Aristotle's sanction of the use of historical names and events in tragedy is based on the credibility they impart to the plot. His reasoning goes as follows: "We find it hard to believe that things that never happened are possible; now it is clear that things that have happened are possible; for if they had been impossible, they would not have happened."[9] And that, as far as Aristotle was concerned, went for fable too, since he made no distinction. But the moderns needed a separate justification for fable, and they found it in a rather offhand remark in chapter 25 of the *Poetics,* in a section devoted to critical objections and replies. If it is objected, says Aristotle, that a poet has depicted things neither as they truly are nor as they ought to be, the answer is: "It is what people say, like the stories about the gods."[10] Common report, then, and general currency lent fables their authority in the eyes of the moderns: "for, having been invented long ago, they are by now so familiar to the spectator that he will not be shocked to see them on the stage."

"All of Ovid's *Metamorphoses* is manifestly an invention; we may draw subjects for tragedy from it, but not invent after that model, unless it be episodes of the same kind." The *Metamorphoses* was the source of Corneille's *Andromède* and of his other soon-to-be-produced extravaganza, *La Toison d'or*. It was also, of course, the treasure house where the Italians had found most of their early operatic subjects and from which the French, beginning with *Pomone* and continuing through the Quinault years and beyond, were to derive most of theirs. A modern classical scholar, in describing the atmosphere of Ovid's *Meta-*

---

8. *Oeuvres,* 1: 74–75 ("Discours de la tragédie et des moyens de la traiter selon le vraisemblable ou le nécessaire," publ. 1660).

9. *Poetics* 9, 1451^{b}16–19. Thomas Twining's footnote to this passage merits citation:

The philosopher might safely have trusted to any reader to find this *proof* of the *possibility* of what *has* actually happened.—A modern writer would certainly have omitted this; and I wish Aristotle had. But it is my business to say whatever he has said. (*Aristotle's Treatise on Poetry,* 2nd ed. [London, 1812], 1: 128n.)

10. 25, 1460^{b}35.

morphoses, could not, it seems to me, have come closer to describing that of the *tragédie en musique* had he intended to do so:

> The world of the *Metamorphoses* . . . conveys an impression of freedom
> and clarity combined with a sense that we are temporarily detached from
> the realms of ultimate seriousness, of normal logic and moral values. . . .
> The distresses of the actors, more frequent than their joys, are often made
> less real by the pervading atmosphere of miracle. They are pathetic for the
> moment, but not tragic. . . . Who weeps for the divine Calypso deserted
> by Homer's Odysseus?[11]

In such an "atmosphere of miracle" anything might happen. The actors might even open their mouths and, instead of speaking, begin to sing.

"Such episodes, however, would not be appropriate to a historical subject." Which is to say, fable and history are so different in the eyes of the moderns that they no longer mesh. They have equal authority but must be kept separate.

The *tragédie à machines* was the French surrogate for opera until the advent of the *tragédie en musique.* The later form made use of the same dramaturgical ingredients, as Dryden's definition makes quite clear:

> An opera is a poetical tale or fiction, represented by vocal and instrumental
> music, adorned with scenes, machines, and dancing. The supposed persons
> of this musical drama are generally supernatural, as gods, and goddesses,
> and heroes, which are at least descended from them, and are in due time
> to be adopted in their number. The subject therefore being extended
> beyond the limits of human nature, admits of that sort of marvellous and
> surprising conduct which is rejected in other plays. Human impossibilities
> are to be received as they are in faith; because, where gods are introduced,
> a supreme power is to be understood, and second causes are out of doors.[12]

Lully's and Quinault's operas gave umbrage to many people for a variety of reasons, but neoclassical doctrine was not prominent among them. A proof of this is that, when Quinault was temporarily forced out by his detractors, they themselves tried to jump into the breach, with the comical result that the author of *L'Art poétique,* Boileau himself, found himself writing the prologue to an opera, while his friend Racine attempted to draft the opera itself. It was to have been based on the fall of Phaëthon, from the *Metamorphoses;* but Quinault's return to favor put an end to the project.

If extraordinary verisimilitude (fable) reigned supreme at the Académie Royale de Musique, common verisimilitude (history) retained its grip on the

11. Wilkinson, 203.

12. John Dryden, *Of Dramatic Poesy and Other Critical Essays,* ed. George Watson (London, 1962), 2: 35 (Preface to *Albion and Albanius,* 1685).

spoken drama. Racine, it is true, took his cue from the immensely successful operas and turned to Greek mythology himself; but his *Iphigénie* and *Phèdre* are treated as history, not as fable. Hippolytus's death, for example, is described by the messenger in vivid detail, so that the scene leaps before the eyes; but Neptune's intervention, when he comes to it, is introduced by "On dit": "They say a god was seen, goading the frenzied horses."[13] It is as if Racine, anticipating the objection that this was neither true nor as it ought to be, had remembered Aristotle's advice. For he quoted him literally ("It is what people say"), and skeptics in the audience were left free to draw their own conclusions regarding superstition and the origin of fables.

WHILE REASON triumphed in France, achieving a neat separation of dramatic genres, in Italy it seemed to have taken a vacation. There, in 1637, the year of *Le Cid,* the fable of Andromeda, set to music and enlivened by aerial displays, had been enacted before opera's first paying public. During the period of adjustment that followed, as the components of opera rearranged themselves to suit the new circumstances, surely no change was more momentous than the gradual shift in subject matter, from fable to history. It first happened in *L'incoronazione di Poppea.* For the first time "real" people—Nero, Poppaea, Seneca —people, that is, who were known to have lived, sang on the operatic stage. The mind of Busenello, who initiated this development, is revealed unmistakably in the preface he wrote to his second historical libretto, *La prosperità infelice di Giulio Cesare dittatore,* which may or may not have been set to music by Cavalli and performed in 1646:[14]

> Whoever has read the life of Julius Caesar in Plutarch, and has studied the ten books of Lucan's *Pharsalia,* can draw up his own Argument to the present Drama, in which Julius Caesar passes from victories over others to the ruin and perdition of himself. You will note that in Act I we are in Pharsalia. In Act II we are in Lesbos. In Act III in Egypt. In Act IV with Cleopatra. And in Act V in Rome. . . . Do not let the changes of place appear strange to you, for he who writes this thinks it no sin to write just as he pleases. And let those who enjoy being slaves to the ancient rules go and seek their satisfactions when the moon is full.[15]

Such was the man who introduced historical subjects into opera. Other librettists followed suit. And now the "arguments" printed in the front were split in two parts: a historical part, in which the librettist could parade all his erudition by

---

13. Act V, scene 6, lines 1539–40.

14. Thomas Walker has questioned whether Cavalli was the composer or indeed whether the work was ever performed. (See his "Gli errori di 'Minerva al Tavolino,' " *Venezia e il melodramma nel Seicento,* ed. M. T. Muraro [Florence, 1976], 16.)

15. Giovanni Francesco Busenello, *Delle hore ociose* (Venice, 1656). This publication contains five librettos, each separately paginated.

citing his learned sources and explaining the factual basis of the plot, and a fictional part, in which he noted the liberties he had taken with his subject—liberties generally so stupendous that one can only wonder why he needed "real" people at all. Here, too, Busenello had led the way. An opera without aerial acrobatics being unthinkable, he had made Mercury fly down to warn Seneca of his impending death and Cupid intervene to save Poppea. He had pioneered also in introducing comic characters, which, if not inconsistent with a historical setting, represented at any rate a crime against neoclassicism's conception of tragedy, against its fundamental separation of the genres.

And so, while in France the two verisimilitudes lived on a more or less amicable footing, each within its own domain, verisimilitude whether singular or plural had vanished utterly from Italian opera. Luckily this did not prevent it from flourishing or Italian composers and singers from attaining new heights of expressiveness and brilliance. But eventually a reform did take place in the Italian libretto.

There seem to have been two forces behind this reform: the literati, now picturesquely banded together as shepherds in an unreal Arcadia, but without the political support their counterparts had enjoyed in France; and public taste, which was thus free to exert its own influence. This public, by 1700, was beginning to feel the impact of French culture in all its forms, an impact that would remain important for much of the remainder of the century. The Arcadians decried it as "infranciosamento" ("Frenchification"); indeed, their crusade to reform public taste was directed as much against contemporary French influence as against the home-grown forms of corruption that in their view had affected Italian letters during the later Seicento.[16] As for opera, the Arcadians were not really interested in reforming it: they would have liked to kill it. Opera stood in the way of the legitimate, spoken tragedy, which they dreamt of reviving; its usurpation of historical plots, the tragic subject matter par excellence, was the last straw. They suggested a return to fable, and to that end they became operatic reformers. Here, for example, is how Pier Jacopo Martello expressed the idea:

> Let these happy dramatists [he means the librettists] derive their
> plots not from history but from fable, mindful that it would be (and in
> fact is) excessively cruel blatantly to distort the truth of events described
> by Livy, Justin, Sallust, and other ancient and revered Authors; which
> would inevitably result from introducing into those histories all the things
> demanded by the composer, the Male Singers, the Female Singers, the
> Architect, the Machinist, the Painter, and the very Impresario. It will any-
> way be difficult but not impossible to satisfy them in a plot based on
> fable, since the versifier will have the same freedom as did our ancestors to
> palm off absurdities and to pile Italian fibs upon the Greek; and he may

16. An amusing example of the anti-"Frenchification" campaign is Scipione Maffei's little comedy *Il Ra-guet*, which pokes fun at the Frenchified speech and affectations then in fashion.

abandon the old for the new. Fables, too, are more capable of machines and spectacle. The French favor them, and so should the Italians. And though [the versifier's] name will not outlive the run of performances, he will at least have the satisfaction of hearing himself addressed at the great courts by the title of Poet, a title as richly deserved by him as that of "virtuosi" is by castratos and female singers.[17]

There was pathos as well as irony in these Arcadian endeavors. It was Italy, after all, that had interpreted Aristotle's *Poetics* to the rest of Europe, Italy that had produced the first examples of "regular" neoclassical drama, both tragic and comic, as well as models for all the newer genres, including, of course, opera. Yet now, in their attempts to link up with a lost tradition and uphold the national honor, no matter where they turned the Arcadians found themselves imitating the French, who had meanwhile adopted, refined, and stylized that same Italian heritage, making it their own. So it was with the Arcadian librettos: while in a sense they may be regarded as attempts to return to the spirit of the original *favole per musica* of the Florentines, more often than not they are imitations of the French *tragédies en musique*.

I will briefly describe some of these librettos, since they have not been viewed in this light before.[18] The earliest of them appears to have been Scipione Maffei's *La fida ninfa,* which, we now know, dates back to 1694, though it was not performed until Vivaldi set it to music in 1732. It contains elements of the supernatural as well as French-style *divertissements* at the end of each act. In Bologna, where French influence was strong, Eustachio Manfredi wrote a *favola boschereccia* entitled *Dafni,* set to music by Aldrovandini and performed in 1696. He described it as a "musical entertainment adapted to the present taste and to the preference of the majority, hence free from the rigorous rules of Poetics."[19] In Bologna, too, Martello himself wrote four such librettos, produced between 1697 and 1699. The first (written in collaboration with Manfredi) was *Perseo,* a frank imitation of Corneille's *Andromède,* complete with flying Pegasus and lavish scenery by the brothers Galli Bibiena. The next two, *La Tisbe* and *L'Apollo geloso,* were both derived from Ovid's *Metamorphoses,* while the last, *Gli amici,* a pastoral on an invented subject, featured "French ballerinas, French and Sicilian choruses, French and Spanish ballets, and scenery by the famous Bibienas."[20]

Even Apostolo Zeno, who later did so much, in the words of Gasparo

17. *Della tragedia antica e moderna* (Bologna, 1735), 128–29. The English version is taken from my "Pier Jacopo Martello on Opera (1715): An Annotated Translation," *The Musical Quarterly* 66 (1980): 387–88.
18. I have, however, reported on what follows in a paper delivered in Venice (Sept., 1981), "Teorie drammatiche e 'infranciosemento': motivi della 'riforma' melodrammatica nel primo settecento," now published in *Antonio Vivaldi: teatro musicale, cultura e società,* ed. Lorenzo Bianconi and Giovanni Morelli (Florence, 1982), 273–96.
19. *Dafni, favola boschereccia per musica* (Bologna, 1696), 5.
20. These are now published in Martello's *Teatro,* ed. Hannibal S. Noce, Scrittori d'Italia, vol. 267 (Rome and Bari, 1980), 1: 1–145.

Gozzi, to "remove the very strange incidents that, especially when unforeseen and unprepared, gave such delight to the common people" and who "drew his subjects from the heart of Greek and Roman history"[21]—even Apostolo Zeno seems to have begun his operatic career as a typical Arcadian. For though his very first libretto, *Gl'inganni felici* of 1695, is based "partly on . . . Herodotus, partly on fiction," the fiction easily outweighs the history and is in fact glaringly —and amusingly—anachronistic (one of his Grecian heroes actually sits down to a harpsichord, "siede alla Spinetta," to accompany his own singing).[22] And in his next two librettos, *Il Tirsi* (a pastoral on an invented subject) and *Il Narciso* (after Ovid), Zeno still showed no signs of embracing the historical subject.

Yet soon he did, like others among his contemporaries. Not French opera, but French tragedy became the model of opera seria. And the Arcadians, disappointed in their hope of reviving the Italian spoken tragedy, had the rueful satisfaction of watching Zeno and Metastasio, two of their most illustrious shepherds, win international acclaim by doing the very opposite of what the reform had originally set out to do: the two poets were pronounced worthy of Corneille and Racine,[23] but their dramas, alas, were *drammi per musica*.

How could two sister nations have started out with the same elements and ended up with two such contrary kinds of opera? The answer, I think, must be sought in the other force I mentioned earlier, the Italian public. Tired of the irrationalities of seventeenth-century opera, conditioned by the new rationalism emanating from France, it nevertheless saw nothing incongruous about a bewigged Mithridates or Julius Caesar singing a grand da capo aria in a scintillating soprano voice, nor had it need of the miraculous atmosphere of fable to explain away such singing. To the Italian public, music was (according to Castelvetro's formulation) one of the "more frequent realities," to be classed not under extraordinary but under common verisimilitude.

And that is how Baroque opera succeeded in living up to both verisimilitudes at the same time: one in Italy, the other in France.[24]

Appendix: Original Versions of the Cited Passages

N.B. Reference numbers refer back to the footnotes in which the sources of the passages may be found.

1. Sono due maniere di verisimili: l'una di quelli che rappresentano le verità le quali avengono per lo più secondo certo corso, e l'altra di quelli che rappresentano le verità che alcuna volta traviano dall'usato corso. . . . Sì che l'un verisimile riguarda l'assai volte della verità, e l'altro le poche volte della verità; e così l'uno come l'altro è verisimile, ma il secondo per la rarità è più maraviglioso.

1. ὥσπερ Ἀγάθων λέγει, εἰκός γὰρ γίνεσθαι πολλὰ καὶ παρὰ τὸ εἰκός.

21. "A' lettori," in Apostolo Zeno, *Poesie drammatiche* (Venice, 1744), 4: v–vi.
22. Act I, scene 16. (See the libretto in Zeno, vol. 7.)
23. J.-J. Rousseau calls them the Italian equivalents of those French poets. (See "Opéra," *Dictionnaire de musique* [Geneva, 1767].)
24. A version of this study was read at the 1981 meeting of the American Musicological Society in Boston.

2. A ce que nous pouvons juger des sentimens d'Aristote sur la matiere du vray-semblable, il n'en roconnoist que de deux genres, le commun, et l'extraordinaire. Le commun comprend les choses qui arrivent ordinairement aux hommes, selon leurs conditions, leurs aages, leurs mœurs et leurs passions. . . . L'extraordinaire embrasse les choses qui arrivent rarement, et outre la vray-semblance ordinaire. . . . Dans lequel extraordinaire entrent tous les accidens qui surprennent et qu'on attribuë à la Fortune, pourveu qu'ils soient produits par un enchaisnement des choses qui arrivent d'ordinaire.

4. Les lois du théâtre bien observées rangent les événements plus irréguliers sous l'un ou l'autre des deux vraisemblables.

5. Je ne m'étendrai pas ici sur la Vraisemblance ordinaire & extraordinaire, . . . personne n'ignore que les choses impossibles naturellement, deviennent possibles & vraisemblables par puissance divine, ou par magie; & que la vraisemblance du Theatre n'oblige pas à representer seulement les choses qui arrivent selon le cours de la vie commune des hommes; mais qu'elle enveloppe en soi le *Merveilleux,* qui rend les évenemens d'autant plus nobles qu'ils sont imprévus, quoi que toutefois vraisemblables.

7. 　　　　　　　　　Prodigiosa loquor veterum mendacia vatum:
　　　　　　　　　nec tulit haec unquam nec feret ulla dies.

8. La fable et l'histoire de l'antiquité sont si mêlées ensemble, que pour n'être pas en péril d'en faire un faux discernement, nous leur donnons une égale autorité sur nos théâtres. Il suffit que nous n'inventions pas ce qui de soi n'est point vraisemblable, et qu'étant inventé de longue main, il soit devenu si bien de la connoissance de l'auditeur, qu'il ne s'effarouche point à le voir sur la scène. Toute la *Mètamorphose* d'Ovide est manifestement d'invention; on peut en tirer des sujets de tragédie, mais non pas inventer sur ce modèle, si ce n'est des épisodes de même trempe: la raison en est que bien que nous ne devions rien inventer que de vraisemblable, et que ces sujets fabuleux, comme Andromède et Phaéton, ne le soient point du tout, inventer des épisodes, ce n'est pas tant inventer qu'ajouter à ce qui est déjà inventé; et ces épisodes trouvent une espèce de vraisemblance dans leur rapport avec l'action principale; en sorte qu'on peut dire que supposé que cela se soit pu faire, il s'est pu faire comme le poëte le décrit.

De tels épisodes toutefois ne seroient pas propres à un sujet historique ou de pure invention, parce qu'ils manqueroient de rapport avec l'action principale, et seroient moins vraisemblables qu'elle. Les apparitions de Vénus et d'Éole ont eu bonne grâce dans *Andromède;* mais si j'avois fait descendre Jupiter pour réconcilier Nicomède avec son père, ou Mercure pour révéler à Auguste la conspiration de Cinna, j'aurois fait révolter tout mon auditoire, et cette merveille auroit détrui toute la croyance que le reste de l'action auroit obtenue.

9. τὰ μὲν οὖν μὴ γενόμενα οὔπω πιστεύομεν εἶναι δυνατά, τὰ δὲ γενόμενα φανερὸν ὅτι δυνατά· οὐ γὰρ ἂν ἐγένετο, εἰ ἦν ἀδύνατα.

10. οὔτω φασίν, οἷον τὰ περὶ θῶν.

13. 　　　　　　　　　On dit qu'on a vu même, en ce désordre affreux,
　　　　　　　　　Un dieu qui d'aiguillons pressait leur flanc poudreux.

15. Chi hà letto Plutarco nella vita di Giulio Cesare, e chi hà studiato Lucano nei dieci Libri della Farsalia formerà da se stesso l'Argomento di questo Drama, nel quale Giulio Cesare passa dalle Vittorie sopra gl'altri, alle ruuine, e perdite di se stesso. Osserverai che nel Primo Atto siamo in Farsalia. Nel Secondo siamo à Lesbo. Nel Terzo in Egitto. Nel quarto con Cleopatra. E nel Quinto à Roma. . . . Nè ti paia strano la mutatione de' luoghi, perche chi scriue non crede di far peccato se scriue à modo suo. E chi gode farsi schiauo delle regole antiche habbia le sue soddisfattioni in Plenilunio.

17. Questi drammatici felici desumeranno dall'istorie no, ma bensì dalle favole i loro argomenti, avvisandosi essere, come in fatti è, troppa crudeltà il deformare sfacciatamente la verità de' successi scritti da Livio, da Giustino, da Salustio, e da qualunque più antico, e venerato Scrittore, lo che saria inevitabile per introdurvi le cose, che vuole il compositore, che vogliono i Cantori, le Cantatrici, che vuole l'Architetto, il Macchinista, il Pittore, e sin l'Impresario. Ciò pure sarà difficile, ma non impossibile nell'argomento favoloso, perchè in ogni caso il versaeggiatore ha tutta la facoltà, che avevano i nostri antenati di dar' ad intendere delle frottole, e di aggiungere bugie Italiane alle Greche, e può, lasciando le antiche, inventarne delle moderne, essendo ancora la favola più capace di macchina, e d'apparenza, e così fanno fortunatamente i Franzesi, e così farà l'Italiano; e come che il nome suo non sia per vivere più oltre delle rappresentazioni, avrà ad ogni modo il piacer di sentirsi chiamato nelle gran corti col titolo di Poeta, titolo così per lui meritato, come per gli castrati, e per le cantanti quello di virtuosi.

19. Un divertimento per Musica addattato [*sic*] al gusto presente, ed al genio della maggior parte, e però dispensato dalle leggi rigorose della Poetica.

21. Esso gli stranissimi accidenti, gran pasto del popolo, massime se sono improvvisi, e senza verun apparecchio, in gran parte levò via; . . . gli argomenti trasse dal cuore della Storia greca, e Romana per lo più.

AN IMPRESARIO AT THE
TEATRO LA PERGOLA
IN FLORENCE:
LETTERS OF 1735–1736

WILLIAM C. HOLMES

LARGE BATCHES of documents recording the day-by-day operations in seventeenth- and eighteenth-century opera houses are extremely rare, and when found they can be a source of much enlightening information.[1] Recently such a body of documents has turned up in Florence, housed in the private archives of the Guicciardini family. It consists principally of the correspondence of Luca Casimiro degli Albizzi (1664–1745), who for many years acted as impresario at the Teatro la Pergola, the opera house run by the Accademia degli Immobili.[2] Although some of the letters are from as early as 1680, by far the largest number of them date from the years 1720–45, the time during which Albizzi was active at the Pergola. The Albizzi archive is divided into two distinct sections: the *copialettere,* which have been put into order, and boxes of letters received, which have yet to be examined.

The Marquis Luca Casimiro degli Albizzi was a member of a prominent Florentine family, and although he is not mentioned in the *Dizionario biografico*

1. For example, the letters and other papers of Marco Faustini in the State Archives in Venice (Scuola Grande di San Marco, Buste 188 and 194) have long been mined in the search for facts about operatic life in Venetian theaters in the mid-seventeenth century. See especially Bruno Brunelli, "L'impresario in angustie," *Rivista italiana del dramma* 14 (1941): 311–41; Remo Giazotto, "La guerra dei palchi," *Nuova rivista musicale italiana* 1 (1967): 245–86, and 3 (1969): 906–33; and Carl Schmidt, "An Episode in the History of Venetian Opera: the *Tito* Commission," *Journal of the American Musicological Society* 31 (1978): 442–66.

2. These letters are recorded in Albizzi's letter books (*copialettere*). Here I wish to thank Dr. Gino Corti for his invaluable assistance in transcribing the letters. I also wish to thank Count Francesco Guicciardini for generously allowing me to have access to his family's archives. Some of Albizzi's letters have recently been published by Gino Corti, "Il teatro La Pergola di Firenze e la stagione d'opera per il carnevale 1726–27: lettere di Luca Casimiro degli Albizzi a Vivaldi, Porpora, ed altri," *Rivista italiana di musicologia* 15 (1980): 182–88.

degli italiani, he is discussed by Luigi Passerini in Pompeo Litta's monumental compilation of Italy's celebrated families and by Ugo Morini in his history of the Accademia degli Immobili.[3] From these sources we have a rather clear picture of this man, who was intimately connected with the Pergola during the waning years of Medici rule in Florence. Further aspects of his character can be gleaned from his very extensive correspondence. During his youth Albizzi was a close personal friend of Ferdinando de' Medici, and he remained on good terms with the ruling family throughout his life. He was rich, and he was very well versed in the complexities of the business of opera. From his many complaints about money it appears that Albizzi was a penurious man when playing the role of impresario, though on occasion he contributed from his own pocket so as to maintain the quality of operatic productions at the Pergola. He was respected by impresarios at other theaters; we know, for example, that during 1735 alone impresarios from Siena, Genoa, and Naples sought his advice on a variety of musical and business matters.[4]

There were a number of theaters active in Florence during the first half of the eighteenth century, and of these the Pergola, run by the Accademia degli Immobili, and the Cocomero, run by the Accademia degli Infuocati, were the most important.[5] The repertories of these two theaters differed in that the Pergola produced only serious and semiserious operas, while the Cocomero presented comic operas and burlettas in addition to the normal fare. Full-fledged ballets and divertissements with dancers during operatic productions were also common in both theaters. In fact, a large part of the Albizzi correspondence is concerned with the hiring of dancers. There were also such extramusical activities as gaming to help raise money for operatic productions.

Carnival activities normally began a few days after Christmastide and ended on Shrove Tuesday. From the listings in the Weavers' *Chronology,* it is apparent that the Pergola would normally mount two or three operas each carnival season. During the carnival of 1735–36, which I propose to discuss here, the two operas performed were *Cesare in Egitto* (libretto by Giacomo Francesco Bussani, music by Giminiano Giacomelli, with alterations by Guiseppe Maria Orlandini)[6] and *Ginevra principessa di Scozia* (libretto by Antonio Salvi, with alterations by Damiano Marchi, music by Antonio Vivaldi).[7]

3. Pompeo Litta and various editors, *Famiglie celebri italiane* (Milan, 1819–75; Turin, 1875–83), series 2, vol. 1, *Albizzi di Firenze.* Table XXI presents a family tree of the Albizzi. Ugo Morini, *La R. Accademia degli Immobili ed il suo teatro "La Pergola"* (Pisa, 1926), 21–23 and 40–46.

4. Florence, Archivio Guicciardini, Albizzi 770, letters of July 9, August 2, and December 27, 1735. All future references will be to letters in Albizzi 770.

5. For a convenient summary of the place of theaters and academies in Florentine life during this time, see Robert L. and Norma W. Weaver, *A Chronology of Music in the Florentine Theater, 1590–1750,* Detroit Studies in Music Bibliography, 38 (Detroit, 1978), 21–59.

6. Weaver and Weaver, 275. Giacomelli is named as composer in the letters of July 1, 4, and August 13. Orlandini's alterations are confirmed in the letter of September 23.

7. Weaver and Weaver, 275–76. Marchi's alterations are mentioned in the letter of September 17.

Although Albizzi began to plan for the 1735–36 season as early as February, 1735,[8] his company of singers was not complete until the following August.[9] Forming the company was no easy task, and while some singers were cooperative in their contractual arrangements, others caused a great deal of trouble. Perhaps most troublesome was the soprano castrato Mariano Nicolini (not to be confused with the celebrated alto Nicolò Grimaldi {"Nicolini"}).

As the correspondence shows, this Nicolini not only had an inflated opinion of his own talents, but also intentionally delayed in his dealings with Albizzi, in the hope of receiving better offers elsewhere. On June 14, Albizzi writes to Nicolini refusing to pay the 300 zecchini demanded by the singer. He informs Nicolini that the Pergola cannot possibly pay such high fees, even to singers of the caliber of Caffariello, and suggests that the singer look to other impresarios (Letter 1).[10] On the same day, writing to his Roman agent, Monsignor Giovanni Luca Niccolini, Albizzi complains bitterly of the castrato's demands, adding that "It seems that this year all the 'castratacci soprani' have sworn to make impossible demands upon me. . . ." Again, he makes a comparison with another, more famous singer: "even Appianino, the best contralto singing today, was ashamed to ask such a sum from me in Bologna. Mariano is not in that class. . . ." However, he tells the monsignor to bargain and sets a limit on the amount of money to be offered (Letter 2). In another letter to his agent, written on June 28, he reports that Nicolini has asked for another fifteen days to make his decision because he is trying surreptitiously to find another, better offer (Letter 3). Obviously, Albizzi was on the verge of canceling all negotiations, as can be seen in his acid letter written to the soprano on the same day. "Dear Signor Mariano, I see that you are thinking only of your own affairs, and I understand. The proverb is trite, but you can't run with the hare and hunt with the hounds. If your discussions with Rome or Milan are more important than those with me, you don't have to deal with me. Nor can I force other sopranos to wait at your whims. . . . I shall expect your definitive answer within a week. . ." (Letter 4). The strained situation collapsed completely by July 12, when Albizzi learned that Nicolini had accepted a position at the Teatro Tordinona in Rome for the next carnival.

Arranging for singers was one problem; acquiring the scores of the operas to be performed was quite another. The first opera, Giacomelli's *Cesare in Egitto,* had been performed the previous year in Milan, and Albizzi wrote there to secure a copy of the score. In the series of six letters sent between July 4 and September 13, one can sense Albizzi's increasing frustration at the seeming lack of cooperation on the part of the Milanese.[11] On July 4, in a letter to the Milan-

---

8. Letter of February 26, 1735 (dated 1734, Florentine style).
9. Letters of August 8 and 13. For the names of the singers, see Weaver and Weaver, 275.
10. The texts of many of the letters cited appear as the Appendix, beginning on p. 134 below.
11. Letters of July 4, August 9, August 23 (two letters), and September 13.

ese impresario Giulio Antonio Lucini, Albizzi requests a copy of the score and four copies of the libretto "at the best price possible." He states, among other things, that if the expenses are too high, he will have to find another opera. On August 9, Albizzi, having heard absolutely nothing from Milan, writes to a friend of his there asking him to look into the matter. He also suggests that if for whatever reason the theater does not want to send the score, perhaps his friend can find a good copyist to make an exact copy of it. As time passed, there was still no affirmative news about the score, although Albizzi learned that the Milanese impresario had been out of the city for a number of weeks and therefore had not received the original request. Albizzi decided to make the request once again and wrote to both the impresario and his friend on August 23. By the end of the month, it was apparently agreed that the score would be sent, but in his letter of August 30, Albizzi complained bitterly to his friend about the long delay. Finally, the score and four copies of the libretto arrived on September 13, and Albizzi wrote a warm note of thanks to his friend.

Perhaps the most interesting part of the 125 letters that make up Albizzi's correspondence for the year 1735 are the twenty-five letters addressed to Antonio Vivaldi.[12] The Vivaldi correspondence is a gold mine of information. It shows how the composer worked with a particular impresario who had commissioned an opera from him and with whom he had had much correspondence in the preceding years, it gives valuable insights into his working methods, and it provides an intimate view of his musical and personal relationship with the singer Anna Giraud (always spelled "Girò" in Italian sources).[13] This is a one-sided correspondence, of course, but many of Albizzi's letters address questions and suggestions originating with Vivaldi.

In the first of Albizzi's surviving letters to Vivaldi in 1735, dated April 16, he speaks of Anna Giraud even before he mentions the possibility of commissioning a new opera for the following carnival (Letter 5). It appears that Vivaldi's first thought was to make certain that his friend would be hired to sing in the company at the Pergola.

> How you are deceived in supposing I am free to choose the artists for the theater in Via della Pergola! Only yesterday the academicians resolved to have operas next carnival. I immediately proposed Signora Annina as prima donna. Oh, how many objections were raised that she is not of the

---

12. Letters of April 16 and 30; June 4 and 18; July 1, 9, 16, 23, and 30; August 6, 13, 20, and 27; September 3 (2 letters), 17, and 23; October 7, 19, and 28; November 5, 12, 19, and 26; December 10.

13. Little is known of Anna Giraud's background. An important source of knowledge about her and her career is Vivaldi's own letter of November 16, 1737, transcr. Adriano Cavicchi, "Inediti nell'epistolario Vivaldi-Bentivoglio," *Nuova rivista musicale italiana* 1 (1967): 66. In it Vivaldi says that he and Giraud have been together for fourteen years, that is, since 1723. The most recent and thorough examination of Giraud and the music Vivaldi composed for her is John Walter Hill, "Vivaldi's Griselda," *Journal of the American Musicological Society* 31 (1978): 53–82. This penetrating study contains an appendix listing the known roles sung by Giraud, most of them in operas by Vivaldi.

caliber of others who have come here, and that she was not successful the last time she sang here![14]

He goes on to say that he argued that Giraud had improved and that he suggested her because he was following the academicians' own instructions to be economical in forming his company. Only then does Albizzi broach the subject of an opera for Florence. He asks Vivaldi to be open and frank about the amount of money he might want. He also mentions Giuseppe Maria Orlandini's close connections with the Pergola, this year principally as an arranger of other people's operas.

Albizzi's next letter, dated April 30, is in answer to one written to him by Vivaldi on April 23 (Letter 6). This opens with a biting comment that Vivaldi apparently is not very busy, since his long list of the honors awarded Anna Giraud must have taken more than a day to write. He then adds a bit more to Giraud's original fee and offers Vivaldi "fifty ducats valued at ten giulios each" for composing the opera, and agrees to pay "whoever plays the first harpsichord." He closes by stating that if Giraud is not satisfied with the proposed arrangements he will find somebody else to sing in her place. In his next letter, that of June 4, Albizzi continues to worry about Giraud's abilities (Letter 7). He says, among other things, that "everybody who returns from Venice says that she cannot be heard at all in [the Teatro] San Samuele." By June 18 everything seems to be in order; Giraud will definitely sing in Florence, for Albizzi has defended her and shouted down her detractors. Furthermore, he has chosen the libretto, Salvi's *Ginevra principessa di Scozia,* and assures Vivaldi that it will be the second opera of the season, not the first (Letter 8).[15] But Albizzi's problems concerning Giraud are not over (Letter 9). On July 1 he writes to Vivaldi,

> I must advise you of what is being said. . . . All of the Florentines who were in Venice for the [Feast of the] Sensa—princesses, ladies, gentlemen, and merchants—with whom I have spoken about Signora Giraud, are in agreement (even though they do not know each other) that she is a fine actress, but that you cannot hear her voice. But let us finish this; I must defend her because I have hired her for carnival. . . . The first opera I shall do for carnival will be *Cesare in Egitto,* done recently in Milan with music by Giacomelli. Signora Annina will sing the role of Cornelia. There are beautiful arias that were sung by Tesi, and they would fit her [Giraud] well. But I shall leave you free to adapt arias to her talents. I cannot send the libretto to *Ginevra* because our poet is adjusting it. . . .

14. Giraud had previously sung in Florence during the carnival of 1728–29, first in Vivaldi's *L'Atenaide* (late December, 1728) and later in Leonardo Vinci's *Catone in Utica* (late February and March, 1729). See also Weaver and Weaver, 255–56.

15. Salvi's libretto had been performed earlier in or near Florence, at Pratolino in 1708 (music by Giacomo Antonio Perti) and at the Cocomero in 1723 (? music by Domenico Sarri).

Suddenly and without warning, Vivaldi decided that the libretto of *Ginevra* should be discarded and replaced by Apostolo Zeno's *Merope,* which he found better suited to Giraud's talents. Albizzi, almost at wits' end, refused to consider the suggestion, saying on July 9 that *Merope* "has been done time and again in Florence, and there isn't a porter in the city who doesn't remember it" (Letter 10). Vivaldi was insistent, but on July 16 Albizzi wrote to him announcing that the academicians refused to hear of any work other than *Ginevra,* the opera first performed at Pratolino in 1708 (Letter 11). The matter was brought to a close once and for all in Albizzi's letter of July 23 (Letter 12).

> *Merope* absolutely cannot be performed in this theater in 1736 because it was given in 1729 with little success. I shall have the poet rearrange *Ginevra* and shall send it to you as soon as possible.[16]

The letter of July 30 and those of August 6 and 13 discuss mainly dancers who might be brought into the company. On July 30 Albizzi sent a copy of the libretto of *Ginevra* with his letter. On August 13 Albizzi announced to Vivaldi that the soprano Francesco Grisi had been engaged, "to whom I shall write so that he can come to an agreement with you about the composition of his part and the arias."[17] Four days later Albizzi wrote to the soprano telling him that the music for *Ginevra* was being composed by Vivaldi, "with whom you can negotiate for your arias and recitative."[18] The four following letters (August 20 and 27, and two on September 3) are entirely devoted to the hiring of dancers, and it becomes clear that Vivaldi was acting in this matter as Albizzi's Venetian agent. Albizzi returns to *Ginevra* on September 17 (Letter 13). After first discussing some dancers, he states that Vivaldi should not alter the libretto of *Cesare in Egitto* at all because the parts have already been copied, and that he will soon send Anna Giraud hers. It is another matter with *Ginevra;* while it is agreed that Giraud may change some of the aria texts of the 1708 libretto, in no case can those already arranged and sent to Vivaldi by the house poet, Dr. Marchi, be touched. That would be an affront.

> I assure you that the Tuscans are vain and will yield to no one in matters of poetry. And I say to you that I am certain that *Ginevra* will not fail, so much is it liked in Florence. If you want to, go right ahead and take out such phrases as *il dado è tratto, o duce il piacerti, duce il vederti,* but do not touch the substance of the libretto or the division of the acts, because I want it as it is.

---

16. For information on the 1729 performance of Zeno's *Merope,* see Weaver and Weaver, 256–57.
17. August 13, "al quale scrivo d'intendersela con Vostra Signoria per la composizione della sua parte e dell'arie."
18. August 17, "con il quale potrà patteggiare lei per le sue arie e recitativo."

On September 23 Albizzi again takes up the subject of the operas (Letter 14). First, dancers are discussed, after which Albizzi informs Vivaldi that Orlandini has made changes in the score of *Cesare in Egitto.* He then states that once Vivaldi has consigned his score to Albizzi's Venetian financial agent he will be paid what was promised. He adds that he himself will not try to find out how many earlier composed arias Vivaldi has inserted in the score, but he reminds Vivaldi that if any of these arias are recognized by the public, it will be embarassing, and some of the singers might feel obliged to change them, "with harm to my purse."[19]

The letters of October 7, 19, 28, and November 5 deal almost exclusively with dancers and the hiring of one new singer for minor roles in the company. The operas are mentioned only once, on October 28. Vivaldi, against Albizzi's earlier instructions, had rewritten some of Giraud's recitatives in *Cesare in Egitto.* Albizzi does not object to this, though he bemoans the fact that he will have to pay additional copyists' charges for the changes.

By November 12 the score of *Ginevra* had arrived in Florence, and most of the singers had received their copied parts (Letter 15). Vivaldi had also enclosed a list of requests regarding the production, and Albizzi promises in his letter to discuss them with the principal violinist, Signor Tanfani. Following this, Albizzi addresses the many changes made by Vivaldi in the libretto. He does not so much mind the changes in the recitative, but he is upset that there are so many in the arias—he counts twelve examples.

> I infinitely abhor those arias filled with similies that really weaken a scene, when instead there should be words of reproof or exhortation or prayer. But enough, I shall see that everything is done according to your wishes.

He then talks about payment for the score and any other expenses Vivaldi might have incurred in Venice. The letters of November 26 and December 10 speak only of money matters. After the latter date there are no more letters sent to Vivaldi until January. When Albizzi and Vivaldi resume their exchange there is no mention of either the season or *Ginevra.* Instead, the principal subject of discussion is Vivaldi's wish to plan a small season at the Cocomero at the time of the Feast of St. John, in late June, 1736.

The *copialettere* furnish only an indirect clue as to how the carnival season went, and this is a reference to *Cesare in Egitto.* On December 27, the day after the opening performance, Albizzi writes to the Neapolitan impresario, enclosing a libretto of the first opera of the season. He remarks in passing that the costumes and dancing were most beautiful. The remainder of the letter mentions possible performers for the Neapolitan carnival of the following year. Ever the impresario, Albizzi begins discussions for a future season elsewhere just as the

---

19. For a list of migrating arias sung by Giraud in Vivaldi's operas, see Hill, "Griselda," appendix, 79–82.

present Florentine season was beginning. Of course, in so doing, he was fulfilling the duties of all impresarios, then and now, and following the very advice he had sent earlier to Giulio del Taia in Siena on July 9, 1735 (Letter 16):

> It is easy for me to find you a very able impresario to run a decent company to do opera during the next carnival. Before doing this I must know how much your academicians are offering, how the quarters will be for all the singers, about food for them, about the lighting of the theater, men to move the scenery, about the extras and the wardrobe. The biggest risk for him is his duty to pay the singers and the orchestra, travel expenses, and through good contracts and box office sales to be able to cover this risk. . . .

Appendix

All the letters contained herein are from Florence, Archivio Guicciardini, Albizzi 770 (1730–36).

LETTER 1 (fols. 475v–476):
to Sig.ᵗ Mariano Nicolini, Roma; *dated,* Firenze, 14 giugno 1735

Q[u]ando scrissi a Vostra Signoria l'altra mia ne' 28 maggio, la credetti a Piacenza, mentre allora non avevo saputo che ella si trovasse a recitare da donna in Roma come poi ne fui avvisato da mons.ᵗ Niccolini, al quale avevo dato incumbenza di sentire se lei era in libertà per il carnevale. Mi càpita ora la sua degl' e sento che per il suo onorario mi chiede zecchini 300. Voglio credere che la sua abilità meriti tale generosità, ma ella non è informato che questo teatro non dà tali paghe, eppure ci ho avuto i primiari [= primari] soprani, come lo stesso Caffariello che è costì puole dirle. Io non avevo cognizione di lei e fu la signora Maria Maddalena Pieri che me la lodò, per avere Vostra Signoria recitato con la medesima a Mantova. Ella si goda dunque i posti vantaggiosi di Roma e di Milano, ché io non fo offerte sopra a dimande simili.

LETTER 2 (fols. 476v–477):
to Mons.ᵗ Giovanni Luca Niccolini, Roma; *dated,* Firenze, 14 giugno 1735

Pare quest'anno che tutti li castrataci soprani abbino fatto congiura di chiedermi spropositi, come ha fatto codesto Mariano Nicolini che recita nel teatro di Tordinona da donna. Vedrete dall'annessa risposta che li faccio ad una lettera che li scrissi a Piacenza ché lo credevo là, e nella sua risposta di costì mi chiede zecchini n° 300, pazzia non più sentita, ed Appianino stesso, che è il migliore contralto che ora canti, ebbe vergogna di farmi in Bologna simile dimanda. Mariano non è in questo rango, però vi prego a mandarli la lettera. Se volete maneggiarvi di trattare l'onorario con lui, vi do l'arbitrio fino a scudi 300 di giuli X; ma se me ne potesse rispiarmiare [*sic*] qualcheduno mi obbligheresti infinitamente. Se non gli vuole, mandatelo a farsi benedire; ma rispondetemi subito perché non voglio che mi scappi un altro che è in Lombardia. Io assolutamente non darei a codesto Giovanni Tedeschi, che pure canta di soprano, scudi 400 o 450, come voi supponete che egli pretenda.

LETTER 3 (fols. 481v–482):
to Mons.̣ Giovanni Luca Niccolini, Roma; *dated,* Firenze, 28 giugno 1735.

Altra lettera mi scrive Marianino da castrato, senza conclusione: vorrebbe trattenermi altri 15 giorni senza risolvere, perché vuole prima fare contratto con codesti e che l'occasion mia non gli scappi. Però letta l'annessa fategliela avere e dirli che se mi risponde con equivoco, intendo d'essere libero. Vi do ben l'arbitrio dai ducati 300 romani di arrivare fino a ducati 350, ma mostrate di essere voi, e maneggiatemeli con più economia che potete.

LETTER 4 (fol. 482):
to Sig.̣ Mariano Nicolini, Roma; *dated,* Firenze, 28 giugno 1735.

Caro Signor Mariano, vedo che lei solo pensa a' fatti suoi e la compatisco. Ma il proverbio è trito, che non si puole tenere i piedi in tante staffe, e se i trattati di Milano o di Roma sono antecedenti al mio, non puole pigliare trattato con me. Né io posso forzare gl'altri soprani ad aspettare i comandi di Vostra Signoria. Sentirà dunque da mons.̣ Niccolini il finale mio sentimento, e se ella ha maggiore vantaggio negl'altri trattati perché non dirmi a dirittura che non mi puol servire, e non mi tenere sempre in dubbio per rispondere poi dopo altri 15 giorni che il trattato di codesto impresario è molto più vantaggioso. Per oggi a otto aspetto il suo decisivo.

LETTER 5 (fol. 457v):
to Sig.̣ Don Antonio Vivaldi, Venezia; *dated,* Firenze, 16 aprile 1735.

Quanto s'inganna Vostra Signoria nel supporre che da me dependa liberamente la scelta de' virtuosi per il teatro di via della Pergola! Ieri solamente risolvettero i cavalieri di farci l'opere il futuro carnevale. Subito proposi la signora Annina per prima donna: ho [= oh] quante mai opposizioni mi furno fatte, che ella non era nel rango di quelle che venivano qua e che non incontrò l'ultima volta che ci stiede [= stette]. M'impegnai a sostenere che non era quella d'allora e che appunto gliela proponevo perché m'impegnavo d'averla con l'economia che i detti signori m'hanno prescritto. Eccoli tutto il fatto sincerissimamente; mi dica se zecchini cento, quartiere e piccolo vestiario fosse cosa per lei, acciò me ne possa spiegare a risposta con detti signori. E per comporre Vostra Signoria un'opera, mi dica sinceramente, ma affatto ristretto, quello che desidererebbe per onorario, essendo tanto legati con l'Orlandini che quando lui voglia sonare una composizione nuova d'altri, non lo leveranno mai dall'orchestra né li scemeranno quello che li dànno ogn'anno, essendo obbligato a rassettare tutte l'opere che si prendono. Dunque Vostra Signoria vede che difficilmente otterrò di fare doppia spesa.

LETTER 6 (fol. 465):
to Sig.ʳᵉ Antonio Vivaldi, Venezia; *dated,* Firenze, 30 aprile 1735

Confesso che la lunga lettera scritta da Vostra Signoria ne' 23 corrente mi fa comprendere che siano molto scarse le sue occupazzioni, giaché per formarla con tutti quei registri di onorari che ha avuto la signora Annina Girò in diversi teatri, vogliono applicato uno scrittorale per più d'un giorno. Quando voglio trattare virtuosi per il nostro teatro, non consulto altro che la propria borsa. Vostra Signoria si formalizza che gl'abbia offerto zecchini cento, e si ricordi che tanti n'ebbe l'altra volta quando ci fu a recitare per seconda donna. Che io gl'offerisca ora la prima parte è per far vedere a questo paese che io ho stima per la medesima con impegnarmi anco contro il genio degli altri cavalieri interessati. Ma facciamola corta: se vuole zecchini dieci di più glieli offerisco, con il quartiere ed il piccolo vestiario per le due opere, di paoli sessanta. Ed a Vostra Signoria offerisco, giaché tiene la borsa divisa affatto dalle medesime, ducati 50 di giuli X, per la composizione intiera d'un opera, dovendo io poi pagare chi suona il primo cimbalo. Se così le piace, me lo dica a risposta che gliene manderò le scritte, dovendo io partire di qua. E se alla signora Girò non sono gradite queste esibizioni, stabilisco con altra e me la riverisca. Ho fatto l'imbasciata alla signora Maria Maddalena, che dice di mandarli per il signor cavaliere Ridolfi quanto ella ha chiesto, giaché il Saletti era partito, e però li rimando la di lui lettera, e l'altra resta consegnata a Valletta, che sarà costì quando questa mia lettera.

LETTER 7 (fol. 471):
to Sig.ʳᵉ Don Antonio Vivaldi, Venezia; *dated,* Firenze, 4 giugno 1735

Appena arrivato ieri qui, fui tormentato dalla signora Maria Maddalena perché volessi mandare a Vostra Signoria e alla signora Annina Girò la scritta, avendomi strappato altri ducati 10 per la di lei persona. Tocca ora a corrispon-dermi con una spiritosa e vivace composizione, giaché ho avuto tutto contrario il paese per questa scelta, e trattenutomi in Bologna sono stato assediato da un mondo di virtuose anco di estimazione grande, per venire a servirmi, ma nulla ho ascoltato perché ci venga la signora Annina, con tutto quelli ritornati di Ven-ezia dichino che ella non si senta punto in S. Semueli [= Samuele]: se ciò fusse vero, sarebbe una grande disgrazia per il nostro teatro. Mi rimandi le contra-scritte.

LETTER 8 (fols. 477v–478):
to Sig.ʳᵉ Antonio Vivaldi, Venezia; *dated,* Firenze, 18 giugno 1735

Oramai è fissata la signora Annina Girò per recitare il futuro carnevale in via della Pergola, e Vostra Signoria per comporre un'opera che sarà assoluta-mente l'ultima e non la prima come Vostra Signoria temeva, credo la *Ginevera* [*sic*] del dottore Salmi, bellissimo libro dove potrà farsi tutto l'onore. Siché non occorre più contrastare dell'abilità della detta giovane, che io ho sostenuto di peso a dispetto di quanti hanno scritto contro di costà, e qui asserito i signori ritornati, portando in aria generalmente la soprano che ora canterà in via del Cocomero con due arie di Vostra Signoria di quelle cantava a Verona la signora Maria Maddalena. Sentirò quali sieno le proposizioni per la medesima signora Maria Maddalena Pieri per il teatro, che lei non mi descrive, ma quando non sia cosa ragionevole e di credito, risolverà forse d'andare a Palermo, e finora vi repugna per il timore del lungo viaggio per mare.

LETTER 9 (fol. 483):
to Sig.ʳᵉ Antonio Vivaldi, Venezia; *dated,* Remole, 1 luglio 1735

Mi compatisca, caro Signore Antonio, se io devo essere più riguardato con Vostra Signoria nell'avvisarla sinceramente di ciò che è detto [h]o scritto della signora Girò, perché lei subito forma de' giudizi temerari né io voglio scrupoli di fumentarli. Non ho né pure parlato ancora a Valletta: veda se lui possa avermi dato le dette relazioni. Quanti erano in Venezia per l'Ascensa fiorentini, principesse, dame, cavalieri e mercanti, con i quali tutti ho parlato della signora Girò, e concordemente senza sapere l'uno dell'altro m'hanno detto che ella è una brava comica, ma che non si sente la sua voce. Finischiamola, ché io devo sostenerla quando l'ho stabilita per il carnevale, e così non se ne parli più. Circa alla signora Maria Maddalena, l'ho lasciata in Firenze invogliatissima di venire con lei per il carnevale in quella città e teatro, dove Vostra Signoria farà l'opere, anco con scapito del suo interesse; ed ha voluto che io scriva martedì in Palermo in forma che assolutamente ne la risposta verrà messa in libertà. Ma se poi li francesi se ne torneranno a casa loro, chi dell'uffiziali collegati manterrà a Vostra Signoria la parola di fare l'opera? Così sarà facile che la detta signora Maria Maddalena si trovi fuori e di Palermo e di Lombardia. Ma ella è incantata di lei, e tutto lascerà per trovarsi in sua compagnia: dunque Vostra Signoria ha ragione di corrisponderli. La prima opera che farò per il carnevale sarà *Cesare in Egitto,* fatto ultimamente in Milano, musica del Giacomelli. La signora Annina farà la parte di Cornelia. Vi sono bellissime arie che ha cantato la Tesi, che giusto li tornerebbero, ma io li lascierò in libertà di mettere l'arie a suo talento. Non posso ancora mandarli il libro della *Ginevra* perché lo fo accomodare dal poeta.

LETTER 10 (fol. 486v):
to Sig.ʳᵉ Don Antonio Vivaldi, Venezia; *dated,* Firenze, 9 luglio 1735

Bisogna confessarla che i musici sono come i predicatori che poco compariscono fuori del loro quadragesimale. Vostra Signoria mi dice nella sua de' 2 che in luogo della *Ginevera* dovrei fare la *Merope* perché la signora Annina meglio comparisse. Questo libro è fatto e rifatto in Firenze, né vi è facchino che non se ne ricordi. La *Ginevera* da Pratolino in qua non è stata mai fatta e bisogna che io varii i libri quanto posso, essendo questo un teatro incontentabile.

LETTER 11 (fol. 490v):
to Sig.^{re} Don Antonio Vivaldi, Venezia; *dated,* Firenze, 16 luglio 1735

Altra pressatura è venuta alla signora Maria Maddalena per un nuovo teatro che s'apre in Lisbona, ma ella l'ha rigettata subito non volendo fare un viaggio sì lungo per mare e star tanto tempo lontana dalla patria. Ella non piglierà
altr'impegni senza che Vostra Signoria lo sappia. Non posso impegnarmi per la
Merope avendo questi signori cavalieri troppo genio per la *Ginevera,* e credo che
Vostra Signoria la sbagli di un'altra moglie di Raimondo, che fu fatta il 1703, e
questa che si vorrebbe far qui fu fatta in Pratolino il 1708. Basta, fra poco li
saprò dire il preciso.

LETTER 12 (fol. 493v):
to Sig.^{re} Don Antonio Vivaldi, Venezia; *dated,* Firenze, 23 luglio 1735

La *Merope* assolutamente non si puol fare in questo teatro per l'anno 1736
perché la feci l'anno 1729 con poca fortuna. Faccio dal poeta rassettare la *Ginevera* e gliela manderò più presto che sia possibile.

LETTER 13 (fols. 521v–522):
to Sig.^{re} Antonio Vivaldi, Venezia; *dated* 17 settembre 1735

Approvo tutto quello che ella ha maneggiato con la sua avvedutezza per le
ballerine Colucci e Barbuzzetti, la quale nella scritta si dice Anna Gobio perché
se ne piccasse, essendo Barbuzzetti sopranome. Infine una sola di queste si vuole,
e prima se sia possibile la Colucci, della quale ha già Vostra Signoria in mano la
scritta, e quando questa non si possa liberare da Verona, eccoli l'altra scritta per
la Barbuzzetta, di 30 luigi d'oro, quartiere ed acconci di teatro, come Vostra
Signoria ha descritto. Avverta bene che delle due una sola ci bisogna. Se mai
avessero licenziate l'opere a Verona, mi dica se alcuno di quei ballerini fusse libero, se ne prenderebbe uno che ancora manca, purché non sia quello che si servì
lei l'anno passato per ultimo di Verona, che è scelerato. Non si puol toccare il
libro del *Cesare in Egitto,* del quale ne sono copiate le parti, e ne manderò presto
quella per la signora Annina. Che nella *Ginevera* ella muti le parole dell'arie del
1708 lo accordo, ma quelle rassette e mandateli dal nostro poeta signor dottore
Marchi non voglio io farli quest'affronto, e le dico che i toscani hanno questa
vanità di non cedere agl'altri nella poesia. E le dico che sono sicuro che la *Ginevera* non precipiterà, tanto è desiderata in Firenze. Che ella levi *il dado è tratto, o
duce il piacerti, duce il vederti* lo faccia pure, ma la sostanza del libretto e la di-
visione degl'atti non li tocchi, perché voglio così. So che ella dice tutto per fa-
vorirmi, ma in Firenze so io ciò che ci vuole. I corni da caccia li ho in orchestra.
Aspetto dunque le sue risposte e che mi rimandi quella scritta che non sarà ser-
vita.

LETTER 14 (fol. 524–524v):
to Sig.ᵉ Antonio Vivaldi, Venezia; *dated,* Firenze, 23 settembre 1735

Comparsami la lettera di Vostra Signoria de' 17, vedo che mi propone un tal Giovanni Chaumont per ballerino molto ragionevole e che volendolo restava stabilito per zecchini di Venezia o ruspi di Firenze in numero 65. Non se li manda la scritta perché essendo stabilito per capo monsù Mijon turinese, si è lasciato a lui la libertà di condurci un altro a suo piacimento. Siché la compagnia tutta è fissata quando sarà di costà venuta la scritta o della Colucci o della Barbuzzetti, ma in tutti i modi si vorrebbe la prima. Già la prima opera del *Cesare in Egitto* venne da Milano, e dal signor maestro Orlandini è stata adattata al mio bisogno, sichè non vi voglio spendere altro denaro. Si vanno dal copista levando le parti e presto verrà quella per la signora Annina. Quando lei averà all'ordine l'opera della *Ginevera* e che l'averà consegnata al signore Cottini, le farò avere quanto l'ho promesso e mi riprometto della sua attenzione, non ricercandole quante arie v'abbia incluso di vecchie, perché ciò dipende dal suo arbitrio. Ma se poi in teatro son riconosciute, sa lei che una tal cosa non le porterà credito, e forse quei tali a chi li toccherà il cantarle saranno obbligati a mutarle, con danno della mia borsa. Ma io li confermo che voglio fare a lei.

LETTER 15 (fol. 539–539v):
to Sig.ᵉ Antonio Vivaldi, Venezia; *dated,* Firenze, 12 novembre 1735

Ho ricevuto lo spartito della *Ginevera* benissimo condizzionato, essendomi venuto per mezzo del procaccio, non già del signor Cottini e mi sarei rispiarmato [*sic*] molto del porto per la franchigia della Corte. Ho letto il suo foglio di considerazioni: saranno da me messe in pratica, e specialmente le concerterò con il Signor Tanfani primo violino. Per le poche parole mutate ne' recitativi, non ci trovo disordini, ma in quelle dell'arie mi pare che si [sia] preso della libertà tanta, contandone 12, ed io abborrisco infinitamente quelle composte di similitudini che infiacchiscono affatto la scena, quando devono essere di rimprovero o d'estorzione o preghiere. Basta, farò che tutto sia eseguito secondo la di lei intenzione e me ne protesterò con il copista. Quando ritorneranno le signore Girò, li consegnerò il suo originale, giaché a lei tanto preme. Suppongo che non manderà altrimenti la parte al signore Canini, così bisognerà che le ne faccia cavare dal copista; ma non voglio che lo spartito esca dalle mie mani. Non m'ha già rimandato il libretto, che m'è necessarissimo perché qua non se ne trovano, e la prego a farlo a risposta. Potrà andare dal signor Anibale della Ciaia, che averà ordine di pagarli ducati 60 di giuli X, che è l'appunto della nostra convenzione. Mi dica poi le spese che li sono occorse tanto della spedizione delle parti ai virtuosi e copia delle medesime, come tutt'altro che io li deva per la carta e legatura, che anco di quelle tali cose sarà rimborsato.

LETTER 16 (fol. 486–486v):
to Sig.^r Cav.^{re} Giulio del Taia, Siena; *dated,* Firenze, 9 luglio 1735

E facile che io possa trovarvi uno capacissimo da farsi impresario per con-
durvi una ragionevole compagnia di virtuosi a fare l'opera nel futuro carnevale.
Per fare questo bisogna sapere cosa offerischino codesti signori, come sarebbe
quartieri per tutti i virtuosi, vitto ai medesimi, teatro inluminato, uomini per
muovimento delle scene, di comparse ed il vestiario. Siché forse l'azzardo del
medesimo, il dovere pagare i musici e l'orchestra ed i viaggi andanti e venuti, e
che le riprese de' viglietti dell'appalti e della vendita de' casini servissero a co-
prire il suo risico. Però rispondetemi a questi quesiti, e poi vi troverò l'impresario, o sia quello di casa Suarez o sia altro, e sarete certamente meglio serviti che
dal Lottini e Santini.

PASTICCIO REVISITED:
HASSE AND
HIS *PARTI BUFFE*
GORDANA LAZAREVICH

THE GERMAN COMPOSER Johann Adolf Hasse (1699–1783), called affectionately by his contemporaries 'il caro Sassone," was one of the pillars of eighteenth-century opera seria. The mellifluousness of his cantilena and the clarity of his predominantly homophonic texture show an affinity with the operatic style that was prevalent among Italian composers in general, and native to those of Naples in particular. The Neapolitan or "southern" musical style was propagated by Hasse in Dresden at the electoral court of Frederick Augustus II, where he and his wife, the prima donna Faustina Bordoni (1700–81), were the focal points of a highly active musical life from 1731 to the beginning of the Seven Years' War in 1756.

In addition to his many operas, Hasse, a prolific composer of sacred and instrumental music, also produced ten comic intermezzos. Whereas the composition of opere serie spanned his entire lifetime, that of comic intermezzos occurred almost exclusively during the last four years of his Neapolitan sojourn of 1722–30.[1] The notable exceptions are the two Dresden intermezzos *Rimario e Grillantea* (1739) and *Pimpinella e Marcantonio* (1741), created for performance at Hubertusburg, Frederick Augustus's hunting lodge outside the capital. Hasse's period of intense involvement with the intermezzo may therefore be seen not only as restricted to a specific locale, but also as falling within the early phase of his musical activities. Table 1 lists his Neapolitan intermezzos.[2]

---

1. Hasse's *Piramo e Tisbe* (Vienna, 1768), an "intermezzo tragico," has nothing in common with the comic genre under discussion in this essay.
2. Table 1 is also available in the preface to my forthcoming edition of three of Hasse's intermezzos in the *Concentus Musicus* series published under the auspices of the German Institute in Rome, ed. Friedrich Lippmann. The works to be included in this edition are *Dorilla e Ballanzone (La serva scaltra)*, *Tabarano e Scintilla (La contadina)* and *Pandolfo e Lucilla (Il tutore)*. The present study is a by-product of the research done for the edition.

TABLE 1

DATE	INTERMEZZO	OPERAS WITH WHICH THE WORK WAS PERFORMED*	SINGERS FOR ALL THE INTERMEZZOS
May, 1726	*Miride e Damari*	*Il Sesostrate*	
December, 1726	*Larinda e Vanesio*** (*L'artigiano gentiluomo*)	*L'Astarto*	
November, 1727	*Porsugnacco e Grilletta*	*Gerone, tiranno di Siracusa*	
May, 1728	*Pantaleone e Carlotta* (*La finta tedesca*)	*Attalo, re di Bitinia*	Gioacchino Corrado
fall, 1728	*Tabarano e Scintilla* (*La contadina*)	*Il Clitarco* (Pietro Scarlatti)	and
carnival, 1729	*Merlina e Capitan Galoppo* (*La fantesca*)	*L'Ulderica*	Celeste Resse
November, 1729	*Dorilla e Ballanzone* (*La serva scaltra*)	*Il Tigrane*	
fall, 1730	*Pandolfo e Lucilla* (*Il tutore*)	*Ezio*	

* All the operas are by Hasse unless otherwise indicated.

** For information about the modern edition of this intermezzo, see n. 3.

These eight works, which demonstrate Hasse's great gift for the *vis comica,* are outstanding examples of the musical idiom of Italian staged comedy before Mozart. Although he did not compose any comic intermezzos after 1741, the genre continued to engage Hasse's attention; throughout the 1730s and '40s he was personally involved with revivals and revisions of his intermezzos and those of other composers.

One may gauge the international acclaim won by Hasse's comic works from their numerous performances in theaters across Europe between 1726 and the late 1750s. Table 2 presents a partial listing of the Italian performances of Hasse's intermezzos as given during the first decade following their date of initial composition.[3]

As Tables 1 and 2 indicate, several sets of singers were associated with Hasse's buffo roles: Gioacchino Corrado and Celeste Resse (1726–30), Cosimo and Margherita Ermini (c. 1734–39), and Domenico Cricchi and Rosa Ruvinetti (c. 1732–52; in 1735 she assumed her husband's family name, Bon). Corrado and Resse, the two singers for whose particular vocal ranges, personalities, and abilities Hasse originally composed the music, were cast in the first performance of all eight of Hasse's Neapolitan intermezzos.

Corrado, as a singer of comic roles at the Teatro di Corte and Teatro di

3. For a list of the performances of *Larinda e Vanesio,* see my edition of the intermezzo in *Recent Researches in the Music of the Classic Era,* vol. 9 (Madison, Wisc., 1979).

TABLE 2

DATE	CITY	INTERMEZZO	SINGERS
1731	Trieste	*Tabarano e Scintilla*	Carlo Amaino, Anna Isola
1731	Treviso	*Tabarano e Scintilla*	Domenico Cricchi, Anna Isola
1731	Venice	*Tabarano e Scintilla*	Domenico Cricchi, Anna Isola
1732	Genoa	*Tabarano e Scintilla*	Domenico Cricchi, Rosa Ruvinetti
1732	Venice	*Dorilla e Ballanzone*	Domenico Cricchi, Rosa Ruvinetti
1733	Naples	*Tabarano e Scintilla*	Gioacchino Corrado, Laura Monti
1733	Genoa	*Tabarano e Scintilla*	Anna Maria Faini, Pellegrino Gaggiotti
1734	Naples	*Pantaleone e Carlotta*	Gioacchino Corrado, Laura Monti
1734	Bologna	*Tabarano e Scintilla*	Domenico Cricchi, Rosa Ruvinetti
1734	Parma	*Tabarano e Scintilla*	Domenico Cricchi, Rosa Ruvinetti
1735	Florence	*Tabarano e Scintilla*	Domenico Cricchi, Rosa Ruvinetti
1739	Venice	*Pandolfo e Lucilla*	Cosimo and Margherita Ermini
1739	Venice	*Larinda e Vanesio*	Cosimo and Margherita Ermini
1739	Naples	*Pantaleone e Carlotta*	not known
1739	Naples	*Dorilla e Ballanzone*	not known
1739	Naples	*Pandolfo e Lucilla*	not known

San Bartolomeo in Naples throughout the first half of the eighteenth century, was one of the rare performers who did not belong to an itinerant opera troupe. The husband-and-wife team, Cosimo and Margherita Ermini, appeared in comic works together and played buffo roles at Dresden for over two decades. Originally from Italy (Cosimo sang buffo roles in Modena as early as 1719),[4] both Erminis began their engagement at the Dresden court in 1725. They came to the Saxon capital with the Comici Italiani, and they received the title "Virtuosi di Camera di S. M. Re di Polonia."[5] During their active careers in Dresden between 1725 and 1744 they performed a number of Hasse's intermezzos. Cosimo died in 1745, Margherita in 1765.

The Bolognese Domenico Cricchi specialized in buffo roles over a period of thirty years. At first, between 1726 and 1735, he sang in such northern Italian cities as Bologna, Venice, Milan, Treviso, Parma, and Florence. Then he joined a company of Italian singers, directed by the bass Pietro Mira, that was bound for the Russian court at St. Petersburg. The evidence gathered from the librettos shows the Bolognese Rosa Ruvinetti (Bon) to have been his singing

4. His name appears in the libretto for a performance of *Lidia e Ircano, amanti campagnoli* given in Modena in 1719; see Ortrun Landmann, "Quellenstudien zum Intermezzo comico per musica und zu seiner Geschichte in Dresden" (Ph.D. diss., University of Rostock, 1972), vol. 1, Table II₇.

5. This title appears in the libretto for the 1739 performance of *Pandolfo e Lucilla* (Washington: Library of Congress, Music Division, Schatz Collection).

partner over a period of two decades. At some point prior to their engagement at
the Russian court (after 1735), the pair was in the service of the prince of
Hesse-Darmstadt.[6] In 1747 they spent one season in Dresden.

During the eight-year period of Italian revivals of the Hasse intermezzos
listed in Table 2, the works in question went through considerable modification
and alteration. Pasticcio-like adaptations of early eighteenth-century intermezzos
constituted standard contemporary practice, but Hasse's intermezzos provide
unusually explicit evidence of the causal connection between singers' needs, audiences' tastes, and the composer's adjustments of his music to satisfy changing
demands.

The eighteenth-century intermezzo repertory has come down to us in the
form of pasticcio variants that exist in the vacuum of anonymity. Faced with this
situation, we have little evidence to help us with such questions as: Who were
the authors of these musical transformations? How big a role did singers assume
in the creation of the pasticcio? How often was the reworking done by the composer himself? And finally, what were the composer's aesthetic views of alterations made to his music? Hasse's documented association with his singers,
therefore, and the long period during which these singers performed his intermezzos—to the point of almost specializing in them (as with the Corrado/Resse
and the Cricchi/Bon pairs)—provide a unique opportunity to study pasticcio
practice in general and Hasse's compositional process in particular. The best examples of Hasse's reworkings are afforded by the Dresden versions of three of
his Neapolitan works that were performed in Dresden in 1734, 1737, and
1738: *Larinda e Vanesio, Tabarano e Scintilla* (known in Dresden as *Il Tabarano*), and *Pandolfo e Lucilla (Il tutore)*. All three were revised in order to adapt
the female vocal part to the alto range of Margherita Ermini, and the result was
a change in the character of some of the music.

Hasse's revision of *Il Tabarano* (original libretto by Bernardo Saddumene)
shows a number of methods. Except for a slight rearrangement in the order of
recitatives at the end of Act II and the substitution of "Pace, si pace" for the
original duet, "Deh ti placa," the text remains unchanged. An attempt was
made to keep as much of the original music as possible, but while most of Tabarano's recitatives and arias were retained, Scintilla's recitatives vary from sections that are direct transpositions of the 1728 version to newly composed
melodic formulas in a range generally a fifth below the original soprano line. Although the new musical settings keep their old rhythmic configurations, the melodic flow of the new setting is often better suited to the inflections of the text.
The incipits given in Table 3 provide a brief chart of the Dresden version of the
intermezzo. Five of Scintilla's six musical numbers are in their original key. In
two of them, "Sul verde praticello" and "Strappami il core," coloratura flourishes composed for Celeste Resse are eliminated. In giving the text of "Sul verde
praticello" a simplified musical setting, Hasse succeeds in lending Scintilla's

6. See the libretto for the performance in Florence in 1735 of Hasse's *La contadina* (Milan: Biblioteca Na-
zionale Braidense, Racc. Dramm. Corniani Algarotti).

quatrain a lighthearted character more in keeping with the meaning of the text. And the aria "Strappami il core" is now structurally more suited to the meaning of the text than was the Neapolitan original. It achieves greater pathos and sincerity by eliminating such mannerisms as the rather blatant two-measure emphasis on the augmented sixth chord at the word *crudeltà*.

TABLE 3. *Il Tabarano*

INTERMEZZO I (ACT I)		INTERMEZZO II (ACT II)	
Tabarano:	"Alla vita, al portamento"—G major	Scintilla:	"Strappami il core"—G major
Tabarano & Scintilla:	"Sul verde praticello"—A major	Tabarano & Scintilla:	"Star allegra"—D major
Scintilla:	"Più vivere non voglio"—E minor (originally in C minor)	Duet:	"Pace, si pace"—D major (substitute duet for the original, "Deh ti placa"—A major)
Duet:	"Vorrei, oh Dio"—G major		

In the duet that closes Act I, the rewritten female part is fitted into a preexisting musical context whose bass line and orchestral parts remain unchanged from the Neapolitan version. The substitute duet put into Act II can be traced back to the 1727 Neapolitan performance of another of Hasse's intermezzos, *Porsugnacco e Grilletta*. Since the key of D major is retained in the reworked version, Tabarano's and Scintilla's parts are reversed in order to adjust the female line to the alto range; that is, she sings his part an octave higher, while he sings hers an octave lower. In this way the orchestral parts need minimal change.

Of the three Dresden reworkings, *Il tutore* was altered the most. In fact, one could say that it received virtually a new musical setting. The recitatives are entirely new, and five of the seven musical numbers show extensive changes (see Table 4). For instance, the new aria "Belle mie calde lagrime" is totally unrelated to the original. Of the two settings, the Neapolitan one has the more lyrical and sustained line; it covers the range of a twelfth (from middle C to G), and its long, sweeping phrases create a flexible and fluid line in the best tradition of an aria seria of the pathetic type. Perhaps the only element to detract from its sensuous beauty is a mannered use of the *alla zoppa* rhythm (Scotch snap),

TABLE 4. *Il tutore*

INTERMEZZO I (ACT I)		INTERMEZZO II (ACT II)	
Lucilla:	"Non ho più genitrice"—E minor (originally in A minor)	Pandolfo:	"Ah perfida"—D major
Lucilla:	"Belle mie calde lagrime"—G major	Lucilla:	"Il vecchio pipistrello"—F major (originally in A major)
Pandolfo:	"Egli e probabile"—F major"	Duet:	"Signor curatore"—G major
Duet:	"Bramo da te"—G major		

prevalent in Naples in the late 1720s. By avoiding coloratura passages, the Dresden "Belle mie calde lagrime" is much simpler than the aria it replaced, and its shorter melodic units have an almost disruptive effect on the flow of the cantilena.

Larinda e Vanesio (original libretto by Antonio Salvi) displays yet a third type of alteration. For the Dresden performance the three acts were contracted to become two, presenting a condensed version of the original. Hasse eliminated the entire first act, retaining only Vanesio's aria "Un marte furibondo." Acts II and III became the main body of the work, with the original final duet, "Che contento," replaced by "Qual tortorella." In this case, the revisions pertain primarily to overall structure rather than to the content of individual arias. Musical numbers are merely transposed rather than transformed. Octave displacement and reversal of parts similar to the duet "Pace, si pace" in *Il Tabarano* occur in the first duet, "Mio dolce amore." Two lutes are added to the instrumentation of the new version.

Thus, each of the three Dresden versions exemplifies a different type of alteration by the composer of a preexistent intermezzo. Interestingly enough, on the occasion of the Dresden performances Hasse chose to rework his earlier intermezzos rather than to provide the court with entirely new comic works. He may have been guided by artistic as well as practical dictates. From the artistic point of view, his methods indicate the care with which he approached these comic works; he treated them as important works in his operatic output rather than as miniatures or bagatelles amenable to being thrown together overnight.[7] On the practical side, Hasse's prolonged absences from Dresden may have placed additional pressures on him during the time he spent at the court, where his obligations included the composition of new large works ranging from cantatas to operas and church music. On one occasion, Hasse received an urgent request to compose "quelque petite operette" for the name day of the queen,[8] and for this task he was left with only five and a half weeks. Hasse did produce a new opera—his *Atalante*—which was performed with the freshly reworked intermezzo *Il Tabarano* on the festive day. There was barely enough time for Hasse to write a full opera, let alone a new intermezzo, but the fact that he reworked the intermezzo himself rather than relegating it to Giuseppe Ristori, the other Kapellmeister at Dresden, is indicative of the care with which he treated his intermezzos.[9]

7. The haphazard approach to intermezzo composition at that time was notorious enough to warrant sharp satire within the genre itself. For example, the libretto for *Don Velasco e Vespetta* by Carlo de Palma, performed in the Teatro de San Bartolomeo (Naples, 1727), pokes fun at the brief time spent by the composer in writing his music, at the lack of originality of subject matter, and at the pasticcio custom of borrowing bits and pieces from a variety of sources to present a "freshly composed" work. The best examples of pasticcio practice in the eighteenth century are the two comic operas *Orazio* and *La finta cameriera*.

8. Carl Mennicke, *Hasse und die Brüder Graun als Symphoniker* (Leipzig, 1906), 385.

9. The autograph *Il Tabarano*, the sole extant source in Hasse's hand, proves the composer's authorship of this new version. The Sächsische Landesbibliothek in Dresden, the repository of the autograph, is planning to publish it in facsimile under the editorship of Ortrun Landmann.

Two of the three revised Dresden intermezzos, namely, *Pandolfo e Lucilla* and *Larinda e Vanesio,* were subsequently given in Venice in 1739, and these performances are directly linked to Hasse's presence in the city at that time. Because of the Saxon court's extended stay in Poland from September, 1738, to April, 1739,[10] musical activities were interrupted in Dresden, and this situation enabled the Hasses to visit Venice and to fulfill their musical engagements there. They were joined by Cosimo and Margherita Ermini, who performed Hasse's two intermezzos at the Teatro di San Angelo during the carnival season. During that time, they sang in three comic works presented alternately with Pietro Chiarini's opera *Achille in Sciro*—the two above-mentioned works by Hasse (in the reworked Dresden version) and Giuseppe Maria Orlandini's *Bacoco e Serpilla* (originally from 1719).[11]

While Hasse's close working relationship with his singers in his opere serie has already been pointed out,[12] few have studied his comic music or raised the question of the influence of his *parti buffe* on his intermezzo revisions.[13] Except for the Erminis, with whom Hasse had close contact in Dresden, Cricchi and Bon seem to have been the pair of singers most involved with performances of his comic works over the longest period of time. Despite the lack of biographical information on the personal relations between the composer and his *parti buffe,* one is able to piece together information that points to a long and even warm relationship between them by examining the published librettos that provide dates and the names of singers.

Hasse's earliest contact with Cricchi and Bon probably occurred during the 1732 carnival season in Venice. It was there, at the Teatro Grimani, that he first presented his operas *Demetrio* (in which Faustina sang the leading female role) and *Euristeo.*[14] Coinciding with this Venetian visit was a performance at the Teatro di San Angelo of his intermezzo *Dorilla e Ballanzone (La serva scaltra),* given during the carnival season with Albinoni's *Ardelinda.* The intermezzo, which was originally composed in 1729 as a three-act work, now appeared in a condensed, two-act version. The first act was omitted, and to the remaining acts was added a new soprano aria, "Son serva son scaltra." The libretto of the 1732 version names Hasse alone as the composer.[15] Since the restructuring of this work follows the same pattern as that of *Larinda e Vanesio* in Dresden two years later, one may deduce Hasse's personal involvement in the Venetian revision of

10. As king of Poland, Frederick Augustus moved his court to Warsaw at regular intervals, and on these occasions he left some of his musicians behind in Dresden. See Mennicke, 386.

11. For further information, see my article "Eighteenth-Century Pasticcio: the Historian's Gordian Knot," *Analecta Musicologica* 17 (1976): 132–33.

12. Frederick A. Millner, *The Operas of Johann Adolf Hasse* (Ann Arbor, 1979).

13. Landmann, 1: 103ff. mentions a number of buffo singers and comments on Hasse's Dresden revisions as they related to Cosimo and Margherita Ermini. Recently, new scholarly work has been done in this area. See Franco Piperno, "Buffe e buffi (considerazioni sulla professionalità degli interpreti di scene buffe ed intermezzi)," *Rivista italiana di musicologia* 18 (1982): 2.

14. Mennicke, 380.

15. The libretto is in the Biblioteca Marciana, Venice.

Dorilla e Ballanzone. And the new soprano aria was created specifically for Rosa Bon.

Hasse's life as *primo maestro di cappella* for the court in Dresden allowed him enough mobility to compose operas for a number of European theaters each year and to be present in those cities during the preparation and at the première of these works. His Dresden duties did not make him feel isolated from the mainstream of musical activity, as Haydn was later to feel at Eszterháza. Throughout their tenure at the Saxon court, both Hasses spent considerable time touring Italian cities, fulfilling their professional commitments while remaining near each other. The first Italian trip (1731–33) during their Dresden period was devoted to engagements in Turin (1731), Rome, Venice, and Naples (1732), and Bologna and Vienna (1733). On their second trip (1734–37) they remained for the most part in Venice, except for Hasse's brief visit to London in late October, 1734. Their third trip (1738–39) was again to Venice, where they had previously rented a house. It is reasonable to assume that Hasse was involved in the addition of new material to those of his intermezzos whose performances coincided with the presence in the above-named cities.

One question of authorship that is of considerable historical interest relates to Hasse's Italian activities in the mid-1730s as well as to those of the singers Cricchi and Bon, and pertains to the particular version of the pasticcio *La contadina.* This work has been misattributed to Pergolesi and is published in Francesco Caffarelli's edition of Pergolesi's *Opera Omnia.* Frank Walker was the first scholar to point out[16] that the "Pergolesi" version is in fact a pasticcio of segments from two of Hasse's intermezzos, *Tabarano e Scintilla* and *Pandolfo e Lucilla,* with the final duet, "Per te ho io nel core," taken from Pergolesi's comic opera *Flaminio.* Up to now we have lacked information about the historical circumstances surrounding the creation of the pasticcio, that is to say, about the occasion for which it was created, the singers who performed it, or the author of this particular adaptation of Hasse's music.

The many extant librettos for Hasse's *Tabarano e Scintilla (La contadina)* can be grouped into three different versions: version 1, the original text as presented in 1728; version 2, the text used in the 1734–35 performances in Bologna, Parma, and Florence; and version 3, the 1737 Dresden version, which adheres to the original text, introducing only a minor variation at the end. The major differences in these texts occur between versions 1 and 2. In version 1, Scintilla, imprisoned by Tabarano, whom she does not recognize in his Turkish disguise, bargains for her freedom and that of her lover Lucindo (a mute part) by promising him treasures owned by a certain Tabarano, whom she proceeds to describe in very unflattering terms. When Tabarano reveals his true identity, a horrified Scintilla, in the duet "Deh ti placa," begs his forgiveness, which he refuses to grant. Only when the servant Corbo (another mute part) runs in after

16. Frank Walker, "Two Centuries of Pergolesi Forgeries and Misattributions," *Music and Letters* 30 (1949): 309–12. The pasticcio should not be confused with *Livietta e Tracolo (La contadina astuta),* by Pergolesi and Tomaso Mariani. See Charles E. Troy, *The Comic Intermezzo* (Ann Arbor, 1979), 43–44.

the final duet and conveys through his gestures that Lucindo has escaped, does Tabarano make a truce with Scintilla. In version 2, Scintilla uses the opportunity of Tabarano's momentary distraction over Corbo's mimed message to pick up Tabarano's dropped sword. In this version of the libretto she assumes the dominant position and places Tabarano in the role of supplicant. Tabarano promises her marriage on her terms, an arrangement which would make her mistress of all his wealth. Their joy at the completion of a successful pact is celebrated in the duet "Sei contento, contento io sono."

Three of the fifteen extant manuscripts of this intermezzo—at Parma (PAc), Florence (Fc), and Brussels (Bc)[17]—follow text version 2, although none of them exactly coincides with it. While the texts to the recitatives in these three manuscripts are identical to those in version 2, the musical numbers in their second acts are arias and duets that substitute for those given in the librettos. Table 5 encapsulates their second-act differences. Librettos following version 2 are dated 1734 and 1735; the manuscripts, however, bear no identifying indications. In the Bc manuscript, a foreign hand has ascribed the whole intermezzo to Pergolesi, whereas the copyists of the PAc and Fc manuscripts correctly attribute only the last duet to this composer.

TABLE 5. *La contadina*

Libretto (version 2):	"Se non credi alle parole" "Il mio error perdona" "Sei contento"
Manuscripts (PAc & Fc):	"Se non credi alle parole" "Oh perfida" (from Hasse's *Pandolfo e Lucilla*) "Per te ho io nel core" (from Pergolesi's *Flaminio*)
(Bc):	"Belle mie calde lagrime" (from Hasse's *Pandolfo e Lucilla*) "Oh perfida" (from Hasse's *Pandolfo e Lucilla*) "Per te ho io nel core" (from Pergolesi's *Flaminio*)

Thus, a text already in existence must have been used as a basis for the performances represented in the PAc, Fc, and Bc manuscripts, in which new musical numbers in Act II replaced those originally given in the 1734 libretto. No new librettos for the productions represented by these manuscripts seem to have been printed, leading one to surmise that the model was either the 1734 libretto (Bologna and Parma) or the 1735 libretto (Florence), both of which belonged to version 2.

Here it is not a question of musical reworkings of arias, duets, and recitatives. On the contrary, one aria and one duet were simply substituted for the

---

17. Library sigla conform to the usage in RISM.

original number. This type of substitution was a common practice in the eighteenth century, with the singers transferring their favorite musical numbers from one intermezzo to another. In this way they could perform the same piece on a number of occasions and not have to learn an entirely new one. So too, the same libretto could be used by audiences, for no new printing was required.

Since the singers in Parma, Bologna, and Florence productions (libretto version 2) were Domenico Cricchi and Rosa Bon, it is likely that they were not only associated with the musical versions reflected in the three manuscripts, but were also responsible for them. The direct relationship between the Bc, PAc, and Fc manuscripts is obvious from the fact that they are the only sources in which the soprano aria "Più vivere non voglio" (Table 3) appears in the key of A minor. The original key is C minor, while the revised Dresden version has it in E minor. This suggests a musical execution by the same soprano voice. In addition, the version of the soprano aria "Belle mie calde lagrime" (Table 5) used in the Bc manuscript is identical with that in the original (1730) performance rather than with the later 1738 Dresden reworking. Moreover, Pergolesi's *Flaminio*, which is the source for the duet "Per te ho io nel core," was completed in the fall of 1735. It is therefore possible to date the pasticcio *La contadina* as 1735 and to associate directly Cricchi and Bon with its genesis.[18] And since Hasse was in the same geographic area as the two singers in the mid-1730s, he probably approved the changes in his original intermezzos or even suggested them.

Another contact between Hasse and the singers Cricchi and Bon occurred after their return from Russia to spend a season in Dresden, where they performed at least four of the composer's intermezzos—*Il Tabarano, La fantesca, Parsugnacco e Grilletta,*[19] and *Dorilla e Ballanzone.*[20] *Il Tabarano* was performed with some changes, further distinguishing it from any of the previous Italian versions of 1728, 1734, or 1735. The original duet "Sul verde praticello" (see Table 3) was replaced by "Colà sul praticello," a duet from Gaetano Latilla's *La finta cameriera,*[21] while two other numbers, "Se non credi alle parole" and the duet "Sei contento," that had been added to the intermezzo during the 1734–35 performances (see Table 5), were retained. Hasse was probably responsible for the revised versions of the intermezzos presented in Dresden on this occasion. He held a virtual monopoly over operatic performances at court,

18. The most likely date is 1735, inasmuch as Rosa Bon was active at the court in St. Petersburg after that year. See R.-Aloys Mooser, *Annales de la musique et des musiciens en Russie au XVIIIe siècle,* 3 vols. (Geneva, 1948), 1: 134.

19. Mennicke, 401, mentions a performance of this intermezzo with the opera *Catone* on August 4, 1747. No libretto for this performance has survived.

20. Although Landmann suggests the possibility of a production of this intermezzo between 1746 and 1748, there is no extant libretto to document her hypothesis.

21. "Colà sul praticello" was a famous aria. It had already been incorporated in the 1745 performance of Hasse's *Il Tabarano* in Hamburg and was later to be included in a Paris performance in 1753 of *Il maestro di musica* (pasticcio).

and as a consequence most of the operas performed there during his tenure were composed by him pursuant to his duties as Kapellmeister.

The Dresden engagement of Cricchi and Bon was followed by their appointment as *parti buffe* to the court of Frederick II at Potsdam, where they entertained the Prussian monarch with Hasse's comic music.[22] Frederick the Great was an admirer of the musicianship of both the Hasses. As early as 1741 he had *La clemenza di Tito* performed in Berlin. At the end of the Second Silesian War in 1745, after the battle at Kesseldorf near Dresden, Frederick spent ten days in the capital city listening to Hasse's *Arminio* and participating in daily chamber music activities with Hasse, Faustina, Bindi, and a string quartet from the royal Dresden orchestra. Later, in 1747, he had *Arminio* performed in Berlin, and from 1748 onward other Hasse operas enjoyed frequent revivals in the Prussian capital. Hasse visited Frederick in 1753. This atmosphere of affection toward Hasse and his music helped to encourage performances of his intermezzos by Cricchi and Bon.

The general popularity of Hasse's intermezzos is demonstrated by the many performances of them over a period of some thirty years. Royalty and commoners alike clamored to hear these comic works. Frederick the Great's enthusiasm was matched by the admiration of the Neapolitan queen Maria Amalia (b. 1724, daughter of the Saxon monarch Frederick Augustus, who married Charles III of Naples in 1738). The affection that had developed toward Hasse at the court in Dresden prompted her to arrange the production of some of her favorite intermezzos in Naples shortly after her arrival in that city.

While performances of Hasse's intermezzos continued in Italy in the 1740s, the demand for them throughout the 1740s and '50s shifted from Italy to cities further north—to Hamburg, Dresden, Potsdam, and Copenhagen. In addition to the singers already mentioned, such touring companies as the Mingotti troupe and the Piccoli Holandesi aided in the spread of Hasse's intermezzos. Three of Hasse's comic works constituted part of the Mingotti company's extensive intermezzo repertoire: *Porsugnacco e Grilletta* (Hamburg, 1745, performed by Pellegrino Gaggiotti and Gaspera Beccheroni); *Il Tabarano* (Copenhagen, 1748, sung by the same two singers; Hamburg, 1745, sung by Allessandro Cattani and Ginevra Magagnoli); and *Il tutore* (Hamburg, 1744, Cattani and Magagnoli).[23]

The Piccoli Holandesi, directed by Nicolini, was a company with a difference: the main actors were children who performed in pantomime. Their period of activity extended from c. 1745 to c. 1770,[24] during which time they ap-

---

22. It is of interest to note that Rosa Bon spent the later part of her life at Eisenstadt where, from c. 1762 to c. 1766, her husband, Girolamo Bon, was involved with productions of Haydn's music at the Esterházy court in his capacities as stage designer, painter, composer, and impresario. See H. C. Robbins Landon, *Haydn: Chronicle and Works*, vol. 1, *Haydn: The Early Years, 1732–1765* (London, 1980), 370–71.

23. Between 1754 and 1758 *Il Tabarano* was presented in Copenhagen a total of twelve times.

24. Landmann, 1: 109. None of the extant sources records Nicolini's given name(s).

peared in Stuttgart, Frankfurt am Main, Munich, Vienna, Prague, Hamburg, and Braunschweig-Wolfenbüttel. The singing in the intermezzos was done by professionals, but it seems that a greater emphasis was placed on the pantomimic potential in the librettos, for the intermezzos were performed with plays acted out in pantomime. Very little is known about the musical activities of this troupe. The surviving librettos, however, indicate that the company had incorporated at least three of Hasse's intermezzos into their repertory: *Il tutore e la pupilla* (Vienna, 1747, with Anna Querzoli Laschi and Filippo Laschi); *Il Tabarano* (Wolfenbüttel, 1750, with Anna Nicolini "di L'Haya nata Van Oploo" and Gaetano Capperoni); and *Merlina e Galoppo (La fantesca)*.[25]

Over a period of roughly thirty years, then, Hasse's intermezzos were presented on European operatic stages both in their original version and in a number of pasticcio-like adaptations. Because of his close association with such *parti buffe* as the Cricchi and Bon pair and the Erminis, Hasse was personally responsible for a number of revisions. This situation allows us a glimpse into his compositional process and into contemporary pasticcio practice. Much of the comic operatic repertoire of the eighteenth century falls within the category of the pasticcio. Unraveling the strands of all these works and identifying their sources would be a task fit for a computer. The only feasible way to deal with the problems surrounding the pasticcio is for the musicologist to chip away at various aspects of the genre in an effort to understand its practices. This process can reveal fascinating glimpses into contemporary singing practices, the musical tastes of the audience, and the composer's attitude toward his work and his singers. In the case of J. A. Hasse, a composer greatly esteemed in his lifetime, and one whose path crossed those of Alessandro Scarlatti, Pergolesi, Handel, Quantz, Metastasio, Haydn, and Mozart, an attempt to understand his efforts in the field of the intermezzo is an attempt to attain an understanding of both the musical style and the aesthetics of his time.

25. Although no libretto has been found to document the date and place of the performance of *La fantesca,* there exists a manuscript copy of the intermezzo with the indication "Al Nicolini" (Weimar: Zentralbibliothek), an indication that supports the conjecture of such a performance.

THE PROBLEM OF
GOETHE'S
DIE UNGLEICHEN
HAUSGENOSSEN

LUISE EITEL PEAKE

Dᴜʀɪɴɢ the 1770s and '80s, at a time when Goethe was writing a number of Singspiel librettos, he corresponded extensively with the composer of his choice, Christoph Kayser. Though he kept assuring Kayser and others that "poetry must be the obedient daughter of music" in the lyric theater,[1] his role as submissive librettist was by no means unambiguous. Kayser was lazy and had little talent, and he needed constant prodding to produce a few settings. Thus along with such general statements as "To me, the opinions of an artist who knows the mechanics of his art are most important, and I place them above all else,"[2] Goethe always included elaborate instructions on what to compose next, how to handle specific passages, what forms and instruments to use, as if he were "Quinault giving orders to Lully."[3] Well versed in current musical styles, Goethe strove to improve the literary quality of existing lyric genres and ultimately to create an opera that combined "German nature with the Italian style," after Mozart's example.[4] Consequently, he often saddled Kayser with problems that could not be solved by him—or perhaps by any composer.

"Observe that there are three kinds of songs," wrote Goethe with regard to his libretto for *Jery und Bätely:*

---

1. Hermann Abert, *Goethe und die Musik* (Stuttgart, 1922), 83. See also Friedrich Blume, "Goethe," *Die Musik in Geschichte und Gegenwart*, 5: 453.
2. Letter to Kayser, Feb. 28, 1786. Johann Wolfgang von Goethe, *Gedenkausgabe der Werke: Briefe und Gespräche* (hereafter cited as GA), ed. Ernst Beutler (Zurich, 1951), 18: 912.
3. Romain Rolland, "Goethe's Interest in Music," *The Musical Quarterly* 17 (1931): 181.
4. Ibid., 189.

First, songs which may be presumed to have been memorized elsewhere by the singing characters and which one introduces into one or another situation. These can and must have their own distinct and well-rounded melodies, which are noticed and easily recognized by everyone.

Second, arias, in which the character expresses the feelings of the moment, and totally lost in this, sings from the bottom of the heart. These must be executed simply, truthfully, and purely, from the gentlest to the most agitated state of mind.

Third comes the rhythmic dialogue, which lends motion to the whole procedure, thus enabling the composer to speed up matters here or to slow them down there. . . .[5]

One might illustrate the first two categories with Gretchen's songs from *Faust,* "Es war ein König in Thule" and "Meine Ruh' ist hin," the first a folksong unrelated to the action, the second an aria charged with the emotion of the moment (even though we know from Goethe's reaction to settings of the famous "Spinning Song" that here too he preferred folksong style). It is not at all clear, furthermore, that Goethe meant "rhythmic dialogue" to be a sort of recitative; he specified that it must be "exactly measured to the course of the action," that it should fit his "almost uniform verse meters," and that Kayser ought to find a "principal theme" to be "brought out again and again in order to lend nuance to individual passages with varied modulations, through major and minor, or with retarded or accelerated tempo."[6]

While Goethe's earliest librettos are plays with inserted songs of the first category, he moved toward Singspiele that have ever more extensive musical components. Recognizing that the main weakness of *Erwin und Elmire* and *Claudine von Villabella* was the relative isolation of the songs within the spoken dialogue, he revised these librettos by providing versified connective passages. The last libretto he was to complete, *Scherz, List und Rache,* was conceived in the spirit of opera buffa, calling for music of an "Italian cast,"[7] through-composed with "Rezitative,"[8] and a comic plot of disguises and intrigues. It failed, no doubt due to Kayser's uninspired score.[9] But Goethe blamed the libretto as "too tight, too belabored," with "too much work for three characters."[10] And since all three characters were villains, he noted a lack of variety in the portrayal of feelings.

5. Letter, Dec. 29, 1779 (GA, 18: 472–73).
6. Ibid., 473. See also Karen Pendle, "The Transformation of a Libretto: Goethe's *Jery und Bätely,*" *Music and Letters* 55 (1974): 79.
7. Letter, Apr. 25, 1785 (GA, 18: 846).
8. Letter, Jan. 23, 1786 (GA, 18: 903).
9. "Italienische Reise," Nov. 1787 (GA, 11: 482).
    Alles unser Bemühen daher, uns im Einfachen und Beschränkten abzuschliessen, ging verloren, als Mozart auftrat. Die "Entführung aus dem Serail" schlug alles nieder, und es ist auf dem Theater von unserm so sorgsam gearbeiteten Stück niemals die Rede gewesen.
10. Letter, Jan. 23 1786 (GA, 18: 902).

With the intention of avoiding such failings in the future, Goethe informed Kayser in December, 1785, "I have started a new one with seven characters. In this I shall also take care of that sentimentality [*Rührung*] . . . which general audiences crave.[11] Entitled *Die ungleichen Hausgenossen,* the book was to include:

> Seven acting characters, living together in one palace, or congregating there from time to time for reasons of family relationship, choice, coincidence or habit. . . . They represent the most diverse personalities, opposed to one another in desires and capabilities, actions and reactions, yet could not get along without each other.[12]

The idea came from Gotter's play *Das öffentliche Geheimnis,* which Goethe had seen in 1781. Based on a translation of Gozzi's *Il secreto pubblico,* which in turn had been adapted from Calderon's *Secreto a voces,* its main dramatic device was a series of anagrammatic verses through which the characters relayed secret messages to each other.[13] Neither Calderon nor Gozzi and Gotter had envisioned music in their respective plays, and it is easy to see that Goethe was attracted largely by the literary challenge it presented. Still, the notion that musical parallels for clever verses of contrasting content could be found—if not in arias and recitatives, then at least in songs in the style of the Berlin school—must also have fascinated him. Since the Lieder of Schulz or Reichardt matched each poem exactly in prosody as well as in affect, it must have seemed reasonable to assume that seven personalities, each represented by a specific song-affect, could interact effectively in a Singspiel.

Many letters to Kayser and Charlotte von Stein from the winter of 1785–86 contain remarks on the progress of the new "operetta." In December he told Kayser:

> My seven personages and their interrelated natures entertain me occasionally, especially when I have to make one-day trips on horseback and have nothing more pressing to think about,[14]

and during the same month he wrote to Frau von Stein in a similar vein.[15] But in January, in an apparent fit of depression, he confessed to her:

> I feel sorry for my poor half-finished operetta, as one might feel sorry for a child that is to be born by a Negro woman in slavery. Under this iron-colored sky!—which I do not scold, since operettas are not an absolute ne-

11. Letter, Dec. 23, 1785 (GA, 18: 896).
12. "Annalen," 1789 (GA, 11: 623).
13. Hedwig Rusack, *Gozzi in Germany* (New York, 1930), 37.
14. Letter to Kayser (GA, 18: 897).
15. Letter to Charlotte von Stein (GA, 18: 893).

cessity. If only I had known twenty years ago what I know now, I would have learned Italian well enough to be able to work for the lyric theater, and I would have forced it somehow. I feel sorry for dear Kayser that he has to waste his music on this barbaric language![16]

Yet Goethe continued undaunted, promising Kayser a scenario as well as some finished segments, and admonishing him to get to work quickly.[17] In the summer of 1786, Goethe traveled to Italy and, anticipating his meeting with Kayser in Rome, seldom failed to mention in letters and diaries up to the fall of 1787 that the "new comic opera" would be worked out then.[18] But after November, when Kayser did arrive, no more was heard of the project. Two years later Goethe was to say:

> I had relegated arias, songs, and ensemble passages from *Die ungleichen Hausgenossen* to my collections of lyric poems, thus making any renewed work on the project impossible for myself.[19]

Kayser must have admitted his inability to compose any music for *Die ungleichen Hausgenossen* on seeing the plan. And from then on Goethe discarded not only this "operetta" but also all further concrete plans for librettos. A serious opera "following the footsteps of Metastasio"[20] was never started, an opera buffa on Cagliostro and the Diamond Necklace Affair (already under way)[21] was converted to a stage play, and the once ardent friendship with Kayser cooled. In all likelihood, the transfer of individual numbers from the opera to poetic collections was suggested by Reichardt, who came to stay with Goethe in Weimar for eleven days in the spring of 1789 principally for the purpose of discussing operatic projects.[22] The tables were then turned, for it was Reichardt who prodded Goethe to write new librettos, and who was always disappointed.

Except for a few fragments (the most significant being a sequel to *Die Zauberflöte* that Goethe wrote more as a study for himself than as a libretto for any living composer), *Die ungleichen Hausgenossen* was Goethe's last practical operatic venture. Since the work embodied the pinnacle of all his efforts in the lyric theater—his ideal combination of comedy with *Rührung,* of "German nature and Italian style"—it is of considerable interest to know what went wrong. Why, for instance, did Reichardt prompt Goethe to destroy the opera by taking out some pieces? Why did he or Goethe himself, who might have called on another composer, see no hope for the future of the promising fragment? From the complete first act, the scenario of the whole, numerous other scenes, and isolated

16. Jan. 26, 1786 (GA, 18: 907).
17. Ibid., 912 and 926.
18. "Italienische Reise," October 27, 1787 (GA, 11: 462).
19. "Annalen," 1789 (GA, 11: 623.)
20. Letter to Kayser, Feb. 28, 1786 (GA, 18: 912).
21. Letter to Kayser, Aug. 14, 1787 (GA, 19: 91).
22. Rolf Pröpper, *Die Bühnenwerke Johann Friedrich Reichardts* (Bonn, 1965), 1: 378.

texts, it is possible to reconstruct the plot, which appears to be eminently suited to music and entirely feasible as a Singspiel.[23] Is it true, then, that in this case "German art has irretrievably lost a great opportunity?"[24]

Act I takes place in the park of a Baron's estate. Rosette enters and sings:

> Ich hab' ihn gesehen,
> wie ist mir geschehen?[25]

Flavio, with whom she is in love, likewise enters and sings, while she hides herself temporarily:

> Hier muss ich sie finden,
> ich sah sie verschwinden ...

Then, in "rhythmic dialogue" and duet passages made up from lines of their respective songs, they discuss the impending visit of the Baroness's sister, the Countess, who, it is hoped, will help the Baron and Baroness settle their marital problems. These are caused by their antipodal personalities, the Baron being a man of action who loves hunting, fighting, and, it is hinted, womanizing, the Baroness being overly sensitive and easily hurt. Next to enter is "the Poet," her protégé, a personification and caricature of her tendencies. As Rosette says of him:

> He feels the beauty of nature right and left, no tree is allowed to green and bloom without admiration. . . . The moon occupies him from the first quarter to the last, and every female sets his tender heart in motion.[26]

While Rosette and Flavio hide, the Poet sings;

> Hier klag' ich verborgen
> dem tauenden Morgen ...

He too quickly hides when his counterpart, Pumper, comes in. Pumper is the Baron's hunter and court jester, as well as his exaggerated image. After his song,

> Es lohnet mir heute
> mit doppelter Beute ...

---

23. Max Morris, "Die ungleichen Hausgenossen," *Chronik des Wiener Goethe Vereins* 18 (1904): 43–48 and 19: 1–9.
24. Ibid., 19: 9.
25. For the full text of this and the other three songs, see the music example in the text (with Reichardt's melodies). The *Ungleichen Hausgenossen* fragment is given in *Goethes Werke,* hereafter cited as WA (Weimar, 1892), 1st section, 12: 225–51. See also "Paralipomena," 392–416. The ensuing summary is partly based on Morris's reconstruction of the plot.
26. WA, 12: 232.

he proceeds to collect some birds he has caught in a snare, thus causing the others to come out of their hiding places and to argue over the fate of the birds (freedom or the frying pan), among other matters. A series of lively ensembles, consisting of lines from each of the four songs, concludes the act.

Act II begins with the Baroness singing an "Arie andantino." Goethe had written this piece on a separate sheet along with a sketched scenario from *Figaros Hochzeit*—probably when his brother-in-law, Christian Vulpius, was preparing a German translation of Mozart's opera for a production in Frankfurt in October, 1788.[27] It is clear that Goethe freely translated in this aria, which begins

> Ach, wer bringt die schönen Tage,
> jene Tage der ersten Liebe . . .

the texts of the Countess's two arias (Acts II and III) from Mozart's opera:

> Porgi amor, qualche ristoro
> al mio duolo, a miei sospir, . . .
> Dove sono i bei momenti
> di dolcezza e di piacer . . .

A marvelously funny scene takes place when the Poet begins rehearsing a tender serenade for the visiting Countess with a woodwind quintet, only to be interrupted by Pumper and his "Janizary Band," who have come to prepare a noisy reveille. As the Poet, hopelessly in love, gets carried away by the delicate sounds of flute, clarinet, etc., he is interrupted by Pumper's shouts, commanding his trumpets and percussions to make more noise. They start fighting, no one being willing to give an inch of ground to the other. Through the Countess's intervention a compromise is reached, and both bands take turns performing to honor the Baron, who happens to be having an anniversary of some kind.

Another, less finished scene shows Rosette alone but faking a dialogue with Flavio and thus provoking the Poet and Pumper, who overhear her from a hiding place, to attack each other verbally and otherwise. In yet another scene the Baron stages a practical joke to be played on Pumper. Throughout the Countess uses her influence (in duets with her sister and the Baron) to heal the wounds and to bring about a general reconciliation in the fifth act. The closing celebration takes the form of a party game with questions and answers framed in elegant verses or songs.

> Was ein weiblich Herz erfreue
> in der klein und grossen Welt?

is answered by the Baroness with a reflection on the constancy of love—con-

27. WA, 12: 393 and 414–16. See also Alfred Loewenberg, *Annals of Opera*, 3rd ed. (Totowa, N.J., 1978), 425.

stancy modified, however, by variety and continual renewal. The Baron replies
to the same question,

> Geh den Weibern zart entgegen,
> du gewinnst sie, auf mein Wort . . .[28]

asserting that quick, bold action must give way to tenderness and consideration
for the feelings of the loved one. Asked about happiness in general, Flavio sums
up variety, strife, and a lighthearted attitude with

> Vielfach ist der Menschen Streben,
> ihre Unruh, ihr Verdruss . . .

while Rosette tells a charming little story of pain in love and speedy recovery,

> Amor stach sich mit dem Pfeile
> und war voll Verdruss und Harm . . .

The Poet, queried in his turn about a "most embarrassing moment," identifies
with Paris, who was forced to make a choice among three beautiful goddesses:

> Paris wat in Wald und Höhlen
> mit den Nymphen nur bekannt . . .

In answering the question "Who has to carry a heavier load than the dumb animal going to the mill?" Pumper takes subtle revenge for the pranks played on
him, revealing a surprising vulnerability and a certain amount of wisdom:

> Wer der Menschen töricht Treiben,
> täglich sieht und täglich schilt . . .

All are perplexed by this, and when Pumper addresses the Baroness with the
question "What is gentler than the path of the moon and softer than a cat's
tread?" Rosette and Flavio break in with:

> Du bist ganz aus dem Geleise,
> gänzlich aus der Melodie!

This altercation, however, is transformed in the spirit of reconciliation, and the
Countess replies,

> Gut, ich nehms als wohl gesungen,
> und ich nehms als wohl gelungen, . . .

28. These lines have entered the repertory of common sayings in Germany. (See Georg Büchmann, *Geflügelte
Worte,* 32nd ed. [Berlin, 1972], 191.)

stating that a clever woman's actions in handling her wayward husband have to be gentler than the path of the moon and softer than the cat's steps.

From these scenes we can see that Goethe thought of his seven personages as human beings rather than as two-dimensional personifications of affects. There is room for development of each character and for the reconciliation of opposites, *Rührung* side by side with situation comedy. A comparison with Mozart's *Figaro* does not seem at all far-fetched. The only feature absent from da Ponte's or any other opera buffa libretto is the artful arrangement of parallel meters, lines, and verse forms, and these seem to constitute the core of *Die ungleichen Hausgenossen*. A skilled composer, say, Mozart or Weber, could possibly have handled the contest scene:

POET	PUMPER
Auf dem grünen Rasenplatze	Auf dem grossen Platz mit Sande,
unter diesen hohen Linden, . . .	in der Läng' und in der Breite, . . .
Übet da die Serenade	Übet mir das tolle Stückchen
die der Gräfin, heut' am Abend	das die Gräfin, morgen frühe
sanft die Augen schliessen soll.	aus dem Schlafe wecken soll.

One might devise two different melodies that first follow one another, then overlap in the heat of the argument and join together in quodlibet fashion. But where there are more than two "opposites" to be joined, as in the party game with similar songs for seven people, one encounters a definite problem. As we saw, the entire first act is built around four songs, one each for Rosette, Flavio, the Poet, and Pumper. Having probably devised all four as parodies of one Lied stanza, Goethe had not given much thought to their musical settings. Clearly, the Poet's melody has to be *empfindsam*—slow, soft, and replete with sighs— whereas Pumper's hunting song calls for loud and fast horn fanfares. Rosette's shy agitation must be handled in a very different way from Flavio's aggressiveness, and even if the lovers' songs could be joined musically, how would they relate to those of the Poet and Pumper? Since everything—melodic contour, rhythm, key, tempo, and dynamics as well as accompaniment—would have to be different in order to express the required affects, there is not one musical way that could parallel the identity of the poetic design. In terms of eighteenth-century song aesthetics, the problem was insoluble.

Kayser's negative reaction is understandable, and when Goethe became aware of his error in judgment his disappointment must have been profound. Though Reichardt too saw no future for the operetta, he was, as we shall see, nonetheless intrigued by it. Goethe's decision to publish elsewhere single "Lieder, Arien, Ensemble Passages" transferred the problem, now in concentrated form, from the lyric theater to the realm of Lied composition. In due time, various solutions were found.

The unproblematic aria inspired by Mozart, "Ach, wer bringt die schönen Tage," which appeared in Goethe's Lieder under the title "Erster Verlust,"[29] was set to music by some forty composers, including Schubert, Mendelssohn, and Verdi ("Chi i bei di m'adduce ancora").[30] On the other hand, no composer ever touched the set of five poems entitled "Antworten bei einem gesellschaftlichen Fragespiel," in which the Baroness, the Poet, the Baron, Flavio, and Pumper have been renamed "Die Dame," "Der junge Herr," "Der Erfahrene," "Der Zufriedene," and "Der lustige Rat," respectively.[31] Without the dramatic context, these verses do not seem to hang together except for their formal features. They look like literary exercises rather than song texts.

The four songs from Act I appeared as "Verschiedene Empfindungen an einem Platz" with Rosette as "Das Mädchen," Flavio as "Der Jüngling," the Poet as "Der Schmachtende," and Pumper as "Der Jäger."[32] It is apparent that Reichardt composed all four but published only three in his *Lieder der Liebe und der Einsamkeit,* explaining in a footnote that "Der Jäger" would be inappropriate in a collection of songs on love and loneliness.[33] Pumper's hunting song then appeared in Reichardt's *Neue Lieder geselliger Freude* with a similar footnote explaining the absence of the other three songs from Goethe's "poem."[34] Ten years later, however, Reichardt did publish all four songs "in the same place" —in his collection *Goethes Lieder, Oden, Balladen und Romanzen* (see Example 1).[35] It is evident that he worked hard to coordinate the four melodies, to observe every detail of proper affective depiction, and yet to show their essential unity. Note, for instance, measures 11–12, where all melodies descend in approaching the word *zurück*—the Girl with an uncertain cadence, the Youth running down the scale, the Pining One gliding around, and the Hunter plunging with a plain triad. Though each tune has its own key, tempo and meter link the first song to the third, and the second to the fourth. The accompaniments, extremely simple, are also tailored to each character. The Hunter's song, as explained in a note, "can also be played by two Waldhorns." Friedrich Himmel, who also accepted the challenge of "Diverse Feelings in the Same Place," fell into the trap unwittingly provided by Goethe: he set all four songs to the same melody.[36] Even though he uses two variants—a gentle one for nos. 1 and 3, a lively one for nos. 2 and 4—the result is not satisfactory. As one reviewer stated:

29. WA, 1: 56; GA, 1: 42–43. The last lines were changed a little in the poetic version, mainly to suggest a shortened da capo form.

30. Willi Schuh, *Goethe Vertonungen* (Zurich, 1953); GA, 2: 672.

31. WA, 1: 37–38; GA, 1: 29–30. These poems, as well as the "Verschiedene Empfindungen an einem Platze," were first published in Schiller's *Musenalmanach* in 1796.

32. WA, 1: 39–40; GA, 1: 31–32.

33. J. F. Reichardt, *Lieder der Liebe und der Einsamkeit,* 1 (Leipzig, 1797): nos. 6a-e.

34. J. F. Reichardt, ed., *Neues Lieder geselliger Freude,* 1 (Leipzig, 1799): no. 6.

35. J. F. Reichardt, *Goethes Lieder, Oden, Balladen und Romanzen,* 1 (Leipzig, 1809): 4–5. A modern edition is available in *Das Erbe deutscher Musik,* vol. 58, ed. Walter Salmen (Munich, 1964), 8–9.

36. F. H. Himmel, *Sechzehn deutsche Lieder* (Zerbst, 1798), no. 8.

EXAMPLE I.

J. F. Reichardt, "Verschiedene Empfindungen an einem Platze," *Goethes Lieder, Oden,
Balladen und Romanzen,* 1: 4–5

M.

ver - ber - get mein Glück.

Jü.

ent-deckt mir mein Glück! ent-deckt mir die Lieb-ste, ent-deckt mir mein Glück!

S.

ver - heh - le dein Glück.

Jä.

es le - be sein Glück!

If music is to express human emotions, the title of the poem should have alerted the composer. Or are we supposed to assume that the same *place* was to be designated by the same melody?[37]

Goethe's good friend Zelter may have tried to grapple with the problem, but eventually turned it over to his talented pupil, Otto Nicolai. Evidently knowing that the "Diverse Feelings" originated as an operatic scene, the latter composed them in a rather effective ensemble.[38] The Girl, the Youth, and the Hunter each sing the first lines of their songs by themselves, and then join in a duet and trio. The Pining One adds his solo lines, then all meet in a quartet. Although the harmonies and the number of measures are the same for each song, which limits expressiveness, the Hunter's fifths and the Poet's sighs are duly preserved.[39] The piece has merits that suggest that Nicolai could perhaps have redeemed the entire Singspiel, but as it stands, one must admit that the abstracted "Diverse Feelings" do not have time to develop in the ensemble. The work sounds like a quodlibet with an odd mixup of tunes, and instead of four feelings there is only one: general hilarity.

Beethoven's pupil Ferdinand Ries found still another solution. Focusing on changeable feelings rather than affects, and by adding other songs at the beginning and the end, he managed to develop the four songs in sequence.[40] A general love song, "An die Erwählte," prepares the way for "Ich hab' ihn gesehen," with short phrases and many rests representing the Girl's shy excitement. The Youth's passionate love song with its exuberant ending seems to conclude a "movement," a process of increasing motion—Andante, Allegretto, Allegro. The song of the Pining One marks a complete break and a new beginning. Slow

37. Anonymous review in the *Allgemeine musikalische Zeitung*, hereafter cited as AMZ, 1 (Dec., 1798): 174.
38. Otto Nicolai, *Verschiedene Empfindungen an einem Platze . . . in Musik gesetzt für 1 Sopran, 2 Tenor, und 1 Bass-Stimme*, Opus 9 (Berlin, n.d.); dedicated to Goethe.
39. Georg R. Kruse, "Goethe, Zelter und Otto Nicolai," *Goethe-Jahrbuch* 31 (1910): 167.
40. Ferdinand Ries, *Sechs Lieder von Goethe*, Opus 32 (Hamburg, c. 1811).

and mournful at first, it brightens in the second half when the Poet recalls his secret happiness. The Hunter picks up with an even happier melody; however, considering Pumper's extreme boisterousness, this is a relatively subdued version of that song. The real feeling of the lines "Es lebe der Jäger,/es lebe sein Glück!" is expressed in the last song of the set, Goethe's "Tischlied: Mich ergreift, ich weiss nicht wie," one of the grandest and most boisterous drinking songs ever.[41]

Had Goethe heard these songs, he would probably not have liked them, because his carefully structured parallelism seems to be quite superfluous here, in fact, an obstacle to the development of musical feelings. The "same place" is merely the togetherness of the songs in one book, or rather—since Ries achieves an essentially romantic chain of songs that engages the listener's empathy and allows his feelings to spill over from one song to the next—a very subtle "same place" in the listener's mind. Though Ries's Sechs Lieder von Goethe are by no means masterpieces, they represent a breakthrough of a kind. Since Ries may have worked on them under Beethoven's direction, it is not surprising that Beethoven should have remembered Goethe's problem and its novel solution.[42]

A poetic parody, Sophie Mereau's "Verschiedene Eindrücke des Frühlings,"[43] allows four persons of different temperaments to share a more poetic common ground than "the same place." This work in turn provided the basis for four poems by Gubitz, "Die Temperamente bei dem Verluste der Geliebten," which was composed as a devastatingly ironic song cycle by Carl Maria von Weber.[44]

It appears that Reichardt all along had also pondered the dramatic possibilities of the song group from Die ungleichen Hausgenossen. The hide-and-seek game from Act I, the songs of Rosette and Flavio, a Janizary band as well as contrasting affect songs of all kinds mingle in a new theatrical genre that he announced rather grandly in 1800 as a kind of reformed Singspiel and a German counterpart of the French vaudeville comedy: the "Liederspiel" made up of "Lied und nichts als Lied."[45] Reichardt says that while working on Goethe's Jery und Bätely he found that the simplest songs, among them some genuine Swiss and French folksongs, were the most effective items in the score. Alas, Herr Goethe could not be persuaded to revise the little opera accordingly.[46] In Reichardt's opinion, German opera was too noisy and complicated, with the result that the best and most deeply felt songs often went unnoticed.

41. Frederick Sternfeld, Goethe and Music (New York, 1954), 112–13.

42. See my essay "The Antecedents of Beethoven's Liederkreis," Music and Letters 63 (1982): 242–60.

43. Sophie Mereau, Gedichte (Berlin, 1801–2).

44. Carl Maria von Weber, Die Temperamente bei dem Verluste der Geliebten, Opus 46 (Berlin, c. 1816). See also Max Friedländer, "Die vier Temperamente: Liederreihe von C. M. von Weber," Die Musik 11 (1912): 228–29.

45. J. F. Reichardt, "Etwas über das Liederspiel," AMZ 3 (July, 1801): 709–17. See also Journal des Luxus und der Mode (Berlin, 1800), 481.

46. AMZ 3: 716. See also Pröpper, 1: 99–100.

I searched for a suitable subject and believe to have found it with a little piece I had prepared a few years ago for an entirely different purpose: a family celebration in my home. I had included songs by Goethe, Herder, and Salis as well as folk songs which were favorites with my family and which everybody could sing, satisfactorily supported by a simple instrumental accompaniment.[47]

Reichardt was fortunate in securing the services of the best actor-singers, and the new Liederspiel, *Lieb' und Treue,* was performed in the Berlin opera house with tremendous success. (It received thirty-two performances in Berlin between 1800 and 1816, and also played in many other cities.)[48] Very reluctantly, Reichardt admitted that his second Liederspiel, in which he meant to combine sentimental songs and a humorous subject, was a failure. The management insisted on changing the title from *Juchhey!* to something less "niedrig-komisch," *Der Jubel,* thus misleading the critics, who misunderstood and were unfair.[49] The work received only three performances, while a third Liederspiel, *Kunst und Liebe,* not mentioned by Reichardt in his essay, never made it to the stage.

The Swiss milieu of *Jery und Bätely,* alpine and rustic, is also that of *Lieb' und Treue.* Father Richard and his children are setting up a birthday party for the mother, and while singing "Wie lieb' ich euch ihr Nachtigallen" (a translated *romance,* "Que j'aime à voir les hirondelles"), recall their former home in France and their friendship with the young nobleman Louis, whom they presume to have perished during the Revolution. A couple of Swiss peasants, actually Louis and his sister in disguise, are invited to the party, and when Louis sings "Im Felde schleich' ich still und wild," Richard's daughter Rose, who was in love with him, recognizes the song. Hiding herself, she sings another song they had shared before their separation, and when Louis answers with still another "test song," his true identity is revealed. The reunion is celebrated along with the birthday, and all members of the cast contribute more songs for the entertainment.[50]

The score has twelve songs plus an overture which is a folksonglike arrangement for a small instrumental ensemble. Besides the *romance,* there are two Swiss or German folksongs as well as three songs previously published in *Lieder der Liebe und der Einsamkeit,* four from other Reichardt collections, and only one specifically composed for the play. The ensembles sometimes consist of alternately sung lines from preceding songs,[51] similar to the "rhythmic dialogues" Goethe had written in the first act of *Die ungleichen Hausgenossen.* The hide-and-seek game as well as the birthday party, we can see now, are merely

47. AMZ 3: 711–12. See also Pröpper, 1: 128–30.
48. Loewenberg, 554.
49. AMZ 3: 715.
50. Pröpper, 1: 137.
51. J. F. Reichardt, *Lieder aus dem Liderspiel Lieb' und Treue* (Berlin, 1800). See also Pröpper, 2: 115–20.

devices to provide a framework for the singing of unrelated songs—"songs which may be presumed to have been memorized elsewhere by the singing character," as Goethe had put it. The characters, thus poised, can sing a love song, a hunting song, a mournful song, and a happy one—in fact, as many songs of diverse affects as one might wish in close succession and in the same place.

The formula did not work again for *Kunst und Liebe,* even though the story was more or less the same and the songs more "deeply felt" and more action-related. An artist's daughter, Marie, here exchanges "test songs" with the young painter, Reinhold, and their little game ends with Marie's "Ich hab' ihn gesehen" and Reinhold's "Hier muss ich sie finden."[52] Ludwig Tieck, of whom Reichardt asked an honest appraisal, gave him a frank criticism: the use of "artists" makes no sense, the action is monotonous and confusing at the same time, the characters are lifeless, and the songs, which in *Lieb' und Treue* grew out of plot development, here seem contrived; moreover, some of Reichardt's best Goethe songs, such as "Kennst du das Land?" seem almost to be travesties in this trivial context.[53]

The weakness of the Liederspiel genre comes out fully in *Der Jubel.* A Janizary march sets the scene in a military camp, and the protagonists are a drill sergeant, soldiers, fishermen, innkeepers, and a "Zithermädchen," part Mignon and part camp follower.[54] For instance, when the sergeant, slightly drunk, sings or bawls "Der Wein erfreut des Menschen Herz," followed by the lovesick zither girl's "Die Lieb' erfreut des Menschen Herz," it seems hardly surprising that critics found the play "niedrig-komisch" and offensive.

Reichardt's intentions were honorable, for he wished to give the "best German songs" a stage setting as well as wider publicity than they would get in song collections. What he did not realize was that this Liederspiel opened the door to mediocrity and lent an air of respectability to pasticcios of popular songs with the plot for an excuse. Himmel, who was altogether less scrupulous than Reichardt, right away, in 1801, produced a Liederspiel, *Frohsinn und Schwärmerei.* Then, adopting some elements of vaudeville comedy, he far outdistanced Reichardt's popular successes with *Fanchon das Leyermädchen* of 1804.[55] Thereafter, with contributions from Karl Ludwig Blum, Karl von Holtei, Carl Alexander Herklots, Georg Friedrich Treitschke, August von Kotzebue, Louis Angely, and various other composers, librettists, and men of the theater, the Liederspiel had a long but artistically less distinguished career, eventually merging with other light operatic genres of the mid-nineteenth century such as burlesque, Posse, or operetta.[56]

---

52. *Musik zu Reichardts Liederspielen,* ed. François Reinhard (Strasbourg, 1804), 44–46 and nos. 8 and 9.
53. Cited in Pröpper, 1: 133–34.
54. Ludwig Kraus, *Das Liederspiel in den Jahren 1800–1830* (Ph.D. diss., Halle-Wittenberg Universität, 1921), 32.
55. Loewenberg, 580. It ran in Berlin until 1853 and was translated into Dutch, Polish, and other languages. "Hit songs" from it continued to be popular up to the twentieth century.
56. Kraus, 33–51.

Goethe probably never knew what he had wrought. He was not on the best of terms with Reichardt between 1795 and 1805; anyway, Reichardt's literary efforts in his Liederspiele would have left him cold. For Goethe, *Die ungleichen Hausgenossen* was by 1800 long forgotten, being merely another failure for German "Spieloper" with a literate text—in short, nothing but an "unheard-of waste of time."[57] Yet even the failures of a Goethe and the honest mistakes of a Reichardt had their repercussions, and if we total these up—from Nicolai's "quodlibet," Ries's pre-Romantic song cycle and its possible influence on Beethoven, to Weber's "Four Temperaments" and its twentieth-century reinterpretation in Hindemith's music, not to mention the many settings of "Erster Verlust" and the consequences of Reichardt's Liederspiel—one has to concede that Goethe's time was not wasted after all.

A rather amusing epilogue might be appended here. In September, 1869, Johannes Brahms was contemplating the composition of an opera and asked Max Kalbeck to write a libretto for him based on Gozzi's *Il secreto pubblico*. He had already copied large portions of the text (Kalbeck does not say whether from Gozzi's Italian play or Gotter's German "translation"), and he was all set to compose certain passages. Brahms was fascinated mainly by "the marvelous opportunity it offered for the presentation of a concert on stage."[58] Understandably surprised, Kalbeck asked Brahms, "How do you propose to express the anagram in music, the essential ingredient of the 'public secret' in such a way that the audience might understand it?" Brahms's answer was gruff: "Just write the text whichever way you like, and let me worry about the rest."[59] About one hundred years earlier, Goethe might have said to Kayser; "Just set to music the songs I send you, whichever way you like, and let me worry about the rest."

57. Rolland, 182.
58. Max Kalbeck, *Johannes Brahms* 3 (Berlin, 1904): 160–63.
59. Ibid., 167–69.

THE END OF
THE ORATORIOS

JOEL SACHS

It was the 1730s and London's Italian-opera world was collapsing in financial ruin. Handel, donning the protective clothing of the oratorio, was about to demonstrate a resourcefulness that would become legendary. Caught between the economic disaster of his operatic speculations and the vogue of ballad opera, which was totally alien to his musical instincts, he sensed a third course—a sacred entertainment that, under certain circumstances, would not suffer from nightly competition. Unfortunately, he misjudged the market. The entertainment-minded wealthy of the city found his oratorios a big bore, and the Puritans found them offensive—an affront to their concept of morality. In view of the spectacular success the Handelian oratorio was to achieve in Victorian England, it is almost inconceivable that Handel had such initial difficulties in "selling" his masterpieces.[1]

Handel's resourcefulness, however, was, as always, his salvation. Urgently needing to recoup his losses, he presented a "benefit" concert at the King's Theatre on March 28, 1738, a grand miscellany of sacred music, along with some secular compositions. By all accounts, the event was a tremendous success, netting Handel a considerable sum of money. But why did he call the evening an "oratorio," when it was actually just a concert? Why did that use of the term —Handel's is the earliest known[2]—become standard practice for nearly a cen-

---

1. Winton Dean, *Handel's Dramatic Oratorios and Masques* (London, 1959), 128–49.
2. Howard Smither, *A History of the Oratorio* (Chapel Hill, 1977), 2: 213. For further information, see Otto Erich Deutsch, *Handel: A Documentary Biography* (New York, 1955), 455, and Paul Henry Lang, *George Frideric Handel* (New York, 1966), 298.

tury? And why did the offshoots of this entertainment terminate abruptly in 1840?

The answers to these questions, and to many others about London's music, can be found not only in the nebulous sphere of "public taste," but also in a suite of offices at St. James's Palace.[3] It was from here that an officer of the Royal Household exercised custodial rights over London's entertainment world. The shades of the Lord Chamberlain of His/Her Majesty's Household can tell us why Handel may have chosen his term, why it lasted so long, and why, if the occupants of that office had had their way, it would have lasted longer.

The Lord Chamberlain wields powers of the royal family, not of the British government. While today his duties largely concern ceremonial occasions (for example, the production of the recent wedding of the Prince of Wales), this crown appointee also possessed, until the middle of the twentieth century, the power of censorship over public entertainment. And until 1843 he had even greater control over theater and music. His duties emerge vaguely from the mists of the seventeenth century, having at least one precedent in a reference to royal prerogative in the Act of 12 Anne c. 23 (1713) for the suppression of rogues, vagabonds, etc. The earliest law alluding to the Lord Chamberlain with respect to the theater is 10 George II c. 28 (1737), another statute dealing with crime. Clarifying some questions that arose after 12 Anne c. 23, this new law extended penalties for vagabond behavior to all persons acting or causing to be acted—whether for gain, hire, or reward—any entertainment on the stage, without authority by virtue of letters patent from His Majesty or of license from the Lord Chamberlain. The Lord Chamberlain's office would be henceforth responsible for theatrical censorship.[4] It is thought that the crackdown of 1737 resulted directly from the sensational success of the *Beggar's Opera* (1728), which had provoked the Puritan faction to attempt to suppress the "immoral" world of the theater.[5]

The power of the crown or of the Lord Chamberlain in restricting or censoring entertainment was not geographically unlimited. It encompassed just the City and Liberties of Westminster[6] and those other places where the sovereign resided, although only during the times when the king or queen was actually in residence. Clearly, the powerful English gentry were prepared to grant such sweeping royal authority only within defined limits—not, for example, where they could be pestered in their country estates. A look at the map, however, shows that these provisions effectively placed under crown control all entertainment in the built-up London of 1737, with the sole and significant exception of

---

3. The surviving documents are in the Public Record Office, London (hereafter cited as PRO).

4. For the original laws, see *The Statutes at Large* 4: 647–48, and 6: 275–77.

5. Dean, 132.

6. The City of Westminster comprised the parishes of St. Margaret's and St. John's; the Liberties comprised the parishes of St. Martin-in-the-Fields, St. James, St. Ann Soho, St. Paul Covent Garden, St. Mary-le-Strand, St. Clement's Danes, St. George Hanover Square, and the Precinct of the Savoy. (See James Elmes, *A Topographical Dictionary of London and Its Environs* [London, 1831], 406.

the City of London (the commercial district), whose guilds jealously guarded their own prerogatives against royal encroachments. Although 10 George II c. 28 was extremely unpopular, it remained in force for over a century.[7]

The term *letters patent* refers primarily to the Drury Lane and Covent Garden Theatres, which operated under a monopoly based on the Killigrew and Davenant Patents (1662). All other aspiring entertainers henceforth would have to apply for licenses from the Lord Chamberlain. The application of his powers as well as the evasion of their stranglehold became a complex and, for us, fascinating affair. Two of its aspects need particular attention here. The first is that under the 1737 act, the Lord Chamberlain could exercise his will "when and as often as he shall think fit."[8] The occupants of his office, therefore, could extend their control over entertainment without the slightest additional statutory confirmation. The other salient point concerns the growth of London as a world metropolis, a development that created an ever increasing market for entertainment, an ever greater number of entertainers ready to profit from that market, and ever stronger pressure on the Lord Chamberlain to intervene on behalf of the Patent Theatres. For in reality his chief obligation was to protect the interests vested in these theaters, in which many wealthy and influential persons had a large financial stake.[9] By the 1820s the Lords Chamberlain found themselves having to reconcile many conflicts between the old Patent Theatres and the more recent entertainment centers that enjoyed considerable professional and community support. The addition of new and articulate interest groups to the ranks of the prosperous complicated the task still further.

However, we are primarily interested in "oratorios." One of the powers wielded by the Lord Chamberlain's office—*office* is an appropriate term because the documents strongly imply that the paid staff was creatively expanding its own powers—was control of Lenten entertainment. This control took two forms: the enforced closing of minor theaters (those without patents) on Wednesdays and Fridays during Lent and in Passion Week, and the restriction of entertainment at the Patent Theatres on those days to "sacred" works. (Even "sacred" dramas had offended the Puritans of Handel's day, since they believed in the fundamental immorality of all theater; but their influence gradually waned.)[10] Impinging as it did on tradition, religion, class conflict, free trade, and royal power, the curious matter of the Lenten restrictions summoned up deep feelings of hostility toward authority. It reminded the British of how the passing of time inexorably transformed law into arbitrary and inconsistent power. Emboldened by the growing divisiveness evident in every aspect of British life, the forces of reform in the 1830s found in these restrictions a new issue around which to rally.

7. Sir William Holdsworth, *A History of English Law* (London, 1938), 11: 547–49.

8. Clause 4.

9. For example, in the form of "property boxes" which could be rented out for a profit by their individual owners.

10. See Dean, chap. 7.

Let us look over the reformers' shoulders as they searched the statute books for a clear definition of the Lenten restrictions. There are no surprises for us: we know that the wording of the fourth clause of the 1737 act—"when and as often as he shall see fit"—rendered superfluous any specific reference to Lent. Indeed, it had placed the shaping of entertainment solely in one person's hands. How this power was exercised depended, of course, on the particular Lord Chamberlain. We might cite the example of the duke of Montrose, who refused to license plays in French in the early 1820s because they had never before been licensed.[11]

The exact beginning of the prohibition of Lenten entertainments eludes discovery; presumably, it was an age-old tradition. That every Lenten day was not included under the ban in Handel's time seems reasonably certain, for operas were performed on some nights.[12] Probably the restriction was already confined to Wednesdays and Fridays as well as to all of Passion Week. We now see how Handel must have used his business acumen in arranging his benefit night of 1738. By giving his concert during PassionWeek, he did not have to fear any competition. But how to get past the authorities? Simply, he made his concert predominantly "sacred" and called it an "oratorio," which most certainly it was not. His gamble paid off amply. Not only was the entertainment allowed, but it also seems to have set a precedent. The date is surely significant, for this was the first Lent after the passage of the 1737 act had given the Lord Chamberlain his enormous power. If Handel had put on his benefit the year before, he might not have had to shield himself with the clever title.

The earliest reference to Lent in the Lord Chamberlain's surviving documents appears fifteen years later in an order of April 11, 1753, prohibiting even oratorios during Passion Week.[13] The messy state of the eighteenth-century ledgers, however, suggests that they may very well contain far from all the decrees of the Lord Chamberlain. The incontrovertible fact is that by the early nineteenth century, the theaters had virtually no flexibility on the prohibited days. Moreover, two other days had slipped away from them: January 30, the anniversary of the execution of King Charles I, and Whitsun Eve in the late spring. The oboist-composer William Thomas Parke recalled in his *Memoirs* how, in 1809, the prohibition concerning January 30 was defied for the first time:

> The 30th of January had hitherto been held so sacred, that no public performance whatever had been permitted. The last season, however, Mr. Ware, the leader of the band at Covent Garden Theatre, ventured to give his benefit concert on that night at the Haymarket Theatre, and it not having been interruped by the authorities, Mr. Ashley, the proprietor of

11. PRO, L.C. 1/42, p. 129 (Jan. 18, 1824).
12. Howard Smither, "Oratorio," *The New Grove* 13: 668.
13. PRO, L.C. 5/162 (Warrant Book 30), fols. 2–3.

the oratorios, this season added it to his former number of performances, and as innovation has seldom any bounds, he afterwards included Whitsun eve.[14]

Parke, whose own imagination also frequently had no bounds, for once had his facts straight. The Covent Garden manager's ledgers show that on January 30, 1809, the oratorio (Messiah) grossed £155.12.0, just a bit below the average receipts for the twelve oratorios given that year.[15]

The plain facts of these ledgers then show that someone had found a golden goose. In 1810, the oratorio receipts jumped tremendously. For the twelve performances in that year (January 30 and eleven times in Lent), receipts averaged just under £500—an increase of 250 percent. The year 1811 was not quite so good, but still lucrative enough to suggest that the oratorio had become quite an attraction.[16] We might credit this situation to the general economic upturn or to the era of spending ushered in by the assumption of the regency by the Prince of Wales. The Whitsun Eve oratorio, by way of contrast, was rarely a success; licenses for it were often recorded as "not used."

The true reason for the success of the oratorios must have been their gradual transformation into a more general musical entertainment far surpassing, in proportion, the small infusion of secular music that Handel had used for "insurance" in 1738. The paucity of surviving programs shields this transitional phase from accurate appraisal. Nevertheless, in 1818 the Quarterly Musical Magazine and Review could report that the oratorios had become "little more than secular performances," which deserved praise for introducing fine music to the poorer people who attended the Patent Theatres. But even oratorios were subject to the vicissitudes of theatrical economy, which was then in a state of depression. For instance, the data from Covent Garden show that receipts fell severely in 1815. Thus in 1818 the Patent Theatres decided to open their doors only on alternate oratorio evenings.[17]

Nevertheless, the oratorio speculators persisted. Describing this phenomenon in the late 1820s, William Stafford referred to their sacred origin—was their origin really sacred? we may ask—but explained that now there were usually two acts of sacred music and one of secular music, unless Messiah was being performed.

By this practice, though variety is provided, some strange juxtapositions, frequently take place, and things sacred and profane are sadly jumbled together. The most eminent performers, vocal and instrumental, are usually engaged; and the high terms which the former demand as a remuneration for their talents, have very materially diminished the profits of these per-

14. William Thomas Parke, Musical Memoirs (London, 1830), 2: 32.
15. The British Library, Mss. Add. 31975 (Charles Kemble's Memoranda Book).
16. Ibid.
17. Quarterly Musical Magazine and Review 1 (1818): 404–5.

formances. Indeed, for several years, the conductors [i.e., the promoters] have been losers. This is much to be regretted, as the oratorios are the cheapest musical performances to which the public of the metropolis have access.[18]

Despite the mixed repertory, the atmosphere of these oratorio evenings was passably sacred. The *Quarterly Musical Magazine and Review,* however, considered them grand miscellaneous concerts with only enough sacred music to preserve a semblance of the original cause of their establishment.[19] Any number of examples could demonstrate the odd mixture. Let us content ourselves with looking at an advertisement in the *Times* (March 24, 1820) that touted a closing oratorio night with a "grand concertante" by Friedrich Kalkbrenner and a *New Grand Battle Sinfonia* by Peter von Winter, played by an "orchestra" (soloists, chorus, and orchestra) of nearly two hundred performers.

Obviously, the Lenten restrictions were not being applied very literally. Inasmuch as the authorities controlled both the statute and the prescribed fines for violation, we must assume that they had chosen to ignore their own rules. Entertainment, after all, was a business. Times had changed, and the language of business was spoken fluently in Britain. But if the authorities were turning a blind eye, the competition was not. In March, 1823, John Ebers, the manager of the King's Theatre (the Italian opera house), detected in the expanding notion of Lenten entertainment a threat to his own monopoly and appealed to the Lord Chamberlain to stop the Patent Theatres from performing Italian operatic excerpts on their oratorio programs.[20] Since the King's Theatre enjoyed the support of some of the most powerful people in Britain, the Lord Chamberlain's office quickly asserted its authority. Thomas Mash, the comptroller for the Lord Chamberlain, apprised the managers of Covent Garden and Drury Lane that:

> As every Theatre is closed on the Wednesdays and Fridays during Lent except for the performance of Oratorios and Sacred Music, it is very objectionable that on those days any other Music should be introduced. My Lord Chamberlain expects that this intimation will render any further interposition of his authority unnecessary and restrain the performance of Italian Opera Music and songs which are not of the description of Sacred or Oratorio Music, such being inconsistent with a due observance of the Season of Lent.[21]

Drury Lane, for one, would not take this dictate lying down. Its subcommittee on oratorios convened immediately—no time could be lost—and replied within four days that the title "oratorio," if construed to mean "sacred," would

18. William C. Stafford, *A History of Music* (Edinburgh, 1830), 366–67.
19. *Quarterly Musical Magazine and Review* 8 (1826): 388–91.
20. PRO, L.C. 1/9, Item 648.
21. PRO, L.C. 1/42, fol. 90 (from Thomas Mash, March 7, 1823).

admit only performances of *Messiah*. In commercial terms, the truth was that nothing sacred but *Messiah* would draw audiences, and even it could be repeated but once or twice a season. Without a realistic attitude on the part of the Lord Chamberlain, the institution of oratorios would have to be abandoned.[22] Ignaz Moscheles's personal experience substantiates this argument. When he attended an oratorio that season (1823), he witnessed the audience storming and stamping because of the deletion of some pieces from Rossini's *La donna del lago*.[23]

The testimony of Moscheles suggests that the Lord Chamberlain prevailed, but even if that were so, his victory was temporary. The restrictions were gradually loosened to the point of allowing performances at some of the minor theaters, where mechanical exhibitions, lectures, and even some comedies brought moral contemplation to Londoners during Lent. The minor theaters could evade the power of St. James's Palace in various ways, but the question remains as to why the Lords Chamberlain tolerated the erosion of their authority. The lack of correspondence in the exceptionally neat early nineteenth-century records suggests that if the duke of Devonshire, the earl of Monmouth, and other holders of this office felt the need for change, they kept their feelings to themselves. Since the duke of Devonshire was Lord Chamberlain for much of this period, we may find some insight into his silence in a remark about him in the *Dictionary of National Biography*, which tells us that in the House of Lords he never spoke out on any of the great issues. He did, however, specialize in behind-the scenes opinions, so we should be careful not to assume that he was simply lethargic. As for the Drury Lane Theatre, it had a surprising protector, who will soon be unmasked.

All the same, the increasing secularization of the oratorios was provocative. *The Athenaeum* reported, as Lent of 1829 approached,

> We have heard that the introduction of Concertos is this Season prohibited by the Lord Chamberlain. We should be glad to learn if this is really a fact, and, if so, the objection.[24]

Was this mere rumor—Mash's impeccable documents do not refer to such a prohibition—or were hints being dropped that the days of toleration were numbered? Unfortunately, extant documents provide no answer, but newspaper reports that year suggest that the oratorios may have taken place at a greatly reduced level.

Nothing promotes change quite so efficiently as public exposure. For better or worse, the power struggle among the theatrical interests and with the Lord Chamberlain came to a head with the parliamentary Dramatic Hearings of

22. PRO, L.C. 1/9, Item 649.
23. *Aus Moscheles Leben*, ed. Charlotte Moscheles (Leipzig, 1872–73), 1: 73.
24. *The Athenaeum* (London), Feb. 29, 1828, 173.

1832, during which a committee, chaired by M.P.-novelist Edward Bulwer-Lytton, tried to discover why the English theater was in such a state of commercial and intellectual doldrums. The hearings must have been the best show in town. They revealed a scandalous situation: nobody really knew exactly what the Lord Chamberlain was authorized to do or how his powers had grown to their current proportions. There was certainly no consensus whatsoever as to whether the Patent Theatres needed or deserved legal protection, and there was even some question as to whether Drury Lane was or ever had been included in the original seventeenth-century patents. Two facts came to light during the hearings, and they were hardly calculated to enhance the prestige of the Lord Chamberlain's office. It was learned that Thomas Mash, the principal officer on the staff and the first witness, was receiving an annual "gratuity" of £100 (recently reduced from £200!) from Drury Lane for watching over their interests and that, moreover, licensing fees were divided among the Lord Chamberlain's staff members, thus making the licensing of anything and everything highly desirable from their point of view. One can imagine the committee's reaction on hearing from Mash that the Lord Chamberlain rarely enforced his prohibitions with legal action.[25]

These revelations posed a potential threat to the Lord Chamberlain, for if he did nothing to clean house and assert his authority, he would soon cease to be needed. The managers, for their part, could not help being provocative in their quest for ways of reviving their sagging box office. Pierre Laporte, Covent Garden's new manager (who, in the 1820s, had found a lucrative escape from the prohibition against French plays) had a stroke of genius that enabled him to fill the house at Lent: he offered a production called *The Israelites in Egypt*, a concoction brewed from Rossini's *Mosè in Egitto* and Handel's oratorio, fully staged and in costume. The proof of the pudding, as it were, is to be found in the ledgers. In a year (1832–33) when Covent Garden's receipts never exceeded £370 per night and when, after February 1, they were always below £150 and sometimes well below £100, the results of eleven performances of this "sacred" show are very instructive:[26]

February 22	£132.15.0	March 15	320.11.0
27	247. 8.6	20	328. 9.0
March 1	256.10.6	22	318. 3.6
6	320.19.0	27	421. 6.0
8	305. 1.0	29	504.13.0
13	311.11.0		

Laporte might well have called the production "The Return of the Golden Goose." But as Alfred Bunn, the manager of Drury Lane, put it, the very suc-

25. The complete transcript is in *Report from the Select Committee on Dramatic Literature with Minutes of the Evidence* (House of Commons, August 2, 1832). The report is reprinted in the Irish University Press Series of Parliamentary Papers, with an intro. and index by Marilyn Norstedt (Shannon, 1968).
26. The British Library, Mss. Add. 23162.

cess of this staged oratorio, probably a first in England, virtually assured that the Lord Chamberlain would not permit it to set a precedent.[27] When, in February, 1834, Covent Garden announced a staging of Handel's *Jephtha* (combined with heaven knows what), the Vice Chamberlain promptly disabused the management of its presumption.[28] According to contemporary accounts, the bishop of London, Benjamin Blomfield, had convinced Queen Adelaide of the moral reprehensibility of performing such music in a theater and she, in turn, instructed the Lord Chamberlain about his duties. Their action·was greeted in the press with a hoot of typically late-1830s ridicule.[29]

Coming at a time when the theaters were on the verge of collapse (and when similar problems lay just around the corner for the concert world), this new prohibition ensured the inevitability of a collision. On the one hand, minor theaters were infringing on the Patent Theatres' monopoly by such clever subterfuges as having only one person on stage at a time (thus rendering the entertainment "nondramatic") or by performing Shakespearian plays with piano accompaniment (thus converting them into "burlettas"). On the other hand, the Lord Chamberlain was doing his part to interfere with the Patent Theatres' freedom of action. In April, 1835, the marquess of Conyngham became Lord Chamberlain, and ensuing events suggest that for Lent in 1836 he cracked down on "nonsacred" presentations. Realizing then how much Drury Lane stood to lose if it were forced to present strictly sacred oratorios, Alfred Bunn seized the initiative. In March, 1837, he petitioned the House of Commons to block the Lord Chamberlain from meddling in Lenten entertainments.[30] This petition must have been the stimulus for a bill introduced on April 17, 1837, a bill which would have amended the century-old licensing act by clarifying the Lenten regulations. Had it passed, it would have prohibited performances in the City and Liberties of Westminster on Sundays, Ash Wednesday, Passion Week, Whitsun Eve, Christmas Eve and Day, and any day set aside for public thanksgiving, fasting, or general mourning. Oratorios, selections of sacred music, and other sacred entertainments could take place on any day but Sunday, Christmas, Good Friday, or the days set aside for thanksgiving, and so on. This change in effect freed the remainder of Lent from restrictions and made totally clear the purview of the Lord Chamberlain's power.[31] But before anything could happen, King William died and Parliament was dissolved. With Victoria on the throne, a similar bill was introduced to and passed by the new Commons, but totally gutted in the House of Lords. A conference committee proved unable to resolve

27. Alfred Bunn, *The Stage: Both before and behind the Curtain, from Observations Taken on the Spot* (London, 1840), 1: 176–78.

28. PRO, L.C. 1/45, fol. 23. According to the wording of the letter, the license may have been available for 1834, but it does not appear that the projected performances of *Jephtha* took place.

29. Dean, 124–25.

30. PRO, L.C. 1/20, Item 1708.

31. Bills Public, 1837 (VII William 4), 4: 469.

the differences, and 10 George II c. 28 not only remained in force but was even strengthened.[32]

This attempt to limit the powers of the Lord Chamberlain was not the first. In 1825 a petition had urged Parliament to abolish his control entirely, which control, let us recall, included censorship; bills proposed in 1833 and 1835 got nowhere.[33] Now, however, momentum was gathering so quickly that a real battle could be expected, and not just because of the ridicule heaped on the Lord Chamberlain after the 1832 Dramatic Hearings. The forces of liberalization finally had a dynamic leader in Parliament, the remarkable Thomas Duncombe, M.P. for Finsbury, a parliamentary district that had been created in 1834 after the Reform Bill had broken some of the power of the landed gentry. Though only forty-three years old, Duncombe was no novice. In 1826 and again in 1830 he had been returned as Whig M.P. for Hertford. But in 1832 Duncombe lost his reelection battle, apparently because of extreme skulduggery by the marquess of Salisbury. "Radicalized" in the process, Duncombe became the spokesman for the extreme reformers. In 1842 he would introduce the great petition of 3,315,752 signatures for the Chartists' Six Points; in 1846 he would purportedly aid the escape of Prince Louis Napoleon from detention at Ham (southwest of London); and he would become deeply embroiled in the Italian revolutionary movement.[34] He served his Finsbury constituency until his death in 1861.

Duncombe, who had brought forth Bunn's 1837 petition in the Commons, was the very opposite of the silent duke of Devonshire. In parliamentary debates he was an absolutely formidable orator. The *Dictionary of National Biography* describes him as

> a good looking and agreeable man, popular alike in society and in his constituency of Finsbury. He had the reputation of being the best-dressed man in the house, and was a fluent, though eccentric speaker. His speeches, without actually being witty, always raised a laugh, and he has been described by an acute observer as being "just the man for saying at the right moment what everybody wished to be said and nobody had the courage to say."

Duncombe had already shown his interest in the theatrical world's plight by introducing Bunn's petition, but there is no record of any formal address by him on the subject. In 1839, however, Duncombe decided to try again. He may

32. Ibid., 473; *Journal of the House of Commons* (1837), *passim*. Bunn (2: 229) says that the legal fees cost him the very substantial amount of £150. According to him, the bishop of London said that the king himself had directed him to "watch the progress of the bill with the utmost caution."
33. Bills Public, 1833, II, 121; *Hansard's Parliamentary Debates*, hereafter cited as *Hansard* (1833), XVI, cols. 561–67; Bills Public, 1835, III, 503: *Journal of the House of Lords*, LXV (1833) and LXVI (1834), *passim*; PRO, L.C. 1/20, Item 1708.
34. *Dictionary of National Biography*. "Thomas Duncombe."

have felt that the young and enlightened queen would be liberal enough to hear
this cry, or perhaps he was galvanized into action by the high-handed treatment
given the 1837 bill in the House of Lords. On February 18, 1839, not long before Lent, the M.P. arose in the Commons and moved the presentation of an
address to Her Majesty,

> that she will be graciously pleased to give directions to the Lord Cham-
> berlain, to sanction on Wednesdays and Fridays during Lent, within the
> city of Westminster, such entertainments as are enjoyed by Her Majesty's
> loyal subjects in every other part of the Metropolis.[35]

Duncombe cleverly avoided the emotionalism latent in the issue of Lent, seeking
only the right of the profession to offer what was offered elsewhere. For, almost
unnoticed, there actually was an "elsewhere." Once comprising virtually the
whole of London (apart from the City of London), by 1839 Westminster was
only a segment of the exploding London metropolitan area. Irrespective of the
merits of the season of Lent, the old geographical limitation on the power of the
Lord Chamberlain now assured unequal treatment under the law. Entertainment
prohibited in Westminster could easily be found elsewhere. If the Patent
Theatres had to present oratorios at a loss, they would be better off remaining
dark. The audiences knew where to seek their pleasures; only the musicians,
actors, dancers, crew, and management would be the poorer.

The House responded furiously, but not to the substance of the motion.
Duncombe's effort failed on a simple point of rules. Not having given the required prior notice of a motion, he was defeated, 160 to 70, in a howl of protest
over the breach of order. In the debate, the angry character of which is easily
sensed from the *Hansard* report, Lord John Russell, Home Secretary, leader of
the majority and a spokesman for official liberalism, expressed his opinion that
Duncombe's motion was more of a private grievance than a matter of parliamentary business.[36]

Time was running out. On February 26, Duncombe was back, hurrying
to accomplish something before another Lent had cost the performers of Westminster more income. This time, having given proper notice, Duncombe wisely
avoided forcing the queen to become a party to the dispute. Such a maneuver
was not easy, considering that the Lord Chamberlain was an officer of her household and not of the state. Duncombe's new resolution, if passed, would assert,

> that it is the opinion of the House, that during Lent no greater restrictions
> should be placed upon theatrical entertainments within the city of West-
> minster, than are placed upon amusements of the same period in every
> other part of the metropolis.[37]

35. *Journal of the House of Commons* (1839), 32.
36. *Hansard* (1839), XLV, cols. 577–83.
37. Ibid., col. 1020ff.

This was a simple enough plea for equal treatment. What a reaction! The acrimonious debate, primarily between Duncombe and Lord John Russell, is a fine specimen of verbal and political class warfare. It fully vindicated the reputation of both men for plain speech and penetrating sarcasm.

First of all, Duncombe demanded just treatment for the theatrical and musical world of Westminster. The restrictions deprived performers of income, whereas the audience could see whatever it liked simply by crossing Oxford Street out of Westminster and into Marylebone, or by crossing the river into the South Bank boroughs. Only the hardworking dramatic profession lost out.

This was merely the preface. Next Duncombe turned to probing the true significance of Lent in England. Imagine the red faces as he described (quoting the *Morning Post*) a great banquet for the Drury Lane Theatrical Fund with plentiful imbibing, during which the Lord Chamberlain himself could be heard singing loudly, on a Wednesday in Lent! Another magnificent party with musical entertainments had numbered the Lord Chamberlain among the guests. And a merry frolic at the deanery of St. Paul's had regaled the elite of the clergy— again on a Wednesday in Lent! Meanwhile, the theatrical and musical professions starved. The restrictions, Duncombe asserted, were dependent on the whim of the Lord Chamberlain; legal opinion held that there was no valid statute. All the while, Duncombe's lengthy disquisition was becoming nastier in tone, spiced with innuendoes such as a pointed reference to the £3000 annual rent paid by the Drury Lane Theatre to the landowner, the duke of Bedford, who made no allowance for the receipts lost on prohibited days.

After the motion was seconded, Lord Russell arose to respond for the Government and the established church. It is not easy to detect his famed liberalism in the speech. First, he relayed the opinion of the bishop of London that entertainments on Wednesdays and Fridays in Lent were disrespectful to church and religion. Furthermore, the practices outside Westminster were illegal, according to Russell, since the magistrates there had only the power to license "music and dancing" and not staged entertainments.[38] Duncombe's proposal would merely spread illegality; and would it not open up Sundays to entertainment? Russell concluded that if Parliament passed the resolution, the Government would not feel bound to abide by it.

As others rose to add their views, the debate heated up still more. Lord Teignmouth predictably sided with Russell, for he may have inherited some of the zeal that had propelled his late father to the presidency of the British and Foreign Bible Society. And of course, as M.P. for Marylebone, Teignmouth represented constituents who benefited from the Lenten restrictions across the street in Westminster. (He probably knew perfectly well that, legal or illegal, the theaters of Marylebone would never be closed up.) J. P. Leader, M.P. for Westminster, supported his own south side of Oxford Street, calling Russell's Sunday-opening argument ridiculous, as it surely was. Sunday, Leader ex-

---

38. Power granted by virtue of 28 George III c. 30 (1788).

claimed at a truly wonderful moment of the debate, was a Protestant holiday; but Wednesday and Friday in Lent were—hear the truth!—Catholic holidays! (Let us recall the acrimonious disagreements over Catholic civil liberties earlier in that decade, with Russell on the side of reform.) Viscount Dungannon, whose title did not bar him from supporting Duncombe the reformer, declared that there was undeniably one law for the rich and one for the poor. But Sir James Graham, a recently lapsed Liberal, pleaded the Lord Chamberlain's responsibility to uphold the law as it stood. Others charged hypocrisy; still other questioned the law. Benjamin Disraeli, a newcomer with only one year behind him in Parliament, reminded his colleagues that the advent of Protestantism in England had been characterized by a relaxation of Lent *and* by the rise of great theater. He would vote with Duncombe. Finally, Duncombe threw in the observation that at Brighton, an area under the Lord Chamberlain's control during a royal residence there, the theater was open on Ash Wednesday in 1838 even though the Lord Chamberlain was actually present in the town. Was this not arbitrary application of the "law"? Apparently so, for Duncombe prevailed by a vote of 92 to 72.[39]

In ecstacy as the new age of freedom dawned over his Drury Lane manager's office, Bunn thanked Duncombe publicly on behalf of his employees. The M.P. replied that it seemed to him.

> impossible that the Lord Chamberlain should any longer interpose his *veto* to the further injury of those who have already suffered by the course which the House of Commons has condemned.[40]

And he graciously observed that the thanks of the theatrical community should also be bestowed on "the common sense of the majority" who had voted with him. Euphoria, alas, had a brief run. Lord John Russell had made his attitude perfectly plain. On March 6, Duncombe furiously accused the government of obstructing implementation of the resolution of February 28 and demanded that Lord Russell, as Home Secretary, "lay on the table" the correspondence between the Drury Lane Theatre and the Lord Chamberlain.[41] Duncombe's suspicions were amply justified, and on the eleventh of the month he introduced a resolution to censure the Government for having directed the Lord Chamberlain "to defeat the manifest object of a resolution of the Commons House of Parliament." Russell replied he did not see that the earlier vote had been so large as to represent a real sense of the wishes of Parliament, since only 164 out of 653 members had voted. (This argument, of course, was specious; a majority is, by

---

39. *Hansard* (1839), XLV, col. 1028; *Journal of the House of Commons* (1839), 67.
40. In an article from an unspecified London newspaper, early March, 1839 (The British Library, Department of Printed Books, 11826.s, vol. 24 [Theatre Cuttings]).
41. *Hansard* (1839), XLV, col. 1318.

law, a majority.) Moreover, Russell claimed he had not interfered; rather he had merely replied to one of the Lord Chamberlain's many requests for guidance.

Then Russell showed his political genius. In an instant, he dissolved the acrimonious mood by admitting that, upon investigation, he had been convinced that Lent was *not* in general observed. His conciliatory remarks obliterated support for Duncombe's censure motion. Aware that he had been outmaneuvered, Duncombe declared that if the Government would promise to introduce remedial legislation, he would withdraw the motion. Russell, now smelling radical blood, would make no such guarantee; Duncombe, virtually admitting defeat, tried to withdraw his motion. No such escape was permitted him; Russell pushed it to a defeat.[42]

And so the motion, and the theatrical lobby, lost. But the debates, publicized broadly and contemptuously, had their effect in consort with external circumstances. In May, 1839, the Government's majority in the House of Commons was reduced to five, and it wisely resigned. As was customary with a change of government, the Lord Chamberlain and other officers of the Royal Household also resigned. Thus was the forty-year old marquess of Conyngham replaced by the forty-year old Henry Paget, earl of Uxbridge. Uxbridge, whom Bunn credits with the kind of liberalism that saved the profession,[43] knew what had to be done. The slate was relatively clean now. Thomas Mash, the Lord Chamberlain's senior officer for so many years and apparently a reactionary in that fashion unique to certain civil servants with decades in their chairs, had retired in some disgrace over the Drury Lane "gratuity." As Lent of 1840 approached, Uxbridge advised the managers of Westminster's theaters that they would be required to close only on Ash Wednesday and in Passion Week.[44] Deregulation had suddenly arrived.[45] Naturally, Uxbridge was bombarded promptly with managerial requests to be allowed to open during Passion Week as well.[46]

Still, the regulations went through one more paroxysm before their demise. Benjamin Lumley, counsel to the Italian opera, had been informed that the annual Lenten lectures at the opera house were illegal because the management's license only permitted operatic events.[47] Onto the field leaped Dun-

---

42. Ibid., XLVI, cols. 229–43; *Journal of the House of Commons* (1839), 49. No vote is given. Presumably the majority for defeat was very large.

43. Bunn, 1: xi. Naturally enough, Bunn's definition of liberalism is conditioned by his vantage point. The marquess of Conyngham was really a liberal in the sense that he opposed the monopoly of the Patent Theatres, but from Bunn's viewpoint, this attitude was extremely dangerous. Uxbridge was a protectionist, but probably far too realistic to fight too hard for the monopoly. On many issues, his stand ended up by benefiting Bunn and his fellow patent-manager at Covent Garden.

44. The theaters in question were: Drury Lane, Covent Garden, Her Majesty's Theatre (formerly the King's Theatre; i.e., the Italian opera house), Adelphi, Olympic Pavilion, St. James's, Lyceum-English Opera House, and the Little Theatre in the Haymarket.

45. PRO, L.C. 1/47, fol. 1.

46. PRO, L.C. 1/47, *passim.*

47. PRO, L.C. 1/47, fol. 2 (Feb. 17, 1840).

combe with a petition of some 1400 "gentlemen of the highest respectability," urging the queen to direct the Lord Chamberlain to allow these traditional lectures on instructive and religious themes. By a vote of 73 to 49, he won.[48]

Essentially, the Lenten closing was a thing of the past. Only three years later, the Lord Chamberlain lost his power to regulate the presentations of any individual theater, and retained only his power of censorship (hardly an insignificant one). He was then given supervisory power over the site selection, construction, and safe operation of all theaters in the kingdom. The entire nature of the theatrical and musical world was basically altered.[49]

Alfred Bunn, whose autobiography reeks of scarcely credible self-righteousness, managed to summarize the preceding tale in an accurate fashion.[50] As a reward for his suffering, this instigator of theatrical liberation deserves to have the last word. Or is it the queen who is really speaking? Bunn reports that his belief that the old regulations were "equally unwholesome and contemptible" was borne out by the fact that "on the very first night of Lent, when the prohibition was taken off, Her Majesty was pleased to visit Covent Garden Theatre, and to sit out the evening's entertainments."[51]

48. *Journal of the House of Commons* (1840), 256 (Apr. 6).
49. 7 & 8 Victoria c. 68.
50. Bunn, 3: 127–52.
51. Bunn, 1: xi. Research in connection with the above essay on the oratorio was supported in part by a grant from the City University of New York PSC-CUNY Research Award Program.

THE RITE REVISITED:
THE IDEA AND
THE SOURCE OF ITS
SCENARIO

RICHARD TARUSKIN

The Rite of Spring was twice "created" by the Ballets Russes. The first production in 1913, with choreography by Nijinsky, was the epoch-making failure that has gone down so resoundingly in history. Diaghilev took another chance at staging the notorious work in 1920, the music having become enough of a cause célèbre to justify the financial risk. A new and very different choreography was commissioned from Massine, and this action raised a question of propriety (one which, needless to say, hardly bothers choreographers today): could a new visual realization be grafted successfully onto a preexistent score without violating the conception of the whole? In an interview given to a Paris arts journal on the eve of the new version's première, Stravinsky met this question head on:

> J'ai composé cette oeuvre après *Pétrouchka*. L'embryon en est un thème qui m'est venu quand j'eus terminé *L'Oiseau de Feu*. Comme ce thème et ce qui en suivit étaient conçus dans une manière brutale, forte, je pris pour pretexte à developpements l'évocation même de cette musique, soit, dans mon esprit, l'époque préhistorique russe, puisque je suis Russe. Mais considerez bien que cette idée vient de la musique et non la musique de cette idée. J'ai écrit une oeuvre architectonique et non anecdotique. Et ce fut l'erreur de l'avoir considerée de ce point oppossée au sens même de l'ouevre.[1]

1. Michel Georges-Michel, "Les deux Sacres du printemps," *Comoedia* (Dec. 11, 1920). Cited from Truman C. Bullard, "The First Performance of Igor Stravinsky's *Sacre du Printemps*" (Ph.D. diss., University of Rochester, 1971), 1: 2–3.

Now there was hardly a word of truth in this, and Stravinsky knew it. The original idea (if we may believe Stravinsky's *Chroniques de ma vie*) had been visual, not musical.[2] The music did in fact "come from the idea," and not, moreover, until the idea had been fleshed out into a more or less detailed scenario with the help of Nicholas Roerich, whose contribution to *The Rite* (the main subject of the present inquiry) was totally slighted by Stravinsky not only here, but also in his subsequent memoirs concerning the ballet.[3] And, finally, Stravinsky did a great and deliberate injustice to Nijinsky, whose choreography he had praised to the skies both in public and in private at the time of the original première.[4]

Motives are not hard to find. Many have accused the composer of "attempting to rewrite the history of the work on the basis of its later success as a concert piece."[5] And one can scarcely blame Stravinsky, caught between conflicting loyalties to Nijinsky and to Diaghilev (with whom the former had broken and who was still so important to the composer) for having sided with the latter. But the motives go deeper. The seven years that separated the two *Rites* were cataclysmic ones for the Ballets Russes and for Stravinsky. The "loss of Russia"[6]—as great a crisis for the composer as for the organization he served— had occurred during that time, and so had the "discovery of the past," signaled within the Ballets Russes first by the *Good Humored Ladies* (1917) and within Stravinsky's output by *Pulcinella,* which was first performed a mere seven

---

2. The well-known passage runs as follows:
   One day, when I was finishing the last pages of *L'Oiseau de feu* in St. Petersburg, I had a fleeting vision which came to me as a complete surprise, my mind at the moment being full of other things. I saw in imagination a solemn pagan rite: sage elders, seated in a circle, watched a young girl dance herself to death. They were sacrificing her to propitiate the god of spring. (Igor Stravinsky, *An Autobiography* [New York, 1962], 31)
   Elsewhere Stravinsky explicitly contradicts his 1920 interview:
   The idea of *Le Sacre du printemps* came to me while I was still composing *The Firebird.* I had dreamed of a scene of pagan ritual in which a chosen sacrificial virgin danced herself to death. *This vision was not accompanied by concrete musical ideas,* however. (*Expositions and Developments* [Garden City, N.Y., 1962], 159–60; italics added)
3. In *Conversations with Stravinsky* (repr. ed. [Berkeley, 1980], 94–95), for example, Roerich's contribution is admitted only as designer, and in a patronizing manner at that, Stravinsky having "chosen" him on account of the favorable impression Roerich's sets for *Prince Igor* had made on the composer ("I knew he would not overload"). Stravinsky owned that he "still [had] a good opinion of Roerich's *Le Sacre*" and that he "became quite fond of him in those early years, though not of his painting, which was a kind of advanced Puvis de Chavannes."
4. In public: "Je suis heureux d'avoir trouvé en M. Nijinski le collaborateur plastique ideal" ("Ce que j'ai voulu exprimer dans *Le Sacre du printemps,*" *Montjoie!,* May 29, 1913; see *Le Sacre du printemps: Dossier de presse,* ed. François Lesure [Geneva, 1980], 15). In private: "Nijinsky's choreography is incomparable. Except for a very few places everything is just as I wanted it" (letter to Maximilian Steinberg, June 20/July 3, 1913; see Boris Yarustovsky, ed., *I. F. Stravinskii: stat'i i materialy.* [Moscow, 1973], 474). Apparently, Stravinsky reversed himself a second time at the end of his life, claiming in a conversation with the Soviet choreographer Yury Grigorovich that Nijinsky's was after all "the finest embodiment of *Le Sacre*" (see Vera Krasovskaya, *Nijinsky,* trans. John E. Bowlt [New York, 1979], 273).
5. Bullard, 1: 3.
6. Cf. *Themes and Episodes* (New York, 1906), 23: "I have had to survive two crises as a composer. . . . The first—the loss of Russia and its language of words as well as of music—affected every circumstance of my personal no less than my artistic life."

months before the new *Rite*.[7] The spirit of French antiromanticism, of Satie, Cocteau, and *choses en soi* had long since begun its rise to dominance in the Diaghilev ballet (e.g., the Satie-Cocteau *Parade*) and in Stravinsky's aesthetic (e.g., the *Pièces faciles* and *L'Histoire du soldat*). From a purveyor of Slavic exotica the Ballets Russes (and with it, Stravinsky) had become a fountainhead of international modernism. *The Rite of Spring,* which contained as much of one as of the other, was therefore a turning point and a particularly touchy matter. So it was a far different composer who spoke to *Comoedia* in 1920 from the one who had spoken in 1913 to *Montjoie!* about "Ce que j'ai voulu exprimer dans *Le Sacre du printemps,*" and it is the outlook of this new Stravinsky, on the threshold of his thirty-year career as "neoclassicist," that has come to dominate conventional thinking about *The Rite* to this day.[8]

But in one matter the interview of 1920 was accurate and revealing—namely, in Stravinsky's insistence that *The Rite of Spring* was not conceived "anecdotally" (which is not necessarily to admit that it was conceived any more "architecturally" than, say, *The Firebird,* with all its thematic relationships and "leit-harmonies"). In this sense, the new ballet had represented a great departure for Stravinsky at the time of its composition, a far greater one than the superficial modernities we admire today. "The whole thing must be staged in dance from beginning to end," he wrote to Nikolai Findeisen shortly after finishing the score. "I have not given a single measure over to mime."[9] This meant he was dropping the balletic equivalent of operatic recitative, that is to say, the narrative element, and this after composing *The Firebird,* which behaves more like an opera than perhaps any other ballet. Stravinsky's new ideal was to be a ballet without plot in the conventional sense, one which would not narrate its content but depict it pure, not represent it but rather present it (to put it as Edmund Gurney might). *The Rite of Spring,* then, would not tell a story of a pagan ritual; it would *be* that ritual. One can detect here a prime tenet of early modernism with its insistence that genres and media not be mixed. But it was no less a derivation from the theurgic aims of Russian symbolism, and however much Stravinsky may later have denied it, his goal was frankly "Scriabinistic" —the communication of ecstasy, of terror. In interviews he gave the St. Petersburg press during a brief visit to his native city in the fall of 1912, he referred to his new work more than once as a "mysterium(!)".[10] He dubbed the new kind of ballet he was pioneering "choreodrama, which is bound to replace the type of

---

7. Cf. *Expositions and Developments,* 128–29: "*Pulcinella* was my discovery of the past, the epiphany through which the whole of my late work became possible."

8. More details on Stravinsky's revisionism with respect to his Russian period are given in Richard Taruskin, "Russian Folk Melodies in *The Rite of Spring,*" *Journal of the American Musicological Society* 33 (1980): 501–6.

9. December 2/15, 1912 (Yarustovsky, 470).

10. M. Dvinsky (M. M. Berman), "U Igoria Stravinskogo," *Birzhevye vedomosti,* No. 13161 (Sept. 25, 1912), quoted in Vera Krasovoskaya, *Russkii baletnyi teatr nachala xx veka* (Leningrad, 1971), 1: 432. This reference also appears in an untitled clipping from *Ogoniok,* Oct. 14, 1912, which is photographed and inset as part of an illustration in *Expositions and Developments* between pp. 72 and 73.

our contemporary ballets,"[11] indebted as they were to the impure principles of "music drama."

Where did these ideas come from? It would be easy, and true enough, to say that they were "in the air" in the Russia of the "Silver Age." But the specific conduit to Stravinsky would seem to have been Roerich, then the titular head of the "World of Art" movement. More than two years earlier than the Stravinsky documents cited above, at the very outset of their soon-to-be-interrupted collaboration, the painter-turned-scenarist gave a press interview which is the oldest surviving description of the project. He emphasized that "the specifically choreographic part consists of ritual dances. This work will be the first attempt [in the theater] to give a reproduction of antiquity without any definite dramatic subject."[12] And in the end it seems the finished product made such an abstract impression (to say nothing of its radical style) that, although many of the Parisian critics who saw the first production were indeed reminded in a general way of the primitivism of Gauguin,[13] few, if any of them, took seriously the subtitle, *Tableaux de la Russie païenne*. "Sur quelles recherches archéologiques se base-t-elle?" sniffed the famous music archivist Henry de Curzon; "je crois inutile de poser la question."[14] That was all right with Stravinsky, of course, who did all he could (and increasingly, as his career went on) to reinforce the impression of abstraction and "baselessness," so well did it accord with the turn his work subsequently took. Even Alexandre Benois, his collaborator on *Petrushka*, believed that "Stravinsky was attracted by the idea of 'reconstructing the mysterious past' chiefly because it gave him free scope in his search for un-

---

11. Krasovskaya, *Russkii baletnyi teatr*, 432.

12. "Teatral'noe ĕkho: balet khudozhnika N. K. Rerikha," *Petersburgskaia gazeta*, No. 235 (Aug. 28, 1910), quoted in Krasovskaya, *Russkii baletnyi teatr*, 1: 429. The impression conveyed in this interview, and its very title, suggest that the original conception of the ballet had been Roerich's and not Stravinsky's. Perhaps it was, at that, the composer's better known (but uncorroborated) side of the story notwithstanding. Benois (see *Reminiscences of the Russian Ballet*, trans. Mary Britnieva [London, 1941], 347), concurred with Diaghilev's regisseur, Serge Grigoriev, that the idea had been Roerich's (see *The Diaghilev Ballet, 1909–29*, trans. Vera Bowen [London, 1953], 79), and in a lecture given in New York in 1922, Roerich stated unequivocally that "I had given the subject for the ballet, taking it from the life of prehistoric Slavs" ("Rhythm of Life," *Adamant* [New York, 1923], 67). The interview in the *Petersburgskaia gazeta* contains interesting testimony about Michel Fokine's collaboration in the early stages of the project: "All three of us are equally fired up by this image and have decided to work on it together" (Krasovskaya, *Russkii baletnyi teatr*, 1: 429). An even earlier announcement in the newspaper *Russkoe slovo* (July 15, 1910), made it known that "the Academician N. K. Roerich, the young composer of the *Firebird* I. F. Stravinsky and the ballet master M. I. Fokine are working on a ballet entitled 'The Great Sacrifice,' dedicated to ancient Slavic religious observances. The subject and the production will be Roerich's" (cited from Irina Vershinina, *Rannye balety Stravinskogo* [Moscow, 1967], 138).

13. Gauguin's influence on the World of Art and on Stravinsky should not be discounted. The painter was cited as an artistic savior by Leon Bakst in his seminal essay "Puti klassitsizma v isskustve" ("Paths of Classicism in Art"), *Apollon* 3 [1909]: 56). Sergei Lifar mentions Diaghilev's enthusiasm for Gauguin as the main motivation behind his decision to produce Stravinsky's and Roerich's "primitive ballet" (*Serge Diaghilev: His Life, His Work, His Legend* [New York, 1940], 199). And last but not least, one of Stravinsky's prized possessions during the *Rite* period was a Gauguin painting given him in 1912 "by an admirer of *Petrushka*." (It may be seen in *Conversations with Stravinsky*, photograph facing p. 33.)

14. "La Semaine: Paris, au Théâtre des Champs-Elysées," *Le Guide musical* 59: 23–24 (quoted from Bullard, 3: 120).

usual rhythms and sounds. Naturally nothing was known of the music of those remote days and Stravinsky felt himself free from all constraints and rules."[15]

But Benois was wrong, as anyone who has read *La Poétique musicale* could easily guess: such an attitude was never Stravinsky's. Suspecting as much, and having established in a previous study the surprising extent of Stravinsky's reliance on authentic ethnic music in composing *The Rite,* it occurred to me that, de Curzon notwithstanding, it might be worthwhile inquiring into the archaeological bases of the scenario of *The Rite.* And once again the investigation did not go unrewarded. A study of the scenario and of the music reveals that Stravinsky's great ballet was a paradigm of the ideals of the World of Art movement (which had initially provided most of the artistic manpower for the Ballets Russes) where "national" subject matter was concerned. According to the precepts of "neonationalism" as defined by art historians today, the artwork sought to justify and, as it were, to validate its stylistic departures by a scrupulous adherence at the conceptual stage to archaeological reality, by combining "ethnographical accuracy and intense imagination."[16] As the great poet Andrei Bely put it in the pages of *The World of Art* itself, "Every artistic form has as its starting point reality and as its finishing point music."[17] *The Rite of Spring* (together with *Les Noces*) stands as a monument to that idea.

Stravinsky's commitment to the "starting point in reality" is evident from the fact that, once he had had his "vision" of the sacrificial virgin dancing herself to death, he was immediately moved to ask Roerich to elaborate it.[18] It was precisely a basis in ethnographical authenticity that he was after, and "who could help me if not Roerich; who if not he is privy to the whole secret of our forefathers' closeness to the earth?"[19] Who indeed? Pagan antiquities were Roerich's known specialty in those days. As Benois rememberd him, he was

> utterly absorbed in dreams of prehistoric, patriarchal and religious life—of the days when the vast, limitless plains of Russia and the shores of her lakes and rivers were peopled with the forefathers of the present inhabitants. Roerich's mystic, spiritual experiences made him strangely susceptible to the charm of this ancient world. He felt in it something primordial and weird, something that was intimately linked with nature—with that Northern culture he adored, the inspiration of his finest pictures.[20]

15. Benois, 347.

16. John E. Bowlt, "The World of Art," *The Silver Age of Russian Culture,* ed. Carl and Ellendea Proffer (Ann Arbor, 1975), 415.

17. "Formy iskusstva," *Mir iskusstva* 2 (1902) (quoted in Bowlt, 417). Bely became one of the central figures in the neoprimitivist movement known as "Scythianism," about which more below.

18. He inherited this commitment from Rimsky-Korsakov, who, though cold to the aestheticism of the World of Art, was nonetheless an avowed neonationalist in his fantastic folk operas beginning with *Snegurochka,* like *The Rite* an allegory of spring, and particularly in the operas, starting with *Sadko* (1897), that he composed for performances by the Private Opera company of Savva Mamontov, the great patron of the neonationalist movement.

19. Letter to Findeisen, December 2/15, 1912 (Yarustovsky, 470).

20. Benois, 347.

The series of paganistic paintings to which Benois refers extended back to the closing years of the nineteenth century. Even some of their titles can give us a heady whiff of *The Rite*'s scenario: "The Elders Gather" (*Skhodiatsia startsy*, 1898), "Idols" (*Idoly*, 1901), "Ancient Life" (*Drevnaia zhizn'*, 1904), "Round Dance" (*Khorovod*, 1904), "The Stone Age (North)" (*Kammenyi vek [sever]*, 1904), "The Prophet Stone" (*Veshii kamen'*, 1905), "Cortège" (*Shestvie*, 1905), "Holy Place" (*Sviashchennoe mesto*, 1907), "Iarilo's Gully" (*Iarilina dolina*, 1908), and "Forefathers of Humankind" (*Chelovech'i praottsy*, 1911; this one may itself have been influenced by *The Rite* project). Stravinsky's vision of the "Great Sacrifice" (*Velikaia zhertva*, the original working title of the ballet), could fit easily into this list. In fact, Roerich responded to their initial meeting in 1910 with a series of sketches bearing that title, one of which he presented to the composer.[21] At that time they worked out a scenario in a single scene. Roerich gave the following brief synopsis of it in the interview cited above:

> The new ballet will give a series of images of a holy night among the ancient Slavs. . . . The action begins with a summer night and finishes immediately before the sunrise, when the first rays begin to show.[22]

One simple, startling fact stands out: in its original conception the ballet was to be a rite of summer, not of spring.[23] And as we shall see, this was entirely accurate from the point of view of ethnology.

Reassignment to spring must have taken place the next year, during Stravinsky's visit to the artist at Princess Maria Tenisheva's estate at Talashkino, where Roerich was designing and supervising the execution of a series of murals and mosaics in "neo-Russian" style for the interior and exterior of her private church.[24] A preliminary scene was added to the scenario, this one depicting the "Adoration of the Earth" in preparation for the "Great Sacrifice." Though no synopsis from 1911 survives, an idea of the order of events and the titles for individual dances formulated (with one exception) by Roerich may be gained from an examination of the headings in Stravinsky's sketchbook for the ballet,[25]

---

21. It is listed as belonging to Stravinsky in the catalogue of works appended to Yurgis K. Baltrushaitis, Alexandre N. Benois, *et al.*, *Rerikh* (Petrograd, 1916), 219. The other two are listed as the property of the painter's wife and of B. G. Vlasiev, respectively. Stravinsky's sketch was lost with the rest of his Ustilug property, as Roerich himself relates: "Then the war came and I heard that one of my sketches on Stravinsky's estate as well as the sketches of 'Sacre' were destroyed" ("Sacre," *Realm of Light* [New York, 1931], 186).

22. Cited from Krasovskaya, *Russkii baletnyi teatr*, 1: 429.

23. So it would seem that despite Stravinsky's account given above in n. 2, his original "vision" probably had nothing to do with the "propitiation of the god of spring," but rather was only an image of a sacrificial dance.

24. John E. Bowlt, *The Silver Age: Russian Art in the Early Twentieth Century and the "World of Art" Group* (Newtonville, Mass., 1979), 45. Princess Tenisheva was, after Mamontov, the most important backer of neonationalism and an early supporter of Diaghilev's enterprises.

25. The sketchbook has been published in facs. (see Igor Stravinsky, *The Rite of Spring: Sketches, 1911–1913* [London, 1969]).

which he began using directly upon returning to Ustilug from Talashkino. In the order of their appearance,[26] the headings are as follows:

1. [*Gadaniia na prutikakh* ("Divination with wands")][27]
2. *Khorovod* ("Round dance")[28]
3. *Igra v goroda* ("The ritual of the camps")[29]
4. *Idut-vedut* ("They are coming, they are bringing him")
5. *Igra umykaniia* ("The ritual of the abduction")
6. *Vypliasyvanie zemli* ("The dancing-out of the earth")[30]
7. *Khorovody, Tainye igry* ("Round dances; secret rituals")
8. *Velichanie—dikaia pliaska (Amozony)* ("Glorification—wild dance [Amazons]")
9. *Diestvo startsev* ("The act of the elders")
10. *Pliaska sviashchennaia* ("Holy dance")

This list differs not only from the headings in the published score, but also from the various synopses prepared by Stravinsky and Roerich in the period leading up to the première.[31] Apart from negligible changes in wording,[32] we should note that *Idut-vedut* became *Shestvie Stareishego-Mudreishego* ("Procession of the Oldest-and-Wisest"), that the four-bar interlude before *Vypliasyvanie zemli* acquired a name of its own—*Potselui zemli* ("The Kiss of the

---

26. That is to say, in the order of the segments in the sketchbook primarily devoted to each respective number, for random jottings out of order do occur.
27. The sketchbook lacks a title for the "Auguries." Possibly there are some missing pages at the front of it, and these may have contained sketches for the Introduction of Part I, which is otherwise represented only by some orchestral drafts near the end of the book. The title is supplied from a letter written by Stravinsky to Roerich (September 13/26, 1911) that is exactly contemporaneous with the sketches. This significance of this letter and this title is discussed below.
28. This number is preceded in the sketchbook by the notation "zapevanie khorovodnoe" ("khorovod incantation"), referring to the passage at no. 48 in the published score (see Taruskin, 515–16).
29. *Goroda* literally means "cities." The title of this dance is usually translated as "Games of the Rival Tribes." Considering the sources of the scenario, however, "camps" seems a better translation.
30. This particular title, Stravinsky's neologism denoting the stamping nature of the dance, is untranslatable.
31. There are three synopses by each of them, and they may be located in published form as follows:
    1. Stravinsky's letter to Findeisen (see n. 19), available in a rough English translation in the booklet that accompanies the facsim. sketchbook (see n. 25).
    2. The *Montjoie!* interview, in which the synopsis is fleshed out with descriptions of the choreography, presumably by the interviewer, Ricciotto Canudo. An excellent English version by Edward Burlingame Hill appears in Vera Stravinsky and Robert Craft, *Stravinsky in Pictures and Documents* (New York, 1978), 524–26.
    3. Stravinsky's final synopsis, prepared for Serge Koussevitzky's performance in Russia in 1914. This document is cited three times in Vera Stravinsky and Craft: on p. 526 in translation from Koussevitzky's program book, on p. 78 as a facsimile of Stravinsky's manuscript draft, and on p. 75 in a translation from the latter, the authors not having noticed that the two translations are identical; in fact, they date the autograph as 1910, an impossible ascription since it calls the ballet by its final name, *Vesna sviashchennaia*, whereas in 1910 the ballet was still called *Velikaia zhertva* ("The Great Sacrifice").
    4. A letter from Roerich to Diaghilev printed in Lifar, 200, and in part in Vera Stravinsky and Craft, 75.
    5. The final draft prepared by Roerich for the program book of the première production, printed in Vera Stravinsky and Craft, 75–76, where it is probably dated a little too early.
    6. A synopsis adapted from No. 5 in the program book for the première, presented in facsim. in Bullard, 1: 241.
32. For instance, *Igra dvukh gorodov* ("Ritual of the Two Camps") for *Igra v goroda*.

Earth")—and that the heading *Vzivanie k praottsam* ("Appeal to the Fore-fathers") was added before *Deistvo startsev*.[33] But these are minor alterations. More significant is the transposition of *Igra umykaniia* from its place before *Vy-pliasyvanie zemli* at the end of Part I to a position much earlier in the scenario, that is, right after *Gadaniia*. We shall return to this matter below, for it has a direct bearing on the matter of the scenario's archaeological authenticity.

In order to gauge the extent of Roerich's fidelity to primary sources in preparing the scenario, one must of course identify them. This can only be done by conjecture, since no documentation survives, assuming it ever existed. While the sources I discovered do not exhaust the store of Roerich's probable models (for example, no authentic prototype for the old woman in the *Auguries* was found), I am sure the following were among them:

1. Alexander Afanasiev, *Poèticheskie vozzreniia slavian na prirodu (The Poetical At-titudes of the Slavs Toward Nature)*, 3 vols. (Moscow, 1866–69), particularly the concluding chapter of the third volume, *"Narodnye prazdniki"* ("Folk Holi-days").

This monumental work was a kind of Slavonic *Golden Bough,* and indeed had been an important source for Frazer. By using comparative and conflation-ary methods, Afanasiev attemped to reconstruct pagan prehistory from contem-poraneous peasant folklore. His interpretations, along with the entire Romantic "mythological school" they represented, have been called into question by later folklorists who complain of the author's "unrestrained conjectures" and of his "enthusiasm for linguistic and mythological assimilation which led to many of the European followers of Grimm to fantastic conclusions."[34] Nevertheless, it remains an indispensable source for anthropologists even today, and it was re-garded as a veritable bible by late nineteenth-century and early twentieth-cen-tury artists in all media, including Rimsky-Korsakov, who drew heavily on it for a number of his operas, notably *Snegurochka* and *Christmas Eve*. Its stock was particularly high during the heyday of Russian symbolism and the World of Art, whose propagators (e.g., Viacheslav Ivanov) saw the creation of myths as the preeminent purpose and function of art.

2. *Nachal'naia letopis' (The Primary Chronicle)* or *Provest' vremennykh let (Tale of Bygone Years)* (c. 1040–1118).

This group of manuscripts had been compiled over the course of three generations by monks of the Crypt Monastery *(Pecherskaia lavra)* in Kiev. In adition to its accounts of the early history of the Kievan state and its dynastic rulers, the chronicle contains a number of rather bilious descriptions of the pagan customs that Christianity was in the process of supplanting.

---

33. In the published score the appellation "Forefathers of Humankind" *(Chelovech'i praottsy)* was added to the title of this number. This reference bolsters the impression that Roerich's painting was directly connected in the *Rite* project.

34. Yury Sokolov, *Russian Folklore* (1941), trans. Catherine Ruth Smith (Hatboro, Pa., 1966), 73 and 69.

3. Herodotus, *The Persian Wars* (Book IV, on the Scyths).

This lengthy and somewhat fanciful account is virtually the sole basis of present-day knowledge about the nomadic, Iranian-speaking people who dominated the Pontic steppes to the north of the Black Sea, ranging as far west as the Carpathians and as far east as what is today called Kazakhstan. As the predecessors of the Slavs over much of what is now Russia, the Scyths were looked upon by the Russians as a kind of mythical, half-human ancestor race—*Chelovech'i praottsy* ("Forefathers of Humankind"), to call them by the title of Roerich's famous painting. Herodotus's description emphasizes their fierceness and brutality (among other things, they used the skulls of their vanquished enemies as drinking bowls and their scalps as napkins and trophies).[35] Hence, for Russian artists at the turn of the century, the Scyths were a prime symbol of all that was elemental, mighty, and seething with primeval forces. The persona of the barbarian, the wild man, was a frequent one in Russian literature and art between the two revolutions, and this figure implied the satiety and fatigue of the existing order as well as apocalyptic premonitions of its demise. "Poets wore themselves out trying to roar like wild animals";[36] the "shamanistic, bogyman style" noted by Simon Karlinsky in the titles of the *Rite* dances[37] was a common affection. Ilya Ehrenberg compared Andrei Bely, when lecturing or declaming poetry, to "a Sybil prophesying or a shaman in ritualistic ecstasy."[38] The word *skifstvo* ("Scythianism") was coined around 1916 in connection with a couple of clamorous poetic miscellanies published during the next two revolutionary years under the title of *Skify;* these contain now-famous work by Valery Briussov, Bely, Alexander Blok, Aleksei Remizov, and Evgeny Zamiatin, among others.[39] But today the term is commonly applied back to works of the preceding decade that embody the elemental and "maximalistic" rendering of primitive antiquity in a shockingly coarse and brutal manner, often with symbolistic, mystical, or theurgic overtones (and often as a flimsy pretext for modernistic effects). *The Rite of Spring,* it scarcely needs saying, was a perfect example of this tendency, called "the new barbarism" in its day.[40]

---

35. *The Persian Wars* 4: 64–65. *Herodotus,* 2, trans. Alfred Denis Godley, (London, 1963): 260–65).

36. Kornei Chukovsky, *Futuristy* [1922] (quoted in Israel Nestyev, *Prokofiev,* trans. Florence Jonas [Palo Alto, 1960], 91).

37. *The Nation* (June 15, 1970): 732 (review of Vershinina, *Rannye balety*).

38. See Stefani Hope Hoffman, "Scythianism: a Cultural Vision in Revolutionary Russia" (Ph.D. diss., Columbia University, 1975), 10.

39. See Hoffman, chap. 1. Remizov was an important contributor to the scenario of *The Firebird.*

40. The term was coined by Maximilian Voloshin, who saw in it "the only path to the art of the future" ("Arkhaizm v russkoi zhivopisi," *Apollon* 5 [1910]: 39). Of course, the real paradigms of musical *skifstvo* were two somewhat meretricious works by Prokofiev: *Scythian Suite* (1915), from an unrealized ballet to a scenario by Sergei Gorodetsky (see below), and the cantata *Semero ikh* ("They Are Seven," [1917]), a setting of an ancient Akkadian spell translated by the symbolist poet Konstantin Balmont and intended to be a direct response to the Revolution. Also worthy of note as a forerunner of these works and of *The Rite of Spring* as well is the symphonic poem *Skify* ("The Scyths" [1912]) by the somewhat older composer and also former pupil of Rimsky-Korsakov, Vladimir Senilov (1875–1918).

4. *Iar'* (1907), a book of "lyric and lyrico-epic poems' by Sergei Gorodetsky (1884–1967).

This collection, a work of imaginative literature rather than of history or anthropology, deserves recognition as a putative "source" for *The Rite,* since it is in many respects the prime examplar of the " 'self-invented,' quasi-Russian mythology" so rife in the literature of the time. The description is that of Prince Dimitry Mirsky, who called *Iar'* "the most interesting monument of its time, when mystical anarchism was in the air, when Viacheslav Ivanov believed in the possibility of a new mythological age, and when the belief was abroad that the vital forces of man's elemental nature were to burst the fetters of civilization and of the world order."[41] To a certain extent Gorodetsky's poems reflect the observation of contemporary folklore—the round dances, games, and songs of the Pskov region, where the poet spent the summers of 1904 and 1905.[42] His response was more aesthetic than mystical, which only brought him closer to the outlook of the World of Art and to Stravinsky, whose Opus 6 (1907–8) is a setting of two poems from *Iar'.* The title is untranslatable. It has been variously rendered in English as "vital sap" or "spring corn," but actually it is a pseudo ur-Slavic root meaning fire (compare the Russian *iarkii* ["bright"], *iaryi* ["ardent"], *iarost'* ["rage"], and so on).

The book is divided into two halves—*Iar'* ("bright") and *Tem'* ("dark") —the halves reflecting the primal myth of the solar cycle and, in more modern terms, the opposition of unspoiled, primeval human nature to the oppression of cities. The root *iar'* is also associated with spring through such archaic Russian words as *iarovoi* ("vernal"), and from it finally comes Iarilo, the name given to the Slavic sun god in the period of his ascendancy. This final extrapolation brings us at last into direct contact with the scenario of *The Rite,* for it is to Iarilo that the "Great Sacrifice" was offered, as is made explicit by some of the early synopses.[43] The three poems printed under the general title "Iarila" *(sic)* in Gorodetsky's book have been cited repeatedly as probable antecedents for *The Rite* or at least for Stravinsky's vision of the maiden sacrifice.[44]

This supposition seems plausible inasmuch as there is no account of human sacrifice among the rituals of the pagan Slavs in authentic anthropologi-

41. Prince Dmitry Svatopolk Mirsky, *A History of Russian Literature* (NewYork, 1948), 473.

42. Memoir material quoted in Semen I. Mashinky's introduction to Gorodetsky's *Stikhotvoreniia i poèmy* (Leningrad, 1974), 10.

43. The last sentence in the printed program book for that fateful evening of May 29, 1913, reads as follows: "C'est ainsi qu'on sacrifie à Iarilo le magnifique, le flamboyant" (see the facs. in Bullard, 1: 241).

44. See Valerii Smirnov, *Tvorscheskoe formirovanie I. F. Stravinskogo* (Leningrad, 1970), 86–87; Mikhail Druskin, *Igor' Stravinskii: lichnost', tvorchestvo, vzgliady* (Leningrad, 1974), 50–51. Lawrence Morton gives the first of them complete, in a rather stilted translation by Avrahm Yarmolinsky and Babette Deutsch ("Footnotes to Stravinsky Studies: 'Le Sacre du printemps,' " *Tempo* 128 [1979]: 10–12). In it a maiden priestess is hacked to death by an axe-wielding wizard in the process of carving an idol of Iarila out of the trunk of a sacred linden tree.

cal and historical literature, though many of the games surviving among the peasantry were thought to embody remnants of such practices.[45] Not only does Gorodetsky describe the sacrifice itself, he even supplies two of *The Rite's* three solo dramatis personae: the maiden and the Oldest-and-Wisest. However, apart from the specific content of Stravinsky's vision—that is, what he himself brought to the first meeting with Roerich—virtually everything in the work's scenario can be found in Afanasiev, Herodotus, and the *Primary Chronicle*. Both the copiousness of the documentation presented below and the specific nature of the relationship between it and the scenario leave no doubt that these were in fact Roerich's sources and that Roerich's scenario reflects the same concern with authenticity as did his costumes, which he based sedulously on peasant originals in Princess Tenisheva's collection.[46]

The songs, games, and rituals of rural Russia chronicled by Afanasiev are organized around a seasonal cycle—a *temporale,* one might say—symbolizing the life cycle of the sun god. The part of the Slavic folk calendar with which we are concerned is summarized authoritatively in George Vernadsky's description of Russian "Sun Worship and Clan Cult":

> The thaw tide is the period of the rapid rise of the sun's ascendency and of the awakening of the forces of procreation. "Ardent" [*iaryi*] is the special epithet of the sun at this stage of its course. In Russian folk-lore the creative ardency of the sun was personified as the image of the god Iarilo [the "Ardent God"].[47]

Afanasiev recounts Iarilo's fundamental attributes as follows:

> The significance of Iarilo is wholly explained in his very name and in the surviving traditions associated with him. The root *iar'* combines within itself the ideas: a) of vernal light and warmth, b) of youthful, impetuous, violently awakening forces, c) of erotic passion, lasciviousness and fecundation: ideas inseparable from the manifestations of spring and its terrifying phenomena.[48]

All this might well serve as the epigraph of the Stravinsky-Roerich ballet. To resume Vernadsky's account:

45. According to Herodotus, the human sacrifices performed by the Scyths were not religious in character. They formed part of the royal burial rite and could be compared to the old Hindu ritual of *suttee*. "In the open space which is left in the tomb they bury, after strangling, one of the king's concubines, his cup-bearer, his cook, his groom, his squire and his messenger . . ." (*The Persian Wars* 4: 71–72; Godley, 268–73).

46. Stravinsky notes this fact both in *Conversations with Stravinsky* (p. 94) and in *Expositions and Developments* (p. 161).

47. George Vernadsky, *The Origins of Russia* (London, 1959), 112.

48. *Poèticheskie vozzreniia slavian na prirodu* (Moscow, 1866–69), 1: 439. Henceforth, references to Afanasiev's volumes will be given following each citation.

Iarilo was in full power between the vernal equinox and the summer solstice. There were two ancient festivals around the summer solstice, one preceding it (the so-called Semik), and the other following it (the so-called Kupala). After Russia's conversion to Christianity, Semik, although not a church holiday, was assigned to the seventh Thusday after Easter, hence its name [*semik* from *sem'*, "seven"]. The Semik thus preceded the Pentecost. Semik was celebrated in the forests and on the shores of lakes and rivers. . . . It was dedicated to the souls of the dead, but actually it was mainly a festival of youth and of prematrimonial love.[49]

The significance of Semik for the conception of *The Rite of Spring* is already known, thanks to the identification of a *semitskaia*, or Semik song, as a source melody for the Spring Rounds in Part I.[50] As for Kupala, it

took place on the day of St. John the Baptist [June 24]. It was dedicated to the "ardent god," Iarilo. . . . This festival is called Jann Nakts among the Letts and "Ion Night" in northern Albania. There it is celebrated as the night of fecundation. A huge bonfire was built at these festivals, often on the bank of a river, or of a lake. A large wooden wheel was kindled at the top of a hill and pushed to roll downhill. Men, women, and maidens danced and sang around the bonfire. Men, young and old, jumped over the fire. This was done because of the belief in the purifying function of the fire. Two effigies, one male and one female, were made of straw that night. The male was called Iarilo, the female Kupala. These figures were burned together.[51]

From the rituals of Semik and Kupala, Roerich fashioned practically the whole of *The Rite*. And since these festivals fell on either side of the summer solstice, it is not surprising that, as we have seen, the scenario was originally conceived in terms of a midsummer night. The emphasis was placed on Kupala, the midsummer festival, rather than on Semik, for it was Kupala that retained the stronger avatars of sacrificial rites. Among the Lithuanians and Letts, as Afanasiev relates, the sacrifice of a white cock to the seasonal deity had been performed within living memory (3:721).[52] The burning of straw effigies also suggests a vestige of sacrificial practices, and such descriptions may be multiplied

49. Vernadsky, 113.
50. Taruskin, 512–19.
51. Vernadsky, 113. Basing his argument on the work of the philologist Fyodor Buslaev, Afanasiev derived the etymology of Kupala from a root word equivalent in meaning to *iar'*: "The names Kup-alo and Iar-ilo had one and the same signification—the fecundating deities of summer" (3: 713).
52. Do we have here an explanation for Stravinsky's otherwise curious reliance on Anton Juskiewicz's anthology of Lithuanian folksongs for evoking "scenes of pagan Russia?" See Morton for a full listing of Stravinsky's appropriations from this source.

from Afanasiev in terms much closer to the scenario, as we shall see.[53] Moreover, the celebration of Kupala was distinguished by its "utter debauchery and shamelessness" (1:444), at least in the eyes of moralizing Christians. In this regard Afanasiev offers a little garland of censorious comments by monkish chroniclers that read like early reviews of *The Rite of Spring;* for example, this one by the *igumen,* or the Father Superior, of Pskov:

> On this holy night [i.e., the feast of St. John the Baptist, coincident with the old Kupala], practically the whole town gathers in the countryside and goes wild. . . . They beat on tambourines, and raise their voices, and saw on fiddles, the women and the maidens flail about and dance, they roll their eyes, from their mouths come revolting howls and yelps, disgusting songs, they give rein to all sorts of mad deviltry, they reel about leaping and stamping. For men and boys there is great temptation and downfall in roaming and gawking among the women and girls at will, likewise for women in the men's unbridled profanity, and for the maidens in seduction.[54]

or this one, from the famous "Hundred Chapters" church code *(Stoglav),* promulgated under Ivan the Terrible in 1551:

> The men, women and maidens all foregather for nocturnal bathing and for scandalous talk and for devilish songs, and for dancing and prancing and for blasphemous acts, and there is profanation by the youths and seduction of the maidens.[55]

These sixteenth-century descriptions, however, are but a pale reflection of the notorious passage from the *Primary Chronicle* in which the great chronicler, Nestor, recounted the pagan practices of his time. When complaining about the lack of proper sacraments among the tribes neighboring on the recently Christianized Russians, he chose as his example the Kupala festival as it was celebrated by the "Radimichi, the Viatichi, and the Severi":

53. However, Frazer's interpretation, like that of his many followers, was rather different. He saw such customs as reflections of the myth of death and resurrection, symbolized by tree worship (see Sir James Frazer, *The Golden Bough: A Study of Magic and Religion,* abridged ed., [New York, 1947], chap. 10 ["Relics of Tree-Worship in Modern Europe"] and chap. 28 ["The Killing of the Tree-Spirit"], both of which use Afanasiev as a major source; see also Jane Ellen Harrison, *Ancient Art and Ritual* [London, 1913], in which she describes Plutarch's account of the spring rites at Delphi that involved the burial and exhumation of a puppet called Charila and also explicitly relates these to the rites of the near-namesake, Iarilo [Bradford-on-Avon, 1978], 40–41).

54. *Poslanie igumena Pamfila vo Pskov* (1505) (cited in Afanasiev, 1: 444).

55. Ibid., 1: 445. This excerpt is also the source for Modest Musorgsky's *Night on Bald Mountain.* Russian anthropologists see survivals of this primitive haetarism (i.e., the ceremonial and seasonal mingling of the sexes) in the custom known as *kumlenie,* one associated with Semik. Moreover, the song that I identified as the basis of Stravinsky's "Spring Rounds" accompanied this specific ceremony (see Taruskin, 514–15).

> Living in the forests like the very beasts, . . . there were no marriages among them, but simply games [*igry*] in between the villages. When the people gathered for games, for dancing, and for all other devilish amusements, the men on these occasions carried off wives for themselves, and each took any woman with whom he had arrived at an understanding. In fact, they even had two or three wives apiece.[56]

But what is this? It is the whole central action of the first part of the ballet: the round dance, the games of the rival tribes ("Games in between the Villages") and the "Ritual of Abduction" or "Game of Chasing a Girl," as Stravinsky preferred to translate it in his late years.[57] The fact that the order of composition reflected in the sketchbook (obviously following the original plan of the scenario) places the rival tribes and the abduction ritual not in the order of the finished ballet, but rather in the order in which they are mentioned by Nestor, seems to leave no doubt that precisely this passage was the source on which Roerich had drawn.[58]

What brings the pseudo-sacrificial ritual of Kupala especially close to Stravinsky's "vision"—and what therefore must have drawn Roerich to this very festival as the basis for his plan of action—was the frequent habit of replacing the effigies mentioned above by a chosen maiden. This common practice is described as follows by the Soviet folklorist Yurii Sokolov:

> Frequently the ceremonial doll, the dummy, is replaced by a tree, a birch. Sometimes, it is true, chiefly in the Ukraine, in the bathing ritual [N.B., Kupala is related etymologically to the Russian verb *kupat'sia*, "to bathe"], the central role is played by a girl, adorned with a garland. Around her choral dances are performed; in her honor songs are sung.[59]

And here is a specific instance cited by Afanasiev:

56. Adapted from *The Russian Primary Chronicle*, trans. Samuel Hazzard Cross and Olgerd P. Sherbowitz (Cambridge, 1953), 56.

57. Robert Craft, "Commentary to the Sketches," published with the sketchbook facs., p. 5 (see n. 25).

58. Some speculation as to the reasons for the transfer of the "Ritual of Abduction" to a point so much earlier in the ballet is offered in Taruskin, 518–19. One explanation may be that Stravinsky noted a thematic correspondence between one of the tunes he derived from Juszkiewicz's anthology and the Semik song alluded to above (from Rimsky-Korsakov's anthology). If taken in the order of the sketchbook, the "Rival Tribes" and the "Ritual of the Abduction" from a well unified pair, and their thematic cross-reference is obscured by the new placement of the latter dance. The passage at no. 43 in the "Ritual of the Abduction" (first sketched on p. 31) is a rhythmic transformation of the main theme of the "Rival Tribes" (two bars after no. 57, first sketched on p. 12). This change into a rapid eighth-note pulse was a momentous development in Stravinsky's technique. It marked his first use of shifting meters based on an equalized value of less than a beat's duration. This device led directly to the ragtime parodies of the late Swiss years and from there to the "Bachianism" of the Sonata and the Concerto for piano. Another unifying device between this pair of dances was the timpani figure appearing first at no. 38 in the "Ritual of the Abduction," but first sketched on p. 20 as part of the "Rival Tribes" (where it may still be heard starting at no. 57). These close correspondences testify to Stravinsky's initial conception of the two dances as a single unit corresponding to the passage cited from Nestor.

59. Sokolov, 196.

Among the Belorussians, with the dawning of St. John's day, the peasant girls choose the most beautiful maiden from their midst, strip her naked, and wind her round with floral garlands from head to toe. Then they set off for the forest, where Dzevko-Kupalo (for that is what the chosen maiden is called) must distribute wreaths among her friends, which have been prepared in advance. She sets about this task blindfolded, while around her a merry maidens' khorovod starts up. Auguries are made on the basis of who gets which wreath. A living wreath vouchsafes a rich and happy married life, while a dead, withered one foretells poverty and an unfortunate marriage. (3:723)

Several themes familiar from both parts of *The Rite* are adumbrated in this: divination by the young maidens, the round dance, the chosen one. The process of choosing the maiden is described elsewhere by Afanasiev in terms reminiscent of Roerich's "Mystic Circles":

At dawn during Radunitsa week [commemoration of the dead following the second Tuesday after Easter], the maidens of the village gather on a nearby hilltop or knoll and form a circle. One of them goes into the middle of the circle carrying bread and a painted egg in her hands, and turning to the east, makes a prayer. And after the prayer she calls a litany to the spring. (3:703)[60]

The next extract from Afanasiev's writing, which depicts the "Burial of Kostroma" (a rite interpreted either as the death of the sun god preceding resurrection or as the death of winter preceding spring), prefigures a large chunk of the action of Part II:

First of all the maidens chose one of their number, who was then obliged to portray Kostroma. They then all bowed down to her, placed her on a plank, and with songs carried her down to the river. There they began to bathe her, the oldest taking part meanwhile making a basket of linden bark and beating on it like a drum. Following this they returned to the village and finished the day with khorovods and games. (3:763)[61]

---

60. According to Afanasiev, a variant of this ceremony entails substituting a dummy for the girl, the dummy being later "burnt amid songs and dances." The "litany to the spring" is related to the singing of the so-called *vesnyanki*, which songs have left important traces in the music of *The Rite* (see Taruskin, 528–33).

61. This passage is quoted by Frazer (p. 318). Frazer describes another ceremony that links the Chosen One even more closely to the idea of human sacrifice (p. 317):

In Little Russia, it used to be the custom at Eastertide to celebrate the funeral of a being called Kostrubonko (= Kostroma), the deity of the spring. A circle was formed of singers who moved slowly around a girl who lay on the ground as if dead, and as they went they sang: "Dead, dead is our Kostrubonko! Dead, dead is our dear one!" Until the girl suddenly sprang up, on which the chorus joyfully exclaimed: "Come to life, come to life has our Kostrubonko! Come to life has our dear one!"

The "Honoring of the Chosen One" is here described in great detail. One even suspects that the passage directly influenced Stravinsky's music: is not the famous 11/4 bar (one measure after rehearsal no. 103, in which four timpani and a bass drum mark each beat in unison) a reflection of the oldest maiden and her wicker basket?

A fourth passage from Afanasiev, describing a ceremony called the "Bride of Iarilo" or the "Bride of Spring" (the name is already suggestive), will in many of its details bring to mind the "Danse sacrale":

> In honor of [Iarilo] the Belorussians celebrate the first sowing season (at the end of April), for which purpose maidens are rounded up in the villages, and one of them having been chosen, she is dressed up exactly as Iarilo is in the imagination of the folk, and she is seated on a white horse. Around the chosen one a khorovod coils in single file. All who take part in the ritual must wear a wreath of live flowers. If the weather is warm and clear, the ceremony culminates in the open field, in the newly sown cornfield, in the presence of the elders. (1:441)

The maiden herself does not perform a culminating dance; rather, one is done around her—in the presence of the elders, as the *Rite* scenario specifies. Moreover, there exists a tradition, which Roerich may have known about, calling for the elders, in their role as shamans, to dance themselves into a trancelike state resembling death:

> The mention in ancient precepts of "whirling dances," that is, apparently a type of shaman's sorcery, and the account given in a chronicle of how "the wonder worker lay and grew numb," that is, brought himself to a fainting condition, is exceedingly interesting. The resemblance of our ancient magicians to the shamans is to be found in the actual process of their sorcery. As the shamans allude to the spirits, so the magicians begin their predictions: "The gods have revealed to us," or "Five gods have revealed this to me." As the shaman falls into a stupor after his dance, so the magician, of whom [the chronicler] Nikon tells, lies "benumbed." The strict prohibition of the "whirling dance" leaves no doubt as to the fact that the magicians are like the shamans also in that method by which they brought themselves to the ecstatic condition.[62]

On the subject of the elders, let us cite a few passages from Afanasiev that seem to contain the seeds of the role of the Oldest-and-Wisest in *The Rite*. The

---

62. Sokolov, 170–71 (his source in this case was E. V. Anichkov, *Paganism and Ancient Russia* [St. Petersburg, 1914]).

ceremony in question here is the lighting of the Kupala bonfire from "living fire":

> The revered elders obtain it from wood by friction, and while this process is going on the assembled populace stands in silent awe. But as soon as the flame bursts forth the whole crowd at once becomes animated and takes up songs of joy. (3:714)

The awesome silence of the "Kiss of the Earth," performed by the Oldest-and-Wisest—perhaps the quietest moment in *The Rite*—gives way to the orgiastic "Dance of the Earth" in just this way. And "Iarilo's Procession," led by a chosen one "who sings and dances," also leads to general revelry in a manner suggesting the "Cortège du sage":

> Iarilo's procession is heralded by the beating of a drum. Circling the village square, [the leader] sings, dances and grimaces, and behind him moves a noisy crowd. The populace gives itself over completely to revelry, and after various games accompanied by singing, music making, and dancing, the crowd divides itself into two sides and begins a fist fight at close quarters. (3:727)

The remaining theme in *The Rite,* the worship of ancestors, is the quintessential "Scythian" theme. Ancestral graves, in fact, were practically the only sites venerated by the Scyths who "made images and altars and shrines for Ares, but for no other god."[63] These gravesites or kurgans (funerary mounds) were the major repositories of the gold artifacts that have made the Scyths famous among art lovers in recent times. The greatest flurry of archaeological digging in such kurgans took place in the late nineteenth and early twentieth centuries, and Roerich was both vitally interested and well informed on the subject. In the end, his set design for Part I of the ballet depicted a Scythian kurgan.[64] We have already noted that the Scyths practiced human sacrifice as part of their royal burial rite. That Herodotus's account of the Scyths provided Roerich with general background for his scenario, then, seems clear enough.

But beyond this there are two instances of specific direct borrowing. One of these concerns the description of Scythian auguries:

> There are among the Scythians many diviners, who divine by means of many willow wands. . . . They bring great bundles of wands, which they

63. Herodotus, *The Persian Wars* 4: 59; trans. (Godley, 258–59).
64. Compare the reproduction of Roerich's set (Krasovskaya, *Nijinsky,* 262) with photographs of Scythian kurgans in *From the Lands of the Scythians: Ancient Treasures from the Museum of the U.S.S.R., 300 B.C.–100 B.C.* (New York, 1975), 23, 27, and 30.

lay on the ground and unfasten, and utter their divinations laying the rods down one by one; and while they yet speak they gather up the rods once more and again place them together; this manner of divination is hereditary among them. (4:67; trans. Godley 264–65)

In a letter written by Stravinsky to Roerich,[65] and in a draft scenario prepared by Roerich for Diaghilev,[66] the "Augures printanières" are called by the name *Gadanie na prutikakh,* that is, "Divination with Wands," as already shown in the list of headings given earlier.[67] Also clearly inspired by Herodotus is the heading "Amazons" that accompanies the sketch for the "Glorification, referred to in the sketchbook as *Dikaia pliaska,* "wild dance."[68] The idea for this came from the story of the mating of Amazons and Scyths in *The Persian Wars* (4:110–16; trans. Godley 308–17), and the reference was evidently a justification of the wild or martial behavior of the women in the Honoring of the Chosen One, as described in the early synopses.

Ancestor veneration and divination (though on a more placid note) occur in Slavic rituals too, of course. Through the rituals of Semik, in large part a commemoration holiday, the theme of "evoking the ancestors" was appropriated from Herodotus and brought into authentic conjection with the dominant theme of *The Rite of Spring.* In Afanasiev's words,

> Together with the awakening to life of nature from its winter sleep (or numbness), the souls of the deceased are also awakened to life, and are condemned to inhabit for a while the sphere of air and cloud. Therefore, the holiday of spring was at the same time a holiday in honor of the departed ancestors, and was generally a time of communion with them, visits to cemeteries, and commemorative feasts [*pominki*]. (3:698)

These public wakes are described in the *Stoglav* in terms close to the "Spring Rounds," particularly in the way the contrasting *Vivo* section at no. 54 interrupts the stately progress of the dance. Could this too have been one of Roerich's sources, and through him an influence on the form of the music itself?

> On Trinity Saturday [i.e., on the third day of the "Green Week" initiated by Semik] throughout the villages and throughout the churchyards, men

---

65. Sept. 13/26, 1911, first published by Irina Vershinina, "Pis'ma I. Stravinskogo N. Rerikhu," *Sovetskaia muzyka* 8 (1966): 60, and later in translation in the booklet accompanying the sketchbook facs., p. 30 (see n. 25).

66. Vera Stravinsky and Craft, 75–76.

67. This correlation was noted and the correct reference to Herodotus given in André Schaeffner, "Au fil des Esquisses du 'Sacre,' " *Revue de musicologie* 57 (1971): 182.

68. Sketchbook facs., p. 50 (see n. 25). In his commentary (p. 14), Craft reminds us that Stravinsky had described the dance as "Amazonian" to Schaeffner in 1931. In view of Schaeffner's identification of Herodotus (see n. 67), one may surmise that Stravinsky mentioned the ancient historian at that time.

and women go out on mourning ceremonies and lament at the graves of the dead, with a great crying. And when the buffoons [*skomorokhi*] begin to perform all kinds of demoniac games, then they cease from their weeping, and begin to leap and dance, and to clap their hands, and to sing satanic songs.[69]

By now, it should be clear that correspondences and parallels between the scenario of *The Rite* and authentic accounts from chroniclers and ethnographers could be multiplied practically ad libitum. The basis of the ballet in "archaic reality" is far more concrete than is generally recognized and certainly more so than Stravinsky wished to acknowledge after 1920.[70] When early admirers exclaimed that the work was "not a ballet, thank heavens; it is a ritual, it is an ancient rite,"[71] they were more literally correct than they could have known.

But to speak of *The Rite of Spring* as an ethnographical work, let alone a "realistic" one, would be literalistic at best. Only a determined and perverse revisionism would seek to emphasize the most old-fashioned of its aspects over all that was so obviously new. Far more important than the initial fidelity to authentic sources was the collaborators' (and in particular Stravinsky's) sovereign freedom in the handling of them. And in this freedom is revealed the profundity of their response to the precepts of the World of Art movement and its reinterpretation of the ideals of Slavic nationalism in art. As the art critic Yakov Tugenhold put it in an article of 1910, "The folk, formerly the object of the artist's pity, is becoming increasingly the source of artistic style."[72]

The Rite of Spring, famous for its total lack of pity, indeed of all "psychology," was a giant step along that path, a path that led directly to the hard-nosed aesthetic modernism of the "neoclassic" period. Folk-derived elements such as had played gaudily on the surface as recently as *Petrushka* were now ruthlessly submerged to work their influence at the deepest levels of structure and harmonic design. This, certainly, is what Stravinsky had uppermost in mind when he exclaimed in a letter to Andrei Rimsky-Korsakov that "it seems that twenty years, not two, have passed since *The Firebird.*[73] For this change to have taken place, for the desired level of abstraction to have been achieved, it was necessary that the sources, both musical and ethnological, be "cachées," not displayed proudly as had been done in Russian music of an earlier time. The result was that *The Rite of Spring* brought some of the finest fruits of the Russian "Silver Age"—the World of Art, neonationalism, *skifstvo*—into the mainstream of

---

69. Quoted in Sokolov, 167.

70. To the end Stravinsky remained hostile to any appraisal of *The Rite* that emphasized its folkloristic content. Many comments indicative of this attitude are strewn throughout the commentary to the sketchbook facsim. (see n. 25), which was published less than two years before his death.

71. Prince Sergei Volkonsky (quoted in Krasovskaya, *Nijinsky,* 243).

72. *Apollon* 10 (1910): 21.

73. Yarustovsky, 467.

Western music and, in so doing, utterly transcended the movements and the sources from which it sprang. It achieved a universality that ultimately rendered its subject superfluous.[74] But how much greater seem both the achievement and the transcendence when we know how concrete and specific the original subject was.

.

74. In Roerich's words, "We cannot consider 'Sacre' as Russian, nor even Slavic—it is more ancient and pan-human" (*Realm of Light,* 188). Nor does it seem an exaggeration to call *The Rite*'s universality "classical," for so it was deemed by some of the poets and painters closest to the World of Art movement. They considered coarseness and maximalism to be both a cleansing force and a harbinger of a new (if not yet "neo") classicism. In his article of 1909 (p. 61; see n. 13), Baskt writes,

Painting of the future calls for a lapidary style, because the new art cannot endure the refined—it has be-come surfeited with it. The elements of recent art have been air, sunlight, greenery; the elements of future art will be Man and and Stone. Painting of the future will crawl down into the depths of coarseness.

Stravinsky too used the word *lapidary* to describe *The Rite* in letters to Findeisen and to Roerich, possibly in unconscious response to these thoughts of Bakst. In any case, Bakst had divined with uncanny prescience not only the nature and the achievement of Stravinsky's masterpiece, but also its then remote aesthetic implica-tions.

THE REJECTION OF
THE AULOS IN
CLASSICAL GREECE

JAMES W. MCKINNON

IT IS A commonplace among music historians that there was a deep-seated aversion to the aulos in ancient Greece. At the root of this alleged aversion lies the identification of the instrument with Dionysos, the god of intoxication and frenzy, an outsider who came to Greece from the wilds of Phrygia. His wailing aulos stands in sharp contrast to the restrained lyre or kithara of Apollo, god of reason and judgment, the quintessential Hellenic deity.

The aulos/kithara antithesis was given its first full exposition at the turn of the century by Hermann Abert in *Die Lehre vom Ethos.* He went so far as to claim that it underlay the origins of the ethos doctrine itself. According to Abert, the neutral-toned kithara, the instrument normally used for accompaniment in Greek musical life, was originally lacking in ethical connotation, but with the eruption of the exciting and sensuous sound of the Phrygian aulos upon sensitive Greek ears, it acquired a positive ethical association with traditional Hellenic virtues. "Thereafter," Abert concluded, "this dualism of the two types of instruments dominated the entire development of Greek art music."[1]

Subsequently Curt Sachs, among others, restated the "radical antitheses" between, as he phrased it, "the immaterial-detached, noble-innocent, 'Apollinian' " nature of kithara music and "the earthy-sensuous, passionate-intoxicated, 'Dionysian' " nature of aulos music.[2] The duality can be traced back, says Sachs, to the very origins of Greek history, with kithara music being derived from the Cretan-Mycenaean side and aulos music from the Phoenician–Asia Minor side.

1. Leipzig, 1899; repr. ed. (Tutzing, 1968), 64–65.
2. *Die Musik der Antike,* Handbuch der Musikwissenschaft, ed. Ernst Bücken, 1 (Potsdam, 1928): 25.

A number of more recent authors have reasserted the antithesis—among them Jacques Chailley, a scholar who differs in some respects from the German tradition.[3] He shares with it the basic conception of a profound and intense opposition between the two instruments; he speaks of "the struggle of the two instruments," which was "long, and by turns cruel, sly, or sordid." What is peculiar to his position is his explanation of the opposition. He sees it as the symbol of "the pitiless struggle" between two modes of civilization, the nomadic-pastoral and the sedentary-agricultural. The lyre, made from such animal materials as a tortoise shell, the horns of a deer, and sheep gut for strings, stands for the nomadic-pastoral society, while the aulos, made from the vegetable material of a reed, stands for the sedentary-agricultural society. This bold notion has a measure of plausibility, but certainly it cannot be sustained in the face of the objection that the aulos was frequently fashioned from the bone of an animal; indeed its Latin name, *tibia,* means "shinbone." One can safely dismiss this explanation and focus here on the mainstream conception of a deep antithesis between the Apollinian and Dionysian principles.

Contemporary music historians might be tempted to dismiss in equally summary fashion the mainstream conception as having been the product of the eighteenth- and nineteenth-century German idealization of ancient Greece, a tendency brilliantly described by Eliza Marian Butler in *The Tyranny of Greece over Germany.*[4] The Apollinian conception of Greek culture, summarized in Winkelmann's famous phrase "noble simplicity and serene greatness," reigned unopposed for nearly a century, until the discovery of the Dionysian principle by Heine and Nietzsche. Within a generation of the publication of Nietzsche's *Birth of Tragedy* (1872) the earlier monistic view was replaced by the new dualism—an "immense antagonism" between the Apollinian and the Dionysian. In turn, music historians like Abert and Sachs applied the new conception to a supposed opposition between kithara and aulos, with the results indicated above. Expedient as it might be simply to operate at the same level of intellectual fashion and ignore their views as the product of romantic imaginings, we must admit that these ideas are too much a part of our musicological heritage to receive so cavalier a treatment. On the contrary, the conventional view that the aulos was rejected on the grounds of an Apollinian-Dionysian conflict ought to be examined in the context of the primary sources.

FIRST, the case for the rejection of the aulos. Perhaps the most important evidence is found in a pair of cognate statements from Plato's *Republic* and Aristotle's *Politics.* The passage from Plato follows immediately upon Socrates's famous rejection of all modes but the Dorian and the Phrygian:

> Then, said I [Socrates], we shall not need in our songs and airs instruments of many strings or [those] whose compass includes all the harmonies.

3. *La Musique grecque antique* (Paris, 1979), 9–12.
4. (Cambridge, 1935); 2nd ed. (Boston, 1958).

Not in my opinion, said he.

Then we shall not maintain makers of the trigonon and pectis and all other many-stringed and polyharmonic instruments.

Apparently not.

Well, will you admit to the city aulos makers and aulos players? Or is not the aulos the most "many-stringed" of instruments and do not the panharmonics themselves imitate it?

Clearly, he said.

You have left, said I, the lyre and the cithara. These are useful in the city, and in the fields the shepherds would have a little syrinx to pipe on.

So our argument indicates, he said.

We are not innovating, my friend, in preferring Apollo and the instruments of Apollo to Marsyas and his instruments.[5]

Since the passage from Aristotle's *Politics* is rather long, only especially relevant excerpts are given here:

> Auloi must not be introduced into education, nor any other professional instrument such as the kithara. . . . Moreover the aulos is not a moralizing but rather an exciting influence, so that it ought to be used for occasions of the kind at which attendance has the effect of purification rather than instruction. And let us add that the aulos happens to possess the additional property telling against its use in education that playing it prevents the employment of speech. Hence former ages rightly rejected its use by the young and the free, although at first they had employed it. . . . But later on it came to be disapproved of as a result of actual experience, when men were more capable of judging what music conduced to virtue and what did not; and similarly also many of the old instruments were disapproved of, like the pectis and the barbitos . . . the heptagon, the trigonon and the sambuca, and all the instruments that require manual skill.

Comment on both passages is reserved for later; it suffices to point out here that Plato and Aristotle clearly propose a ban of some sort upon the aulos. The passage from Aristotle concludes with a reference to a myth that is another central element in the evidence for the conventional view:

> The tale goes that Athena found an aulos and threw it away. Now it is not a bad point in the story that the goddess did this out of annoyance because of the ugly distortion of her features; but as a matter of fact it is more

5. *Republic,* 399c–e; trans. Paul Shorey in *Plato: The Collected Dialogues,* ed. Edith Hamilton and Huntington Cairns (New York, 1963), 644. All translations quoted here will be altered in one respect: terms for musical instruments will be given in transliteration as opposed to such common misleading renderings as flute for aulos and harp for kithara.

likely that it was because education in aulos-playing has no effect on the intelligence, whereas we attribute science and art to Athena.[6]

Aristotle alludes here to just one episode in the myth. Equally relevant to our subject is the famous one about the musical contest between Apollo and Marsyas. The mythographer Apollodorus succeeded in narrating the oft-told tale with all its essential elements in a relatively brief passage:

> Apollo also slew Marsyas, the son of Olympus. For Marsyas, having found the auloi which Athena had thrown away because they disfigured her face, engaged in a musical contest with Apollo. They agreed that the victor should work his will on the vanquished, and when the trial took place Apollo turned his lyre upside down in the competition and bade Marsyas do the same. But Marsyas could not. So Apollo was judged the victor and despatched Marsyas by hanging him on a tall pine tree and stripping off his skin.[7]

The story differs in detail from mythographer to mythographer. Certain of these variations are relevant to the point at issue and will be cited later. For now, one need mention only the most fundamental of them: in Ovid's version Marsyas is replaced by Pan, and Marsyas's punishment is replaced by one for the sole judge of the contest who dared to vote against Apollo. The judge was Midas, who for his error grew the ears of an ass.[8] This of course, is the version of the myth that is marvelously celebrated in J. S. Bach's *Der Streit zwischen Phoebus und Pan* (BWV 201).

Another key element in the case for the conventional view is the fascinating anecdote of Alcibiades's rejection of the aulos. It is best told in the rather lengthy version of Plutarch:

> At school, he usually paid due heed to his teachers, but he refused to play the aulos, holding it to be an ignoble and illiberal thing. The use of the plectrum and the lyre, he argued, wrought no havoc with the bearing and appearance which were becoming to a gentleman; but let a man go to blowing on an aulos, and even his own kinsmen could scarcely recognize his features. Moreover, the lyre blended its tones with the voice or song of its master; whereas the aulos closed and barricaded the mouth, robbing its master both of voice and speech. "Auloi, then," said he, "for the sons of Thebes; they know not how to converse. But we Athenians, as our fathers say, have Athene for foundress and Apollo for patron, one of whom cast the aulos away in disgust, and the other flayed the presumptuous aulos-

---

6. *Politics*, 1341a-b; trans. Harris Rackham, *Aristotle: Politics*, Loeb Classical Library (London, 1932), 667–69.

7. Apollodorus 1. 4. 2; trans. James Frazer, *Apollodorus: The Library*, Loeb Classical Library (London, 1921), 2: 29–31.

8. *Metamorphoses*, 11: 144–93.

player." Thus, half in jest and half in earnest, Alcibiades emancipated himself from this discipline. . . .[9]

The final element in the case for the conventional view concerns the part played by Pythagoras. There are two sources from late antiquity that refer to his preference for the lyre over the aulos. They may strike the reader as having a somewhat different flavor from the previous passages. The Neoplatonic philosopher Iamblichus (d. A.D. 325) said in his biography of Pythagoras that "he used the lyre, but maintained that the sound of the aulos was ostentatious and suited to festivals, but in no wise suited to a free man."[10] Again the roughly contemporary music theorist Aristides Quintilianus tells us that

> Pythagoras likewise advised his students who had heard the sound of the aulos to cleanse themselves as if stained in spirit and to chase away the irrational desires of the soul with melodies of good omen played on the lyre. For the former instrument serves to rule the active part of the soul while the latter is dear and pleasing to the management of the logical part.[11]

The documents cited above comprise the principal evidence upon which modern scholars base their idea of a profound antithesis between the Apollinian lyre or kithara and the Dionysian aulos. The case against it is of a somewhat different nature, for it does not consist in a similar series of extended passages but rather of many shorter references. One must first establish a chronological perspective on the issue and analyze the relevant texts.

As FOR the matter of chronological perspective, the conventional view maintains that the antithesis goes back to the very origins of the Greek people; after-all, if the antithesis is so deep-rooted, so elemental, it cannot be an ephemeral thing. However, the evidence cited above is chronologically very restricted; with the exception of the references to Pythagoras, it is all confined to the Classical period of the fifth and fourth centuries B.C. Also it is confined regionally to Athens. There have been attempts to present earlier evidence, but at best it would cover a period antedating other sources by only a century or so. The two references to Pythagoras are a case in point. Music historians tend to accept them quite literally as authentic Pythagorean sayings.[12] One could, for the sake of argument, acquiesce in this conclusion, which distorts only minimally the chronological perspective suggested here. But surely a more plausible view is that these references, which postdate the lifetime of Pythagoras by nearly a millennium, are a manifestation of Neopythagorean thinking. They therefore combine echoes of

---

9. *Alcibiades*, 2: 4–5; trans. Bernadotte Perrin, *Plutarch's Lives*, Loeb Classical Library (London, 1916), 4: 7–9. See also Aulus Gellius, *Noctes atticae*, 15, 17.

10. *De vita pythagorica liber*, [25] 111; ed. Michael von Albrecht (Zurich, 1963), 116.

11. *De musica libri tres*, 2: 19; ed. Reginald Pepys Winnington-Ingram (Leipzig, 1963), 91.

12. For example, Helmut Huchzermeyer, *Aulos und Kithara in der griechischen Musik bis zum Ausgang der klassischen Zeit* (Emsdetten, 1931), 52–53; Annemarie J. Neubecker, *Die Bewertung der Musik bei Stoikern und Epikureern* (Berlin, 1956), 77.

the Classical Athenian notion of the "free man" with Neopythagorean preoccupation with the purity of the soul.

There are two other possibly relevant sources that do predate the time of Plato and Aristotle. One is a fragment by Pratinas of Philus, who was active in Athens around 500 B.C. It asserts that "Song's queen Muse hath made; the aulos, he must dance second as becometh a servant."[13] Helmut Huchzermeyer interprets this to mean that Pratinas "is altogether averse to the noisy music of the aulos."[14] This, however, is an unwarranted inference, and one must agree with Warren Anderson, who argues that "Pratinas was presumably not condemning the instrument itself" but rather "felt outraged by virtuoso displays on the aulos at the expense of the text."[15] The second source is a poetic reference by Critias to Anacreon, an Ionian lyric poet active in Athens toward the end of the sixth century. Critias, a Sophist and early associate of Socrates, describes Anacreon as "an antagonist of the aulos and a friend of the barbiton."[16] Huchzermeyer takes Critias at his word and cites Anacreon as the only Ionian poet who preferred strings to the aulos and the man who "embodied in his person the kitharodic reaction against aulos music."[17] Although this is a defensible interpretation, one must consider the possibility that Critias's remarks are anachronistic.

There exists, then, a scattering of uncertain references to antagonism toward the aulos from the century preceding the time of Socrates and Plato. Each of them is open to serious question, but even if all were authentic, they would have only a relatively minor effect on the chronological limitations suggested here. On the other hand, a massive body of evidence points to the honorable status of the aulos in Greek musical life during the centuries preceding the Classical period.[18] In Homer, it is true, the aulos plays a subsidiary role and the lyrelike phorminx has pride of place, but by the time of Alcman (fl. 654–611 B.C.) the aulos was firmly established in Sparta as the principal accompaniment instrument of choral lyrics. Among the Ionian poets the aulos occupied a similar position, and it was only on Lesbos that strings seem to have been preferred. One notes that there is no question of opposition here, but simply that strings were cited more frequently than the aulos in Lesbian verses, and further that the strings generally mentioned are the pektis and barbiton, both excluded later on by Aristotle along with the aulos.[19] But the lyric poet whose references have the most relevance to our subject is the Boeotian Pindar; no less than six times does he cite aulos and lyre or phorminx together, as when he alluded to the brave soldiers of Aegina, "celebrated on the phorminx and in the harmony of the

13. Fragment 1; ed. and trans. John Maxwell Edmonds, *Lyra Graeca*, Loeb Classical Library (London, 1959), 3: 51.
14. Huchzermeyer, 54.
15. "Pratinus of Philus," *The New Grove* 15: 203.
16. Hermann Diels, *Die Fragmente der Vorsocratiker*, 6th ed., ed. Walther Kranz (Zurich, 1951), 2: 376.
17. Huchzermeyer, 42.
18. The references are set forth with admirable thoroughness in Huchzermeyer.
19. On Lesbos, see Huchzermeyer, 40–42.

many-voiced aulos."[20]

In fifth-century Athenian drama, as is well known, the aulos occupied a position of nearly exclusive usage. And not only was it used; it was also occasionally referred to with fondness by the great dramatists of the time. To Sophocles it was "sweet" and "pleasant-sounding,"[21] and to Euripides it was "blended with light laughter."[22] With Aristophanes the situation is somewhat more complex. In general it can be said that he fails to convey to us any evidence of serious antagonism toward the aulos in the Athens of his time. This constitutes something of an *argumentum ex silentio* against the conventional view because Aristophanes otherwise has so much to say about music. Surely if Athenians had been all that aware of an antithesis between kithara and aulos, there would have been some allusion to it in the scene in the *Frogs* where Dionysos weighs the respective musical merits of Aeschylus and Euripides. The only reference to the aulos in Aristophanes that can be construed as at all negative is of an entirely different nature. In the *Acharnians,* a Boeotian, who speaks in dialect and seems meant to be something of a bumpkin, mentions his compatriot aulos players.[23] We are reminded, of course, of Alcibiades, who exclaimed, "Auloi, then, for the sons of Thebes."

To summarize, there is little trace of antagonism toward the aulos or of opposition between it and the kithara up to the time of Plato and Aristotle. Before discussing their views, the historical context must be made complete by a brief survey of the following centuries. Aside from the two references to Phythagoras given above and repetitions of the Athena-Apollo-Marsyas myth, later authors are similarly silent on the subject. This is particularly significant when one considers the character of a gossip-inclined historical work like the *Musica* of Pseudo-Plutarch. He mentions the aulos again and again but not once with reference to a Greek rejection of it. The situation with Athenaeus, the author of the massive *Deipnosophists,* is only slightly different. There are two rambling passages in his lengthy work that cite the aulos on virtually every page.[24] It is fair to say that he looks on music with consistent favor or at least with benign curiosity. Moreover, the aulos figures as one of the most prominent specific objects of his praise. Nonetheless, there are a few references that might be construed out of context as supporting the conventional view. For instance, he cites Athena's discarding of the aulos and in a nearby citation Pratinas's injunction that it not get out of hand in exercising its accompaniment function.[25] One had best consider this an echo of Classical Athens, keeping in mind Athenaeus's tendency to quote each and every reference he can muster. Moreover, he has Telestes immediately step into the breach with a spirited defense of the aulos.

20. *Isthmian,* 5: 27; see also *Nemean,* 9: 8; *Pythian,* 10: 39; *Olympian,* 10: 94; *Olympian,* 7: 12; *Olympia,* 3: 8–9.
21. *Ajax,* 1202, and *The Woman of Trachis,* 640.
22. *Bacchanals,* 380.
23. *Acharnians,* 860–66.
24. *Deipnosophists,* 4: 174–85; 14: 616–39.
25. *Deipnosophists,* 14: 616–17.

On a related point, Athenaeus discusses the *harmoniae* and their ethical character.[26] What is noteworthy from our point of view is that while he and other writers of late antiquity show some consistency in the ethical qualities they attribute to the two principal *harmoniae,* the Dorian and the Phrygian, they show no such consistency in associating the kithara with the former and the aulos with the latter, and thus no consistency in assigning ethical character to the two instruments. For instance, Lucian speaks of Harmonides as a performer who wishes to display on his aulos the "enthusiasm of the Phrygian and the restraint of the Dorian";[27] and Apuleius tells of Antigenidas, who performed on his aulos the "religious Phrygian and the warlike Dorian."[28]

To summarize the situation in the later centuries: aside from the troubling Pythagorean references, one detects no general awareness of an antithesis between kithara and aulos but, at most, an occasional echo of the Classical period's rejection of the aulos.

WHAT precisely was the character of that rejection? Since it had its most explicit expression in Plato's and Aristotle's exclusion of the instrument from their ideal states, an examination of the question ought to begin with this. The first point to establish is the context of the exclusion. We can keep matters in perspective if we recall that Plato and Aristotle are philosophers describing utopian societies, not active political figures seriously advocating that the aulos be banned from contemporary Athens. Indeed the context is still more narrow, for they do not propose a general ban on the aulos in their ideal states, but only in education. Aristotle, especially, is quite explicit on this point, excluding the aulos and all modes but the Dorian from education while allowing them in other areas of society. "It is clear that we should employ all the modes," he writes, "but use only the most ethical ones for education." He goes on to cite some of the beneficent uses of exciting music for adults—in the dithyramb, the tragedy, and "sacred melodies" *(ieroi meloi)*—all accompanied by aulos; such music has the effect of purgation and of harmless pleasure. At the same time he notes in Plato's *Republic* the inconsistency of Socrates, who, while excluding the aulos, admits the Phrygian mode into education along with the Dorian, whereas "the Phrygian mode has the same effect among harmonies as the aulos among instruments."

On this distinction between Aristotle and Plato, Warren Anderson makes the important point that, while in Aristotle's view education is meant for youth alone, in Plato's view it extends to the entire life of a citizen.[29] One might argue, then, that his ban on the aulos was absolute. However, it defies historical good sense to claim that Plato's one brief remark in the *Republic* should be applied with inexorable logic to his views throughout his life. Indeed he supplies explicit

---

26. *Deipnosophists,* 14: 624–26.
27. *Harmonides,* 1.
28. *Florida,* 1: 4.
29. *Ethos and Education in Greek Music* (Cambridge, Mass., 1966), 137–38.

evidence against such an interpretation when later, in the *Laws,* he provides for judges at aulos-playing contests.[30]

Another point of contrast with Plato is Aristotle's more pragmatic and tolerant approach. This is of some relevance because we are seeking to define general Athenian attitudes more than those of an individual. That Plato's views should be taken as somewhat eccentrically intolerant is warranted by his proposed legislation against the changing of rules in children's games.[31]

Whatever the extent of Plato's and Aristotle's proposed ban on the aulos, the reasons underlying it are another matter. Was it primarily that they felt that a deep ethical antithesis existed between the aulos and string instruments? This, it must be said, is the aspect of the conventional view that finds the least support in the sources. Plato does indeed exclude the aulos while retaining the lyre and the kithara, but he also allows the syrinx "to shepherds in the fields" and excludes the trigonon, the pectis, and "other many-stringed instruments." Aristotle destroys the antithesis completely when he excludes not only a host of string instruments such as the pectis, barbiton, trigonon, heptagon, and sambuca, but also the kithara itself. This is perhaps the crucial point: he retains Apollo's lyre and excludes Apollo's kithara! Why? He tells us simply enough that "the aulos must not be admitted into education nor any other professional *(technikos)* instrument like the kithara." And again, at the end of the list of string instruments given above, he adds "and all those requiring manual skill." Thus he excludes instruments that require professional skill—indeed, virtually all instruments.

Plato implies similar motivation in his strictures. He excludes "many-stringed and polyharmonic instruments" and goes on to cite the aulos as the "most 'many-stringed' of instruments," in fact, the one that the polyharmonic instruments imitate. The context of his remarks is a discussion of modal ethos. Plato objects to instruments that have the capacity to play all the modes without retuning and mix the modes within a single composition. Professional virtuosos were doing this in the new music of the late fifth century, both on the versatile aulos and on the string instruments of the time, to which strings were being added in an effort to keep pace with the aulos. The kithara had evidently undergone this sort of development by the time of Aristotle. Such instruments, then, were out of place in the musical education of well-born Athenian youth.

This antithesis between vulgar professional and genteel amateur is altogether more authentic than any antithesis between aulos and lyre as such. It lies at the very heart of the Classical conception of "liberal" education: skills which tradesmen and technicians exercise to earn a living are merely tolerated, as opposed to those prized intellectual pursuits whereby the "free man" improves himself. Indeed this is the central point of Aristotle's doctrine of education as presented in Book VIII of the *Politics* and provides the context of his views on music.

30. *Laws,* 764c–e.
31. *Laws,* 797b.

Once it is established that antiprofessionalism is the primary motive behind Plato's and Aristotle's position concerning the aulos, there remains a chance to accept various elements of the conventional view as secondary motives. Plato does, after all, conclude the above-quoted passage with the afterthought that "we are not innovating . . . in preferring Apollo and the instruments of Apollo to Marsyas and his instruments." And Aristotle closes with a similar reference when he invokes the same legend and goes so far as to say that the aulos contributes nothing to intelligence *(dianoia)* whereas science *(epistēmē)* is an attribute of Athena. Now it can be said that there is a suggestion of the Apollinian–Dionysian antithesis in these references. On the one hand, Athena and Apollo are easily identified as copatrons of both Athens and reason, while, on the other, Marsyas, the Phrygian satyr, is a devotee of Dionysos. It would be wrong, however, to take Plato and Aristotle further than they themselves went and to attribute to them anything like a profound aversion to the orgiastic aulos of Dionysos. We have already seen that Aristotle acknowledged the usefulness of orgiastic music.[32] Plato's attitude is more complex, perhaps ambivalent, or even contradictory. While it is clear that he prized reason above all else, it cannot be said that he rejected religious frenzy outright. "Divine madness" is his general term for such manifestations, which he describes with apparent approval in the *Phaedrus.*[33] A passage of special relevance appears in the *Symposium,* where Alciabiades in a eulogy of Socrates compares him to Marsyas. He exclaims that Socrates had in his speech the same marvelous effect as had Marsyas in the aulos tunes of divine origin with which he charmed mortals.[34] In short, to claim that either Aristotle or Plato rejected the aulos because of its association with religious frenzy is at best a caricature of their authentic views. To claim, on the other hand, that they betrayed an occasional trace of uneasiness over this kind of association is at least an arguable position.

Now to turn to a direct consideration of the Athena-Apollo-Marsyas myth. Its various versions offer many indications that the Greeks failed to read into it the sort of antithesis in question here. Consider the roles taken in it by the deities involved. Athena throws away the aulos in this particular myth because it distorts her appearance, and yet she is frequently associated with the aulos in others. She gave an aulos as a present at the wedding of Cadmus and Harmonia;[35] she actually invented it, according to Pindar;[36] and, according to Corinna, she taught none other than Apollo to play it.[37] Telestes takes an interesting approach to the subject in denying outright that Athena discarded the aulos; she

32. In support of this point, see Jeanne Croissant, *Aristote et les mystères* (Liège, 1932), repr. ed. (New York, 1979).

33. *Phaedrus,* 244d–e; see Ivan M. Linforth, "Telestic Madness in Plato, Phaedrus 244de," *University of California Publications in Classical Philology,* 13/6 (1946): 163–72.

34. *Symposium,* 215b–c.

35. Diodorus Siculus, 5: 49, 1.

36. *Phythian,* 12: 19–24; see also Diodorus, 3: 58, 2.

37. See Ps.-Plutarch 14; indeed, in the same passage Soterichus maintains that Apollo himself invented the aulos.

was a virgin, he argues, and therefore had no reason to worry about her appearance.[38] To add a final note of contradiction on Athena, Diodorus Siculus cites Marsyas as her closest associate and adds, still more surprisingly, that he was admired for his intelligence and chastity.[39] Regarding the musical aspects of the contest between Apollo and Marsyas, the more commonly expressed view among the ancients is that Marsyas was superior! And how did Apollo win then? By trickery. We observe, for example, in the version of Diodorus given above that Apollo played his lyre upside down, a feat that could hardly be matched by Marsyas with his aulos. Here is what the goddess Hera has to say to Apollo's mother, Leto, on the subject:

> You make me laugh, Leto. Who could admire one that Marsyas would have beaten at music and skinned alive with his own hands, if the Muses had chosen to judge fairly? But as it was, he was tricked and wrongly lost the vote, poor fellow, and had to die.[40]

The anecdote about Alcibiades similarly fails to support the sort of ethical antithesis set forth in the conventional view. Although one finds a clearly expressed preference for the lyre over the aulos, perhaps the most unambiguous in the literature, the motives fail to match. Central again is the context of education, and accordingly the aulos is seen to be "illiberal" (aneleutheron); the translation nicely captures the proper connotation when it declares the instrument to be unbecoming to the bearing and appearance of a "gentleman" (eleutheros). The whole issue is described as a light rather than a profound one: "Thus, half in jest and half in earnest Alcibiades emancipated himself from this discipline." Finally, there is the nasty remark about the countrified Thebans mentioned above: "Auloi, then, for the sons of Thebes: they know not how to converse." If one is to summarize the unifying motive of Alcibiades, it is snobbery, not ethos.

IN DRAWING conclusions here, one may recognize some claims that can be accepted with a fair degree of confidence—for example, that the Hellenic animus against the aulos is not perennial but, rather, confined almost exclusively to the Athens of the Classical period. Again it seems clear enough that the principal reason for the phenomenon was the antiprofessional bias in the Athenian educational ideals. Contributory to it were the disdain of Athenian "free men" for mercenary activity of any sort, a disapproval of the rapid musical development of the time, and a touch of prejudice against the contemporary virtuosos who hailed from rural Boeotian. Still, one does detect a measure of unease in Classical Athens concerning the orgiastic associations of the aulos, even if not an

38. Athenaeus, *Deipnosophists*, 14: 617.
39. Diodorus, 3: 58, 3.
40. Lucian, *Dialogues of the Gods*, 18 (16); trans. M. D. Macleod, *Lucian*, Loeb Classical Library (London, 1969), 7: 327; see also Diodorus, 3: 58, 2–6. The one version that clearly gives the musical victory to Apollo is that of the Roman poet Ovid. *Metamorphoses*, 11: 165–74.

unequivocal disapproval. It is difficult to measure this element precisely—it seems more to lurk below the surface than to be expressed—but it can at least be said that the conventional view greatly exaggerates it.

To engage for the moment in somewhat less guarded speculation, let it be said that music historians must be disabused of any notion that the Athenian rejection of the aulos, particularly in the form it takes with Plato, amounts to anything like a positive, noble statement on behalf of the perennial Apollinian principle in music. For all its artistry of expression, it is a negative and essentially antimusical position. We must associate it with Plato's own strictures against poetry, with the Neoplatonic Augustine's scorn for practicing musicians,[41] with the twelfth-century humanist John of Salisbury's criticism of polyphony,[42] with the classical scholar Johann August Ernesti's disapproval of Bach, and, yes, to at least some extent with the artistic control exercised by twentieth-century totalitarian regimes.[43]

As for Nietzsche's "immense antagonism" between the Apollinian and the Dionysian, whatever its merits per se, enough has been said to demonstrate the invalidity of its application by German musicologists to an antithesis between kithara and aulos.[44] We English-speaking music historians, incidentally, would do well to note an analogous Victorian influence on our thinking.[45] In particular, Benjamin Jowett's much-read translations tend to give Plato's remarks on subjects like the aulos and ritual frenzy more the tone of nineteenth-century religiosity than Athenian musical conservatism.[46]

It is not my intent here to deny totally a role in this subject to the historical imagination. Once the simplistic application of the Apollinian–Dionysian antithesis is set aside, there remains room for more plausible dualistic conceptions. It is interesting to note that Sachs came to reject the Apollo–Dionysos antithesis and proposed instead an antithesis between *ethos* and *pathos*, from which stems a tendency in Western art to oscillate between classic and romantic poles.[47] And Walter Wiora has recognized the emergence of an Apollinian ideal in Classical Greece alongside the existence of a more primitive artistic vitality. He denies, however, that the Greeks looked upon the two as absolute opposites; rather, they cultivated both in an undogmatic manner.[48] It is not for us here either to accept or to reject such speculations. While expressing admiration for them, we have undertaken the more pedestrian task of indicating that they are applied at peril to a subject as specific as the Greek attitude toward the aulos.

41. *De musica*, 1: 4.
42. *Polycraticus*, 1: 6.
43. In citing this relationship it is not necessary to go so far as to ally oneself completely with the bitter anti-Platonic revisionists of the twentieth century such as Karl Popper, *The Open Society and Its Enemies* (1945), 5th ed. (Princeton, N.J., 1966).
44. On this aspect of the subject, see Martin Vogel, *Apollinisch und Dionysisch* (Regensburg, 1966).
45. See Richard Jenkyns, *The Victorian and Ancient Greece* (Cambridge, Mass., 1980).
46. Compare, for example, Jowett on *Republic*, 399a–e, *Laws*, 669d–70, and *Laws*, 700a–b, with more recent translations.
47. *The Commonwealth of Art* (New York, 1946), 199–206.
48. *The Four Ages of Music*, trans. M. D. Herter Norton (New York, 1965), 74–75.

SINE LITTERA AND *CUM LITTERA* IN MEDIEVAL POLYPHONY

ERNEST H. SANDERS

THE COORDINATION of text and music has often presented transcribers and editors of Medieval polyphony with uncomfortable problems. Indications of the dilemmas that confronted them are manifest in one way or another in published articles and editions. The following examination of primary evidence is put forth as an endeavor to clarify the issue.

The earliest description of mensuration in polyphony, contained in the first part of the *Discantus positio vulgaris,* associates it with a system of melismatic notation.[1] The relevant sentences in the treatise establish (1) that rhythmic meaning is conveyed by ligatures; (2) that these constellations are characteristic of the upper voice (duplum) in the discant settings of chant melismas in organa, with each note of a melisma sustaining a standard of two successive notes in the duplum, i.e., a long and a short (2:1), the only mensurable units; (3) that each odd-numbered note of the discant voice (duplum) is generally consonant with the coincident note of the cantus firmus (the term *odd-numbered* being used even if more than one note intervenes between two contrapuntal intervals); and (4) that the intervening notes can be and usually are more dissonant. The first reper-

---

1. Ultra mensuram sunt que minus quam uno tempore et amplius quam duobus mensurantur. . . . Quandocumque due note ligantur in discantu, prima est brevis, secunda longa. . . . Item consonantia est diversarum vocum in eodem sono vel in pluribus concordia. Inter concordantias autem tres sunt ceteris meliores, scilicet unisonus, diapente et diapason. . . . Preterea notandum quod omnes note plane musice sunt longe et ultra mensuram, eo quod mensuram trium temporum continent. Omnes autem note discantus sunt mensurabiles per directam brevem et directam longam. Unde sequitur quod super quamlibet notam firmi cantus ad minus due note, longa scilicet et brevis, . . . proferri debent, que etiam convenire debent in aliqua dictarum consonantiarum. . . . Sciendum insuper quod omnes note impares, he que consonant melius consonant, que vero dissonant minus dissonant quam pares.
Hieronymus de Moravia, O. P. Tractatus de musica, ed. Simon M. Cserba, Freiburger Studien zur Musikwissenschaft, 2nd ser., no. 2 (Regensburg, 1935), 190–91.

toire to exhibit many such passages is the *Magnus liber organi,* whose author was Leoninus.

This book, says the English author known as Anonymous IV, "fuit in usu usque ad tempus Perotini Magni, qui abbreviavit eundem et fecit clausulas sive puncta plurima meliora, quoniam optimus discantor erat."[2] In editing and modernizing the *Magnus liber organi* Perotinus gave greater preponderance to discant style, thus tightening and abbreviating the Leoninian originals, including many of their organal passages.[3] The rapid consecution of syllables, inevitably becoming more frequent in the process, necessitated adjustments in the melismatic ligature notation of discant, which on the whole had not been tampered with till then.[4] The 156 snippets of discant polyphony collected in the fourth and fifth

2. Fritz Reckow, *Der Musiktraktat des Anonymus 4,* Beiträge zum Archiv für Musikwissenschaft, 4 (1967), 1:46.

3. In a recent article ("The Problem of Chronology in the Transmission of Organum Duplum," *Music in Medieval and Early Modern Europe,* ed. Iain Fenlon [Cambridge, 1981], 1: 365–99), Edward Roesner has set forth arguments suggesting the inadequacy of the traditional view that the known versions of the *Magnus liber organi* attest to an evolution from preponderantly organal style to its diminution in favor of discant style. One leg of his argument stands on his understanding of the term *abbreviavit* as "made a redaction" (p. 378). But *abbreviare* was never used in this sense. Its known Medieval meanings are: to abbreviate, to shorten, to reduce, to abridge, to write down or record, the latter in the sense of an original inditing or inscribing or rendering of a brief account (see *Mittellateinisches Wörterbuch* [1967], 1: col. 15; *The Dictionary of Medieval Latin from British Sources* [1975], fasc. 1: 3). Hence, any Medieval redaction described as *abbreviatio* is, in fact, a reduction. And Roesner's claim that "Anonymous IV uses *abbreviatio* in the sense of 'a writing, treatise' " rests on a passage in which the author of the treatise merely presents his reader with the unsurprising information that verbal instruction became more concise as notational symbols became more precise.

More crucial to the issue are Roesner's numerous stylistic interpretations and hypotheses in support of his statement that "Ludwig's hypothesis is too simple" (p. 369). A comparison among the three versions of organa preserved in the manuscripts commonly referred to as W_1, F, and W_2 (see n. 5 below) reveals three major categories of change in certain passages: (1) discant over grouped (unpatterned) long notes in the tenor as opposed to discant over a modally patterned tenor; (2) discant over grouped longs in the tenor as opposed to discant over grouped double longs; (3) organal setting versus discant setting, the latter over grouped longs, grouped double longs, or rhythmic patterns. As to (1), for obvious reasons no argument has ever been presented to the effect that irregular grouping of notes in the tenor should be regarded as more progressive than their rhythmic patterning. Patterned tenors are extremely rare in the W_1 version of the *Magnus liber organi;* they are quite a bit more common in W_2 and especially in F—a good many of them taking the place of more old-fashioned discant settings in W_1. Since the former often set more than one statement of the tenor, the more modern versions frequently turn out to be longer than the comparable passages in W_1. Relatively few cases exemplify category (2). When the three manuscripts do not agree in the use of longs versus double longs in the setting of identical tenor passages, the double longs are always in F and/or W_2, such settings therefore being twice as long as the others. Chains of double longs are very rare in W_1 (see Ernest H. Sanders, "The Medieval Motet," *Gattungen der Musik in Einzeldarstellungen: Gedenkschrift Leo Schrade* [Bern, 1973], 1, n. 14). The cases belonging to category (3) are by far the most numerous. On the one hand, there are very few instances of discant setting in W_1 versus organal setting in one or both of the other sources (e.g., two passages in Ó 29 and one in M 13), thus demonstrating the probability that W_1 cannot be the Leoninian original. And on the other hand, examples of the reverse situation are very numerous, with discant sections over unpatterned tenors (longs or double longs) about twice as frequent as those over patterned tenors. With few exceptions, the settings of these passages in F and W_2 are significantly shorter than those in W_1. All in all, then, the versions of the *Magnus liber organi* in F and W_2 certainly contain many abbreviations in comparison with W_1.

4. It is well known that before Johannes de Garlandia's time no system of differentiated single notes existed that could denote durations. The need for such a system arose only with the totally syllabic genre of the motet. For all the evidence concerning the priority of melismatic, as against syllabic, rhythmic notation, see Erich Reimer, *Johannes de Garlandia: De mensurabili musica,* Beiträge zum Archiv für Musikwissenschaft, 11 (1972), 2: 52–53.

EXAMPLE I

a(1). F, No. 2297 (fol. 178v)   a(2). W₁, fol. 28 (24)

b(1). F, No. 2354 (fol. 180v)   b(2). W₁, fol. 18 (14)

c(1). F, No. 2359 (fol. 180v)   c(2). W₁, fol. 40v (34v)

d(1). F, No. 2412 (fol. 182v)   d(2). W₁, fol. 18 (14)   d(3). W₁, fol. 20v (16v)

d(4). W₁, fol. 39v (33v)   d(5). W₁, fol. 47 (41)   d(6). W₁, fol. 27v (23v) = 46v (40v)

e(1). F, No. 2371 (fol. 181)   e(2). F, No. 2329 (fol. 179v) groups of the fifth fascicle of MS F,[5] most of which are extremely concise alternatives to long organal passages in the *Magnus liber organi* and were therefore presumably meant to serve as abbreviate substitutes,[6] for the first time require and exhibit a notation systematically adapted to incidences of syllabic change. The notation of such passages, with its profuse syllable strokes (rendered, for purposes of demonstration only, as apostrophes in the examples) as well as its unusual ligations and plications arising from frequent syllable changes, can be easily shown to result from adjustments to actual or at least to conceptual melismatic models (Example 1).[7]

5. For manuscript symbols as well as numerations of organa, clausulae, etc., see Rudolf Flotzinger, *Der Discantussatz im Magnus Liber und seiner Nachfolge*, Wiener Musikwissenschaftliche Beiträge, 8 (1969).

6. They should not be referred to as clausulae, since, with few significant exceptions, they are not sections constituting defined and formed entities (see Sanders, "The Question of Perotin's Oeuvre and Dates," *Festschrift Walter Wiora* [Kassel, 1967], 242f.). Roesner (p. 377f.) has expressed strong doubts that they were written to abbreviate organa. But Anonymous IV, in identifying Perotinus as *optimus discantor*, credited him with two distinct activities: he shortened the *Magnus liber organi*, and he composed a great many clausulae. (As to their probable functions, see Sanders, "Medieval Motet," 505ff.) For evidence that many (all?) of the snippets in the fourth and fifth groups of the fifth fascicle of F are likely to have been composed by Perotinus for the purpose of abbreviation (and modernization) of Leoninus's organa, see Sanders, "Medieval Motet," n. 14, and Frederick W. Sternfeld, ed., *A History of Western Music*, vol. 1, *Music from the Middle Ages to the Renaissance* (London, 1973): 107. Most of them link up quite well with the musical environment for which they seem to have been intended. In any case, for what other purpose could they possibly have been designed? That only relatively few of them appear in our sources of the *Magnus liber organi* can be ascribed to the disappearance of sources, the rapidly increasing vogue for patterned tenors, the fact that the substitutes could easily be learned and incorporated from a separate collection, and so on. In any event, in view of the evidence presented here and in n. 3 above, the W₁ version must be regarded as stylistically anterior to F and W₂.

7. It therefore turns out that the entire collection still exhibits only premodal rhythms, inasmuch as it contains no second-mode patterns (see Sanders, "Question of Perotin's Oeuvre," 244). The term *premodally trochaic*, which I have used on occasion to describe the rhythm prevailing in discant sections of early Notre Dame organa, is not really appropriate, since it was only the motet's first mode that made those rhythms trochaic (see Sanders, "Medieval Motet," 512, and Sternfeld, 114). In melismatic discant such rhythms are more properly called premodally iambic (i.e., not in the sense of second mode, but closer to the original Greek meaning). It is in the nature of this conception of rhythm that the first duplum note of some discant passages is written occasionally as a *virga*, rather than as the first note of a ligature, even though no repeated notes are involved; see for instance, Ex. 1a(2) and the last phrase of Ex. 6, both taken from W₁, where such cases still occur more frequently than in the other sources. The two notations of Ex. 7 reveal a related aspect of this situation.

The existence of the "original" ("alternate") third mode invalidates all the examples of mixed rhythmic modes given by Gordon A. Anderson, with the exception of those in the La Clayette manuscript (see "Johannes de Garlandia and the Simultaneous Use of Mixed Rhythmic Modes," *Miscellanea Musicologica* 8 [1975]: 11–27, specifically 20–26). It cannot be emphasized too strongly that no evidence exists for the rise of the system of rhythmic modes prior to the time when clausulae and some of the organa tripla were written; see Sanders, "Duple Rhythm and Alternate Third Mode in the 13th Century," *Journal of the American Musicological Society* 15 (1962): 283. In that article I concluded that originally the first of the two breves in the third-mode pattern was doubled (pp.269–71 and 278–85). This conclusion is strengthened further by a passage in the treatise of "Dietricus," regrettably overlooked by me at the time. After enumerating and defining the six modes, this theorist adds, "Isti tamen modi frequenter ad invicem miscentur; fit enim mutatio de primo in tertium vel in quintum et sic de aliis . . ." (see Hans Müller, *Eine Abhandlung über Mensuralmusik* [Leipzig, 1886], 5). That the second mode, in yielding to copious ornamentation, often transmuted itself into the sixth has long been recognized (the second and sixth modes being "the others," since the author reported the fourth mode as not *in usu*). But his failure to associate the third mode with the second is both unique and significant. In his subsequent discussion of ligatures, "Dietricus" instructs his reader (ibid., 6) that the notes of any ternary ligature have to be performed as long, short, and long: "nisi forte caudata precedat tres ligatas . . . et tunc de tribus ligatis prime due sunt breves. . . ."

Similar rules are given by the author of the *Discantus positio vulgaris* (Cserba, 190) and, in a more com-

Only one of these substitutes exhibits, as it proceeds, melismatic notation at a point of change in syllables (Example 2). Presumably, the phrase should have been written as in Example 3. This disregard of the proprieties of the syllabically adjusted notation, while singular within any of the short substitutes, is encountered often at the close and occasionally at the end of subsections (Example 4).

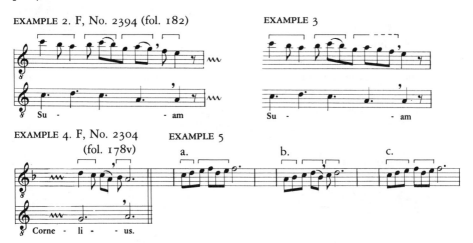

EXAMPLE 2. F, No. 2394 (fol. 182)   EXAMPLE 3

Su -   - am   Su -   - am

EXAMPLE 4. F, No. 2304   EXAMPLE 5
(fol. 178v)   a.   b.   c.

Corne -   li -   - us.

Particularly significant is the notation of a concluding formula that was used almost constantly, at least in the substitutes. The two notations given in Examples 5a and 5b always apply to melismatic and syllabic contexts respectively. The melismatic notation in Example 5c is favored in W_1 (where the formula is far less frequent than in F); for example, at the end of M 13, fol. 31v (27v)—its notations in F and W_2 are as in Example 5a—and at the end of the respond of M 37, fol. 41 (35). This notation occurs occasionally in F; for example, at the end of the substitute, No. 2439 (fol. 183) and before *et ponam* in M 54, fol. 141v. While a scalar descent in breves was easily written with *coniuncturae*, scalar ascents produced what William Waite, whose standard was modal notation, called irregularities, since an ascending *quaternaria* was awkward to write.[8]

prehensive way, by Amerus (*Practica artis musice* [1271], Corpus Scriptorum de Musica, vol. 25, ed. Cesarino Ruini [American Institute of Musicology, 1977], 99). Even though "Dietricus" had previously defined the *nota caudata* as a long, his use here of the term *caudata* rather than *longa*—in contrast to the other two writers—may well justify the application of this rule to the fair number of cases that are like the above-mentioned phrase in Ex. 6 as well as to the Perotinian "augmentation" of that rhythm ("third mode") presumably meant by "Dietricus." Subsequently, in Garlandia's time (probably the 1250s), the practice arose of transposing the values of the two breves in the third mode, thus making it compatible with the second rather than with the first (see Sanders, "Consonance and Rhythm in the Organum of the 12th and 13th Centuries," *Journal of the American Musicological Society* 33 [1980]: 277–80).

8. William G. Waite, *The Rhythm of Twelfth-Century Polyphony*, Yale Studies in the History of Music, 2 (New Haven, 1954), 105. The melismatic notation of the formula (Ex. 5a) is easily accounted for by the notators' traditional tendency to involve a *quaternaria* in order to indicate motion in breves. In this case it was most conveniently written after an initial *binaria*. For similar seven-note groups with the same rhythm, whose different contours permitted more conventional notation—that is, with an initial *quaternaria*—see Ex. 1d.

Examples 2, 4, and 5b represent an exceedingly common situation in Notre Dame polyphony prior to the rise of the motet—that is, the appearance after a syllable stroke of a two-note ligature *(binaria),* the constituent notes of which are respectively dissonant and consonant with its coordinate tenor note.[9] The widespread modern interpretation of such ligatures as isolated second-mode events forming appoggiaturas not only bespeaks an "optical illusion,"[10] but also produces a jarring anachronism of style. Manfred Bukofzer cited one instance (from M 53) to show that Waite himself, in whose pioneering edition such *binariae* ordinarily appear as appoggiaturas with second-mode or occasionally fifth-mode rhythm, felt compelled to interpret them as components of a rhythmically homogeneous melismatic chain, regardless of any syllable change. A good many more such examples can be cited.[11] On the other hand, cases in which Waite let "optical illusion" prevail are far more numerous.[12] Especially revealing is a passage in O 13. Waite's transcription (Example 6) obscures the sequential design

EXAMPLE 6. Waite, 30

by misinterpreting the stroke as a long rest; see *(Johan)nes e(rat)*. But one of the cardinal rules in this notation is that a stroke signifying a change of syllable rarely has a mensural meaning as well.[13] Even in purely melismatic contexts a stroke does not necessarily denote a rest; at times it can be nothing more than a subordinate phrase mark, a function lacking mensural significance, as in the melisma on *(acces)se(runt)* in M 17 (Examples 7a, 7b, 7c).[14] The notation of both voices of this passage in MS F (see Examples 7a [also Plates I and II], 7b,

9. Theodore Karp has called attention to the problem of the interpretation of this "cadential *binaria*" (see "St. Martial and Santiago da Compostela: An Analytical Speculation," *Acta Musicologica* 39 [1967]: 152f.).

10. Manfred F. Bukofzer, Review of Waite, *The Rhythm of Twelfth-Century Polyphony,* in *Notes* 12 (1955): 236.

11. See especially the discant passages mentioned in Karp, n.16.

12. Waite, p. 6: *de ce(lis)* in O 2; p. 26: *(et cepe)runt* in O 11; p. 73: *reve(lavit)* in M 1; p. 91: *(ma)nere* in M 5; p. 119: *(et) confi(tebor)* in M 12; p.123: *(do)mine* in M 13; p. 124: *quoni(am)* in M 13; p.143: *et te(nuerunt)* in M 17; p.161: *edi(ficabo)* in M 31. See Ex. 10 below. Waite's predecessors and successors in this practice are too numerous to list.

13. According to Anonymous IV, "Nullum tempus significat, sed ponitur propter divisionem syllabarum" (Reckow, 1: 61). For an alternative transcription, see Sanders, "Medieval Motet," 500, Ex. 7.

14. Waite, 143. "Pausationum vel tractuum quedam dicitur ... suspiratio. ... Suspiratio est apparentia pausationis sine existentia," as Garlandia puts it (Reimer, 1: 66–67). For a similar formulation by Anonymous IV, see Reckow, 1: 61. The function of the stroke as a *suspiratio* to indicate phrasing occurs in other contexts as well (e.g., in *caudae* of conducti and in *copulae* of organa). Though he does not cite the theorists' rule, Karp has offered transcriptions of some of the latter, based on musical common sense ("Toward a Critical Edition of Notre Dame Organa Dupla," *The Musical Quarterly* 52 [1966]: 358ff.).

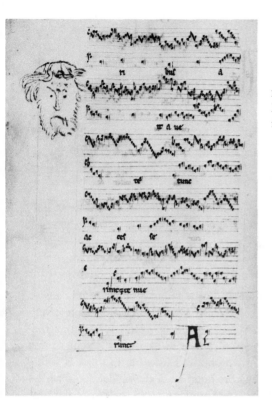

PLATE I. Wolfenbüttel, Herzog August Bibliothek, 677 (Helmstedt 628), W₁, fol. 33v (29v)

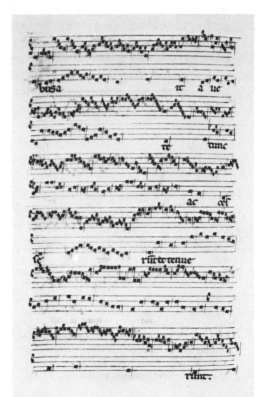

PLATE II. Florence, Biblioteca Mediceo-Laurenziana, Plut. 29.1, fol. 111v

and 7c; barlines are added in Examples 7b and 7c for clarification) does without
the strokes and thereby significantly alters its sequential phraseology.

EXAMPLE 7.

a. W₁, fol. 33v (29v); F, 111v   b. Articulation of the tenor in W₁

c. Implied articulation of the tenor in F.

(F: No strokes in either voice)   (Bar lines added for clarification)

Telltale remnants of this scribal habit can be found in quite a few clausulae, and similar notational quirks crop up in early Notre Dame motets preserved
in later sources; for instance, clausula No. 2148 (F, fol. 164v), a setting of the
melisma *Johanne* from *Alleluia: Inter natos,* ends as in Example 8. None of the
motet sources[15] managed to notate the two phrases marked in Example 8 without distorting or changing either the ligature notation or the modal declamatory
pattern, though certainly it would have been simple to avoid the first of the two
problems by applying the principles of syllabic notation initially demonstrated in
the corpus of substitutes in MS F. Stemming from the historical primacy of melismatic notation of rhythm, the apparent practice of Notre Dame composers to
precede the writing of motets with the conception and composition of their melismatic models in melismatic notation (clausulae)[16] apparently caused both the
composers and scribes to retain, more or less uncritically and unconsciously certain particularly conventional remnants of melismatic notation in syllabic contexts.

EXAMPLE 8. F, No. 2148 (fol. 164v)

Johan   - ne.

15. See Friedrich Gennrich, *Bibliographie der ältesten französischen und lateinischen Motetten,* Summa Musicae Medii Aevi, 2 (Langen bei Frankfurt, 1957), 35f. For facsimiles of the clausula and three of the motets,
see *The New Grove* 12: 622f. (figs. 1–4).

16. Sanders, "Medieval Motet," 508f. In view of the thinking that led to Franconian notation, the clausula
and the syllable stroke became unnecessary and were no longer discussed in the treatises written after that of
Anonymous IV, except by the St.-Emmeram Anonymous, who in his distress at some of the new tendencies
clung to many of Garlandia's formulations.

The notation in a duplum of a *binaria* preceded by a stroke and coincident with a new syllable is particularly common at the end of organal phrases, often those immediately before a discant passage. In such cases, alternative notations in concordant sources will at times help to demonstrate the proper reading of these *binariae* (see Example 9). Moreover, purely melismatic passages similar or identical to phrases with syllabic change are plentiful. For instance, the setting of *quoniam* (cited in n. 12 above) exemplifies the occurrence of a concluding *binaria* with syllable change at the end of a discant passage. A similar entirely melismatic phrase occurs in M 42 (Example 10). In view of the usually rather wide distance between changes of syllable in "Leoninian" organa,[17] the absence of a consistent notational orthography to account for them is hardly surprising.

EXAMPLE 9. F, fol. 84v; W₂, fol. 58v   EXAMPLE 10
a. W₁, fol. 31v (27v); Waite, 124

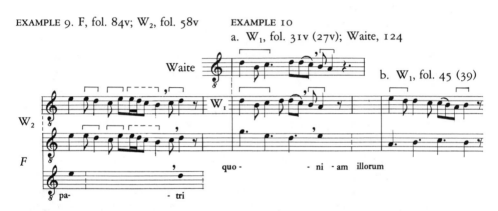

b. W₁, fol. 45 (39)

A reasonable chronology of treatises presumably written in the eighth decade of the thirteenth century can be founded on the following considerations. First, the fact that Anonymous IV mentions Franco of Cologne does not warrant the conclusion (see Anderson, Review of Reckow, *Die Copula,* in *Music and Letters* 54 [1973]: 455) that the latter wrote his treatise before the former finished his. In fact, the only informative passage regarding Franco in the anonymous treatise states that he and someone else "had begun, each in his way, to notate differently in their books of music, for which reason they taught other special rules appropriate to their books" (see Reckow, *Der Musiktraktat,* 1: 46; with one exception—namely, Boethius—Anonymous IV refers to a book of music when he writes *liber*). Nothing indicates that Franco had already written his treatise; that he had yet to do so is made more likely by Anonymous IV's use of *tractatus,* a word that always refers to a treatise that did exist (i.e., Garlandia's *De mensurabili musica*).

Second, there is no compelling evidence to sustain the argument (see Anderson, ibid.) that Lambertus wrote his treatise only after Franco's had become known. Third, so late a date as Wolf Frobenius assigns to the treatise by Anonymous IV is quite unnecessary ("Zur Datierung von Francos Ars cantus mensurabilis," *Archiv für Musikwissenschaft* 27 [1970]: 122–27, specifically 124), since (a) the St.-Emmeram Anonymous might have known the Englishman's treatise; (b) the Paris version of Garlandia's treatise is likely to have originated well before the last quarter of the thirteenth century, when Jerome of Moravia must have copied it, perhaps in the 1260s; and (c) other treatises, now lost, may well have contained an explication of *ordo* in the rhythmic modes (see Reimer, 1: 31).

Hence, the treatises may be dated as follows: Anonymous IV, 1273 or shortly thereafter; Lambertus, a year or a few years before 1279; St.-Emmeram Anonymous, November 23, 1279; Franco, c. 1280 (see Frobenius). The latest stage of notation, that of Petrus Picardus, represented in Jerome of Moravia's treatise allows the dating of the latter as c. 1290. For a different approach to this issue, see Kenneth Levy, "A Dominican Organum Duplum," *Journal of the American Musicological Society* 27 (1974): 184, n. 3.

17. That is, those versions—mostly in W₁—that seem oldest from the point of view of style.

Concluding *binariae* with syllable change likewise occur frequently in the examples of, and in the organa appended to, the Vatican Organum Treatise, and these are closely related in style to the older organa of the *Magnus liber organi*,[18] except that the upper voice contains no ligature patterns guaranteeing fixed rhythms. One third of the 251 short passages constituting the main body of examples coordinate the syllable change at the end with a ligature in the upper voice, preceded by a stroke. By far the most common case is that of a final *clivis* (71 percent),[19] and in well over half the cases its first note forms a unison with its predecessor, the antepenultimate. In most of the remaining cases of a concluding *clivis*, it is preceded by a form of *climacus* ("coniunctura," to make anachronistic use of Franco's term). Taken together, these two groups account for over ninety percent of all final *clives*. Of the eleven cases of concluding *pedes*, only one does not fall into either of these two main groups. These facts strongly suggest the following conclusion: endings with a *binaria* whose last note produces consonant counterpoint, rather than endings with a single note, are often a matter of notational convenience or compulsion.[20] Endings with ligatures may also suggest an unselfconscious tradition of melodic and notational flourishes or gestures.

The manuscripts transmitting the *Magnus liber organi* have all the appearance of carefully prepared copies. The music of the Vatican Organum Treatise, however, like that in most sources of polyphony prior to Notre Dame, looks far less orderly, since the spatial coordination of the successive stages of writing was planned with less care.[21] The distribution of the notes shows that some syllables were written either too far to the right or too far to the left to accommodate the music neatly. More obvious is the drawing of more or less vertical lines which, as in the Notre Dame sources, are symbols of allocation, coordination, delimitation, and grouping for units of melismatic and syllabic events; more often than not, these lines are curved and bent—evidence that their function was not taken into account when the music was written. The untidy—in fact, often chaotic—look of the pages shows that the lines or strokes were drawn later, though quite possibly by the same hand that had notated the music.

The same or similar procedures can be observed in other polyphonic sources preceding the *Magnus liber organi*, such as the Codex Calixtinus,[22] GB-

---

18. Frieder Zaminer, *Der Vatikanische Organum-Traktat (Ottob. lat. 3025)*, Münchner Veröffentlichungen zur Musikgeschichte, 2 (Munich, 1959), 33ff., 88ff., and especially 159. The Notre Dame closing formula singled out above appears among its examples (e.g., Nos. 45 and 308).

19. It also occurs quite frequently in the organa, where the final *pes* is quite rare, though it constitutes thirteen percent of the concluding ligatures in the examples.

20. Similarly, the numerous *binariae* in the duplum at ends of phrases involving syllable change in W_1 organa can almost always be demonstrated to be clearer than any conjectural alternative for the notation. In fact, the rare substitution of two *virgae* for a final *binaria* (e.g., *domi(nus)* in M 1; see Waite, 70) seems clumsy and *gestaltlos* in the original notation.

21. The question as to whether the manuscript is an autograph (see Zaminer, 32–33) is of no consequence in this context.

22. Some of its repertory is thought by Zaminer (pp. 148 and 150) to be related to the tradition represented by the Vatican Organum Treatise.

Lbm Add. 36881 (the latest of the polyphonic "St. Martial" manuscripts),[23] GB-Cu Add. Ff. 1.17, and a polyphonic version (composed c. 1100 and preserved in an Apt manuscript) of a monophonic *Benedicamus* substitute in F-Pn lat. 1139 (the earliest of the manuscripts preserving Aquitanian polyphony).[24]

For the most part, the older Aquitanian sources of polyphony do not exhibit any added lines of division.[25] Both their absence in these manuscripts and their presence in the others compel the conclusion that the notation is basically descriptive of the compositional process and only loosely prescriptive for the singer, whose musicianship must have been adequately served by this elliptic stenography. The notation conveys the impression of more or less florid counterpoint fitted to the notes of *cantus prius facti*, but not to the words—a procedure seemingly characteristic of most contrapuntists anytime. The composers' customary indifference to text in their concern for contrapuntal design is well exemplified in the discant passage from the *Alleluya: Hic Martinus,* appended to the Vatican Organum Treatise (see Plate III),[26] shown in Example 11. Chiefly, their response to text seems to have been their recognition of its syntactical structure as determining the main divisions of the music.

EXAMPLE 11. I-Rvat Ottob. Lat. 3025, fol. 49

If, then, the conception of such counterpoint *cum littera* generally was not neumatic, but rather purely melismatic (regardless of the incidences of syllables), the declamation of the text by the upper voice may well have been, and presumably often was, unconstrained by the ligations. When a scribe has provided syl-

---

23. In both manuscripts the division lines were added after text and music had been written (see Peter Wagner, *Die Gesänge der Jakobusliturgie zu Santiago de Compostela,* Collectanea Friburgensia: Veröffentlichungen der Universität Freiburg [Schweiz], Neue Folge, no.20 [Freiburg, 1931], 112, n.1; Sarah Fuller, "Aquitanian Polyphony of the Eleventh and Twelfth Centuries" [Ph.D. diss., University of California, Berkeley, 1970], 331, n. 33).

24. See Wulf Arlt, "Peripherie und Zentrum," *Forum Musicologicum* 1 (1974): 169–222.

25. Occasionally they are omitted in such later sources as the Vatican Organum Treatise and the *Magnus liber organi.* In nearly all those cases in W_1, Waite's transcription requires the singer of the duplum to break the final ligature of a passage, except in the rare instances of the editorial addition of a stroke followed by a second-mode appoggiatura; see, for instance, Waite, 190: *(Au)di filia* in M 37.

26. Karp's categorical systemization (p. 147f.) of rhythm in twelfth-century polyphony seems too speculative and insufficiently supported by evidence (see Fuller's critique, 321ff.). The controversial subject of the rhythmic organization, if any, of polyphony before the *Magnus liber organi* cannot be dealt with here.

Ex. 11 is very similar to the discant setting of *mea* in M 54 (W_1, fol. 40v [34v]; see Plate IV). Roesner's identification of the latter passage as modern (p. 370) rests on an interpretation of the strokes that seems to me to be quite inapplicable; it leads him to ascribe to it a quasi-hocket technique, which is anachronistic and by no means inevitably warranted by the notation.

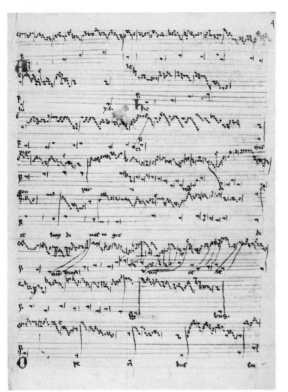

PLATE III. Rome, Biblioteca Apostolica
Vaticana, Ottob. Lat. 3025, fol. 49

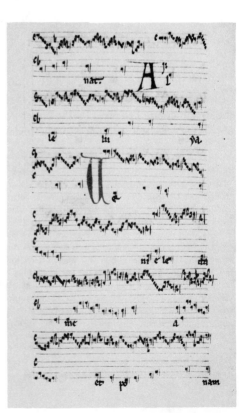

PLATE IV. W₁, fol. 40v (34v)

lable strokes subsequent to writing the music, he has placed them in each case as close as convenient and possible to the note on which the singer of the upper voice, simultaneously with his partner, is to pronounce a new syllable.[27] Thus syllabication would in principle seem to have been one of the many "accidental" elements not precisely specified or specifiable by the notation, and hence one left to be worked out in rehearsal, rather like the choice of *b mi* or *b fa*.

No medieval treatise prior to Johannes de Garlandia's, the first to use the terms *sine littera* and *cum littera,* provides us with any information about the way text and counterpoint other than "first species" were coordinated. It is essential, however, to stress that the fundamental condition of polyphony had been and still was consonance (and so continued to be until the early twentieth century). The evidence we have makes it most unlikely that notation at any time indicated a fairly consistent departure from this condition only in conjunction with the articulation of syllables in counterpoint other than "first species."[28] In view of the persistence until the mid-thirteenth century of significant notational customs, it is hardly surprising, and therefore has long been recognized, that in earlier polyphony *cum littera* the notation of more or less florid counterpoint generally shows the last note of a ligature to form a proper consonance with the appropriate note of the *cantus prius factus* (although sometimes, usually at the beginnings of phrases, the first note of a ligature provides the consonance). To be sure, the polyphonic art of the twelfth century and of the early thirteenth century as well is not to be straitjacketed by rigid procedures, and its notation is often far less than clear, reliable, and uniform.[29] However, the very lack of notational uniformity, whenever it arises between concordant versions of passages of a piece, can help us arrive at more reliable transcriptions at the same time as it shows that matters of syllabication often played no role in the design and notation of the upper part. This observation can be demonstrated with examples from the *Magnus liber organi*[30] as well as from the Aquitanian repertoire. Tran-

---

27. Rudolf von Ficker, "Probleme der modalen Notation," *Acta Musicologica* 18–19 (1946–47): 12f. Ficker's observation preceded both Bukofzer and Karp (see nn. 9 and 10 above).

The early practice of successive notation—that is, of notating polyphony by writing the counterpoint after the *cantus prius factus* and equipping it with the text of a separate stanza (see Fuller, "Hidden Polyphony—A Reappraisal," *Journal of the American Musicological Society* 24 [1971]: 169–92), in no way contradicts the conceptual process posited here. In her dissertation Fuller had written that "reading from successive notation, the singer of the lower voice cannot instantly tell if the upper voice has a large melisma against one note of his, *as he can in score notation,* or if three notes in his part are to be synchronized with five in the other" ("Aquitanian Polyphony," 119). But the manuscripts, regardless of whether their polyphony is notated successively (as is also the case with the double motets in F and W₂) or by superimposition ("in score"), provide very little information for performance; coordination is left to him who "knows the score." Fuller's deletion from her article ("Hidden Polyphony," 174) of the clause italicized by me seems to indicate that she must have reached the same conclusion. Not even the syllabic three-voiced cantilenae composed in fourteenth-century England were written as precisely aligned scores, even though many of them were conceived apparently from the outset in three-part harmony, are chordal in texture, and have rhythms paralleling those of the poetry.
28. See also Karp, 151.
29. Ibid., 144.
30. Sanders, "Consonance and Rhythm," 272, Ex. 1.

EXAMPLE 12

F-Pn lat. 3549

F-Pn lat. 3719 (I)   *MS:E

F-Pn lat. 3719 (II)

GB-Lbm Add. 36881

scriptions of four versions of one short passage in *Veri solis radius*,[31] offered with all due caution, are cited in Example 12 to support the point.

Thus the performance of polyphony written in the twelfth century and shortly thereafter appears to require rather frequent breaking of ligatures[32] in order to maintain the counterpoint and declamation apparently intended by the composer.[33] This procedure has been considered, advocated, or adopted repeatedly in recent years,[34] on the grounds of common sense.

31. F-Pn lat. 3549, fol. 149ff.; F-Pn lat. 3719, fol. 16vff. and 54ff.; GB-Lbm Add. 36881, fol. 5vff.

32. It may be apposite to mention the analogous practice of many modern editors of vocal music to beam groups of two or more notes (eighth notes, sixteenth notes, etc.) for the sake of convenience and clarity, even if their rendition requires the pronunciation of more than one syllable.

33. These considerations therefore strengthen the improbability of the curious noncoincident syllabication evidently envisioned by Bukofzer (p. 236), hesitantly preferred by Karp (p. 150; but see n. 34 below), and prescribed by Heinrich Husmann (see *Christie dei forma* and *spiramen* in his transcription of the *Kyrie Cunctipotens* from the Codex Calixtinus in *Die mittelalterliche Mehrstimmigkeit* [Das Musikwerk, vol. 9], 15; with manifest inconsistency he chose the dissonant appoggiatura in his transcription of *(confite)mini* in the organum *Hec dies* from the *Magnus liber organi* in the same volume, 20). In my review of Flotzinger's *Der Discantussatz* (*Die Musikforschung* 25 [1972]: 338–42), I still adhered to the same view (p. 341).

34. For example, Flotzinger, 165; Ian D. Bent, "A New Polyphonic 'Verbum Bonum et Suave,' " *Music and Letters* 51 (1970): 238; Margaret Bent's edition of a fourteenth-century English setting of *Gaude virgo* in the Music Supplement for *Early Music*, 1/3 (1973), see the pertinent note; my edition of *Prima mundi* from GB-Lbm Add. 36881 in Sternfeld, 96; Wulf Arlt and Max Haas, "Pariser modale Mehrstimmigkeit in einem Fragment der Basler Universitätsbibliothek," *Forum Musicologicum* 1 (1974): 247; Karp, "Text Underlay and Rhythmic Interpretation of 12th Century Polyphony," *Report of the Eleventh Congress of the International Musicological Society, Copenhagen 1972* (Copenhagen, 1974),2: 483). As early as 1958 Gilbert Reaney had sug-

Florid organum and moderately elaborated discant are *musica instrumentalis* in a quite particular way; though vocal and involving text, they are originally and essentially not "musica verbalis," at least not in the twelfth century. The decorative function of such counterpoint goes hand in hand with its basically melismatic conception and notation. Even though as early as the fourteenth century a treatise on polyphony defines as ligatures those notes that "in cantando attribuuntur uni sillabe,"[35] nonetheless, the instances of polyphonic passages that force the performer to break ligatures so as to pronounce the text are too numerous to cite. They continued to occur in the thirteenth century and throughout the fourteenth and fifteenth as well.

It must be stressed, however, that twelfth-century polyphony, of course, was not regimented by an absolute system of consonant counterpoint. The excerpts in Example 13, taken from Perotinus's conductus *Salvatoris hodie* (c. 1200?),[36] demonstrate incidences of dissonance produced by the coordinate, though relatively independent, melodic drive of three voices to contrapuntal cadences.[37] Similarly, Wulf Arlt, in his meticulous and detailed study (cited in n. 24 above), repeatedly calls attention to cases where the melodic design of the upper voice in certain Aquitanian polyphonic compositions seems to be preeminent and therefore responsible for passing dissonant simultaneities with the lower.[38] But his assertion that contemporaneous theory provides no evidence for such procedures[39] disregards pertinent passages in the treatise written by Johannes Affligemensis.[40] As the latter so nicely put it, "diversi diverse utuntur."

---

gested the existence of similar situations in the conductus repertory ("A Note on Conductus Rhythm," *Bericht über den siebenten Internationalen Musikwissenschaftlichen Kongress, Köln* [Kassel, 1959], 219–21). His reference to a St. Victor conductus, however, is inappropriate, since texted passages immediately following the excerpt given in his Ex. 3 contain imperfect ligatures, ligatures which must therefore be performed with the first note on the beat. Referring to him as well as to others, Karp some years later (in "Text Underlay," cited above in this note) gave other conductus passages and adduced a rule from the treatise of Anonymous IV in support of the melismatic interpretation of upper-voice *binariae* in syllabic context. But the pertinent context and wording in this section of the treatise leave no doubt that the rules concern *discantus cum littera* (i.e., motets), insofar as they demonstrate the didactic process of equating (*reducere*) the notes and rhythms of this novel syllabic polyphony to constellations familiar from the ligature notation of melismatic discant.

35. Higinio Anglès, "*De cantu organico:* Tratado de un autor catalán del siglo XIV," *Anuario musical* 13 (1958): 19. I thank Clovis Lark for bringing this document to my attention as well as for spurring me to reexamine the treatise by "Dietricus" (see n. 7 above).

36. W₁, fol. 95 (86); LoA, fol. 86v; F, fol. 201; Ma, fol. 111v; W₂, fol. 31.

37. Such passages, which are not so rare as one might expect, clearly convey implications for performance (tempo and dynamics).

38. Arlt, 181–82, 186–87, 200ff., 206, 207, 209ff., and 221f. Despite his infinitely careful workmanship, Arlt occasionally bases conclusions on what appear to be inconsistent interpretations of the evidence. For instance, his statement (p. 210) that a certain passage consists of a chain of thirds requires the assignment of structural contrapuntal weight to the last note of one ligature and to the first note of the next. In another case (p. 209), such function is assigned to all but two of the first notes of ligatures and, in addition, once to the penultimate note of a five-note ligature. (The exceptions are dissonances.) That middle notes of ligatures should have such significance seems most unlikely.

39. Ibid., 211.

40. For the most recent discussion of this work, see Fuller, "Theoretical Foundations of Early Organum Theory," *Acta Musicologica* 53 (1981): 52–84, specifically 67–73.

EXAMPLE 13

candida - - - tur

domi - ni

inve - - - nit

Nevertheless, it seems clear that most of the florid polyphonic works composed up to the time of Leoninus are based on a pervasive standard of consonant counterpoint, with the notation of the upper voice indicating an originally melismatic conception. Only with the rise of the motet in the first quarter of the thirteenth century—excluding the necessarily short-lived conductus motet—does each of the voices in a polyphonic composition gain its full, "lettered" individuality and definition.[41] Literally, the upper voices of other polyphonic genres are *sine littera* in the manuscripts.[42]

41. For a more extensive discussion, see Sanders, "Medieval Motet," 522–23.
42. When viewed in this light, Garlandia's assertion, as phrased in the generally very trustworthy Bruges version, that "figura aliquando ponitur sine littera et aliquando cum littera; sine littera ut in caudis et conductis, cum littera ut in motellis" (Reimer, 1: 44) quite plausibly may be understood *ut iacet* and not as referring only to the *caudae* of conducti. Reimer bases his assertion to the contrary (2: 51, n. 30) on his edition of this sentence from the Vatican version, which he presumably interpreted in the light of the analogous, but modified, statements by Garlandia's successors. Even they, however, continue to associate specifically only the motet with the category *cum littera,* though withholding the conductus from the opposite category. Anonymous IV's elliptical remark that notes "sine litera coniunguntur in quantum possunt vel poterunt; cum litera quandoque sic, quandoque non" (Reckow, 1: 45) may also reflect the conceptual and notational changes associated with the rise of the motet.

Though polyphonic notation in the early twelfth century doubtless resulted from a growing need for prescription, its flexibility (or imprecision) still
reflects the customary function of freezing the products of unwritten musical
tradition for mnemic purposes; i.e., to provide reminders of a systematic referential order.[43] Variants in the rendition of such music, both in writing and in
performing, are thus an inevitable aspect of this art.[44] Gradually the relative
cursiveness—or linearity, to use Charles Seeger's term—of such descriptive notations gave way to the increasing use of discrete symbols characteristic of prescriptive requirements.[45] (Total fixity and specificity, of course, are possible only
in electronic music, which is intrinsically notationless.) The motet's decisive step,
in the mid-thirteenth century, toward comparative notational precision reflects a
new standard of strict coordination of text and musical symbols denoting both
pitches and durations.[46] It is symptomatic of the Gothic tendency toward greater
structural rationality.

43. In an article published after the completion of this paper Leo Treitler suggests historical, systematic, and
phenomenological aspects of such stages in the development and uses of notation ("Oral, Written and Literate
Process in the Transmission of Medieval Music," *Speculum* 56 [1981]: 471–91).
44. This observation still applies to the *Magnus liber organi* (see Sanders, "Consonance and Rhythm,"
272ff.).
45. "Prescriptive and Descriptive Music-Writing," *The Musical Quarterly* 44 (1958): 185f.
46. Declamatory propriety, however, continued to be far from inevitable. As I suggested recently (*Journal of
the American Musicological Society* 33 [1980]: 611), it was only in the course of the fifteenth century that, in
beginning to pay increasingly strict attention to accurate declamation, composers of polyphonic music gradually propelled it into a new age, in which it was not merely attached to text (or vice versa), but was more inte-
grally bound up with it as an agent of declamation and explication.

MARTIN AGRICOLA AND THE EARLY THREE-STRINGED FIDDLES

ELIAS DANN

*I do believe no instrument to be
So like the human voice in melody,
As are the fiddles . . .*

Martin Agricola (1545)[1]

ONE WHOSE opinion of fiddles was so high, so long ago, deserves to be read with care, especially in this case, for it was during the mature years of Martin Agricola's lifetime that the violin separated itself from its ancestors and from collateral branches of the string family to enter upon a life of its own. In the several editions of *Musica instrumentalis deudsch*, the first published in 1529 and the last in 1545, Agricola left a record of his knowledge and thoughts about most of the instruments of his time, including the various types of fiddles. His description of the latter is a tantalizing one, incomplete in many ways and difficult to interpret, but it nonetheless provides a record covering the crucial years of the emergence of the violin family.

Any attempt to understand Agricola's text is beset with problems, among which the obscurities of sixteenth-century German and the varied and ambigu-

---

1.

             Ich halts das kein instrument sey
             Den menschen stim mit melodey
             Se ehnlich/ gleichsam die Geigen . . .

(*Musica instrumentalis deudsch,* last ed. [Wittemberg, 1545], fol. 36.) In the text the last edition is indicated in brackets by its date, 1545, followed by the relevant folio references. The same procedure is followed for the first edition (Wittemberg, 1529). Both editions are available in *Publikation älterer praktischer und theoretischer Musikwerke,* vol. 20, ed. Robert Eitner (Berlin, 1896), facs. repr. (New York, 1966).

ous nomenclature for instruments of the time are the most obvious. The entire body of the treatise is written in rhyming couplets, in a mostly irregular metrical scheme, that give on the whole the impression of doggerel. (One suspects there are instances when finer shades of meaning have given way to the rhyming word.) The treatise was a popular one, and its popularity might be ascribed in part to its clever rhymes and humor. Cast in the vernacular for the benefit of students, amateur musicians, and music lovers, it is one of the earliest such works to deal with instruments and performance methods. In spite of some apparent inconsistencies, redundancies, and moments of naive poetic license, Agricola's verses, if carefully read, can throw a great deal of light into that quarter-century when the basic technique of the violin family was being established. It is with regard to the technique of playing the instruments and to their tunings that Agricola's information is most valuable. For information about the appearance and construction of the instruments one must look elsewhere.[2]

Fortunately, the existence of the violin is established by pictorial evidence from the years under consideration. The most convincing—and best known from their numerous reproductions—are the paintings of Gaudenzio Ferrari (c. 1470–1546). In an altarpiece at the Church of San Cristoforo in Vercelli, reliably dated 1529, an angel child is seen playing a lovely three-stringed instrument, clearly a violin judging from the shape and manner of performance. In Gaudenzio's great fresco in the dome of the Sanctuary of the Madonna dei Miracoli at Saronno, completed in 1536, there appear among fifty or more instruments of all types in an angelic concert three instruments which can be classified as the soprano, alto-tenor, and bass of the violin family—surely a preview of the later, fully developed violin, viola, and cello.[3] Iconography can supply many details of construction not to be found in a written account where the main subjects are how to tune and how to play the instruments. At the same time, a painting cannot indicate that strings are tuned in perfect fifths; neither can it provide instructive details of fingering, nor is it likely to hint at the use of vibrato. All these matters are discussed by Agricola, and they are matters of major importance closely associated with the development of the violin.

In the first edition, that of 1529, Agricola describes a set of small fiddles (*kleine Geigen*) usually without frets, each with three strings that are tuned by fifths. He clearly distinguishes these instruments from two types of previously described viols (*grosse Geigen*) and from the rebecs (also called *kleine Geigen*) that he discusses several pages later in the treatise. The tunings for the small fiddles are as follows: discant, g–d'–a'; alto-tenor, c–g–d'; and bass, F–c–g (1529, fols. 49–50v). The pitches are the same respectively as the lower three strings of the violin, the viola, and the obsolete tenor violin. These small fiddles, then, might be classified as belonging to a transitional stage—as perhaps more rebec

2. The illustrative woodcuts in the treatise are likely to be more confusing than helpful.
3. See Emanuel Winternitz, *Gaudenzio Ferrari: His School and the Early History of the Violin* (New York, 1967), 11ff.; David Boyden, *The History of Violin Playing from Its Origins to 1761* (London, 1965), 7–8.

than violin—were Agricola's emphasis on the difficulties of playing without frets not so strong. The rebec, of course, had been without frets for centuries, but no one seems to have fussed about it. Agricola, however, was seriously concerned about the technique of fingering without frets on both the three-stringed fiddles and the rebecs. When discussing the *kleine Geigen,* he says that they are usually found without frets, and for this reason it is difficult to grip the strings properly. But the student is not to give up, he says—if at first he uses frets, he will master the technique very well; if thereafter he wishes to be rid of the frets, he can cut them away with a knife and then fiddle to his heart's content (1529, fol. 49). This advice may indicate the historic moment when performers, seeking a more elaborate and artistic method on an instrument without frets, were prompted to abandon the rebec in favor of the violin family.

The edition of 1545 provides important new information. Here Agricola writes about three types of fiddles: *Welsche, Polische, und kleine dreyseitige Geigen.* The *Welsche* (meaning Italian in this context) are the old *grosse Geigen* or viols; the Polish *Geigen* are three-stringed fiddles without frets whose strings are stopped by the fingernails; and perhaps the *kleine dreyseitige Geigen,* later referred to as *Handgeiglein,* are slightly more mature versions of the little fiddles of 1529 (1545, fol. 35vff.).

Once again, the reader is warned about the problems of playing without frets and receives the same advice about learning with frets and dispensing with them later. Agricola makes much of understanding the secrets of a new kind of fingering and then refers the reader to the diagrams of the necks of the instruments that appear later in the treatise (see Plates I, II, and III). These diagrams are perfectly clear fingering charts that apply equally to the Polish fiddles and to the *Handgeiglein.* Whereas the discant and alto-tenor tunings remain the same as they were on the small fiddles of 1529, the bass now has four strings tuned F–G–d–a (1545, fols. 46, 47, and 47v). The three top strings are the same as those on the modern cello; the fourth seems not to have been fingered at all, and in all probability it served merely to extend the range down one tone, thereby reaching the same pitch as the bottom string of the bass instruments of 1529. Alongside the diagram of each neck one finds the most salient information—the fingering. These markings demonstrate the use of the first finger for two half steps, the second finger for two half steps, and the third finger for one further half step—in all, a rise to a perfect fourth above the open string. No provision is made for the next half step. Since Agricola does not mark a stretch for the third finger or show the use of the fourth finger, one can assume that the chromatic scale of the diagram, in each case, lacks the half step just below the pitch of the open string. One other idiosyncrasy should be noted: the two larger instruments have no letter marked at the half step above the lowest fingered string (i.e., the alto-tenor has no C♯, the bass no G♯). These omissions are not accidental; they probably indicate the difference between normal and abnormal hand positions on an instrument where the strings are stopped "with the fingernails."

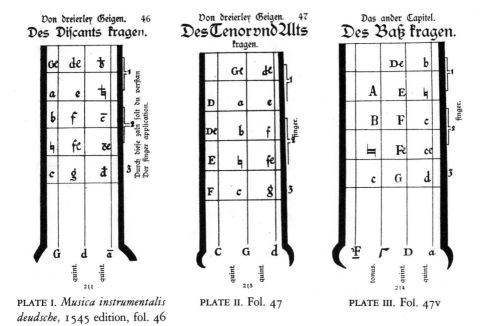

PLATE I. *Musica instrumentalis*   PLATE II. Fol. 47   PLATE III. Fol. 47v
deudsche, 1545 edition, fol. 46

Agricola's reference to touching the strings of the Polish *Geigen* with the fingernails merits close attention. His words are:

> die Seiten . . . werden auff ein ander art/Gegriffen . . ./Mit den negeln rürt man sie an/Drumb die seiten weit von ein stan . . . (1545, fol. 42v)

> (The strings . . . are stopped in a different way . . . One touches them with the nails; therefore they are set wide apart . . .)

The idea of stopping strings "with the fingernails" on any but the most primitive of instruments seems so strange to the twentieth-century string player that one is not surprised to find that modern scholars either misinterpreted Agricola's text or else avoided drawing any conclusions from it. Curt Sachs readily admitted that the allusions to the *Polnische Geigen* had caused him many headaches. He surmised that Polish fiddlers had remained true to the old Slavic and Asiatic custom of approaching the string from the side and forming an "artful" fret with the nail and, therefore, that the strings were set wide apart in order to facilitate this sideways approach.[4] Gerald R. Hayes was equally frank about his quandary over this problem. Discussing the "Polish players," he wrote:

---

4. *Handbuch der Musikinstrumentenkunde,* 2nd ed. (Leipzig, 1930), 173.

This passage gave me a vast amount of trouble to understand, though it is really perfectly simple. . . . This form of stopping notes is much more common than I had supposed; for example, it is used on the Greek and Cretan lyra (rebec), where there is no fingerboard.[5]

David Boyden, at the end of his summary of the new material found in Agricola's final edition, confined himself to the following hypothesis:

The fingernail fashion of playing may have been specifically Polish, and the manner of playing may account for the phrase "Polish violins."[6]

There exists another reference to Polish fiddles. In 1619, Michael Praetorius mentioned them, and it is apparent that he considered them synonymous with the violin family. However, he too wondered why they were called Polish. In a passage on string instruments in *De organographia,* Praetorius stated:

Musicians . . . [call] the *Violn de gamba* viols but they call *Violn de bracio Geigen,* or *Polnische Geigeln.* Perhaps this type first came here from Poland, or outstandingly excellent performers on these fiddles were found there.[7]

Any assumptions regarding Agricola's meaning in his description of the use of the fingernails on the strings cannot possibly be valid unless they entail a technique that can be reconciled with everything else he says about the instrument. For example, there would seem to be no way that a player can stop a string with the curved surface or edge of a fingernail and also produce a vibrato. And Agricola is very clear about the use of vibrato when he says:

> Auch schafft man mit dem zittern frey,
> Das süsser laut die melodey
> Denn auff den andern geschen mag . . . (1545, fol. 42v)

The implications of this passage relate to the violin family and its characteristic use of vibrato (greater or less, narrower or wider) from 1545 to the present day. Agricola's assertion about creating "with free vibration" a sweeter sound than is possible on the "others" (*grosse Geigen*) sets up a classic comparison between violins and viols. Since all fiddles sound beautiful ("so like the human voice") and Polish fiddles sound more beautiful than viols, it is incongruous to take the little *Geige* to be an odd instrument on which the fingernails

5. *Musical Instruments and Their Music, 1500–1750,* vol. 2, *The Viols, and Other Bowed Instruments* (London, 1930), 165, n. 3.
6. Boyden, 28–29.
7. *Syntagma musicum,* 2, *De organographia* (Wolfenbüttel, 1619); facs., ed. Wilibald Gurlitt (Kassel, 1958), 44.

are pressed against the sides of the strings. Still, Agricola seems to be describing a new family of instruments. He says they sound quite clear ("lauten gantz rein") and produce a far more delicate, artistic and lovely resonance than do the viols ("viel subtiler sein/Künstlicher und lieblicher gantz/Dann die Welschen mit resonantz"). The problem is that one cannot ascertain exactly what these words mean or how many of his statements were based on firsthand experience with the instruments in question. Nonetheless, if we take into account all of the information he provides and reinforce it with a few discretely performed experiments, we may arrive at some measure of the truth.

Before considering any experiments using fingernails on strings, it would be well to list the pertinent statements made in the passage on "das fundament der Polnischen Geigen" (1545, fols. 42v–43): the fiddles are common in Poland; their strings are tuned by fifths and are stopped by the fingernails in a way different from the one previously learned; the strings are set wide apart; the fiddles have a more limpid and lovely sound than do the viols; a string touched by the fingernail produces a brighter tone than one stopped with a soft fingertip because the sound is not muted by pliable touching; the vibrato results in a sweeter sound than is possible on the viols; and since the fiddles lack frets, it is more difficult to apply the fingers and to move them properly over the strings.

The serious musician of the time who played the viol may very easily have been lost without frets to guide him, and to the lack of "feel" on a fretless fingerboard was added the problem of the tuning by fifths. A viol tuning, in which there occurs no interval larger than a perfect fourth and each semitone is set off by a fret, presents no fingering problems in first position; each finger has one fret—open–1–2–3–4 will cover the interval of a major third chromatically, and the following semitone will be the next higher open string. With a tuning in fifths, a diatonic scale is possible without using any one finger on more than one stop. To play different diatonic scales or any chromatic succession, however, a technique must be learned whereby each finger is prepared to stop either of two adjacent semitones assigned to it or sometimes both in succession. Considering the care with which Agricola labeled pitches on the diagrams of the three-stringed fiddles as well as his elaborate air of elucidating what was presumably a mystery to the uninitiated, one is inclined to believe that he relished the opportunity to disclose what he knew about these new and fascinating instruments. One can only wish that he had spent some time describing just how the fingernails were applied to the strings.

Agricola's words will remain merely a literary reference (and a confusing one at that) unless one executes some carefully controlled experiments. If what he says has any value—and Agricola is a credible witness—it should be possible, on some bowed string instrument, to produce at least a satisfactory tone, with vibrato, while the fingernail stops the string.[8] Since it is unlikely that authentic Polish *Geigen* will ever be discovered or that reasonable facsimiles can be built

---

8. I conducted such experiments and found that the results clarify the problem of fingernail technique.

today, the experiment will have to be performed with materials and methods chosen to simulate conditions that existed in Agricola's time. Although the *Geige* is not available, its components are. This instrument had gut strings and was played with a horsehair bow. The strings were of equal length, the freely vibrating length extending from some sort of bridge to a nut at the pegbox end. There had to be a fairly uniform fingerboard surface; whether it was an integral part of the neck or a separate piece glued on like a modern fingerboard is unimportant. As is true of any fingerboard today, it must have been close enough to the strings so that a string could be depressed and stopped against it without pulling the string so far from its resting position that the increased tension would put it noticeably out of tune. All these conditions can be met by the modern violin strung with gut—to be precise, with the E, A, and D strings of pure gut and the conventional silver-wound G (gut of proper thickness for a violin G string is not readily obtainable).

Initially, the experiment may be restricted to the A and D strings. If a modern bow is used, the hair should be quite tight to minimize the spread along the string that results from the greater amount of hair in use today. One should hold the bow in such a way that fairly strong pressure can be exerted by the index finger. The fingernails of the left hand ought to be short, but not overly so; only the first, second, and third fingers are to be used. Place the fingers on B, C♯, and D on the A string (Example 1) so that in each case both the flesh of the fingertip and the nail stop the string, the actual point of the stop being exactly where the string emerges from under the fingernail.

EXAMPLE 1

The entire hand should be brought to a position that allows one to hold all three fingers down at once, each finger in the position just described. It is cumbersome to achieve this position on the modern violin unless the neck is allowed to rest on the loose flesh between thumb and forefinger, but the position is a little more comfortable on the old thicker neck. Raise and lower each finger, making sure that the nail makes contact each time a finger descends until it is possible to play the exercise shown in Example 2 with reasonable rapidity.

EXAMPLE 2

Practice vibrato with each finger in turn while the other fingers are raised but not removed so far from the strings that the newly developed position is destroyed. One should try to maintain a small, rapid vibrato, because in these circumstances the modern wide vibrato is neither possible nor desirable. The procedure outlined thus far may be duplicated at the pitches shown in Example 3, and at all the corresponding pitches on the D string.

EXAMPLE 3

The same exercises, on the G string, will demonstrate that the silver G responds in much the same way as do the gut strings. At this point, all the stops diagramed by Agricola on the neck of the *Discant Geige* have been used.

To continue the experiment, play everything at various dynamic levels, exerting especially strong pressure during the forte. Compare the sound of playing slowly or rapidly, with or without vibrato, forte or piano, with the sound achieved by the usual modern methods on the same strings. Repeat parts of the experiment on individual strings tuned lower and higher than normal (perhaps as much as a third each way) in order to cover a wide range of string tensions, since we do not know the exact tensions on the Polish fiddle. Remove the E string from the fingerboard and play on the A string to approximate the conditions that would exist if the fingerboard were wider and the strings quite widely separated; one can also remove the A and play on the D string, or remove the D and play on the G string. With the edge of the nail and the edge of the fingertip stopping the string, finger action is facilitated when the rest of the flesh of the fingertip can rest solidly on a fingerboard area unhampered by the proximity of another string.

From the evidence of all these experiments, one can make some observations and draw some tentative conclusions. To achieve the stopping of the strings in this manner, the hand is drawn into a position over the strings with the fingers fairly tightly curled and the final phalanges of the fingers more or less perpendicular to the fingerboard or, in the extreme, sometimes past the ninety-degree angle with the first knuckle almost over the next lower string. Most of the flesh of the fingertip will be resting against the fingerboard between the string being stopped and the next higher string—in Agricola's words, "die Polacken zwar/Greiffen zwischen die seiten gar" (1545, fol. 45v). Indeed, Agricola pointed out that the fingernails touched the strings and that the fingers gripped between the strings; he did not say that *none* of the flesh of the fingertips touched the strings. Moreover, the little scale ascending and descending on each string can be played with remarkable clarity. The fingernail stops the string exceptionally well so long as it is backed up by the pressure of a small amount of hard-packed fingertip just behind it. Trills are especially clear, the greatest surprise being the sound of the trill on the open string—either the half-step or the whole-step trill. Today, violinists almost never perform such a trill, partly because it is hard to do with modern hand position but mostly because it sounds so bad, the difference between the tonal quality of the open string and that of the tone above being so great.

The application of this technique, including rapid fingering and vibrato, sounds better when the strings are tuned higher than normal; more tautly stretched strings, therefore, seem preferable. And since there was no particular standard of pitch when such instruments were used alone, one may assume that they were tuned to a fairly high pitch or at least to a pitch that was relatively high for the thickness and length of the strings. This assumption is corroborated by Agricola, who, when dealing with the tuning of a family of fiddles at several points in both editions, suggests beginning by drawing the top string of the discant instrument as high as it will go without breaking (1529, fols. 47 and 49; 1545, fol. 43).

The vibrato that can be produced by starting with the fingernail tightly stopping the string is so impressive that it should be heard rather than described. The undulation of the finger raises the nail so slightly that the pitch variation is kept to a minimum. More accurately described, the rocking back of the fingertip raises the nail just enough to create the minute change of pitch between the stop made by the fingernail and the stop made by the flesh behind it. Assuming that the fingernail is stopping the desired pitch, one cycle of the vibrato consists of rolling the fingertip back slightly, just enough to clear the stop made by the nail, and then rolling forward again to the solid stop of the nail. The usual speed, or number of cycles per second, of the modern vibrato is easily achieved. Moreover, the pitch accepted by the ear is the highest one heard, the one returned to again and again as the fingernail makes its most solid contact.[9]

One additional factor needs to be considered here. Vibrato is not only a variation in pitch; it is also a series of variations in intensity. The fluctuation of intensity in the vibrato with fingernail stop appears to be perfectly synchronized with the variation in pitch: the sound seems to be loudest at the moment of highest pitch, when the fingernail completely stops the string, and softer while the flesh of the fingertip forms the stop. Assuming a continuous and unvarying bow speed and pressure, the change in intensity (or amplitude of vibration) will be determined entirely by the movement of the fingertip. All other things being equal, the string will vibrate most widely when the stop is hardest, less so when there is a bit of rounded fingertip intruding ever so slightly on the vibrating length. A carefully controlled vibrato, produced as described, adds a surprising silvery resonance to the tone.

By playing at various dynamic levels, one can understand the relationship

9. In spite of the widely held view that vibrato consists of a slight wavering of the tone alternately above and below the correct pitch, I am firmly convinced that the ear accepts the reiterated high points of the undulation as the correct pitch. See Samuel B. Grimson and Cecil Forsyth, *Modern Violin-Playing* (New York, 1920), 5–6; Ivan Galamian, *Principles of Violin Playing and Teaching* (Englewood Cliffs, N. J., 1962), 42.

between finger and bow pressure—that is to say, the weaker stopping of the string (the use of softer flesh or less finger pressure) does not allow the use of strong bow pressure; on the contrary, the string will stop its regular vibration and the sound will become impure and scratchy. The stronger the finger pressure, the stronger the possible bow pressure before the vibrating string buckles. In short, the well-produced tone with fingernail stopping has a solidity of sound never quite equaled by fingertip-flesh stopping.

Despite its value for tone production on the Polish *Geige,* the fingernail method has some intrinsic disadvantages. Since each of the three useful fingers approaches the string at a slightly different angle, it seems that the development of an advanced technique with consistent passagework would have been quite arduous. It is possible, of course, to apply the first, second, and third fingers with nails stopping the string, but the hand position which results is such that the fourth finger cannot be applied in a similar manner. Why Agricola's fingering diagrams show no use of the fourth finger is quite understandable. Indeed, long after any technique necessitated by the Polish *Geige* had disappeared from violin playing, the use of the fourth finger was often avoided.

Perhaps a more developed technique was achieved on the three-stringed *Handgeiglein* of 1545. They were presumably like the Polish *Geigen* in all respects except that they did not call for the fingernail technique. But according to Agricola, the fingers still had to be above the strings, indicating a more or less vertical descent of the fingertips: "Die finger müssen oben sein/Auff den vorgnanten Geiglein," (1545, fol. 45v). This technique, on the one hand, could have been a variant, or a development, of the fingernail technique described above. Anyone adept at playing the Polish *Geige* could have relaxed his left hand slightly, making the stop with the hardest part of the fingertip just behind the nail. On the other hand, the problem of solidly stopping the strings of a strong-voiced little violin that had no frets could have led to the fingernail method of playing on the Polish fiddles. And on the new *Handgeiglein* this technique may have given way, perhaps with some adjustments of bridge and fingerboard, to strong stopping with the flesh of the fingertips at a point very close to the nail. The fingers would then descend in a nearly vertical alignment, the stop would be still quite strong, and left-hand facility would be greatly enhanced.

This kind of execution might represent the beginning of true violin technique, a technique that would have pleased Leopold Mozart, who said, two hundred years later:

> The fingers must not be laid lengthwise on the strings but with the joints raised, and the top parts of the fingers pressed down very strongly. If the strings are not pressed well down, they will not sound pure.[10]

10. *A Treatise on the Fundamental Principles of Violin Playing,* trans. Editha Knocker, 2nd ed. (London, 1951), 60.

Nor had things changed after another one hundred and fifty years. In the early twentieth century Leopold Auer, the teacher of Heifetz, Elman, and Zimbalist, wrote:

> The left arm should be thrust forward under the back of the violin so that the fingers will fall perpendicularly on the strings, the fingertips striking them with decided firmness.[11]

Agricola, Mozart, and Auer agree in recommending a basic principle of left-hand technique—a technique applicable from the time of the three-stringed *Handgeiglein* to the first quarter of the twentieth century.

On the basis of the evidence, interpretive and experimental, it does not seem unreasonable to construe Agricola's treatise as testimony for the beginnings of a technique for playing on an instrument without frets. This artistic technique, once established, was to make its contribution both to the evolution of the members of the string family and to the development of their idiomatic musical style.

---

11. *Violin Playing As I Teach It* (New York, 1921), 32.

CHRISTIAN ULRICH RINGMACHER (1743–1781): HIS HERITAGE, HIS FIRM, AND HIS CATALOGUE

BARRY S. BROOK

The Published Thematic Catalogue in the Eighteenth Century

B ETWEEN 1761 and 1830 some forty thematic catalogues were published, most of them only one to four pages long and limited either to a single composer or to an individual genre.[1] Four of them, however, are extensive multicomposer, multigenre catalogues of unusual value for dating works, identifying composers, and illuminating the process of music dissemination. All four were commercial sales catalogues put out by publishing, copying, or bookselling firms during a thirty-year period, 1762–1792, when the rate of distribution of music in prints and manuscript copies was expanding rapidly. All were sold rather than distributed gratis. All were published separately rather than as supplemental pages to editions of music. In chronological order, they were:

1762–87: Breitkopf, Johann Gottlob Immanuel (1719–94)
Catalogo delle sinfonie, [partite, overture, soli, duetti, trii, quattri e concerti per il violino, flauto traverso, cembalo ed altri stromenti,] che

---

1. See Barry S. Brook, *Thematic Catalogues in Music* (New York: Pendragon, 1972), xxvi–xxvii, where all extant pre-1830 published catalogues are listed chronologically. Extant thematic catalogues in manuscript from before 1830 number over 110 (see ibid., xxi–xxv). Before 1761, only two thematic lists were printed, the first in William Barton's *The Book of Psalms in Metre* (London, 1645), the second as a supplement to Johann Caspar Kerll's *Modulatio organica* (Munich, 1685); see Barry S. Brook, "The First Printed Thematic Catalogues," in *Festskrift Jens Peter Larsen*, ed. Nils Schiørring, Henrik Glahn, and Carsten E. Hatting (Copenhagen, 1972), 103 and 112.

*si trovano in manuscritto nella officina musica di Giovanno Gottlob
Immanuel Breitkopf, in Lipsia.* (Leipzig, 1762–87). Six parts and
sixteen supplements (titles vary). 888p. (Eight or nine complete
sets extant.)

1768–74: Hummel, Johann Julius (1728–98) and Burchard (1731–97)
*Catalogue thématique ou commencement de touttes les oeuvres de musique que
sont du propre fond de J. J. & B. Hummel, publié à la commodité des amateurs, par où ils pourrant voir, si les pièces qu'on leur presente pour original,
n'ont pas déjà été imprimées.* NB. Le supplément de ce catalogue consistant
en une feuille de nouveautez, paroitra chaque anné (Amsterdam, 1768–
74). Catalogue and six supplements. 72p. (Scattered copies, no complete
sets known; a seventh supplement advertised in 1778 has not been located, nor has a thematic list announced in 1783 been found.)

1772–75: Ringmacher, Christian Ulrich (1743–81)
*Catalogo de' soli, duetti, trii, quadri, quintetti, partite, de' concerti e
delle sinfonie per il cembalo, violino, flauto traverso ed altri stromenti
che si trovano in manoscritto nella officina musica de Christiano
Ulrico Ringmacher libraio in Berelino.* MDCCLXXIII (Berlin,
1773). 112p. (One copy extant; two heretofore unreported Ringmacher catalogues, discussed below, have never been found.)

1792: Imbault, Jean-Jérôme (1753–1832)
*Catalogue thématique des ovrages de musique mis au jour par Im-
bault Md de musique au Mont d'Or Rue S. Honoré près l'Hôtel
d'Aligre no. 627 a' Paris* (Paris, c. 1792). 141p. (One copy
known.)

Hummel and Imbault were advertising engraved works they themselves
had published. Breitkopf was offering handwritten *Musikalien* that would be
copied out on order at his premises from his stock of manuscript (and later also
printed) masters. Ringmacher was a bookseller who also sold printed and
handwritten music obtained from various sources.

As indicated, altogether only about ten complete copies of these four catalogues survive. All except the Imbault were published in several parts or with
supplements; even odd copies of individual supplements are very rare. It is pertinent, and rather strange, that the sole extant copy of the Imbault catalogue,
published in Paris, is to be found in a Berlin library, while the Ringmacher,
published in Berlin, can be found only in Brussels. And as will be described
below, Ringmacher also published two other thematic catalogues that have not
survived at all. There are several explanations, some conjectural, for the extremely low survival rate of such catalogues:

To begin with, a high percentage of all the published and manuscript
music from the eighteenth century has been lost through fires, floods, bombing,

etc. Second, the plates used for engraving music in this period could not, as a rule, produce more than 250 or 300 copies. Initial runs of 10 to 25 copies at a time were quite common.[2] Since paper was expensive, publishers employing the engraving process would usually print—and reprint—only according to anticipated demand. There is no evidence of how many copies of the two engraved catalogues (Imbault and Hummel) were printed. As for the two catalogues (Breitkopf and Ringmacher) printed from movable type (a technology capable of producing many more copies), Breitkopf states in the "Nacherinnerrung" to Parte 1ma of his catalogue (p. 30), after discussing how difficult it was to be accurate in such works, "Ich habe deswegen nur eine kleine Anzahl Exemplaren von diesem ersten Versuche gedruckt, und den Nutzen der Liebe zur Richtigkeit gern aufgeopfert." Third, the cheaper the paper used (and paper of poor quality was probably customary in relatively expendable catalogues), the less likely that copies would survive the rigors of time.[3] Fourth and most relevant is the factor of a catalogue's loss of function soon after its issue. Just as an eighteenth-century symphony score became superfluous once the parts for it were printed or copied out (very few such scores survive, since additional parts could more easily be re-copied from parts than from the score), similarly a catalogue was simply discarded when it no longer served its function as a purchasing medium.

It should be pointed out that of the four catalogues just discussed, three —Breitkopf,[4] Hummel,[5] and Imbault[6]—have been reprinted in recent years in response to a growing awareness of the importance of such documents for musical scholarship.[7] With the forthcoming reprint, under the present author's editorship, of the Ringmacher catalogue (Leipzig: Peters; New York: Pendragon, 1984), the fourth and last major published thematic catalogue surviving from the eighteenth century will become available in facsimile. It has been reproduced from the sole extant copy in the Library of the Brussels Conservatory.

2. Printing music from movable type could not operate on this on-demand basis because of the greater time and expense required to set a page into type and the need to reuse the type elements for other compositions, probably even for other sheets of the same composition. The relatively inexpensive engraving plates, on the other hand, could easily be stored and reused, even for decades, until they became worn out. See also Anik Devries, *Édition et commerce de la musique gravée à Paris dans la première moitié du XVIIIe siècle: les Boivin et les Le Clerc* (Geneva, 1976).

3. The practice of printing small runs from engraved plates according to need made the occasional use of cheaper paper eminently feasible. Evidence for this practice can be found in announcements of works for sale at two different prices, depending on the paper used. See, for example, Ringmacher's "Nachricht" (p. 112) of his *Catalogo*, trans. on p. 260 below.

4. Barry S. Brook, *The Breitkopf Thematic Catalogue: The Six Parts and Sixteen Supplements, 1762–1787,* with introduction and indexes (New York, 1966).

5. Cari Johansson, *J. J. & B. Hummel Music-Publishing and Thematic Catalogues* (Stockholm, 1972).

6. Jean-Jérôme Imbault, *Catalogue thématique des ouvrages de musique* (Geneva, 1972).

7. A fifth major sales catalogue with incipits, that of Christian Gottfried Thomas (1748–1806) of Leipzig, was made available in manuscript in 1778. Although announced for publication, it was never printed. Its description closely resembles that of the Breitkopf catalogue. No copy survives. See Barry S. Brook, "Piracy and Panacea in the Dissemination of Music in the Late Eighteenth Century," *Proceedings of the Royal Music Association,* 102 (1975–76): 13–36; published in German as "Piraterie und Allheilmittel bei der Verbreitung von Musik im späten 18. Jahrhundert," *Beiträge zur Musikwissenschaft* 20/3 (1980): 217–39.

The Ringmacher Heritage

CHRISTIAN ULRICH RINGMACHER has long been a shadowy figure in eighteenth-century studies. Although his thematic *Catalogo* of 1773 is cited frequently by scholars, his name appears in none of the standard dictionaries of music. Even in the histories and directories of German publishers and book dealers, he receives only the briefest mention or none at all. In short, he has been known almost entirely through his catalogue. Information about his background, his date and place of birth, etc., and about the activities of his firm has been limited to a few references, the first of which may be found in Johann Nicolaus Forkel's *Musikalische Almanach* of 1782 (p. 161): "Herr Christian Ulrich Ringmacher, Buchhändler in Berlin, hält ebenfalls eine Musikalienhandlung, und ist zugleich Verleger von geschriebenen Musikalien."

Arthur Georgi, in *Die Entwicklung des Berliner Buchhandels bis zur Gründung des Börsenvereins der deutschen Buchhändler 1825* (Berlin, 1926), lists Ringmacher as being in business during the years 1770–81, but provides no additional data. And Robert Eitner refers to him thus: "Ringmacher, Christian Ulrich, Buch- und Musikhändler in Berlin gab 1773 einen Lagerkatalog von 110 Seiten heraus, bestand noch 1781."[8]

As Rudolf Elvers points out in his excellent article "Musikdrucker, Musikalienhändler und Musikverleger in Berlin 1750 bis 1850: eine Übersicht,"[9] "breitet sich über die eigentliche Entwicklung des Musikverlagswesen seit etwa 1750 in der ehemaligen preussischen Hauptstadt noch ein fast undurchdringliches Dunkel." The "Dunkel" is due in part to the destruction during the Second World War of virtually all archives in Berlin relating to music publishers. However, it has been possible to shed some light on Christian Ulrich Ringmacher, the man and the music dealer, by searching through regional biographical dictionaries, which in turn led to archival family records in cities other than Berlin, and by perusing Berlin, Leipzig, and Hamburg newspapers of the period for the announcements he placed in them.

The evidence that has emerged, although hardly devoid of blank patches, includes a detailed family tree, a clear outline of the workings of the Ringmacher firm, and an understanding of Ringmacher's role in the dissemination of music in the eighteenth century.

In tracing the family, one first finds the Ringmacher name in Christian Gottlieb Jöcher's *Allgemeines Gelehrten-Lexikon, 6. Ergänzungsband* (Bremen, 1819 [repr. ed., 1961], cols. 2195–96), where a Daniel Ringmacher is said to have been born on August 8, 1662, in Isny, to have studied in the Gymnasium at Ulm, and to have received the *Magisterwürde* in Leipzig. We are told that he

8. "Buch- und Musikalien-Händler, Buch- und Musikaliendrucker nebst Notenstecher, nur die Musik betreffend, nach den Originaldrucken verzeichnet," *Beilage zu den Monatsheften für Musikgeschichte* 36 (1904): 189.

9. *Festschrift für Walter Gerstenberg,* ed. Georg von Dadelsen and Andreas Holschneider (Wolfenbüttel and Zurich, 1964), 37–44.

was then named *Professor der Moral* in Ulm and that he held a series of church positions (*Pfarrer, Diakon, Prediger,* etc.) in various German cities. We also learn that Daniel Ringmacher published some twenty-seven books in German and Latin (all are carefully listed), mainly religious and philosophical tracts except for one work, entitled *Gottgeheiligte Singübung* (Ulm, 1717, 1723, 1737, 1747, and 1761), which also appeared with the title *Alte und neue evangelische Kirchenlieder mit vielen nützlichen Anmerkungen und Historien.* He was sufficiently well known to have been the subject of three copperplate engraved portraits. He died on August 8, 1728, at exactly sixty-six years of age.[10]

The invaluable *Moniteur des dates, contenant million de renseignements biographiques, généalogiques et historiques* by Édouard-Marie Oettinger (Dresden, 1867) lists two other Ringmachers:

> Ringmacher (Daniel), deutscher Theolog, Prediger in Isny (Württemberg), geb. zu Ulm (Württemberg) 4. October 1699, gest. zu Isny 24. Juli 1761.

> Ringmacher (Johann Elias), Bruder des Daniel R. (s.d.), deutscher Rechtsgelehrter und Theolog, Pfarrer in Nernstetten (Württemberg) geb. zu Ulm im J. 1696, gest. 6. Juli 1772.

The relationship of these three gentlemen to our Ringmacher was finally established in the Stadtarchiv at Isny, where the Ringmacher family ancestry could be traced back to the sixteenth century.[11]

The first of the two Daniel Ringmachers (1662–1728) mentioned above was Christian Ulrich's grandfather; the second (1699–1761), his father. As the references cited above tell us, the highly respectable Ringmacher family was made up of theologians, lawyers, professors, city officials, and merchants.[12] The Isny archives carry Christian Ulrich's lineage back five generations to Sebald Ringmacher senior, *Spitalmeister* in Nuremberg, who died in 1576. His son, Sebald junior (1554–1607), was a *Handelsmann,* also in Nuremberg. The latter's son, Johann (d. 1635), moved to Ulm, where he became a *Weinschreiber* and where his son, Daniel senior, Christian Ulrich's grandfather and the fifth of nine children, was born.

10. The notice from which these facts were drawn (Jöcher, 1819) appears also in Albrecht Weyermann, *Nachrichten von Gelehrten, Künstlern und andern merkwürdigen Personen aus Ulm* (Ulm, 1798), 445–46. Weyermann in turn refers back to an even earlier edition of Jöcher (not seen) which served as his source.

11. I would like to express my profound thanks to Frau Margarete Stützle, archivist, Bürgermeisteramt, Isny im Allgäu, who kindly provided the carefully drawn Ringmacher family tree as well as the drawing of the Ringmacher coat of arms reproduced below.

12. This is true not only of Christian Ulrich's direct ancestors but of members of other branches of the family who do not appear on his family tree. They may have been descendants of Conrad Ringmacher (d. 1575), whose name is listed beside that of his brother, Sebald Ringmacher, senior, at the head of the family tree. For example, a Hans Ringmacher (active c. 1590) is listed by A. M. Hildebrandt in the *Vierteljahrsschrift für Wappen-, Siegel-, und Familïenkunde* 39 (1911): 196. Also the name Hanss Christoff Ringmacher appears under the date of July 8, 1681, in Immanuel Kammerer's *Regesten der Urkunden des Spitalarchivs Isny* (Karlsruhe, 1960) for the year 1698; the same name is found in Carl-Hans Hauptmeyer's *Verfassung und Herrschaft in Isny* (Göppingen, 1976).

Daniel junior was born in Ulm, the fourth of six children. He became rector and *Pfarrer* in Isny,[13] where he married Rosina Susanna Feuersteinin (1710–79), a local merchant's daughter. Daniel junior's career was similar to his father's, but somewhat less distinguished. He wrote only two books (one in Latin and one in German) and was honored by only one engraved portrait.[14] Christian Ulrich, his sixth and youngest child, was born in Isny on June 30, 1743. He died in Berlin, unmarried ("ledig") on June 7, 1781.[15]

The Ringmacher family had its own coat of arms (Plate I).

PLATE I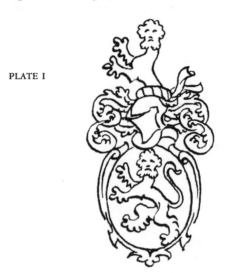

Wappen: in Weiss ein bärtiger roter Mannslöwe. Derselbe wachsend auf
            dem bewulsteten Stechhelm.
Quelle: Siegel auf einer Urkunde von 1751 im Ev. Kirchenarchiv Jsny
            (1751—Daniel Ringmacher V.D.M./Verbi Divini Magister/in
            Jsny.)
            Das Grabmal der Ringmacher auf dem Friedhof zu Jsny zeigt im
            Wappen statt des Mannslöwen einen Leopard mit einem Ring im
            Maule, denselben wachsend auf dem gekrönten Stechhelm.[16]

13. A small city about 100 kilometers south of Ulm and close to Germany's border with westernmost Austria.
14. See Albrecht Weyermann, *Neue historisch-biographisch-artistische Nachrichten von Gelehrten und Künstlern* (Ulm, 1829), 423.
15. See *Eintrag in den Kirchenbüchern der Ev. Pfarrgemeinde* (Isny), 6: 139, and 13: 12.
16. Stadtarchiv, Isny, Wappensammlung, Wappen Nr. 318.

The Ringmacher Family Tree

Conrad Ringmacher   und dessen Bruder   *Sebald Ringmacher,*
Spitalmeister zu Nürnberg   sen. ebenfalls
gest.1575   Spitalmeister in Nürnberg,
                                              gest.daselbst 1578

Sebald Ringmacher,
geb.1554, Handelsmann,
gest.5.VIII.1607 in Nürnberg,
verh. 10. Jan.1579   Anna Seufferheldin
                                gest. 30. April 1629

Johann Ringmacher,
Weinschreiber in Ulm,
gest. 1635
verh.21.Nov.1620   Anna Maria Baumgärtner
                                von Dinkelsbühl
                                geb.13.Sept.1593
                                verh.sich in 1.Ehe mit
                                Johann Jakob Schaffter
                                Handelsmann in Ulm,
                                welcher am 3.Juli 1619 starb

1.	2.	3.	4.	5.
Anna Maria	Elisabeth	Johannes	Anna Catharina	*Daniel*
geb.24.II.1656	geb.1.Sept.1657	geb.9.Dez.1658	geb.2.IV.1660	geb.8.Aug.1662
				gest.8.Aug.1728
6.	7.	8.	9.	verh.1695 mit
Johann Sebald	Michael	Phil. Conrad	Johann Christoph	Maria Magdalena
geb.25. Sept.1664	geb.2.I.1666	geb.27.X.1667	geb.20.Aug.1671	Faulhaberin,
			städt. Werkmeister	geb.1675,
			in Jsny, gest, ledig	+ 20. Juli 1727
			7.März 1744	(in Ulm Rev. Minist.
				Schol. et Senior)

1.	2.	3.	4.
Johann Elias	Joh. Christoph	Joh. Matthäus	*Daniel*
geb.21.II.1696	geb.3.III.1697	geb.10.V.1698	geb.4.X.1699 Pfarrer
Advokat, verh.			zu Jsny gest.24.Juli 1761
in Karlsruhe			verh.23.I.1730
mit Elise			Rosina Susanna Feuersteinin,
Remingerin, Tochter			Tochter des
v. Joh. Reminger,			Ulrich Feuerstein,
Handelsmann zu Ulm			Handelsmann zu Jsny,
			gest.31.Juli 1711.
5.	6.		Seine Frau Jakobina verh.
Philipp Jakob	Conrad Selbald		sich wieder nach dem Tode
geb.30.V.1707	geb.1713		ihres 1.Mannes U.F. mit
gest.Juli 1772	Kauf- und		Leonard von Eberz,
Pfarrer im	Handelsmann im		Bürgermeister von Jsny
Ulmischen	Westfälischen		

Kinder des Daniel Ringmacher, Pfarrer zu Jsny, geb.1699,Okt.4., gest.1761, Juli 24.
und der Rosina Susanna Feuersteinin, geb.1710.Nov.1., gest.1779,6.Jan.

1.	2.	3.	4.
Jakobina	Daniel	Maria Magdalena	Christoph Leonhard
geb.16.II.1731	geb.5.Sept.1732	geb.15.XII.1734	geb.25.XI.1735
verh. mit	Posamentier,	verh. mit Johann	Kaufmann
David Gaumer,	Notar, Landgerichtsprokurator,	Jakob Rau, Pfarrer	
Chirurg und	verh. in 1.Ehe am 27.X.1760	im Ulmischen	
St. Leonhards-	Susanna Dorothea Funkin		
Pfleg-Einzieher	von Kempten + 26.V.1779		
	2.Ehe mit Barbara Bechtingerin		
	gest.6.III.1792		
	3.Ehe mit Jakobina Ursula		
	Eggingerin am 7.X.1793		

5.	6.
Christoph	*Christian Ulrich*
geb.3.X.	geb.30.VI.1743 in Jsny
1740	Buchhändler
Strumpfwirker	gest. ledig, in Berlin
	am 7.VI.1781

Christian Ulrich Ringmacher: A Summary of His Life

ALTHOUGH we now know a good deal about Christian Ulrich Ringmacher's
ancestry and, as will be seen below, about the activities of his firm, we still have
to rely on conjecture and negative evidence regarding his early life. Born on June
30, 1743, in Isny, son of a clergyman and a merchant's daughter, he undoubtedly went to a local Gymnasium. He seems not to have studied at either of the
two universities, Leipzig[17] and Tübingen,[18] attended by his ancestors. Neither

17. A search of the Matrikel of the University of Leipzig did not reveal his name. His grandfather and uncle
are listed as follows: "Ringmacher,—erus, Dan. [Daniel] Isnen. [Isny] (Ulmen.) 16 gr. i [inscriptus] S [om-
mersemester] 1682 B 19, b,a, und m [agister] 28.I.1686. Ringmacher, Joh. Elias Ulmen. Franc. [Francus]
prom. [promisit] i[nscriptus] S[ommersemester] 1717 B 37." See *Die jüngere Matrikel der Universität Leipzig 1559–1809. Als Personen-und Ortsregister bearbeitet. Im Auftrage der Königlich Sächsischen Staatsregierung herausgegeben von Georg Erler*, vol. 2, *Die Immatrikulationen vom Wintersemester 1634 biz zum
Sommersemester 1709* (Leipzig, 1909), 361. Also *Die jüngere Matrikel der Universität Leipzig 1559–1809.
Als Personen- und Ortsregister bearbeitet und durch Nachträge aus den Promotionslisten ergänzt. Im Auftrage
der Königlich Sächsischen Staatsregierung herausgegeben von Georg Erler*, vol. 3, *Die Immatrikulationen vom
Wintersemester 1709 bis zum Sommersemester, 1809* (Leipzig, 1909), 331. Furthermore, in his *Alte Allgäuer
Geschlechter*, vol. 5, *Allgäuer auf hohen Schulen* (Kempten, 1939), Alfred Weitnauer lists all "Allgäuer" he
found in "Matrikelbüchern" of universities. Only grandfather Daniel Ringmacher is named (p. 53), as having
studied in Leipzig and received the "bacc. art et mag. 1686."
18. An examination of *Die Matrikeln der Universität Tübingen*, vol. 2, *1600–1710*, and vol. 3, *1710–
1810*, ed. A. Bürk und W. Wille (Tübingen, 1953), shows the following:
    27470   Daniel Ringmacher Isna-Ulmensis 24.4.1679 inscripta 90 Prof. d.Moral in Ulm
    31157 9.10.1713 inscr. Johan Elias Ringmacher Ulmensis
    31297 23.4.1715 Johannes Christophorus Ringmacher Ulmensis
    31481 13.10.1716 Daniel Ringmacher ex gymnasio Ulmensis 29 Rektor in Isny
    32336 24.3.1725 Philippus Jacobus Ringmacher Ulmensis 48 Pfarrer in Grimmelfingen
    32842 15.5.1730 Philippus Jacobus Ringmacher Ulmensis

did he follow in the footsteps of his forebears by choosing the law or theology as his profession. He may well have apprenticed himself to a bookseller, for whose trade, although a departure from family tradition, his home environment provided a reasonable background.

At the age of twenty-six or twenty-seven, he founded his own bookselling and music business in Berlin. The year was 1770, a time of great acceleration in the book trade in Germany and soon thereafter in the music business as well.[19] Our knowledge of Ringmacher's musical background is limited to the fact that his grandfather, Daniel senior, published the previously mentioned collection of sacred songs, "mit vielen nützlichen Anmerkungen und Historien." His interest in music, however, is apparent from the inclusion of musical items in his very first announcement as bookseller and from his increasing involvement with the sale of music throughout his career.

That Ringmacher was an enterprising merchant is seen (1) from the evidence (presented below) of the sales announcements he placed in newspapers of three cities; (2) from his active participation in the Leipzig book fairs, from his efforts to obtain salable musical items from Mannheim and probably also from Paris; and (3) from his publication of three thematic catalogues.

He died at the age of thirty-seven on June 7, 1781, at a time when his business was apparently at its height.

The Ringmacher Firm

THE SHORT-LIVED history of Ringmacher's firm (1770–81) can be gleaned from the notices ("Anzeigen") he placed in the following newspapers (the titles are preceded by abbreviations to be used henceforth):[20]

BN   *Berlinische Nachrichten von Staats- und gelehrten Sachen*
BZ   *Königlich Berlinische privilegirte Staats- und gelehrte Zeitung*
LZ   *Leipziger Neue Postzeitung*
HC   *Staats- und gelehrte Zeitung des Hamburgischen unpartheyischen Correspondenten*

Although no advertisements have been found in Berlin newspapers before 1773,[21] it is not impossible that the firm was already in existence there in 1769. The first notices seem to have been published in Leipzig in 1770 in order to reach purchasers attending the book fair there. In the earliest one (LZ, May 14, 1770, p. 401), Ringmacher referred to himself as a "Buchhändler von Berlin."

---

19. See Barry S. Brook, "Piracy and Panacea," 13–16 (German version, 217–19).
20. Relatively few libraries or archives in Germany possess holdings of these newspapers, and then almost invariably in broken runs, complicating the researcher's task immeasurably. The author would like to thank particularly the staffs of the Regierungsbibliothek, Schloss Ansbach, and the Landesbibliothek, Dresden, for their assistance during visits to these libraries.
21. Some issues from these newspapers have not been seen.

He advertised the availability, at his Leipzig depot in the "Nicolai-Strasse in der goldenen Hand," of a varied group of nine books plus two music collections, "Burmann's neue Lieder zum Singen beym Clavier à 8 Gr." and "Ptolomäus und Berenice, mit Melodien fürs Clavier, à 4 Gr."

Two years later (LZ, May 14, 1772, p. 430) he made a special appeal to music lovers and announced a "vollständiger thematischer Catalogus 22 Gr." for the first time:

> Der Buchhändler Ringmacher aus Berlin macht den Musikverständigen und Musik-Liebhabern hierdurch bekannt, dass diese Jubilate-Messe bey ihm allhier zur goldenen Hand in der Nicolai-Strasse die neuesten geschriebenen Musicalien von den berühmtesten Meistern um sehr billige Preise zu haben sind, welche mehrentheils in Solos, Duettos, Trios, und besonders Quadros, Sinfonien & Concerts, auf allerley Instrument, als für die Violine, Flöte, Flügel, Bratsche, Violoncell, Basson, Hoboe u.a. bestehen. Das neue Verzeichniss davon wird daselbst umsonst ausgegeben, das thematische aber kostet 4 Gr. ein ganz vollständiger thematischer Catalogus 22 Gr. und ohne Themas 3 Gr.

Ringmacher's Leipzig depot was located in the same premises as that of the Buchhändler C. A. Reussner von Quedlinburg, who also advertised both books and music (LZ, Oct. 5, 1772, p. 896).

On April 1, 1773 (BN, No. 39, p. 202), Ringmacher announced that he had moved from his previous lodgings in Berlin (address unspecified) and had transferred his shop "in der Poststrasse in des Herrn Martinets Hause." He stated further

> dass bey ihm ein neuer gedruckter thematischer Catalogus von den geschriebenen neuesten Musikalien für alle Instrumente, welche allhier, und diese Jubilate in Leipzig, die Messe über, zur goldenen Hand in der Nikelstrasse in seiner Niederlage um billige Preise verkauft werden, à 16 Gr. zu haben ist.

This new catalogue "à 16 Gr." (rather than "à 22 Gr." for the catalogue offered a year earlier in Leipzig) is apparently the only one that has survived. A similar announcement was published in Hamburg (HC, No. 60 [Apr. 14, 1773], p. 4), stating that the catalogue could be obtained "bei H. C. Grund am Fischmarkt" and again two weeks later (HC, No. 68 [April 28, 1773]) with the reference to H. C. Grund omitted.

Three times in the autumn of the same year, Ringmacher, calling himself in one announcement "Buchhändler und Musikverleger," offered his musical wares, including the catalogue "à 16 Gr.," to his Hamburg customers. He asked them to order by mail, and added, "Wer Musikalien lehnen will, dem stehen solche auch zu Diensten, wofür vierteljährlich 3 Rthlr. pränumeriret, und 5 Rthlr. Pfand gelassen wird." (HC, No. 144 [Sept. 8, 1773], p. 4; No. 160 [Oct. 6], p. 4; and No. 176 [Nov. 3], p. 4.)

In Berlin, in January of 1774, Ringmacher offered the "2te Theil" of his thematic catalogue, with the newest engraved and hand-copied works from Mannheim, for eight Groschen:

> Bey dem Musikhändler Ringmacher allhier in der Poststrasse wohnhaft, ist nunmehro der 2te Theil seines thematischen Catalogi von den neusten gestochenen und geschriebenen Musicalien für alle Instrumente, welche besonders dieses Jahr in Mannheim herausgekommen sind, fertig geworden, und kostet 8 Gr. Desgleichen sind daselbst zur ietzigen Winterlustbarkeit gedruckt à 8 Gr. zu haben: Ein Dutzend neu componirte Englische Tänze und Quadrillen für zwo Violinen, Flöten, und Bass von Herrn Grosse in Potsdam. (BN, No. 6, [Jan. 13, 1774], p. 26)

For the Leipzig fair of April 1774, Ringmacher, "in der Nicolai-Strasse . . . logirend" advertised (LZ, Apr. 26, 1774, p. 363) "ein neuer thematischer Catalogus à 8 Gr." (obviously the same "2te Theil" announced in Berlin in January), adding that "ein ganz vollständiger aber kostet 1 Thlr." He also listed nine individual works for sale, including two books on how to win the "Lotterie," one on "Cabballistische Tabellen," one entitled "Geheime Punktierkunst und Geomantie," and four music items—"Burmanns kleine Lieder für kleine Mädchen, in Musik gesetzt von J. G. H. *** à 6 Gr.; Grosses, Englische Tänze und Quadrillen für zwey Violinen, Flöten, und Bass. à 8 Gr.; Komische Opern, à 18 Gr.; und Umschläge zu Musicalien, sehr sauber gestochen, à 1 Gr. der Bogen."

A "Dritter thematischer Catalogus von den neuesten Musicalien, a 12 Gr." is advertised as available in Ringmacher's Leipzig lodgings (LZ, May 15, 1775, p. 436). Fourteen other works are listed including music items by Henning, Christian Cannabich, Haueisen, and Karl Joseph Toeschi.

One year later, one can read in the *Leipziger Zeitung* the following typical notice:

> Bey dem Buchhändler Ringmacher von Berlin, in der Nicolai-Strasse zur goldenen-Hand logirend sind diese Messe folgende Neuigkeiten zu haben: Komische Opern, 3r Theil. 18 Gr. Der Goldmacher-Catechismus, 4 Gr. Der Teufels-Beschwörer P. Gasser, 2 Gr. Schreibers venerische Krankheiten, 2te Aufl., 4 Gr. Six Trios di Cannabich, 1 Thlr. 14 Gr. Six Sonates par du Boulay. 1 Thlr. 4 Gr. nebst noch mehrern neuen Musicalien. (LZ, May 6, 1776, p. 428)

For the Jubilate-Messe of 1777 Ringmacher gave his Leipzig residence as "hinter der Nicolai-Kirche in Banquier Fregens Hause, 2 Treppen hoch." The advertisement mentioned seven items, only one of them musical: "Sterkel VI. Sonatas pour le clavecin, à 2 Thlr. 12 Groschen"(LZ, Apr. 28, 1777, p. 390).

In 1778 Ringmacher became involved, with other booksellers, in the sale of a major publication, "Der allgemeinen synchronistischen Weltgeschichte oder Zeitungen aus der alten Welt, von Alexander dem Grossen bis auf den Octavianus Augustus." (BN, No. 10 [Jan. 22, 1778], p. 54; No. 54 [May 5, 1778], p. 278; No. 140 [Nov. 21, 1778], p. 676). He also began to sell sermons by his father (BN, No. 141 [Nov. 24, 1778], p. 680). No music is included in these advertisements.

In the last notice that has been found (BN, Apr. 20, 1779, p. 224), Ringmacher again offers a varied group of items for sale, all nonmusical except for two compositions by Carl David Stegmann. A collection of his father's sermons, with a portrait, is included on the list.

On November 1, 1781, five months after his death in Berlin on June 7, Ringmacher's stock of "Verlags- und Sortimens-Bücher, wie auch Musicalien" from both Berlin and Leipzig was officially auctioned off ". . . den 1sten Decbr. 1781, Nachmittag um 2 Uhr, . . . in der Poststrasse, in des Verstorbenen Laden . . . J. G. Böhme, Königl. Bücher-Auctions-Commissarius" (BN, No. 134 [Nov. 8, 1781], p. 871; notice repeated on Nov. 15 and 29 and on the Dec. 13 and 15). In June, 1782, the bookdealer, Friedrich Maurer announced that he was then established in business "in der Postrasse, in Martinetzschen Hause ehemaligen Ringmacherschen Laden" (BN, No. 67 [June 4, 1782], p. 510).

In summary, it is evident that Ringmacher operated a modest book- and music-selling establishment in Berlin for eleven or twelve years, 1770-81. To judge from the advertisements placed in newspapers in three cities, he maintained a varied and at times esoteric stock of books as well as a wide assortment of music, first in manuscript, and after 1774 also in engraved editions, designed to suit the taste of his clientele. He also made music available on rental. He kept a depot in Leipzig from at least 1772 until his death, taking advantage of the selling opportunities offered by its book fairs. With some rare exceptions, he was not himself a publisher except for his own book and music catalogues. His most important contribution to music history is undoubtedly his one surviving thematic catalogue. While there is no specific evidence that he also sold manuscript copies of music items in his stock at so much per *Bogen*, as did Breitkopf and Thomas,[22] it is entirely possible that he did so. Forkel spoke of him as both "Buchhändler und Verleger von geschriebenen Musicalien"; the term *Verleger* in this period was often also applied to the head of a copying firm (e.g., to Breitkopf and Thomas). It is doubtful that Ringmacher actually published any music other than his own thematic catalogues. The latter were printed from movable type similar in process to that of Breitkopf, but quite different in the design of their individual type segments.

22. See n. 7.

The Ringmacher Thematic Catalogue

ALTHOUGH only one of his thematic catalogues has ever been found, Christian Ulrich Ringmacher published at least three such catalogues and some supplementary lists as well. Newspaper advertisements (documented above) show the following:

1772 I   "Ein ganz vollständiger thematischer Catalogus 22 Gr."
     Ia   The same but "ohne Themas 3 Gr."
     Ib   Verzeichniss of [only] "die neuesten geschriebenen Musicalien . . . wird umsonst ausgegeben"
1773 II   "Ein neuer gedruckter thematischer Catalogus . . . 16 Gr."
1774 IIa ". . . der 2te Theil seines thematischen Catalogi von den neuesten gestochenen und geschriebenen Musicalien für alle Instrumente, welche besonders dieses Jahr in Mannheim herausgekommen sind . . . ist nunmehro . . . fertig geworden, und kostet 8 Gr."

CATALOGO

de'

Soli, Duetti, Trii, Quadri, Quintetti, Partite, de' Concerti e delle Sinfonie

per il

CEMBALO
VIOLINO, FLAUTO TRAVERSO
ed altri Stromenti

che

fi trovano in Manoſcritto nella
Officina muſica

di

CHRISTIANO ULRICO RINGMACHER
Libraio in Berolino.

PLATE II. The title page of the Ringmacher thematic catalogue (1773)

MDCCLXXIII.

IIb "ein neuer thematischer Catalogus ... à 8 Gr. ... [ob-
viously the same as IIa] ein ganz vollständiger aber kostet
1 Thlr" [probably II and IIa sold together].

1775   III   "Dritter thematischer Catalogus von den neuesten Musicalien à 12 Gr."

The sole surviving catalogue is No. II listed above. We can be quite certain of
this because the date on the title page (1773) corresponds to the date of the
newspaper notice.

It contains 112 pages (105 pages with incipits), and 627 incipits by 148
composers. The catalogue is organized by genre and, within each genre, alpha-
betically by composer. The title page (see Plate II and p. 244), in its very wording, its use of the Italian language, and its general layout, is an obvious imitation
of those used by Breitkopf for the sixteen supplements (1766–87) to his six-
part thematic catalogue. Other comparisons are in order. Internally, Ringmacher's organization by genre and then by composer is also very similar to that
of the Breitkopf supplements. The contents of his catalogue may be seen from
the following outline (the number of incipits for each genre is given in parentheses followed by the pages on which they appear):

CEMBALO

Soli a Cembalo (22)	3–6
Duetti a Cembalo (2)	6
Trii a Cembalo (with various instruments) (36)	7–12
Quadri etc a Cembalo (5)	13
Arie a Cembalo (12)	14–15
Concerti a Cembalo (38)	15–22
Opera a Cembalo (15)	22–24
Arie a Cembalo (8)	24–26
Operette tedesche a Cembalo (8)	26–27
Cembalo Soli (6)	27–28
Trii a Cembalo (3)	28
Quadri a Cembalo (2)	29
Concerto a Cembalo (1)	29

VIOLIN

Violino Solo (16)	29–32
Duetti a Violino (3)	32
Trii a Violino (a due Violini con basso) (69)	32–44
Quadri (due Violino, Viola, e Basso) (53)	44–52
Quintetti (Tre Violino, Viola, e Basso) (53)	53
Partite (2)	53
Arie (1)	53
Le Miserere (per il Violino e Basso) (1)	54
Concerti a Violino (17)	54–56

FLUTE

Soli a Flauto (18)	57–59
Duetti a Flauto (10)	60–61
Trii a Flauto (55)	61–70
Partite a Flauto (3)	70–71

Composers in the Ringmacher Catalogue

THERE ARE approximately 150 composers represented in the Ringmacher catalogue, all of whom are listed by their last names only (see Plate III). The following list includes first names in all cases where identification has been possible.

PLATE III. A typical page of the
Ringmacher catalogue

Those Bachs, Bendas, and Grauns that have not as yet been sorted out are entered with a question mark, as are several obscure names, such as Heil, Lizka, Roth, and Ude. A number of works listed in the catalogue as anonymous have been identified and are given here under their rightful names. Following each name is the total number of works (given in parentheses) by that composer. (The forthcoming facsimile edition of the Ringmacher catalogue will provide references justifying the identification of the incipits and, where possible, source references for extant copies of the specific works.)

Anonymous (11)

Abel, Karl Friedrich (9)
Adam, Johann (3)
Agrell, Johann Joachim (8)
Agricola, Johann Friedrich (2)
Aspelmayr, Franz (2)
Aubert (1)

Bach [?] (5)
Bach, Carl Phillip Emanuel (16)
Bach, Johann Christian (9)
Bach, Johann Christoph Friedrich (3)
Beck, Franz (1)
Benda [?] (6)
Benda, Franz (4)
Benda, Georg (1)
Bertram, Balthasar Christian Friedrich (1)
Binder, Christlieb Siegmund (1)
Boccherini, Luigi (6)
Böhm, Gottfried [?] (1)
Breidenstein, Johann Philipp (1)
Brennessel, Franz (3)
Bümler, Georg Heinrich (1)
Burmann, Gottlob Wilhelm (1)

Campioni, Carlo Antonio (16)
Cannabich, Christian (4)
Cirini [= Cirri?] (1)
Cohn, see Kohn
Cramer, Wilhelm (1)

Die durchs Geld erworbene Heyrath (1)
Dietzel, Jean Nicolas (1)
Diezel, see Dietzel
Dittersdorf, Karl Ditters von (2)
Doebbert, Christian Friedrich (1)
Doethel, Nikolaus (2)

Fasch, Carl Friedrich (3)
Feo, Francesco (1)
Filtz, Anton (13)
Fischer, Ferdinand (8)
Fischer, Johann Christian [?] (1)
Förster, Christoph [?] (1)
Fränzl, Ignaz (1)
Frederic (1)

Frenzel, see Fränzl
Freymaurer Lieder (1)

Galuppi, Baldassare (3)
Gavinies, Pierre (2)
Gewey, Carl (1)
Giardini, Felice de (4)
Giraneck, see Jiraneck
Glösch, Carl Wilhelm (1)
Graf, Friedrich Hartmann (7)
Graff, see Graf
Graun [?] (19)
Graun, Carl Heinrich (29)
Graun, Johann Gottlieb (10)
Gros (Gros e Gloesch) (2)
Guerini, Francesco (6)

Händel, Georg Friedrich (1)
Haindl, Johann Sebastian (1)
Hartmann, Christian Karl [?] (1)
Hasse, Johann Adolf (14)
Haydn, Franz Joseph (39)
Heil (1)
Heinichen, David [?] (1)
Hendel, see Händel
Henichen, see Heinichen
Hertel, Johann Wilhem (5)
Hien, Ludwig Christian (1)
Hiller, Johann Adam (5)
Höckh, Carl (2)
Hoffmann, see Hofmann
Hofmann, Leopold (16)
Holzbogen, Johann Georg (1)
Honauer, Leontzi (1)
Houpfeld, see Hupfeld
Hupfeld, Bernard (2)

Ivanschiz, Amandus (3)

Janitsch, Johann Gottlieb (11)
Jiranek, Anton (1)
Josefsky, see Abel
Jvanschiz, see Ivanschiz

Kirmair, Friedrich Joseph (1)
Kirnberger, Johann Philipp (4)
Kleinknecht, Jakob Friedrich (11)
Kloeffler, Johann Friedrich (12)

The catalogue's untitled prefatory note and concluding "Nachricht," both brief, provide clues as to the functioning of the Ringmacher firm and the enterprise of its director. In translation, they read as follows:

[PREFACE]

With great pleasure, I publish herewith, for music lovers, the present thematic catalogue of my music holdings [*Musikalien*] because I see that my small efforts [with his first catalogue] have not turned out to be in vain. I will, therefore, pursue this work with much diligence henceforth and do hereby present my compliments for your future goodwill.

Ringmacher

NACHRICHT

In addition to the symphonies shown here, there is a quantity of four- and six-voice symphonies by almost all possible composers which I have still to catalogue thematically. Also available are music folders [*Umschläge*], printed by copper engraving on large music paper; the cost is 1 Rthlr. per book, but only 16 Gr. on writing paper. Music can also be had on loan, which costs 12 Gr. per month, but not more than one piece at a time may be borrowed. To avoid costs of postage, I will send 6 pieces to nonresidents, but for that there must be prepayment of at least 3 Rthlr. for 3 months, and 5 Rthlr. deposit, which will be returned when one stops borrowing.

The value of the Ringmacher catalogue for authentication and dating may be stated briefly and provisionally thus:

1. The catalogue contains a number of incipits that do not appear in any other eighteenth-century reference source. (A rough comparison with the Breitkopf catalogue, for example, indicates that about three-fourths of the Ringmacher entries are not duplications.) For those incipits that are to be found in other catalogues, old or recent, Ringmacher can provide corroborative evidence of authorship, especially in instances of doubtful or multiple attributions. The Ringmacher catalogue may ultimately prove to have a higher percentage of correct attributions than does the Breitkopf; the latter was based to some extent on sets of incipits sent to Breitkopf in advance by persons, including professional copyists, seeking to sell their wares, while in Ringmacher's case, the music was apparently on hand before he put their incipits in his catalogues.

2. As for its significance as a dating tool, comparison with Breitkopf shows that for the approximately 140 duplicated entries found thus far, Breitkopf's dates are earlier for all but about ten works, sometimes by as much as a decade. This corroborates the already well known significance of the Brietkopf catalogue as a dating tool. However, for the more than four hundred unduplicated works, Ringmacher may, in many instances, provide the only available date.

Conclusion

CHRISTIAN ULRICH RINGMACHER played a modest though vital role in the musical life of his time: modest because of the size of his business and the brevity of its existence, vital because he was part of a process of dissemination without which music would stagnate. In the past two decades many monographs and catalogues have appeared to help document the music publisher's role in this process. The part played by music dealers, copying firms, commission merchants, and so on, has been studied relatively little. Ringmacher was one of hundreds of such dealers plying their trade throughout Europe in the second half of the eighteenth century. His claim to special historical consideration stems from his publication of a thematic catalogue of his wares, a document valuable for purposes of identification, authentication, and dating as well as for our understanding of the process through which music was disseminated.

A SYSTEMATIC
INTRODUCTION TO
THE PEDAGOGY OF
CARL CZERNY
ALICE LEVINE MITCHELL

Carl Czerny (Vienna, 1791–1857) is best known today as the composer of thousands of études for the piano that have been dispensed in doses by generations of piano teachers as though to immunize their pupils against the technical ills lurking within much of the piano music of the nineteenth century. Modern researchers, however, have been showing a renewed interest in Czerny as a reliable witness to and a candid reporter of the appropriate performance of many compositions of Beethoven in particular[1] and a rich original source of early Romantic performance practices in general. In the wake of this increasing scholarly respect for Czerny's contributions to historical perspectives, performing musicians are likewise seeking to revitalize any of his compositions that might show evidence of aesthetic qualities hitherto unnoticed or misunderstood. Considering the well over one thousand numbered works, not to mention the additional unnumbered ones still in manuscript and awaiting perusal,[2] this quest will undoubtedly prove fruitful to some degree. Yet it is safe to assume, after all is said and done, that Czerny's overwhelming contribution to nineteenth-century stud-

---

1. See esp. Czerny, *On the Proper Performance of All Beethoven's Works for the Piano*, ed. Paul Badura-Skoda (Vienna, 1970).

2. A catalogue of Czerny's works through Opus 798 and a listing (as of 1848) of unnumbered works, editions, arrangements, and works in manuscript or in progress appear in the English edition of Opus 600 (see Czerny, *School of Practical Composition* [London, 1848].) This catalogue is extended through Opus 861 in Franz Pazdírek, *Universal-Handbuch der Musikliteratur* (Vienna, c. 1904–10). A brief description of unprinted works and other manuscripts housed in the archives of the Gesellschaft der Musikfreunde is found in Eusebius Mandyczewski, *Zusatz-Band zur Geschichte der K. K. Gesellschaft der Musikfreunde in Wien* (Vienna, 1912).

ies will be recognized most fully in his monuments of pedagogy. In fact, he occupies the position—still unchallenged—of the first musical pedagogue of
modern times.

The broad array of his writings signals an intellect of remarkable versatility, practicality, and "dexterity" such as he sought elsewhere. It also offers a
wealth of data and insights pertaining to such matters as nineteenth-century
concert life, trends in programming, the special requirements for the public performer (as distinguished from the cultivated amateur), the varied styles of improvisation that were considered to be appropriate and that were therefore
eagerly anticipated by audiences of the time, the proprieties of performance in
Beethoven's compositions, and the diverse performing techniques that have
helped to crystalize our comprehension of the different schools—the successive
waves of pianism—in the Vienna of the nineteenth century.

There is indeed hardly a musical subject of general interest or specific necessity that Czerny does not address somewhere in his numerous pedagogical
works, which range in size and scope from the modest to the formidable, from
the merely thorough to the encyclopedic. Aside from the profusion of etudes, the
pedagogical legacy consists of Opus 200, a *Systematic Introduction to Improvisation on the Pianoforte,*[3] Opus 300 (designated by Czerny as a continuation of
Opus 200), *The Art of Preludizing: 120 Examples of Preludes, Modulations, Cadenzas, and Fantasies,* Opus 400, a *School of Fugue-Playing* (dedicated to Felix
Mendelssohn), Opus 500, the *Complete Theoretical and Practical Pianoforte
School* (four volumes), Opus 600, a *School of Practical Composition* (three volumes), and Opus 815, *Umriss der Ganzen Musik-Geschichte bis 1800,* a set of
chronologically organized historical tables that can be considered the prototype
for Arnold Schering's *Tabellen.* One may well be amused by the studied pattern
that emerges from the numbering scheme of his "schools," which, given the
implausibility of happenstance, reveals what may very well be the only discernible vanity in an otherwise remarkably modest individual. (One cannot help but
ponder the possibility of premeditation even in the fact that Opus 815 was
published in the year 1851, though this conjecture probably goes too far.)

There is also his *Exercises on Harmony and Thorough Bass.* Problems of
thorough bass are addressed in a treatise as well as in "letters" on the subject. In
these discussions thorough bass is viewed through the distorting lenses of the
nineteenth century, for the focus had long since shifted from practical procedures
set out for the use of the improvising keyboard accompanist of the eighteenth
century to pedantic presentation of fairly well preserved principles of musical
grammar. Incidentally, the *Letters on Thorough Bass* contain essentially the substance of the treatise on this subject but now simplified, abbreviated, and addressed to ladies, seemingly adhering to a tradition of differentiating between the
sexes in levels of communication. The same distinction can likewise be inferred

3. The present author's English translation and commentary was published by Longman, Inc., in 1983.

from the relationship between Czerny's great pianoforte school and his *Letters to a Young Lady on Playing the Pianoforte.* All the same, since we know that Czerny was an "equal opportunity" piano teacher, it is entirely possible that he was focusing on the amateur of either sex when writing "letters" to "ladies" on subjects of musical importance and focusing on the professional in the works he called "schools."

Today Czerny's études are appreciated for reasons other than their immediate usefulness or original intentions, for they, along with his pedagogical writings, reflect the two new waves of pianism that characterize Viennese musical activities during the early decades of the nineteenth century—the first cresting with Beethoven, Czerny's teacher, and the second with Liszt, Czerny's pupil. In fact, a study of the technical barriers that the études are designed to overcome, of the various levels of student they address, and of the diversity of subject matter regarded as essential for the preparation of the performer bring into sharp focus the critical changes in keyboard technique that determined the future course of the piano's history and literature.

Always hovering over Czerny's études and teaching pieces (a designation even included in some titles)[4] are the new technical horizons of this age of virtuosity, the new technical and expressive possibilities of the nineteenth-century piano, and the recently won role of the pianoforte as the favorite solo instrument for salon as well as public concert hall. For example, his Opus 335, the *Legato and Staccato Exercises,* of which Book I is designated as a sequel to his best-known opus, 299, the *School of Velocity,* is conceived as a direct result of the capabilities of the then modern piano at Czerny's disposal. In this regard he recalls in his memoirs that legato playing was one of the new and important techniques that he had begun studying with Beethoven.[5] His pairing of legato and staccato in the same collection indicates that with the conceptual clarification and subsequent realization of a legato style, a truly staccato, and not merely "non legato," technique emerged as a corollary.

The technical skill required of the virtuoso gave rise to études exploiting chromatic scales with alternate fingerings (Opus 244), études for thirds in all keys (Opus 380), and études for scales in thirds (Opus 245). Studies for the strengthening and improvement of the left hand (Opera 399 and 718)[6] reflect the latter's increasing technical and textural responsibilities generally and its noteworthy release from former bondage as a mere accompaniment. Etudes on embellishments (Opera 151 and 355), on bravura playing (Opus 365), on octaves (Opus 552), and on rapidly repeated notes (throughout the "schools") round out the picture of technical urgencies. Although the opus numbers cited above refer to collections that concentrate exclusively on the individual techniques mentioned, other études and collections explore these as well as other technical difficulties.

4. For example, Opus 268 is entitled *Grande Sonate d'étude* and Opus 92 is a *Toccata ou exercice.*
5. "Recollections from My Life," trans. Ernest Sanders, *The Musical Quarterly* 42 (1956): 302–17.
6. Czerny's Tenth Sonata, Opus 268, can be added to this list.

Virtually no problem that the student pianist, on whatever level, might encounter is left untouched by the meticulous pedagogue. There are very easy studies for small hands (Opus 748) and rather more difficult ones (Opus 749), stylistic études (Opus 785), études in the *brillant* style (Opus 753), études for duet (Opera 239, 495, and 751) and for two pianos (Opus 727). All in all, the diversity and the dimensions of these materials are mind-boggling.

For the researcher the task is to arrange this profusion in some kind of order, a challenge that at times appears insurmountable but is nonetheless irresistible. A profile of the seemingly endless list of works can possibly delineate these truths: that the very notion of *Geläufigkeit* and its myriad of corollary requirements (as exploited in Czerny's *School of Velocity,* Opus 299), crystalize the technical essence of the so-called first Viennese school of pianism; that the virtuoso pyrotechnics that constitute both the notion and the realities of *Fingerfertigkeit* (as exploited in Czerny's *School of Dexterity,* Opus 740) parallel the salient characteristics of the second Viennese school; that the remarkably broadened technical, stylistic, and expressive facets that now represented the *sine qua non* of the Romantic pianist's technique had necessitated a systematic, progressive, and all-encompassing method of building this technique from earliest childhood, above and beyond any other studies that led to a cultivated musician. This last circumstance, perhaps taken for granted nowadays, must have been perceived as rather a novel necessity in Czerny's time, and his comprehension of this situation prompted him to return repeatedly to composing collections of systematic and progressive études for the young. Moreover, the comments in his treatises as well as the problems addressed in many of his "systematic methods" indicate that, for Czerny, the "young" who were the focus of his prolonged and intense interest were envisioned by him mainly as the budding predecessors of blossoming virtuosos.

The pattern of frequent appearances of these new collections in the body of his works, a pattern of consistency which differs remarkably from what appears to be spurts of interest in other forms of composition or other techniques to be exploited, not only suggests something close to an abiding preoccupation on Czerny's part but also exposes one of the richest veins of his genius as pedagogue.

While the building of technique through progressive études and repetitive exercises was the main theme of Czerny's output, it was a systematic study of soloistic fantasylike improvisation that launched his formal career as a musical pedagogue. Czerny was clearly aware that success for the executant musician of his day could be ensured only by the combination of a virtuoso technique and an ability to extemporize before the public. One is even tempted to speculate that his premature retirement as a public performer was not merely the result of his heavy teaching schedule from the time he was fifteen years of age or just a consequence of his poor health. His retirement may very well have been caused as well by his lack of inspiration (or an inability to abandon himself to it during improvisation). For Czerny the very preciseness of his playing, which had earned

him the respect of one such as Beethoven, may have proved incompatible with
the sort of abandonment that was one of the earmarks of successful fantasylike
improvisation.

It is hardly possible to find any program by a professional pianist during
the first half of the nineteenth century that does not include the improvisation
(usually at the end) on either an original or a "given" theme—often one
"given" by the audience. Indeed, the improvisation in fantasy style became the
vehicle for the performer's display of inventiveness, inspiration, and, most important, originality.

Despite Czerny's well-earned reputation for practicality, despite the very
elusive nature of solo improvisation, a subject that most other musicians may
have regarded as unteachable,[7] Czerny nevertheless embarked on his maiden
voyage into formal pedagogy with the Opus 200, *Systematische Anleitung zum
Fantasieren auf dem Pianoforte*. Judged from the pace at which his works were
appearing, Opus 200 was probably written within a year or two after Beethoven's death, but it was not published until 1836. This work had been preceded
by some of his more serious and successful compositions (including nine of his
piano sonatas, of which the first, Opus 7 in A♭, was one of Liszt's favorites to
perform) and a good number of individual études and collections. However,
Opus 200 is the first formal pedagogical essay, complete with "reserved" opus
number, descriptive and prescriptive text, and musical illustrations. Whether
this first attempt exposes a streak of raw courage or just plain foolhardiness on
Czerny's part is a moot consideration. He had responded to this particular necessity in the preparation of the performer in the same manner as he had to all
others that he recognized, namely, with a systematic introduction.

From Opus 200 we learn that the sort of improvisation that earned a
crown of distinction for the virtuoso was born of inspiration and executed spontaneously, "on the spur of the moment." Although these fantasylike improvisations could depart from the more stringent principles of formal construction,
Czerny cautions that they must nevertheless be rational and organized into a coherent totality. Because of its multifaceted nature and its inherent capability of
supplying complete sonorities, the piano above all other instruments is recognized by Czerny as the one on which improvisation can be elevated to the level
of true artistry.

While Czerny's writing style is generally as dispassionate as his études, he
now and then offers lovely descriptions, such as his comparison of a "fantasy
well done" with a "beautiful English garden, seemingly irregular, but full of
surprising variety, and executed rationally, meaningfully, and according to
plan." Should our flights of fancy soar a bit out of control, Czerny provides bal-
last by listing the prerequisite attributes and attainments for improvising,

---

7. Czerny's Opus 200 is the only treatise on fantasylike improvisation during the entire first half of the nineteenth century. André-Ernest-Modeste Grétry's *Méthode simple pour apprendre à préluder* (1802) is retrospective in comparison with Czerny's work.

namely, natural aptitude, a thorough knowledge of theory, and a virtuoso technique. As though aware that many readers might be instantly discouraged by these demands, he adds that they are the necessary prerequisites for those who aim to improvise in public with artistic integrity, but that other "qualified performers" can still profit from the substance of his essay.

Czerny's ideas are now so completely performer-oriented that his differentiation between improvisation and composition (at the beginning of the treatise, and once again in his concluding remarks) implies more of a hiatus between them than seems appropriate, especially for a composer such as he was. This separation of functions and of professions must, at least in part, reflect the thought of his contemporaries, despite the fact that both roles were still often assumed by the same individual. Czerny does admit that fantasy and composition are closely allied, but his remarks imply that they coexist rather than that they are manifestations of one set of attributes. An examination of his musical illustrations, however, clarifies this initially puzzling distinction, for a remarkable number of passages are conceived as patterns of finger activity that are elaborated with virtuoso complexities. In fact, dispersed throughout the essay are comments to the effect that the fingers are not merely agents for the expression of ideas but also the very source of some of them.

The nine chapters of Opus 200 are organized by gradations of difficulty and of artistic sophistication and, in accordance with Czerny's systematic approach, represent the order in which the student must learn the styles and techniques. Therefore, short preludes, more elaborate preludes, embellished fermatas, and (most surprisingly for the twentieth-century musician) cadenzas for concertos are designated by him as essential yet merely preparatory beginnings for artistic, full-fledged improvisation in fantasy style. Thus prepared, the student improviser is led through the catechism of "genuine" extemporizing, beginning with fantasies first on a single theme and then on several themes. These steps are followed by the distinguishing characteristics of and special problems encountered in improvising the potpourri, variations, and fantasies in strict (contrapuntal) and fugal style. The Parnassus of Opus 200 is the improvisation of capriccios.

For each of these categories Czerny both composes musical illustrations and also cites works by other composers (along with his own) as models for further study. Included are references not only to his own contemporaries (Beethoven, Ignaz Moscheles, Ferdinand Ries, Johann Nepomuk Hummel, Luigi Cherubini, Muzio Clementi, Friedrich Wilhelm Kalkbrenner, and Johann Ladislaus Dussek) but also to composers of the recent past (Mozart, Haydn, and C. P. E. Bach) as well as the more distant past (J. S. Bach and Handel). As an indication of Czerny's lack of insularity, these further citations are in themselves commendable; also they reflect the broadening musical horizons of musicians of his time. They are of greatest interest, however, in that they help remove any lingering ambiguities concerning each species of improvisation and the styles associated with it. Moreover, they shed light on how the compositions referred to were actually viewed at that time. Beethoven's Fantasy in G minor, Opus 77, for example, is designated by Czerny as a model for the capriccio, in spite of its title. As examples for further study of the fantasy on a single theme, Czerny cites the Beethoven Fantasy for Chorus and Orchestra, Opus 80, the finale of the Ninth Symphony, and Bach's *Art of the Fugue*. This last reference, particularly, constitutes not a misconception by Czerny but rather a signal to those who know the work by Bach of the sweeping dimensions of the category described as the fantasy on a single theme.

The scope of subject matter that Czerny includes under categories for improvisation and the stylistic caricatures that emerge from his musical illustrations prompt the twentieth-century musician to regard the piano literature of the nineteenth century in a new light—namely, that shed by Czerny's crystalizing of the musical vocabulary of improvisation. The fact that Czerny was not particularly distinguished for originality lends greater importance to his contribution in this instance, for the chances are good that at least some of his illustrations emulate or perhaps even parody the improvisations of his teacher Beethoven (who was "unsurpassed" in this style of playing, according to Czerny himself), as well as those of other great improvisers who impressed him, such as Hummel, Moscheles, and his pupil Liszt.

That Czerny was a past master of stylistic caricature is proved repeatedly in Opus 200. His chapter on the fantasy on a single theme, for example, contains illustrations of various manipulations of a brief theme, not in the abstract style of symphonic development but rather into an allegro as a first movement, a serious adagio, an allegretto grazioso (adorned in gallant style and unadorned), a scherzo presto, a rondo vivace, a polacca, a theme for variations, a fugue and canon, and a waltz, écossaise, and march—representing a tour de force of this kind of art. Further illustrations of this uncanny mastery are found in the keyboard recitative among the "longer and more elaborate" preludes, in the gossamerlike elaborations at fermatas, and in his examples of returns to the final tutti after a concerto cadenza.

From his caricatures we learn to recognize many of the external characteristics of the improvisatory style: the uneven figuration in accompaniments and extended scale passages; the swift shifting from one expressive style to another, with rough edges smoothed out through gradations of tempo and dynamics; thematic material heavily adorned with garlands of embellishments; and unexpected changes in harmonic direction at conveniently unstable diminished-seventh chords.

In Opus 200, Czerny covers the entire musical and circumstantial gamut of improvisation as it was known in his day. He discusses proprieties for shorter and longer preludes and also points out where no prelude at all would be appropriate. He explains that attempting exact repetitions is incompatible with the realities of improvising, since the performer in the heat of the situation can seldom remember the precise details of what has been improvised earlier. He offers tips on how to avoid the embarrassment of being unable to continue in the midst of extemporizing, on how to discreetly try out an unfamiliar instrument, on how to arouse the attention of an audience that is becoming bored, and on what types of improvisations to select (and to avoid) depending on the nature of the audience and other circumstances. In short, no facet of the subject that can conceivably be taught is left untouched.

As a brief postlude to this discussion, a comparison of Czerny's first pedagogical work with his last, Opus 815, brings into sharp focus the extent to which the interests of the times had changed. It is quite difficult to discern whether Czerny's own interests had also changed or whether the chronological, historical, abstract "tables" of his *Umriss* are actually an indication that he was responding to new necessities in precisely the same manner as always—with a "systematic introduction." The latter possibility seems more likely. What, in 1851, could have been a more systematic introduction to the then new field of music history than a set of historical tables?

JOSEPH W. DREXEL
AND HIS MUSICAL LIBRARY

SUSAN T. SOMMER

THAT MUSIC AND CIVILIZATION form a fragile but inextricable web was a lesson often heard in the seminars of Paul Henry Lang. A corollary of this axiom, that great libraries are a means of preserving that web and bringing the past into the future, was implicit in a Columbia education. A great library, in turn, depends for its development on generations of individuals—men and women whose taste, means, and concern have contributed to the particular collection of books and written materials preserved there. It may be instructive therefore, to examine one such person whose private collection has had a profound effect on the musical resources of the past available in New York today.

Although it is not yet a century old, The New York Public Library includes one of the world's most comprehensive collections of music and music literature, in the research collections established by the Astor, Lenox, and Tilden Foundations in 1895. The foundation for the library's Music Division was laid in the mid-nineteenth century in the extraordinary music library assembled by Joseph William Drexel, the only American philanthropist of his time to interest himself in music collecting. Who was Joseph Drexel, what world did he come from, and what was the nature of the collection he bequeathed to New York?

The nineteenth century in America was an age of expansion. The frontier was pushed westward, while at home the industrial revolution created new products, new markets, and new demands. The new industries needed capital, and great houses of investment banking arose to serve them. In this rapidly expanding economy there were opportunities for enterprising men to acquire great personal fortunes. One thinks immediately of John Jacob Astor, the fur trader who at his death in 1848 was the wealthiest man in the United States, J. Pierpont Morgan, the most powerful of bankers, Andrew Carnegie, who rose from humble beginnings to amass a fortune in rails and steel, and many others.

Making money, however, was not enough for most of these men; they had also to spend it. Hard-headed businessmen became connoisseurs of art, transforming vast sums of money into paintings, books, precious furniture, and other treasures. Some of the most valuable collections now available to the public, the Morgan Library and the Frick Museum, for example, were once the personal property of these capitalist entrepreneurs.

Among the most powerful dynasties profiting from America's expanding economy was the Drexel family of Philadelphia.[1] Founded by a former portrait painter, Francis Martin Drexel, the Drexel banking interests were furthered by his three sons, Francis, Anthony, and finally Joseph William, a man whose cultural and philanthropic interests outweighed his business ones and whose music collection, the largest and most significant in America, eventually came to The New York Public Library.

Francis Martin Drexel, born in 1792, was the son of an Austrian merchant who encouraged his son's artistic interests by sending the boy to Italy to study art and languages. When financial reverses during the Napoleonic wars ruined his family, young Francis traveled about Europe, supporting himself by painting portraits. In 1817 he set sail for America, landing in Philadelphia, where he remained for ten years, painting, teaching, and establishing himself in the community. In 1826, married and with two infant sons, Drexel quarreled with his brother-in-law, and leaving his family behind, set off for South America. During the next decade he traveled extensively, painting, making friends—he was aparently a most congenial man—and demonstrating his business ability by collecting a considerable amount of capital through trading in the money market.

Business triumphed over art, and after a short period with his own brokerage firm in Louisville, Kentucky, Francis Martin returned to Philadelphia to establish the firm that was eventually to become the internationally known investment bankers, Drexel & Co. Securities and currency in the United States were at this time in a chaotic condition, and Drexel's connections and experience in matters of exchange put him in a good position to capitalize on this situation. Loans made to the government during the Mexican War and resourceful banking during the Gold Rush consolidated the financial position of the house.

From the beginning the elder Drexel trained his sons in the intricacies of banking and the value of hard work. "No one in his employ worked longer or

1. Chief sources for the history of the Drexel family are Edward Hopkinson, *Drexel & Co. over a Century of History* (New York, 1952); Drexel & Co., Philadelphia, *A New Home for an Old House* (Philadelphia, 1927); Will Bowden, "Anthony Joseph Drexel," "Francis Martin Drexel," and "Joseph William Drexel," *Dictionary of American Biography* 3 (1930): 455–57; Drexel Institute of Technology, *Service in Memory of Anthony J. Drexel* (Philadelphia, 1896); Katherine Burton, *The Golden Door: The Life of Katherine Drexel* (New York, 1957). For further information about Joseph Drexel, see the *National Cyclopedia of American Biography* 2 (1899): 366.

harder hours than his three boys," says a memoir of Drexel & Co. "When closing time came, it was the employees who went home; Mr. Drexel and his sons remained at their counters and desks."[2] In 1847, when his two oldest sons were twenty-three and twenty-one, the father took them into the firm as partners. Anthony, the second of these, was the real genius of the family, the one who was to pilot the firm to greatness in the second half of the century.

Joseph William, Drexel's youngest son, born in 1833 and thus seven years Anthony's junior, seems never to have been as thoroughly involved in banking as his older brothers. After a clerking apprenticeship with the firm, Joseph went abroad to continue his education and to establish contacts with European bankers whose interests coincided with those of Drexel & Co.

There is no doubt that these travels gave Joseph a command of languages and a cosmopolitan taste in culture. The whole family was musical; Anthony's tastes included "a strong inclination to art, especially music,"[3] while Francis built a pipe organ in his front hall for the enjoyment of his family. But Joseph, of whom it was said "there was scarcely a musical instrument on which he could not perform,"[4] was surely the most devoted to this art, and it was probably in the brilliant musical atmosphere of the mid-century continental courts and salons that his taste was formed.

Returning home, Joseph served for two years, from 1861 to 1863, with a branch of the family bank in Chicago, coming back to the headquarters in Philadelphia following the death of his father. In 1865 he married Lucy Wharton, a girl from Philadelphia society, and three daughters were born in the three succeeding years.[5] In 1869 Joseph went to Paris to represent the firm in the newly merged Drexel, Harjes & Co., maintaining a regular liason between Philadelphia and the European banking community.

In 1871 a friend and colleague of the Drexel family, the London banker Junius S. Morgan, was anxious to establish his promising son J. Pierpont in a profitable partnership. Anthony Drexel was equally anxious to have a New York representative. He called Pierpont to Philadelphia, and in one evening, with a contract consisting of a few figures scribbled on the back of an envelope, the firm of Drexel, Morgan & Co. came into being. Joseph and his family moved to New York to join the new firm, but now as before Joseph took a back

2. Drexel & Co., New Home, 39.

3. Hopkinson, 23

4. National Cyclopedia 2: 366.

5. The Drexels had four daughters: Catherine, who married Charles Penrose and who later donated an additional fund to The New York Public Library for the acquisition of current music materials; Lucy, who married Eric P. Dahlgren, brother of John (see below), and settled in St. Paul; Elizabeth, first married to John Dahlgren and widowed shortly after the birth of their son Jack, and whose later unhappy marriage to fortune hunter, possible transvestite, and darling of New York and Newport society, Harry Lehr, is related in her King Lehr and the Gilded Age (Philadelphia, 1935); and Josephine, mentioned only in Leslie's History of the Greater New York (New York, n.d.), 3: 114. The extent of the fortune Drexel left his family can be measured by a report of Elizabeth Lehr to the effect that, besides assuming "household expenses," she could allow her second husband $25,000 annually as spending money (King Lehr, 42).

seat in the direction of the business. A sound conservative investor, he built up his own fortune considerably, but he lacked the dynamism and drive that were to bring the younger Morgan to the forefront of his profession.

Six years later, in 1877, Joseph William Drexel retired from active business concerns at the age of forty-four. Freed from these responsibilities, Drexel devoted himself to philanthropy and numerous cultural activities. His musical interests found an outlet in the Philharmonic Society of New York, of whose governing board he was president from 1881 to 1888. He also became a director of the newly formed Metropolitan Museum of Art, and formed a distinguished collection of etchings which he later presented to that museum. Other cultural institutions with which he was connected included the Metropolitan Opera, the Academy of Natural Sciences, the American Geographical Society, and the New York and Saratoga historical societies. A close friend of General Ulysses S. Grant, he gave the ex-president the cottage at Mount MacGregor where Grant subsequently died.

In addition to his great interest in cultural activities, Drexel shared with his contemporaries an impulse toward philanthropy. His benevolent enterprises took several forms. The most ambitious of these was his establishment of two model communities in Maryland and Michigan, which made modest farms available to buyers at reasonable prices. On each tract Drexel also provided a school, a meeting house and music hall, and some light industry. In New Jersey Drexel started a proto–job corps, taking from fifteen to twenty unemployed men at a time and feeding, clothing, and instructing them in farming until they found employment. Two distinct failures were Drexel's establishment of free coffeehouses for the poor, an enterprise on which he lost $15,000 because nobody ever came, and the distribution of free coal tickets, a project that was thwarted by bureaucratic corruption. Other charitable efforts with which he associated himself were the Society for the Improvement of the Condition of the Poor, the Cancer Hospital Society, of which he was treasurer, and various enterprises to aid prisoners and their families.

Joseph William Drexel died during the blizzard of 1888 at the relatively early age of fifty-five, from heart trouble and Bright's disease. By the terms of his will his music collection was to go to the Lenox Library in New York, "on the express condition that the said trustees of the Lenox Library shall sign and deliver an agreement to keep the same separated from all other books or collection of books, and to preserve the same in separate shelves or cases to be labeled *Drexel Musical Library*."[6] In the event the Lenox Library could not meet these requirements, the collection was to go to the Astor Library, or thence under the same conditions to the Mercantile Library of the City of Philadelphia.

The trustees of the Lenox Library voted to accept the bequest on June 7,

6. New York Public Library, Astor, Lenox & Tilden Foundations, *Book of Charters, Wills, Deeds, and Other Official Documents* (New York, 1905), 66.

1888. An alphabetical catalogue of the book portion of the library was published as *Lenox Library List XI*, but apparently nothing much happened to the collection until the Lenox and Astor libraries consolidated with the Tilden Trust to form The New York Public Library in 1895. Then Drexel's books and music were sorted, arranged according to the new Billings classification scheme, and assigned permanent numbers from 1 to 6013. These numbers, some of which represent several titles once bound together, signify a fixed location in the collection, since by terms of the will nothing can be added or taken from the Drexel Collection. Each volume bears a bookplate reading "Drexel Musical Library." Much of the collection was rebound in uniform red buckram in 1939, but many valuable old bindings were retained. The collection has been stored together, following Drexel's wishes, first in the main stacks of the Forty-second Street library, then in a small basement room in that building, and finally in more spacious, air-conditioned stacks in the Special Collections of the Music Division in the library's building at Lincoln Center.

The story of how the eponymous Drexel assembled his musical library must be pieced together from various sources. On the whole, Drexel seems to have relied on concentrated bursts of acquisition, buying whole libraries or bidding heavily at important sales. It seems likely that the nucleus of Drexel's collection was formed by the library of Henry F. Albrecht, a German musician who had come to the United States in 1848 with a group of his fellow countrymen determined to succeed as a resident orchestra.[7] Calling itself the Germania Society, the orchestra tried valiantly to introduce Beethoven and Mendelssohn to audiences in Boston, Baltimore, and Philadelphia, but was often reduced to playing popular Auber overtures and the light dances the populace of these cities demanded. After the orchestra disbanded in 1854, Albrecht, a former viola and clarinet player, settled in Philadelphia, where the younger Drexel was able to purchase his collection.

The library Drexel acquired from Albrecht was an impressive one, especially for an itinerant musician. In 1854, when he was in Newport, Rhode Island, Albrecht had written out a catalogue of the books in his collection, dividing them up by language.[8] Numbering some 477 titles in 661 volumes, the library was particularly strong in eighteenth-century theory; it contained works by most of the important German writers of the day—Friedrich Wilhelm Marpurg, Johann Mattheson, Johann Friedrich Reichardt, Johann Christoph Kellner, and Daniel Gottlob Türk. Although Albrecht's copies of C. P. E. Bach's *Versuch über die wahre Art das Clavier zu spielen* of 1753 and Johann Walther's *Musicalisches Lexicon* of 1732 qualify as rare books today, Albrecht owned few early or unusual books for his time, Athanasius Kircher's monu-

---

7. H. Earle Johnson, "The Germania Musical Society," *The Musical Quarterly* 39 (1953): 75–93; Henry Albrecht, *Skizzen aus dem Leben der Musik-Gesellschaft Germania* (Philadelphia, 1869).

8. Henry Albrecht, "Alphabetisch geordnetes Verzeichnis einer Sammlung musikalischer Schriften," manuscript (Newport, R.I., 1854).

mental *Musurgia universalis* (1650) being perhaps an exception. English books were also well represented, for Albrecht continued to collect contemporary publications throughout his active musical life. We possess no index of the music that Albrecht passed on to Drexel; however, it seems certain that a good proportion of the many early nineteenth-century chamber works, the Beethoven and Mozart scores, and the popular piano arrangements now in the collection stemmed from this source.

After acquiring Albrecht's library, Drexel felt, with good reason, that his collection was weak in the area of French sources, and he remedied this deficiency by buying another library, that of Dr. René LaRoche, a distinguished Philadelphia physician of French parentage.[9] This was undoubtedly the source of the Berlioz writings and of the works by Rousseau, Rameau, André Grétry, and François-Henri-Joseph Castil-Blaze that grace the Drexel Collection today.

In 1869 Joseph Drexel published the first part of a never completed catalogue of his collection.[10] The preface, written in Drexel's somewhat rhetorical German, states that he is issuing the work at the demand of many friends of music who, having heard that he possessed the most complete and valuable music collection in America, are anxious to learn just what the collection contains. Part I—all that was ever published—is a list of writings on music. Preceded by a tabular breakdown by language and subject very similar to the one in Albrecht's earlier manuscript, the catalogue reveals an impressive and well-rounded collection of books. Within two years Drexel had compiled lists of the manuscripts and the music in his library as well, but the move to New York and the pressure of additional duties apparently interfered with his plans to publish them.[11]

A comparison of these catalogues with the Drexel Collection today shows that the library Drexel passed on to posterity was substantially formed by 1870 —at least in terms of volume and direction. But even though there are some very fine items—for example, a one-page sketch for Beethoven's quartet Opus 18, No. 2, Franchino Gafurio's *De harmonia* (1518), Morley's 1608 edition of the *Plaine and Easy Introduction,* and letters of Haydn, Weber, Mendelssohn, and Liszt—the collection still lacked the jewels that would make it shine with international luster for years to come.

The opportunity for Drexel to acquire these treasures arose in 1877, a year of tremendous activity on the collector's part. Several sales enriched his library, but unquestionably Drexel's finest hour came in July, 1877, at the auction of

---

9. LaRoche (1795–1872) was also a good amateur musician. Among other accomplishments, he conducted the first American performance of Haydn's Mass No. 3 with orchestra in Philadelphia (see his entry in the *Dictionary of American Biography* 6 [1930]: 3–4).

10. Joseph William Drexel, *Catalogue of Jos. W. Drexel's Musical Library,* Part I, *Musical Writings* (Philadelphia: King & Baird, 1869).

11. Joseph William Drexel, "Catalogue of a Collection of Autograph Letters, Documents, and Music" and "Catalogue of Music for the Church, Theatre, Concert Room & Chamber," manuscripts (Philadelphia, 1871).

the library of Edward Francis Rimbault, English antiquarian and collector of note.[12] Rimbault's vast library—2359 lots in a four day sale—reflected its owner's enthusiasm for early English music, a field he had championed in his writing, editing, and lecturing throughout his life. In a generation of distinguished collectors, Rimbault was still outstanding. Among the treasures he owned were a number of remarkable manuscripts from the late sixteenth and early seventeenth centuries: John Gamble's Commonplace Book of some 250 English songs; the Sambrooke Book of madrigals and motets, an anthology we now know to have been scored by Francis Tregian, the incarcerated assembler of the Fitzwilliam Virginal Book; the Mulliner Book of early English keyboard music by John Redford, William Blitheman, Thomas Tallis, and others; also two later unnicknamed collections of music for the virginals; a superb set of part books with music by Byrd, Bull, the Ferraboscos, and Orlando Gibbons; and over two dozen other manuscripts containing music from the same general period.[13]

Rimbault's collection of printed materials included unique copies of parts from Thomas Morley's *First Booke of Consort Lessons* (1599) and Philip Rosseter's *Lessons for Consort* (1609);[14] the sole remaining copy of the engraved *Parthenia In-violata* (1615),[15] and numerous prints of John Playford's seventeenth-century song anthologies and instruction manuals. Among the other sale lots were such extraordinary items as number 593, a group of three incunabula —Gafurio's *Theorica musica* (1492), his *Practica musica* (1496), and the *Elementorum musicalium* (1496) of Faber Stapulensis—and number 1011, a copy of the *Balet comique de la royne* by Balthasar da Belgiojoso, with the autograph of Ben Jonson, a former owner.

Drexel's agent at the sale was the future bibliographer of Americana, Joseph Sabin, a fellow Philadelphian who had established himself as a distinguished and effective European representative for several American book collectors. Sabin bid hard and long, and when the sale was over he had acquired 281 lots for Joseph Drexel, among them virtually all the recognizable treasures in addition to a wealth of contemporary literature. Only the Mulliner Book escaped his grasp; and while Sabin had acquired the Sambrooke Book for £21, his rival W. H. Cummings had to bid up to £82 to secure this handsome keyboard manuscript.

12. The story of the sale can be read in *The Musical Times* 18 (1877): 427–28, and A. Hyatt King, *Some British Collectors of Music* (Cambridge, 1963), 62. A marked copy of the *Catalogue of the Valuable Library of the Late Edward Francis Rimbault . . . which will be Sold at Auction by Sotheby, Wilkinson & Hodge, July 31, 1877* (London, 1877) has the shelfmark Drexel 1012.

13. Further bibliographical details about the manuscripts purchased by Drexel, including citations to later literature, can be found in Susan T. Sommer, "Drexel Collection," *Die Musik in Geschichte und Gegenwart* 15: cols. 1846–49.

14. Described in Carleton Sprague Smith's Foreword to *The First Book of Consort Lessons Collected by Thomas Morley, 1599 & 1611,* reconstructed and ed. Sydney Beck (New York, 1959), xi–xiv.

15. Published in facs., *Parthenia In-violata* (New York, 1961).

In the case of the Rimbault sale, a marked catalogue in the Drexel Collection lets us follow the dramatic progress of Drexel's purchases. It is harder to know what he may have acquired from the distinguished library of Edmond de Coussemaker, but the presence of two volumes bearing the historian's book plate—a lovely 1516 edition of Aristoxenos and a copy of Vincenzo Galilei's *Dialogo* (1581) with contemporary annotations—demonstrate Drexel's participation in the Brussels sale of April 17–20, 1877.[16] The same year also saw a Sotheby sale on July 24, at which Drexel instructed Sabin to "pay *fair* prices for books marked" in the catalogue of H. A. Ouvry's library that he had supplied,[17] and several other minor auctions where catalogues in Drexel's library indicate his participation.

Since Drexel retired in 1876, one might expect that the decade before his death in 1888 would have seen even more dramatic developments in his library, but such was not the case. After the concentrated buying of 1877, Drexel seems not to have continued his collecting in any systematic way. The last burst of recorded activity took place in 1880, when Drexel paid his New York dealer, F. W. Christern, $320.97 for fifty items from the Munich antiquarian Ludwig Rosenthal's *Catalogue XXVI*, over half of which were rare music books, among them Ludovico Fogliani's *Musica theorica* (1526) and Giovanni Terzi's *Intavolatura di liuto* (1593).[18] Several volumes of more peripheral musical interest from the same source, among them the famous medieval Latin dictionary of Charles Du Cange (1681) and a particularly handsome copy of *Margarita philosophica* (1503), also ended up in Drexel's Musical Library.

Certainly Drexel no longer bought contemporary books or music in any number. One has to search hard to find 1880s imprints in his collection, and those that exist—works by Frédéric Louis Ritter and William Smyth Rockstro, for example—may have been gifts from the authors. Although Drexel attended the opera regularly—on Saturday afternoons with his daughters and on fashionable Monday evenings with his wife—and though from 1880 to 1888 he was president of the Philharmonic Society, he did not buy the new music that he heard there. Although the Philharmonic played Dvořák, Bruckner, Brahms, Saint-Saëns, and Philipp Scharwenka, only the first symphony by Saint-Saëns is represented in Drexel's library. He bought librettos but not scores for *Die Meistersinger, Die Walküre,* and *Carmen,* and nothing at all for Arrigo Boïto's *Mephistophele* and Karl Goldmark's *Königin von Saba,* which were popular with the New York public. Rossini, Bellini, Donizetti, Halévy, Meyerbeer, and Spohr had earlier found a place on his shelves; for Liszt and Schumann the piano arrangements predominate over the larger scores.

Drexel, a serious man with a sense of responsibility about his wealth, de-

16. Drexel's library includes a catalogue of the sale as Drexel 956.
17. Drexel 909.
18. Drexel 1015, which is a copy of *Bibliotheca musica, theatralis, saltatoria: Catalogue XXVI* (Munich, 1880), contains a manuscript bill, from Christern to Drexel, dated June 19, 1880.

voted long hours to his philanthropic work. However, he did not lose interest or pride in his musical library. Correspondence with the American music historian Frédéric Louis Ritter reveals that Drexel was happy to share his own knowledge and ready to lend the writer books from his collection (which Ritter was ungraciously slow to return).[19] Perhaps, had he lived longer, Drexel would have returned to the development of the musical library he had assembled.

The Drexel Musical Library has withstood the test of time. In the 1980s scholars and students daily request items from the century-old collection. Later acquisitions by The New York Public Library have enriched areas where Drexel laid the foundations for significant collecting—theory, Elizabethan and Jacobean music, and early nineteenth-century opera. New generations are benefiting from the old. Meanwhile, Drexel's bust, looking like a bearded Roman senator in a white marble toga, gazes benevolently down on the readers of his collection, adding an old-fashioned note to the austerely modern reading rooms at Lincoln Center.[20]

If Joseph Drexel was not the best-known collector and philanthropist of his day, it was because he had many rivals. In the field of music, however, he is outstanding as the only American collector of note. He bought at a time when treasures were still available, and musicians and scholars will always be grateful to him for bringing together such a rich and rewarding collection.

19. Correspondence between Drexel and Ritter in the Special Collections, Vassar College Library, Poughkeepsie, N.Y., and posthumous correspondence regarding return of the books in the Music Division of The New York Public Library. (I am indebted to Professor Mary Jane Corry of the State University of New York at New Paltz for the former information.)
20. Drexel's marble bust was executed by J. Q. A. Ward, one of the foremost American sculptors of the late nineteenth century.

TCHAIKOVSKY AS
A TEACHER

ALFRED MANN

IN A DISCUSSION of nineteenth-century musical thought, Paul Henry Lang addresses himself to a phenomenon that has dominated the musical scene well into our time. He describes the beginnings of a modern phase in the teaching of composition and points out that "the number of non-professionals advised by Mattheson and the other eighteenth-century theoretical writers reached such proportions as made detailed personal instruction impossible, calling for class and mass instruction"; and he observes that the respected teachers of the nineteenth century taught "a métier, not an art."[1]

What renders this fundamental change in artistic standards complex is that it involved the active interest of the great composers. Beethoven welcomed the change from Haydn's to Albrechtsberger's tutelage because of its methodical approach, and Schubert sought to fill gaps that his studies under Salieri had left by turning to Sechter.

This situation established a new norm in the relationship of student and teacher of composition, a norm marked by the inferior stature of the teacher; the association of Wagner and Weinlig and that of Marxsen and Brahms serve as further outstanding examples. Yet when Beethoven called Emanuel Aloys Förster his "old master," he spoke of a mentor who was no mere theorist but an experienced composer whose versatility in the idiom of the string quartet and whose neighborly advice—he and Beethoven had temporarily lived in the same Viennese apartment house—provided the latter with decisive guidance.[2]

1. Lang, *Music in Western Civilization* (New York, 1941), 973–74.
2. See Alexander Wheelock Thayer, *Life of Beethoven,* ed. Elliot Forbes (Princeton, 1964), 1: 262.

The time-honored "actual practice, under the direction of active masters in their workshops,"[3] to which Lang refers by way of comparison to the traditional instruction in the fine arts, was not completely gone, as is perhaps best shown by the example of Mendelssohn's study with Zelter. What had changed—and what had prompted the change in artistic training—was the workshop. In the environment of the Berlin Singakademie a commitment to the past took precedence over one to the present, and this influence made itself felt in a guarded and self-conscious attitude that began to becloud the spontaneous creative expression. As the separation between the roles of composer and interpreter grew, apprenticeship in the traditional sense became the exception; its last stronghold, curiously but not surprisingly, was in the aristocracy. Beethoven refused to accept any composition students, with one notable exception—Archduke Rudolph.

One of the most interesting vestiges of the old system by which an eminent composer served as teacher for a novice in the profession is the correspondence of Tchaikovsky with Vladislav Albertovich Pakhulsky, the son-in-law of Tchaikovsky's benefactor Nadezhda von Meck. Between the years 1883 and 1891, Pakhulsky sent various samples of his writing to Tchaikovsky, and in a series of letters that have remained unpublished the aging composer made detailed comment accompanied by copious music examples.

These letters are preserved in the Library of Congress. Acquired from the Rachmaninoff estate in 1968, they were originally bought from a descendent of Pakhulsky in Paris, and the Russian text was transcribed, as is noted in the Library of Congress folder, by A. V. Fessenko in January, 1969, and translated into English by Robert V. Allen of the library's Slavic and Central European Division. Jay Leyda of New York University, in consultation with Georg Knepler of the University of Berlin, examined the entire material during the past decade, adding English translations of two further Tchaikovsky letters owned by the Heinemann Foundation, New York. I am indebted to Professors Leyda and Knepler for making their copies available to me as well as to my colleague Professor Alexander Wieber of the University of Rochester for advice on details of the original text.

A NINETEENTH-CENTURY document of unusual quality emerges from Tchaikovsky's remarks. Asked for advice, he doubtless felt an obligation to comply with the request, but it is also evident that his artistic interest and sympathy were aroused. Much of his comment shows the voice of the authoritative master of the craft. Nevertheless, there is a pervading tone of perplexity in these letters, due not only to the personality and the increasing depression of the composer, but also to the problematic nature of the didactic situation that more and more seems to have entered his awareness.

3. Lang, 974.

The letters, dated mostly by both the Julian and the Gregorian calendars, begin with an extensive exposé written April 10/22, 1883, in Paris. As becomes explicit later in the correspondence, Tchaikovsky had known the young man's work for more than five years, but it was apparently at this point that a somewhat formal situation of instruction was established. Pakhulsky had submitted to him a choice of compositions representing various genres; together with an overture, a march, and a quartet, however, he had also sent him some fugues. Were the latter included at Tchaikovsky's suggestion and because of his skeptical view of the young composer's technique? Tchaikovsky goes to the heart of the matter:

> Vladislav Albertovich! First of all, I will talk with you about your contrapuntal works. What is counterpoint? It is a word that sounds loud, frightening, and the ignorant imagine that it is some sort of musical hocus-pocus.

He then defines counterpoint, saying that actually nothing could be simpler. Taking his point of departure from the exclusive use of consonances (unison, fifth, third, sixth, octave—in the tradition represented by Fux, Tchaikovsky omits the fourth), he proceeds to "more complex situations, arising from melodic and rhythmic animation of the voices"; here dissonances enter, as he explains, in two ways: (1) on the accented beat, as syncopation, "known in the modern school as suspension"; and (2) on the unaccented beat, as passing or auxiliary tones.

> All these dissonances give to contrapuntal texture an inexpressible beauty and life, but only on the condition that they are naturally resolved into consonance. It was long before any other combinations of musical sound were tolerated. Eventually citizenship was given to the chord of the dominant seventh, and it grew so independent that its intervals were given the significance of consonances.

It becomes clear that Tchaikovsky uses *consonance* here in the sense of *tonal function*. He adds that the components of the dominant seventh chord should be used within strict limits, "always observing the rules of resolution"; yet he takes his extension of the basic contrapuntal law one step further:

> When counterpoint crossed over from the realm of vocal music into that of instrumental music, little by little, chromaticism and total freedom of modulation penetrated harmony. Beyond this, counterpoint cannot, and must not, go.

It is interesting both to find Tchaikovsky viewing the practice of his time from the basis of the principles of strict counterpoint and to see where he draws the line. He dismisses the conflicts arising from this view and holds to the absolute rule of consonance.

> Nevertheless, in our times we occasionally encounter contrapuntal works in which the basic law of counterpoint is completely ignored. You can find dissonances in them in abundance, unprepared, unresolved, and even enjoying such honor and significance as if the whole thing were based on them—as if natural consonant combinations were an unavoidable evil which the composer would willingly skirt if possible. I do not say that your counterpoint is an example of such extraordinary prevalence of dissonances,[4] but you are not far from it. At each step, as I go through your fugues, I come upon such clashing of voices as to pass my understanding.

Tchaikovsky speaks of a counterpoint for the eye, not for the ear, and he refers to the "inner ear" that constantly demands that the listener "stop to seek what *shadow* of chord had brought together such voices seemingly alien to each other —and at times even the stop does not help."

More intricate is Tchaikovsky's criticism of the student's fugal structure. As he uncovers fundamental weaknesses of execution, he also substantiates his earlier objections, namely, that the prevalence of dissonance serves to hide a lack of skill and structural logic. And he blames, as well as recommends, the model of the academic fugue.

> It is only your fugues that cannot be considered successful. They are all so terribly long, with so many interludes and inserted episodes which at some points are too bare of modulation, i.e., too dependent upon the tonic, and at others go so far to the other extreme that they eventually have to return to the tonic in an unnatural manner and end abruptly and without preparation. . . . How pleased I should be to find among your fugues just one, one small one, with no more than three expositions, but bright, clear and simple, with irreproachable part writing (I have even had to mark many *fifths* and *octaves!*), with a well-balanced form—in short, the sort of fugue befitting a young man trying to purify his style and learning to build solid, sound forms from modest materials in admissible and positively beautiful consonant combinations. . . . The fugue with an inversion of the theme (in F major) may seem unarguable in theory, but there, too, I came upon *eleven dissonances in a row,* followed by one accidentally consonant chord, and then four more *dissonances*—in all, a sequence of sixteen configurations of sound with only one chord to rest the ear!!!!

Tchaikovsky's critique is modified by one sentence which, at the same time, summarizes his stand:

---

4. Tchaikovsky's text reads "consonances" here, evidently due to an error.

Of course, your fugues contain some very nice, piquant and pretty passages and details, and I certainly do not want to say that everything, without exception is bad—but I do wish that you would hurry up and learn to write with dexterity and simplicity.

The latter remarks—and a comparison between them and Tchaikovsky's subsequent comments—show that he is compelled to speak from two different levels—that of the instructor of conventional theory and that of the eminent composer. And while in the role of the former, he speaks with some *engagement* —even in later instances—it is evident that his role as an adviser of the young colleague does not come into its own until the discussion moves from studies to compositions. In the end he himself unwittingly draws the distinction between teacher and composer as he defers judgment on matters of basic technique; he says that he has placed question marks at numerous spots, but that the marked places are far from being the only ones that "looked strange and incomprehensible"—in fact, had he marked them all, he would have splattered the manuscript so as to make it unrecognizable—and he asks whether Pakhulsky's teacher was at fault for guiding him without sufficient severity, or whether his own nature was such that elasticity, wholesome vitality, clarity, and simplicity in part writing would come to him only with difficulty. Thus, the discussion of fugal studies ends at an impasse, and Tchaikovsky moves on to Pakhulsky's compositions proper.

Some of these had evidently either appeared in print or were about to be published at the time they were submitted to Tchaikovsky (see pp. 286-88 below, letters 4 and 5), but this does not seem to apply to the pieces discussed in this initial letter.

Regarding the first of them, an overture, Tchaikovsky writes:

Much of its music is very nice; for example, the first theme (in Mendelssohn's spirit) is very much to my liking. The transition from the first theme to the second is too clumsy. You say too much with the first theme, all at once and fully, adding even a quasi-cadential turn [Example 1] and then, as if it were something quite new, you begin the second theme. Of course, this is possible, for in music everything is possible, but if your aim was to write an overture in classical form—then this was a mistake.

EXAMPLE 1

As Tchaikovsky begins to devote his attention to general matters of style, he nevertheless deals with specific technical detail. He says that the end of the piece, being "influenced by Wagner," would be considerably more effective if its orchestration were not so heavy as to blur the main idea. He concludes that Pakhulsky is not sufficiently versed in matters of orchestration and strongly advises him to practice writing for small orchestra, i.e., without trombones and with sparing use of trumpets. He remonstrates that there are passages that are virtually impossible to play and points out that in some cases notes not contained in the ranges of the respective instruments are involved. His principal objection is to an excess of detail that would frustrate even the closest attention and deprive the orchestral sound of power and clarity. An earlier formulation of Tchaikovsky's criticism returns here:

> Won't you be disappointed to hear the performance of passages that are beautiful for the eye but inadequate for the ear? Yet this is the lot of young composers. Very few are endowed with such a flair for orchestration that they show mastery without study.

The second piece of the group, a march, offers fewer problems in this respect. Tchaikovsky comments that the orchestration is here "much better," but he singles out a number of spots for a detailed critique. He points out how crude it would sound to have two trumpets play the theme (Example 2) and how

EXAMPLE 2

awkward the distribution of parts would sound in another passage (Example 3).

EXAMPLE 3

Why, he asks, should the bass part be played solo by the first bassoon two octaves above the double bass—one could not hear it (and he adds, "and if one could, would it be desirable?"). A somewhat related problem is the combination of trombones playing a high and a low E while the bass instruments of the string section play D and D♯ on the respective beats (Example 4). Tchaikovsky remarks, "In the deliberate tempo of the march this is very unattractive."

Turning to the trio of the march, which is "good, but terribly short," he takes exception to the distribution of chord tones in the brass parts for the final

EXAMPLE 4

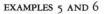

cadence. He quotes what appears in the score (Example 5) and then writes out what the total sound should be (Example 6)—"When the whole orchestra is playing, the middle must be full."

EXAMPLES 5 AND 6

Tchaikovsky's reaction to the last piece in the group is in remarkable contrast to his appraisal of Pakhulsky's qualifications for orchestration and part writing—particularly since that piece posed the special challenge of quartet texture. He writes that it pleases him more than anything else the young composer had sent him—"in both ingenuity and form it is mature and solid." And he adds that, having quibbled with so much, he must not spoil the impression of this praise by pointing out any mistakes in the quartet—it is so difficult to write in this genre. He expresses the hope that they may see each other during the following summer, so that they might discuss all these compositions at greater leisure.

> And now, good Vladislav Albertovich, I beg you not to be embarrassed, not to be hurt, and not to blame me for offering more reproof than praise. From experience I know how tender a composer's feelings can be—and I realize how harshly I have touched the sensitive strings of your composer's heart. But if my praise is to have any value, I *must* tell you the truth. What good would compliments be to you? No matter how cruel my judgment may be, such cruelty is more useful than reticence on defects. Now I must say: be sure that I shall be very, very happy when I shall be able, with full honesty, to approve of some future compositions by you without any reservation whatsoever. If you have an urgent inner feeling that you must compose music, you will not—not even for a moment—be weakened or discouraged by such comments as mine. The more severe these comments the more sincere and friendly are the thoughts that guide me in examining your work.

The second and third letters in the series, written on August 16 and August 31, 1885, from the village of Maidanovo near Moscow (Tchaikovsky's country retreat), show scant reference to Pakhulsky's work, but they contain Tchaikovsky's mention of a symphony—presumably the "Manfred" Symphony —on which he himself was working at the time.

Apparently Pakhulsky had taken the mentor's advice to heart, for Tchaikovsky writes:

> I fully approve of your intention to learn the art of orchestration from the classics. And in general, in our days, when music has departed so far from initial simplicity and clarity of ideas and form, it is good to come back to old days and to try to imbue oneself with the spirit of soberness of the great masters of the past.

Conversely, he admits that in his own new symphony he has been extremely immoderate in the choice of orchestral means, remarking that among the existing instruments there does not seem to be a single one that would not appear in the score; one becomes aware of what may have been a considerable artistic struggle:

> Never before have I written such a complicated, difficult piece as the symphony I am writing now. I will probably finish it in the middle of September, and then I shall make some short trip for distraction and rest.

Thus the weight has shifted somewhat; Tchaikovsky takes the young composer into his confidence in discussing his own concerns. This impression is strengthened by the fact that from this point on the correspondence also touches upon performance and publication of Pakhulsky's works. In the letter of August 16 Tchaikovsky writes, "I am interested in the result of the tryout of your orchestral work. Please write a few words about how you were pleased with the performance." And the letter of August 31 contains the following passage:

> It is very useful and good for you to have had an opportunity to hear your works played by a decent orchestra. I am sorry you had to be disappointed in some respects, but such disappointments are the lot of every artist who strives for perfection, and nobody could do without them.

One may, in fact, conclude that the wording of the latter remark subtly refers to the prediction Tchaikovsky had made two years earlier when he was commenting on the excess of detail in Pakhulsky's orchestration.

The fourth letter, dated February 27/March 11, 1890, and written in Florence, was prompted by Tchaikovsky's survey of a series of songs Pakhulsky had sent him, and as before, Tchaikovsky makes mention of the work in which he himself is engaged. He apologizes for delaying his comments since he happened to be occupied with an extremely difficult opera scene (the work is evidently *Pique-Dame,* to which Tchaikovsky specifically refers in a subsequent letter), and he explains that he wanted to study the songs when he had regained some peace of mind. He says that, in sum, the songs please him very much. "Undoubtedly they are the most mature of all your compositions known to me. There is poetry and sincere feeling in them, in spots very beautiful harmony." He modifies this observation somewhat, because at times the harmony seems forced to him. He says that the songs capture the vocal medium well and that the connection between music and text is continuous, though he has found some deficiencies of prosody. Then he turns to details, discussing the songs one by one.

In his remarks about the first song Tchaikovsky comments on the awkward setting of the accompaniment at the beginning and the end.

> In the Allegro moderato it is difficult for the right hand to play all four notes of the chord; if you had in mind that the lower two notes should be played by the left hand, it would be better to indicate this, i.e., to add the letters m.s. for mano sinistra (left hand). Even so, it remains somewhat clumsy.

His next remark is concerned with prosody; he suggests that Pakhulsky write out the second stanza if he is planning to publish the song and to apply a slight rhythmic change to avoid a false accent (Example 7). He points out that here

EXAMPLE 7

o   ne   top-chi
[oh,   don't tram-ple]

the accent must be on the syllable *chi* and that the diction of the phrase might accordingly be adjusted in the second stanza (Example 8). He further recommends that the song, which is "pretty and heartfelt," should receive a little more of an ending, an ending that is not "somehow chopped off."

EXAMPLE 8

svet-ley - ut ne - be - sa_____ o   ne top - chi   ikh
[the skies   are bright-en - ing,   oh, don't tram-ple   them]

The second song is, as Tchaikovsky writes, very close to his heart because of its warmth and spontaneity. He has special praise for the attractiveness of a particular suspension (Example 9) and shows how it may be used again in the final cadence (Example 10). At the same time, his criticism returns to elementary flaws in part writing: "Well then, a teacher of harmony is forever within me, and I can't help but persecute *octaves* and *fifths*. It is a different matter if they are used intentionally. . . ." As examples for such use, Tchaikovsky mentions two passages from the last song in the group (which, however, he does not copy out in the text of the letter). But, he continues, instances of such parallel progressions which he sees on paper without discerning their *purpose,* he "must put to death." And Tchaikovsky speaks to the same point again in his discussion of the next song.

> Perhaps this is just an eccentricity of mine, but I have a certain right to it because I positively avoid fifths and octaves myself, except for cases where it is obvious to everyone that they are used intentionally for the sake of a characteristic effect.

There may be a special ring of intensity in this admonition for the very reason that such lapses are out of keeping with the quality Tchaikovsky recognizes in these songs. The third song is "again a very fine one"; in the fourth song "the gloomy mood of the words is successfully expressed and sustained"; the fifth song (the last in the group) is "very successful, with very beautiful harmonies in the beginning."

EXAMPLE 9   EXAMPLE 10

Tchaikovsky's suggestions concern minor points—in accordance with the proper word accent of *ocharovanny* ("enchanted") the stress should be shifted from the syllable *va* to the syllable *ro;* a note should be changed to avoid an "unattractive spot" in the bass; a detail of the accompaniment should be more fully understood in terms of pianistic texture. But in general, Tchaikovsky's reaction is positive and heartening. His comment on the last song is a single sentence of praise, after which he adds:

> Here, Vladislav Albertovich, is my sincere opinion of your songs. If you are going to publish them, please check the part writing once more, so that nobody like me could cavil at anything.

An additional song is discussed in the fifth letter, mailed from Florence only two weeks later (March 11/26, 1890). Unlike the earlier ones, this song does not meet with particularly favorable response from Tchaikovsky:

> It starts well but ends with a melodious turn which I dislike very much because it has become a cliché of a Russian song style [Example 11].[5] Couldn't you change it, Vladislav Albertovich? I would advise you strongly to do so. Invent something like the following: [Example 12].

EXAMPLE 11

EXAMPLE 12

Tchaikovsky also takes exception to the fact that the rhythmic motion of the accompaniment gives way occasionally, and without any ostensible reason, to simple chords—"as if from laziness (forgive me)." Such a change, he says, is particularly unfounded if it conflicts with the momentum of the vocal part. Then he refers to the opposite situation—a passage in which simple chords are highly suitable because of the "prayerful meaning of the words"—and, finally, his criticism returns once more to part writing.

> Further, by an old habit, I could not refrain from fussing at your writing octaves in the outer voices. Please, correct this! Such octave passages can be good if they appear for a special reason in a whole series of chords, but here (in the second measure of your third page) they shook me terribly.

Concerning another composition Tchaikovsky had received with this song he writes: "The little violin piece is charming. Is there a whole series of such Bagatelles in print or just one at present? If others exist, please send them, too." In

5. Tchaikovsky adds the footnote: "So ends the famous *Red Sarafan*."

closing the letter, Tchaikovsky assures his correspondent once again of his ever "friendly advice and friendly captiousness."

With these five letters, the series of Tchaikovsky's didactic commentaries preserved in the Library of Congress collection is exhausted. There is, however, a further letter, written on July 3, 1890 (see Plate I), from Tchaikovsky's new home in the village of Frolovskoye and contained in the Heinemann Collection, New York, which seems to form the conclusion of Tchaikovsky's advice to his young colleague.

A different tone rules in this letter and suggests that Pakhulsky's work must, in fact, have matured considerably during the years in which the correspondence took place. Tchaikovsky's remarks are now concerned with more general questions of design. The pieces he reviews are evidently orchestral works conceived on a fairly large scale; they are identified, in turn, as *Andante largo, Le Matin,* and *Bolero.*

It is interesting, though to be expected, that Tchaikovsky is confused by the first of these titles; he says that "grammatically it is correct" but that "there is some contradiction here." He comments that there is mood and color in this piece but that it suffers from a certain abruptness—something which, as he puts it, is not quite articulate.

> One forever expects that eventually the *real gist* of the thing will appear, for which one has been rather prepared by a contrapuntally oriented introduction of this theme [Example 13], but the expectation is in vain. At the end there is a passage that is very fine both with regard to invention and instrumentation [Example 14]. But this pretty little episode can make no impression upon the listener, for its origin is unknown; we do not understand what organic connection it has with what has gone before. In vocal music the text can justify a lack of musical logic. But instrumental music invariably requires themes and development of these themes.

EXAMPLE 13

EXAMPLE 14

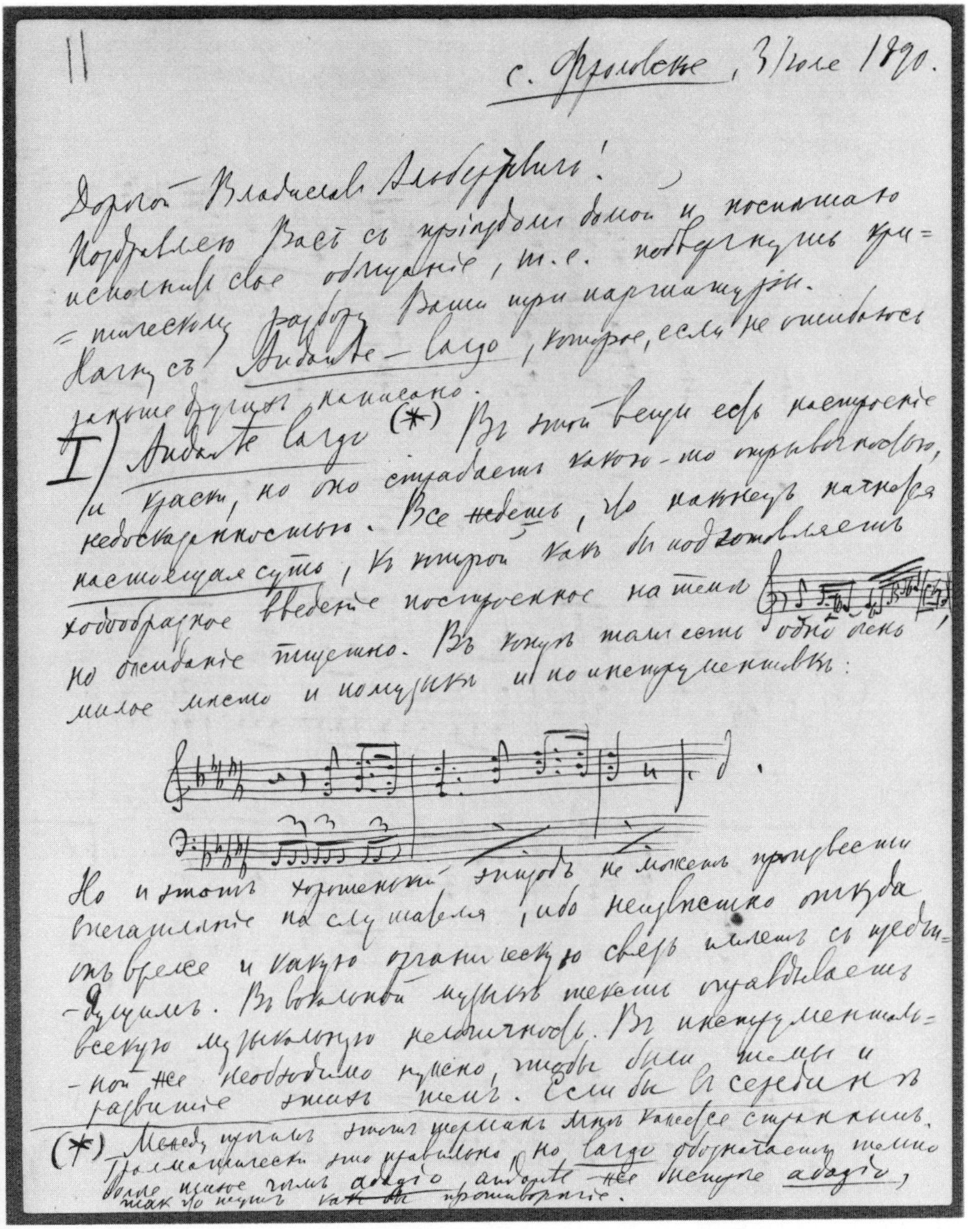
с. Фроловское, 3 июля 1890.

Дорогой Владислав Альбертович!
Поздравляю Вас с прибытием домой и посылаю
исполнив свое обещание, т.е. подвергнув кри=
=тическому разбору Вашу партитуру.
Начну с Andante-Largo, которое, если не ошибаюсь
раньше других написано.
I) Andante largo (*) В этой вещи есть настроение
и краски, но оно страдает какою-то отрывочностью,
недосказанностью. Все ждешь, что наконец начнется
настоящая суть, к которой как бы подготовляешь
ходообразное введение построенное на теме
но ожидание тщетно. В нем там есть одно очень
милое место и по музыке и по инструментовке:

Но и этот хорошенький эпизод не может произвести
впечатление на слушателя, ибо неизвестно откуда
он взялся и какую органическую связь имеет с предыду=
=щим. В вокальной музыке текст оправдывает
всякую музыкальную нелогичность. В инструменталь=
=ной же необходимо нужно, чтобы были темы и
развитие этих тем. Если бы в середине
(*) Между прочим этот термин мне кажется странным.
Грамматически это правильно, но largo обозначает темп
более медленный, чем adagio, andante же быстрее adagio,
так что термин как бы противоречие.

PLATE I. Tchaikovsky's letter to Pakhulsky, July 3, 1890; New York, Morgan Library, Dannie and Hettie Heinemann Collection

He adds that if, after the introduction for the *Andante largo*, the piece were to contain a passage such as he suggests (Example 15), the conclusion of the work could be made more impressive.

EXAMPLE 15

The second piece, *Le Matin*, is "the most complete and the best" of the three compositions.

> Both your principal themes are successful. A little more development and cultivation of them would be desirable. In your structure, seams are noticeable. For example, in the passage before the return of the second theme in a minor key where the brass instruments echo each other [Example 16], the writing is too brief and the harmony too stiff. The conclusion is too sudden, and there is no life in the orchestra.

EXAMPLE 16

To bear out this last point, Tchaikovsky observes that most of the instruments have rests in the coda, although it is marked fortissimo. His advice is couched in purely practical terms: it is uncomfortable for the orchestra player to count rests "instead of participating in the final bustle," and the experienced orchestrator speaks in the remarks that at this point "everything must be working" and that "one is more inclined to worry about a shortage in the orchestra's personnel than about an excess of instruments." He also says that the orchestra, especially the string section, does not show enough animation or impetus and quotes a spot where he senses a lack of sixteenth notes, suggesting a specific change (Example 17). Again he objects to the omission of thirds in a chord, to another instance in

EXAMPLE 17

which a four-part texture is suddenly reduced to a two-part texture, and to parallels; he singles out parallel fifths between the second and fourth French horns in a passage of *Le Matin*, returns to the *Andante largo* once more where his eye had caught parallel octaves (Example 18), and finally spots another case of octaves in *Le Matin* (Example 19), with the words "But I will stop pestering you with my mania to root out *fifths* and *octaves* everywhere."

EXAMPLE 18   EXAMPLE 19

On the last of the three pieces, *Bolero,* Tchaikovsky offers a special point of advice. He says that the work, having been conceived with an orchestral texture in mind, would gain greatly if it were written in D major rather than half a tone lower; Berlioz, he notes, transposed Weber's *Invitation to the Dance* from Db major to D major when he undertook its orchestration, being guided by the consideration that the desired brilliant orchestral sound called for a key involving sharps. The string section in particular would sound muffled and unsatisfactory in a key with five flats. Tchaikovsky goes on to say that, as a matter of fact, the string section is slighted in the instrumentation of Pakhulsky's piece, since it has a merely accompanimental task and the main theme never appears in the violins.

Further details on orchestration follow with a summary review of Tchaikovsky's critique containing remarkably specific points of advice:

1. I repeat that I should like more motion and rhythm in the string section, especially when the whole *mass* is playing, in codas, strettos, finales.

2. You use trombones with commendable restraint, but it is very strange that you do not give the bottom part to the bass trombone but to one in the middle of the group. Of course, such a constellation is possible (in music everything is possible, nothing can be positively prohibited), but with you the *exception* appears more often than the *rule*.

3. If the French horn has a melody in a low register, it should not be played by the first or third but by the second or fourth player, because they can make the necessary adjustment with the so-called *embouchure*.

And so again, dear Vladislav Albertovich, I am generous with reproof and sparing with my praise. Your musical organism has something sickly that requires treatment, and it is my opinion that the best remedy would be to rid yourself entirely of the pressure of modernism and saturate yourself in classicism. I advise you to try a symphony with modest orchestra, and in a strictly classical form. This may give your composer's nature that balance which it needs. I have known you as a composer for more than twelve years; of course, in this time you have made considerable progress even though you seldom work regularly and steadily. But your technique still suffers from immaturity and lack of purity. I notice that you do not tackle big problems, and you write quite purely and irreproachably so far as harmony is concerned. Your Second Bagatelle (I don't remember whether I wrote you about it) pleases me very much, and as I played it I was very happy that there was positively nothing for me to quibble about. Thus before beginning to write works in the modern vein (and you show an inclination in that direction), you should work on quite simple symphonic forms in a classical spirit. I hope that you are now well and that you have a desire to work; if so, I shall be very glad to receive from you a symphony (or a quartet, if you wish)—not a large one, not a profound one—but one that would have not one place for me to criticize. . . .

Again I beg you not to be grieved by my criticism.

A postlude to the exchange between Tchaikovsky and Pakhulsky is formed by two letters which no longer touch upon questions of composition but which have rare value as documents of biography; the first, written on March

13/26 [*sic*], 1891, from Paris, is preserved in the Library of Congress; the second, dated June 6, in Moscow, is contained in the Heinemann Collection.

In the fall of 1890, Tchaikovsky's benefactor, erroneously advised of impending bankruptcy, had suddenly discontinued her financial support and all communications; thus the correspondence with Pakhulsky remained the only contact between his mother-in-law and Tchaikovsky. Even Pakhulsky's messages had become sparse, and the first letter opens with an expression of Tchaikovsky's gratitude for writing again and with his assurance that there is no thought of blaming Pakhulsky for his long silence. Tchaikovsky speaks of great changes that have taken place in his plans. He reports that he has accepted an offer to go to New York to conduct a large music festival (the opening of Carnegie Hall), and that he has also been engaged for a concert in Cologne. He says he does not know whether to rejoice or to be unhappy at the prospect of traveling and that he has agreed to the journey mostly in order to be distracted from the adverse circumstances into which his life has fallen—with everything in a seeming state of collapse, he had been greatly offended by both imperial theaters, because his operas had been taken out of the repertory: "One has to go somewhere far away to recover oneself." In a postscript to the letter he says that he has been evicted from his home in Frolovskoye and that he does not know where he will live.

The second letter reveals Tchaikovsky's complete despair. He says that he has made every effort to resume regular correspondence with N. F. [Nadezhda Filaretovna von Meck] and that he cannot believe that she should be so ill, weak, or nervously upset as to be unable to write to him as before. He retraces the grievous events of the past year and says that when he was informed that his benefactor's financial condition had become too precarious to allow any further material support to him, he had answered that he wanted, he needed, that there should be no change in their personal relations. All his efforts having come to naught, he admits to being deeply hurt and embarrassed at a situation which gives the appearance of his having broken with the friend as soon as he "received no further money from her."

He writes that during the past autumn, in the country, he had read her letters again, and it seemed as though nothing—neither illness nor sorrow nor material difficulty—could alter the feelings expressed in them. "It seemed more possible for the world to break into tiny pieces than for N. F. to change toward me." His faith and his repose are shattered:

I have never felt so humiliated, so wounded in my pride as I do now. Worst of all, with N. F.'s present ill health, I am so afraid to grieve or upset her that I cannot tell her what is tormenting me. I cannot unburden myself—and only this could ease my mind. But enough of this. Perhaps I will regret having written all of it—but I had to find some outlet for all the bitterness that has filled my soul.

Not a word of this to N. F. If she should wish to know what I am doing, tell her that I have safely returned from America, that I have settled in the village of *Maidanovo* and that I am working. I am well.

Don't answer this letter.

P. Tchaikovsky

The question of whether the end of Tchaikovsky's life, two years later, was due to suicide is still a matter of debate.[6] The testament he left in his letters to the young composer who had become his confidant shows him in some respects to be torn, frustrated, and distressed as much in his role as a teacher as in his personal life. And yet, the reader cannot help but be touched by the artistic integrity expressed by it.

6. See the articles in the *New York Times,* July 28 and August 9, 1981.

PROXY WARS
AND HORNS OF PLENTY:
ON MUSIC AND THE HUNT
AT THE TIME OF
FRANCIS I

ALEXANDER L. RINGER

THE REMARKABLE transformation of hunting—from a crude pursuit in search of food as a condition of sheer survival to a carefully staged, lavishly equipped, and commensurately expensive pastime of the leisure classes—was essentially a French phenomenon that had its tentative beginnings during the Carolingian era, gained considerable momentum as the Middle Ages drew to a close, then quickly reached its apogee under the Valois kings. Within a few years after Francis I was crowned "sacré roi de France," only his army confronted the princes of Europe with a greater challenge than did his splendid hunting establishment. Though justly renowned as a healthy, manly sport, the hunt with running hounds owed its central place among noble diversions to a variety of considerations well beyond the realm of mere entertainment. As a peacetime test of courage, skill, and endurance it was held in particular esteem by that relatively small group of noblemen upon whose physical as well as mental alertness and tactical imagination court and country ultimately depended in time of war. Baldassare Castiglione, whose *Il cortegiano* appeared while he served at the court of that other noble hunter, Emperor Charles V, ascribed its broad appeal to the undeniable fact that "ha una certa similitudine di guerra."[1] And this view was still echoed by Henry III, who, in an ordinance signed December 10, 1581, declared the hunt to be "chose plus que nulle approchante le faict des armes et bien séante à la noblesse."[2]

---

1. See Jean Jules Jusserand, *Les Sports et jeux d'exercise dans l'ancienne France* (Paris, 1901), 194.
2. Ibid.

In the temporary absence of real warfare—the ultimate hunt—any properly equipped Renaissance lord could thus wage private proxy wars on the beasts of the wild, in particular the prized stag, and enjoy "all those pleasures of which he was so fond: the outdoors, violent action, the handling of weapons."[3] In these respects alone, not to speak of its inherent dynamics and the collective effort involved, a properly conducted hunt far outdid jousting or, for that matter, any kind of formal duel, as a sport capable of simulating the conditions of actual warfare, the bloodiest and most manly entertainment of all. Indeed, war and hunt were but two sides of the same psycho-cultural coin, to the point where large-scale hunts took place even between battles. Besides a welcome change of pace, the chase with running dogs afforded ample opportunity for disciplined demonstrations of continued good physical condition, while ensuring the maintenance of a psychological momentum that was always in danger of slackening to the point of outright boredom. Given the lack of outside stimulation, unoccupied warriors existing from day to day in the roughest of physical environments were bound to take to drinking, wenching, and generally making nuisances of themselves. Bringing the stag to bay, on the other hand, involved not merely ever-present risks of serious injury and a ubiquitous smell of blood, but also the typical state of organized confusion and, conversely, the careful strategic planning so crucial in time of war to the surprise and ultimate defeat of an opposing army. To be sure, Renaissance France, which celebrated the king's formal entrées into the principal cities of his realm as colorful mass events, presaging in many ways the *son et lumière* spectacles of today, also enjoyed the hunt as a sophisticated if cruel ritual replete with fixed moves executed by large numbers of men and animals, as well as with informal aleatoric episodes that required the foresight and extrasensory perception of a brilliant chess player. Chess was, of course, the favorite indoor game of some of the same lords who missed no opportunity to participate in one of these magnificent proxy wars known as royal hunts. In earlier days, moreover, chess had often been attended by violence of the sort that continued to mark the hunt well after the game of kings had been sublimated into a quiet contest of sheer wit and intelligence.[4]

The extent to which hunting, warfare, and chess appealed to the same underlying passions is made clear from the graphic account of "a ball in the manner of a tournament" that François Rabelais gives in the fourth book of *Gargantua and Pantagruel*. Accompanied by two sizable bands of musicians, we are told, thirty-two young persons performed intricate moves and countermoves on a "large piece of velveted white and yellow checkered tapestry, each checker exactly square, and three full spans in breadth."[5] The two opposing groups lined up so that four rows of squares between them remained empty. Each group,

3. Ibid., 191.
4. Alexander Cockburn, *Idle Passion: Chess and the Dance of Death* (New York, 1974), 98.
5. As reprinted in *The Chess Reader: The Royal Game in World Literature,* comp. Jerome Salzmann (New York, 1949), 66ff.

"the one with orange coloured damask, the other with white," backed by eight musicians and following the rules of the game, tried to outsmart the other to sounds "played on different instruments most harmoniously, favoring in time and measure the figure of the dance required." On both sides participants began to fall ("the fight was obstinate and sharp . . . the battle was doubtful and victory hovered over both armies") until "the silvered king" carried the day and was musically acclaimed by all. "And thus the first battle ended to the unspeakable joy of all the spectators." Benjamin Franklin, for one, might have enjoyed such a massive, lively, and aggressive version of the royal game. For him too the hunt was "the image of human life, and particularly of war; in which, if you have incautiously put yourself into a bad and dangerous position, you cannot obtain your enemy's leave to withdraw your troops, and place them more securely; but you must abide all the consequences of your rashness."[6]

Such, of course, was precisely the predicament of the stag unfortunate enough to make a wrong move while trying to elude his pursuers. And, as in the case of Rabelais's human chess figures, decisive tactical moves of the hunt were musically communicated with the help of an expanding repertory of horn signals that supplemented and eventually supplanted at least a portion of the age-old dog calls with which the hunting masters, the *piqueurs*, controlled their faithful hounds. By the time Francis I ascended the throne of France, the chasse had engendered functional musical materials numerous enough and of such inherent quality as to furnish the motivic substance of several extended sonorous canvasses, polyphonic minidramas inspired, it seems, by the hunting exploits not only of the king of France but also of the Holy Roman Emperor Charles V, his long-time political foe, who fully shared his fierce devotion to the noble sport.[7]

History knows of few sovereigns less compatible in attitude or similar in appearance than Francis I and Charles V, whose perennial struggles for hegemony determined the political fate of much of Europe throughout the first half of the sixteenth century. Profoundly devout and scrupulous, physically rather inconspicuous, the emperor seemed to have little in common with the dashing Frenchman, except a glutton's taste for power and a lasting devotion to the pleasures of the hunt. Characteristically, the lugubrious emperor, though generally lacking Francis's knack for splendor and luxury, readily matched his hunting expenditures. What distinguished him from his rival in this respect, however, was that he rarely spent what he could not afford, whereas Francis disregarded all rules of prudent management where his greatest passion was concerned, even at a time of severe crisis such as that which racked French finances in 1523. Nor did the royal hunting budget cease to increase as the years went by. Still limited to 40,000 crowns in 1535, by 1546 it had reached

---

6. See Ralph K. Hagedorn, *Early America: A Review of the Literature* (Philadelphia, 1958), 17.

7. For a general survey of the history of the hunt in music, see the present author's 1955 Columbia University Ph.D. dissertation written under Paul Henry Lang and entitled "The Chasse: Historical and Analytical Bibliography of a Musical Genre."

150,000.[8] In addition, the king lavished fortunes on related building projects. His favorite hunting retreat, Fontainebleau, was completed in 1528. And even though he had already declared war on Charles V and things were going badly for him in Italy, he kept pushing his architects and draftsmen to get on with "the castle of Madrid and two other castles at Livry where the said Lord wishes to be able to enjoy the pleasures of the hunt."[9] Whether or not Clément Janequin composed *La Chasse* specifically for the inauguration of Fontainebleau may never be conclusively documented. But it seems quite plausible. He had, after all, glorified the battle of Marignano, which he may or may not have witnessed in person, in a similar piece, and it stands to reason that he seized the opportunity to do homage to the king's second major cause for pride. Moreover, both the battle piece and the hunting piece saw their initial publication in the same Attaignant collection of 1528.

A year later the king had concluded the Paix des Dames, the treaty of Cambrai, which brought temporary peace, and was able to devote himself with still greater abandon to the ladies, to poetry and art, to science and music, and, needless to say, to the hunt. Even during the difficult negotiations of July, 1529, however, he had spent most of his time in the forest of Coucy, where news from the negotiating table was relayed to him for his comments, so that he might not have to forgo a day's hunt.[10] And yet these negotiations involved, aside from the fate of Burgundy, nothing less than the freedom of his children held hostage by Charles V. Francis, to be sure, hunted the stag also the morning after his second wedding and while traversing Spain as the emperor's prisoner. And it was after returning from a hunt, at Rambouillet in March, 1547, that he died.

During his lifetime and beyond, French culture reflected this royal predilection in countless ways. Janequin's *Chasse* had barely appeared when the great humanist Guillaume Budé contributed a little Latin treatise, *De venatione,* that set a general pattern that obtained until Jacques Du Fouilloux produced *La Venerie,* a work as poetically written as it is practical and as widely translated as it was plagiarized.[11] Meanwhile, the finest French artisans wove royal hunts into their magnificent tapestries, and François Clouet was commissioned to paint his royal patron seated on his favorite horse. Under these circumstances, France's foremost musical talent, Clément Janequin, who was anything but averse to such secular pleasures, could hardly be expected to stand by idly and miss an obvious chance to curry favor at court. That he paid homage to the king with unprecedented musical evocations of the terrors and rewards of both a victorious

8. William Leon Wiley, *The Gentleman of Renaissance France* (Cambridge, Mass., 1954), 137.

9. See the *lettres patentes* of Aug. 1, 1528, quoted in Dunoyer de Noirmont, *Histoire de la chasse en France* (Paris, 1867–68), 1:160.

10. René Guerdan, *François Ier: le Roi de la Renaissance* (Paris, 1976), 284.

11. For a complete bibliography of editions, see Jacques Du Fouilloux, *La Venerie et l'adolescence,* ed. Gunnar Tilander (Karlshamn, 1967), 9–12.

battle and a successful hunt reveals acute understanding of the close affinities of these twin components of royal existence and a political acumen which, in the event, generated an entirely new genre. Michel Brenet, in her pioneering study of the so-called program chanson, was careful to stress its descriptive features.[12] Yet "descriptive," though quite to the point with regard to stylistic detail, fails no less than the customary "program" to convey the substance of an action-packed and hence intrinsically dramatic type of music. Unlike much later program music, Janequin's *La Chasse* does not follow a story. Instead, it recreates a full day's hunt stage by stage, from the early morning call, urging grooms, hunting masters, and dogs to search the woods, to the final horn consort hailing success and good fortune. Between these two poles, the introduction and the postlude, unfolds a minidrama sustained by furious action that is further highlighted, rather than alleviated, by an occasional lyrical interlude. There is no narration: the *dramatis personae* and, indeed, *dramatis bestiae,* address each other directly, alternating encouragement with disappointment, differences of opinion with seemingly extraneous personal experiences, but always in single-minded pursuit of their goal, the entrapment and eventual destruction of the stag. Well-known personalities and the names of famous places and dogs associated with the royal hunting establishment pass in review, as does the unique professional jargon of the hunters, their vocal calls and horn signals, the barking of the excited hounds pressing forward or temporarily losing the scent, all to achieve an exceedingly re-alistic portrayal of a largely preordained series of events, which in purely musical terms abounds with premonitions of the Italian *dramma per musica* as it emerged nearly three generations later. Janequin's extended declamatory pas-sages on a single sustained harmony, in particular, uncannily point to the *stile concitato,* while the compression of so many conflicting occurrences into a per-fectly balanced four-movement chanson of less than fifteen minutes' duration furnishes what is perhaps the first effective demonstration of the unique power of music to manipulate man's sense of "real" or clock time. Some of the poly-textual passages, in which as many as four opposing views may be in contention, not only serve admirably to portray the excitement and/or misgivings of a group of hunters pursued by bad luck; they also anticipate techniques characteristic of much later operatic ensembles. Janequin's dramatic polyphony, at any rate, pro-duces a temporal-spatial sensation of multidirectionality that was not only beyond the reach of the spoken word but also without musical precedent.

The musico-dramatic procedures of *La Chasse* alone reveal an innovative mind that was anything but satisfied with the mere reinterpretation of extant quodlibet techniques.[13] But in addition this minidrama makes use of allusion and metaphor in ways not more broadly explored even in Claudio Monteverdi's lifetime. A case in point is the class consciousness that pervades *La Chasse* but

12. Michel Brenet, "Essai sur les origines de la musique descriptive," *Rivista musicale italiana* 14 (1907): 725–51; 15 (1908): 457–87 and 671–700.
13. The quodlibet connection was made first by Brenet, 15: 465.

did not come to the fore in opera until the rise of opera buffa in the eighteenth century. Representatives of the lower classes, such as the *piqueurs* who form the vanguard, searching the forest and paving the way with the help of their highly trained dogs, are depicted here typically as either superstitious or weary. In two polytextual passages they ascribe their lack of success to early morning encounters with a magpie and a hunchbacked old woman. Later on, conflicts of interest arise between the commoners, who think "it's time to turn back" and "it's folly to go on searching," and the king and his noble friends, whose personal stake in the enterprise prompts them to select a temporary resting place instead. Significantly, the suggestion to abandon the search is made by an upper pair of voices. The lower voices simply ignore their warning that "the hour is already late." Considering the later operatic convention of assigning the parts of kings and noblemen to baritones and basses, Janequin's social identification of voice ranges marks a first important step on the long road toward musical class characterization.

When Charles V crossed France in the winter of 1539–40 on his way to the troubled Flemish provinces, his royal host made the most of their common passion. After a brief hunting prelude at Lusignan—as Martin and Guillaume Du Bellay relate in their memoirs—Francis received the emperor at Amboise and Blois and finally at Fontainebleau, "auquel lieu pour estre maison que le Roy avoit bastie pour les chasses et deduicts, le festoya et luy donna tous les plaisirs qui se peuvent inventer, comme des chasses royales, tournoi, escarmonges. . . ."[14] The emperor may well have been accompanied on this historical trip—possibly for the last time—by his court musician Nicolas Gombert, who had followed him previously all over his far-flung domains. While nothing points specifically in this direction, the possibility of a personal meeting between Janequin and Gombert cannot be entirely discounted. They may even have met the year before at Aigues-Mortes, where the musicians of pope, emperor, and king reportedly engaged in a series of artistic competitions while their masters weighed the fate of Europe. Whatever the case, in 1545 Tylman Susato of Antwerp, the most important early sixteenth-century printer of music north of Paris, published his "Dixiesme Livre contenant la Bataille a Quatre de Clement Jannequin, avecq la Cinquiesme partie de Phili. Verdelot Si placet, Et deux Chasses de Lieure a quatre parties, & le Chant des oyseaux a troix . . ." (see Plate I). The first hunting piece appeared anonymously, but the second, like the *Chant des oiseaux,* as the work of Gombert.

Gombert's topic, the hare hunt, was a far less spectacular affair than the stag hunt depicted by Janequin. By the same token, Jacques Du Fouilloux calls it the most pleasant and high-spirited of all, "the more so, as it affords pleasure at all hours and at little expense."[15] In contrast to a massive stag hunt, he tells

14. See Dunoyer de Noirmont, 162.
15. Jacques Du Fouilloux, *La Venerie,* facs. of the 1st ed. (Angers, 1844), fol. 63v.

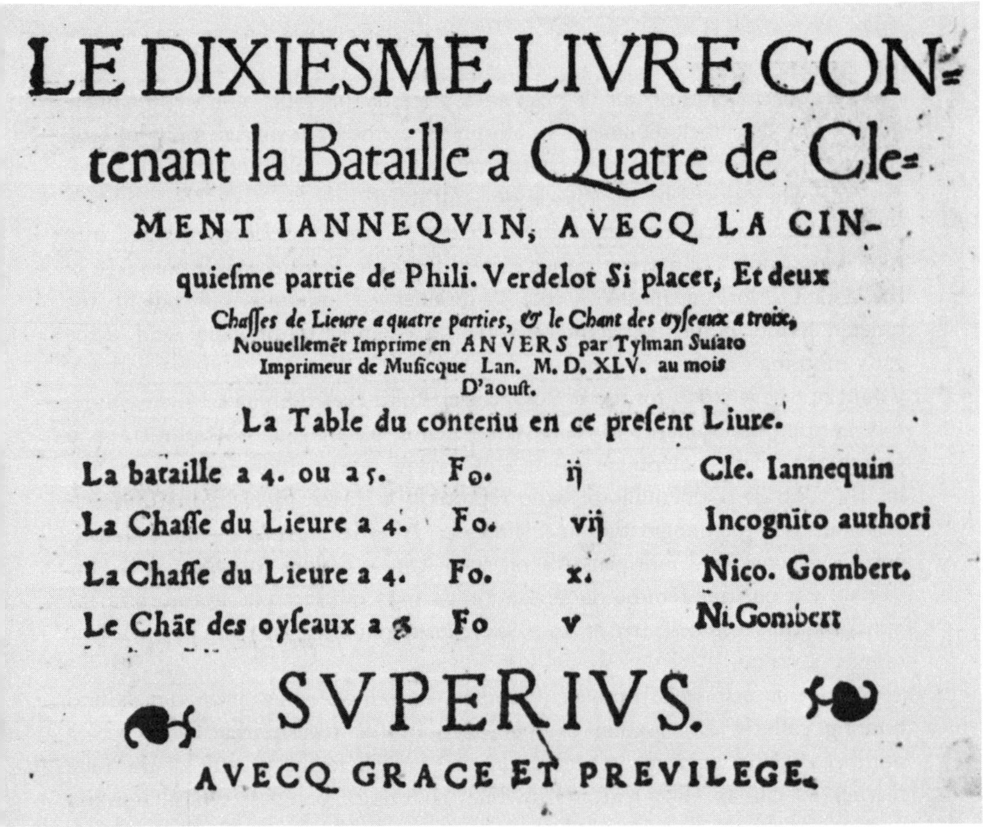

PLATE I. Title page of the superius part from Susato's Tenth Book, 1545

us, it involved optimally no more than two or three hunters at a time. Accordingly, Gombert's chasse nowhere mentions royalty. The hunters are simple people who wind up the day with a celebration at the village inn. After gorging themselves on their prey, they have every intention of making merry in the most uninhibited fashion possible. Moreover, having no cash on hand, they propose to pay with an IOU. In every way, the scenes depicted here recall the lusty canvases of a Brueghel rather than the regal art of French tapestry.

That Gombert was thoroughly familiar with Janequin's hunting piece, which had been reprinted several times by then, is beyond question. Certainly his more descriptive passages betray the unmistakable influence of Janequin's staccato technique. By and large, though, the piece carries the imprint of a northern composer well versed in sacred polyphony. A feeling of structural solidity prevails even at the very height of dramatic excitement, inevitably at the expense of more strictly coloristic effects à la Janequin. Gombert, according to his German contemporary Heinrich Finck, was unequaled in "all the subtleties of imitation."[16] And his chasse displays a textual refinement, a contrapuntal art-

16. See Joseph Schmidt-Görg, *Nicolas Gombert, Kappellmeister Kaiser Karls V.: Leben und Werk* (Bonn, 1938), 227.

istry, that seems almost out of place in a piece of this type. The web of finely interwoven, long melodic lines is as admirable as the tight motivic unity of long stretches governed by ingenious transformations of a simple motive of the third, undoubtedly inspired by the typical dog-call third.

Unlike Janequin's composition, that of Gombert is clearly divided into four parts (more appropriately four scenes), each devoted to a different stage of the action. Not unexpectedly, the "subtleties of imitation" prevail at the quieter, lyrical moments, beginning with the assembly traditionally held in the early morning "under trees, near a spring or creek." Possibly because Charles V would not have stood for it, the Rabelaisian spirit that dominated such obligatory hunting preliminaries in Renaissance France has been all but submerged in Gombert's solidly polyphonic prelude exhorting "every amorous heart" to join in. By contrast, Du Fouilloux, who reportedly fathered fifty children himself, leaves little to the imagination in this respect. After listing various kinds of wine and food considered indispensable on such lusty occasions, he goes on to say: "Et s'il y a quelque femme de réputation en pays qui face plaisir aux compagnons, elle doit estre alléguée et ses passages et remuement de fesses, attendans le rapport à venire."[17]

As this first scene unfolds, Gombert introduces a few horn signals and hunting calls in anticipation of the Janequin-like realism that permeates a number of later passages, especially in part 3, where the pursuit of the hare reaches its climax. The text, meanwhile, continues to reflect typical hunting concerns of the peasantry, including a warning to hold on tight to the dogs' collars and leashes, "lest they damage the woods." Few noble hunters, their daily existence not depending directly upon agriculture and forestry, exerted such caution. Quite to the contrary, their massive pursuits evinced, as a rule, tragically little respect for the natural environment. That the rhythmic excitement of part 3 nowhere quite matches that of Janequin's corresponding passages may, in turn, be due to the greater intimacy of a hare hunt, which not only involved fewer men and smaller animals, but covered less ground than a royal stag hunt. Possibly this accounts also for the sparseness of instrumental signals until the finale. Only when the dogs are finally recalled do the hunters sound their horns to their hearts' content. It is true, of course, that custom precluded at least the use of the higher harmonics (le gresle) during the earlier stages of the hunt, except when the dogs had to be reassembled unexpectedly or a sudden change in direction was indicated.[18] But then Gombert, true polyphonist that he was, hardly worried about every last realistic detail. In fact, he chose to conclude his piece in the same imitative chanson style that marks its beginning, very much in contrast to Janequin's veritable symphony of horn signals on the syllable *tronc*.

When Franz Commer first published the anonymous "chasse du lièure" from Susato's Tenth Book in the twelfth volume of his collection of Netherlan-

17. Du Fouilloux, fol. 34v.
18. Ibid., fol. 66.

dish music, he blithely ascribed it to Janequin, even though the original unequivocally states "incognito authori." Ambros subsequently compounded the
confusion by referring to Janequin as the author of a "chasse du lièure" only.[19]
While it is admittedly difficult to see what prompted Susato to withhold the
composer's name, Janequin's authorship must be ruled out on external as well
as internal grounds. Surely no publisher of Susato's generation would have neglected to cash in on Janequin's enormous popularity as a secular composer.
And since he is clearly identified as the author of *La Bataille,* which appears in
the same collection, it would have made little sense to refuse him credit for a
companion piece. Paris or Lyon publishers would certainly have hurried to print
their famous compatriot's works before the ink had quite dried, and a century of
research in French sixteenth-century musicography has produced no evidence
substantiating Commer's rash assumption.

Stylistically, the anonymous chasse (see Plates II and III) stands halfway
between the stylized conception of Gombert and the coloristic realism of Janequin, since it pays relatively little attention to learned contrapuntal procedures.
This holds true even for the introductory portion that Gombert turned into such
a splendid display of his polyphonic genius. Nor does the anonymous composer
bestow upon his harmonies anything like Gombert's wealth of modal progressions. Instead, he relies in far greater measure on the three principal tonal functions. His rhythmic declamation, on the other hand, while sustaining interest
throughout, does not quite achieve Janequin's dynamic power. Utilizing a text
that is in the main identical with Gombert's, the chanson retains Gombert's division into four parts. Janequin's influence is, however, strong enough to
prompt the use of additional hunting calls and onomatopoetic materials for the
sake of climactic excitement. Relative closeness to Janequin's social milieu is
suggested by the respectful "Sire" with which the hunters address their master.
But the social stratification according to voice ranges is not carried out consistently. The aristocratic setting probably precluded anything like the boisterous
finale with which Gombert had to contend. Even so, the piece ends almost too
inoffensively, with a general exaltation of the noble sport after a mere hint at the
culinary pleasures awaiting the ravenous hunters.

The "modern" harmonic tendency of the anonymous chasse is reinforced
by its motivic characteristics. Thus the continued use of a rising skip of a fourth,
with which the superius begins, serves to enhance the frequent dominant–tonic
progressions. The concerto-like juxtapositions of voice pairs in ever-varying combinations, on the other hand, are reminiscent of procedures just then being developed in Italy by Willaert and the Venetian school. Intriguing features such as

19. August Wilhelm Ambros, *Geschichte der Musik* (Leipzig, 1881), 3: 344. More recently, the editors of
Janequin's complete chansons, far from clarifying the situation, managed to muddle it further with their erro-
neous identification of Gombert as the author of the anonymous "Chasse du lièure" printed in Commer's
Collectio operum musicorum batavorum. See Clément Janequin, *Chansons polyphoniques,* ed. A. Tillman Merritt
and François Lesure (Paris, 1965), 182.

PLATE II. Superius of the anonymous *Chasse* from Susato's Tenth Book, fol. 6v

these inevitably add to one's desire to solve the mystery of anonymity, admittedly no rarity in the case of Susato, who was a composer of merit himself and had included some of his own work in earlier printed collections. Although it seems rather unlikely, given sixteenth-century practice, he may have run into difficulty on this count. At any rate, his preface to the *Vingt et Six Chancons musicales,* published in 1544, amounts to nothing less than an apology to the effect that he contributed compositions of his own not for personal glory but rather to demonstrate his qualifications as an editor of music composed by others. Perhaps he found it more profitable the following year to drop his claim to authorship altogether, reasoning that in the case of this particular chanson, in the distinguished company of similar pieces by Janequin and Gombert, anonymity was bound to increase public interest. Or he may simply have exploited the psychological value of anonymous publication after commissioning a hunting piece in the manner of Janequin from one of the numerous regional talents in the service of a church closely supervised by imperial agents. Susato's ortho-

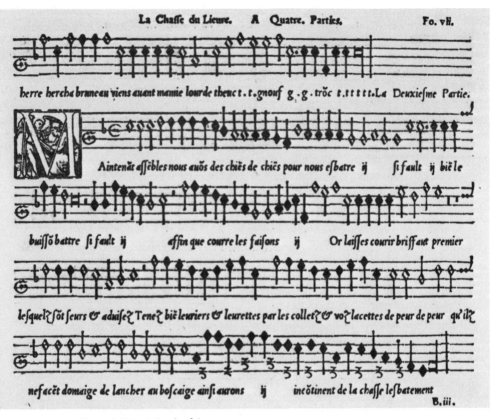

PLATE III. Susato's Tenth Book, fol. 7

doxy appears to have been questioned at one time[20]—reason enough for the clergy to avoid open identification with him or his publications.

All three compositions closely follow contemporaneous textbook outlines of the hunt and employ standard hunting terms like "vez le ci," "parci," and "outre a lui," that go back to the medieval treatises of Guillaume Twici and Gaston de Foix. Similarly, dog names like Gerbaud, Marault, Briffault, and Cléraud were part of a longstanding tradition that Jacques Du Fouilloux merely recapitulated for the benefit of his sixteenth-century readers. Typical, too, were the endearing appellations "brother," "friend," and "my love," which the hunters addressed to their animal companions. Since direct vocal contact with the dogs was preferred at all times, and the horn was used only when the dis-

---

20. See Paul Bergmans, *La typographie musicale en Belgique an XVI* siècle (Brussels, 1930), 16, for an affidavit dated Sept. 18, 1546, in which three respected Antwerp burghers attest to Susato's unblemished record as a good Christian "in no way infected by heresy and conscientious in the fulfillment of his religious duties."

tance exceeded the carrying range of the human voice, in neither the theoretical treatises nor the three principal hunting compositions of the era do instrumental signals abound. Modern attempts to read such signals into certain repetitive rhythmic patterns are in fact without historical foundation, unless they occur explicitly on the syllable *tronc* or *tran*.[21] Vocal calls, it seems, produced better results, perhaps because the instrumental abilities of the average hunter, irrespective of social standing, were greatly limited. The role of the horn was in many ways ceremonial rather than functional, hence capable hunter-players were urged to improvise freely in accordance with their individual skills.

The three polyphonic hunting frescoes that have come down to us from the time of Francis I, though hardly representative of French Renaissance music generally, nevertheless typify an era of relentless conflict and change, an era from which France emerged as the cultural fountainhead of modern Europe. Janequin's descriptive chansons managed, in the words of Paul Henry Lang, to restore "a heroic epic touch to a lyrical genre which had not known the heroic since the times of Roland."[22] Indeed, *La Chasse* successfully projects the entire heroic ritual of a royal hunt by way of a minidrama that thrives on novel melodic, rhythmic, and harmonic techniques capable of communicating the full impact of sustained dynamic action involving large groups of people and animals under ever-changing physical and psychological conditions. No extant visual or literary work probes the tensions and despair that accompany the bringing to bay of the quarry with anything like the power of Janequin's or, for that matter, Gombert's music. Nor did any other type of vocal music echo the ferocious noises and lusty cries, with which the forest resounded, in a comparably realistic manner. Historically, therefore, these three compositions, together with a few similar pieces, must be regarded as direct, if somewhat distant forerunners of the late sixteenth-century Italian madrigal comedies of Orazio Vecchi and Adriano Banchieri, as well as Monteverdi's *stile concitato*. Needless to say, it was the very nature of the subject matter that mandated sophisticated declamatory procedures in a relatively simple but expressive harmonic context of a sort rarely found in the more extended and essentially modal works of the period. It is true that functional tonality was by then firmly ensconced in the French chanson, but this was the case primarily in relatively brief, often dancelike pieces. One would certainly be hard put to find significant contemporary parallels for the kind of striking harmonic progression that marks the climax of Gombert's chasse shortly before the end of the third of its four parts: the hare has just been killed, and the hunter responsible so informs his companions—on a repeated E♭ chord—requesting their immediate assistance, lest the excited dogs tear it to pieces; as he starts to express this very real fear, the harmony abruptly changes to A minor in root position, thus causing the bass part to drop a diminished fifth

---

21. In this matter Kurt Taut, in his valuable study *Beiträge zur Geschichte der Jagdmusik* (Leipzig, 1927), unfortunately failed to proceed with the necessary caution.
22. Lang, *Music in Western Civilization* (New York, 1941), 219.

from E♭ to A, whereas the alto rises chromatically from E♭ to E♮. A progression such as this would have been considered commonplace some fifty years later with Luca Marenzio, Carlo Gesualdo, or Monteverdi in the saddle, but it must have sounded quite extraordinary to Charles V and his contemporaries, who, like Heinrich Finck, thought of Gombert as the master of subtle imitation.

The extent to which the declamatory and coloristic devices, the yielding of polyphonic complexity to an irristible rhythmic drive, betray a peculiarly French attitude (discernible as early as the thirteenth century in the polytextual Parisian motet and as recently as the 1950s and '60s in works of Pierre Boulez) is revealed by the most cursory comparison with contemporaneous hunting pieces from the German-language area. Maximilian I was as avid a hunter as his successor Charles V (unlike the latter, he took care to have his views and his knowledge preserved in writing).[23] Nor did other German princes and noblemen disdain the royal sport. Quite the contrary is true. Yet, given musical evidence only, one would hardly be able to tell, even though a number of *Jegerlieder* appeared in polyphonic collections over some four decades from Part II of Georg Forster's *Frische Teutsche Liedlein* of 1540 to Melchior Schramm's *Neuwe ausserlesene Teutsche Gesäng,* dedicated to Charles II in 1579. Generally, these pieces make no attempt to depict the hunt stage by stage, let alone step by step, and hence are largely devoid of real drama. In a single instance, the anonymous *Wohlauf, Wohlauf* in Forster's collection, the traditional assembly, search, and pursuit are alluded to in three brief sections replete with dog calls of a third, dogs barking in response, and even an occasional duet between groups of hunters. But the rhythmic frenzy and onomatopoetic variety of Janequin, who clearly provided the model in this case, are totally lacking. Although one may not agree with Kurt Gudewill, the modern editor of the volume in question, that "the tenor retains its leading position," his comment that *Wohlauf, Wohlauf* seems to "straddle the border between Lied arrangement and the French motetlike setting of a songlike text" is quite to the point.[24] Admittedly, speech rhythms prevail to a greater extent here than in most *Tenor-Lieder,* and their characteristic structural rigidity has been substantially mitigated. Still, the anonymous composer demonstrably stopped short of the ultimate step toward a dramatic type *sui generis.* If an unprecedented degree of tonal definition has been achieved nevertheless, it is thanks to clever short-range imitations of motivic materials emphasizing tonic and fifth. Due largely to the skillful adaptability of quodlibet techniques, moreover, there are moments of vocal excitement, however brief. In the end, this piece, which may or may not be attributable to Ludwig Senfl or Heinrich Isaac, is more readily identified with slightly later works of

---

23. See *Kaiser Maximilian's I. geheimes Jagdbuch,* ed. Theodor Georg Karajan (Vienna, 1858). Interestingly enough, this somewhat haphazard compilation of hunting hints and information refers to the hunt also as an effective vehicle for closer contact between a ruler and his subjects (ibid., 25).

24. Georg Forster, *Frische Teutsche Liedlein,* 2nd part (1540), ed. Kurt Gudewill and Hinrich Siuts, *Das Erbe deutscher Musik* 60 (Wolfenbüttel and Zurich, 1969): v.

Orlando di Lasso and others following directions indicated by the conventional French chanson as well as the Italian madrigal.[25]

As for Janequin's seminal composition, its great popularity throughout the sixteenth century is attested by a remarkable publication record that extends over a period of more than thirty years from its first appearance in 1528, among the *Chansons de maistre C. Janequin,* to 1559, when Le Roy and Ballard issued the *Verger de musique contenant partie des plus excellents labeurs de maistre C. Janequin* posthumously. Perhaps because he realized belatedly that the traditional four voices could not possibly do full justice to the sonorous ramifications of his subject, the composer eventually wrote three supplementary voices for the Secunda Pars, which contains the actual hunting sequence, from the assembly to the final horn medley. Their primary function is to reinforce the onomatopoetic aspects, but they also serve to intensify the impression of hopeless confusion, as dog calls go out in all directions and hunters get into fierce arguments. It is this seven-part version that Attaingnant printed in his 1537 collection, devoted exclusively to Janequin's descriptive works. Eighteen years later Nicolas Du Chemin selected *La Venerie, autrement dit la Chasse* for separate publication, a signal honor indeed, suggesting strongly that Janequin's masterful minidrama, so sorely neglected in modern times, once enjoyed the status of a true best-seller, a fact that may well have contributed to Jacques Du Fouilloux's decision a few years later to publish *La Venerie,* a book destined to reach similar fame. If so, this was possibly the first, though by no means the last, instance of a literary best-seller inspired by a highly successful piece of music.[26]

25. On the question of possible authorship, see Ludwig Senfl, *Sämtliche Werke,* 6, ed. Arnold Geering and Wilhelm Altwegg (Wolfenbüttel and Zurich, 1961): 100.

26. The author wishes to thank his friend and colleague Herbert Kellman for a most cogent critical reading of this article.

MARCO DA GAGLIANO, *FILLI, MENTRE TI BACIO,* AND THE END OF THE MADRIGAL IN FLORENCE

EDMOND STRAINCHAMPS

In 1602 the young Florentine musician Marco da Gagliano, who was just twenty years old, brought out his first publication, a book of five-part madrigals for voices alone. He thereby began a career that would soon lead to his being regarded as one of the best Italian composers of his generation; indeed, within six years his name would be familiar well beyond the city of Florence, and the grand duke of Tuscany, Ferdinando de' Medici, would appoint him to the dual posts of *maestro di cappella* of the court and *maestro di cappella* of Santa Maria del Fiore, the Florentine duomo. Thus, at the age of twenty-six, he would be set for life as the official chief musician of the city.

It is not surprising that Gagliano began with the publication of a book of madrigals, for in 1602 the madrigal was probably still the most favored secular genre throughout Italy—certainly it was in Florence. Present-day musicological writings, with their understandable enthusiasm for searching out historical roots and precedents and for emphasizing progressive tendencies, have exaggerated the relative weight of the borning opera and monody in Florentine culture during that watershed period, the last decades of the sixteenth century and the first of the seventeenth. Evidence of the madrigal's prevailing popularity in Florence is found variously. Young Florentine noblemen, for example, when they studied music, studied counterpoint, and when they composed and published music, it was almost always madrigals.[1] In addition, several of the most important of the

---

1. Among those who may be cited in this regard are Neri Alberti, Antonio Bicci, Alberto del Vivaio, Lodovico Arrighetti, Piero Strozzi, Lorenzo, and Giovanni del Turco. All published madrigals as guests in the books of professional composers; Giovanni del Turco, in addition, brought out two books of his own (in 1602 and 1614). The last four named published in Gagliano's books and were probably all students of his.

patrons who sponsored musical salons or *camerate* at the time seem to have preferred the performance of five-part, unaccompanied madrigals over any other
kind of music.[2] And it will be recalled that in the Florentine Accademia degli
Elevati, whose constitution dates from the first decade of the century, admission
to membership depended upon the acceptance of two madrigals composed by
the candidate, and that when the academy planned at one point to publish
compositions by its members, it was to be an anthology of their madrigals.[3]

There is much that might be said about Gagliano's *Primo libro de madri-
gali* from 1602—about the general character of the book, the texts he set, the
poets he favored, the diverse and sometimes discrete stylistic elements that are
featured from one madrigal to the next.[4] But here it is enough to let a single
madrigal draw our attention. *Filli, mentre ti bacio* from Gagliano's first madrigal book sets a text by Antonio Ongaro (1560?–1600?), a poet who is chiefly
remembered for his *Alceo* (1581), a drama that adapts Torquato Tasso's pastoral *Aminta* to the piscatorial mode (and that was subsequently dubbed *Aminta
bagnato*), and for a book of poems published in 1600.[5] *Filli, mentre ti bacio,*
which appears in Ongaro's *Rime,* is as follows:

Filli, mentre ti bacio,	Filli, while I kiss you
Dalle tue labbr' amorosette e care	From your dear and amorous little lips
Bevo d' ambrosia un mare;	I drink a sea of ambrosia;
Si che sommerso il core	So that my heart, drowned
Fra le dolcezze amaramente more.	In sweetnesses, bitterly dies.
Hor s' ancidi col mele,	Now, if you kill with honey,
Con l' assentio, che fai, Filli crudele?	With wormwood, what do you do, cruel Filli?

With its seven lines and seven or eleven syllables per line, this is a favorite
kind of text for late madrigalists, an epigram in which the last lines give an unexpected and wittily sarcastic twist to the poem. In his 1602 setting of the text
Gagliano reinforces the importance of the two final lines by devoting more than
half of his madrigal to them.[6] The first five lines of the poem are set in thirty
measures; the last two take thirty-six. What at first glance might seem to be an
ill-proportioned musical treatment must have seemed to Gagliano an appropriate formal response to the sense of Ongaro's poem.

2. Most notable of these is Cosimo Cini, about whose patronage more will be said below.

3. These matters are fully detailed in Strainchamps, "New Light on the Accademia degli Elevati," *The Musical Quarterly* 62 (1976): 507–35.

4. A general description of Gagliano's madrigal style appears in the article on him in *The New Grove* 7:
81–87.

5. *Rime d'Antonio Ongaro, detto l'Affidato Accademico Illuminato. . . . In Farnese, per Nicolò Mariani, MDC.
. . ,* which is extant in the New York Public Library, seems to be an edition not known to students of Ongaro's work.

6. The complete madrigal appears in the Appendix, pp. 318–22 below. The transcriptions given in the Appendix retain as much of the original prints as possible and introduce only such regularizing changes as are customary in modern scholarly practice.

A closer examination reveals something of what is achieved by Gagliano's approach. The madrigal's first thirty measures, those in which the first five lines of the poem are presented, break down into two sections: the first with its settings of lines 1–3 of the poem; the second with lines 4 and 5. In each of these sections, the text is presented line by line with distinct motifs chosen for each, and with sufficient dovetailing that full stops are reached only in measures 16 and 30—that is, at the ends of sections 1 and 2, as they are labeled here (see Table I). These correspond to the partial stop in the poem itself at the end of line 3 and the full stop at the end of line 5.

TABLE 1. *Filli, mentre ti bacio*, 1602

SECTIONS	1	2	3	4
Text lines	1–3	4–5	6–7	6–7
Measure numbers	1–16	17–30	31–43	44–66
Number of measures	16	14	13	23
Harmonic plan	G–B♭	B♭–D	G–D	D–G

Gagliano's treatment of lines 6 and 7 of the poem contrasts with the through-composed setting given those preceding by presenting both lines in measures 31–43 (section 3) and by expanding—or developing, as it were—this material to make measures 44–66 (section 4). Further contrast exists in the textural extremes within each of these final sections: line 6, set simply and homophonically, is followed by an inventive and elaborate polyphonic treatment of line 7. Indeed, the setting of line 7 alone in the two final sections comprises thirty measures of music—nearly half of the entire piece.

The formal scheme, ABCC′, is supported by a plan that can be readily described in the anachronistic but pragmatically useful terminology of modern tonal theory. Section 1 moves from its tonic beginning, G minor, to B♭; section 2 starts there and passes on to D; section 3 then retraverses this same tonal distance, I–V; and section 4, reversing the motion of section 3, moves from its start on D in measure 44 to a close on G at measure 66. This scheme, which guarantees harmonic continuity, links section 1 to section 2, and section 3 to section 4 by having the second of these, in each case, open where the first has closed. But between sections 2 and 3 an important difference occurs: the closing dominant harmony of section 2, which coincides with the end of line 5 in the poem, is not continued into the next section; instead, the dominant close of section 2 functions as preparation for the third section, which begins on the tonic. The important demarcation point in the poem, the beginning of line 6 (the witty moment where the poem's epigrammatic twist sets in), is thus supported by the important grounding in harmony on G that Gagliano provides at that point. Thus, the madrigal's harmonic scheme helps to define and to clarify the pacing of textual matter as Gagliano presents it in this setting of *Filli, mentre ti bacio*.

Within this scheme, the madrigal is, of course, contrapuntal in both its conception and its working out. Each verse of the text is set to a carefully chosen motif that is nearly always passed through the entire ensemble so that the individuality and the equality of the voice parts are for the most part maintained. Most of these motifs demonstrate how preoccupied Gagliano is with correct declamation and prosody: speech rhythm and, to a lesser degree, speech melody have shaped many of the motifs. Only at the oxymoronic lines 5 and 6, where the text speaks of being submerged in sweetnesses and dying bitterly, does the emphasis on sustained dissonant harmony break the rapid, almost parlando-like delivery of words. But the melodic contour, the slowed rhythm, the dissonant suspensions, and the unexpected prolongation on A-major harmonies are all for text-illustrative purposes—a concentrated moment of madrigalisms in a madrigal that otherwise shows very little interest in such matters.

There are a few awkwardnesses. At some moments, for the sake of support or for filling out the harmony, the smoothness of the part writing suffers (as at measures 54–55 in the tenor, or at 62–64 in the alto). Sometimes the harmonic flow is not entirely felicitous, though the many cross relations may be regarded as calculated choices; they are simply a sound Gagliano liked (they appear with some frequency in other of his madrigals also). And motivic play is occasionally weakened by the adjustments made in response to the exigencies of rhythmic activity or continuity. For instance, in the opening measures the several forms of the "mentre ti bacio" phrase weaken the passage, and the focus is not so sharp as it might be. But these are minor matters, and not surprising in a young composer's Opus 1.

After the 1602 publication Gagliano brought out five more books of five-part madrigals: Books II, III, IV, and V came out in quick succession, and then, after a gap of nine years, *Il sesto libro* appeared in 1617. In this book is found another *Filli*. This *Filli,* with exactly the same text as that of 1602, is not a new setting, however; it is instead a reworked version of the earlier piece.[7]

Gagliano's gains as a composer are at once evident. The opening, for example, has been tightened and made more musically pointed. After the chordal salutation, the motif for "mentre ti bacio" is now nearly the same for each voice part—the same melodic contour and only a slight rhythmic variation. And the deliberately paced movement within the harmony on G at the opening of the first *Filli* (in the first four measures the upper parts singing—at the rate of one measure for each harmony—I–V and, with the bass joining in, V–I), is replaced by a concise harmonic statement that, including the bass voice from the outset, establishes G minor and at once moves on to introduce the words "dalle tue labbr' amorosette e care." Gagliano's greater command of contrapuntal technique allows him to use the same motif at each level of its presentation through all five voices—at least in the crucial opening notes of the phrase. No longer does the quinto voice detract from the imitative point here by a less interesting

---

7. The complete madrigal appears in the Appendix, pp. 323–25 below.

variant of the motif opening on "dalle tue . . . ," as it did in measure 5 of the earlier *Filli*.

Then, after the briefest appearance of this phrase, the singers move directly into the next, "bevo d' ambrosia," with its fine counterpoint of contrasting motifs—a musical contrapposto, as Einstein would have termed it. And almost at once they move into the next, and then into the next. Indeed, the speed and succinctness with which the text is delivered is nearly dizzying. This is the madrigal as a telegraphic communication—a *madrigale-telegramma,* if you will.

In fact, the second *Filli* is considerably shorter than the first. Again four sections may be spoken of, with the layout of textual lines the same as before (see Table 2). And in much the same manner as before—but with some crucial differences—the harmonic plan supports a formal design based on textual presentation. The harmony in the first section once more works its way from G to B♭; the second, linked to it by a mediant opening, moves on to a close on dominant (and again with that important "applied dominant" A-major area—now considerably shortened through the diminution by half of all rhythmic values that set text lines 4 and 5).

TABLE 2. *Filli, mentre ti bacio,* 1617

SECTIONS	1	2	3	4
Text lines	1–3	4–5	6–7	6–7
Measure numbers	1–11	12–21	22–28	29–37
Number of measures	11	10	7	9
Harmonic plan	G–B♭	B♭–D	D–D	G–G

Now, though, a very decisive change occurs. In this later setting, section 3 is linked to section 2 (as section 2 was to 1) by opening harmonically where the last has closed—that is, on D. Section 3 also closes on D; and then comes the return to G for section 4. The seven measures of dominant in section 3, functioning as preparation for the return to tonic, are now balanced by a nine-measure section 4 on G. Note that Gagliano arranges this harmonic alteration not by extensive rewriting of sections 3 and 4, but simply by reversing them: section 4 of *Filli* II is made from section 3 of *Filli* I, and vice versa.

The reduction of sections 3 and 4 taken together—those sections that set text lines 6 and 7 (the epigrammatic twist) from 36 measures in the 1602 madrigal to only 16 measures in the 1617 version—is the result of a considerable musical abbreviation. To be precise, this occurs chiefly in Gagliano's treatment of line 7. Why has he so curtailed the presentation of this line, the punch line of the poem? Perhaps in 1617, as an experienced dramatist—after having written *La Dafne* of 1608 and a number of other staged works—Gagliano no longer wanted to belabor the joke by extending it beyond the point of surprise, thereby weakening the psychological whole through excessive reiteration. But this explanation does not account for everything here. Something much more telling has occurred, and it is something with broad implications for Gagliano's altered thinking about the entire genre.

The abbreviated presentation of line 7 is so striking as to capture one's attention first, but Gagliano has not only shortened this final line, he has trimmed *Filli* I throughout to produce *Filli* II. And the trimming, the shortening, the abbreviation, have resulted from his reducing vocal display, from his reining in of vocality itself. Gagliano's musical-aesthetic values as manifested in *Filli* II indicate that in 1617 he preferred clarity over display, balance of the musical structure, and succinctness of utterance over expressivity. The madrigal as musical embodiment of text, as expressive of text—and this is the very heart of the genre—is replaced by a musical construction, refined and abstract, that happens to set text. This is, of course, a contradiction in terms, since at the core of the madrigal is its balance of textual-musical factors. If text no longer stands in this relationship within the stylistic boundaries of the genre (even though equality of voices and the a cappella ensemble remain), then it is a dead issue. Certainly it had become this for Gagliano.

The two versions of *Filli, mentre ti bacio* are in themselves fascinating examples of how over a fifteen-year period one composer altered his thinking about a single text. (There are very few examples from this period in which such comparisons are possible.)[8] Beyond this, the two pieces may be fitted into the pattern of evidence to demonstrate the development of style and technique that brought about the dissolution of the genre in Florence. Indeed, pieces called "madrigal" were written after 1617 by Florentines and others, but they are for the most part no longer part of a living tradition; they are embalmed representations of the deceased organism. (Perhaps we should acknowledge that, as with Masses and motets, there are also *stile antico* madrigals.) Vital and evolving creative energies of Florentine composers had moved into other genres—monody, oratorio, and opera.

Marco da Gagliano, the best Florentine-born composer of madrigals the city ever had, lived twenty-six years more, but so far as is known, never wrote in the genre after 1617. He is, historically speaking, a figure at the watershed of style and procedure that music history, along with other disciplines, denotes (and tends to dichomotize) in the terms *Renaissance* and *Baroque*. Italian Renaissance attitudes concerning musical construction, expressivity, and all the stylistic artifice accompanying these, are met in their purest form in the latter half of the sixteenth century and the first years of the seventeenth in the madrigal. But the new, more immediate, subjective, and dramatic style of the emerging Baroque precludes further usefulness of the madrigal. Gagliano's development as a composer, as a musical intellectual, and as a musician responsive to fashion-minded patrons must have left him no choice but to abandon it.

8. It is noteworthy that among the few additional examples that might be cited are madrigals by Giovanni del Turco, Gagliano's student, which appeared originally in 1602 and were republished in his 1614 book in reworked versions.

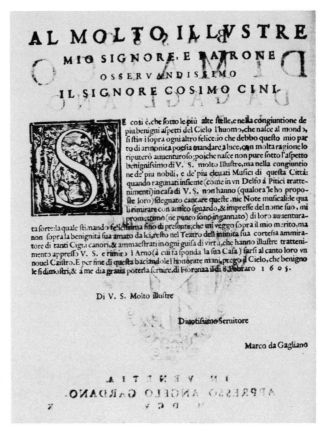

PLATE I. The dedication page of Gagliano's Third Book of Madrigals; Bologna, Civico Museo Bibliografico Musicale

In fact, it seems that Gagliano as early as 1606 recognized the madrigal as a genre without a future. In the dedication of his Third Book of Madrigals from that year[9] (see Plate I), he praised its dedicatee, Cosimo Cini, and the musical evenings held at Cini's palace on the Arno river at which "the most elevated musicians" of Florence were in attendance.[10] Gagliano continued by recalling with gratitude the many *cigni canori*—singing swans—who had performed his madrigals on those occasions, and he closed by declaring that the madrigal singers at such times turned the Arno, which banked on Cini's palace, into a new Caÿster. Thus, in a twisted image, Gagliano linked the madrigal to those Lydian swans of Greek mythology whose sudden and extraordinary singing at the point of death has given us in our own language the expression "swan song."[11]

9. The dedication, dated in Florence on February 8, 1605 *(stile fiorentino)*, is, according to our calendar, from February 8, 1606.

10. The particular words Gagliano uses here—*de' più elevati musici*—encourage the notion that a direct link may exist between Cini's informal gathering of musicians—his camerata—and the Accademia degli Elevati (the Academy of the Elevated Ones), founded by Gagliano and others in the summer of 1607. There is, however, no documentary evidence now known to permit more than speculation on the point.

11. In other forms this paper was presented at the University of Louisville, on October 13, 1979, at the forty-fifth annual meeting of the American Musicological Society in New York City, on November 4, 1979, and at Bryn Mawr College, as the "Class of 1902 Lecture," on March 4, 1980.

Appendix

Filli, mentre ti bacio, 1602

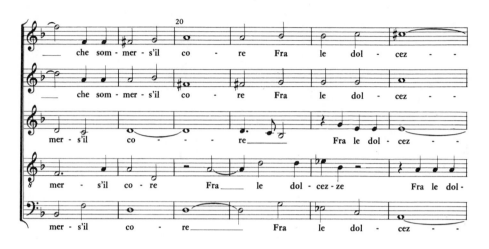

Filli, mentre ti bacio, 1617

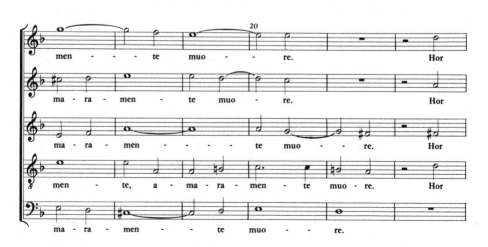

THE SACRED MUSIC OF FRANCESCO BARTOLOMEO CONTI: ITS CULTURAL AND RELIGIOUS SIGNIFICANCE

HERMINE WEIGEL WILLIAMS

THE FIRST DECADES of the eighteenth century were extraordinary ones for Viennese culture. The Turks had been decisively, if not wholly, defeated in 1683; southern Germany and Austria had been largely rid of the Protestant menace. It was a time when the Hapsburg monarchy, represented by the emperors Leopold I, Joseph I, and Charles VI, initiated the monumental rebuilding of Vienna. Joyous expression of the restored power and wealth of church and state was made manifest by abbots and noble families in the building of churches (Karlskirche), monasteries (Melk), and palaces (Belvedere).

In this Baroque environment of artistic magnificence, music for court entertainment and religious edification was created by three important composers in the employ of the Hapsburgs: Johann Joseph Fux, Antonio Caldara, and Francesco Bartolomeo Conti. Of these three, only Conti has suffered considerable neglect by music historians. Although biographical information about Conti and a study of his operas have been available for some time,[1] his music remains unpublished. Yet he is a composer whose works dominated both the secular and the sacred realms of Hapsburg life from 1706 to 1732 and a musician whose performances as a theorbist gained for him a reputation as the world's foremost exponent of that instrument.[2]

Francesco Conti was born in Florence, Italy, on January 20, 1682. Few details are known about his early life except that he developed into a virtuoso

---

1. See Hermine W. Williams, "Francesco Bartolomeo Conti: His Life and Operas" (Ph.D. diss., Columbia University, 1964). See also entries for "Francesco Conti" and "Ignazio Conti" in *The New Grove*.
2. Ludwig von Köchel, *Johann Josef Fux* (Vienna, 1872), 226.

theorbist by the age of nineteen, a fact evidenced by his appointment as theorbist to the court of Emperor Leopold I in 1701.[3] The position of theorbist at the Hapsburg court was an important one throughout the reign of Leopold I, and it continued to be so during the subsequent reigns of Joseph I and Charles VI. It was therefore an honor to receive this appointment, an honor which Conti readily accepted. He left the city of his birth and moved to Vienna. Catterina Angela Conti, a sister of Francesco, may also have accompanied him at this time, for she was closely associated with Francesco's household in Vienna throughout his entire career.

The theorbo was used as both a solo and a basso continuo instrument. In the latter capacity, it either substituted for a keyboard instrument or shared the continuo part with the cello and harpsichord. Since the theorbo formed an essential and versatile part of the orchestral palette, Conti did not lack opportunities to perform. He participated in large-scale secular and sacred works as well as in the smaller chamber compositions.

What Conti did lack, however, was regular payment for his services at the court. Although his position entitled him to a reasonable stipend of 1200 florins, the resources of the Hapsburg monarchy were inadequate to keep pace with the financial obligations of the court payroll. Soldiers were seldom paid on time, and musicians waited as much as a year to receive their stipends and housing allowances. While some resorted to revolts and strikes to call attention to their plight, Conti took a more peaceful approach, writing petitions to his superiors, including the emperor.

The stresses within the imperial realm, however, were but a small matter as compared to the growing tensions between the emperor and the papacy. The hereditary claims of the Hapsburg family to Spain and the kingdom of Naples were being challenged by the king of France, and both claimants put pressure on Pope Clement XI to decide the issues. The pope attempted to remain neutral, urging diplomatic solutions to the territorial arguments. But as the imperial army led by Prince Eugene encroached further and further onto territories north of Rome and extracted exorbitant amounts of tribute from the residents along the way, Clement XI became increasingly anxious over the security of his own realm. Just when events seemed to present no viable alternatives for the pope, Emperor Leopold I died.

Although Leopold I had ruled as one faithful to the doctrines of the Roman Catholic Church, he nevertheless had exerted undue political pressures upon the papacy. Is it any wonder, then, that Pope Clement XI welcomed the change in leadership that the emperor's death occasioned? It was the pope's sincere desire that his peace initiatives would find a more receptive audience at the court of the new emperor, Joseph I.

Conti must have been thinking somewhat along the same lines with re-

---

3. Vienna, Staatsarchiv, "Hofprotokollbuch: 1700–1709," fols. 201v–202v. See also Vienna, Finanz- und Hofkammerarchiv, "Hofrechnungsbuch: 1702," fols. 193v–210v.

spect to his own private battle for payment of his stipend. At least this is a possible explanation for the new dimension assumed by Conti's musical career in 1706, the year in which two of his major works—one secular, the other sacred —were performed before the imperial court. The secular work, the opera *Clotilde*, was presented during carnival season in February, 1706. The sacred work was the oratorio *Il Gioseffo*, which had a text obviously chosen to honor the new emperor, whose coronation occurred on March 19, 1706. The title page reads: "Il Gioseffo / Oratorio / Cantato / Nell' Augustissimus Capella / Di / Giuseppe i / Imperatore / De Romani / Sempre Augusto / L'Anno 1706. / Posto in Musica dal Franc:° / Conti."[4] Although only the year, 1706, appears on the title page of the oratorio manuscript, it is entirely possible that the oratorio was sung in the month of March, which coincided with the Lenten season, the time when oratorios were most frequently performed.

Any expectations that Conti and Pope Clement XI may have had that the new emperor would be more favorably inclined to their respective concerns were soon disappointed. Conti received no additional benefits, such as an increase in his stipend or a court promotion; Clement XI found himself dealing with a very arrogant ruler, quite unlike the youthful, innocent emperor he had expected. Not only did Joseph I have the audacity to ask the papal nuncio, Davia, to leave Vienna, but he also ordered taxes levied against Italian territories considered by him to be imperial fiefs, and he demanded of the pope free passage through the Papal States for the sole purpose of annexing the kingdom of Naples.[5] In short, Joseph I openly defied pronouncements from the papacy, including threats of excommunication directed against Prince Eugene.

The exasperation felt by the pope when his various communications and pronouncements went unheeded by the Hapsburg court is evidenced in the papal brief, here quoted in part, which Clement XI wrote to Joseph I on June 2, 1708:

> The action of your Majesty's troops in throwing garrisons into the Pontifical States and unfurling their banners as in a conquered territory . . . is contrary to equity and reason, as well as to the regard due to the Holy See and the rights of the Church. . . . Withdraw without delay your foot from where your soul would find certain damnation . . . take heed lest you stain the first-fruits of your flourishing youth by scandalizing the whole Christian people and begin your reign by offending the Church. . . .[6]

Undaunted by these words from the pope, Joseph I proceeded to publish his own manifesto, a document considered by some to be one of the harshest

---

4. A manuscript score for Part I is in A/Wn: 18148; no score for Part II is known. Parts for violins, viola, and cello are available in manuscript for both Parts I and II in A/Wn: 18149.
5. Ludwig, Freiherr von Pastor, *The History of the Popes,* trans. Dom Ernest Graf, 33 (London, 1941): 38–39. See also Owen Chadwick, *The Popes and European Revolution* (London, 1981), 273–94.
6. Pastor, 49–50.

statements ever directed by the Hapsburgs against the papacy. Dated June 26, 1706, it declares the papal brief quoted above to be null and void, and it expresses the belief that the emperor has a rightful claim to all Italy.[7]

It would be incorrect to conclude from this evidence, however, that the imperial realm was becoming less religious. Rather, there was developing in Vienna at this time an exciting new *via media* between the Protestant left and the somber Counter-Reformation right. Sincere Catholic piety was by no means lacking, but it assumed a different form—a form that seldom bowed to the wishes of Rome. The question therefore arises: did this imperial defiance of Rome have any significant effect upon music as an expression of religion in Vienna and upon Conti's career as it related to the writing and performing of sacred music?

In seeking answers to the first part of the question, one contemporary document, the *Wiener Diarium,* proves particularly helpful. This biweekly publication, first issued in 1703, provides information about services of worship and religious celebrations that might otherwise escape notice. For example, entries in the *Wiener Diarium* mention more than once that Ambrosian chant was usually sung at services in the cathedral, St. Stephen's.[8] Was this use of Ambrosian chant, the authorized chant of the cathedral of Milan, a matter of aesthetic preference, or was this a conscious attempt to call papal attention to the political ties between the Hapsburgs and the duchy of Milan?

The *Diarium* further reports that music for double choir was performed for festive occasions in the cathedral and that trumpets and timpani were commonplace among the instrumental resources available to many of the churches within the imperial city. The *Diarium* also makes it clear that oratorios were presented within the framework of a Thursday afternoon Lenten service, complete with a sermon preached in Italian:

> 1724—Donnerstag/den 30 Martii. Nachmittag wurde bey Hof in der Kaiserl. Capellen ein Italiänisch-gesungenes Oratorio, (welches der *David* benahmset und von dem Herrn Apostolo Zeno, Kaiserl. Poëten und Historico, verfasset und die Music hierüber von Herrn Francesco Conti, Kaiserl. Tiorbisten und Cammer-Compositoren gemacht ware) wie auch die gewöhnliche Italienische Predig gehalten.

According to a letter that Apostolo Zeno wrote to Pier Caterino Zeno in 1728, the sermon was delivered between the two sections of an oratorio.[9] Is this not reminiscent of the practice observed in the Lutheran services of Germany, in which a sermon was positioned between the two halves of a cantata or some other musical composition? In the Lutheran service, there was usually a direct

---

7. Pastor, 52.
8. Vienna, Stadtarchiv, *Wiener(isches) Diarium.* See, for example, the entry for July 25, 1708.
9. Apostolo Zeno, *Lettere,* 2nd ed., 4 (Venice, 1785): letter no. 739, dated May 1, 1728.

correlation between the sermon and the text of the musical work. Whether or not a similar correlation took place between the Italian sermon and the text of the oratorio performed in the Hofburgkapelle is not entirely clear from the evidence at hand. If indeed this were the case, the oratorio could have been a powerful vehicle for commenting upon imperial authority.

Perhaps this is exactly what Conti attempted to do in his second oratorio, *Il Martirio di San Lorenzo,* performed first in 1710 and again in 1724. This work represents the single example of an oratorio by Conti based upon the life of a saint. St. Lawrence was a deacon of the church in Rome during the first half of the third century. According to a tradition set forth in martyrologies as early as the fourth century, St. Lawrence was asked by the prefect of Rome to hand over the treasures of the church. But in reply to this request, St. Lawrence took the treasures and gave them to the poor, whom he then presented to the prefect, saying, "These are the treasures of the Church."[10] It was for this defiance of Roman authority that St. Lawrence was martyred in the year 258, a few days after the martyrdom of Pope Sixtus II.

The performance of *Il Martirio* in 1710 occurred at a time when Joseph I was spending money far beyond the means of the imperial court.[11] In fact, he found it necessary to levy taxes against the clerics in the territories conquered by Prince Eugene and to demand great sums of money from the pope and the Catholic Church in order to keep the imperial treasury solvent. Was it pure coincidence that the libretto of this oratorio underscored the financial tug of war between church and state?

Of the ten extant oratorios Conti composed for the imperial court,[12] all are in two structural parts, and with but two exceptions, their librettos are drawn from stories in the Old Testament.[13] The casts for these oratorios vary from four to seven singers; the majority of them, though, require five. Only in *Gioseffo che interprete i segni* is there a *testo,* or narrator's part. At least one alto, one bass, and two sopranos are included in each of the ten works. The tenor role, however, is not consistently present; it is eliminated whenever the soprano roles are increased to three. The singers assigned to these oratorio roles were the very same singers who filled Conti's operatic roles. In other words, the soprano roles were divided between the female singers and the castrati, whereas the alto roles were sung only by the castrati.

---

10. *The Oxford Dictionary of the Christian Church,* ed. Frank L. Cross, 2nd ed. (London, 1974), 804.

11. The performance on March 23, 1724, also occurred at a time when Charles VI was spending money far in excess of the resources of his treasury.

12. On page 142 of Ursula Kirkendale's *Antonio Caldara* (Graz, 1966), a libretto is listed, entitled "Sara in Egitto," written by Domenico Cavanese and published by Vangelisti in Florence in 1708. Among the numerous composers named in the libretto are Alessandro Scarlatti, Antonio Caldara, and Francesco Conti fior [entino]. This may indeed be F. B. Conti, whose absence from the imperial court during this period would have given him an opportunity to work on this score (which is no longer extant). Conti may have returned to his native city often, for he owned a house there on the Strada nel corso de' Barbari.

13. One has an allegorical text; the other, cited earlier, is based upon the life of St. Lawrence.

Throughout these oratorios, the da capo aria predominates. Ensembles (duets, trios) are used sparingly or not at all. The chorus, however, constitutes a regular feature. What is not regular is the position that the chorus occupies. Unlike Fux's oratorios, in which the chorus regularly appears at the end of Parts I and II,[14] the oratorios of Conti lack consistency in the positioning of the chorus. Sometimes the oratorio opens and closes with a chorus; at other times, the chorus appears at the end of Part I and again at both the beginning and the end of Part II. Rarely does the chorus become involved in the internal design of the libretto. Fugal writing forms an important part of the fabric of these works; from the contrapuntal movements of the overtures to the choral finales, Conti's mastery of this compositional technique is readily apparent.

One aspect of Conti's oratorios that deserves more than passing notice is the variety of instrumentation in his scores. The instrumental resources at Conti's disposal were exceptionally fine; indeed, the court took great pride in the number of first-rate musicians it employed. Joseph I had been extravagant in this regard, so much so that immediately upon his death, in 1711, the empress-regent, Elenora, quickly intervened in the affairs of the state to curb court spending. As one might expect, she advocated sharp reductions in luxury items, and as a result, the number of active court musicians was reduced.

This reduction was carried out by a committee appointed by Ernest Graf Mollart, the Director of Music. The committee, consisting of Marc' Antonio Ziani, Johann Joseph Fux, and Kilian Reinhardt, evaluated not only the credentials of each musician on the court payroll but also their respective positions. In their opinion, for example, three organists were sufficient to carry out the duties of the daily chapel services, and twenty-four singers, six to a part, were sufficient to perform the current repertoire of court music.[15]

Through the actions of this committee, almost every instrumental section was reduced by at least one member, and in one instance, the entire section was eliminated. The number of instrumentalists in the "Hofprotokollbuch" for December, 1712, is the smallest recorded at any time during Conti's association with the Hapsburg court. This reduction in the staff, however, was only temporary for the empress-regent's decree could do nothing to prevent the next ruler from spending large sums of money on the musical affairs of the court. Thus, by 1721, the number of musicians serving Charles VI had increased significantly, as

As accurate as the court records are, they do not necessarily convey a true picture of the instrumental potential for court performances. Noticeably lacking from the court payroll are musicians credited with playing the harp, chalumeau, flute (traversière), baryton, and mandolin; yet Conti's scores require these instruments. Actually all five instruments cited are included in the scoring for Conti's opera *Il trionfo dell'amicizia e dell'amore* (1711, 1723). Obviously extra

14. Howard E. Smither, *A History of the Oratorio,* 1 (Chapel Hill, N.C., 1977): 409.
15. "Hofprotokollbuch: 1700–1713," fol. 218.

TABLE 1

INSTRUMENT	APRIL 1712*	DECEMBER 1712**	APRIL 1721†
Violin-Viola	18	18	23
Violoncello	4	3	4
Violone	3	2	3
Gamba	3	2	1
Theorbo	1	1	1
Lute	1	1	1
Organ	4	3	6
Cornett	2	2	2
Corno da caccia	0	2	1
Oboe	9	4	5
Bassoon	4	3	4
Trumpet	6	8	16
Trombone	5	4	4
Tympanum	1	0	2
	61	53	73

* "Hofprotokollbuch: 1700–1713," fols. 215–26. April, 1712, represents the time of reevaluation before the actual reductions took place.
** "Hofprotokollbuch: 1700–1713," fols. 401–5v.
† Köchel, *Johann Joseph Fux*, 225.

musicians were hired from time to time for special situations. Just as obvious is the fact that help from outside the court was not always needed, for many court musicians were adept at playing more than one instrument.

Evidence of this is demonstrated by *Il Gioseffo*. In this work Conti has scored Noafa's aria "Bramo un core" for mandolin, violins, viola, and cello. Given Conti's interest in the mandolin (as evidenced both by his music for solo mandolin and by his treatise on the playing of the instrument),[16] it would appear that he incorporated the mandolin into the score as a way of involving himself in the performance.

That his intentions may have been governed primarily by dramatic considerations and only coincidentally by opportunities to perform is suggested by another of his oratorios, *David* (1724). At the point of dramatic climax in Part II, when David appears before Saul, Conti composed a sequence of three numbers, each featuring the theorbo: an instrumental prelude, a *recitativo stromentato*, and an aria. The first number sets the mood for David's soliloquy; the second has arpeggio figuration for the theorbo to simulate the music of the ancient kinnôr, which David is said to have played for Saul; the third highlights the theorbo as a solo instrument with an extensive instrumental introduction.

Whether Conti was scoring a sacred or a secular work, he paid the same special attention to instrumental variety. Sometimes he varied the scoring by introducing solo instruments such as the chalumeau, bassoon, or trombone; at

16. Josef Zuth, "Die Mandolinhandschriften in der Bibliothek der Gesellschaft der Musikfreunde in Wien," *Zeitschrift für Musikwissenschaft* 14 (1931): 89–99.

other times, he varied the sonority through particular instrumental combinations, as exemplified in arias accompanied solely by woodwinds[17] or solely by the lower strings such as baryton 1, baryton 2, "violone e contrabassi,"[18] or by interesting combinations of both with bassoon 1, bassoon 2, and cellos.[19] In each instance, there seems to be a direct correlation with the dramatic action.

Conti had presented several major works at the Hapsburg court before 1712, but he was not officially granted the title of "Hof-Compositor" until the reign of Charles VI. The stipend for this new position, together with the one he already earned as court theorbist, brought Conti an annual income exceeding that paid to Kapellmeister Fux. In addition, Conti's household received the earnings of the court's prima donna, for both his second and third wives held this coveted appointment.

Wealth, fame, and honor were enjoyed by Conti during his lifetime, and one would have thought that history would remember him most for his major dramatic works. But oddly enough, after Conti's death in 1732, his fame as a composer was perpetuated not by the music he wrote for the Carnival season or the Lenten season, the birthdays and namedays of the imperial family or the wedding celebrations, but by the music he composed for liturgical use in services of worship. Unlike the prescribed and very limited occasions when his dramatic works were performed, the liturgical music was heard repeatedly, year after year, far into the next century. Evidence of this comes from the covers of the part books on which later generations of musicians have recorded the dates when this music was used for services in the Hofburgkapelle and in the Schottenkirche on the Freyung.

One of these works, which was frequently performed as late as 1753, is an instrumental *Sinfonia a 4*, listed as No. 8 of the "Hofcapelle musica opus 261."[20] This particular sinfonia had already served a quite different purpose before it became associated with the service music for the imperial chapel, for it is none other than the three-movement overture to Conti's opera *Pallade trionfante*.[21] But whereas the opera seemed to bloom and fade all within the year of its creation, 1722, the overture, once placed in its new surroundings, continued to serve a useful purpose for at least the next thirty years.

Conti wrote a number of vocal works designed for liturgical use, ranging in scope from the brief four-part settings of ten Latin hymns to his grandiose double-chorus setting of the Mass. While each of these works is interesting and worthy of attention, two are singled out here for discussion. The first is Conti's *Te Deum,* written for a ten-voice double chorus (SSATB) and a seven-part instrumental ensemble consisting of clarini, timpani, violins, viola, and organ/

17. See *Il martirio di S. Lorenzo,* Part I, aria "I tormenti son."
18. See ibid., Part II, aria "Adorato di tante faville."
19. See *Il Gioseffo,* Part I, aria "Tergi pur l'umido."
20. Nine of the twelve part books are in A/Wn. No score is contained in this particular Hofcapelle collection.
21. My analysis of Conti's instrumental music, including this sinfonia, appears in *The Symphony, 1720–1840,* ed. Barry S. Brook, Series B, vol. 2 (New York, 1983).22.

continuo. Although no date is indicated on the manuscript, the extensive proportions of this *Te Deum*[22] lead one to surmise that it was composed to celebrate an important event in the imperial city. From its triumphal homophonic statements to its introspective a cappella sections, from its antiphonal exchanges between choirs and instruments to its majestic multivoiced fugues, this is indeed a glorious tribute to God and to the emperor.

No less magnificent are Conti's settings of the Mass currently housed in the archives of the Schottenkirche, the church where Johann Fux was organist for a number of years. One of these, the *Missa Sancti Pauli,* is the only composition by Conti that can claim performances spanning a period of approximately 150 years. This particular work belongs to a unique category of musical settings of the Mass known as "Credo" Masses.[23] The category derives its name from the fact that the word *credo* is repeated over and over again against the exposition of the text of the creed, a practice at variance with the Roman Catholic rite. The reiteration of this very word *credo* draws attention to the juxtapositioning of tensions that lay behind the facade of imperial splendor. On the one hand, it expresses the affirmation of a jubilant nation fresh from its victorious encounter with the Turks; but on the other, it reflects the firm determination of the Counter-Reformation to prevent Protestant domination of the empire.

Francesco Conti's contribution to the Hapsburg court is as significant as it is varied. In this respect, his career bears a marked resemblance to that of his more illustrious contemporary, Johann Bernhard Fischer von Erlach. Just as Fischer von Erlach combined a seemingly infinite variety of contrasting styles to create his own unique architectural designs, so too did Conti feel free to experiment in the musical expression of religious ideas. In a certain sense, Conti is not unlike Hanswurst, the stock character created by Stanitzky, who freely commented upon the thoughts and actions of the nobility but did so in the accepted artistic forms of his day.

By no means does this essay intend to provide a definitive appraisal of Conti's religious works. Rather, its purpose is to spark musicological interest in a composer worthy of taking his rightful place with the other composers who served the Hapsburg court at the beginning of the eighteenth century. It is hoped that this brief glimpse into the life of Francesco Conti as a composer of sacred music will serve to honor him on this, the three-hundredth anniversary of his birth.

22. A manuscript score is in A/Wgm.
23. Georg Nikolaus Reichert, "Zur Geschichte der Wiener Messenkomposition" (Ph.D. diss., Vienna, 1935), 31–42.

RAVEL AND FALLA: AN UNPUBLISHED CORRESPONDENCE, 1914–1933

ARBIE ORENSTEIN

"Arrivé à Paris il y a cinq ans, je garderai toujours une profonde reconnaissance pour la bonté avec laquelle les maîtres Isaac Albeniz, Claude Debussy, et Paul Dukas ont bien voulu m'encourager et s'intéresser à mes travaux. J'ai aussi des motifs d'une sincère gratitude amicale et artistique pour Ricardo Viñes, Maurice Ravel et Florent Schmitt."—From an unpublished letter, dated November 15, 1912, written by Manuel de Falla to the French musicologist Jules Ecorcheville.

MAURICE RAVEL (1875–1937) and Manuel de Falla (1876–1946) were introduced in the summer of 1907 by the distinguished Catalan pianist Ricardo Viñes.[1] Falla had just arrived in Paris from Madrid, ostensibly for a brief visit. As it turned out, he remained in the French capital for seven years.[2] He met many compatriots in Paris, among them Pablo Casals, Joaquín Turina, who was studying with Vincent d'Indy at the Schola Cantorum, and Pablo Picasso, who

---

1. Viñes (1876–1943) was Ravel's closest friend at the Conservatoire. Blessed with a prodigious memory, he introduced a wide variety of contemporary music, including virtually all the piano music of Debussy and Ravel. Falla added the orchestral part to *Nights in the Gardens of Spain* at his suggestion and dedicated the piece to him. Viñes's diary is a document of extraordinary interest (see Nina Gubisch, "Le Journal inédit de Ricardo Viñes," *Revue internationale de musique française* 1/2 [June, 1980]: 154–248).

2. Gilbert Chase has provided an astute summary of the seminal role played by Paris: "When the history of modern Spanish music comes to be written, a full chapter should be devoted to the role that Paris played in its development. All that a great, noble, generous, and beautifully civilized city could do for the promotion of art was done by Paris, the modern Athens, in those decades before and after the first World War.... On the material side, the great majority of works by modern Spanish composers were first published in Paris, and in the concert halls of that capital these works always found a cordial welcome" (*The Music of Spain*, 2nd rev. ed. [New York, 1959], 185). Of course, a fruitful artistic symbiosis existed between the two nations, inasmuch as the exotic lure of the Iberian peninsula stimulated some of France's outstanding achievements—Bizet's *Carmen*, Lalo's *Symphonie espagnole*, Debussy's *Ibéria*, and Ravel's *Rapsodie espagnole*, to name but a few.

would later design the drop curtain, décor, and costumes for *The Three-Cornered Hat*. In a commemorative article printed in *La Revue musicale* in 1939, Falla recalled his first meeting with Ravel. As Falla described the incident, Ravel and Viñes were reading through the *Rapsodie espagnole,* which had just been published in its original version for piano, four hands, and which would soon be introduced at a concert of the Société Nationale de Musique. Viñes's observations on the problems of achieving clarity in several passages of the four-hand version gave rise to the idea of an orchestral setting. In this way, Falla explains, began the

> wonderful series of transcriptions from piano to orchestra, whose ingenuity and virtuosity have never been surpassed. But how could I explain Ravel's subtly authentic Hispanic quality, knowing, by his own admission, that he had but neighboring relations with our country, being born near its frontier? I rapidly solved the problem: Ravel's Spain was a Spain ideally presented by his mother, whose refined conversation, always in excellent Spanish, delighted me, particularly when she would recall her youthful years spent in Madrid.[3]

Thus through his mother Ravel retained a lifelong interest in Spanish music, and Falla, for his part, would discover a second musical homeland in France. Falla's account includes a reference to Ravel's musical achievement as a "bold art of supreme distinction and rare perfection"[4]—a characterization that could just as well be applied to Falla's own achievement.

When Falla left Paris for Madrid, because of the outbreak of World War I, he left behind many good friends and warm memories. He had attended innumerable recitals, private orchestral rehearsals, and musicales in middle- and upper-class salons. Above all, he had received informal counsel from Debussy, Dukas, and Ravel.[5] Shortly after returning to Madrid, Falla wrote to Ravel,[6]

---

3. Falla, "Notes sur Ravel," trans. Alexis Roland-Manuel, *La Revue musicale* 20 (Mar., 1939): 83.

4. Ibid., 81.

5. One may note the spiritual imprint of Ravel's *Five Greek Folk Songs* on Falla's *Seven Spanish Folk Songs,* and that of Debussy (*Ibéria*) and Ravel (*Rapsodie espagnole*) on *Nights in the Gardens of Spain.* Falla composed brief homages following the deaths of Debussy (*Homenaje,* for guitar, which quotes *Soirée dans Grenade*) and Dukas (*Hommage,* for piano, which contains several references to Dukas's Piano Sonata).

6. Eighteen letters (four from Falla to Ravel and fourteen from Ravel to Falla) dating from 1914–33 have come to light. Three autographs of Falla are in the music division of the Bibliothèque Nationale, and the remaining autographs, or reproductions of them, are in the private collection of Señora Maria Isabel de Falla de García de Paredes, Falla's niece, whom I wish to thank for her kind cooperation. I am also grateful to Madame Alexandre Taverne, the present inheritor of Maurice Ravel's estate. With one exception—Ravel to Falla, Jan. 2, 1919, reproduced in Manuel Orozco's *Falla* (Barcelona, 1968), p. 32—all the letters have remained unpublished. It is clear from the correspondence that other letters were exchanged that have not yet been recovered. Three letters are printed as part of the main text of the present essay, and thirteen letters, referred to by number, are printed in the Appendix, beginning on p. 343 below. Two letters have been omitted from this study: a typewritten letter from Ravel to Falla dated Jan. 25, 1924, which contains virtually the same information as the letter of Jan. 11, 1924, and a post card from Falla to Ravel dated July 14, 1931, in which Falla wrote that he was staying at the Hôtel de Bourgogne et Montana in Paris and hoped to see Ravel soon, either in Paris or at Montfort l'Amaury.

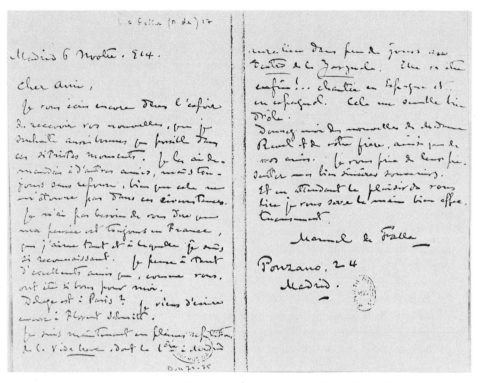

PLATE I. Falla's letter to Ravel, November 6, 1914; Paris, Bibliothèque Nationale

expressing his concern about the lack of news from friends, his feeling of gratitude toward them, and his amusement over the fact that *La vida breve* would finally be performed in Spain and in Spanish (Letter 1, see Appendix, p. 343; see Plate I).[7]

7. Although the opera *La vida breve* won first prize in a national competition in 1905, it was first performed, in a revised version, at the Municipal Casino in Nice in 1913. In a review of a performance at the Opéra Comique in Paris in Jan., 1914, Ravel made the following observations:

At the present time, they [Falla and Enrique Granados] are the two composers who appear to affirm most profoundly and elegantly the distinctly national character of the modern Spanish school. Together with Mr. Turina, . . . they are the most brilliant disciples of Isaac Albeniz. Exempt from the clumsiness, frequent monotony, and the laborious workmanship that often encumber the initiator's work, they inherited, in return, his sensitivity for rhythm, harmony and color.

Among his compatriots, Mr. Falla offers the closest affinity with present-day French musicians. His origin is revealed, however, in his slightest compositions, to the point that certain individuals perceive a shortcoming in this respect: *La vida breve* has been reproached for the frequent recurrence of certain melodic turns, which are characteristic of Andalusian song. One might just as well deplore the fact that the performers are adorned in embroidered shawls, or have their heads covered with mantillas. . . .

Furthermore, it would be wrong to conclude that local color is obtained solely by means of these melodic turns, or that local color alone accounts for the importance of this work. Undoubtedly, the composer has most brilliantly taken advantage of the picturesque episodes, which happily possess very little plot: the march of the fruit peddlers, a folk wedding, and gypsy dances. But, in the scenes that call for other talents, one discovers a sincerity of expression, as well as an abundance and freshness of inspiration that are thoroughly charming. (*Comoedia illustré* [Jan. 20, 1914], 391)

In his reply (Letter 2), Ravel sent his good wishes for the forthcoming performance, adding a gently ironic observation: "you will thus be discovered by your compatriots after having been appreciated abroad; that's always the fate of artists." In addition Ravel reports that whereas his brother Edouard was serving in the ambulance corps, his own application for military service had been rejected because he was underweight by some four pounds.

Ravel did finally manage to enlist, and so he witnessed the horrors of war. His worsening bouts of insomnia and especially the death of his mother in January, 1917, led to a long period of depression and painful readjustment. He wrote very little during the war, and in the postwar years he would find it increasingly difficult to compose. In a post card sent to Falla in January, 1919, from the isolated mountain resort of Mégève in France's Haute-Savoie, Ravel mentions his innermost fear—that of being unable to work (Letter 3).

Falla's war years, spent in Madrid, were, in comparison with Ravel's, artistically productive and personally unadventurous. He completed *El amor brujo, Nights in the Gardens of Spain,* and *The Corregidor and the Miller's Wife,* the first version of *The Three-Cornered Hat.* In July, 1919, Falla was in London for the Ballet Russe production of *The Three-Cornered Hat,* but he hastily returned to Madrid upon learning that his mother was gravely ill. His subsequent bereavement called forth from Ravel a message of condolence that is certainly one of the most poignant and revealing letters he ever wrote:

St Cloud   19/9/19

Mon cher ami,

Aubry[8] m'avait appris votre présence à Londres; je l'avais chargé de vous transmettre le souvenir de mon amitié, et depuis, je n'avais plus aucune nouvelle de vous.

Et voici que Strawinsky m'apprend l'affreux malheur qui vous a obligé de quitter Londres précipitament.

Je vais raviver votre douleur, et pourtant je ne veux pas vous laisser croire à mon indifférence. Je n'ai pas oublié la lettre affectueuse, à laquelle j'ai répondu si tard, que vous m'avez envoyée dans les mêmes circonstances.

C'est une chose terrible qui nous est arrivée, mon cher ami. Dès ce moment, la vie est transformée. On peut encore en ressentir les joies, les émotions, mais plus de la même façon; un peu comme lorsqu'on n'a pas dormi, ou qu'on a la fièvre. Peut-être cela finit-il par s'apaiser à la longue.

Moi, je ne me suis pas encore repris. Bien que mon séjour dans les montagnes m'ait fait grand bien, et que ma santé soit à peu près rétablie, je n'ai pu encore me remettre au travail, et pourtant je sens que ce serait là, sinon l'oubli, que je ne désire pas, du moins le meilleur adoucissement.

---

8. The French critic Georges Jean-Aubry (1882–1949) was a close friend and ardent supporter of both composers.

Tâchez d'être plus fort que moi, mon cher ami. Je vous le souhaite de tout mon coeur, en vous envoyant mon plus profond sentiment de sympathie.

Maurice Ravel

Ravel spent the winter of 1919 in Lapras, a village in the Cévennes mountain range some 350 miles southeast of Paris (Letter 4). In an admittedly "extreme" attempt to shake off his lethargy, he worked in total isolation at the country home of an old friend, André Ferdinand Hérold.[9] Ravel succeeded in recapturing his creative enthusiasm, and in the spring of 1920 he returned to Paris with a new work, *La Valse.*

The completion of Ravel's Sonata for Violin and Cello in 1922 marked the beginning of creative impasse that lasted for more than two years. During this period Ravel traveled extensively, which seems to have aggravated the crisis rather than resolve it. In 1922 he concertized in London, Amsterdam, and Milan. In a post card sent in early 1923 from St.-Jean-de-Luz in the Basque territory of France, he apologizes to Falla for having allowed his correspondence to lapse (Letter 5). Shortly after writing this message, he set out on a concert tour that took him to Italy, England, and Belgium.

Falla's remarkable marionette play, *El retablo de Maese Pedro (Master Peter's Puppet Theater)*, was commissioned by Princess Edmond de Polignac,[10] and the first staged performance, conducted by Vladimir Golschmann, was given at her elegant home in Paris on June 25, 1923.[11] Unable to attend the performance because of a painful foot inflamation, Ravel wrote to Falla the next day, inviting him and the princess to come to Le Belvédère[12] for lunch (Letter 6). Falla was about to leave Paris, however, and so the composers did not meet on this occasion (Letter 7).

After many changes in schedule, Ravel concertized in Madrid and Barcelona in the spring of 1924, this being his first trip beyond the Basque provinces of northern Spain. At the invitation of Madrid's Philharmonic Society he conducted *La Valse* and his transcriptions of Debussy's *Sarabande* and *Danse* on May 5.[13] On May 18 the Chamber Music Society of Barcelona presented an all-Ravel program with the participation of the composer, soprano Marcelle Gerar,

9. Hérold was the translator of *La Cloche engloutie* (based on Gerhardt Hauptmann's *Die versunkene Glocke*), an operatic project that never materialized, although Ravel had worked on it intermittently between 1906 and 1914.

10. Among the many works she commissioned were Ravel's *Pavane pour une infante défunte*, Satie's *Socrate*, and Stravinsky's *Renard*.

11. The first concert performance had taken place in Seville on March 23, 1923, with Falla conducting the newly formed Bética Chamber Orchestra.

12. In 1921, Ravel moved to Montfort l'Amaury, a tranquil village some thirty miles west of Paris. Le Belvédère, his final official residence, has been preserved exactly as he left it and is now a national museum open to the public.

13. Other highlights of the program included *Le Tombeau de Couperin* and *Alborada del gracioso*, conducted by Perez Casas. In another recital, at Madrid's French Institute, Ravel performed several of his piano pieces, sharing the program with Joaquín Turina.

pianist Robert Casadesus, violinist Marius Casadesus, and cellist Maurice Maré-chal.[14] Ravel had told Falla of his plans (Letter 8), but as circumstances worked out, Falla was in Granada, a twenty-two-hour train ride from Madrid, and thus the composers missed seeing each other again.

Ravel's inability to speak Spanish led to a "disastrous" incident in Madrid: upon asking for some stationery at his hotel, he was served hot chocolate! Despite the problems of communication, the orchestral rehearsals went well, thanks to the skill and enthusiasm of the musicians (Letter 9).

In July, 1924, Falla wrote a gracious letter of introduction on behalf of Ernesto Halffter (b. 1905). Herein he reiterates his high regard for Ravel's artistic counsel. In addition, the letter bespeaks Falla's own good judgment and modesty, as well as his genuine concern for the young composer who would ultimately prove to be his most distinguished disciple.[15]

Granada   le 7 juillet [1]924

Cher ami,

Ernesto Halffter me demande une lettre de présentation pour vous, et je la lui envoie avec un vif plaisir.

Il s'agit, comme vous le savez, d'un garçon doué pour la musique d'une façon bien peu commune.

Il a pour vous la plus grande admiration—ce qui, d'ailleurs est tout naturel; mais cela est encore une raison de ma sympathie pour lui.

Faites lui bon accueil. Il a besoin de vos si précieux conseils.

J'ai grand espoir dans l'avenir de Halffter, car indépendamment de ses dons naturels, il a la ferme volonté d'en profiter autant que possible, les développant par des études sérieuses.

Il est aussi le chef du nouvel *orquestra Bética de camara* que nous avons organisé à Seville.[16] Je vous en ai déjà parlé. Ils travaillent d'ailleurs votre admirable *Mère l'oye* avec enthousiasme.

Combien vivement j'ai regretté ne pas vous voir pendant votre séjour en Espagne, et combien aussi j'ai été ému par la grande bonté que vous avez eue pour moi à cette occasion.

Merci de coeur, cher ami, avec mes très affectueuses amitiés.

Votre

Manuel de Falla

14. Robert Casadesus played *Gaspard de la nuit* and performed in the Trio in A minor. Ravel provided the piano accompaniments for *Shéhérazade, Ronsard à son âme,* and *Sur l'Herbe,* as well as performing the *Berceuse sur le nom de Gabriel Fauré* and *Tzigane.* The program also included the Sonata for Violin and Cello. Another program in Barcelona, devoted to choral music, included Ravel's *Trois Chansons pour choeur mixte sans accompagnement,* and works by Janequin, Palestrina, and Debussy.

15. Falla and Halffter were introduced by the Spanish musicologist and critic Adolfo Salazar in Madrid in 1923. At Falla's request Halffter orchestrated the accompaniments to the *Seven Spanish Folk Songs,* and he later completed *Atlántida,* the imposing posthumous oratorio that Falla had worked on during the last eighteen years of his life.

16. The Bética Chamber Orchestra traveled throughout Spain, introducing audiences to works by Monteverdi, Alessandro Scarlatti, and Haydn, as well as by Stravinsky, Ravel, and the modern Spanish school.

Although the initial drafts of Ravel's *L'Enfant et les sortilèges* were composed in 1920, only three scenes of Colette's libretto had been set to music by the autumn of 1924. About this time the director of the Monte Carlo Opera, Raoul Gunsbourg, visited Le Belvédère and told the composer that his *L'Heure espagnole* had been performed with great success at Monte Carlo. Urged on by his enthusiastic prodding, Ravel agreed to have a new opera ready for the coming season. But he fell far behind schedule and was further delayed by a bout of influenza coupled with food poisoning. In a letter written to Falla toward the close of 1924, Ravel mentions these troubles (Letter 10). All ended well, however, as the opera was completed in an extraordinary burst of speed. Ravel spent the opening months of 1925 in Monte Carlo retouching his score and supervising rehearsals. The première, conducted by Vittorio de Sabata, was given on March 21.

During the 1920s the positions of leadership achieved by Ravel and Falla became increasingly apparent to the public and the press alike. The composers continued to work slowly, Ravel at Le Belvédère and Falla in Granada, and their composing was interrupted by occasional concert tours presenting their own music in London, Paris, and other European cities. In an unusually prompt reply to a post card sent from Granada, Ravel wrote to Falla on February 2, 1927, expressing pleasure at having heard from his colleague and suggesting that they try to keep in touch more often (Letter 11; see Plate II).

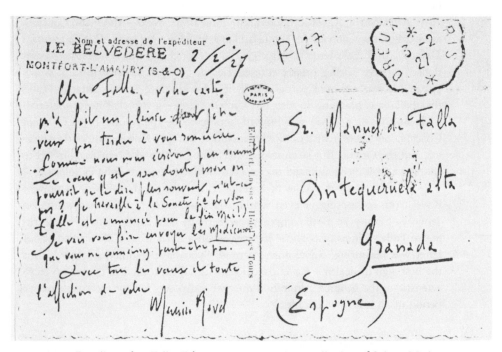

PLATE II. Ravel's card to Falla, February 2, 1927; private collection of Señora Maria Isabel de Falla de Garcia de Paredes

In March, 1928, the Opéra Comique presented a triple bill consisting of *La vida breve, El amor brujo,* and *El retablo de Maese Pedro,* and on March 19, Falla participated in a recital devoted to his music at the Salle Pleyel. Before an appreciative audience that filled the hall Falla performed as soloist in his Harpsichord Concerto and accompanied Ninon Vallin in his *Seven Spanish Folk Songs.* In reviewing this concert, Henry Prunières made the following perceptive comments:

> Long unappreciated in his own country, M. de Falla has seen his work, little by little, arouse the most enthusiastic admiration, at first in France, and finally throughout the world. His name today is almost a symbol of Spanish music. . . . Ever dissatisfied with himself, seeking perfection, he revises over and over again.[17]

At this time Ravel was in the midst of an exhilarating four-month coast-to-coast tour of the United States and Canada. Upon returning to France in late April, 1928, he composed the *Boléro* for Ida Rubinstein, and in November, together with mezzo-soprano Madeleine Grey and violinist Claude Lévy, he undertook an exhausting tour in Spain, appearing in nine cities within some eighteen days. The arrangements for the highly successful recital in Granada were made by Falla (Letter 12), and the composers enjoyed a warm, albeit very brief reunion.

After *Boléro,* Ravel composed only three more works—the Piano Concerto in G major, the Concerto for the Left Hand, and his swan song, *Don Quichotte à Dulcinée.* In Ravel's letter of March 6, 1930 (Letter 13), the concertos are mentioned together with a project entitled *Dédale 39* ("an airplane in C"), which apparently was not even partially sketched. In addition, Ravel's letter indicates that Falla was planning to visit the United States—a trip that never materialized. At this time Ravel was himself hoping to be the soloist in his G-major Concerto on a tour that would have included Europe, North and South America, and the Orient. But because of his declining health, the tour was limited to Europe, and Ravel conducted the concerto with Marguerite Long as soloist.

During 1933 the onset of a debilitating terminal disease was to prevent Ravel from composing or even writing. His last letter to Falla was written in January of that year. Both composers had recently been indisposed. Ravel, learning of Falla's illness, was about to write when a letter from Falla arrived. Your letter was reassuring, Ravel notes, because "you have resumed work, which is the best sign of health." Ravel concludes with an expression of friendship characteristic of the genuine admiration the two composers felt for each other over a period of almost three decades.

17. *New York Times,* Apr. 8, 1928.

Le Belvédère   6/1/33
Montfort l'Amaury

    Cher Falla,
    Roland Manuel[18] m'a inquiété en m'apprenant que vous aviez été
souffrant.
    J'allais vous écrire: vous me devancez, et me rassurez puisque vous
avez repris le travail, ce qui est le meilleur signe de santé.
    Moi-même, je commence à peine à m'y remettre. L'accident n'était
pourtant pas très grave: froissement du thorax et quelques blessures de la
face. N'empêche que j'étais incapable de faire quoi que ce fût, sinon de
dormir et de manger. Il ne me reste plus guère qu'une terreur animale des
taxis dont je n'use qu'à la dernière extrémité.[19]
    A bientôt, cher Falla: aurai-je la joie de vous revoir sur la côte, vers
l'automne, sinon avant? En attendant, trouvez ici les souhaits les plus affectueux de votre

                                    Maurice Ravel

Appendix

LETTER 1

Ponzano, 24   6 Nov[em]bre [1]914
Madrid

    Cher ami,
    Je vous écris encore dans l'espoir de recevoir vos nouvelles, que je sou-
haite aussi bonnes que possible dans ces si tristes moments. Je les ai de-
mandées à d'autres amis, mais toujours sans réponse, bien que cela ne
m'étonne pas dans ces circonstances.
    Je n'ai pas besoin de vous dire que ma pensée est toujours en France,
que j'aime tant et à laquelle je suis si reconnaissant. Je pense à tant d'excellents amis que, comme vous, ont été si bons pour moi.
    Delage est à Paris? Je viens d'écrire encore à Florent Schmitt.[20]
    Je suis maintenant en pleines répétitions de la *Vida breve,* dont la 1ère à
Madrid aura lieu dans peu de jours au *Teatro* de la *Zarzuela.* Elle va être,
enfin! . . chantée en Espagne et . . . en espagnol. Cela me semble bien
drôle.

---

18. The distinguished French musicologist and critic Alexis Roland-Manuel (1891–1966) was a close friend
of both composers.
19. On Oct. 9, 1932, Ravel was injured in a taxi collision in Paris, suffering several facial wounds and chest
bruises. Although he endured considerable pain, his condition was not serious, and in December he felt well
enough to participate in a concert devoted to his works given in Basel.
20. The composers Maurice Delage and Florent Schmitt were among Ravel's closest associates.

Donnez moi des nouvelles de Madame Ravel et de votre frère, ainsi que de nos amis. Je vous prie de leur présenter mes bien sincères souvenirs.

Et en attendant le plaisir de vous lire je vous serre la main bien affec-tueusement.

Manuel de Falla

LETTER 2

4 Avenue Carnot   15/12/14
Paris

Cher ami,

je suis ravi d'apprendre que la *Vida Breve* va enfin être jouée en Espagne, et suis certain de son succès. Vous allez donc être découvert par vos compatriotes, après avoir été apprécié à l'étranger; ce qui sera toujours le sort des artistes. Nous venons de rentrer à Paris, après un séjour de 4 mois à St Jean de Luz plein d'agréments, comme vous pensez. Voici les nouvelles des amis: *Delage* engagé volontaire avec l'auto de son père, a passé quelque temps à Bordeaux. Il est envoyé maintenant en mission. Son quartier général est à Fontainebleau où je dois aller le voir un de ces jours. Je ne sais son adresse exacte. *Schmitt* est au *41e territorial 16e Cie. Toul.* Sur son désir, il a été envoyé sur le front, mais je pense que les lettres envoyées à l'adresse ci-dessus lui parviendront. Mon frère, engagé dans les autos sanitaires, ne nous donne que trop rarement de ses nouvelles. Quant à moi, je me suis présenté à Bayonne, et j'ai échoué, parce qu'il me manque 2K[ilo]g[ram]s. Je ne songe plus qu'aux moyens efficaces de recom-mencer. Ma mère n'est pas très bien portante. Ses angoisses, en ces circon-stances, expliquent son état. Donnez-moi bientôt de vos nouvelles et de celles de votre oeuvre.

Maurice Ravel

Votre frère est-il à Paris?

LETTER 3

Hôtel du M[on]t Blanc   2/1/19
Mégève (H[au]te Savoie)

Cher ami,

excusez-moi de mon long silence: je suis si détraqué depuis ma réforme. Les médecins m'ont envoyé ici pour me soigner. Ce n'est pas très gai; il fait un froid terrible, et je dois y rester au moins 3 mois. Enfin, si au bout de ce temps je puis me remettre au travail . . .

Recevez, mon cher ami, les voeux les plus cordiaux de votre

Maurice Ravel

LETTER 4

Lapras par Lamastre   16/12/19
Ardêche

    Mon cher ami,

    excusez-moi: je n'ai pas encore répondu ni à votre carte du mois dernier, ni même à votre lettre d'octobre. Je n'avais pu encore reprendre le travail, et la correspondance elle-même me semblait demander un effort surhumain. Je suis enfin arrivé à secouer cette torpeur; j'ai pris les grands moyens: j'ai quitté Paris et suis venu m'enfermer dans une grande maison à peu près isolée, au milieu des Cévennes. Je ne vois personne. Cette solitude que je redoutais tant autrefois me semble délicieuse. Je vis davantage avec ceux qui m'ont quitté. Je travaille comme cela ne m'était pas arrivé depuis 5 ans. Il faudra remettre mon voyage à Madrid, et pourtant l'espoir de connaître cette ville me remplit d'un bonheur nostalgique: n'y ai-je pas vécu toute ma jeunesse au milieu des souvenirs évoqués journellement par mon père et ma mère?

    Je serais heureux d'avoir quelquefois de vos nouvelles, mon cher ami. Je vous envoie une affectueuse poignée de main.

                                      Maurice Ravel

LETTER 5

St-Jean-de-Luz   4/3/23

    Cher Falla,

    je semble bien mériter vos reproches. Pourtant, je ne vous oublie pas. Mais depuis près d'un an, je ne cesse de voyager. Cela ne m'empêche pas de m'ennuyer formidablement, d'autant plus que je me persuade que je ferais jamais plus rien. Pardonnez-moi et donnez-moi souvent de vos nouvelles. Je tâcherai de secouer mon cafard et de vous répondre.

    Affectueusement à vous

                                        Maurice Ravel

LETTER 6

Le Belvédère   26/6/23
Montfort l'Amaury

    Cher Falla,

    ainsi que je l'écris à la princesse de Polignac, il m'a été vraiment impossible, quoique je l'aie espéré jusqu'au dernier moment, d'aller entendre votre oeuvre hier soir. J'espère que vous voudrez bien m'excuser, et que vous n'allez pas repartir sans me voir. Je ne pourrai certainement pas bouger d'ici à Samedi. Ne pourriez-vous pas venir un de ces jours partager un déjeuner qui ne sera même pas frugal, à cause de la mauvaise saison? Je prie la princesse de vous accompagner. Si elle ne le pouvait pas, et que votre auto soit en réparation, vous n'avez qu'à prendre à la gare des Invalides le train de 9ʰ13 (consultez l'horaire) et, à la gare de Montfort l'Amaury, l'auto-car qui vous conduira à la ville. Donc, à très bientôt, n'est-ce pas? et bien affectueusement à vous

Maurice Ravel

LETTER 7

Paris   le 1ᵉʳ juillet [1]923

Très cher ami,
Je reçois votre gentille invitation qui m'a fait le plus grand plaisir. Je suis, malheureusement, sur le point de partir, or je dois me priver de la joie de passer chez vous ces quelques heures. J'espère qu'une autre occasion plus favorable pour moi se présentera bientôt, ici *ou à Grenade,* où j'aurai, moi aussi un repas frugal avec ma très affectueuse amitié à vous offrir.
Bien cordialement votre

Manuel de Falla

LETTER 8

Le Belvédère   11/1/24
Montfort l'Amaury

Mon cher ami,
bien avant de recevoir vos bons souhaits, je devais vous écrire. J'attendais pour cela des nouvelles de l'*Associacio de Musica da Camera* de Barcelona avec qui je suis en pourparlers depuis quelques semaines au sujet d'un concert dont la date avait été fixée primitivement au 24 Février, mais que je désirais reculer de quelques jours. Un télégramme reçu à l'instant m'avise que l'on a reporté ce concert au 27 Février.
Je serais très heureux si vous pouviez arranger quelque chose à Madrid vers cette époque; aussi près que possible de cette date, car si l'Espagne est le pays que je désire le plus vivement connaître, et singulièrement la ville à qui je dois tant (en ce moment, je ne lui en ai aucune reconnaissance), je préfère attendre des jours plus favorables pour m'y attarder.
A partir du 15 Février, je suis en balade: Londres, Bruxelles, etc. J'ai tout de suite accepté pour Barcelone parce que ça tombait dans la période que je m'étais fixée pour le repos. Je pensais terminer ma Sonate pour V[io]lon et piano vers les 1ers jours de Février. Je viens de l'abandonner. La parenthèse ci-dessus vous en donne la raison principale: le cafard a

repris de plus belle. Tout ce que je puis faire est de mettre en musique une Epitaphe de Ronsard, qui correspond assez à mon état d'esprit. Prunières[21] en sera ravi, d'ailleurs, car je ne lui avais donné qu'un faible espoir de collaborer à son numéro de *Ronsard*. Seulement, j'avais promis à Londres la 1re audition de ma Sonate![22]

J'attends impatiemment de vos nouvelles, mon cher ami, et vous envoie toute l'affectueuse pensée de votre

Maurice Ravel

et aussi tous mes souhaits, non moins affectueux, bien que tardifs.

LETTER 9

Hôtel de Paris 30/4/24
Madrid

Cher ami,
vous savez que je suis à Madrid. Ne devez-vous pas y venir ces jours-ci?

Je voudrais bien aller vous voir, mais vraiment 22 h[eures] de chemin de fer, c'est beaucoup. D'autant plus que le 18, je dois être à Barcelone et que, grâce à un retard de 3 heures, j'ai dû passer 2 nuits en chemin de fer, dont je suis encore abruti.

Je viens de faire répéter "la Valse", "Sarabande" et "Danse" de Debussy, que j'ai orchestrées. Heureusement que l'orchestre est composé d'excellents musiciens très gentils; sans quoi je ne sais comment je pourrais m'en tirer avec les quelques mots d'espagnol d'italien et de nègre que je puis rassembler.

A l'hôtel, ça donne des résultats désastreux: quand je demande du papier à lettres, on m'apporte un chocolat. Enfin, ça se tassera . . .

J'étais chargé d'une foule de choses aimables de la part des Coppeley-Harding et d'Aubry, lequel a dû vous écrire, d'ailleurs.

J'espère tout-de-même vous voir. En attendant, trouvez ici toutes mes pensées les plus affectueuses.

Maurice Ravel

21. Henry Prunières (1886–1942), the editor of *La Revue musicale,* commissioned two brief works that were published by the journal and subsequently by Durand: the *Berceuse sur le nom de Gabriel Fauré* (violin and piano), for an issue (Oct., 1922) honoring Fauré, and the song *Ronsard à son âme,* for an issue (May, 1924) commemorating the four hundredth anniversary of the poet's birth.

22. At a Ravel festival given in London on Oct. 18, 1923, the following notice appeared in the program:
Daniel Mayer Company Ltd. beg to announce that they have arranged with M. Maurice Ravel to give a concert of his own works with the composer at the piano at the Aeolian Hall, on January 15 [1924] at 8:30. The first performance in the world will be given on that occasion, if ready, of the composer's new Sonata for Violin and Piano.
The sonata was not ready, and three more years were to elapse before its completion.

LETTER 10

Le Belvédère   12/11/24
Montfort l'Amaury

 Mon cher ami,

 on m'apprend que vous êtes souffrant. Ce n'est peut-être pas vrai, et
j'espère en tout cas que ce n'est pas grave. Mais je suis tout-de-même in-
quiet, et si vous aviez un moment, je serais bien heureux que vous me ras-
suriez d'un petit mot.

 Moi, je sors d'une grippe qui s'est compliquée d'intoxication. Maintenant, c'est passé; mais cela m'a fait perdre plus de 3 semaines . . . et j'étais
déjà terriblement en retard: "l'Enfant et les Sortilèges" doit passer à
Monte-Carlo cet hiver, et l'ouvrage est loin d'être terminé.

 A bientôt de vos nouvelles, si possible, et croyez, mon cher ami, à toute
l'affection de votre

             Maurice Ravel

LETTER 11

Le Belvédère   2/2/27
Montfort l'Amaury

 Cher Falla,

 votre carte m'a fait un plaisir dont je ne veux pas tarder à vous remer-
cier. Comme nous nous écrivons peu souvent. Le coeur y est, sans doute,
mais on pourrait se le dire plus souvent, n'est-ce pas? Je travaille à la Sonate p[ian]o et v[io]llon (elle est annoncée pour la fin Mai!)[23]

 Je vais vous faire envoyer les *Madécasses,* que vous ne connaissez peut-
être pas.[24]

 Avec tous les voeux et toute l'affection de votre

             Maurice Ravel

LETTER 12

Gran Hotel Oriente   13/11/28
Zaragoza

 Cher Falla,

 j'aurai donc la grande joie de vous revoir bientôt. Je crains bien de ne
voir de Granada* que la gare et la salle de concert. Et même pas la gare:

23. Georges Enesco, a classmate of Ravel at the Conservatoire, gave the first performance of the sonata with
the composer at the piano in a recital sponsored by Durand on May 30, 1927.
24. Commissioned by the American Maecenas Elizabeth Sprague Coolidge, the *Chansons madécasses* were
composed in 1925 and 1926. Based on the poetry of Evariste-Désiré de Parny (1753–1814), the song cycle
had recently been published by Durand.

comme vous avez fixé le concert à 4ʰ et que le seul train de Malaga où nous jouons la veille arrive trop tard, il nous faudra une automobile qui vienne nous chercher de très bonne heure le 21 au matin, soit à Malaga, soit à Bobadilla, comme vous le jugerez le mieux — une grande auto, pour 3 personnes et beaucoup de bagages. Nous serons à Valencia, hôtel Reina Victoria, du 15 au 18 et y attendrons de vos nouvelles.

Une auto de Malaga à Granada ne devant pas être "al ojo",[25] tâchez de nous la trouver dans les meilleurs conditions.

A bientôt, et toute l'affection de votre vie[i]l [!] ami

Maurice Ravel

*Nous devons quitter Granada le soir même du concert à 8ʰ½ pour Madrid, où nous jouons le lendemain.[26]

LETTER 13

Le Belvédère   6/3/30
Montfort l'Amaury

   Cher Falla, . . .[27]

En effet, un concert d'orchestre est toujours en Amérique un double-concert, à quelques jours de distance.

Donc, vous allez là-bas. Je pense que c'est pour la saison 30–31. C'est aussi à cette epoque que je comptais y promener mon concerto. Mais rien ne m'assure qu'il sera terminé à temps, d'autant plus que je travaille en même temps à un 2ᵉ concerto (pour la main gauche) et à *Dédale 39* (comme vous le devinez, c'est un avion — et un avion en *ut*).

Il y avait bien longtemps que je voulais vous écrire: je me précipite sur l'occasion. Si vous avez un moment, envoyez-moi deux mots. Toute l'affection profonde de votre

Maurice Ravel

Si vous aviez besoin de nouveaux renseignements, ne craignez pas de m'écrire directement.

---

25. Literally, in Spanish, "to the eye," meaning that the car should not be "too expensive," but rather priced as reasonably as possible.

26. This letter contains a postscript written by Madeleine Grey, in which she asks Falla to make sure that the texts of Ravel's songs and their Spanish translations appear in the programs. Otherwise, she writes, the audience will understand nothing. The songs in question were *Ronsard à son âme, Nicolette, Ronde*, the child's aria from *L'Enfant et les sortilèges*, Concepcion's aria from *L'Heure espagnole, Deux Melodies hébraïques*, and the *Chanson hébraïque*.

27. The opening paragraph of this letter concerns the receipt of a telegram whose contents are undisclosed.

THE CASE FOR PERCY GRAINGER, EDWARDIAN MUSICIAN, ON HIS CENTENARY

DAVID JOSEPHSON

ONE HUNDRED YEARS after his birth in a Melbourne suburb, Percy Grainger continues to puzzle. Following a fitful musical training in Frankfurt,[1] he established himself as pianist and composer during a fourteen-year sojourn in Edwardian London. At the outbreak of the Great War he fled to America, where for over a decade he enjoyed a notable career. But that career unraveled during the 1930s, declining steadily until his death in 1961. While the past fifteen years have seen a resurgence in the study and performance of Grainger's music, a firm critical stance eludes us.[2] Awash in a sea of sensitive biographical and tangled musical documents, we have yet to chart our way surely through them and take his measure. A welter of recent amateur studies, and special pleading as well, has only confirmed the standard history of modern Western music that ignores a fascinating man.

---

1. Peter Cahn,"Percy Grainger's Frankfurt Years," *Studies in Music* 12 (1978): 101–13; John Bird, *Percy Grainger* (London, 1976), 26–41; Thomas Armstrong, "The Frankfort Group," *Proceedings of the Royal Musical Association* 85 (1958–59): 1–16.

2. The bibliography in *The New Grove* 7: 618–19, covers writings through 1977. Since then there has appeared a valuable catalogue (marred, however, by the absence of an index) of Grainger's music in the Grainger Museum: Kay Dreyfus, *Percy Grainger Music Collection, Part I: Music by Percy Aldridge Grainger* (Melbourne, 1978). Other recent works include five articles in *Studies in Music* 12–14 (1978–80), as well as the following: Kay Dreyfus, "The Adelaide Grainger Collection Transferred to the Grainger Museum, University of Melbourne," *Miscellanea Musicologica* 9 (1977): 49–71; Frank Strahan *et al., Objects, Documents and Pictures to Reflect Upon, Selected from the Grainger Museum and the Archives Collection of the University of Melbourne* (Melbourne, 1978); and Rachel Lowe, *A Descriptive Catalogue with Checklists of the Letters and Related Documents in the Delius Collection of the Grainger Museum, University of Melbourne, Australia* (London, 1981). Discographies and other articles are found in the *Grainger Journal*, published since 1978 by the Percy Grainger Society (England).

Australians have claimed Grainger for themselves, finding reflections in his music of that nation's pioneering spirit and vast spaces.[3] It is an argument difficult to sustain in any but the most general terms. Among the small number of works Grainger associated with his homeland are the early sketches for *Bush Music* (first sketched in 1900), *Train Music* (first sketched in 1900–1901), *Free Music* (first sketched in 1907), and *Sea-Songs* (1907), which were never developed beyond a preliminary stage; an *Australian Up-Country Song* (1905), eventually absorbed into *Colonial Song* (1911–12); *"The Gum-Suckers" March* (1905–14); and the *Marching Song of Democracy* (1901–17), with its acknowledged debt, however, to that most American of nineteenth-century poets, Walt Whitman. In none of these works would we recognize an Australian association had not Grainger evoked one in words. Nowhere among them can we find such pointed debts as those, for instance, in *Random Round* (1912–14) to Rarotongan improvisation; in *Tribute to Foster* (1913–16) and *Spoon River* (1919–22) to American song; or in *The Rival Brothers* (first sketched in 1905) and *The Merry Wedding* (1912–15) to Faeroe Island texts.

A second claim places Grainger in the European mainstream, based on his few serious large-scale works and suites: the two versions of *Hill-Song* (1901–2 and 1907); *Youthful Suite* (first composed in 1899–1901) and *"In a Nutshell" Suite* (compiled in 1916 from works composed in 1908–1912); *The Warriors* (1913–16), which owes much to *Petrushka; The Power of Rome and the Christian Heart* (1918–43), with its model in Strauss's symphonic poems; and *Lincolnshire Posy* (compiled in 1937 from works begun as early as 1906). Whatever their individual merits, these works betray Grainger's inability to sustain large formal structures, and the mainstream has proceeded without them.

A third claim is based on Grainger's experiments: irregular meters in *Love Verses from "The Song of Solomon"* (1899–1900) and the *Hill-Songs;* free rhythms in the *Bush* and *Train Musics;* chance procedures in *Random Round;* the visionary beatless, pitchless *Free Music;* and the innovative choices and uses of instruments. But these remained scattered attempts. Grainger did not see any of them through, with the exception of *Free Music,* and even that work remained an unfulfilled vision at his death. The avant-garde, like the mainstream, has ignored him.

A fourth claim is British. Grainger spent his most productive years in England. His British folksong collections and settings are his largest body of work and arguably his finest achievement. But though this work (unlike the later Danish folksong research) is well known, our narrow concentration on it has yielded a distorted and partial view of his debt and contribution to English music.

None of these claims, or these bodies of work seen in their usual light, has secured Grainger's name. The standards governing our chronicle of Western music allow us to disregard him. But if his music seems not to belong to our

3. See, for instance, Roger Covell, *Australia's Music: Themes of a New Society* (Melbourne, 1967), 88–103.

chosen legacy, where does it belong? Admittedly, it is not a consistent body of work, or a steadily developing one. His training was too uneven, his temperament too restless, his spirit too twisted, and his later professional distractions too frequent to have allowed him to integrate his elcectic habits into a firm personal idiom. Yet Grainger was not the only composer of his generation who failed to forge a convincing personal style from the wreckage of late nineteenth-century music, and at least he did not retreat into the harmonic perfumes and frail conceits of his pre-Raphaelite colleagues. He was nothing if not adventurous; he tried whatever was at hand. Still, his music is not a compendium of unrelated styles. Most of it bears a characteristic quality arising from none of the influences usually cited, but rather from one that writers have failed to acknowledge. In tune, habit, and sonority, Granger's is an art music rooted in the popular expression of prewar England: the drawing-room ballad of his mother, the folksong of the old men in rural workhouses, the music-hall fare of their working-class descendants, and the musical comedy of the Edwardian London bourgeoisie.

This insight allows us to connect what have seemed unrelated characteristics of Grainger's life and music. It explains the disconcerting similarity between many of his folk-music settings and original works attributed to a nonexistent folksong style. It helps to account for his preference for and mastery of short forms; his peculiarly free scoring suggestions and his invitation into the concert hall of "vulgar" instruments; his attraction to Kipling's verse; a sentimentality that he attributed, misleadingly, I suspect, to his Australian blood; and his discomfort with the social cost of his career as a concert pianist. It may even help us understand, in part, the eventual failure of his reputation.

Typical of many attributions to a folksong style is the following assertion: Grainger "wrote a few original pieces for various media in a style that sounds distinctly English for the good but then novel reason that it was founded on folk-song."[4] One of the works then cited as an example, *Mock Morris* (1910), is noted elsewhere as the genuine (folksong) article.[5] But Grainger, in a note in the published score, took pains to state otherwise: "No folk-music tune-stuffs at all are used herein. The rhythmic cast of the piece is Morris-like, but neither the build of the tunes nor the general lay-out of the form keeps to the Morris dance shape." *Mock Morris,* for string sextet, is musical comedy transferred to the concert hall. The tune, Grainger wrote in an autobiographical sketch, "came to me in bed, the morning after seeing 'The Arcadians' . . . & [is] based upon the motto of the song (but not its music) sung by Grossmith: 'I've got a mother, always merry & bright.' "[6] Aside from a few measures "cribbed unwittingly" from a *Magnificat* by Cyril Scott, the work is entirely original. But the style is

---

4. Frank Howes, *The English Musical Renaissance* (New York, 1966), 197.
5. Thomas Slattery, "The Wind Music of Percy Aldridge Grainger" (Ph.D. diss., University of Iowa, 1967), 94.
6. MS sketches for "The Life of My Mother and Her Son," 40.

bracingly comedic. The original title, *Always Merry and Bright,* paid homage to a song that was a hit from the day it appeared in 1909.[7]

Mock Morris is not alone. "Gay but Wistful" (the second movement of *"In a Nutshell" Suite)* was described by Grainger in the preface to the score as "an attempt to write an air with a 'Music Hall' flavor embodying that London blend of gaiety with wistfulness so familiar in the performances of George Grossmith, Jr., and other vaudeville artists." We must also ascribe to music hall the charming offspring of this elegant work, *Children's March, "Over the Hills and Far Away"* (1916–19). *English Waltz* (composed 1901, completed 1943; from *Youthful Suite),* wrote Grainger, "reflects, to some extent, popular English waltz-types of the Eighteen-nineties."[8] Modest words; it positively evokes the salons of a lost era. Of a series of five English dances planned around the turn of the century, three were completed: *English Dance* and *Rustic Dance,* which were first composed for orchestra in 1899 (with the latter work being eventually incorporated into *Youthful Suite),* and *Zanzibar Boat Song,* written in 1902 for three pianists at one piano.[9] Both *Colonial Song* for theater orchestra and *When the World Was Young* for two pianos (1910–11), the only two of a projected set of *Sentimentals,* are associated with the popular culture. Finally, the piano trio *Handel in the Strand* (1911–12), a reworking of materials originally intended for variations on Handel's *Harmonious Blacksmith,* is doubly identified with Edwardian popular music: the Strand was the home of musical comedy in London, and the original title of the work was *Clog Dance.*

Two arrangements are from the popular culture: the American song *The Rag-Time Girl* (1900) and a sketch for whistlers and strings of *After the Ball Was Over* (1901), a ballad sung in the halls.[10] Several other related works were sketched and abandoned: a "music hall tune" written at the turn of 1911–12; *Oh My Little Sailor Boy,* "a tune heard in Chelsea . . . sung by a working man"; *Pritteling, Pratteling, Pretty Poll Parrot,* sketched for guitars in 1911;[11] and *Who Built de Ark?* for voices and guitar, also from 1911. Grainger also left a piano sketch for a "cakewalk smasher" entitled *In Dahomey,* "prompted" by a performance of the all-Negro musical of that name in London in 1903.[12]

It was in the music hall (where he once met his estranged father at a per-

7. *The Arcadians,* with lyrics by Arthur Wimperis and music by Lionel Monckton and Howard Talbot, opened at the Shaftesbury Theatre on April 28, 1909. Grossmith's role was created by Alfred Lester. See Brian Rust, *London Musical Shows on Record, 1897–1976* (London, 1977), 28.

8. "Program-note" to the published score, January, 1949.

9. Written as "English Dance No. 5," its title was changed for publication. *Rustic Dance* was originally the fourth, *English Dance* the first. The second and third have not been located. Dreyfus, "Adelaide Grainger Collection," 52–53.

10. Colin MacInnes, *Sweet Saturday Night* (London, 1967), 107.

11. Perhaps modeled on, or taken from, the Victorian music-hall standard, *Pretty Polly Perkins,* mentioned in ibid., 137.

12. *In Dahomey,* with lyrics by Paul Dunbar and Alex Rogers and music by Will Marion Cook, opened at the Shaftesbury Theatre on May 16, 1903 (Rust, 144). A photograph of "the grand cake walk at the darkies' ball in Gatonville" is reproduced in Raymond Mander's and Joe Mitchenson's *Musical Comedy* (New York, 1970), photograph 44.

formance by the famed Harry Lauder) and musical comedy that Grainger found a novel use of massed instruments: a flexible ensemble ranging from one or two pianos to an orchestra with augmented percussion, in which parts were interchangeable and orchestration was a matter of adapting to the players and instruments at hand. Grainger took to this pit band at once and used its principles and practices in much of his later music. Retroactively he attributed the practice to his belief in "musical democracy," a music in which any or all could participate—an Australian form of orchestration, he suggested. Yet the impulse was not Australian but English, and musical democracy was not a personal dream but a music-hall reality.

Grainger stretched the boundaries of the practice, however, and the added instruments were, characteristically, popular ones. *Shallow Brown* (first composed in 1910) calls for guitars, harmonium, mandolas, mandolins, and ukeleles; *Scotch Strathspey and Reel* (1901–11), for concertina, guitars, and harmonium; *English Waltz,* for chimes, handbells, marimba, vibraharp, and others. He frequently used these instruments, as well as celesta, xylophone, glockenspiel, banjo, tambourine, and musical glasses. Unfortunately, however, the "elastic scoring" of his musical democracy hurt his name. Exposing his music to an unlimited assortment of musical groups encouraged performances by the most conventional of them. As a result, we hear most of his work without the striking sonorities that give it its special charm and claim.

Music hall is the most palpable link in the chain of affinities connecting Grainger with Kipling, some three dozen of whose poems and ballads he set. Kipling explored the halls and absorbed the vulgar speech he heard there; and from the experience came his *Barrack-Room Ballads* (the book from which Grainger borrowed texts most frequently), with its Cockney dialect and heavy speech rhythms. It was through his mastery of the ballad, the popular expression of the late Victorian working classes and their folk ancestors, that Kipling became a popular poet, even as his reputation among critics suffered a steady decline. By his death he had been dismissed as a balladmonger. In 1941, T. S. Eliot attempted a posthumous rehabilitation of Kipling by assessing him as a writer not of bad poetry but of good verse, a painstaking craftsman who had "the inspiration and refreshment of the living music-hall," to be defended against the charges of being "a popular entertainer" and of "writing jingles."[13] While taking issue with Eliot, whose essay had provoked a storm, George Orwell also invoked the music hall, and called Kipling instead a "good bad poet" whose work was vital, vulgar, vigorous, memorable, and given to sentimentality.[14]

13. *A Choice of Kipling's Verse* (Garden City, N.Y., 1962), 12, 33, and 8, respectively.
14. "Rudyard Kipling," *Kipling and the Critics,* ed. Elliott L. Gilbert (London, 1966), 74–88. A sharper response to Eliot, Boris Ford's "Case for Kipling," publ. in 1942 and repr. in ibid., 59–73, has much that can be applied to Grainger, notably the discussion of the spiritual isolation, sexual abnormality, and inner disorder of *fin-de-siècle* writers, "whose real nature they fought to conceal" (p. 65); and the lack of emotional growth in Kipling's *oeuvre* (p. 67). Also interesting is Colin MacInnes's "Kipling and the Music Hall," *The Age of Kipling,* ed. John Gross (New York, 1972), 58–61.

Virtually every word here applies to Grainger. Like Kipling, he was a co-lonial who sought acceptance in the mother country and attempted to articulate an expression of popular values. He too wanted to be a popular artist, he was technically facile, he accepted perhaps too easily the formal attitudes he found in the popular marketplace, and he was attacked for his lowbrow tone. Like Kipling, he loved popular machines—phonographs, player pianos, vacuum cleaners, electronic devices, successively—and he used them in his work. Like Kipling, he flowered and declined early; both men were, long before the end, isolated and creatively depleted.

THE LONDON YEARS are most often associated in the secondary literature with Grainger's folksong activities. And it is here that our thesis is most firmly tested, for nothing was more distasteful to the folksong collectors than the popu-lar music of their day. In 1905, Grainger attended a lecture given by Lucy Broadwood on folksong collecting.[15] While this was not his first encounter with folksong, Miss Broadwood's lecture was a revelation because it offered an ap-proach to collecting that was seemingly professional and free of cultural con-straints. That summer he went to Lincolnshire and joined other collectors in transcribing a few songs in the usual manner, noting by hand a simplified ver-sion of what he had heard.[16] The following year he returned, this time armed with a phonograph, and recorded the singers. He transcribed with extraordinary fidelity what the recording had captured and published the results, along with a lengthy introduction, in a magnificent article in the Folk-Song Society's journal in 1908.[17] While earlier transcriptions had yielded straightforward tunes ripe for the amateur singer, Grainger's were a riot of notes and ornaments, accompanied by instructions, warnings, and analyses. To sing these tunes again would be im-possible. His litter of information was not prescriptive but descriptive. Grainger was attacked for his use of the suspect recording machine and for the complexity of the results.[18] The article was to be his only major publication on folksong. He

15. "On the Collecting of English Folk-Song," *Proceedings of the Royal Musical Association* 31 (1904–5): 89–109.

16. Four, including *Brigg Fair*, were published in the *Journal of the Folk-Song Society* (hereafter cited as *JFSS*) 2 (1905–6): 79–81.

17. "Collecting with the Phonograph," *JFSS* 3 (1908–9): 147–242.

18. Bird paraphrases and quotes from a letter from Sharp to Grainger, dated May 23, 1908, which ends, "The question is, is it worth doing at all?" (*Percy Grainger*, 113–14). Patrick O'Shaughnessy mentions briefly a doubting letter from Sharp, but does not give its date ("Percy Grainger: The English Folk-Song Collection," *Studies in Music* 10 [1976]: 21). Other letters from Sharp to Grainger, now in the Grainger Museum, may well bear on the subject; they are dated Mar. 11 and Oct. 25, 1906, and May 23, 24, and 29, 1908. Mar-garet Dean-Smith mentions among the Broadwood papers an unpublished article by Anne Gilchrist, one of the original collectors, rebutting Grainger ("Letters to Lucy Broadwood," *Journal of the English Folk Dance and Song Society* 9 [1960–64]: 254). A most delicate cautionary note by the Editing Committee of the society was inserted into Grainger's article (*JFSS* 3 [1908–9]: 159); since it disputes not only Grainger's dependence on the phonograph but also his conclusions concerning mode in folksong, conclusions that upset Sharp's char-acteristically cleaner and simpler modal theories, we may be certain that Sharp had a strong voice on that committee. Fuller Maitland and Kidson were also opposed to the use of the phonograph. Among Grainger's colleagues, only Broadwood seems to have been open to it. As the unpublished evidence is brought to light, the sharp divisions will be seen more clearly.

continued for a while, but for all intents and purposes his serious work as a collector of English song was finished by 1910, five years and more than three hundred songs after it had begun. A final rebuff on the eve of his departure from England in the summer of 1914 marked the end of his active participation in the society.[19] When he returned to the field in the 1920s, it was to collect Danish folksong.

The hostility of some colleagues and the indifference of the others surely hastened the end of Grainger's English work. For he knew that rejection of the phonograph was also a rejection of its musical documentation. Grainger's transcriptions reveled in the "baffling, profuse characteristics" of his gifted singers' performances.[20] He would not accept folksong " 'simplified' (generally in the process of notation by well-meaning collectors ignorant of those more ornate subtleties of our notation alone fitted for the task) out of all resemblance to its original self."[21] But that is precisely what is found, by the hundreds, in the pages of the society's journal. The issue was not in fact the phonograph. Occasional transcriptions from recordings, sometimes "corrected" (Vaughan Williams's word), were tried by his colleagues, and they bear little resemblance to Grainger's.[22] The arguments over a machine were really arguments over what was to be done with folksong. And these were not susceptible to resolution, for they hid a fundamental issue on which agreement was impossible. The issue was class. The old folksingers were very much of one class, and their attitudes found expression in their song. The collectors were solidly of another class, and their attitudes were of another order entirely. Grainger alone among the collectors respected the crucial class difference.[23] That respect accounted for the distinction of his collections and settings as well as for his premature removal from the society of collectors.

Miss Broadwood had galvanized the early collectors by founding the Folk-Song Society in 1898. Among her cofounders and colleagues were three of the great Victorian composers, Sir Hubert Parry, Sir John Stainer, and Sir

19. In 1914 Grainger "had approached the committee with a view to having the soundtracks transferred from his wax cylinders on to a more durable medium, but had been rebuffed" (O'Shaughnessy, 22).

20. Grainger, "The Impress of Personality in Unwritten Music," *The Musical Quarterly* 1 (1915): 422.

21. Ibid., 417. Note in contrast Kidson's distrust of the phonograph transcription as "complex and confusing," with its "excessively elaborate rhythms and shifting tonality" (Frank Kidson and Mary Neal, *English Folk-Song and Dance* [Cambridge, 1915; repr. ed., Totowa, N.J., 1972], 49).

22. See, for instance, *JFSS* 3 (1908–9): 267, 268, 292, 298, and 311; *JFSS* 4 (1910–13): 30, 47, 49, 304, and 334. For different transcriptions of the same song, compare Sharp's *Six Lords Went Ahunting* (*JFSS* 5 [1914–17]: 79) with Grainger's *Six Dukes Went Afishin'* (*JESS* 3 [1908–9]: 170–74), or Broadwood's *Bold William Taylor* (*JFSS* 5 [1914–17]: 69) with Grainger's (*JFSS* 3 [1908–9]: 214–17 and 219).

23. As, for instance, in this statement written by Grainger in 1952 and published in the foreword to his setting of *Bold William Taylor*:

> The greatest crime against folksong is to "middle-class" it—to sing it with a "white collar" voice production & other townified suggestions. Whether it be true, or not, that the ballads originated in the knightly & aristocratic world, one thing is certain: they have come down to us solely as an adjunct of rural life & are drenched through & through with rural feelings & traditions. To weaken any characteristics of this rusticness—in collecting, arranging & performing folksongs—is, in my opinion, to play false to the very soul of folksong.

Charles Villiers Stanford; the music critic of the *Times,* J. A. Fuller-Maitland; the Rev. Sabine Baring-Gould; and Frank Kidson, a musical antiquary. There was disagreement among them about what to do with the songs they found, with their crude texts and their irregularities of key, mode, rhythm, and phrasing. Broadwood and Kidson asserted their obligation to copy the tunes more or less as they found them, while their more orthodox colleagues insisted upon expunging the musical crudities and rewriting the tunes. About the rest, however, there was broad agreement. Vulgarities of verse were to be excised and the tunes set in good taste, because this music was a national treasure to be reclaimed in its purity and simplicity, and not least for the benefit of the middle and lower classes. There was, in other words, behind this activity a broad moral and social agenda.

That agenda was articulated best by two younger men who joined the committee of the society in 1904: Cecil Sharp, an energetic school teacher who would shortly take control of the society and set its course, and Ralph Vaughan Williams, who was to become the emblem of its success. Sharp outlined his vision in the influential *English Folk Song: Some Conclusions,* published in 1907. The recovery of English folksong would lead to the founding of a great national school of composition, ending the monopoly by continental musicians of English concert life. The vehicle would be education. Folksong was to be introduced into the curriculum at the elementary level since it satisfied the two conditions of an ideal school song: it was "natural, pure and simple," and it was "attractive to children, easily comprehended, and easily learned by them." If the songs were chosen and graded carefully, if they were English, and if the words were adapted to young minds,

> no other musical pabulum will be needed until the child has reached the age of ten or eleven years. By that time folk music will have served its purpose, and the child will be prepared to make a wider excursion into the realms of art music.[24]

Folksongs were to be used to cleanse the streets of music-hall tunes, at which Sharp threw no end of epithets: coarse, vulgar and vulgarizing, poverty-stricken, deluding, and uneducative. It was "impossible to exaggerate the harmful influence upon character" of these tunes. But good songs, provided they were sufficiently attractive and "catchy," would drive out the bad, and purify the minds of children as well as of musically illiterate adults. Such a result "will make the streets a pleasanter place for those who have sensitive ears, and will do incalculable good in civilizing the masses."[25]

At the end of his argument, Sharp turned in an afterthought to the ques-

24. Cecil J. Sharp, *English Folk Song: Some Conclusions,* 4th ed., prepared by Maud Karpeles (Belmont, Calif., 1965), 171–72.
25. Ibid., 172 and 173, respectively.

tion of the intrinsic musical value of folksong. Is it, he asked, "beautiful in itself, judged as music?" Here at last he foundered.

> This is a question of taste rather than of argument. . . . There are not so many fair things in the world that no room can be found for more. In a material age, too, such as the present, there is an especial need for fostering the growth and development of those things which, like good music, exercise a purifying and regenerative influence.[26]

That is, folksong is beautiful because it purifies, and it purifies because it is beautiful. His entire argument had collapsed in this tautology. But it made no difference; his program of social reform, reactionary and futile though it was, remained intact. Indeed, it held sway within the society from the time he wrote the book until his death in 1924. The Board of Education adopted his curricular ideas. And he has continued to direct the society from the grave, through the voices of his disciples, one of whom, recalling Sharp's "vision of the streets being flooded with folk tunes," lamented recently that "this happy circumstance" has not yet come to pass.[27]

It is no accident that the home of the society is Cecil Sharp House, nor that its archive is the Ralph Vaughan Williams Library. In an essay on folksong first published in 1934, Vaughan Williams added his authority to Sharp's program. He defined folksong as intuitive, oral, and purely melodic; that is, he gave it an entirely musical definition. He then offered it as the answer to the dilemma of the modern composer, who would achieve a national voice by absorbing folksong and its idiom into his vocabulary. Folksong had passed the Darwinian test; having evolved through "a real process of natural selection and survival of the fittest," it had become the link between the composer and his national audience. But beyond the composer, "it is the ordinary man for whose musical salvation the folk-song will be responsible." And the working man needed saving:

> There are thousands of men and women naturally musically inclined whose only musical nourishment has been the banality of the music-hall. . . . It never occurred to them to listen to what they called "classical" music, or if they did it was with a prejudiced view determined beforehand that they would not understand it.[28]

What was Grainger to make of these arguments? One in particular must have alienated him deeply. If the reason for collecting folksong was to create a school of national composers, the very legitimacy of his collecting work was

---

26. Ibid., 179.
27. Ibid., xvi.
28. Ralph Vaughan Williams, *National Music and Other Essays* (London, 1963), 32 and 38–39, respectively.

called into question, for alone among the collectors he was not an Englishman. He must have found the other arguments unsettling as well. He knew well that unembellished folksong "is far too complex" for "the general educated public."[29] It could not be used to overcome English musical inferiority. It was not to be used and graded as school song to prepare children for a life of art music, to improve their character, to purify their minds, or to inculcate in them notions of good taste. It was not to provide salvation for the working man, certainly not from the banality of the music hall. It was neither pure nor simple. Certainly it was not pabulum.

If it did not occur to working people to listen to art music, or if they listened to it only with prejudice, Grainger understood why. Such music did not address itself to them, nor was it meant for them. Everything about its creation, dissemination, and presentation was bound up with the values, the manners, the language, and the accent of privilege. Vaughan Williams and Sharp, like the class they represented, were bewildered by the vulgarity and potential power of the urban working class. Indoctrinate these people with your values, and you might remove their threat to your privilege while you saved their souls; never mind that you would or could not share with them the realities and symbols of that privilege.

Sharp and Vaughan Williams, like the rest of Grainger's colleagues in the society, could not see that the economic and technological history of Victorian England had put their program beyond reach. Industrialization had destroyed the old rural culture and its music with it, creating in its stead a managerial and clerical middle class and a vast urban proletariat. These new classes had developed distinctive musical cultures—the shop ballad and later the musical comedy of the middle class, the music hall of the working class—even as the academics, professionals, and aristocrats maintained their older habits, needing no new ones. But the growth of a new popular culture was lost on the folksong collectors; it had no aesthetic validity because for them its social roots were unacceptable and, in some vaguely perceived way, threatening.

Sharp had noted that no one under sixty or seventy had the songs he wished to collect. He concluded, therefore, that "the chain of tradition had snapped" around 1840, and he found nothing of interest beyond that time.[30] His colleagues concurred. All of them but Grainger. Only twenty-four when his landmark article was published, Grainger was by far the youngest of them. He was the only one born and trained in foreign lands and, with Vaughan Williams, he was the only truly professional musician among them. For these reasons perhaps, his attitudes were less enchained to the ruling social order, his mind more open to music artistry wherever he might find it. Like Kipling, he recognized that "the transfer of writers and audience from the broadside to the music hall carried with it very much of the folk tradition."[31] Music hall and

29. Grainger, "Impress of Personality," 417.
30. Sharp, *English Folk Song,* 151.
31. J. S. Braxton, *The Victorian Popular Ballad* (London, 1975), 25.

musical comedy were the folksong of his time, therefore he saw in them equally legitimate sources of expression. His music, like theirs, is vigorous, direct, given to dialect and colloquial language, and concerned with story and mood rather than with abstract ideas and structures. His tunes are easy, his forms brief, his titles colloquial, and his instructions in clear English.

Since folksong and music hall were the expression of the same class, one could not be used to wean people from the other. Vaughan Williams's narrowly musical definition of folksong was irrelevant; its essential feature was not its antiquity, its anonymity, or its oral transmission, but rather its "presentation of the common denominator of feeling and experience in the community to which it belongs."[32] Just as one could not apply the dying rural song to the needs of modern society, one could not apply modern criteria of taste to the old song. And so Grainger preserved the folksong as he found it, taking pains in his transcriptions to retain the asymmetries and peculiarities of the songs and their singers. He published biographies of the singers and donated his royalties to them, for he considered the songs to be their property. His settings of what he had collected were not only polyphonic renderings of the tunes, but were also musical portraits of "these . . . kings and queens of song,"[33] with their "instinct for untrammeled and criticised and untaught artistic self-expression,"[34] "whose individualistic excrescences and idiosyncrasies . . . [are] a precious manifestation of real artistic personality."[35] In these marvelous words lies the answer to the question of folksong's intrinsic value that Sharp, for all his missionary zeal, could not locate.

So while the amateur folksong treatments of a Sharp or the masterly ones of Vaughan Williams evoke a haunting past with its innocents inhabiting an idealized countryside, Grainger's settings fairly stink of the earth, of hard life and violent death, of work and sex and love. He romanticized nothing, refusing to sanitize texts or diatonicize rough tunes or to fashion trite accompaniments for tender sensibilities. His range of expression, characterization, and sonority was enormous. To name a few settings among many, *The Merry King* (first composed in 1905–6), *Rufford Park Poachers* (1937), *Scotch Strathspey and Reel* (1901–11), *Shallow Brown* (1910, revised 1923–25), and *Six Dukes Went Afishin'* (1905–12), stand out as musical treasures of the English folksong movement, just as Grainger's recordings of his singers stand out, along with the society's journal, as its greatest document.

GRAINGER left England for good in 1914. Whatever the reasons for his flight—and a flight it was, undertaken apparently in secret, not a departure[36]—

---

32. Ibid., 7.
33. Grainger, "Program-note" to *Lincolnshire Posy* (New York, 1940), 1.
34. Grainger, "Impress of Personality," 418.
35. Ibid., 421.
36. Bird accepts as "simple and logical" Grainger's later explanation for his departure at the war's outbreak that he had "wanted to emerge as Australia's first composer of worth and to have laid himself open to the

it was the beginning of the decline of his creative life. There is a surface reason, and there is a deeper one. The surface reason is simply stated. In England there had been a delicate balance between his careers as a concert pianist, a composer, and a collector. The tension between the necessity of making a living for himself and his invalid mother, of performing the music of the classical repertory for affluent audiences, and of trying to maintain a creative imagination rooted in another world entirely, was kept somehow in equilibrium. But in America the balance was shattered. He was a pianist first and always; recognition as a composer was secondary and lukewarm.

On a deeper level, Grainger was cut off in America from the soil of his inspiration, and while he continued to compose, the new society and its popular musical expression were different from what he had known. Try as he might, he could not find creative nourishment in them. But even had he remained in England, it might have made little or no difference. There the Great War and its chaotic aftermath changed forever the structure, mood, and expression of the land and its working classes. Cinema replaced music hall, and American jazz and dance rhythms changed the character of popular music. In America Granger would still identify with the common man in *The Power of Rome and the Christian Heart.* He would collect black music and cowboy songs. He would befriend Cowell, admire Ellington, and arrange Gershwin. But whereas his London work had been modern and authentically rooted, now his music became old-fashioned. Ironically, the most famous piece of his American years would be a setting of a morris-dance tune collected by Sharp, *Country Gardens* (1918). As early as 1917 he wrote of his *Marching Song of Democracy,* "It is the *kind* of music I like. . . . I like it better than 'modern' music."[37] His music never again reflected his society, and it never grew. Henceforth he devoted himself largely to the completion and revision of work begun before the war.

---

possibility of being killed would have rendered his goal unattainable" (*Percy Grainger,* 152). Perhaps, but not likely; Grainger's memories of earlier events were often distorted and self-serving, and they must be treated gingerly and checked against those documents contemporaneous with the events in question. His explanation in this case does not ring true. There was more to it than Grainger subsequently allowed. The pertinent documents are in the Grainger Museum.

37. Grainger's letter to Balfour Gardiner, December 12, 1917. The Gardiner–Grainger correspondence is particularly valuable, for of all Grainger's English friends Gardiner understood him best. One example must suffice—the passage from a letter of April 5, 1923, in which Gardiner encourages Grainger to keep exploiting popular sonorities, even though he himself cannot abide them or their class associations:

I have been thinking about your use of harmonium, muted trumpet, whistlers, organ tremolo, etc. . . . These sounds are, to people like Delius and myself, ghastly; in fact, everybody I know is agreed about it; but then the difference between our point of view and yours is due to the fact that we are bound to certain traditions of culture and association from which you are entirely free. . . . You can exploit instruments that we cannot touch. You will find your public, also; not much in the old countries, perhaps, but in the new ones where traditional feeling is weak or non-existent. In Delius and myself the means you employ, and the feelings you exhibit in employing them, arouse, as you say, the "wildest" antagonism. You must disregard us, and go your own way. It is unfortunate, from our personal point of view; and moreover, as we see it, the employment and acceptance of such procedures implies a decadence of taste which we cannot but regret—the world seems to us all the worse for it. But you cannot put aside your feelings for ours, and it is obvious you will not do so.

These letters, originally deposited in the Library of Congress, are now housed in the Grainger Museum.

We must treat Grainger, then, as an Edwardian composer, though also as one alienated from the professional, educational, and social goals of his colleagues. His music is as idiosyncratic as was his personality, as wide-ranging as his adventurous mind, as perplexing at times as his troubled spirit. While rooted in the popular expression of a people, it was not written for, nor in its sophistication could it appeal to, that group. It would succeed or fail as art music, and the judgment would be made by the consumers of art music. Few of these people—few of us—would take seriously, however, its manner of expression. Using the privileged standards of our own class values, we have judged Grainger a failure. But his music does have a claim on us; it is a precious and exquisitely wrought document of a faded people and their era—the men and women of Edwardian England. It will be recognized, and Grainger's contribution adequately assessed, only when we have broadened the bases of our judgment and overcome the stubborn cultural biases that we bring to bear on the musical record of the past.[38]

---

38. A preliminary version of this paper was read as the annual Grainger Lecture at the University of Melbourne on July 28, 1978. Revised in its present form, it is nonetheless incomplete in its documentation, since the University of Melbourne has not made available copies of all the relevant sources deposited in the Grainger Museum at the university.

SHOSTAKOVICH, SOVIET CITIZEN AND ANTI-STALINIST

BORIS SCHWARZ

ON APRIL 22, 1962, Paul Henry Lang published one of his provocative Sunday articles in the *New York Herald Tribune* entitled "Soviet Dragon, Profit Motive." It was a barbed response to an essay by Dmitri Shostakovich, "The Composer's Mission," originally published in *Pravda* in January of that year and distributed in translation by the Soviet embassy to further "a broader mutual understanding." What aroused Lang's anger was the hollow rhetoric of the party line, the reiteration of pompous platitudes under the guise of "Socialist Realism."

> Soviet art fulfill[s] its principal function—to be an instrument of Communist education of the people. . . . To serve people today means to take active part in the implementation of the policy of our party.
>
> The confusion of ideas that holds sway in the capitalist world today, with its undercurrent of despair, fear, and overhanging doom . . . is responsible for the large number of current trends in art, so far removed from the requirements of the people. . . . We cannot be too emphatic in stressing the fact that all these anti-humanistic trends are entirely alien to Socialist realism.[1]

Lang's reaction was predictably and justifiably negative. He dismembered Shostakovich's flowery prose and concluded,

---

1. Dmitri Shostakovich, "The Composer's Mission (On the Tasks of Soviet Composers in the Light of the Program Accepted by the XXII Congress of the CPSU)," *Pravda,* Jan. 17, 1962. Excerpts translated and quoted by Paul Henry Lang; see n. 2.

Mr. Shostakovich has produced a piece of writing which if presented with the same solemnity in this country would be hooted down as completely vapid and unworthy of an artist of integrity. . . . It is still sadly difficult for us to watch this Russian composer's astonishing capacity for changing his position, his habit of always testing the political wind and then submitting obsequiously to its direction.

And Lang deplored "the unhappy spectacle of self-abasement by someone who undoubtedly knows better."[2]

It seemed a harsh indictment at a time when many considered Shostakovich a victim of cultural persecution in his own land. Yet there was this essay (and several others in a similar vein) published under his name which read like propaganda leaflets straight out of agitprop. What was one to believe?

Twenty years later, Shostakovich's son Maxim—by now a defector living in New York—told me emphatically, "All his life my father wore a *mask of loyalty*. He never wrote the stuff that was issued in his name; it came ready-made from the Composers' Union. He merely accepted it. . . . " It is an explanation that is a shade too simple. Granted, he did not author the pompous prose—what compelled him to endorse it, at a time when there was no outside coercion? To understand his motivation, one must place his essay within the context of events leading up to it.

Let us briefly summarize his career prior to 1962. Born in 1906, he belonged to the first generation of Russian composers educated under the Soviet regime. He grew up during the 1920s, when there was a revolutionary fervor that gripped workers and intellectuals alike. "Art belongs to the people," was Lenin's dictum. Young Shostakovich lived up to it, not by cheapening his own art, but by elevating the audience to his standards. In 1927 he celebrated the tenth anniversary of the Revolution with his Second Symphony, *To October,* trying to combine modernism and Marxism. He remained a Leninist at heart, though he abhorred Stalinist terror.

Twice during Stalin's rule, he was the victim of party-inspired attacks— the first time in 1936 (the well-known *Lady Macbeth* debacle), the second time in 1948, when he and other leading Soviet composers, including Sergei Prokofiev and Nicolai Miaskovsky, were castigated for their "antisocial" modernistic music. In 1936 he stood alone and was frantic with fear; in 1948 he gritted his teeth and remanded his serious compositions to his desk drawer while writing film scores. His apologia, if any, was perfunctory, while other intellectuals were wallowing in mass recantations and self-abasement. It literally came down to a matter of life and death. The writer Ilya Ehrenburg was asked by a younger colleague, "How is it that you survived?" And the answer: "I shall never know."[3]

2. Paul Henry Lang, "Soviet Dragon, Profit Motive," *New York Herald Tribune,* April 22, 1962.
3. Ilya Ehrenburg, *Memoirs: 1921–1941,* trans. Tatiana Shebunina and Yvonne Kapp (Cleveland, 1963), 429.

The next key date is March 5, 1953: Stalin died in the morning, Prokofiev in the afternoon. In the turmoil of the day, the dictator's death dominated the world news, while the composer's death remained unreported for days. For Shostakovich, that day had a twofold significance: he had lost his most hated enemy, whom he considered a murderer, and he had inherited the mantle of Prokofiev as the premier Soviet composer.

With the death of Stalin, Soviet literature and art entered a phase of liberalization that lasted almost ten years and is usually described as "the thaw," after a short novel by Ehrenburg published in May, 1954. It reached its peak with the publication, in November, 1962, of Solzhenitsyn's novella *One Day in the Life of Ivan Denisovich* and came to an abrupt halt a month later. This decade requires special scrutiny if we are to understand Shostakovich's pattern of behavior.

The Soviet intelligentsia had breathed a collective sigh of relief in March, 1953, which grew to muted jubilation after the arrest (July 10) and execution (December 23) of the hated police chief Lavrenti Beria. While Soviet literature proceeded cautiously to test the limits of the new "tolerance," music went its own way. In the summer of 1953, Shostakovich began to compose a new symphony, his tenth; it was completed by the end of October and was first performed on December 17 of that year in Leningrad. "In this composition I wanted to express human emotions and passions,"[4] said the composer, cutting off all discussions about a possible programmatic content. We now know that the prickly and evil-sounding scherzo is a musical portrayal of Stalin. But the symphony was subjected to much criticism during a three-day discussion in the Composers' Union, particularly because of its prevailing pessimism—a cardinal sin in Soviet aesthetics. Ultimately, however, it won approval and indirectly paved the way for other Soviet composers to encompass a wider gamut of expression.

The following year, 1954, Shostakovich received the highest artistic honor —he was named People's Artist of the U.S.S.R. Creatively, it was a quiet period that produced only one conventional piece, the *Festive Overture*. But Shostakovich was putting the finishing touches on several compositions that had been hidden away during the Stalin freeze: the song cycle *From Jewish Folk Poetry* (composed in 1948, first performed on January 15, 1955) and the Violin Concerto No. 1, Opus 77 (composed in 1947–48 and first performed on October 29, 1955, in Leningrad, followed by a Carnegie Hall performance on December 29 by David Oistrakh and Dimitri Mitropoulos). The Jewish cycle was delayed because of Stalin's virulent antisemitic drive, while the violin concerto was considered "too modern" for its time. Even in 1955 the work was judged problematic in Moscow, though not in New York, and it took many months for a favorable opinion to begin to crystallize.

---

4. *Sovetskaya muzyka* 6 (1954): 120.

Thus, the "thaw" did not proceed consistently, but it reached a culmination in 1956 when Nikita Khrushchev, the new man in power, unmasked Stalin in his famous seven-hour speech before the Twentieth Party Congress meeting in a closed session. It was a courageous step that must have impressed Shostakovich. The jovial Khruschchev, while not posing as a "liberal," knew how to flatter the intelligentsia and dispel lingering doubts about a possible revival of Stalinism. In April, 1957, the Composers' Union met in a congress (its first meeting since 1948) and heard an address by a high party official, Dmitri Shepilov, who promised a return to Leninist principles of dealing with the arts: no more "high-handed commands and petty tutelage."[5] Shostakovich spoke up in the debate and argued for a public discussion of ideological differences. Interrupted by applause, he concluded, "Unfortunately, the Composers' Union has done more to freeze discussion than to encourage it."[6]

At this point, Shostakovich may have felt obligated to make a positive contribution toward the gradual relaxation. His next symphony, No. 11, a historic fresco subtitled *The Year 1905,* used the first revolution as a topic. It was first performed in honor of the fortieth anniversary of the October Revolution (1957) and was received with deep satisfaction—the paradigm of great Socialist art. In writing a work with a programmatic content, Shostakovich remained true to his longstanding conviction that program music had an important place in serious composition. This was not a passing fancy; his next three symphonies were either programmatic (No. 12) or word-connected (Nos. 13 and 14). Symphony No. 11 was panned abroad, but was defended by at least one British critic, Peter Heyworth, who ridiculed its almost automatic rejection:

> Soviet critics have only to herald a work like the Eleventh Symphony. . . . as a masterpiece of Socialist Realism, for some of their Western confrères to dismiss it with Dulles-like promptitude as a propaganda piece. . . . [7]

In Moscow, the rapprochement between party officials and artists proceeded unabated. In February, 1958, Khrushchev gave a reception at the Kremlin "in honor of the Soviet People's intelligentsia." He recommended to the artists "greater daring in their quests, more attention to life and people." Shostakovich answered on behalf of the musicians: he praised the "material care given to the Soviet composers by the Party and the government" as well as the "constant, paternal, attentive, and thoughtful guidance of our music." He concluded with a toast to "the Communist Party and its Leninist Central Committee, the Soviet Government, and the Soviet People."[8]

5. Trans. in *Current Digest of the Soviet Press* 9/13 (May 8, 1957): 15ff.
6. Ibid., 11–12.
7. "Music and Musicians: Shostakovich and the Party," *The Observer* (London), Jan. 31, 1960.
8. Boris Schwarz, *Music and Musical Life in Soviet Russia, 1917–1970* (New York, 1972), 310.

It is obvious that, with Stalin and Stalinism removed, Shostakovich felt more at ease with the party hierarchy. His use of the word *Leninist* is indicative of his belief that the abuses of Stalinism were a thing of the past. This opinion was confirmed later that year, when the Communist Party took an unprecedented step: it admitted "blatant errors" in the past condemnation of Soviet composers, including Shostakovich, and exonerated them all. In the meantime, two had died—Miaskovsky and Prokofiev—and others had suffered great harm to their professional careers. The new decree, dated May 28, 1958, and entitled "On Rectifying Errors," provided a curious explanation:

> Some incorrect evaluations in the decree [of 1948] reflected J. V. Stalin's subjective attitude to certain works of art. . . . As we know, a very adverse influence was exercised on Stalin in these matters by Molotov, Malenkov, and Beria. . . . [9]

There was no mention of Zhdanov, the true villain of the 1948 purge.

Shostakovich's reaction, prominently published in *Pravda,* was somewhat diffident, as if he had not himself been a victim of that cultural massacre.

> The Central Committee's Resolution of May 28, 1958, made me happy, first and foremost because it stresses the high place Soviet music rightly takes in the promotion of Socialist culture. The resolution wipes out the unfair and sweeping appraisals of various Soviet composers, and opens up wonderful prospects for the further advance of Soviet music along the path of realism. . . . [10]

The cultural exchange agreement between the United States and the Soviet Union was signed in 1958, and Shostakovich visited the United States in the fall of 1959 as a member of a composers' delegation. The group was controlled with an iron grip by Tikhon Khrennikov, the "boss" of the Composers' Union. Those of us who saw Shostakovich in New York remember his tenseness and his unwillingness to communicate. After a forum held in California on modern American music, a correspondent complained, "Shostakovich's views can be best described as cautious and noncommittal. . . . All six [Soviet] musicians exhibited a conformity of thought in discussions of representatively contemporary music."[11] Asked about a trend toward twelve-tone music in Russia, Shostakovich stated flatly, "There is none."

More and more, Shostakovich seemed to parrot the party line. On July 17, 1960, the Soviet intelligentsia was once again invited to the Kremlin in an

9. *Current Digest* 10/23 (July 16, 1958): 3.
10. *Pravda,* June 13, 1958, trans. Schwarz, 312.
11. *Musical America* (Dec. 1, 1959): 6.

atmosphere of "cordiality, unity, and elation." Pictures of the event show Khrushchev in shirt-sleeves and Ekaterina Furtseva, the new culture commissar, surrounded by leading composers, among them Shostakovich. The gathering of writers and artists was addressed by Mikhail Suslov, a veteran ideologist, who stressed the need for Socialist content in art. Most of the musicians expressed their approval informally, but the reaction of Shostakovich was published by *Pravda* on September 7, 1960, giving it the weight of a major policy statement. Entitled "The Artist of Our Time," it is Shostakovich's commitment to the party. Never before had he sounded quite so much like the "composer laureate" of the Soviet regime: "Now that the country has entered the era of building the Communist society, the mission of the Soviet artist has become great and exalted."[12]

A week later, on September 15, the official TASS announced the discussion and approval of Shostakovich's candidacy for membership in the Communist Party. After having been a "fellow traveler" (and a reluctant one at that) for most of his life, Shostakovich at age fifty-four, took the decisive step of seeking a formal affiliation with the ruling party. Writing in the late 1960s, I ventured this explanation: "Shostakovich may have felt that the new Party attitude toward the arts, initiated after Stalin's death and gathering strength under Khrushchev, promised a definite turn toward liberalization."[13] Even now, after having read the controversial *Memoirs*,[14] I continue to believe that Shostakovich's step was dictated not by opportunism (he had nothing to gain by it in 1960), but by his growing belief that a coexistence between art and politics was possible and even desirable. His next major work stressed this point: the Twelfth Symphony, subtitled *The Year 1917* and dedicated to the memory of Lenin, was (like its predecessor) a programmatic symphony. He had stated openly early in 1961,

> The creative failures in the genre of program music are regrettable. The positive role of program music in musical education is well known, for this music is understandable to mass audiences. . . . Program and text-related genres have a special democratism. But this does not mean that we must neglect other genres of symphonic and instrumental music. . . ."[15]

The Twelfth was greeted with elation by the Soviets and with consternation by Western critics. It was first performed in Moscow on October 15, 1961, in honor of the Twenty-second Party Congress. This congress, incidentally, liquidated the "cult of personality"; it was decided to remove Stalin's embalmed re-

12. *Information Bulletin,* Soviet Composers' Union (Moscow), 1960, No. 3: 38–47.

13. Schwarz, 334.

14. *Testimony: The Memoirs of Dmitri Shostakovich,* ed. Solomon Volkov, trans. Antonina W. Bouis (New York, 1979).

15. *Information Bulletin* (Moscow), 1961, No. 2: 4–5.

mains from the Lenin mausoleum on Red Square—a symbolic action that must have pleased Shostakovich, the eternal Stalin hater.

A very different kind of satisfaction was provided by the première, so long delayed, of the Fourth Symphony. It was composed in 1935–36, but withdrawn by Shostakovich prior to its scheduled first performance in 1936 because of the *Lady Macbeth* controversy, and had been hidden away for twenty-five years. As recently as 1953, he had called it "a very imperfect, long-winded work that suffers from 'grandiosomania.' "[16] On December 30, 1961, the work was played in Moscow under Kyril Kondrashin. It was received with profound respect and recorded in Moscow soon thereafter.

We have reached January, 1962, when Shostakovich's essay "The Composer's Mission" appeared in print. In retrospect, we can see that it was by no means an opportunistic tack taken for the "political wind," but a logical outgrowth of a psychological change within Shostakovich that can be traced back to Stalin's death—a gradual melting away of his bitterness and resentment, a peacemaking process with the powers that be, a reaching out toward his country and the people he so loved. The Twelfth Symphony, memorializing the ascent of Lenin, was meant as a social message to his compatriots and co-Leninists, though to British ears it sounded like a "monumental triviality."[17]

Shostakovich's anti-Stalinist sentiments were not extinct, however, and with obvious relish he selected five poems by Yevgeni Yevtushenko—all with an anti-Stalinist slant—to use for his Thirteenth Symphony, subtitled *Babi Yar*. It was performed on December 14, 1962, and I can still remember the stunned silence followed by a wild outburst of approval at the end of that première in the packed conservatory hall in Moscow. The following morning, the work was withdrawn "for revisions." The cultural honeymoon had ended, the "thaw" was refreezing. The intelligentsia tried to fight back, but in vain; whether in music, literature, or art, the hard-liners took over, and "The Heirs of Stalin"[18] regained power.

Yet, the struggle for liberalization had not been entirely in vain. The eyes and ears of the public had been opened, the pressure for change became stronger. The avant-garde may have been forced underground, but it did survive. And it was Shostakovich who helped it survive—not by his words but by his music. Gradually, he widened the gamut of permissible dissonance, of expressive violence, of structural and instrumental experiments. He who had denounced dodecaphony used in 1968, a twelve-tone theme in his Violin Sonata, Opus 134, and dodecaphonic devices in his Twelfth Quartet. The following year, he achieved another breakthrough with his strongly expressionistic Symphony No. 14, on texts by mostly foreign poets. It was received with more re-

16. Schwarz, 170.
17. *New York Times*, Sept. 5, 1962.
18. The title of a poem by Yevtushenko, 1962.

spect than acclaim by the Moscow establishment. With these works, Shostakovich had detached himself from Socialist Realism and smoothed the way for the younger generation. He himself continued to compose until his death in 1975; his late works—the Fifteenth Quartet, the Michelangelo Sonnets, the Viola Sonata—are among his best.

In retrospect, it can be seen that the year 1962 signaled the culmination of Shostakovich's adherence to the cultural policies of the Soviet regime. It explains the dogmatic tone of the statement that aroused Lang's objection. By December of that year, the official policy suddenly hardened, and one of the first casualties was Shostakovich's Thirteenth Symphony, censured not because of the music but because of the texts by Yevtushenko. By March, 1963, Khrushchev had declared war on "ideological coexistence," a reversal of his former flexibility and a concession to the neo-Stalinist wing. It no longer mattered; by October, 1964, he was out of power.

Shostakovich's last official speech was given in May, 1968, when he retired as chairman of the Russian Composers' Union, giving his failing health as the reason, and passing his position to his former student Georgi Svirdov. Once he was removed from the public platform, Shostakovich's statements became rarer and less dogmatic. Asked about "new means of expression in music," he answered,

> As for the use of strictly technical devices borrowed from such musical systems as the twelve-tone or the aleatory . . . everything is good in moderation. . . . The use of elements from these complex systems is entirely justified if it is dictated by the idea of the composition. . . . [19]

He confirmed this point of view to an American interviewer in October, 1973: "If a composer feels that he needs this or that technique, he can take whatever is available and use it as he sees fit. It is his right to do so."[20] Such statements can rightfully be interpreted as a call for creative freedom; they supersede whatever he may have said in 1962.

19. *Yonust'* 5 (1968), trans. in condensed form in *Current Digest* 20/24 (July 3, 1968): 1.
20. Royal S. Brown, "An Interview with Shostakovich," *High Fidelity* (Oct., 1973): 8.

STEFAN WOLPE'S
BERLIN YEARS

AUSTIN CLARKSON

DURING THE YEARS of extreme social and economic tension that afflicted Germany between World War I and Hitler's coming to power, artistic modernism blazed up with hectic brilliance. The vitality and diversity of German modernism, suppressed during the reign of Wilhelm II, were released when the first German Republic struggled out of the ashes of war. In spite of inflation, depression, and public unrest, the capital of the new republic supported a culture of unprecedented richness. Having managed to survive war, hunger, and disease, a new generation of German musicians born around the turn of the century fell heir to a city of four million inhabitants that came to have three opera houses, twenty concert halls, three dozen theaters, hundreds of chamber groups, choruses and orchestras, and more than one hundred music publishers of international repute. Superb composers and performers returned to Berlin or came there for the first time. Ferruccio Busoni was invited to return to teach a master class at the Akademie der Künste, and when Busoni died in 1924, Arnold Schoenberg was called back to Berlin to replace him. Franz Schreker came from Vienna to direct the Hochschule für Musik, and a number of younger composers, including Paul Hindemith, subsequently taught there. The Weimar Republic proved to be considerably more receptive to new music than had the Wilhelmine régime. The Staatsoper (formerly the Court Opera) presented twelve new operas between 1919 and 1932 and gave Alban Berg's *Wozzeck* twenty-three performances following its première in 1925. The Kroll Oper under Otto Klemperer produced many other contemporary works, including scores by Stravinsky, Schoenberg, Hindemith, Janáček, and Weill, and the Städtische Oper gave Ernst Křenek's *Jonny spielt auf* in 1927 with great success. Jonny, the un-inhibited American jazz fiddler who lures the introverted, angst-ridden German composer to the West, links Berlin's tradition-bound bourgeois culture to the rowdy life of its pubs and cabarets dancing to the jazz styles brought over from America. But Germans also looked eastward. In the aftermath of the war, cut off from European countries to the west, Germans sought inspiration for new initiatives from Russia as well as from America. Radical elements were especially receptive to the Bolshevik ideals of collectivism and constructivism, and German artists and writers responded enthusiastically by founding such institutions as the Bauhaus, the Novembergruppe, the *Melos* Gemeinschaft, theater collectives, and book clubs that supplied cheap editions of quality fiction. The products of the avant-garde received wider currency than ever before. Supported by the Weimar government, German artists did not so much liberate the modern movement as "shift it onto a new, much wider and less personal plane where for the first time it could affect the lives of whole communities, not just small cul-tural elites."[1] Composers were caught in the tension between maintaining the transcendence and autonomy of the aesthetic realm and attempting to communi-cate to wider audiences than ever before. Some responded with societies for the private performance of new music, while others saw their task as the liberation of music from the control of the bourgeoisie. A few tried to hold the tension of the opposites so that art would not be sacrificed to ideology, nor ideology to art. Stefan Wolpe was one of that few.

Born in Berlin on August 25, 1902, Stefan Wolpe was the third of the four children of David Wolpe and Hermine Strasser.[2] As a young man his father had emigrated from Moscow to the Prussian capital; his mother had been born in Vienna, although her family was Hungarian and had come from Trieste. De-spite their very comfortable circumstances (David Wolpe had developed a suc-cessful manufacturing business), Stefan's parents had no use for literature or the arts and did little to encourage his musical gifts, which must have emerged early. Though Hermine Wolpe did play the piano a little, she was dominated by an authoritarian husband whose interests seem to have extended no further than commerce and who wished his elder son to go into the family business. Never-theless, Stefan must have had piano lessons quite early, for by the age of four-teen he was beginning theory instruction at the Klindworth-Scharwenka Conservatory—harmony with Alfred Richter (1846–1919) and counterpoint

---

1. John Willett, *Art and Politics in the Weimar Period: The New Sobriety, 1917–1933* (New York, 1978), 12.

2. This account of Wolpe's early years has been compiled from biographical information given in the follow-ing articles: Marion Bauer, "Stefan Wolpe," *Modern Music* 17 (1940): 233–36; Clare Reis, *Composers in America* (New York, 1947), 389; Abraham Skulsky, "Stefan Wolpe: Liberation from Enslavement of the Twelve-Tone System," *Musical America* (Nov. 1, 1951): 6f.; Joan Peyser, "Wolpe: A Thoroughly Modern Maverick," *New York Times*, Sunday, Feb. 6, 1972. The several inconsistencies in these accounts have been checked with information obtained from interviews with Mrs. Irma Wolpe Rademacher (recorded Nov. 20, 1975, and Oct. 4, 1976), Mrs. Hilda Morley Wolpe, Dr. Leopold Last (recorded Dec. 14, 1979), Mr. Mor-dechai Ardon (recorded Nov. 27, 1979), and Dr. Hans Heinz Stuckenschmidt (Dec. 5, 1979).

and composition with Otto Taubmann (1859–1929). A venerable descendant of the illustrious musicians of the Leipzig Thomaskirche in that his father served as cantor there, Richter was not the ideal teacher for a precocious boy who wanted only to compose.[3] Stefan's frustration with Richter's pedagogy surfaced in the form of a musical collage that combined a scurrilous gutter tune with a Bach fugue. When he presented this symbol of his rebellion to Richter, the worthy professor slapped him in the face and threw him out.[4] At about the same time, in 1918, Stefan and his younger brother William, who wanted to be a painter, left home; no longer were they to tolerate their father's bullying. They joined a commune of young artists and survived as best they could doing odd jobs. (This was the year of the November Revolution, which deposed the kaiser and brought an end to the German empire and the war. "Revolt against the fathers" was in the air, and young people were leaving home in droves to cluster in the bands of Wandervögeln that roamed about the country in hopes of recovering the ideals of the German spirit destroyed by Prussian militarism.) Having cut himself off from his family, Stefan was fortunate to find a patron in about 1919.[5] She was Frau Else Schlomann, the wife of a wealthy Jewish attorney who did much to help young artists. She took an especial liking to Wolpe and treated him almost like a son, giving him the use of a studio with a piano in the basement of her mansion in the Berlin district of Dahlem. Wolpe continued to use this studio until he had to flee Berlin in 1933.

Wolpe's formal academic schooling had suited his nature no better than his musical studies. He attended the Theodor Mommsen Humanistisches Gymnasium, a classical grammar school in the upper-middle-class district of Charlottenburg, but he was too free a spirit to submit to the authoritarian regime, and his studies suffered accordingly. He finally dropped out in 1919 or early 1920 before completing the *Abitur* that would have qualified him for entrance to a university.[6] In the spring of 1920 Wolpe applied to the Staatliche Hochschule für Musik for admission to the diploma course in composition. He was admitted, and in the fall of the year began studies with Paul Juon (1872–1940), a Russian-born composer who wrote copiously in a late Romantic vein. Juon had Wolpe write nothing but fugues, a discipline that soon palled. Not finding what he was looking for at the Hochschule, Wolpe, like Křenek and Weill shortly before him, did not reenroll for a second year.[7]

Liberated from formal schooling, Wolpe was free at last to satisfy his avid curiosity for everything new in the arts, and 1920 became a year of exploration

3. Bauer (p. 233) quotes Wolpe as saying that by the age of fourteen he had written "a complete opera, an octet for winds and several piano pieces," but no trace of these works remains.
4. Wolpe recounts this story in his "Lecture on Dada" (unpublished).
5. Mr. Mordechai Ardon was one of the young artists befriended by Mrs. Schlomann. He recalls meeting Wolpe at the Schlomann house when he went there for the first time in 1919 (recorded interview).
6. Dr. Leopold Last attended the Gymnasium from 1915 until 1921 and was in Wolpe's class until 1920. He recalls that Wolpe was held back a term before he left the school (recorded interview).
7. Dr. Thomas Martin Langner reported to me that Wolpe was registered as a regular student at the Hochschule from October, 1920, to Easter, 1921.

and discovery. As he passed from his eighteenth to his nineteenth year he came in touch with the Bauhaus at Weimar, with the Dadaists of Berlin, with the *Melos* Circle around Heinz Tiessen and Hermann Scherchen, and with Ferruccio Busoni. This was also the year from which come his earliest surviving compositions and in which his first published work appeared in print. It was a year of experiences that set a pattern for Wolpe's entire creative life.

He made the first of his many visits to the Staatliche Bauhaus in Weimar shortly after it was founded in 1919 by Walter Gropius. This institute was designed to train artists and craftsmen dedicated to returning to first principles in the search for design with universal validity. There they sought to build the "cathedral of socialism" by bringing the arts and crafts into creative relationship with modern social conditions and industrial technology. Gropius brought to Weimar many of the finest artists and teachers of the day: Lyonel Feininger, Paul Klee, Oskar Schlemmer, Johannes Itten, and László Moholy-Nagy, to name only those with whom Wolpe developed a particularly warm relationship. "The Bauhaus was the place in which modern art was being taught and experimented on, and we all travelled there like pilgrims to Jerusalem or Mecca."[8] Wolpe not only attended lectures but actually participated in the Preliminary Course of Johannes Itten, the course all incoming students had to take before being apprenticed to one of the masters.[9] Itten's teaching methods were highly innovative. He gave equal value to the students' discovery of their own artistic individuality and to expanding their aesthetic awareness. He believed that the mind and body must be properly prepared for creative activity and led his students in movement, breathing, and chanting exercises before beginning the day's classes. He assigned texture studies in which contrasts of qualities (large–small, thick–thin, much–little, etc.) were approached through nonrational and then through rational means and finally through a creative synthesis of both approaches.[10] For Wolpe the Bauhaus was a revelation. He found there what his earlier teachers had been unable to offer—belief in the value of the individual imagination, in experimentation, in a nonauthoritarian teaching attitude, and in the artist's mission to build a new society. He also found there a group of young artists who became lifelong friends. His first wife, the painter Ola Okuniewska, whom he married in 1927, was one of Itten's students from Vienna.

At about the same time in 1920, Wolpe became associated with the Berlin Dadaists.[11] Richard Huelsenbeck had arrived in Berlin in early 1917 with the message of Zurich Dada, and in early 1918 he delivered the first German Dadaist manifesto, a furious attack on all "isms"—Expressionism, Futurism,

---

8. Wolpe, "Lecture on Dada."

9. In the "Lecture on Dada" Wolpe describes his participation in the lectures of Paul Klee, but it is clear from the context that he means Johannes Itten. He undoubtedly attended lectures by Paul Klee also, but Mr. Ardon confirms that Wolpe took part in Itten's preliminary course (recorded interview).

10. See Johannes Itten, *Design and Form: The Basic Course at the Bauhaus and Later* (New York, 1975), 9 and 34.

11. See Hans Richter, *Dada: Art and Anti-Art* (New York, 1965), 102ff.

Cubism, Abstractionism, *et al.*[12] This aroused Raoul Hausmann, Johannes Baader (the self-styled *Oberdada*), the Herzfeld brothers, Franz Jung, Georg Grosz, and Hans Richter to release their pent up fury at the suffering and carnage of the war and the insanity of the culture that had led to it. These men were considerably older than Wolpe, but they found him suitably free of spirit and thus qualified to contribute to their exhibitions. One of his offerings—surely one of the earliest musical "happenings"—consisted of eight gramophones playing recordings of eight different kinds of music (waltz, march, symphony, etc.) at varying speeds. At the same time a girl holding a dripping water hose recited a Shakespeare sonnet.[13] After 1923 the Berlin Dadaists went their several ways, but Wolpe remained friends with Hans Richter and later associated with the Hanover Dadaist Kurt Schwitters. In 1929 Wolpe set to music Schwitters's celebrated Dada poem *Anna Blume* for a tenor seated on a (presumably stationary) bicycle. The singer on occasion blows a siren, and the pianist, in the midst of a wild, atonal accompaniment, at one point joins the singer in the recitation. Wolpe may have accompanied the sound-poet and collagist on at least one of his reading tours.[14]

The year 1920 also marks the beginning of Wolpe's contact with Ferruccio Busoni. Busoni returned to Berlin in the fall of that year after a wartime stay in Zurich and was assigned a master class of composition students by the Akademie der Künste. Although Wolpe was not a member of that class, which included such composers as Kurt Weill and Vladimir Vogel, he visited Busoni on several occasions and later recalled having played his music for the master and receiving encouragement and helpful counsel.[15] Busoni was at the time campaigning against Expressionism, which in his view gave up formal coherence for extravagant emotion. His ideal was a music that invests recent experimental developments with strong and beautiful forms. He wished to rescue melody from the fragmented melodies of the Expressionists and restore to it its role as bearer of the musical idea and of harmony. He also wished to renounce subjectivity and unbridled sensuousness for a new serenity. For this aesthetic he coined the term *Junge Klassizismus.*[16] Busoni advised Wolpe to moderate his tendency to extreme Expressionism, and several of Wolpe's compositions from the next few years show the imprint of Busoni's influence. Busoni was the first musician Wolpe met who won his unreserved admiration and respect.

During this period Wolpe also came into touch with Hermann Scherchen and the *Melos* Circle of leftist Expressionists. Scherchen—composer, conductor, editor, and tireless promoter of new music—had returned to Berlin from war-

---

12. Wolpe, "Lecture on Dada."

13. Ibid.

14. In the "Lecture on Dada," Wolpe recounts a Schwitters reading at the University of Jena. The context suggests that Wolpe was on tour with him.

15. Irma Wolpe Rademacher: "He (Wolpe) adored him. He just had no words when he thought about Busoni, about the greatness of Busoni as a pianist. And as a composer he asked Busoni for advice" (recorded interview). See also Peyser.

16. Busoni, *The Essence of Music and Other Papers* (New York, 1965), 19–23.

time internment in Russia to found in 1919 the Neue Musikgesellschaft, the Scherchen Quartet, and *Melos,* the provocative monthly journal for new music. The first issue of *Melos* appeared early in 1920, and the December issue that year carried an Adagio for Piano by Wolpe.[17] Assisted by Heinz Tiessen and the pianist and composer Eduard Erdmann, Scherchen in 1921 founded the *Melos* Gemeinschaft, which presented concerts that brought to Berlin performances of Schoenberg, Bartók, Malipiero, Kodály, Hindemith, Milhaud, and many others. Scherchen and Tiessen thought highly of Wolpe and gave him much encouragement.[18] The following year he was admitted to the ranks of the Novembergruppe, an association of artists and writers formed in the wake of the November Revolution of 1918 for the purpose of popularizing modern art and reforming the cultural policies of the German government. These "revolutionaries of the spirit" wished to free the arts from exploitation by the bourgeoisie and return them to the people.[19] The musical evenings of the Novembergruppe were first organized by the composers Max Butting, Philipp Jarnach, and Heinz Tiessen, but soon other musicians joined: George Antheil, Hanns Eisler, Jascha Horenstein, Hans Heinz Stuckenschmidt, Vladimir Vogel, Kurt Weill, and—the youngest of the group—Stefan Wolpe. Wolpe contributed to the Novembergruppe concerts as both composer and pianist.

> In the concerts of the Novembergruppe he astonished listeners with the cyclopean power of his piano playing, which he put to the service of his own and others' works. Wherever new musical ideas were developed and planned one saw this tall, lanky young man with closely cropped hair and burning eyes.[20]

1920 is also the year from which come Wolpe's earliest surviving compositions. He destroyed everything he wrote before 1923 save for sixteen pieces from 1920. These reveal that unlike most of his contemporaries, whose fledgling compositions are steeped in the sound world of Brahms or Wagner, Strauss or Reger, Wolpe did not go through a post-Romantic weaning period, or if he did, the phase did not last long. Fourteen of the sixteen pieces from 1920 affirm that his mother tongue was free atonality. The two tonal pieces of the group are charming *jeux d'esprit* in the spirit of Erik Satie, which, far from depending on nineteenth-century Romanticism, are jaunty ostinato pieces with more than a touch of ragtime. The atonal pieces deploy a wide palette of sonorities ranging from simple triads to bitonal, bimodal, and quartal structures with dense layerings of varied interval complexes. Tertian chords are not construed as tonally

---

17. *Melos* 1/21 (Dec. 16, 1920). The composition is printed in facs. of the composer's manuscript.
18. See Stuckenschmidt, "Heinz Tiessen—der Freund," in Manfred Schlosser, ed., *Heinz Tiessen 1887–1971* (Berlin, 1979), 11; and Herman Scherchen, *Alles hörbar machen* (Berlin, 1976), 217 and 219.
19. See Willett, 44, and Helga Kliemann, *Die Novembergruppe* (Berlin, 1966).
20. Stuckenschmidt, "Musik und Musiker in der Novembergruppe," *Anbruch* 10 (1928): 293–95. This and succeeding translations are mine.

functional. The opening measure of *Vöglein Schwermut,* a setting of a moody lyric by Christian Morgenstern on the black bird of death, sounds Gb major, but the second measure unfolds a melody drawn from the whole-tone hexachord [0, 2, 4, 6, 8, 10] (Example 1).[21] The accompaniment in the second measure confirms the extinction of tonal function by adding the tones of the complementary whole-tone hexachord {1, 3, 5, 7, 9, 11}. Triads are taken as just one more type of interval complex with a particular color. These pieces show a remarkable grasp of possible means for achieving coherence in the atonal idiom. In *Kleiner*

EXAMPLE 1.[22] *Vöglein Schwermut* (June 13, 1920), mm. 1–2

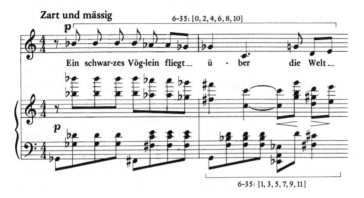

Erfolg, one of the two songs in which Wolpe set his own texts, there is an ostinato figure consisting of three minor sixths that, taken together, form the hexachord 6-Z46 (Example 2). During the slower second section, while this ostinato

EXAMPLE 2. *Kleiner Erfolg* (Summer, 1920), mm. 1–2

21. The integer notation designates pitches as follows: C is O, C# is 1, . . . B is 11. The pitches within square brackets constitute a pitch-class set. The naming of pitch-class sets follows the system set forth by Allen Forte in *The Structure of Atonal Music,* 2nd ed. (New Haven, 1977). A Z-related pair of pitch-class sets is a pair of sets that share the same interval content, but not the same structure.

22. All the musical examples except No. 6 are reproduced by permission of Mrs. Hilda Morley Wolpe and Mrs. Katharina Wolpe Leonard. The manuscript sources are in the Stefan Wolpe Archive, New York, New York.

is in the left hand of the piano part, the vocal line and the piano right hand introduce the pitches of the complementary hexachord 6-Z24. The coda of the song repeats the melody of the second section, but now in ragtime style. The presentation of an ostinato by one of a pair of complementary Z-related hexachords while the other member of the pair is deployed in the melody reveals a lively ear and constructive imagination for atonal ordering principles. The textures of the atonal songs are mainly chordal, the rhythms are controlled by the declamation of the vocal line, and the voice mostly maintains a distinct part undoubled by the piano.

Wolpe's early Expressionistic style is revealed more fully in the instrumental compositions from 1920, five Adagios for piano, four of which are dedicated to his patron Else Schlomann. Long, arching, continuously elided phrases (there are very few rests) are upheld by densely voiced chords, rather stiff rhythms, and strong dynamic contrasts. These Adagios avoid ostinato figures and clear reprise structures in favor of through-composed extension and variation of motives and the free association of ideas; at this early stage in his career they already demonstrate Wolpe's gift for instrumental lyricism and his ability to sculpt characteristic, richly modeled, and colorful shapes. The opening phrase of the Adagio printed in the first volume of *Melos* is typical (Example 3a). The phrase opens and closes on G major, but G major does not control the tonality of the piece. It seldom recurs, although it does reappear at the beginning of the final phrase (Example 3b). However, the final C♯ of the piece effectively neutralizes the sense of a G center.

EXAMPLE 3. Adagio for Piano (September 27, 1920)

a. Mm. 1-2

b. Mm. 71-72

Wolpe's compositions from 1920 reveal an eighteen-year-old with a musical imagination of remarkable originality and technical resourcefulness. He navigated the little-charted realm of free atonality with the confidence born of a

powerful lyric impulse, a discriminating ear for sonority, and an ability to manipulate a very wide range of chordal structures. Although the rhythms and textures lack differentiation, his music is as open to vernacular styles and
extraverted playfulness as to lofty expression and intense seriousness. Above all,
this music reveals an authentic voice not given to imitating models. Wolpe took
to free atonality as naturally as a duck to water. It is small wonder that he
learned more from the modern masters he played continually on the piano—
especially Skriabin, Mahler, Schoenberg, Bartók, and Hindemith—than from
his conservatory mentors.[23]

Wolpe was very self-critical even as a youth, and he later destroyed much
of the music he had composed before 1925.[24] Some clue to the considerable
amount of music he disposed of is given by the opus numbers he assigned his
compositions. The first series of numbers extends at least to a cello sonata composed before April, 1925, and given the number 21. Three compositions exist
in whole or in part from the first series: Three Piano Pieces, Opus 5b (1923), a
fragment of *Music for a Shadow Play,* Opus 8 (1923), for three women's voices,
and a set of *Arrangements of East Jewish Folk Songs,* Opus 14 (1925), composed
for the singer Rahel Ermolnikof. Titles for pieces now lost turn up in various
concert programs. On June 24, 1923, he performed Piano Pieces, Opus 5a, at
the Frankfurt Kammermusikwoche organized by Paul Hindemith, and Studies
for Piano, Opus 16, at the Sixth Evening of the Novembergruppe, January 22,
1924; a Violin Sonata, Opus 20, and the Cello Sonata, Opus 21, are listed on
the program of an all-Wolpe concert in the Meistersaal, April 27, 1925.

The second series of opus numbers begins with the Five Songs from Friedrich Hölderlin (1924, 1927), Opus 1, and extends to an Opus 31, from
around 1938. Of the second series only fourteen numbers are assigned to known
compositions. The seventeen unassigned numbers may have been given to compositions not completed, or to those lost or destroyed. The music that does survive from the Berlin years is principally for the voice. The few instrumental
works—some solo piano pieces and the Violin Duo—are dwarfed by the March
and Variations for Two Pianos, composed just before he left Berlin. The Duo for
Two Violins (1924), Opus 2, is an offspring of Bartókian barbarism with two
fast movements given to motoric rhythms, mixed meters, and harsh bitonal dissonance (Example 4). The incomplete third movement, a Romanze, has a legato
section of dissonant counterpoint followed by a bitonal passage with the instruments in D and E♭, respectively.

23. Stuckenschmidt, *Zum Hören Geboren* (München, 1979), 87: "He was a phenomenal piano player and enlivened with his explosive expressivity the late sonatas of Skriabin and the piano works of Bartók we both admired, the Suite, Opus 14, and the Sonatina." In an interview in Berlin (Dec. 5, 1979) Stuckenschmidt
related how Wolpe enjoyed playing Schoenberg's piano music, especially Opus 11 and Opus 19: "He played,
analyzed and talked about Opus 19. He was impressed by the concentration of form, especially of the last one.
He played it at least ten times one after another."

24. Bauer (p.234) reports that Wolpe destroyed all his early music in 1923, but he did keep the sixteen
pieces that survive from 1920.

EXAMPLE 4. Duo for Two Violins (December, 1924)

a. First movement, mm. 1–9

b. Second movement, mm. 1–3

The Five Songs from Friedrich Hölderlin mark a decisive step in the evolution of Wolpe's lyric style. Written in the years of the poet's final illness and madness, the verses are meditations on nature, love, and life's journey expressed in language of utter serenity, lucidity, and detachment. They provide the perfect framework for Wolpe's emerging skill at reconciling Expressionism with Young Classicism in his music. Busoni, who died the year the songs were written, would surely have approved of them. The voice part is not doubled by the piano and seldom falls below the pitch of the uppermost line of the accompaniment. The vocal lines spin out long-breathed, richly inflected phrases that imply an eventful harmonic background. The accompaniment rhythmically complements the vocal line, intensifying its phraseology with a newfound flexibility of rhythmic motion and melodic cursus, and with a more open texture. Motives are woven into phrases rather than being splintered and fragmentary, and there are no obviously illustrative images, recitativelike declamations, ostinato patterns, or long-held pedal sonorities. The forms are clearly articulated by means of subtle variations of phrases and some use of large-scale reprise. Of the four songs composed in 1924, two are quite brief: No. 1, *Hälfte des Lebens* (Example 5a), a lyrical work that has great rhythmic freedom and contains a single varied reprise, and No. 4, *Der Spaziergang* (Example 5b), a rhythmically more symmetrical narrative, nearly tonal in idiom, which is dedicated "to the sacred memory of Busoni." The two lengthier songs are No. 3, *Diotima,* a dramatic alternation of hymnic and stormy elements, and No. 5, *Zufriedenheit,* an exaltation of the loftiest idealism through varied strophic correspondences and intensive expressivity.

As is usual in Wolpe's atonal music of this period, in these songs the complete chromatic vocabulary is cycled with considerable speed. Vocal phrases often use all twelve tones or nearly all, and when pitches of the entire chromatic spectrum are omitted from the voice part, they are usually sounded in the piano.

EXAMPLE 5. Five Songs from Friedrich Hölderlin

a. No. 1, *Hälfte des Lebens* (1924), m. 1

b. No. 4, *Der Spaziergang* (1924), mm. 11–13

c. No. 2, *An Diotima* (1927), mm. 1–4

The second song, *An Diotima,* is anomalous. Composed three years later than the other four, it is the briefest of the set and contains Wolpe's earliest twelve-tone melody. In the first of the two long vocal phrases, all twelve tones are used without repetition (Example 5c), but the second phrase, although it begins with the same five tones as the first, changes the order of the remaining pitches. The melody is accompanied by a colorful assortment of triads and seventh chords that have little discernible structural connection with the melodic line. Wolpe took great pride in his Opus 1. Of all the vocal music from the Berlin years, it was the Hölderlin songs he selected to revise for performance in Palestine in 1935.

In 1925 Wolpe composed two pieces for piano that are totally divergent in nature, though both manifest a reaction to Expressionism. The *Early Piece for Piano* is an essay in pure C-Aeolian. Its agile, mercurial lines are based on both tertian and quartal complexes. Mainly in two-part counterpoint, with a dynamic level that seldom rises above mezzo forte and a narrow tessitura, its sotto voce intimacy is couched in a highly articulated structure. The opening Andante (Example 6) is followed by an Allegro and a canonic duo based on the theme of the

EXAMPLE 6. *Early Piece for Piano* (1925), mm. 1–3

Copyright 1955 by Josef Marx Music Company. Reproduced by permission.

Allegro. The piece concludes with a literal reprise of the Andante. And yet, as Stuckenschmidt notes, "the ecstatic undercurrent lives on beneath the classically quieted surface."[25] At the opposite pole from this example of Young Classicism lies *Stehende Musik,* a study in dissonant sonorities being repeated in asymmetric rhythmic patterns in all registers and with the dynamics reaching quintuple forte. Through repetition of dynamic, rhythmic, and textural elements in place of melodic and harmonic processes, it creates a monumental, sculptural object, a music of stasis. The principal sonority of the first movement combines a seventh chord with a quartal trichord (Example 7a), while the incomplete second movement begins with a bitonal sonority (D major plus D♯ minor with added sixth) that makes up the hexachord 6-Z44. This sonority is soon combined with its Z-related hexachord 6-Z19 scored as a structure of fifths with an upper third (Example 7b). The sonorities remain virtually unchanged throughout the movements. *Stehende Musik* was performed by Else C. Kraus at a concert titled *Stehende Musik* given on May 2, 1927, as the Nineteenth Evening of the Novembergruppe. The concert, which included a sonata by Hans-Jörg Dammert played by Franz Osborn and a sonata by H. H. Stuckenschmidt played by Wolpe, caused a scandal. The program note explicitly cites Schoenberg's Orchestra Piece, Opus 16, No. 3, and Stravinsky's *Piano Rag Music* as models in which formal tensions and relaxations are obtained from the principle of repetition rather than the principle of variation.[26] It is worth noting that hexachord 6-Z19 also plays an important role in the Schoenberg score.[27]

25. Stuckenschmidt, "Ein Berliner Komponist wieder in Berlin," *Melos* 24/6 (June, 1957): 184f.
26. Stuckenschmidt, *Zum Hören Geboren*, 94–96.
27. Forte, Ex. 152.

EXAMPLE 7. *Stehende Musik* (1925)

a. First movement, mm. 1–4

b. Second movement, mm. 1–17

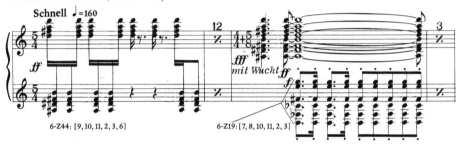

During 1925 and 1926 Wolpe continued to compose songs to poetry by culture heroes of the youth of Weimar Germany. Following the Hölderlin cycle, he wrote Three Songs after Heinrich von Kleist (1925), a setting of a Klopstock ode (1925), Nine Songs from the Gitanjali of Rabindranath Tagore (1926), a Cantata for Baritone, Viola, Cello, and Contrabass on Five Songs of Rilke from 1914 (1926), and Two Fables for Baritone and Piano on Texts of Hans Sachs and Jean de La Fontaine (1926).[28] In these songs Wolpe works out a new synthesis of Expressionism and Young Classicism. While still composing atonally, he now varies the rate at which the total chromatic is cycled. At some points the rate is slow enough to give the impression of a tonal center. In the first Kleist song (Example 8)—"Very even, in steady rhythm"—the treatment of sonority, phraseology, rhythm, and melodic cursus is more measured than in the Hölderlin songs. The music is more tightly drawn and coherent, the use of materials more economical, the aesthetic attitude more objective and distanced. The shift in style reflects the prevailing reaction to Expressionism and the move to the aesthetic of *Neue Sachlichkeit,* the New Sobriety (or New Objectivity). The Kleist songs may have been affected by Hindemith's *Marienleben,* which Wolpe must have heard in 1923 at the Bauhaus Week in Weimar. Wolpe was moving away from the introverted Expressionism which attempted "to recapture the religious

---

28. The Kleist and Hans Sachs songs are the only ones that survive complete. The Klopstock Ode, the Rilke Cantata, and the Fontaine Fable are incomplete, and the Tagore Songs were extremely severely scorched in the fire that swept Wolpe's New York apartment in 1970.

EXAMPLE 8. Three Songs after Heinrich von Kleist (1925), No. 1, *Der Engel am Grabe des Herrn*, mm. 1–7

(or quasi-religious) ecstasy of the Middle Ages."[29] Indeed, two of Wolpe's songs from 1920 set poems taken from medieval Minnelieder. The youthful hope after the war that mind and spirit could change the world had been dashed. "The world of brotherly love of which they had dreamt was farther away than ever."[30] Many young artists felt that it was not enough to remain closeted, dreaming new art forms; one had to become engagé. And so in 1925 Wolpe, together with his brother and his closest friend, Max Bronstein (later Mordechai Ardon), joined the Communist Party of Germany (KPD). Ostensibly the party of the workers, the KPD attracted young bourgeois artists and intellectuals, who found there a sense of a growing movement with a social mission. These young "revolutionaries of the spirit" could see their gifts put to use to strike down the old standards of bourgeois art so as to make way for a new art of the people. Joining the KPD was like entering a monastic order. The postulants studied Hegel, Marx, and Lenin in a Marxist Workers' School, read the approved papers (the *Arbeiter-Internationale Zeitung* and *Die rote Fahne*) and attended Piscator's theater productions, the Soviet cinema, and concerts by workers' choruses.[31] But 1925 was also the year of the première of *Wozzeck,* an event with as far-reaching consequences for Wolpe's musical development as joining the KPD was for his politics. Wolpe obtained the vocal score some weeks before the pre-

29. Walter Lacqueur, *Weimar: A Cultural History, 1918–1933* (London, 1974), 118.
30. Ibid., 117.
31. Willett, 204.

mière and, together with his friend tne composer and later critic and musicologist Hans Heinz Stuckenschmidt, played through it day and night until they both knew it well.[32] The impact of *Wozzeck* can be seen in the two chamber operas that are Wolpe's principal compositions from 1927 and '28.

Schöne Geschichten (1927–29) is a collection of seven scenes that spoof science, religion, justice, education, love, philosophy, and patriotism, in cabaret style. The music for each of these fast-moving and bitingly sardonic comic scenes is scored for eight-man jazz band and owes much to the spirit of *Wozzeck*. The highly active, motivically generated instrumental parts are fragmented by driving agogic rhythms and open, linear textures. Principal and secondary motives are labeled *Haupt-* and *Nebenstimme,* and the voices make liberal use of Sprechstimme. The second opera, *Zeus und Elida* (1928), is a more ambitious work, with an orchestra of twenty-five players. The single act is set in the Berlin of the day and recounts the adventures of Zeus, who lands in the Potsdammer Platz looking for a nice girl friend, only to find Elida, a tough streetwalker. The complications of this *Zeitoper* culminate in a rather too obvious satire of bourgeois morality and civil authority. The music is organized around a series of stylized jazz numbers, including a Charleston, Tango, Boston, and Foxtrot, proceeding to a Concerto and Variations, a Blues Solo and Duet, a Czardas, and a closing Potpourri. The tonal popular idioms are deftly spliced to his vigorous, caustic, atonal style.

In 1929 Wolpe became more and more engrossed in the theater. He composed incidental music for a production of *Hamlet* at the Renaissance Theater and for Walter Mehring's play *Troilus und Cressida.* But he also became involved with the agitprop troupes that sprang up as the political situation became increasingly polarized. Inspired by the Soviet troupe, the Blue Blouse, that visited Berlin in 1927, numerous German groups emerged and were formed by the KPD in 1928 into the German Workers' Theater League (ATBD). The following year the International Workers' Theater League (IATB) was formed in Moscow. Wolpe composed anthems for both the ATBD and the IATB[33] and numerous songs for such agitprop troupes as Roter Wedding, Roter Stern, and Rote Falken. But he found it difficult to compose in the simple diatonic style needed for these *Massenlieder.* "It took an enormous effort on my part to overcome and uproot my organic creative condition to write a simple song."[34] Nevertheless, he composed much *Kampfmusik* between 1929 and 1933 to texts by such Communist authors as Lenin, Mayakovsky, Erich Kästner, J. R. Becher, Ernst Ottwald, and Ludwig Renn. Most of these pieces are brief songs with a straightforward piano part, but a few are heroic utterances in Wolpe's most flamboyant style. Mayakovsky's *Decree No. 2 to the Army of Artists* is a diatribe

32. Stuckenschmidt, *Zum Hören Geboren,* 87.

33. *Wir kommen aus Fabriken (Lied des IATB)* and *In Fabriken und Gruben (Lied des ATBD)* reprinted in Inge Lammel, ed., *Lieder der Agitprop-Truppen vor 1945* (Leipzig, c. 1959), 10–13.

34. Herbert Sucoff, "Catalogue and Evaluation of the Work of Stefan Wolpe" (M.A. thesis, Queens College, 1969), vii.

against bourgeois culture in which the poet laureate of the Russian Revolution calls for a new proletarian art to be raised on the ashes of the old. The poem ends, "Comrades, give us a new art so we can pull the republic out of the filth!" Wolpe's setting is suitably pungent, hard-driven, and dissonantly atonal. The gestures are furious and biting, and the imagery is often onomatopoetic. In one passage Wolpe seems to point beyond free atonality toward twelve-tone principles. At the words " 'Give us new forms!' all things roar," the voice sings a hexachord that is immediately answered in the piano by its twelve-tone complement (Example 9). This suggests that for Wolpe the revolutionary new musical art might be founded on twelve-tone principles, despite the fact that colleagues such as Hanns Eisler then regarded Schoenberg as a bourgeois composer and the twelve-tone method as unsuitable for proletarian music. But this was no time for formalistic concerns, and Wolpe continued to compose tonal songs for the revolution. He did not come to terms with twelve-tone music until after he had left Berlin and settled in Palestine.

EXAMPLE 9. *Decree No. 2 to the Army of Artists* (1929), mm. 65–69

In the spring of 1931 Wolpe collaborated with the author Ludwig Renn and the choreographer Jean Weidt to produce the dance drama *Passion eines Menschen*.[35] The closing chorus is "Es wird die neue Welt geboren!" a song that became very popular and has been reprinted many times (see Plate I). Wolpe's touch can be heard in the prominent augmented second and tritones, the asymmetric fifth beat as the last phrase rises on a defiant minor sixth, and the rhythmic displacement by a sixteenth of the final cadential chord. The song is reported to have been sung by the members of the international brigade during the Spanish Civil War, and it still appears in East German songbooks as a classic agitprop song.[36]

35. The circumstances surrounding the preparation and production of this work are recounted by Jean Weidt in *Der rote Tänzer: Ein Lebensbericht* (Berlin, 1968), 16–18.
36. It is printed in *Mit Gesang wird gekämpft: Lieder der Arbeiter-Bewegung* (Berlin, 1967), 64f., and arranged for SATB in *Brüder am Werk*, 2, 4th ed. (Leipzig, 1973): 76f. For a historical and analytic account of the German workers' song see Inge Lammel, *Das Arbeiterlied* (Leipzig, 1980). "Es wird die neue Welt geboren" is included on pp. 176–77.

PLATE I. "Es wird die neue Welt geboren!"; Berlin: Verlag für Neue Musik, 1932

In August, 1931, Gustav von Wangenheim, an actor, director, and playwright who had worked for Max Reinhardt and Erwin Piscator, formed a group of unemployed Communist actors into the first professional agitprop theater company, Die Truppe 31. As music director of the company Wolpe composed the scores, led the band, and played the piano for the three productions mounted during the next two years. The first, *Die Mausefalle,* opened in December and, although financed on a shoestring, was a critical success.[37] It went

37. The plays are printed in Gustav von Wangenheim, *Da liegt der Hund begraben und andere Stücke aus dem Repertoire der 'Truppe 31'* (Hamburg, 1974). See also Klaus Kändler, *Drama and Klassenkampf* (Berlin, 1970), 238–43. The director's wife, Inge von Wangenheim, a member of the Truppe 31, gives an account of the work of the troupe in her autobiography, *Mein Haus Vaterland* (Halle/Saale, 1976), 380–90.

on to play over three hundred performances in Berlin and on tour through Germany and Switzerland. With a deft use of montage techniques and trenchant citations from Goethe and Shakespeare, this satirical *Lehrstück* dramatizes Marxist doctrine as it affects the life of a white-collar worker in a Taba (read Bata) shoe factory. The more than thirty musical numbers scored for violin, saxophone, trumpet, piano, and percussion include a Blues, a Tango, a Lullaby, a Waltz, and several rousing march songs, of which the best known was the "Lied vom Nebenmann." The music is tonal, but the chords are often gritty with dissonance and the rhythms concise. Wolpe's theater music shuns the epidemic ostinatos and vamp patterns in the proletarian style of his contemporaries, which he referred to as "the diatonic barrel organ of the revolution."[38]

The second play presented by Truppe 31, *Da liegt der Hund begraben,* was written and rehearsed too quickly and did not last long, but the third was another critical success. *Wer ist der Dümmste?* opened in February of 1933 soon after Hitler became chancellor and was closed on March 4 by edict of the Nazi chief of police. The instrumentation had to be reduced to piano alone, because, as Wolpe noted on the title page of the score, the troupe's funds were low during the last few months before Hitler.

The music of Wolpe's Berlin years does not end with these pieces for the theater. While working for the Truppe 31, he began composing a March and Variations for Two Pianos, h s most important piece of instrumental music up to that time. Begun in 1932 and completed the following year, it is both a culmination of the *Kampfmusik* he had been composing for the revolution and a reaffirmation of the value of purely instrumental music. The theme is an athletic, determined marching tune—"Lively, energetic, taut"—in purely diatonic C♯ minor (Example 10a). The nine variations that follow fall into two groups. The first four are formed on the familiar model in which motivic work, counterpoints, figural rhythms, and increasingly rich harmonies are added in an intensifying succession. After the fourth variation there is a long pause, signifying a break between the more traditional variation procedure and the developmental variations that follow. Variation 5—"Very fast, turbulent, triumphant"—shifts to triple meter and transforms the theme into an atonal sequence of broken triads (Example 10b). Variation 6—"Controlled (armed)"—is a fantasy on the transformed theme that exploits chordal texture and mixed meters. The seventh variation—"Mobile, light, and quick"—is a brilliant development of textural contrasts in which the atonal theme is refracted into a number of countermoving trajectories, and the eighth variation—"Very broad and tenacious"—is an eight-minute essay on the dark side of the struggle. Its opening figure (Example 10c) molds the tonal theme into a repeated gesture of utmost heaviness and weariness. The middle section is a powerful, threatening slow march played

38. Wolpe, "Diary No. 2," 382. He wrote this after attending a performance of the Brecht/Eisler play *Die Massnahme* in late 1931.

marcatissimo and "with bitterness." It closes after a varied reprise with triple-forte open fifths on F♯, from which emerges the final variation—"Fast, and with a joyful swing." It opens diatonically in the tonic major with the beginning of the original theme doubled in parallel thirds (not unlike the ring motive in Wagner's tetralogy). It is an image of man no longer marching alone but going forward in harmony after the struggle is won (Example 10d). The original theme is not heard complete. Instead, there is a strettolike concatenation of motivic elements that concludes in a tumultuous coda, a pandiatonic celebration with tolling bells and general rejoicing.

EXAMPLE 10. March and Variations for Two Pianos (1932–33)

a. Theme, mm. 1–15

b. Variation 5, mm. 1–8

c. Variation 8, mm. 1–2

d. Variation 9, mm. 1–4

The March and Variations derives its power from the tension between the straightforward, diatonic, monophonic theme and the dynamic process by which each variation develops out of the preceding one. The atonal theme of the fifth variation is a kind of Doppelgänger that leads the theme to progressive degrees of disembodiment as split-off motives are themselves developed and recombined. The foursquarely diatonic theme is not heard again in full after variation 4. When it reemerges in variation 9, after the crisis of variation 8, it is transformed into a utopian, pandiatonic condition. Wolpe wrote of the piece:

> New degrees of assent and affirmation are used as elements of the élan of a 15-bar, one-voice theme. The prevailing character is intentionally heroic. The characters of courage, looming consciousness and faith are expounded as intense emotional principles.[39]

The March and Variations is as close as Wolpe comes in a major work to the ethos of socialist realism. The tonal framework, the optimistic conclusion, the triumph of major over minor, and the glorification of the new man and the social reality that *should* be might have recommended the work to Stalin's cultural commissar A. A. Zhdanov. But the piece would surely have been banned because of the complexity of its technique and structure and the individuality of the authorial voice. Wolpe achieves a purely musical drama of transformation in which the thematic protagonist undergoes severe trials by textural, tonal, rhythmic, and formal distortion, dissolution, and complication before achieving a final resolution. Wolpe, like Brecht, did not suppress his expressionistic nature to please the ideologues. He provokes and distances the listener with the richness of his imagery, the forcefulness of his address, and the intense accumulation of musical values.[40] The March and Variations compensated for all the *Massenlieder* and the collective music making by celebratiang the transcendence and autonomy of art and the artist's right to his own voice. In this work Wolpe achieves in the purely instrumental medium what Herbert Marcuse calls "the individualizing of the social."[41] It is a goal for which Wolpe continued to strive, even though he later employed technical means of greater complexity and a higher level of abstraction.

When the barbarians descended on the "army of artists" in March of 1933, intense emotional principles were little match for rifle butts, and the KPD and the Socialists caved in without a fight. The storm troopers at once concen-

---

39. The program notes were prepared for reading at the American première, Feb. 11, 1940, at a League of Composers Concert in The Museum of Modern Art. The performers were Irma Wolpe and Edward Steuermann.

40. Mrs. Irma Wolpe Rademacher notes various elements in the work: "There are several streams meeting there in this March and Variations. There is the march idea from his proletarian phase, and then there is the Great Fugue, Beethoven last period. This was an obsession with him (Wolpe). The energy, this ten thousand volt, or a hundred thousand. And Mahler, maybe—the last movement" (recorded interview, Oct. 4, 1976).

41. Herbert Marcuse, *The Aesthetic Dimension: Toward a Critique of Marxist Aesthetics* (Boston, 1978), 25.

trated their attentions on such Communist enclaves as the blocks of flats on the Südwest Korso, known locally as "Der rote Turm," where Wolpe had his little apartment. His brother William was picked up and beaten so brutally that he lost an eye. When Stefan saw his brother in this condition, he was at last convinced that a Jewish–Communist–avant-garde musician was no longer welcome in his beloved Berlin. But he was penniless and would have been unable to escape had he not been helped by the Rumanian pianist and Dalcroze teacher Irma Schoenberg. She found him a place to stay near her home in a bourgeois part of the city and went herself to Wolpe's Dahlem studio to retrieve his music. She bought him a new suit of clothes so that he could pass as a businessman, threw away his Communist literature, and put him on a train for Czechoslovakia. She then left Berlin with the manuscripts, and they rendezvoused in Zurich.[42] In May Wolpe, along with the members of the Truppe 31, was invited to attend the International Workers' Theater Olympiad in Moscow.[43] He was elated by the feelings of freedom and brotherhood he found there and was strongly tempted to stay in Russia. But some instinct prompted him to attend to the inner needs that he had so long neglected, and in July he wrote to Anton Webern to ask whether he could study with him.[44] This was a crucial turning point. Eisler, who had studied with Schoenberg as a youth in Vienna, later turned away from the "bourgeois" music of his master to devote the remainder of his career to providing music for the proletarian revolution. In the belief that all music should teach Marxist doctrine and that a scenario or verbal text is necessary to make the doctrine clear, Eisler gave up writing chamber music and purely symphonic works.[45] Wolpe, by contrast, had not had the advantage of tuition from a master when he was young (by the time Schoenberg came to Berlin in 1926 Wolpe was already engagé), and he now felt the need to attend to basic compositional technique after so many years at the front. Circumstances allowed him only four months with Webern, but this was sufficient time for him to focus on the core of his own aesthetic nature, and it opened the way to his encounter with twelve-tone music.

Wolpe's Berlin years were over. He went into exile with an artistic nature formed by the most radical and vital aesthetic movements of the time, though he had not achieved recognition on the national or international scene. Unlike

---

42. This account is based on the interview with Mrs. Irma Wolpe Rademacher, recorded Oct. 4, 1976.

43. See Ludwig Hoffmann and Daniel Hoffmann, *Deutsches Arbeitertheater, 1918–1933* (Munich, 1973), 386–404.

44. The letter Webern sent in reply is dated Maria Enzersdorf, Aug. 28, 1933. Webern wrote that he is most interested in Wolpe's plans, that he would very much like to see his music, and that he is already willing to work with Wolpe if he so desires. Also see Hans and Rosaleen Moldenhauer, *Anton von Webern: A Chronicle of His Life and Work* (New York, 1979), 376 and 506 for Wolpe's recollections of his contact with Webern.

45. Hanns Eisler, "Our Revolutionary Music" (1932), in Manfred Grabs, ed., *Hanns Eisler: A Rebel in Music* (New York, 1978), 59: "All music forms and techniques must be developed to suit the express purpose, that is, the class struggle. . . . The most important requisite of revolutionary music is to divide it into music for practical performance: songs of struggle, satirical songs and so on, and music to be listened to: didactic plays, choral montage, and choral pieces with a theoretical content."

Hindemith, Eisler, Křenek, and Weill, he did not have a great popular success during the Weimar years. By the time his colleagues left Germany, they had found the path they would later follow. Hindemith turned to neo-Baroque *Gemeinschaftsmusik,* Křenek to a systematic exploration of serialism, Weill to the legitimate musical theater, and Eisler to unwavering service to Marxist ideology. But Wolpe's way was still obscure, and he himself was little known. His music had not been programmed by the International Society for Contemporary Music or the Allgemeine Deutsche Musik Verein. His *Kampflieder* had been printed in Berlin and Moscow, but none of his serious works was published. As Vladimir Vogel recalls, "He was an outsider who belonged to none of the then fashionable schools."[46] But Stuckenschmidt sensed then that Wolpe was a force to reckon with. He put his finger on Wolpe's unique qualities in a profile that appears in his report on the musicians of the Novembergruppe that appeared in the 1928 volume of *Anbruch:*

> Stefan Wolpe, the youngest of the group, is a special case. Plunging from ecstasy to ecstacy, from extreme to extreme, passionately investigating the materials and ideology of his art, he has demonstrated in numerous works of all kinds a more than exceptional talent that awaits maturity. Ideologically I would place him between Antheil and Eisler. I attribute decisive technical influences to Erik Satie, Arnold Schoenberg, and Josef Matthias Hauer.[47]

Stuckenschmidt's portrait is as apt for Wolpe's later career as it is for the Berlin years. It recognizes the depth and intensity of Wolpe's commitment, both to musical means and to social ends. Placing Wolpe ideologically between Eisler and Antheil suggests that he was not as doctrinaire politically as Eisler though more socially engagé than Antheil, and that he combined the pugnacious, *kämpferisch* attitude of Eisler and the brash, reckless fantasy of Antheil. His resonance with Satie (influence is perhaps too strong a word) surfaces in Wolpe's whimsy, his Dadaism, his hilarious takeoffs of popular styles, and his unerring knack for the unexpected. The impact of Schoenberg is evident in the early atonal music, but the influence of Hauer is not yet apparent. Only when Wolpe begins to develop his own approach to twelve-tone technique in the mid-thirties does his debt to Hauer emerge in his treatment of the set as a mode as well as a series. But as early as 1928 or even before, he must have indicated to Stuckenschmidt a strong interest in the writings, if not the music, of the cofounder of twelve-tone music. Above all, the sketch conveys Wolpe's total dedication to his calling, his passionate commitment to an exploration of the aesthetic structure and the cultural function of his art.

46. Letter to the author, dated May 15, 1981.
47. Stuckenschmidt, "Musik and Musiker der Novembergruppe," 293–95.

After Wolpe reached Palestine in 1934 and recovered from the first shock of exile, he returned to atonal music, his mother tongue, and set out to evolve his own approach to twelve-tone music. He continued to write tonal songs and theater music as the occasion arose, but the balance of his oeuvre shifted decisively to the purely instrumental media of the piano, the chamber ensemble, and the symphony. Although Wolpe never gave up his populist sympathies, he moved away from socialist realism to abstract expressionism, and as his mature music took shape, he investigated its structural and expressive foundations in a series of compositional studies and articulated them in a number of lectures.[48] The constructivist method and imaginative content of these researches give unmistakable evidence of his early experiences with Busoni, the Dadaists, and, most especially, the masters of the Bauhaus. Indeed, Wolpe remained an apostle to that vital, though tragically curtailed, culture of aesthetic liberation and radical populism, the culture of Weimar Germany.[49]

48. For a brief survey of Wolpe's later works see my *Stefan Wolpe: A Brief Catalogue of Published Works* (Islington, Ontario, 1981). The published lectures reveal the impact of the Bauhaus and also give indispensable insights into his later music: "Thinking Twice," in Elliott Schwartz and Barney Childs, eds., *Contemporary Composers on Contemporary Music* (New York, 1967), 274–307; "Thoughts on Pitch and Some Considerations Connected with It," *Perspectives of New Music* 17/2 (Spring–Summer, 1979): 28–57.

49. I came in touch with Stefan Wolpe when I attended his private class in analysis between 1960 and 1962 while studying musicology at Columbia University. It has taken many years to bring together what I gained from the graduate program directed by Paul Henry Lang with my growing involvement with the life and work of Stefan Wolpe, and I offer this essay in tribute to both my valued teachers.

MUSICAL FORM
AND MUSICAL IDEA:
REFLECTIONS ON A
THEME OF SCHOENBERG,
HANSLICK, AND KANT

PATRICIA CARPENTER

Language is the mother of the idea.[1]

WHEN A COMPOSER—I have in mind Arnold Schoenberg—maintains that music is not some kind of entertainment, but some kind of discourse, a musical poet's or thinker's representation of musical ideas, what does he mean by "idea"? Schoenberg uses the word *Gedanke* ("thought"), yet denies any connection between musical concepts and the concepts of ordinary language. Rather, he affirms (with Schopenhauer) that the true nature of music is irrational, and its language, a language that reason does not understand: ineffable, immediate, yet unmistakable in meaning. A musical idea is strictly musical.

For Schoenberg the musical idea is central to the being of the musical work and the ground for its coherence: the composer envisions and materializes the idea; the listener apprehends it. Musical form articulates it. In all the arts, but especially in music, he says, form aims at comprehensibility (SI, 215).

Although musical ideas are unrelated to the concepts of reason, according to Schoenberg, they must correspond to the laws of human logic and thus are part of what man can apperceive, reason, and express. They are comprehensible because they are fit in a certain way to the comprehending mind. Schoenberg likens the satisfaction felt in the comprehension of an idea to the pleasure that attends the apprehension of beauty: "The relaxation which a satisfied listener ex-

---

1. Karl Krauss, quoted in Schoenberg, *Style and Idea: Selected Writings of Arnold Schoenberg*, ed. Leonard Stein (New York, 1975), 369. References in the text (SI) are to page numbers. The translations have been altered in some instances.

periences when he can follow an idea, its development and the reasons for such development is closely related, psychologically speaking, to a feeling of beauty" (SI, 215). That is to say, he conceives of the true musical experience, like any true experience of art, as a kind of cognitive harmony. In his striving for truth-fulness the artist may attain beauty without willing it, but his goal is expression of the aesthetic idea. Art is the truth.

Schoenberg echoes an old idea—Kant's characterization of the pleasure felt upon the contemplation of beauty (as pure form) as a kind of heightened cognition resulting from the free and harmonious interplay of the two cognitive powers, imagination and understanding, harmonious because of a certain fitness of the form of the aesthetic object to the mind of the apprehending subject. In-deed, Schoenberg has taken a further step along the path of traditional Idealist aesthetics toward the transformation of pleasure to comprehension and of beauty to truth, now applied specifically to music.

His immediate predecessor in this line of thinking about music was the critic Eduard Hanslick. For Hanslick, as for Schoenberg, the idea generates the work: "The object of every art is to clothe in some material form an idea which has originated in the artist's imagination."[2] The musical idea is projected from the imagination of the artist to that of the listener; proper listening is the con-templation and comprehension of the idea. Hanslick, like Schoenberg, links pleasure and comprehensibility—pleasure follows comprehension: "The most important factor in the mental process accompanying the apprehension of the musical work, and that which converts true listening into a source of pleasure, is the mental satisfaction which the listener derives from following and anticipating the composer's intentions" (BM, 98). Like Schoenberg, Hanslick attributes that satisfaction to a certain fitness of subject and object.

Hanslick also considered music to be in some ways like a language. Lan-guage and music are both artificial products, he maintains, in that neither exists ready-made in nature; each has been gradually formed and must be specifically learned. We may infer that our musical system, like language, will be enriched by new forms in the course of time and undergo changes. "If, for instance, the system were widened by the 'emancipation of the demisemitones' (of which a modern authoress professes to have found adumbrations in Chopin's music), the theories of harmony, composition, and musical aesthetics would become totally changed" (BM, 108).

It is significant, Hanslick says, that we apply to music terms of discourse: we speak of 'thought' (Gedanke) in regard to a musical composition; we speak of a completed musical phrase as a sentence when it comes to logical closure; we speak of both meaning and logical sequence in musical works, but use these no-

---

2. Hanslick, Vom Musikalisch-Schönen (Leipzig, 1854), trans. Gustav Cohen, The Beautiful in Music (Lon-don, 1891), repr. ed. Morris Weitz (New York, 1922), 52. Because the translation distorts Hanslick's mean-ing in the direction of an extreme formalism, I have on occasion used my own translation. References in the text (BM) are to page numbers.

tions in a musical sense (BM, 50). He too opposes musical ideas, which are immediate, to the ideas of ordinary language, mediated by concepts. Music is expression, a language we speak and understand but cannot translate.

I

N o w if music is a language, then form, on the traditional view of language, can be conceived separately from content, the structure of the sentence abstracted from its meaning—what it is and how it is done, as Schoenberg put it to Rudolf Kolisch. Further, the concepts of ordinary language are clear and distinct, definite and determinate. Because in music there are no such concepts, tradition has held that if music is a language, it is the language of the emotions and its content is feeling. Schopenhauer, for instance, carries this view to an extreme. Musical language, he says, is not unclear or indistinct; on the contrary, it is the most powerful language, directly understandable without mediation of concepts. It externalizes for contemplation the most basic affect, the cry, and in externalizing the cry it clarifies and defines the feeling.

Both Hanslick and Schoenberg reject this view. They maintain that the ultimate content of music is not feeling, but musical ideas, and that, because the musical idea is sheerly musical, there is no separation of form and content.

Hanslick speaks against those who make vague analogies between music and ordinary language, which have their centers of gravity at different points; sound in speech is only a means for the expression of something quite distinct from its medium, whereas sound in music is the end, the absolute object in view (BM, 67):

> We must free ourselves from the notion that the beautiful melody and skillful harmony do not charm us in themselves, but only by what they imply: the whispering of love or the clamor of ardent combatants. The whispering, true, but not the whispering of love; the clamor, undoubtedly, but not the pugnacity. Music can whisper, storm, roar—tenderness and anger are carried only in our own hearts (BM, 20).

Music is not a language of emotions, but a logic of sound in motion. The true content of music, as of any art, is the aesthetic idea (BM, 48). Musical form, the completely materialized musical idea, thus means itself.

Schoenberg also aims for a work in which content and form are completely taken up in the materialization of the musical idea. For example, he attributes the

> almost unexampled objectivity of Mahler's music to the fact that his sound never comes from ornamental additions, but from the idea or message itself. . . . Where it soughs, it is the theme which soughs; the themes have such a form and so many notes that it immediately becomes clear

that soughing is not the *aim* of this passage, but its form and its content (SI, 463).

For Schoenberg, a true comprehension of a work is neither the apprehension of mere form nor the understanding of content, but the comprehension of the specifically musical meaning, the artist's message.

For both Schoenberg and Hanslick, a composer is one who thinks and speaks in music. The musical work is an utterance, in which idea and form arise together in externalizing and thus clarifying the idea. Musical language is not sound plus meaning, but meaningful sound.

II

BOTH MEN stress the cognitive aspect of music (as of all art). Music is coherent, they maintain, because of the logical presentation of ideas and their objective consequences. It has meaning because it is part of the logical makeup of man and comprehensible by the alert and well-trained mind. Such logic is not that of ordinary language. Yet they have transformed the traditional dichotomy of form and the expression of feeling into a dichotomy of form and the articulation of ideas. Each reconciled this separation in his own way.

Schoenberg, throughout his career, felt compelled to defend his music against reproaches of both intellectuality and incomprehensibility and himself against the charge that he composed with his head, not his heart. "I have often wondered," he writes, "whether people who possess a brain would prefer to hide this fact" (SI, 122). In "Heart and Brain in Music," Schoenberg speaks, as creator, against the opposition between those who create cerebrally—philosophers, scientists, mathematicians, inventors—and those who create "artistically," who should not admit the influence of a brain upon their emotions, between those who seek for direct and sober language and those who circumscribe an idea or a fact, befogging both. This opposition, he says, is misconceived. Art is not a dream without sleeping.

> It is not the heart alone which creates all that is beautiful . . . nor is it the brain alone which is able to produce the well-constructed, the soundly organized, the logical, and the complicated. Everything of supreme value in art must show heart as well as brain (SI, 75).

"Heart and Brain" is an anguished cry of a man alone, "a human being painfully stirred by the search for inner harmony,"[3] a cry against the traditional bifurcation of human nature and human experience. If there exist two irreconcilable faculties, sense and reason, and reality is shaped by a common sense and a

---

3. From a letter written by Schoenberg to Gustav Mahler, Dec. 12, 1904. Quoted in Willi Reich, *Schoenberg: A Critical Biography,* trans. Leo Black (New York 1971), 43.

common rational language, this is the language of objectified knowledge. Who then speaks the ineffable language of art? In the Idealist tradition it is the pivotal role of art to mediate the dichotomies that structure other modes of awareness. And indeed, for Schoenberg, although these may be in tension in the world around him, they are in balance in the work.

III

THE MODERN locus for the tension between aesthetic form and aesthetic idea I take to be the *Critique of Judgement* by Kant.[4] Its framework is the bifurcation of human experience that Schoenberg renounces with such anguish.

Kant maintains that the central aesthetic phenomenon is beauty, which he explicates both as mere form and as the expression of aesthetic ideas. The simplest explanation for this contrast would seem to be that Kant looks at the aesthetic experience from two sides—that of the observer, who makes a judgment of taste, in which beauty is purely formal (CJ, 1–22), and that of the producer, the theory of genius, in which beauty is expressive of aesthetic ideas (CJ, 43–60). I think, however, that the dichotomy that structures Kant's thought in this *Critique* and provokes the apparent paradox generating his work is a more interesting ground for these two views of beauty, because he resolves his paradox (at least on one level) by rethinking the relationship between aesthetic form and aesthetic ideas. He thereby bequeathed to his followers not only a crystallized dichotomy between form and expression, but also the means for its resolution.

Therefore, I shall begin, as does Kant, with his dichotomy. The mind, as he sees it, has three different modes of awareness: cognition, the feeling of pleasure and pain, and desire. The opposition he sees between the first two—he formulates it as logic versus aesthetic—is brought into sharp focus by the judgment of taste. Here is his paradox:

> We have a faculty of judgement which is merely aesthetic—a faculty of judging of forms without the aid of concepts, and of finding in the mere estimate of them, a delight that we at the same time make into a rule for everyone, without this judgement being founded on an interest, or yet producing one (CJ, 42).

Now a judgment, for Kant, is basically an assertion. If I assert that something—this sonata, for example—is beautiful, in contrast to "I like it," I have made a judgment of taste. Kant finds something peculiar about it because, according to him, I claim for that statement a universal validity, that it "may exact the adhesion of everyone" (CJ, 29). That is, I have in some sense made Schoenberg's claim that art is the truth. My assertion therefore sounds like an objective

---

4. *Kritik der Urteilskraft* (Berlin, 1790), trans. James Creed Meredith, *The Critique of Judgement* (Oxford, 1952). References in the text (CJ) are to Kant's section numbers.

judgment, an "is the case" statement, instead of an aesthetic judgment, an "it seems to me" statement. Since judgments are classified according to their determining grounds, mine is an aesthetic, not a logical judgment, because it is based, Kant maintains, upon my own feeling of pleasure. A logical judgment refers a concept to an object; an aesthetic judgment refers a representation only to the subject and its feeling of pleasure or displeasure. The determining ground of the aesthetic judgment is subjective (CJ, 1).

For Kant, aesthetic means "of the senses" and carries two meanings that ought to be distinguished: feeling and sense impression. Sense impressions, although subjective, may be referred to an object: "This is red." Feelings are referred only to the subject. Sense impressions are therefore available for cognition, whereas feelings are not.

> Every reference of representation is capable of being objective, even that of sensations. . . . The one exception to this is the feeling of pleasure or displeasure. . . . To apprehend a regular and appropriate building with one's cognitive faculties, be the mode of representation clear or confused, is quite a different thing from being conscious of this representation with an accompanying sensation of delight (CJ, 1).

The grounds for communicability and hence for universal and necessary validity, Kant says, are only in cognition. But a judgment of taste is not cognitive. How then can I claim universal assent for this judgment?

IV

PERHAPS I have exacerbated the problem by framing my judgment of taste in regard to music. Music, however, exacerbated the problem for Kant himself: on the one hand, it is exemplary of pure beauty; on the other, it is the most intense language of the emotions. Although music is merely the play of sensation and speaks without concepts (CJ, 52), it must nevertheless permit of universal communication. Kant therefore questions whether music can indeed be said to be a fine art. This predicament of music has to do, I think, with its problematic relation to concepts and hence to truth.

TRUTH, on one view, is the correspondence between the idea and the real, the content of the mind and its correlate in the world. But music, as Hanslick, for instance, so strongly emphasizes, has no ties in the external world, no visual images, forms, or shapes with which to represent it, no concepts with which to describe it. "The relation subsisting between music and nature discloses the most pregnant truths in respect of musical aesthetics, and on the just appreciation of this relation depends the treatment of its most difficult subjects and the solution of its most debatable points" (BM, 104). If art is the truth, the predicament of music stems partly from its peculiar objectivity and partly from its nonverbal, nonconceptual nature.

A traditional Scholastic formula defines truth as the relation between thought and reality: "veritas est adaequatio rei et intellectus" ("truth is the adequation of things and the intellect"). Thomas Aquinas, whose formulation this is, says this equation may be looked at two ways, depending on whether the nature of the thing is the cause of knowledge in the intellect or the intellect is the cause of the thing's nature.

> [Where] things are the measure and rule of the intellect, truth consists in the equation of the intellect to the thing . . . but when intellect is the rule or measure of things, truth consists in the equation of things to the intellect. So a product of human art may be said to be true when it accords with the artist's plan or intention.[5]

We hear an echo of this view in Kant's "Genius gives the rule to art."

Three possible interpretations of this traditional formulation have been elaborated by Albert Hofstadter in his thinking about truth and art.[6] I shall follow these here. Truth involves a kind of knowledge, he says, and the clue to it is to be found in human understanding of existence. Language is the articulation of that understanding. "Taken generally, the perfection of language lies in the adequacy with which it performs the work of articulating human being" (TA, 90). Hofstadter develops three forms of linguistic adequacy (or truth or validity), distinguished according to that aspect of man's being which language tries to articulate, the cognitive, practical, or spiritual. He elaborates the three possible interpretations of the old formula as follows: (1) truth of statement (the adequation of intellect to thing); (2) truth of things (the conformity of the thing with the concept held of it); (3) truth of spirit (the mutual adequation of the two, which unites thing and concept in their mutual conformity). Central to all three concepts of truth is the identity between what is intended in the concept and what *is* in the thing. Truth of statement is the identity of what is meant (the thought), with what is (the existence). Truth of things is the agreement of the thing as it is with the concept of what it ought to be—the thing is right. In truth of spirit the thing realizes in its actuality the concept itself. Our concept is equally the thing's concept; hence the thing itself is intentionalistic, "purposive." This last, says Hofstadter, is the concrete unity of the concept and objectivity. In its appearance the thing must show itself as being what we ourselves intend as understanding of truth.[7] Art achieves this kind of truth.

5. *The Summa Theologica*, trans. The Fathers of the Dominican Province (London, 1912–36), question 16, arts. 2 and 3.

6. *Truth and Art* (New York, 1965). References in the text (TA) are to page numbers.

7. Hofstadter says that this notion of truth is best expressed by Hegel: "Truth in the deeper sense consists in the identity between objectivity and the concept [*Begriff*]. It is in this deeper sense that we speak of a true state, or of a true work of art. These objects are true, if they are as they ought to be, i.e. if their reality corresponds with their concept" (TA, 141). Carl Dahlhaus points out the dependency of Hanslick's notion of Idea ("immer den in seiner Wirklichkeit rein und mangellos gegenwärtigen Begriff") upon Hegel's definition of *Idee* as "Einheit des Begriffes und der Objektivität" ("Eduard Hanslick und der musikalische Formbegriff," *Die Musikforschung* 11 {1965}: 146).

CONSIDER now one side of the traditional truth relation, the idea.

An idea is a content of the mind or a mental object. In its oldest sense *(eidos),* it transliterates a Greek word meaning "to see" and therefore carries a possible meaning of visible aspect or shape, that is, form. But it also means an object seen by the eye of the mind—a conception or thought, abiding (unlike the physical thing) and grasped by reason.

There is then a basic tension in the notion of 'idea,' as object of conceptual thought or representation of perception, concept or percept, ideas of intellect or ideas of sense. Confusion over the term generally has to do with this distinction. 'Concept' is a fairly definite mental content, determined by consideration of instances abstracted from sense experience, a universal; 'percept' refers to particular perceptions in space and time.

In the balance between ideas of intellect and ideas of sense, truth has generally been on the side of intellect. Kant's immediate predecessors drew the distinction very clearly: the ideas of the intellect are clear and distinct and therefore true; the ideas of sense are confused and obscure.

KANT maintains the distinction between intellect and sense, using 'idea' strictly, in the Platonic sense, to mean something beyond sense experience and different from 'concept.' It is fundamental to his thought that all cognition presupposes perception, but he takes these to be two irreducibly different faculties. Concepts either are abstracted from sensations (a posteriori) or else order sensations in a certain way (a priori). 'Ideas', in contrast to concepts, are not applicable to perception; further, they must not be abstractions from sense or composed of such abstractions, and thus they are of all mental contents the furthest removed from sense experience. Such, according to Kant, are the ideas of reason and the aesthetic ideas. Ideas of reason are concepts to which no intuition can be adequate; they are indemonstrable. Aesthetic ideas, by analogy, are representations of the imagination to which no concept of ordinary language can be adequate; they are ineffable.

Kant held to the traditional formulation of truth, the accordance of a cognition with its object ("truth of statement"), but effected what he himself characterized as a "Copernican revolution" in the theory of knowledge.[8] Concepts that have been abstracted from perception are returned to objects, so to speak, conforming to them. But is it possible that in applying nonempirical concepts to objects in perception, objects are made to conform to the concepts, thus transforming perception in some way? As early as 1772 Kant wrote with excitement about this possibility to his friend and former pupil Marcus Herz.[9] Here would be grounds for what Hofstadter terms "truth of things."

Since Kant's "revolution," knowledge can no longer be considered passive recording, but is seen as a dialectic between subject and object.

8. Preface to 2nd ed. of the *Critique of Pure Reason* (Riga, 1787).
9. Quoted in Stephán Körner, *Kant* (Harmondsworth, 1955), 29.

Cognitions and judgements must, together with their attendant convictions, admit of being universally communicable; for otherwise a correspondence with the object would not be due them. They would be a conglomerate constituting a mere subjective play of the powers of representation. . . . But if cognitions are to admit of communication, then our mental state, that is, the way the coAnitive powers are attuned for cognition generally . . . must admit of being universally communicated, as, without this, which is the subjective condition of the act of knowing, knowledge . . . would not arise (CJ, 21).

If the judgment of taste is only subjective and in no way cognitive, what is our experience of an aesthetic object?

V

ALTHOUGH for Kant cognition presupposes perception, he works with an obsolete faculty psychology which dichotomizes perception and cognition, sense and understanding. Sense perception is the faculty of apprehending particulars given in space and time. Judgment, an act of understanding, is the faculty of thinking through concepts. Sense is passive reception of perceptions; judgment, active application of concepts to what we perceive.

The acquisition of knowledge requires first of all a certain subjective condition, a harmonious interplay of the two active cognitive faculties, understanding and imagination. This mental state of readiness can be called a state of cognition in general. Aesthetic judgment arises here. "The quickening of both faculties (imagination and understanding), to an indefinite, but yet . . . harmonious activity, such as belongs to cognition generally, is the sensation whose universal communicability is postulated by the judgement of taste" (CJ, 9). Thus, although Kant maintains that the judgment of taste is not cognitive, it feels as if it were.

Knowledge is achieved by the application of concepts. Sensation provides the raw data—a stream of impressions, such as colors and noises. Imagination collects and unifies the data. Understanding synthesizes them under a concept, thus determining a specific object. The object of an aesthetic judgment has unity, but no determining concept.

Judgment in general, according to Kant, is the faculty of thinking the particular as being contained in the universal. He distinguishes two ways in which this takes place: "If the universal (the rule, the principle, the law) is given, then Judgement which subsumes the particular under it is determinant. If however, the particular is given, to which Judgement is to find the universal, then it is merely reflective" (CJ, Intro., Sec. IV). In a determinant judgment, given a concept, I search for an object, a particular synthesis of representations to subsume under it. If I succeed, I achieve knowledge. In a reflective judgment, given a variety of particular representations—this conglomerate of visual impressions, say, or this stream of sounds and silences—I search for a concept under which they may be synthesized. A judgment of taste is reflective, but it involves no concept. If I find a unifying principle, I feel pleasure. The object is not judged with respect to any concept, but only according to whether the contemplation of it produces in me a feeling of pleasure or displeasure.

In ordinary cognition Kant distinguishes between perceptual judgments, such as "This stone seems heavy to me," and objective judgments, such as "This stone is heavy." Although subjective, even a perceptual judgment, he says, unifies representations into concepts, for it contains concepts abstracted from perception (for example, 'stone' and 'heavy'), but such a judgment merely expresses a relation of these two impressions to the same subject. An objective judgment requires a further unification, an application of an a priori concept, involving the manner in which specific concepts are ordered—in other words, a category—which confers objectivity and generality on perceptual judgments. For example, in "This stone is heavy," the category applied is that of existence, substance-plus-accidental properties. The unification of a manifold by means of a determinate concept produces an object in perception. The application of a category confers the characteristic of objectivity. These are two aspects of the same process; objective experience of reality requires both. For example, the application of a category without a concept results in an undetermined object-as-such.

The object of an aesthetic judgment, "the beautiful," would seem to be an object-as-such, undetermined by a concept. But further, no existence is posited of that object; no category is applied. I am concerned only with its appearance. In my apprehension of it representations are referred by the imagination to my own feeling of pleasure or displeasure. But the pleasure it evokes is without subjective interest. "Taste," says Kant, "is the faculty of estimating an object by means of delight or aversion apart from any interest whatsoever" (CJ, 5).

The musical object would seem to be a paradigm for such an object. A sensible instance of a concept has location in space or time or both, but where or when does the sonata exist? How do we apprehend that object, and how as "beautiful" or aesthetic? This is not Kant's primary concern in his third *Critique,* but two of his strategies, used on the way to more profound problems, are relevant here. First, we behave as if the aesthetic judgment were objective, not subjective; we attend only to the communicable aspect of the object, its form. Second, we behave as if that judgment were cognitive: there is some kind of a concept involved. Kant characterizes it as "indeterminate."

How do these two, form and idea, work together in the apprehension of the aesthetic object?

VI

KANT maintains that in apprehending an object as aesthetic, I attend only to its form. And, although a judgment of beauty is of a particular object—*this* rose, *this* melody—the form, he says, is its structure, abstracted from the material supplied by sense. In cognition the imposition of order on the manifold of raw data is the work of the understanding. Only the form of a cognition, then, is objective for all percipients, whereas matter is subjective. Only the forms of our experience are communicable and thus the concern of aesthetic judgment—in painting and sculpture, the design abstracted from color; in music, the composition, not the qualities of tone (CJ, 14).

However, although in the judgment of taste I attend only to the objective aspect of things, the ground for this judgment, according to Kant, is not in the object. Because there is no subjective interest in an aesthetic judgment, beauty seems to be a quality of the object and the judgment seems to be an objective, logical one, one that is therefore universally communicable and valid. But if the ground for beauty were in the object, he says, our pleasure would be of that object and thus an interested pleasure. Beauty is not that which gratifies in sensation but that which pleases by means of its form alone.

Pleasure in the object follows the judgment of beauty. "The purely subjective (aesthetic) estimation of the object . . . is antecedent to the pleasure in it, and is the basis of this pleasure in the harmony of the cognitive faculties" (CJ, 9). The ground which determines the judgment of beauty is not an objective concept, but a subjective feeling: the pleasure that derives from the quickening of the mental powers, unbounded by an imposed concept; the pleasure in finding "purpose" in the manifold of perception.

Ordinarily an object is produced in perception by a determining concept or rule, the "purpose" of the object. In order to apprehend a unity, a synthesis under the concept must always be possible. The rules or principles by which we apprehend an empirical unity "must be considered . . . as if an understanding (though not ours) had given them for our faculties of cognition," that is, as if nature is fitted to our mental capacities (CJ, 58).

In aesthetic experience, I am confronted with a conglomerate of sounds and silences, with no concept to bring it together as a determined object. Nevertheless, I proceed as if that passing stream were organized for cognition. The imagination "attunes itself to the faculty of concepts in general," and unifies the data. I am in subjective readiness for knowledge. I behave as if the particular representations were indeed designed for my cognition, reflecting upon them to discern whether they are organized in a purposeful manner, whether they can be seen as if they were rule-governed, looking for structure and formedness. I expect them to "make sense." I expect a synthesis.

Because there is no concept involved, Kant says, the determining ground for synthesis in the aesthetic judgment can be only structure or relation. The object is called purposive on the basis of its form alone. It has only the mere form of purposiveness.

Kant distinguishes the object of this pure judgment of taste as "free" beauty, which presupposes no concept of what the object should be, in contrast to "adherent" beauty, which does presuppose a concept. In nature, flowers,

many birds, and a number of crustacea are free beauties. So too are arabesques
and music without words, which have no intrinsic meaning, pleasing freely on
their own account (CJ, 16). These two kinds of beauty are the objects of two
different attitudes. For a natural object, there is indeed a concept involved, but
in making a judgment of taste, I abstract from that concept and judge the object
only on the basis of its form, as if there were no determinate concept of flower or
bird. My mental powers are released from that purpose and instead delight in
the object in their free, harmonious interplay, in my own sense of quickened
mentality. The imagination is "at play in the contemplation of outward form,"
in the expectation that the object is so constructed that it fits my powers of cognition.

Now suppose the manifold of sense impressions is a piece of music, which
was in fact designed to harmonize with my mental powers. I move toward apprehending it in the same fashion as I would a free beauty of nature, expecting
to find it purposive. On what basis do I "attune" to such an "object"? How am
I justified in proceeding as if it will make sense, fit itself to my mental capacities?
Kant's answer to this is the means by which he resolves his paradox: he makes a
distinction between determinate and indeterminate concepts.

A concept, a general representation of that which is common to many objects, is determinable by means of predicates that have been borrowed from
sense experience. There are "marks" or criteria in the manifold, says Kant, that
lead us to subsume the object under the concept (CJ, 59). An indeterminate
concept is not determinable through such predicates of sensible intuition; it is
supersensible, beyond sense experience. That indeterminate concept, nevertheless, is the source of my expectation that the given manifold of impressions will
make sense, even though there is no reason to assume that the flower or the sonata was in fact designed for my cognition. The indeterminate concept that underlies aesthetic experience is the principle—subjective, not objective—that
nature and mind harmonize; therefore there can be unity and synthesis. It is to
this determining ground of the aesthetic judgment that I appeal in my claim of
universal validity for the judgment.

What we discover in uncovering this principle at the basis of aesthetic experience, according to Kant, is a result that makes it seem as if the world of our
experience, the empirical world, were designed for our faculties. In maintaining
that music is comprehensible because it fits our mental makeup, Schoenberg and
Hanslick are, I believe, calling upon this notion of indeterminate concept.

VII

K A N T does not intend to say that aesthetic experience is mere delight in empty
forms and that the aesthetic object has no content (CJ, 52). Art is communication, and form the means by which it communicates. The contemplation of mere
form is essential to art, disposing the soul to ideas, making it thus susceptible of

aesthetic pleasure in greater abundance. The matter of sensation, he says, is not essential. "Here the aim is merely enjoyment, which leaves nothing behind it in the idea, and renders the soul dull, the object in the course of time distasteful, and the mind dissatisfied with itself" (CJ, 52).

Beauty (whether it be of nature or of art) is the expression of aesthetic ideas. Fine art is the production of beauty through the medium of a concept. In order to apprehend a beauty of nature, as such, I do not need a concept of what sort of a thing it is intended to be; I attend only to its form. Art, however, always presupposes an end in the cause; a concept of what its product is intended to be must always be laid at its basis (CJ, 48). However, the purpose in the product of art, intentional though it be, must not have the appearance of being intentional; rather it must seem like nature by virtue of "a perfect exactness in the agreement with rules prescribing how alone the product can be what it is intended to be, but without a sense of the artist having always had the rule present to him and of its having fettered his mental powers" (CJ, 45).

Genius is the talent which gives the rule to art (CJ, 46). Since artistic beauty cannot be derived from any rule that has a concept for its determining ground, nature in the individual—his subjectivity—must give art its rule. The source of this rule, unattainable by concept and beyond sense, lies in the supersensible substrate of all his faculties at the point of reference for the harmonious accord of all the faculties of cognition (CJ, 55, Remark I).

Therefore, artistic beauty is only possible as a product of genius, which produces that for which no definite rule can be given. Originality is the primary property of genius. Genius is irrational, for it cannot indicate logically how it brings about its product. It is inspired; the artist himself does not know how the ideas have entered into his head. But although the idea is inspired, the form is not; it is the product of a slow and even painful process of improvement, directed at making the form adequate to the thought (CJ, 48)—that is to say, "true."

WHAT is the relation between the indeterminate concept of aesthetic judgment and the aesthetic idea? Perhaps this can best be understood in terms of function. Both lie beyond the bounds of sense experience. Both provide the ground, in a noncognitive experience, for the mutual harmony of the cognitive powers. Both are the means by which purposiveness and unity are achieved in that experience.

Ideas, in the most comprehensive sense of the word, are for Kant representations referred to an object according to a certain principle (subjective or objective), insofar as they can never become a cognition of it. They are either referred to a concept according to an objective principle and called rational ideas, or referred to an intuition, in accordance with the merely subjective principle of the harmony of the cognitive faculties, and called aesthetic ideas. A rational idea is a representation for which no sensible intuition can be adequate. An aesthetic idea is its counterpart, a symbol, which Kant defines as "that representation of the imagination which induces much thought, yet without the possibility of any definite thought whatever, that is, the concept, being adequate to it, and which language consequently can never get quite on level terms with or render completely intelligible" (CJ, 49).

For Kant the idea (indeterminate concept or aesthetic idea) generates the work, in the sense that it makes possible the comprehension and comprehensibility of the work. The artist *presents* a specific image, what Kant calls the "aesthetic attribute," because he cannot present something beyond sense. The image spreads out, drawing to it associations and related concepts. The artist *expresses* the aesthetic idea. A central idea functions as if it were a concept in ordinary perception, unifying the manifold and synthesizing it into an "object"; but because the idea is supersensible, it overflows any concept.

Genius thus attempts the impossible: to present in sensuous form something that is beyond sense; to make real and hence objective a concept of reason; and to go beyond the limits of experience, creating a second nature with a completeness of which there is no example in nature.

We can see now where Hanslick and Schoenberg stand in relation to Kant's notions of aesthetic idea and aesthetic form. In regard to function, they agree: the idea generates the work; the form makes it comprehensible. But they have concretized and objectified both idea and form. Kant opposes form, as abstract structure, to the aesthetic idea, beyond sense. Hanslick takes form to be a sensuous embodiment, that is, objectification, of the idea. Schoenberg, in a sense like Kant, considers form to be that aspect of the aesthetic object which makes the idea comprehensible.

VIII

I HAVE SUGGESTED that if, for Kant, pure beauty is only form, the objective aspect of things, music would seem to be its paradigm. Yet he considers music to be mere play of sensation.

Now a musical object is not like things of external sense. "The systematic succession of measurable tones we call 'melody,' " Hanslick emphasizes, "is not to be met with in nature, even its most rudimentary form" (BM, 105). Of all the arts music would seem to be the most inner and furthest from the real, its material most ethereal and ideal. Music, says Hegel, cancels objectivity and takes the subjective as such for both form and content, remaining even in its objectivity subjective.[10]

We can suppose a reversal in the traditional view of the world, suppose a view in which the real is the subjective. Indeed Schopenhauer, using music as pivot, turned around the relationship of reality and rationality and held that reality is the inner, nonphysical, nonrational, and music the most real of the arts.

Richard Wagner's writings (at one time) reflect this view: "Music has

10. G. W. F. Hegel, *Aesthetics,* trans. Thomas Malcolm Knox (Oxford, 1975), 1: 880.

nothing in common with the seizure of an idea . . . [for the latter] is absolutely bound to a physical perception of the world." We must clearly see within, he says, for the true idea is the essence of the thing, not merely an expression of its objective character. Wagner maintains that the idea is visual, a representation of the outer light world, against which he sets another, real, inner sound world.

> Besides the world that presents itself to sight, in waking as in dreams, we are conscious of the existence of a second world, perceptible only through the ear, manifesting itself through sound; literally a *sound world* beside the light world, a world of which we may say that it bears the same relation to the visible world as dreaming to waking.

Music originates in this world. From the most terrifying dreams we wake with a scream, the immediate expression of the anguished will, which makes its first entrance into the sound world, only then to manifest itself without. That cry, in all the diminutions of its vehemence, as root element of every human message to the ear, is the archetype of music.[11]

Hanslick vehemently opposed this view, seeing *Tristan und Isolde* as a total destruction of musical form, reminiscent of a boundless flood, governed not by the musical idea but by the word.[12] In his theory of musical beauty he objectifies musical form, the melody, externalizing it for contemplation.

IX

HANSLICK, like Kant, takes beauty to be the central aesthetic phenomenon. We cannot generalize to beauty, he says; each art has its own. His purpose is to investigate a specifically musical beauty, that which inheres in the combinations of musical sounds and is independent of all alien, extramusical notions (BM, 5).

A curious tension between music objectified for contemplation and music as expressive of musical ideas evolves in his doctrine, I believe, because his general aesthetic stems from Kant's *Critique*. Hanslick takes beauty to be mere form: "The beautiful, strictly speaking, aims at nothing, since it is mere form, which . . . has, as such, no purpose beyond itself" (BM, 9). But, as we have seen, in his thinking it is the aesthetic idea that generates the work. The unity of these two aspects of the work, form and expression, is the basis for his investigation of the beautiful in music: "A work of art embodies a definite idea as beauty in sensuous appearance [*Erscheinung*]. This definite conception, its embodiment, and the unity of both are the conditions of the concept of beauty with which a critical examination into every art is indissolubly connected" (BM, 20).

Inconsistencies in Hanslick's dogma are enhanced if it is forced into a formalist mold; for him art is expressional. Music is mere form, but not only form; it is also expressive of musical ideas.

11. "Beethoven," in *Richard Wagner's Prose Works*, trans. William Ashton Ellis (London, 1896), 5: 65–75.
12. Hanslick, *Music Criticisms, 1846–99*, trans. and ed. Henry Pleasants (Baltimore, 1950), 222.

LIKE KANT, Hanslick begins with the opposition between aesthetic and logic and a version of Kant's paradox applied to music. All beauty, as all phenomena, affects us first through our senses (BM, 10), and every work of art appeals in some way to our emotions (BM, 13). But there is no invariable and inevitable nexus between musical works and certain states of mind, the connection being, on the contrary, of a far more transient kind than in any other art (BM, 15). If the essential nature of music is to represent or arouse emotions, then music is essentially subjective and there are no grounds for necessary judgments about music.

Like Kant, Hanslick takes the aesthetic experience, what he calls "proper listening," to be contemplation. His analysis of musical beauty paraphrases Kant's four moments in the Analytic of the Beautiful. "The most essential condition for the aesthetic enjoyment of music is that of listening to a composition for its own sake" (BM, 100). If the contemplation of something beautiful arouses pleasurable feelings, this effect is distinct from the beautiful as such. Contemplation of music is more difficult than contemplation of any art; nevertheless, even in the experience of music, pleasure follows the judgment of beauty. Music too is the object of universal delight, not agreeable only to me. Those enthusiasts who enjoy music as they would a warm bath or a glass of wine lower the dignity of music (BM, 91).

The contemplation of a melody is such a disinterested and free delight, sheer appearance, which "pleases for its own sake, like an arabesque, a column, or some spontaneous product of nature—a leaf or a flower" (BM, 71). Hanslick cites the arabesque as an example of how music may exhibit pure forms of beauty: "Imagine . . . an arabesque, not still and motionless, but rising before our eyes in constantly changing forms"—or a kaleidoscope, which brings forth a profusion of forms all logically connected with each other yet all novel in their effect, forming as it were a complete and self-subsistent whole (BM, 40 and 48).

Such pure forms are purposive without purpose: the organic completeness and logic or the absurdity and unnaturalness of a group of sounds are intuitively known without the intervention of a definite logical concept; the logical connection of musical elements, which produces in us a feeling of satisfaction, rests on certain elementary laws which nature has laid in both the human organism and the phenomena of sound, instinctively felt by every experienced ear (BM, 51). "The beauty of an independent and simple theme appeals to our aesthetic feeling with that directness which tolerates no explanation except, perhaps, that of its inherent fitness and the harmony of parts" (BM, 71).

Kant's strategy had been to locate the ground for beauty in the subject (in contrast to his predecessors, who sought to formulate the qualities of the beautiful object). Hanslick reverses this ploy; the locus of the beautiful is in the object. "The beautiful is and remains beautiful though it arouses no emotion whatever, and though there be no one to look at it. In other words, although the beautiful exists for the gratification of an observer, it is independent of him" (BM, 11).

Thus Hanslick's first step in the objectification of musical form is its externalization as musical beauty.

HANSLICK reinterprets the dichotomy between logic and aesthetic. His quarrel (we hear an adumbration of Schoenberg's "Heart and Brain") is ultimately with the separation of objective and subjective knowledge in the names of science and art.

Kant distinguished the arts according to the mode of expression of ideas —the arts of speech, the formative arts which present ideas as sensuous intuition or semblance, and the arts of the play of sensation (CJ, 51). Hanslick takes issue with this distinction. Formerly, he says, the arts have been contrasted according to the possibility of presenting to the mind either a determinate concept or form (as in the poetic and plastic arts) or mere form (as in music) (BM, 9). This division rests on the old view of the structure of faculties which, he says, is incorrect. "It is rather curious that musicians and the older writers on aesthetics take into account only the contrast of feeling and intellect, quite oblivious of the fact that the main point lies halfway between the horns of this supposed dilemma" (BM, 11).

A more accurate contrast, he maintains, is that between intellect and feeling (both determining, abstracting faculties), on the one hand, and sensation (which deals with the concrete), on the other. Like Kant, he believes that the distinction between feeling as sensation and feeling as emotion should be made more precisely. But, unlike Kant, he does not see them both as subjective. Feeling as emotion is the consciousness of some psychic activity and thus is knowledge, though subjective knowledge; sensation, the act of perceiving some sensible quality, is objective knowledge. Certainly all art begins with sensation, as does all perception; but no art is mere sensation.

All art involves the understanding, but the traditional distinction between understanding and feeling has been made too strongly, says Hanslick, for both are abstract. Emotions have no isolated existence in the mind. Only by means of ideas and judgments can the indeterminate drift of the mind become a definite feeling; upon abstracting concepts from consciousness only a vague sense of satisfaction or dissatisfaction remains (BM, 21). A definite emotion can only be communicated through the medium of definite concepts, and so it is mediated knowledge. To speak of representing an abstract concept or emotion is a contradiction in terms. Hanslick maintains Kant's distinction of concept and idea, but general ideas, like definite concepts, are not the content of art. The primary aim of all art is the production of the concrete (BM, 23).

The organ that apprehends beauty, according to Hanslick, is the imagination, which contemplates beauty with intelligence, immediately. He broadens the notion of the imagination, which no longer applies only to visual processes, but also to the function of the other senses. It is in fact eminently suited to represent the act of attentive hearing, which is a mental successive inspection of musical images. Beethoven did not compose for the tympanum, he says, but for the ear of the mind (BM, 11 and 26). The beautiful in music is the aural image, the aural arabesque, "the ingenious co-ordination of intrinsically pleasing sounds, their consonance and contrast, their flight and reapproach, their increasing and diminishing strength—this it is which, in free and unimpeded forms, presents itself to our mental vision" (BM, 47).

All art, then, is the immediate knowledge of the concrete real. The specific arts, Hanslick says, are differentiated by their content *(Inhalt)* and mode of handling *(Gestaltung)*. Each has its own range of ideas, which it presents through its own material and according to its particular manner of shaping. In music these are all immediate ideas associated with audible changes of strength, motion, and ratio. The differences among the arts are a natural consequence of the dissimilarities of the senses to which they variously appeal. It is superfluous to assure us that music is unable to express abstract concepts; no art can do this, for only concepts which have become "living" are the substances of artistic embodiment (BM, 24). Each art presents an object not to a particular sense, but to the imagination for contemplation. The issue, then, is neither emotions nor represented subject matter, both of which are mediate and therefore secondary to all the arts, but rather the true content of all art, the concrete aesthetic idea.

X

THROUGH the notion of the concrete aesthetic idea Hanslick concretizes musical form, thus overcoming the dichotomy between percept and concept. The melody serves for him (as it did for gestalt theory of perception) as a paradigm of concrete form.

Hanslick rejects Kant's notion of indeterminate concept and supersensible idea. To utilize an indefinite feeling or concept as subject matter any art would, first of all, have to solve the problem: How will it be formed? The function of art consists in individualizing *(prägen)*, in impressing the definite out of the indefinite, the particular out of the general (BM, 37f.).

Furthermore, Hanslick rejects Kant's notion of form in music as abstract design. The locus of the beautiful in music, he says, is not the architectonic, and not organization at the level of an entire structure. It is true that in looking at a composition in the aggregate, particularly musical works of great length, we are in the habit of speaking of form and subject. What we call the "form" of a symphony is the architectonic combination of the units and groups of units of which it is made up, the symmetry of the successions, their contrasts, repetitions, and general working out. However, musical enjoyment cannot be fully accounted for by the pleasure derived from mere regularity and symmetry, for the most insipid theme may be perfectly symmetrically built. Symmetry is a relational concept and leaves open the question: What is it that appears here as symmetrical (BM, 64 and 122)?

Music is not mere play of sensations, opposed to the "objective" aspect of cognition, form. In music form is immediately figure. "It is extremely difficult to define this self-subsistent and specifically musical beauty. . . . What in any other art is still descriptive, in music is already figure." (BM, 50). Wherever form cannot be conceived separately from substance, says Hanslick, there can be no question of an independent substance. Now in music, substance and form, the subject and its working out, the image and the realized conception, are mysteriously blended in one undecomposable whole, a complete fusion exclusively characteristic of music. Thus music is *essentially* concrete, whereas in other arts it is possible to abstract form from content (BM, 121f.).

Hanslick reconciles Kant's apparent separation of form and expression with respect to music by rejecting the opposition of form as objective and matter as subjective. Confusion regarding form, Hanslick says, arises when one does not make clear what is taken as correlative to 'form'; in music the difficulty is compounded because form and that which is formed are inseparable in thought (BM, 118f.). He distinguishes three levels at which form may be discussed in relation to music: as correlative to matter, as correlative to content, or as identical with substance. Beginning with the correlative pair *Form* and *Inhalt,* he distinguishes *Inhalt,* on the one hand from *Materiel* or simply tones (that is, material constituents), and on the other, from *Gehalt* or, more specifically, *geistlich Gehalt* (that is, substance). The difficulty, he says, lies with *Inhalt,* which in its broadest sense means everything that a thing contains *(enthalten),* everything it includes within itself *(in sich halten).* In this sense the tones out of which a piece is constituted are themselves the *Inhalt* (BM, 161). "Der Inhalt der Musik sind tönend bewegten Formen."[13] And if we ask what the tonal material expresses, the answer is: musical ideas (BM, 59).

This definition is usually dismissed, he says, as a truism, and *Inhalt* is confounded with *Gegenstand* (subject matter). Music has no *Inhalt* in the sense of subject matter; its *Gehalt* is the unity of everything the composer shapes (BM, 121f.).

Thus does Hanslick reconcile form and content and explicitly objectify the unity that results. The function of the composer, he says, like that of any artist, is a constructive one. Unlike the sculptor or architect, for instance, who has to mold unwieldy rock, the composer works with a material more ethereal and subtle than that of any other art, a material which adapts itself with great facility to any idea the composer may have in mind. He works with memory and understanding—the ulterior effect of past sounds and the possibility for continuity and coherence (BM, 51f.). But like the sculptor or architect, the composer aims at giving objective existence to his musical idea and casting it into a pure form (BM, 52). For Hanslick music, unlike other arts, is essentially concrete; like other arts, it is the objectification of spirit *(Geist),* which is its true content (BM,

---

13. See Geoffrey Payzant, "Hanslick, Sams, Gay, and 'Tönend Bewegte Formen,'" *Journal of Aesthetics and Art Criticism* 40 (1981): 41–48, for a discussion of the "material," that is, the tonal aspect of the musical idea.

124). And I maintain that if a work successfully articulates that content, it can be said to be true.

XI

HANSLICK, like Kant, does not intend to say that music is mere form without content. Composition is a working of spirit in material capable of receiving it. Since the combination of sounds in a work is an act of free imagination, the spiritual energy and character of the particular mind that made it will impress itself upon the creation. A great composer will call into being forms of music that are seemingly conceived at his pure caprice and yet, for some unaccountable reason, stand to each other in a necessary relation. Such compositions, in their entirety or fragments of such, may without hesitation be said to contain the "spark of genius" (BM, 58). Sounding forms, says Hanslick, are not empty, but filled, not the envelope enclosing a vacuum, but *Geist* taking shape from within. Music, as compared with the arabesque, is a picture, but a picture whose subject we cannot define in words or include in any category of thought (BM, 50).

Now *Geist,* according to Kant, is the animating principle of the mind; it quickens the psychic substance, its proper material, by setting into swing the mental powers, thus generating the play which lies at the heart of the aesthetic situation. This interplay is set off by the aesthetic idea. "Geist is nothing else than the faculty for presenting aesthetic ideas" (CJ, 49).

LET ME ASK again my first question: What is a *musical* idea? All three—Kant, Hanslick, and Schoenberg—use the term in its traditional sense, a musical figure or theme. For Hanslick, it is the melody; for Schoenberg, those elements of the melody that project the work; for Kant, the figure that expresses the dominant affect of a piece.

Kant contrasts musical language to ordinary language, but grants to music a universal communicability: "Just as modulation is, as it were, a universal language of sensations intelligible to every man, so the art of tone wields the full force of this language wholly on its own account, namely, as a language of the affections, and in this way, according to the law of association, universally communicates the aesthetic ideas that are naturally combined therewith." But because, he goes on to say, the aesthetic ideas expressed in music are not like the concepts of ordinary language, there is no separation of form and content in music:

> But . . . inasmuch as those aesthetic ideas are not concepts or determinate thoughts, the form of the arrangement of these sensations (harmony and melody), taking the place of the form of a language, only serves the purpose of giving an expression to the aesthetic idea of an integral whole of an unutterable wealth of thought that fills the measure of a certain theme forming the dominant affection of the piece (CJ, 53).

The basis of the "essential concreteness" of musical form as the total materialization of the idea, maintained by both Hanslick and Schoenberg, can be found in this passage.

HANSLICK and Schoenberg each draw upon Kant's theory of genius: genius is original, irrational, and inspired. For both, as for Kant, the idea, the inspiration of genius, generates the work.[14] The initial force of a composition, says Hanslick, is the invention of a definite theme, which, thanks to that primitive and mysterious power whose mode of action will forever be hidden from us, flashes on the composer's mind. The origin of this first germ cannot be explained, but must simply be accepted as a fact (BM, 52 and 57). Schoenberg also echoes Kant: the composer is one who envisions musical ideas; the aesthetic idea is the message the artist has to convey to humanity. "A creator has a vision of something which has not existed before this vision. And a creator has the power to bring his vision to life, the power to realize it" (SI, 215). The idea is inspired, always new, and pursued for its own sake. "One thinks only for the sake of one's idea. He who really uses his brain for thinking can only be possessed of one desire: to resolve his task" (SI, 124).

Hanslick describes the musical idea as originating in the composer's imagination, taking root, and forthwith beginning to grow and develop. This idea is the principal theme of a composition, a systematic correspondence of melody, rhythm, and harmony (BM, 27), the center around which the branches group themselves in all conceivable ways, and are yet always related to it. Like the chief character in a novel, it is the source of everything the piece contains. As the composer develops it, more and more crystals coalesce with it, until by imperceptible degrees the whole structure in its main features appears before him. Nothing then remains to be done but to examine the work, regulate its rhythm, and modify it according to the canons of the art (BM, 52, 57, and 123).

Schoenberg, along the same line of thought, advised his students to wait patiently for an idea. It may strike one as a rhythm, a melody, or a harmony, he said, but it consists of all three. It is the source of the work, which will display under changing circumstances the life of its basic idea. "An idea is born; it must be modeled, formulated, developed, elaborated, carried through and pursued to its very end. The artist will be ceaselessly occupied with doing justice to the idea" (SI, 124). "He is sure that, everything done which the idea demands, the external appearance will be adequate" (SI, 121).

For Hanslick as for Kant, the idea is inspired, but the process of "getting it right" can be slow: "The slowly progressing work of molding a composition,

14. In discussing the creative process (and in relation to Schoenberg's notion of the musical idea), Hofstadter elaborates four elements of the idea: "The idea of the work is the unity of all four: the particular material occasion, the substantive will, the formal understanding, and the spiritual concern. It is the unity of the first three under the persuasion of the fourth" (TA, 194).

which at the outset floated in mere outlines in the composer's brain, into a structure clearly defined down to every bar," requires much subtle and quiet thought (BM, 72). And for Schoenberg, "Alas, it is one thing to envision one's idea and another to realize one's vision by painstakingly connecting details until they fuse into a kind of organism . . . and yet another to organize this so that it becomes a comprehensible message 'to whom it may concern" (SI, 215).

Hanslick sees the unity of an idea as deriving from the unity of the mind that made it. "The soul and talent for musical construction are bound up in one inseparable whole. Melody and harmony issue simultaneously in one and the same armor from the composer's mind. . . . The theme was conceived with *that* harmony, *that* rhythm, and *that* instrumentation." Its spiritual validity, he says, stems from the union of all these factors (BM, 56). He seems to be unable, however, to explicate several levels of musical form in relation to the musical idea. As we have seen, he does not want to apply the terms *form* and *content* to a work in the aggregate, as a whole consisting of parts; rather these should be used in relation to the work's ultimate and aesthetically indecomposable germ *(Kern)* (BM, 123). Thus, although he seems to imply a notion of a unity generated by the idea as single cell, Hanslick objectifies the musical idea only at the level of the theme.

Schoenberg extends the notion of concrete form, objectifying what he calls the "musical space," conceived as both discourse and perceived gestalt, and serving as matrix for the musical idea. As composer he created techniques, in both theory and practice, for enhanced unity at all levels of organization of the work.

XII

I HAVE attempted to develop here a notion of form which would adequately account for two aspects of the musical work: that which the composer creates and that which the listener apprehends. I take that form to be the articulation of the musical idea. As the composer thinks, speaks, and writes in music the realization of the form of his expression makes determinate what the idea is; the realized form, the concrete object, is grasped by means of the idea that generated it. Further, I want the notion of that idea to be adequate to the object itself—as Wagner put it, not merely an expression of its objective character, but the true idea, the very essence of the thing. The Expressionists speak of objects in this manner. Wassily Kandinsky writes of the form as the husk of the object which allows its inner sound to be heard.[15] Schoenberg describes sound as radiation of ideas which are light, powerful enough to penetrate the hull of the form (SI, 138).

15. Kandinsky, "The Problem of Form," in Victor H. Miesel, ed., *Voices of German Expressionism* (Englewood Cliffs, N.J., 1970), 53; first appeared in *Der blaue Reiter* (Munich, 1912).

I began with a notion of this unity of form and content which I take to be common to both music and language—not language conceived as sentence structure plus a separate meaning, but as meaningful sound. Schoenberg describes such form very clearly:

> One may let oneself be carried by the language, but it carries only the man who would be capable, if it did not exist, of inventing it himself. "Language, mother of the idea," says Karl Kraus—as wrongly as if he had said the hen is there before the egg. And as rightly. For that is how it is in the real work of art: everything gives the impression of having come first, because everything was born at the same moment. Feeling is already form, the idea is already word (SI, 369).

AS CREATOR Schoenberg rejected the traditional dichotomy between aesthetic and logic. Construction, he said, is not necessarily a product of the brain; difficult passages can be produced by either heart or brain, or both. "It would not occur to me to deny one of the greatest virtues of my music: that it really is well worked-out, that for all the freedom and for all the wealth of shapes, images, figures, themes, motives, transformations, I am still able to ensure coherence and unity" (SI, 107).

One must absolutely trust one's fantasy. Freedom and coherence come about, he says, because inspiration is always present. Whether the source of his expression be heart or brain, it is always inspired, compulsively inspired. "I believe art is created from the 'I must,' not the 'I can' " (SI, 365). The inspiration is the idea. The composer speaks coherently in music because he thinks coherently. The basis of the freedom and coherence of his music, he says, is the self-evident nature of his musical logic. Proof of the logic inherent in the initial inspiration is that modifications of the idea, stemming from the wide-awake, conscious mind, usually spoil the inspiration. The idea, that is to say, is a single concrete musical thought.

The idea shapes the work from the smallest germ to the whole.[16]

> What I sense is not a melody, a motive, a bar, but merely a whole work. Its sections: the movements; their sections: the themes; their sections: the motives and bars—all that is detail, arrived at as the work is progressively realized. . . . The inspiration, the vision, the whole, breaks down during its representation into details whose constructed realization reunites them into the whole (SI, 107).

For Schoenberg there is no form without logic and no logic without unity. Unity has to do with ideas, their consequences, and their logical progression. He aims at a form in which the idea is totally concretized:

16. Charlotte M. Cross explores the multileveled nature of Schoenberg's notion of idea in "Three Levels of 'Idea' in Schoenberg's Thought and Writings," *Current Musicology* 30 (1980): 24–36.

I wish to join ideas with ideas. No matter what the purpose or meaning of an idea in the aggregate may be, no matter whether its function be introductory, establishing, varying, preparing, elaborating, deviating, developing, concluding, subdividing, subordinate, or basic, it must be an idea which had to take this place even if it were not to serve for this purpose or meaning or function. . . . There should be no space devoted to merely formal purposes (SI, 407–8).

He describes such a musical form as a unity of body: "The work of art is like every other complete organism. It is so homogeneous in its composition that in every little detail it reveals its truest, inmost essence. When one cuts into any part of the human body, the same thing always comes out—blood" (SI, 144).

And he describes such form as a unity of thought:

The two-or-more dimensional space in which musical ideas are presented is a unity. Though the elements of these ideas appear separate and independent to the eye and the ear, they reveal their true meaning only through their cooperation, even as no single word alone can express a thought without relation to other words. All that happens at any point of this musical space has more than a local effect. It functions not only in its own plane but also in all other directions and planes, and is not without influence even at remote points (SI, 220).

The unity of the musical space demands an absolute unity of perception. In this space, says Schoenberg, "as in Swedenborg's heaven" (SI, 223), there is no absolute up or down, right or left, forward or backward. Every musical configuration must be comprehended primarily as a mutual relation of sounds. Just as I recognize a knife or bottle, regardless of its position, even so a musical creator's mind can operate with a row of tones, regardless of their direction (SI, 225).

Now Kant has maintained that we recognize a knife or bottle by means of our determinate concept of it. And indeed, we may see the least characteristic aspect of a bottle—say, the dislike bottom—or the most characteristic profile, but we only "see" the whole with the eye of the mind. I believe that Schoenberg ultimately conceives of the musical idea in its Platonic sense, like Kant, as beyond sense experience. The musical space is the space of thought; the musical idea is an "idea of intellect," not a perceptual image. It sets the mental powers into swing, puts us into a state of cognitive readiness, brings the object into perception, makes it apprehensible, as if "purposive."

XIII

IN HIS ESSAY "Brahms the Progressive," Schoenberg shows us something of what he means by the function of the idea to effect coherence in a work. "The most important capacity of a composer," he says, "is to cast a glance into the most remote future of his themes or motives. He has to be able to know before-hand the consequences which derive from the problems existing in his material, and to organize everything accordingly" (SI, 422). Among the examples he uses are references to Beethoven's String Quartet in F minor, Opus 95. "I cannot renounce the opportunity to illustrate the remoteness of a genius's foresight" (SI, 423). I shall use this quartet as an example here of how Schoenberg's conception might work.

First of all, the musical idea is sheerly musical. "There is an assumption abroad that a piece of music must stir up images of some kind, and that if such images are lacking, the piece of music either wasn't understood or was worth-less. . . . From no other art do we demand anything like this; rather we content ourselves with the operations of its own material" (SI, 141).

The idea is a musical operation, a function. Schoenberg compares an aes-thetic idea to the idea of a pair of pliers.

> In comparison with all our developments in mechanics, a tool like a pair of pliers might seem simple. I have always admired the mind which invented it. In order to understand the problem which this invention had to over-come one must imagine the state of mechanics before its invention. The idea of fixing the crosspoint of the two crooked arms so that the two smaller segments in front would move in the opposite direction to the larger segments at the back, thus multiplying the power of the man who squeezed them to such an extent that he could cut wire—this idea can only have been conceived by a genius (SI, 123).

The idea that Beethoven's quartet is "about," I think, is the function $\flat$II/$\flat$VI.

Schoenberg speaks of the musical idea as pertaining to both the smallest element in a piece and to the unity of the whole. "In its most common meaning, the term idea is used as synonym for theme, phrase, or motive." He too follows this use, for he considers the main theme of a work to be the basic shape or *Grundgestalt* from which all else is to be derived. But he continues: "I myself consider the totality of the piece as the idea: the idea which its creator wanted to present. But because of the lack of a better term I am forced to define the term idea in the following manner." He goes on to describe the way in which, in a tonal piece, a state of unrest or imbalance is developed. "The method by which balance is restored," he says, "seems to me the real idea of the composition" (SI, 123). These two senses of "idea" would seem to correspond to Hanslick's dis-tinction between *Inhalt* and *Gehalt*.

Here I shall begin with the broadest sense of idea, its function within the entire musical space, which I take to be the tonal space: a nexus of relationships, a dynamic complex of strains and stresses, a structure of ways through the tonal-ity. The tonality—what Schoenberg calls "monotonality"—includes in the single key all pitches, so long as their relationships are made clear to the ear. Precisely, this is the relationship of each scale degree (and its transformations) to the tonic, as single pitch, as triad or root function, and as key area or "region." In the *Harmonielehre* Schoenberg describes this structure as a complex of fifth- and third-relations mapped onto the circle of fifths; in *Structural Functions of Harmony* he presents it in a "chart of regions." Here I shall use the circle of fifths, which I have extended and set up for Beethoven's quartet, with F major/ minor at the top (see Example 1).

EXAMPLE I

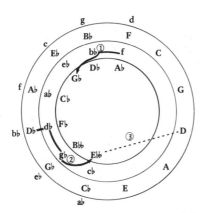

The ♭II/♭VI relation exploited in this quartet is one of Beethoven's favor- ite ideas, which he develops in many ways, one of the most straightforward being the "Apassionata" Sonata, Opus 57. Here in Opus 95 the game is the ambiguity of D♮ (♮6 of F) and E♭♭ (♭6 of G♭, the Neapolitan region). I have sketched on the circle the three relations that underlie the basic idea:

1. the Neapolitan (or ♭II), says Schoenberg, is derived as ♭VI of the subdominant minor, two fifths counterclockwise from the tonic around the circle.
2. by analogy, E♭♭, the Neapolitan of the flat submediant (D♭), is derived from its subdominant minor (G♭), taking us to the farthest point in the circle opposite the tonic;
3. the enharmonic equivalence of E♭♭ and D throws us back a quarter of the circle toward the tonic.

It is this ambiguity that I want to explore.

Now let us return to the first theme (Example 2). Schoenberg cites within the theme the three-note succession D♭–C–D, indicates its retrograde, and dem- onstrates several motivic occurrences of the forms throughout the first movement (SI, 423f.). These three notes present in the tonic the basic function, the cross- related forms of the 6th degree, D♭/D.

EXAMPLE 2. From Schoenberg, "Brahms the Progressive"

Schoenberg analyzes a melodic theme into motivic elements of interval and rhythm. Here (Example 3) I shall concentrate on pitch motifs: the modal third (x), the fourth of the key (y), and the leading tone (z), which is picked up to create the continuity of the contrasting phrase of the theme in measure 3. As is his habit, Beethoven condenses the motivic material in the bridge to the second theme (beginning in measure 21), where a complex of the three motifs produces a combination which will generate much of the thematic material for the remainder of the quartet (Example 4). The B♭♭ in measure 22 (♭6 of the contrasting key area D♭) is a premonition of things to come.

EXAMPLE 3. Motivic elements

EXAMPLE 4. The basic motivic combination

For Schoenberg tonality is a struggle between centripetal and centrifugal forces—the idea, the means by which balance is restored (and, I assume, imbalance brought about). I emphasize the unity of the musical space: melodic and harmonic aspects are two dimensions of the tonal whole. The continuing statement of the first theme is on the ♭II (G♭), returning to the tonic by way of its dominant D♭. This region, the flat submediant of the tonic, becomes the contrast area of the movement. The ♭II/♭VI function has taken us away from the tonic, creating the imbalance.

How is balance restored? Notice in measure 38 the striking turn to the ♭VI of D♭ (B♭♭/A) and its sequence on the ♭II (E♭♭/D) in measure 49 (Example 5). Now compare the corresponding passage in the recapitulation on D

EXAMPLE 5

in measure 107 (Example 6). If this were the expected return of the passage a fourth higher, it would be E♭♭, but no, it is indeed a real D, ♮VI, moving in the sequence to II and on to V—a transposition of an augmented third. What a trick!

EXAMPLE 6

Then what about the motif Schoenberg cites in measure 41? Is that A or B♭♭? In measure 110 it returns as a clear statement of the basic cross relation D/D♭♭.

Look now at the second movement, in D, the (natural) submediant of the tonic, F minor. There are two groups of thematic material, the first (measure 5ff.), an elaboration of the material of the first movement (Example 7); the second (measure 35ff.), a fugue based on the combination we saw in the bridge of the first movement. This melodic material is framed by three statements of a descending scale passage, the first and last in the key of this movement (D), in which the cross relation becomes G/G♯ on the fourth degree; and in the center

EXAMPLE 7 Second movement

of the movement (measure 65), a descent at the original pitch level (A♭–C), here at the tritone, reached as the subdominant of the ♭II (E♭). In the last sequence the ♯4 becomes A, returning us to the tonic D (Example 8). Except for this curious tonal twist, the movement is quite straightforward—but is it in D or E♭♭?

EXAMPLE 8

The third movement, the scherzo, returns to the tonic F minor, and the motivic work seems clearly derived from the basic combination of the bridge, resulting in a theme shaped from the scalewise descent, Ab–C (in this form containing the [natural] 6, D; Example 9). In the trio of this movement, however,

EXAMPLE 9. Third movement

Beethoven shows us how he has been playing this game. In measure 41 he moves, by the semitone F–Gb, to the region of bII, the contrast key area for the trio. And in measure 64—there it is! By the "same" semitone, F–F♯, he flips us into the bVI of the bII, Ebb/D. So that's how it was done! At the return in measure 145, in case we missed it, there again is D, now as (natural) VI of the tonic (Example 10). I am reminded of Hanslick's kaleidoscope.

EXAMPLE 10

In the fourth movement we hear the intense motivic cohesion and gradual untangling of the complex of the original three motifs, into an innocent rondo theme (measure 12) which, in combining all three, brings out the subdominant minor, the source of the web of tonal relations Beethoven has unfolded (Example 11). And in the coda (measure 133) the dénouement: the F♯/G♭ is revealed

EXAMPLE 11. Fourth movement

as F♯ and we are a quarter of the way around the circle toward home (Example 12).

EXAMPLE 12

If my understanding of the musical idea and its role in the musical work accurately reflects Schoenberg's ideas of musical coherence, he conceives of a kind of musical object that not only fits with harmony and purpose to the mind of man, but also bears that same harmony and purpose within itself. Schoenberg often maintains that such musical logic need not be conscious. "A composer who is sure of himself, of his sense of form and balance, can renounce conscious control in favor of the dictates of his imagination" (SI, 424). It is not easy to reconcile his insistence on the logic of music with his sense of its irrationality:

> Schopenhauer said, "The composer reveals the world's most inward being and expresses the deepest truth in a language his reason does not understand, just as a mesmerized sleepwalker gives information about things of which, when she is awake, she has no concept." In so doing, he said something truly comprehensive and thorough about the nature of music. The true nature of music is irrational (SI, 141–2).

I believe he would agree with his friend Karl Kraus that although the source of the idea is in the fantasy, truth lies in the reconciliation of fantasy and reason— that not only the creator, but also the beholder, in the true experience of art, is "a human being painfully stirred by the search for inward harmony."

TONALITY AND THE STYLE
OF PALESTRINA

SAUL NOVACK

TONALITY IS REGARDED generally as a phenomenon first appearing in the seventeenth century. Its beginnings are somewhat hidden in the baffling network of modal theory and practice in Renaissance polyphony. The usual view of this facet of stylistic differences between Renaissance and Baroque music is summarized thus by Manfred F. Bukofzer:

> Tonality may be defined as a system of chordal relations based on the attraction of a tonal center. . . . It is no mere metaphor if tonality is explained in terms of gravitation. Both tonality and gravitation were discoveries of the baroque period made at exactly the same time.[1]

Bukofzer goes on to explain that in Renaissance music chord progressions were dictated by the melodic laws of part writing, which were governed individually by modality. In the time since Bukofzer wrote these words there have been some changes of view, but the basic dichotomy between modality and tonality has been sustained generally. Despite some important initial studies that have begun to explain the gradual evolution of tonality, a widespread acceptance of these evolutional views has been slow in coming.[2]

Tonality is a concept, not a system. It relies on a principle of composition

---

1. Manfred F. Bukofzer, *Music in the Baroque Era* (New York, 1947), 12.
2. See especially Edward E. Lowinsky, *Tonality and Atonality in Sixteenth-Century Music,* 2nd ed. (Berkeley, 1962). Important contributions concerning problems of tonality in the Medieval and Renaissance eras are to be found in vols. 1 and 2 of *The Music Forum* (New York, 1967 and 1970) in articles by Felix Salzer, Carl Schachter, Peter Bergquist, William J. Mitchell, and Saul Novack.

wherein one scale degree is more important than any other, and wherein the subservience of all tones in a composition to the centrality of this scale degree can be discerned; thus we can find within any tonal composition a background upon which are based the relationships of tones creating the force of a central tonality. In considering sixteenth-century composition, the chief problem rests with the theories of mode as they are applied to both earlier and contemporaneous practice. The theorists explain it in their ways. Our ears tell us differently.[3]

The music of Palestrina lies in a central position in sixteenth-century music. His Masses and motets are usually regarded as "conservative," though beautifully formed, typifying the ideal of Renaissance sacred polyphony. The predominant view holds that the great body of his music is written within the modal system. Since some of the theorists generally accounted for modes in polyphonic writing by considering the tenor only, the results of their thinking bear no relationship to the compositional process. Yet scholars have recently made notable progress in modal analysis based upon a number of factors.[4] A number of works are problematic, and it may not always seem persuasive to identify the final as the principal note (a concept phrased thus for those fearful of using the term *tonality*). In an analysis of Palestrina's *Vestiva i colli*, Harold Powers makes a convincing point about the difficulty of assigning a mode to that work. He offers no conclusive solution, but rather an unorthodox suggestion.[5] Knud Jeppesen provides a helpful overview of mode in Palestrina.[6] He accepts only five modes as pertinent to Palestrina's music: Dorian, Phrygian, Mixolydian, Aeolian, and Ionian. He considers the Lydian mode with the flat signature to be primarily Ionian. For Jeppesen, the final becomes the basic indicator of the principal tone of the composition, hence its relevance to the mode; he also considers the beginning of a composition as an important criterion. In a more recent study Powers provides a formidable survey of the complexity of modal categories.[7] Evaluating the contributions of Siegfried Hermelinck, Bernhard Meier, and Carl Dahlhaus, Powers constructs a system based on specific combinations of cleffing, ambitus, and finals, and he provides a number of tables to describe the tonal plans in modally organized cycles by Cipriano de

3. I do not dismiss the importance of the theorists, but I cannot ignore what our ears hear. See Edward E. Lowinsky, "Canon Technique and Simultaneous Conception in Fifteenth-Century Music: A Comparison of North and South," in *Essays on the Music of J. S. Bach and Other Divers Subjects: A Tribute to Gerhard Herz*, ed. Robert L. Weaver (Louisville, 1981), 181–222, esp. his perceptive comments on p. 184.

4. Siegfried Hermelinck, in *Dispositiones modorum* (Tutzing, 1960), assigns a mode identification for individual works of Palestrina through a different system of analysis. For a critical discussion of his theories as well as an appraisal of the difficulties involved, see Harold S. Powers, "The Modality of *Vestiva i colli*," in *Studies in Renaissance and Baroque Music in Honor of Arthur Mendel*, ed. Robert L. Marshall (Kassel and Hackensack, 1974), 31–34.

5. Ibid.; see particularly the concluding paragraph. The entire study underlines the problem of describing sixteenth-century polyphony in modal terms.

6. "Problems of the Pope Marcellus Mass: Some Remarks on the Missa Papae Marcelli by Giovanni Pierluigi da Palestrina," in the Norton Critical Score of Palestrina's *Pope Marcellus Mass*, ed. Lewis Lockwood (New York, 1975), English trans. by the ed., 99–130. See esp. pp. 100–109.

7. Harold S. Powers, "Tonal Types and Modal Categories," *Journal of the American Musicological Society* 34 (1981): 428–70.

Rore, Tielman Susato, Orlandus Lassus, and Palestrina. The empirical evidence admirably produced by Powers reveals clearly the inadequacy of mode identification purely in terms of the traditional church modes and Heinrich Glarean's extension of them. (The title of the study, while valid for the purposes intended, may be misleading, since "tonal types" bear no direct relation to tonality.)

Thus complexity surrounds any application of modal theory to the music of Palestrina and his contemporaries. If we work our way through this labyrinth of sixteenth-century theorists and musicological etiologists, the total picture, while fascinating, speculative, and instructive, offers us no insight into the compositional matrix. Consequently, further consideration of mode per se is not germane to the purpose of this essay.

Several attempts have been made to find in Palestrina's music the "harmonic" factors that do not contradict mode identity. One study has determined the frequency of chords and the characteristics of cadences by means of statistical survey.[8] Another has examined the frequency of immediate chordal relationships and the patterns of movement formed by them in a specific Mass.[9] Both these studies fragment the object of study. While they provide us with information, they do not offer us a unified contextual analysis of a given work, a view of the work as a whole. Jeppesen's *Style of Palestrina* is universally acknowledged to be a monumental achievement in analysis; and the painstaking thoroughness of his exposition is quite admirable.[10] While Jeppesen gives some introductory attention to other facets of Palestrina's style, the great bulk of his study is given over to the treatment of dissonance. Central as the dissonance is to the expressive elements in Palestrina's style, it is seen here as though through a microscope. Each type of melodic construction and intervallic combination is examined and accounted for with numerous examples, with small fragments being excerpted from the works, and all the types being categorized. It is impressive scholarship, yet we are never given large or complete units of music.

The largest single study of the overall style of Palestrina is the well-known work by H. K. Andrews.[11] The primary facets of Palestrina's music considered are mode, rhythm and time signature, melodic line, consonance and dissonance (treated in great detail), contrapuntal techniques, i.e., fugue, canon, and inversion, followed by texture, form and structure, and, finally, word setting. Each topic is minutely dissected, not with the surgical precision of Jeppesen, but still in considerable detail. Many excerpts are given as examples of various techniques. To close, one complete composition is examined—a motet 166 measures long. The study of this motet has as its purpose the identification of melodic-rhythmic motives (labeled a^1, a^2, b^1, etc.) and the changes in textures. The result is a mere description rather than an analysis; neither mode nor tonal-

8. Andrew C. Haigh, "Modal Harmony in the Music of Palestrina," in *Essays on Music in Honor of Archibald Thompson Davison* (Cambridge, Mass. 1957), 111–20.
9. Richard Bobbitt, "Harmonic Tendencies in the Missa Papae Marcelli," *The Music Review* 16 (1955): 273–88.
10. *The Style of Palestrina and the Dissonance,* 2nd ed. (Cambridge, 1946; repr. New York, 1970).
11. H. K. Andrews, *An Introduction to the Technique of Palestrina* (London, 1958).

ity is mentioned. Thus, Andrews's book, while well-organized and detailed, is surgical and sterile, and lays out no unified approach to a conceptual evaluation of the art of Palestrina's compositions. The study of the *Pope Marcellus Mass* by Lewis Lockwood in the Norton Critical Score series merits special recognition as a meticulous approach to both a historical and a musical analysis of the work as a whole.[12] Lockwood provides a rewarding analysis of the setting of Kyrie I. Yet there are important features of integration that go unmentioned. These will be discussed below.

ERNEST NEWMAN once said:

> Fux's book, as the reader will not need to be reminded, is one of the landmarks of music history; directly or indirectly, it is the fountain of practically all the methods of teaching counterpoint during the last two hundred years.[13]

While Newman is hardly a leading authority on music theory, here he is echoing the sentiments of composers and music teachers of the eighteenth and nineteenth centuries. It is well known that Johann Joseph Fux supposedly based his theories of counterpoint on the art of Palestrina, as is openly stated in his foreword to the reader in *Gradus ad Parnassum*.[14] Fux has had a profound influence on the study of counterpoint up to the present day, and his work has been a vehicle for the continuation of the Palestrina legend.[15] There are many noteworthy texts based on Fux's principles, primarily the species system, and these works have played a contributory role in establishing the notion of Palestrina's style as representing the ideal of sixteenth-century contrapuntal art.[16] While Fux believed that he was abstracting the art of Palestrina, even to the extent of casting his ideas in the form of a dialogue in which he identified himself as the pupil of the master Palestrina, he allowed some characteristics of early eighteenth-century style to creep into the contrapuntal web. Jeppesen's counterpoint text eliminated these imperfections, and his examples are quite true to the pure linear flow and to the intervallic consonant–dissonant relationships to be found in Palestrina. Yet these studies do not reflect Palestrina's considerations of tonality as a unifying force. They fail to account for the nature of the important outer voices. Thus, species counterpoint as traditionally expounded, whether by Fux, Bellermann, or Jeppesen, among others, has no stylistic relevance to Palestrina, or to any other composer, for that matter. Therein lies the value of species counterpoint. By limiting itself to the principles of linearity and intervallic relationships

---

12. See esp. 91–93 and the chart on p. 94.
13. London *Times*, Aug. 21, 1938.
14. *Steps to Parnassus*, trans. and ed. Alfred Mann (New York, 1943).
15. See Paul Henry Lang, "Palestrina across the Centuries," in *Festschrift Karl Gustav Fellerer zum sechzigsten Geburstag am 7 Juli 1962*, ed. Heinrich Hüschen (Regensburg, 1962), 294–302.
16. Most noteworthy are the works of Johann Georg Albrechtsberger, Heinrich Bellermann, Heinrich Schenker, Hermann Roth, Jeppesen, and, most recently, Salzar and Schachter.

based on a systematic temporal organization of consonance and dissonance, species counterpoint becomes applicable to all music based on triadic tonality, without any considerations of style. This is not my main concern here, though I will return to Palestrina's concepts below. I now turn directly to the music.

Opening Imitation

THERE IS A direct and important relationship between quasi-fugal beginnings in Mass movements or motets and tonal functions. The following example seems quite complex (Example 1a). Its thematic incipits commence on the following notes:

m. 1	altus	g
3	bass	c
5	cantus	c′
7	tenor	f
9	bass	B♭
10	altus	g (quasi-entry)
12	cantus	f′ (some altered durations)
15	tenor	f
16	altus	f (rhythmically altered)

EXAMPLE 1. *Missa brevis,* Kyrie I

a.

b. Reduction

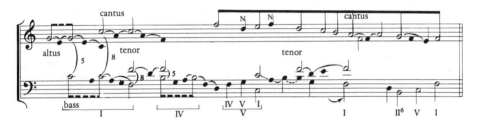

Such a series of successively descending fifths from g to B♭ might be regarded as beginning in a foreign area distant from the main "mode." For this
there is, however, a logical explanation. It is obvious that nine interphonic statements within a total of nineteen measures reflect a tightly knit design. The incipit is a complete four-bar unit characterized by a division into two equal and
contrasting parts terminating, in its first four appearances, with a stepwise descent from the fifth degree to the root of a triad. While the successively descending fifths are not a usual practice, the choice of the intervals is dictated by the
shaping of the tonal organization. The shape of the first part of the incipit is
important; basically a movement down a third and a return to the initial tone, it
permits the second voice to enter a fifth below at the moment of return to the
initial tone at measure 3. This relationship of entry at the fifth is possible with a
voice below the altus, not above it, for then the entry on c′ would have resulted
in the prohibited fourth (Example 1b). The cantus entering at measure 5 is at
the octave, the only possible tone; entering on g would have been possible initially, but its prolongation to measure 7 would have produced a dissonant ninth
above the bass, the determinant and dictating voice in the drive toward F, the
tonic, at measure 7. The added entry of the bass at measure 9 on B♭ is imaginative—far more dynamic than the possible entry on F. The alterations and adjustments in the succeeding entries are readily understood within the context of
the direction of the voices in the complete tonal organization.

The exactness of imitation does not appear to be a criterion in this example. While the later terminology, *real* and *tonal,* may seem applicable, the connotations of these terms is quite different. I prefer the terms *exact* and *inexact.*[17] The entry on B♭ is inexact, as are the succeeding altered entries. The two entries of the bass determine the tonal structure of the entire movement. Its entry at measure 3 affirms the tonic in its stepwise descent through the triad, completed at measure 7. Its second statement, following almost immediately after, prolongs the IV chord (B♭), and it is altered so that it arrives to fit in with the beginning of a definitive IV–V–I progression of the dominant, which is attained at measure 14. The entire harmonic progression is shown in the example. It is clear that the shape of the incipit, the order of the succession of the voices, and the time factor between entries all combine to determine the initial tones, the degree of exactness, and the relationship to the entire tonal structure. Although the initial tone, g, is neither the root nor the fourth or fifth of the final, F, it is not "out of key." It is part of a totally integrated beginning within F Ionian. The total clarity of the succession of entries is not only affirmed by the bass entries but also by the added entry in the uppermost voice at measure 12. The statement is augmented, thus delaying the motion to the third tone, e′, which falls as a result on the important V chord (measure 14). It continues to the close of the movement in a descent outlining in stepwise motion the entire octave f′ to f, by this means affirming the tonality.

Bass Motion

I N M A N Y of Palestrina's compositions the lowest voice has a double responsibility, not only sharing with the other voices the statements of melodic units, but also providing the foundation for tonal unity. This occurs not alone at cadential points but throughout units and in large-scale dimensions. Neither Fux nor Jeppesen discusses bass motion in his treatise, and motions in fifths rarely appear in their examples other than at cadences. In the four-voice examples they are more frequent, but they do not have harmonic impact. Andrews calls attention to the "special treatment of the bass," but the discussion is very brief, superficial, and incorrect; it concludes with the statement "Palestrina's basses, however slow moving and disjunct, still preserve the essential character of the pure polyphonic line."[18] In Example 2 the words "suscipe deprecationem nostram" are represented through a motion from the A chord. This chord, in terminating the preceding text phrase "Qui tollis . . .," is minor, attained through its own dominant, the E-major chord, with G♯ stipulated (measures 72–75), and then becomes A major at measure 81. The A-major chord is prolonged through a series

---

17. Modes are undeniably a factor in these relationships, but this is a separate topic. For additional comment on Palestrina, see Lowinsky, *Tonality and Atonality,* 31.
18. Andrews, 59.

EXAMPLE 2. *Missa Sicut lilium inter spinas,* Gloria, mm. 73–86

a.

b. Reduction

of successive descending fifths, A–D–G–C–F, followed by a quickly rising motion to A. It is here that, so as to conclude the phrase, the A chord, still major,
resolves as a dominant to the D chord. Even at this point the D, as a major
chord, moves strongly into the next text phrase, "Qui sedes . . .," which commences with the G chord. The strong harmonic character of these successive
fifths, intensified by constant leading tones with the necessary accidentals stipulated, must be recognized. Earlier, in the same Gloria, the articulation of "Lau-
damus te. Benedicimus te. Adoramus te. Glorificamus te" is strengthened by a
similar succession of fifths, each motion contained within each text unit, and all
unified through the large-scale prolongation of the A chord, the section as a
whole terminating on the A-major chord. The stipulated raised third is a concluding sonority factor, as is shown by the immediate appearance of the A-minor
chord that begins the next text phrase (Example 3).

EXAMPLE 3. *Missa Sicut lilium inter spinas,* Gloria, mm. 8–17

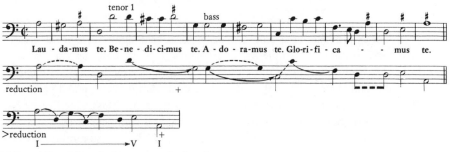

N.B.: *All accidentals shown are stipulated.*

Bass motions sometimes take on a character that truly foreshadows the personalities of bass lines in early seventeenth-century music. They are unlike the upper voices. Although a bass line may begin a section as an interphonic repetition or first statement, preceded or followed respectively by an upper line, it will change its shape in such fashion as to direct its motion to a specific tonal goal, especially a cadence. Sections from a Credo by Palestrina are quoted to illustrate this point (Example 4). The descending motions to the dominant and to the tonic are used repeatedly. The pattern at measure 218 is not unlike a characteristic Italian dance type of the early seventeenth century. At measure 225 the polyphony of the last section of the Credo is supported by a bass motion which descends through the entire octave, c to C. The boundaries of the bass in the entire Credo lie within the octave c to C, the lower C always attained through a V–I progression or through a descending linear motion.

EXAMPLE 4. *Missa Ave Regina coelorum,* Credo, m. 180ff.

The bass in the succeeding Sanctus expresses the significance of the descent even more strongly (Example 5). In measures 2–6 the bass descends by step from c to G. In measures 11–15 the bass is repeated exactly, but commencing on F and falling to C. Thus the c–C octave is divided into two equal parts with design repetition. The setting of the Osanna in the same Mass, *Ave Regina coelorum,* is entirely on four statements in the bass of a complete octave, as in the Credo example, from c to C, with complete or partial stepwise motions divided into several harmonic parts.

EXAMPLE 5. *Missa Ave Regina coelorum,* Sanctus, mm. 2–18

It is thus evident that the frequent octave ambitus of the tonic, and its divisions, sometimes clearly profiled by thematic repetition, defines the causal role of the bass.[19] Melodic repetition, whether within the same voice or in different voices, is well controlled and fused with tonal organization, as is shown in Example 6, from Palestrina's *Missa Ascendo ad Patrem.*

EXAMPLE 6. *Missa Ascendo ad Patrem,* Kyrie I, mm. 12–19.

The concluding motive of Kyrie I is first stated by the lowest voice at measure 12 in such a way as to move from the tonic C to the dominant G. At the moment of arrival on this G the cantus enters with the motive, beginning on d′, which not only permits the motive to be prolonged within the G chord but also prepares the entry of the lowest voice with the motive again at measure 16. The bass, too, starts on the tone D, but in its descent its goal is the D chord, a full-fledged major triad with stipulated f♯. This chord, V of V, strengthens the attained dominant that closes the movement. The concluding short section (not shown in the example) lies within the C chord. This does not function as the tonic. Rather, it is a neighbor IV chord lying within the prolongation of the dominant, G, and functioning as the so-called plagal IV. The section is tonally open-ended, with the final dominant leading into the Christe setting, which begins in the tonic.

Sequences intensify motion through the repetition of melodic units that commence on successive pitches. Palestrina employs descending sequences in stepwise order, which thus move very strongly toward a goal, as can be seen in Example 7.

19. Such tonal-defining functions are not new. In the works of Palestrina they are frequent and clear in their function. For a fascinating example in Josquin Des Prez, see Saul Novack, "Tonal Tendencies in Josquin's Use of Harmony," in *Proceedings of the International Josquin Festival-Conference,* ed. Edward E. Lowinsky in collaboration with Bonnie J. Blackburn (London, 1976), 330–33; my article provides an analysis of an entire motet, *Levavi oculos meos in montes,* organized by variations of descending bass motions.

EXAMPLE 7. *Missa brevis*, Kyrie II, mm. 45–51

Tonal Prolongations

THE IDEAL of the art of counterpoint attributed to Palestrina rests primarily
on the flow of consonance and dissonance and on smooth linear motion. Chords
are regarded as incidental to these factors, without any functional significance.
We have already seen that this is an incorrect view. Harmonic functions are expressed in V–I motions, in other fifth relationships, and in their expanded harmonic progressions, not necessarily confined to cadences. Chord prolongations
frequently guide the voices. Consequently, the linear flow of contrapuntal activity is controlled by the sense of a chord or chords being sustained over a time-
space determined by the tonal processes. The simplest examples are to be found
in codas, which almost consistently create the prolongation by means of combined neighbor motions and voice exchange, as is evident in Example 8. The
prolongations in the example are only a schematic representation of two types.
In actual composition the number of measures involved and the techniques used
vary.[20] The previously examined Kyrie I of the *Missa brevis* serves as a good ex-

EXAMPLE 8

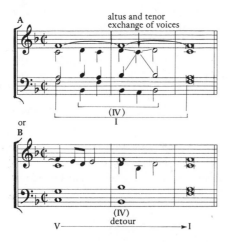

20. See, for example, the various endings to the sections in the *Pope Marcellus Mass*, particularly the seven-
voice Agnus Dei II. The texture of seven voices imposes a relatively more intensive requirement of prolongation control on the individual voices.

ample (see Example 1). The interphonic incipit is triadic, terminating with a fall to the root. The bass entry at measure 9 begins a prolongation of the B♭ triad starting on the first degree. The continuation is altered to preserve the prolongation of the chord. The voice leading at measures 13–14 is conditioned by the harmonic motion IV–V–I of the dominant, C. Triadically conditioned neighbor-tone and passing motions are found in all the voices in terms of the prolongations and/or harmonic goals.[21]

The Uppermost Voice

THE UPPERMOST voice has a special character in addition to its melody-carrying role. Its ambitus, partly conditioned by the mode, frequently defines the central tone that is being prolonged, both in small and large units. Palestrina is far from consistent in exploiting this concept, but it manifests itself often enough to merit our attention. The line created by the top voice is generally a descending one, hence a literal exhibition of the quality of gravitation to which Bukofzer refers. While it occurs most frequently in the drive towards the cadence, it is present elsewhere as well, thus fusing with the lowest voice in defining units. This stepwise motion of descent fills in the octave, scale steps 8 to 1, or the fifth, 5 to 1, or the third, 3 to 1. Palestrina most often uses the established cadential figure in which 2 moves to 1 by way of the leading tone. In Example 6 above, the cantus descends an entire octave, g'–g, in the prolongation of the dominant, G. Units of text frequently are marked not only by units of bass motion, but also by descents of the uppermost voice to the first degree. This voice may also play a role in the molding of form. In the Credo of the *Missa brevis* (an example too long for quotation) the line falls in each unit, but does not reach the first degree except at the end of the text phrase "per quem omnia facta sunt" (measure 41). At the end of the Credo, however, the setting of "Amen" is characterized by an extended sequential descent of the outer voices in parallel tenths, the inner voices joining in quasi-fauxbourdon style, so that all serve as a fitting climax to the form of the movement as a whole.

The contribution to form made by a descending line is shown in the following example from Palestrina's *Missa De Beata Virgine*. The closing section of the Kyrie II setting is divided into two parts by (a) polyphonic repetition, (b) harmonic motion (IV–V and I–V–I), and (c) reiteration of the descending line. The harmonic motion and the descending line in the cantus together create a

21. An excellent example of tonal prolongation in Palestrina's music is provided in Felix Salzer and Carl Schachter, *Counterpoint in Composition* (New York, 1969). In a detailed analysis of Agnus Dei I from *Missa Veni sponsa Christi* (pp. 413–17), the contrapuntal motions and the activities of the voices within the prolongations of the chords are represented graphically. The final reduction (p. 417) indicates the background of the mainly contrapuntal prolongations within the basic harmonic framework, I–IV–V–I. While there may be some reluctance to accept the final Schenkerian reduction, the forces of tonality in its extended form and the individual chords projected beyond the immediate are made obvious through the analysis.

beautiful inner form characterized by interruption: instead of falling from 2 to 1 at measure 42, the top voice, together with the other voices, commences again, the second time falling to the final tone by way of the leading tone. The extension leading to the resolution in the second statement attains through this artistic delay a lovely realization of the terminus.

EXAMPLE 9. *Missa De Beata Virgine,* Kyrie II, mm. 37–48

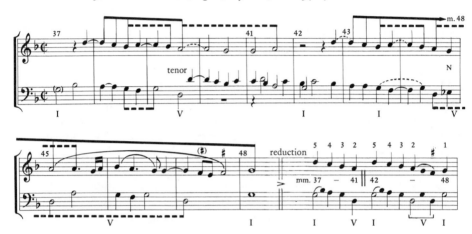

The endings of the uppermost lines after the descent has occurred are at times somewhat misleading. Palestrina is fond of superimposing a third over the first degree, either almost directly at the final cadence or indirectly through subtle preparation in the penultimate measures. This procedure of substitution is intended to secure a desirable sonority on the final chord, the third usually being major, either as a diatonic note or as a stipulated accidental. In such cases the continuation of the descending line from 2 to 1 is most frequently transferred to the altus.

Harmonic Function

IT IS NOT necessary at this point to illustrate the various types of harmonic function used by Palestrina, both at internal and final cadences and in large-scale prolongations of various chords, including chords such as the subdominant and dominant, which not only function as structural harmonic chords but also are themselves prolonged harmonically. (See, e.g., the discussion of the Kyrie of the *Missa brevis,* Example 1.) Successive fifths as major chords via stipulated raised thirds, and applied dominants are often used. These functioning chords combine with the direction of the voices and repetitions of design to create inner form and a strong sense of tonality.

In closing, attention can fittingly be given to the previously cited study by

Lewis Lockwood.[22] In his very informative discussion and analysis of Kyrie I of the *Pope Marcellus Mass,* Lockwood describes the larger layout of this movement and its divisions, considering the facets of rhythmic, linear, contrapuntal, and harmonic elements. He accepts the role of C as the tonic, "solidly planted" at measure 9, though he views the preceding measures as ambiguous. A few additional observations may help to explain the fusion of tonality and melodic design. (Since this Mass is available in a number of editions, Kyrie I is not reproduced here.)

1. The opening interphonic statement of the initial motive ("point of imitation") is closely related to the tonal organization. The leap of the fourth after the repeated tone constitutes the essential motive. The succeeding portion is not repeated other than in some form of descent. Bass 2 and bass 1 follow each other significantly. The entries are as follows:

    a. tenor 2, on d;
    b. cantus, above the tenor's d, on d′, an octave above by necessity;
    c. bass 2, entering below d and d′, on G, a fifth below, by necessity;
    (The shape of the bass now determines the shaping of the other voices. After the leap of the fourth to c it falls stepwise and returns to G, the other voices joining together in the G-major chord.)
    d. altus, entering on g, an octave above bass 1, foreshortening the motive after the leap and resolving on b, the third of the G chord;
    e. tenor 2 and bass 1 entering successively within measure 5 at d and G, both within the prolonged G chord.

2. The G chord is prolonged within measures 1–4. Each voice is controlled by this prolongation, not only in entry but also in shape. The cantus moves down an octave; the altus, from g to b, with c as an incomplete neighbor tone; tenor 1 prolongs d with an outline of the intermediate C chord (g–e–c). The C chord in measure 3 should not be construed as the tonic. In the succession of the chords, G–C–G, the C chord functions as a neighbor, subservient to G, which is being prolonged for four measures. The motion is outlined in Example 10:

EXAMPLE 10

3. The prolongation of G is continued through measures 5–8 with the same motion as in measures 1–4, bass 1 providing the structural foundation. Again each of the voices above moves within the chords in a directed fashion, outlining the prolonged G–C–G. Significantly the uppermost voice elaborates the neighbor-tone

22. Cited in n. 6 above; see esp. pp. 91–94.

motion, d′–e′–d′. This neighbor motion pervades the Kyrie I setting and can be considered a unifying motive.

4. At measure 9 bass 2 enters for a second time, beginning now on C. It is at this point that the resolution of measures 1–8 is finally achieved and, as Lockwood states, C as the tonic is "solidly planted." Thus, the opening measures, while possibly exhibiting tonal ambiguity, really serve as an artistic preparation for measure 9. The shape of the theme and the interphonic continuity demand this open beginning. The initial leap, d–g, answered by g–c was necessary. Had Palestrina begun on g, the order would have been g–c followed by c–f, which would have thrown the motion toward the subdominant. Obviously, Palestrina preferred gaining C at measure 9. (While such preparatory openings may appear to be deceptive, tonal structure like this is a possibility to be found in music of all styles.) From measure 9 on, the tonic is asserted without any doubt. The F-major triad at measure 10 is incidental to the prolongation of the C triad.

5. The close of the form of Kyrie I is attained with the support of chords that function harmonically. At measure 17 the tonic moves through ii$^6_5$ to V to I (measure 18). A repetition for the close of the form occurs through measures 18 and 19, with an extension delaying the final resolution for several additional measures— actually until measure 21. It is at this point that the coda begins.

6. The coda, measures 21–24, is typical. The sustained tone in the uppermost voice is the first degree, the tonic. It is similar to the schematic representation previously cited (see Example 8). In later usage this double neighbor-tone motion is realized above the sustained tonic via the well-known $^{6-5}_{4-3}$ device and its expansions.

7. Throughout the entire Kyrie I it is apparent that the basic tonal structure has conditioned the flow of the voices. The tonal division of the entire setting is in three parts:

A   measures   1–8, V;
B   9–16, I;
C^1 16–18, I–ii^6–V^7–I; the dissonant 7 is passing;
C^2 19–21, repetition with extension of the close;
coda   21–24, I prolonged (I–[IV]–I).

8. The outer voices provide the framework. The cantus in each statement moves within an ambitus that defines the prolongation. On a larger scale its motion of tonal definition is fused with design, as the closing phrases indicate. The motion of the cantus is as follows:

measures 10–12   C chord prolonged, terminating on e′;
         13–15   same motive, terminating on d′;
         16–18   concluding motive terminating on c′;
         18–21   concluding motive repeated and extended terminating on c′
                 through the leading tone.
measures 10–21   e′–d′ // e′–d′–c′ (e′–d′–c′ repeated) //
                 I–V // I–ii^6–V–I   //

9. The linear flow of the voices has been guided by the prolongations of the chords that function in the dividing of the Kyrie. Each of the voices individually can be accounted for in these terms.

This brief essay on an enormous subject is not offered as a comprehensive study. Through a few examples I have sought only to focus on a handful of points which seem appropriate. A study of these examples suggests the need for a reassessment of Palestrina's style. The evidence of the music itself is that it is tonal, and the tonality is based on the triad, major and/or minor. Tonality and modality are different phenomena; the former does not evolve from the latter. While the ultimate major and minor modes proved to be the most successful modes for the projection of triadic tonality, other modes have always retained the capacity to prolong a central tone, with varying degrees of success depending on the art of the composer, and with varying degrees of intensity related to the admission of nonmodal tones through stipulation and *musica ficta*. There are tonal composers of the twentieth century who do not use the major and minor modes or the triad. Nor have the major and minor modes been pure, for in their history they have taken on various types of mutations and mixtures. In the music of the sixteenth century the harmonic factors constitute only one ingredient of the tonal process.

I have tried to point out some of the compositional factors that contribute to the tonal process in Palestrina's music. They vary considerably, and further study is needed to show the differences between various types. In the movements of the Mass, for example, Kyrie settings offer ideal examples of abstract music, since there are only two words in their text. This is also true for the Osanna. Gloria and Credo movements have a different kind of orientation, as do motets and madrigals. There are differences in prolongation techniques of the individual lines related to the number of voices involved. Special problems arise with respect to Masses based on another composer's work, but at the same time these pieces provide fascinating material for a detailed study of Palestrina's compositional techniques, the matrix being present before the composition. Another area to be examined concerns the relationships of tonality to the various modes and "tonal types." We also must review the relationship of Palestrina's style to the continuum of sixteenth-century composition.

Fux's species concept still remains a brilliant achievement of great value to the study of counterpoint and to the analysis of contrapuntal principles in all styles based on triadic tonality. It is not, however, an exposition of the music of Palestrina. The rules and exercises in Jeppesen's admirable text on counterpoint do not contradict the connective techniques in individual measures and small extensions within Palestrina's music, but it is a connection constructed of small mosaics and does not offer us a key to the organic compositional style of Palestrina. We demean Palestrina's art by concentrating on them. Finally, I believe that a consideration of the principles and points I have raised will contribute to revealing Palestrina to be an even greater master than is universally acknowledged.

WHAT'S IN A WORD?
INTERPRETING
VICENTINO'S TEXT

MARIA RIKA MANIATES

THIS STUDY of Nicola Vicentino's treatise, *L'antica musica ridotta alla moderna prattica* (Rome, 1555),[1] is an exploratory one—a test case for textual exegesis that will be reworked extensively in a book on the relationship of this treatise to Gioseffo Zarlino's *Istitutioni harmoniche* (Venice, 1558). Consequently, the ideational background of the treatise receives cursory treatment in order to focus on problems in Vicentino's writing. It still needs to be said in the course of these prefatory remarks that there can be no doubt as to Zarlino's firsthand knowledge of the earlier book.[2]

Assuming, as do I, that interpretations of a text can produce valid reconstructions of authorial intent, it follows that such reconstructions are in turn valid exercises in history of ideas.[3] But history of ideas also subsumes textual significance, and while the latter need not and often cannot be severed artificially from the former, it is better evaluated after one has arrived at a reasonably accurate adjudication of primary meaning. Within the purview of any critical assessment of significance there fall the author's own ideas in this regard and those of his contemporaneous readership, as well as the longevity of the work and modern scholarship concerned with any or all of these matters. The length of this

---

1. Facs., ed. Edward E. Lowinsky, Documenta Musicologica, 1st Series, vol. 17 (Kassel, 1959).

2. Maria Rika Maniates, *Mannerism in Italian Music and Culture, 1530–1630* (Chapel Hill and Manchester, 1979), chaps. 9, 11, 12, and 15. Karol Berger, *Theories of Chromatic and Enharmonic Music in Late 16th Century Italy* (Ann Arbor, 1980), chap. 2.

3. See Maria Rika Maniates, "Applications of the History of Ideas to Music (II)," *The Musical Quarterly* 69 (1983): 62–84.

essay permits but a few tentative probings as to the significance of what Vicentino had to say even in the context of the text itself, let alone other contexts in which the text lived as text.

My title asks, "What's in a word?" and the word is *maniera,* especially insofar as it signals specific notions about stylistic ideals in music of the mid-sixteenth century. The answers here assayed, however, entail the interpretation of two key words in Vicentino's text—*modo* and *maniera*—taking into account their explicit and implicit meanings. Historians of music's sister arts have had much to say about *maniera* in primary sources pertaining to their specialized fields. On comparing their documentation with my findings, I discovered that references to *maniera* in writings on music are more numerous and more provocative.[4] To put the issue of interpretation in very brief terms, scholars have identified two main uses of *maniera.* The first—an absolute one—simply means manner, style, or fashion. But more often the word becomes a portmanteau for a second intricate meaning that connotes stylization, modishness, or stylish style. Contrary to the first sense of the word, the second engenders relative value judgments, and these can sometimes be adduced from the motley collection of adjectives assigned to *maniera—buona, cattiva, bella, ridiculosa, antica, moderna.* Individual partialities arise from aesthetic norms of one kind or another, norms often implicit in didactic treatises. They should not be overlooked because they justify the technical precepts recommended by a theorist.

When it comes to interpreting the details of a single text, certain problems must be kept in mind, and I refer to problems that hamper overly categorical readings; at the same time, these problems should not encourage unreliable readings. Theorists may adumbrate either the technical or the aesthetic precepts without using the word *maniera,* or they may choose instead any number of alternatives, such as *sorte, arte, prattica, stile,* and *modo*—this last being the most common word in Vicentino's text. Quite apart from its frequency, *modo* raises another controversial issue for music historians, for like its doppelganger it can appear to have a neutral sense, one meaning nothing more than how, way, or kind. And two musicologists have concluded that *maniera* too has precisely this routine explanation.[5] But interpreting this word is not quite so simple a matter as they would have us believe.

As we shall see, neutral cases usually function as components of normal grammatical phrases where they acquire syncategorematic meaning. After these have been collected, a relatively easy task, they can be set aside. As for substantive or categorematic usage, the interpreter must deal with four possibilities.

4. Surveys of the primary literature in music can be found in chap. 15 of my book as well as in James Haar's article "Self-Consciousness about Style, Form and Genre in 16th-Century Music," *Studi musicali* 3 (1974): 219–27.
5. Helmut Hucke, "Das Problem des Manierismus in der Musik," *Literaturwissenschaftliches Jahrbuch des Görres-Gesellschaft* 2 (1961): 224; Hellmut Federhofer, "Zum Manierismus-Problem in der Musik," *Renaissance-Muziek 1400–1600: Donum Natalicium René Bernard Lenearts,* ed. Jozef Robijns (Louvain, 1969), 108–9.

First, neutral cases which, like grammatical ones, present no ambiguity of meaning. Second, cases where neutral and technical meanings overlap, "technical" understood here as denoting instructions on an assortment of musical methods. Third, cases that shed neutrality by indicating unequivocally either a technical or an aesthetic pronouncement. Fourth and most treacherous of all, the ambivalence of technico-aesthetic resonances whose simultaneity muddies interpretive waters. The last possibility is especially troublesome because the sources seldom exhibit mechanical distinctions between a battery of advanced techniques and a stylistic norm whose aesthetic at once encompasses and transcends them. And so we find that *maniera,* a word capable of fusing both meanings, is employed interchangeably by one author in one treatise, in one chapter, and even in one sentence.

How do these possibilities operate, then, in Vicentino's text? The ensuing tables provide taxonomic guides to language structure, whereas my discussion deals with the linguistic and conceptual contexts of instantial usage. It must be said that in some respects, Vicentino emerges as a careless writer—*vide* his inconsistent dialectics and sloppy exposition of data or programs pertaining to systems (e.g., tuning and solmization). And yet his pedestrian, even redundant prose is a blessing in disguise for the interpreter.

TABLE 1. *Modo* and *Maniera*[6]

MODO	TM	PM I	PM II	PM III	PM IV	PM V	TOTAL
Grammatical	1	3	2	3	3	4	16
Substantive	23	44	89	63	112	29	360
Total	24	47	91	66	115	33	376

MANIERA	TM	PM I	PM II	PM III	PM IV	PM V	TOTAL
Grammatical	0	1	0	1	3	0	5
Substantive	0	1	0	3	8	3	15
Total	0	2	0	4	11	3	20

The tabulation of all cases of *modo* and *maniera* (Table 1) offers some initial coordinates; for instance, the high incidence of *modo* as opposed to the limited use of *maniera,* and the small proportion of grammatical cases as opposed to substantive ones. Even though these statistics in all likelihood indicate routine addictions, it is not insignificant that they draw attention to Book IV of the *prattica musicale,* a book on designs, genres, and styles labeled "Musica poetica" by Henry Kaufmann.[7] Let it be said, for readers unfamiliar with the treatise, that the *Libro della theorica musicale* deals with theories of mathematics and

6. In the tables, TM stands for *Libro della theorica musicale* and PM for *Libri della prattica musicale,* numbered from Book I to Book V.
7. *The Life and Works of Nicola Vicentino* (American Institute of Musicology, 1966), 147.

the other four books of the *prattica musicale* treat the following topics: I—melodic intervals with diatonic, chromatic, and enharmonic sizes; II—rudiments of intervallic progressions and combinations; III—the three ancient genera and their use in modern practice as exemplified by Vicentino's compositions; V—the two tuning systems for the archicembalo. Before investigating the different classifications, it should be stated that the relative length of various sections seems not to account for the proportionate use of either *modo* or *maniera*, except for the *theorica musicale*, which is considerably shorter than any of the other books.

TABLE 2. Grammatical Uses of *Modo* and *Maniera*

SPECIES	TM	PM I	PM II	PM III	PM IV	PM V	TOTAL
A. di/in/nel modo che	1	3	2	3	2	4	15
B. fuore di moto	0	0	0	0	1	0	1
C. di maniera che	0	0	0	1	3	0	4
D. di tal maniera che	0	1	0	0	0	0	1
Total	1	4	2	4	6	4	21

It is evident that the grammatical cases given in Table 2, being quite simple, require little commentary. All but one involve phrases that may be translated as "in (such) a way that" or "in (such) a manner that" or merely as "so that." The sole exception (Species B) acts as an adverb meaning "exceptionally."

TABLE 3. Substantive Uses of *Modo*

SPECIES	TM	PM I	PM II	PM III	PM IV	PM V	TOTAL
A	19	32	33	29	63	19	195
B	2	1	24	15	4	4	50
C	2	8	31	11	24	4	80
D	0	2	0	1	6	1	10
E	0	0	1	1	0	0	2
F	0	1	0	3	4	0	8
G	0	0	0	3	11	1	15
Total	23	44	89	63	112	29	360

A. *Modo* alone or with: *alto, certo, che, lor, medesimo, mio, qual/che, quel, questo, questo notato, sopradetto, sopra notato, sopra scritto, sotto scritto, suo, tal/e, uno et altro*
B. *Modo/modi* with cardinal or ordinal numbers: e.g., *tre modi, il primo modo*
C. *Modi* alone or with: *alcuni, altri, diversi, loro, molti, quanti, questi, sopra detti, tali, tanti, variati, varij*
D. *Modo* with: *facile, sicuro*
E. *Modo* with: *buon/et cattive*
F. *Modo* with: *alla moderna, antico, commune, moderno, non/troppo/moderno, nuovo*
G. *Modo* with: *bel, bellissimo*

To all intents and purposes, the first three species of *modo* in the substantive genus (Table 3) are identical in that *modo/modi* occurs either by itself or else modified by specific numbers as well as by such vaguer words as "this, various,

many, diverse," and so on. The most accurate reading for these cases is
"method/s," although "how, way/s, kind/s" may be equally appropriate, indeed more natural in certain kinds of phrases. Pedantry is not an alluring prospect. Nonetheless, a lexical choice of syntactical grounds ought not to confound
the issue of distinguishing neutral from technical meanings. Here are some of
the interpretive problems.

"Kind/s" has a decidedly neutral sense, and a meticulous study of the text
shows that it pertains to but one case of *modo* (Book V, chap. 1): "Twelve different kinds *(modi)* of leaps of a third." Otherwise Vincentino indicates the
kinds of something by employing *sorte/sorti,* a word used seventy-one times in
contexts corresponding to the first three species of *modo/modi.* On the other
hand, "in this way" or "thus" seem especially apt whenever *à/in questo modo* (a
belabored expression) precedes an illustration of some sort. If the illustration is
rudimentary—a note shape, for example—the meaning is surely neutral. But if
the illustration is, say, a cadential formula or a contrapuntal device, then neutral
and technical meanings carry equal weight. Most contexts suggest a technical
sense, one that is clearly seen in books dealing with scientific or procedural matters; for instance, such chapter titles as "Modo d'accordar l'Archicembalo"
(Book V, chap. 5) or "Modo di comporre le cadentie" (Book III, chap. 25). For
the sake of brevity and idiomatic English there is nothing wrong with starting
such titles with "How to . . ." so long as these criteria are not mistaken for perfunctory evidence of neutral meanings.

An instructive context for Vicentino's use of *modo* as technical method is
provided by the chapter prefacing his exposition of musical rudiments (Book II,
chap. 1). Vicentino begins by outlining three basic methods *(modi)* for suave
and harmonious composition (note the performative adjectives). The first *modo*
governs the linear succession of intervallic species, be they tense or soft. The second *modo* regulates suitable consonances and dissonances, and the third *modo*
does the same for rates of motion. To elucidate his cardinal injunction that all
three *modi* are mutually complementary, Vincentino then describes six other
modi, each pair producing effects that range from bad through indifferent to
perfect. Bad effects result from the method of combining antipodal elements;
e.g., tense intervals with slow tempo. Indifferent effects ensue when the method
is one of constant variety, e.g., mixing major and minor (tense and soft) imperfect consonances *(pace,* Zarlino). But if all elements interact to enhance the
words, then the method achieves perfect effects. There are fifteen cases of *modo/
modi* in this chapter alone. Each of them addresses a specific technique, but their
selection depends on a hierarchy of values dictated by Vicentino's implied aesthetic, one made explicit elsewhere in the book—to wit, perfect vocal polyphony
is both depictive of the text and suasive for the listener.

A similar interpretation applies to Species D, as the adjectives "easy" and
"secure" indicate. All cases of *sicuro* and four of *facile* describe purely mechanical matters like writing notes or reading clefs. In addition, *modo facile* appears
three times in discussions in Book IV of various contrapuntal techniques. The

first of these is a simple summary of more detailed recommendations concerning voice leading (chap. 32). The second occurs during a polemic on extempore counterpoint, a practice disliked by Vicentino, who finds it either too dull or cacophonous. His comment on the easy method grants that it avoids clashes (as others he describes do not), but also notes that it is monotonous and inexpressive (chap. 23). Improvisatory facileness here entails a derogatory judgment. In the case of premeditated facility the opposite view prevails. This point concerns the concluding section of a work (chap. 16). If the composer has in mind the mode for the end of the piece when he begins, says Vicentino, the unfolding of his themes will lead easily *(con modo facile)* to a proper conclusion. His advice, of course, refers to church music, which must have a strong ending on the main mode. And even though *con modo facile* is an adverbial construction, its connection to facile or effortless technique must be considered significant, its significance here concealed beneath the primary meaning of an apparently guileless phrase.

We come now to Vicentino's assessment of good versus bad and modern versus ancient methods (Species E and F). The first pair of polarized concepts discloses a sharp division between acceptable and unacceptable methods of handling dissonances (Book II, chap. 5), as well as modal freedom in *musica participata & mista* (Book III, chap. 18). The second pair indicates an unequivocal preference for modern techniques in syncopated cadences whereby those with small note values emanate neoteric stylishness (Book III, chaps, 24 and 34). The some bias appears in Vicentino's description of written counterpoint on a cantus firmus (Book IV, chap. 23), where he differentiates between *modo non moderno* (counterpoint using motives from the cantus firmus) and *modo moderno* (freely composed points of imitation). Once again, the interpretable meaning of *modo* refers to Vicentino's elucidation of specific techniques; but the critical significance of the word implies an aesthetic equivalency between modern methods and stylish flair.

This implication becomes explicit in *bel modo* (Species G), a term designating canons of grace, order, and fluency. That the majority should occur in Book IV is not surprising. Three cases pertain to methods of logical disposition, one for changing orders on the manuals of the archicembalo (Book V, chap. 65) and two for writing balanced counterpoint (Book IV, chaps. 14 and 26). The central topic of modal variety and its role in the tripartite structure of a composition (beginning, middle, ending) occasions five appearances of *bel modo* (Book IV). Of these, one case concerns a basic rule—namely, that the fourths and fifths of the main mode should not be disturbed (chap. 18). This requisite of modal centricity is elsewhere amplified to accommodate subtleties of one kind or another (chaps. 15 and 16). With regard to church music, Vicentino insists that compositions must begin and end on the principal mode. But this rule is less inflexible than one might expect, for he also says that other modes may be introduced between the juncture points of a work's three sections. Just how far and exactly where a composer is allowed to stray from the main mode is a moot question, given Vicentino's chromatic motet *Hierusalem convertere*.[8] For secular music Vicentino recommends more frequent and extreme changes of mode at any point, even at the end of a piece, so long as these aberrations imitate the words. It is true that Vicentino stresses the need for *bel modo*, the proviso stated twice for each style. And yet it is equally true that he goes far beyond the principles of logic and coherence to embrace ideals of grace and elegance, which in themselves may transgress against the rules, not to mention the chromatic and enharmonic extravagances of his madrigals and Latin compositions.[9]

Vicentino's interest in stylishness also surfaces in the exposition of the cadences possible in the twenty-four generic modes (Book III, chap. 32). Here *bel modo* occurs alongside such words as *bel procedere, buon ordine, gratia,* and *varieta.* The first three phrases can be construed as defensive ploys against anticipated disapproval of methods promoting chaos and anarchy; the last two reinforce the interpretation of *bel modo* as a method leading to stylish style.

The last two cases of *bel modo* appear in Book III, chap 15. The ostensible subject of this chapter is the first, or Dorian, mode but much of it is devoted to a comparison between music and the visual arts, promoted no doubt by an analogy to the Doric order of classical architecture as described by Vitruvius.[10] Vicentino likens the modes to columnar scaffolding in architecture and linear design in painting, both of which may be decorated *con bel modo.* Similarly, musical inflections may embellish the basic structure or design of a composition. On the level of primary meaning, these cases correspond to the interpretation given to previous instances of *bel modo.* Vicentino's comparison to art, however, introduces other tantalizing notions that include important cases of *maniera,* and therefore they will be examined in the latter context.

TABLE 4. Substantive Uses of Maniera

SPECIES	TM	PM I	PM II	PM III	PM IV	PM V	TOTAL
A	0	1	0	0	2	2	5
B	0	0	0	3	4	0	7
C	0	0	0	0	2	1	3
Total	0	1	0	3	8	3	15

A. *Maniera* alone or with: *altra, diversa, tal*
B. *Maniere* with: *differenti, diverse, molte*
C. *Maniera* with: *bella*

It would greatly simplify matters if all the substantive uses of *maniera* meant style (Table 4). But they do not. One case from Species B must be in-

8. The work is transcribed and analyzed in my book, pp. 189–92; for other modern editions, see my book's "Bibliography of Primary Sources."

9. Modern editions of these works are listed in *ibid.* Their titles are as follows: *Dolce mio ben, Madonna il poco dolce, Soav'e dolc'ardore, Alleluia haec dies, Hierusalem convertere,* and *Musica prisca caput.*

10. The significance of this passage has already been remarked on by Karol Berger and myself (see n. 2 above).

cluded in the neutral classification (Book III, chap. 48). In his exposition of the generically inflected intervals available within the stable limits of a fourth, Vicentino lists *diverse maniere de gradi confusi,* a phrase in which *modi* or *sorti* ("kinds") would have been equally appropriate. The equivocal adjective *confusi* merits a parenthetical comment. Its meaning, "confused" or better "turbulent," touches a Vicentino's aesthetic apology on behalf of rhetorical music—namely, that unexpected, even prohibited intervals produce marvelous effects. But in the restricted context of this chapter his aim is to show that the proper deployment of *gradi confusi* does not destroy logical coherence. Of course, what seemed to Vicentino to be a reasonable norm was condemned as a ridiculous one by his adversaries, most notably by Zarlino.

Two other cases of *maniera* (Species A) concern the tuning of instruments, and they both vacillate between neutral and technical meanings (Book I, chap. 6, and Book V, chap. 3). *Maniera* also appears with technical overtones (Species B) in an introductory chapter consisting of a list of topics wherein *modo/modi* occurs five times (Book IV, chap. 1). In such a context, then, *diverse maniere di comporre varie fantasie da sonare, & da cantare, sopra i canti fermi, & figurati, con varij Canoni* incontrovertibly calls for "different methods/ways . . . etc." The ensuing interpretation of *maniera* in the chapter of canons will show that Vicentino considers them to be too cerebral even in terms of the limited capacity for textual depiction characteristic of ordinary style. Needless to say, canons are entirely out of place in rhetorical style. I mention this value judgment here because it lurks behind the word *fantasie,* a term that always alludes to the abstract invention of melodies or harmonies which do not derive their disposition from the nature of the words.

Yet two other cases of *maniera* (Species A and C) parallel *modo* and *bel modo* insofar as they fuse technical and aesthetic meanings in the course of a description of the archicembalo tuned in the first of two systems, the one underlying virtuosity in microtonal music.[11] To start off, Vicentino states derisively that everybody plays in the same tuning and compensates for this defect by relegating individuality to picayune idiosyncrasies in performance practice (Book V, chap. 1). His instrument, on the other hand, offers limitless potential for *rara & maravigliosa prattica,* and specifically for *la maniera diversa del procedere piu dolce con le fughe diverse.* The latter phrase can be read in two ways. The first equates *maniera* with method: "a different manner of sweeter procedure by means of diverse imitative points." The second, which I prefer, distinguishes *maniera* from technique: "a different, sweeter style of proceeding with diverse imitative points." Admittedly, the immediate context offers little help in deciding one way or the other. I submit, however, that my reading is reinforced by Vicentino's advice to the archicembalist to strive for *bella maniera* when mixing the genera (Book V, chap. 5). One could counterargue in this case that *bella*

11. Maria Rika Maniates, "Vicentino's *'Incerta et occulta scientia'* Reexamined," *Journal of the American Musicological Society* 27 (1975): 335–51.

maniera means the same thing as *bel modo*—that is, elegant or polished method. But Vicentino has already explained the *bel modo* of switching orders, the playing technique itself. It does not seem far-fetched, therefore, to interpret *bella maniera* as signifying the stylistic results of a technique rather than the mechanics of handling the instrument. Smooth manipulation of the orders on the manuals enables the player to mix the genera in such a manner as to achieve *bella maniera*. And *bella maniera* arises from marvelous diversity in fugal counterpoint, this diversity involving unexpected microtonal mixtures.

Then there are the three cases of *maniera* (Species A and C) in the exposition of canonic devices (Book IV, chap. 37). Considering Vicentino's loathing of all artifices, it is natural for him to condone solely those canons with rich harmony and *bella maniera di procedere*. But he decides that canons resist these demands and consequently suggests adding free parts to camouflage their inherent defects, thus attaining *maniera del procedere*. It is tempting to view his disdain as a clue to inferior craftsmanship. Be that as it may, Vicentino's stipulated reasons tally with his general aesthetic position, for he points out that canons please the intellect and bore the ear because they fail to imitate the words. Moreover, those which succeed in this regard are worth a hearing, but few, he concludes, are composed *di tal maniera*. The interpretation of the first and third citations as synonymous with *bel/modo* cannot be discounted altogether, even though I find this reading to be grounded more on syntactical than on lexical reasons. The middle one denotes stylishness on both counts. And in my opinion, all three cases imply the desideratum of varied harmonic effects that reflect the conceits and affects of the words. Thus they in turn reflect Vicentino's most exalted ideal for vocal polyphony, an ideal founded on oratorical eloquence whereby abstract logic cedes to blandishments of imitating the text.

Earlier in this essay I examined two cases of *bel modo* with reference to an analogy between art and music (Book III, chap. 15). To recapitulate it, the foundation of a musical edifice is the main mode because its structural intervals function like pillars in architecture and design in painting. Vicentino explains that in the former medium a good architect introduces decorative variety by mixing elements from different orders. During these remarks, *diverse maniere* (Species B) appears twice in connection with styles or stylizations in classical architecture. The point of this comparison is as follows: the composer should likewise use his judgment to mix intervals from different modes. To demonstrate exactly how this is to be done Vicentino again separates church music, in which the principal mode must dominate, from secular music, in which greater variety occurs. And even though the context is somewhat garbled, it is evident that harmonic adornment in secular music encompasses the most unorthodox generic inflections to represent the words. These microtonal inflections appear to be comparable to the varied shadings or colorings imposed on the linear design of a painting. So far, so good.

But Vicentino's ensuing diatribe brings up a contentious point requiring some clarification. Since even restrained variety depends on slight mixtures of the genera, the pure diatonic genus, Vicentino maintains, has been supplanted by *musica participata & mista;* in this style the arsenal of true diatonic intervals is adulterated by the semitones and thirds proper to the chromatic and enharmonic genera, a fact blithely ignored by most of his contemporaries.[12] On account of its limited variety this music deserves to be called *musica communa,* an uncomplimentary epithet used by Vicentino to isolate the commonplace style "that all music professionals practice today." *Musica communa* can be stylish up to a point, especially if composers follow Vicentino's advice for spicing it up. But his sympathy lies emphatically with an extraordinary style whose unbridled capacity for sonal variety and rhetorical illusion permits it to project graphically the nature of the words and so to excite the listener. This is the style he elsewhere calls *la Cromatica & Enarmonica Musica riserbata . . . ad uso delle purgate orrechie* (Book I, chap. 4).[13] Vicentino's manifesto can be tied to his admiration of the miraculous realism in painting where objects are depicted on a flat surface. Indeed, we may conclude that he views *musica communa* as a rather flat, insipid style in comparison with the excitement and novelty of "musica reservata." And while his exposition is not a little jumbled, there emerges from it a sense that his definition of two styles in music develops as a loose corollary to the *diverse maniere* in ancient and modern art.

Stylistic ideals also underlie three other cases of *maniera* (Species B) in an intriguing chapter on the abuses of singers (Book IV, chap. 42). Here Vicentino complains that singers are lazy creatures of habit who stick to their sole personal *modo* in complete disregard of the *differenti maniere* of the pieces they are called upon to perform. He warns them in stern tones to learn to vary their *modi di cantare* according to the *diverse maniere di compositioni.* Only then will they be respected as masters of *molte maniere di cantare.* Vicentino thus implies that their singing will become a work of art whose stylishness and propriety can be appraised much like a composition. Far from being accidental, his division between *modo* and *maniera* is consistent enough to warrant associating the former with method and the latter with style. This interpretation receives support from further details in the same chapter concerning singers' *molti modi di cantare.* From among these many improvisatory techniques Vicentino singles out four: the general disposition of ornaments, the purpose of *accenti* and vocal timbres, changes in dynamics, and changes in tempo. All share one set of interrelated goals—to intensify the intelligibility and passions of the text, a recreative task guided by the written composition. To the extent that accomplished singers can use their techniques to bring a piece of music to life and thus move the audience, they deserve to be called orators in Vicentino's estimation. And it goes without

---

12. Vicentino's definition of the genera was the central issue in his public debate with Vicente Lusitano in Rome in 1551. Vicentino rehashes the arguments in his treatise (Book IV, chap. 34).

13. "Chromatic and Enharmonic Music reserved . . . for the delectation of refined ears." Vicentino felt so strongly about the strict diatonic genus that he composed a polyphonic piece without a text to show how crude and harsh the genus sounds in counterpoint, so crude that he could not set any words to it. The work is transcribed in Kaufmann, 183–84.

saying that their most promising vehicle is the *maniera* that embraces ideals of rhetoric.

Before looking at the last case of *maniera* it might be helpful to review Vicentino's concept of stylistic decorum, for it engenders his recurrent invocations of judgment *(giuditio)* with respect to standards of variety. It is apparent that judgment works in two affiliated ways. On the one hand, judgment seems to be a faculty of the musician's intelligence, and in this role it controls selection and management of techniques, the pragmatic jurisdiction of professional expertise. On the other hand, it is also a less transparent factor in the aesthetic sensibility of the intellect to stylistic norms, and as such it governs in a more contemplative manner the manifestations of its own practical operation.

Giuditio, then, amounts to recognizing under what circumstances a style is stylish and how to achieve its appropriate measure. Vicentino talks about style on many levels, and these are not always adequately delineated in the text. On the most prominent and ubiquitous level his concept of styles congeals into two broad groupings—sacred and secular. The former he associates with traditional *musica participata* or *musica communa*. Here criteria of logic and coherence curtail the variety of available techniques, but there still remains a degree sufficient to impart a modicum of flair to the basic design of a well-formed structure. The latter, of course, is the domain of *musica participata* rendered stylized. Here variety runs rampant even to the point of severely weakening any intrinsic design. Not only does Vicentino not apologize for this negative effect, he rather ostentatiously parades it, partly, one suspects, because he enjoys playing the radical, but mainly because he is firmly convinced that iconoclastic techniques are mandatory for graphic depiction and rhetorical projection of the text. And my word for *maniera*—that is to say, stylization—echoes the preciosity and artificiality of radical practice recognized by Vicentino himself when he confines it to aristocratic surroundings and refined audiences. It is this second stylization of music into an imitative art that occasions his most extreme polemics. Vicentino does discuss gradations of decorum in the Mass, motet, canzona, madrigal, and so on. Yet in the end he generalizes these forms in terms of music for the church and for the chamber, cautioning musicians to keep their discriminatory judgment finely honed (Book IV, chap. 26). And in spite of his many illuminating comments on sacred music Vicentino's aim is to publicize his innovative ideals and their concomitant rejuvenation of the *mirabili segretti* hidden in the ancient genera (Book III, chap. 52). Weighed in this balance, received practice is found wanting and dwindles to a pallid, if not hackneyed language appropriate for public festivals and the pleasure of common ears (Book I, chap. 4).

My digression on stylistic decorum (an idea borrowed from rhetoric) elucidates several important issues. First, the two styles in question are connected because, in Vicentino's view, they both adapt the ancient genera to modern practice. Second, the two are distinct inasmuch as received practice admits but a small number of generic intervals which, although commonly misconstrued,

nevertheless make up the elements of conventional resources; stylized style includes all generic intervals, and these are the ingredients of a radical and hence
marvelous vocabulary invented by Vicentino. Third, both styles have a common
objective—to enhance the text—and they therefore share certain rational rules
concerning the intelligibility of the words. Fourth, stylized style is unique, surpassing all others—even the fabled excellence of classical practice—in its extraordinary arsenal of imitative-affective devices, imitative because they represent
conceits and images, affective because they represent the passions.

These similarities and differences aid us in unraveling the tangle of rhetorical values that clutters Vicentino's precepts for setting the text (Book IV, chaps.
29 and 30). One facet of this subject, *modo della bella pronuntia,* or "technique
of elegant pronunciation," must be put into practice in both styles, and Vicentino gives detailed rules for observing the correct prosody of different languages.[14] The other facet, imitation of the passions, occasions a labyrinthine
excursus. What one gleans from it is that effective projection of the text expands
prosodic considerations to include the accurate imitation of linguistic and emo-
tive inflections. And inflections, according to Vicentino, comprise the principal
means whereby the passions and affections are expressed in speech and in music.

For this reason, Vicentino presents an incredibly long list of affective words
and images that should be represented meticulously by means of melodic, harmonic, and rhythmic figures. These three kinds of figures, incidentally, take up
the strands of his three basic *modi* of perfect composition. Rhythmic figures
aside, it is the myriad novel sounds of totally generic music that expedite the
consummation of this ideal. Vicentino's cardinal manifesto can be inferred from
the sentence that opens the list mentioned above: "for music setting words is
made for no other [reason] than to express the conceit, and their passions and
affects with harmony" (chap. 29). It is statements like this one that implicitly
demote *musica communa* to an imperfect vocal style.

The sentence including *una bella maniera di comporre* (Species C), the last
case under scrutiny, immediately follows the list of figures, and at best it is ambiguous in the extreme. Vicentino here criticizes those composers who translate
selected vowels from the text into solmization syllables under the delusion that
this is "an elegant manner of composing." One's initial reaction is that he could
just as well have said *un bel modo di comporre.* And yet, the syntactical connection
of this phrase to the preceding description of truly rhetorical style suggests another interpretation. Could it be that Vicentino appended this critique at this
point because solmization puns had a connection with rhetoric, primarily with
the art of memory, and earned their admission, in Italian at any rate, from the
use of *figure* for "notes"? If this is so, then Vicentino is condemning a pseudo-
rhetorical masquerade that debases the aesthetic premises of *bella maniera* or ele-

14. See Don Harrán, "Vicentino and His Rules of Text Underlay," *The Musical Quarterly* 59 (1973): 620–
32.

gant stylization. It is pertinent to recall that elegance of style in rhetoric was the province of *decoratio* or *elocutio,* the branch of the discipline concerned with vivid figures of speech—in Vicentino's terms, of course, vivid figures of music. His organization of this chapter is rather slipshod, and he passes over the reference to *bella maniera* to go on to an explanation of the proper treatment of vowels. Hence the primary meaning of this case appears to be inconsequential. But Vicentino's haste should not prevent us from considering the implied significance of his statement. Like canons, solmization puns are misdirected intellectual games that do nothing for the listener's reaction to the text; by way of contrast, *bella maniera* in secular music invites the kind of imitative puns that create the illusion of oratorical eloquence. And as he elsewhere says, the more graphic and novel the illusions, the more marvelous are the effects on the listener.

My final interpretation is, I am well aware, somewhat strained, relying as it does on a reverse reading from contextual arguments which I am not able to document fully in this essay. Ambiguities notwithstanding, it is still feasible to conjecture that, with certain exceptions duly noted, Vicentino's substantive uses of *modo* and *maniera* are intended to convey two meanings. *Modo* refers mainly to various methods or techniques in composing and performing music. *Maniera* refers mainly to stylishness and stylization, concepts defined by the antinomy characteristic of traditional and radical attitudes towards a perennial tension: the exigency of intrinsic logic in vocal music versus its purported capacity to be an art of rhetoric. Zarlino too recognized this tension, but his solution was substantially different from the one advocated by Vicentino. It can be shown, moreover, that Zarlino was prompted to propose his own concept of stylishness *(maniera)* by what he was distressed to see as dangerous aesthetic ideals in Vicentino's treatise.

Despite the present essay's obvious shortcomings that come from compacting a great deal of material in so short a space (e.g., unduly narrative exposition and fragmented or generalized exegesis), it may perhaps persuade some readers that there is something to some words—a meaning to be interpreted and a significance to be evaluated.

APOLLO AND DIONYSOS:
MUSIC THEORY AND
THE WESTERN TRADITION
OF EPISTEMOLOGY

JAMIE CROY KASSLER

THE BEGINNINGS of music theory are to be found deep in Western mythology, where an antithesis is established between order and disorder.[1] Order
was the domain of Apollo, who radiated multiple functions from his godhead.
As preserver of the harmony of life, Apollo purged the soul of man from guilt
and cleansed the body of its ills, thus becoming the god of purification (*kath-
arsis*). His regular movement through the heavens produced order in the universe by imparting harmony and rhythm of form; wherefore, he was not only
leader of the Muses but also god of poetry, dancing, and music. His widespread
legal activity embraced everything in religious and secular life that could be
brought under rules and regulations, and so, as god of law and order, his
maxims enjoined limit, moderation, and obedience to authority. But most important, among those Greek divinities who were chiefly personifications of cosmic forces Apollo symbolized rational powers and represented pure intellect.[2]

Apollo was a Greek god, but his antithesis, Dionysos, was a foreign god.[3]
The many different names for Dionysos outside of Greece[4] suggest that he stood
for the "wet element" in nature—that is, wine, the juicy sap of plants, the life

---

1. I am investigating this antithesis in a book in progress, *The Role of Music in the Transformation of Knowledge.*
2. For the various attributes of Apollo, see William Keith Chambers Guthrie, *The Greeks and Their Gods*
(London, 1950), 183–204; Bruno Meinecke, "Music and Medicine in Classical Antiquity," *Music and Medicine,* ed. Dorothy May Schullian and Max Schoen (Freeport, 1971), 47–52.
3. See Guthrie.
4. The most common name for Dionysos is Bacchos, a name denoting both the deity and the devotee (see
Guthrie, 174 and 181).

blood of animals, semen, and, by extension, creative powers. By the time his cult was introduced into Greece, however, disorder was the domain of Dionysos, who symbolized the cosmic forces of irrationalism and represented sensuous appetites. His rites were intended to lead to a final state of ecstasy (*ekstasis,* standing outside oneself) and divine possession (*enthousiasmos).*[5] Indeed, the most characteristic parts of the Dionysian *orgia* were music and dancing, for they led to ecstasy, to a temporary sense of union with the godhead, and to the power of seeing visions.

The intelligible, determinate, and mensurable domain of Apollo's order, then, was opposed to the fantastic, vague, and shapeless domain of Dionysos's disorder. These two domains were further distinguished by the music and musical instruments associated with each. On the one hand, Apollo's concordant music quelled the passions, and his instrument was the kithara or Greek lyre. Dionysos's dissonant and "barbarous" music, on the other hand, raised the passions, and his instrument was the aulos or Greek oboe. Moreover, the kithara became the model of proportionate tuning systems based on rational numbers, but the aulos, requiring air pressure to produce its sounds, involved tempered systems based on irrational numbers.[6]

The antithesis of Apollo and his kithara and Dionysos and his aulos formed the basis of the Greek theory of the soul, for the Greeks held that to achieve its purpose the soul had been endowed with a dual nature. First, there was its rational nature, a divine, incorporeal element concerning itself with reason. Then there was its irrational nature, concerning itself with the corporeal body through sensuous desire.[7] This twofold division—with its hierarchy of higher (rational) and lower (irrational) orders—was retained and amplified not only in most Western theories of knowledge, but also in most Western theories of music after myth began to give way to science, for two different philosophies were established—the one rationalism, based on the intellect, the other empiricism, based on the senses. The resulting two types of knowledge were then distinguished as objective and subjective knowledge.[8]

The objective nature of musical knowledge was stressed by the Pythagoreans, who held that the principles of music are founded on certain general and universal laws, into which all that we discover in the material world of harmony,

---

5. Guthrie, 147ff. See also Eric Robertson Dodds, ed. and trans., Euripides's *Bacchae,* 2nd ed. (Oxford, 1960).

6. The problem of tuning is implied in James W. McKinnon's interesting article "Aulos," in *The New Grove* 1: 699–702. Further regarding this problem, see Jamie Croy Kassler, "Music as a Model in Early Science," *History of Science* 20 (1982): 103–39.

7. For a brief survey of Greek theories of the soul, see Karl R. Popper and John C. Eccles, *The Self and Its Brain* (Berlin, 1977), chap. P4, sec. 46 ("The Mind–Body Problem in Greek Philosophy"), 159–71.

8. Insofar as rationalism dominated Western thought until about the end of the sixteenth century, empirical evidence was mustered occasionally, and only to verify or demonstrate a priori propositions. Moreover, the sway of rationalism led to the study and development of the logic associated with it, namely, deductive logic. Only after 1600, when empiricism began to assert itself, were investigations undertaken into the nature of its particular logic, induction. This change coincided with the rise of psychology and aesthetics as specialized disciplines.

symmetry, proportion, and order are resolvable.[9] That is, it was supposed that music's principles, like the principles of all other things, were founded on mathematical truth and resulted from some general and universal laws of nature—laws, of course, that were conceived as divinely ordained. Therefore, the excellence of music was thought to be inherent, intrinsic, and absolute—in short, resolvable into number, weight, and measure.[10] This hypothesis, the basis of most later "formalist" doctrines about music, was adopted in the seventeenth century by the experimental philosopher Robert Hooke, and in the eighteenth century by the mathematician Leonhard Euler, among others.

In contrast to the objective approach of the Pythagoreans, there was the subjective theory of Theophrastos, which was subsequently developed into a systematic theory of music by Aristoxenos.[11] Theophrastos argued that hearing is the sense that most deeply stirs our emotions and that music is a movement of the soul whereby we are freed of the evils ensuing from passion. And yet the soul is moved by divinity; this belief is clearly seen in Theophrastos's idea that what a musician composes is not his own work but rather a message or dispensation from the gods, especially the Muses. The musician is thus the instrument through which the Muses speak, a mouthpiece of the gods; possessed by a divine spirit, he becomes frenzied and communicates this state to his audience.[12] For Theophrastos, then, the first cause of music is divinity, but the second cause is emotion, namely, inspiration, pleasure, or pain. Any of these emotions may so change the character of the voice that it loses its customary form and becomes musical. This hypothesis, which is the basis of most later "expressionist" theories of music, was adopted by the eighteenth-century philosopher Jean-Jacques Rousseau and by the nineteenth-century psychologist Herbert Spencer, among others.

If we take the theory of inspiration and frenzy and discard its divine source, we arrive at a theory of art as self-expression or, more precisely, self-inspiration and the expression and communication of emotion. This modification replaces the gods or God with the hidden nature or the essence of the artist. Hence, since the artist is thought to inspire himself and since the source of inspiration is unconscious and therefore irrational, the theory is open to the charge of

9. The main Pythagorean texts on music are the Euclidean *Sectio canonis* and Ptolemy's *Harmonika* (see Thomas J. Mathieson, "An Annotated Translation of Euclid's Division of the Monochord," *Journal of Music Theory* 19 [1975]: 236–58; Ingemar Düring, ed., *Die Harmonielehre des Klaudios Ptolemaios*, Göteborgs Högskolas Arsskrift, vol. 36 [Göteborg, 1930]; Edward A. Lippman, *Musical Thought in Ancient Greece* [New York, 1964], chap. 1).

10. Number, weight, and measure were the principal formal categories of early science to about the end of the sixteenth century (see Kassler, 126ff.). Although they remained in use after 1600, these categories were replaced, for instance, by the Cartesian categories of number, motion, and extension, and later by the Newtonian categories of mass, length, and time.

11. See Friedrich Wimmer, ed. and trans., *Theophrasti Eresii opera . . . omnia* (Paris 1866; repr. ed., Frankfurt am Main, 1964); Henry S. Macran, ed., *The Harmonics of Aristoxenus* (Oxford, 1902); Lewis Rowell, "Aristoxenus on Rhythm," *Journal of Music Theory* 23 (1979): 63–79. None of the extant fragments of Aristoxenos's work deals directly with the origins of music.

12. The two favorite models for this process of communication were magnetism and sympathetic resonance.

subjectivism. Such a charge has been made by one of the most eminent philosophers of science in the twentieth century, Sir Karl Popper. Born in Vienna in
1902, Popper left Austria in 1937, at the time of the Nazi ascendancy; during
the Second World War he held a lectureship at Canterbury College, Christ-
church, New Zealand. After the war he made his home in England, where since
1945 he has been professor of logic and scientific method at the London School
of Economics. In 1964 he was knighted.

Popper believes that questions like "What is art?" are never genuine questions, since they can lead to the theory of art as self-inspiration. This subjectivist
theory had a resurgence during Popper's student days in Vienna in the so-called
Expressionist movement, one of whose central figures was the composer Arnold
Schoenberg.[13] According to Schoenberg,

> a work of art can produce no greater effect than when it transmits the
> emotions which raged in the creator to the listener, in such a way that they
> also rage and storm in him. . . .
>
> [Indeed,] there is only one greatest goal towards which the artist strives:
> *to express himself.* If that succeeds, then the artist has achieved the greatest
> possible success; next to that, everything else is unimportant. . . .[14]

Popper argues that such a theory is vacuous, because everything a man or animal
can do is, among other things, an expression of an internal state, of emotions, or
of personality. This holds trivially true, according to Popper, for all kinds of
human and animal languages. For this reason he concludes that the important
question to ask about art is: "What makes a work interesting or significant?"
Popper maintains that one should focus on the artwork itself, for only in this
way can an objectivist theory of art be achieved.

Popper does not deny self-expression in art, but he stresses its utter triviality. He argues that the really interesting function of an artist's emotions is not
that they are to be expressed, but that they may be used to test the success or
fittingness of the impact made by the objective work. The artist may use himself
as a kind of test body, and he may modify his artwork or even discard it whenever he is dissatisfied by his own reaction to it. Thus does Popper adumbrate a
theory of art not as the product of artistic inspiration but as the result of self-
criticism. According to Popper, such a theory would be objective inasmuch as it
is the artwork itself that is responsible for the emotions of the artist and not the
reverse.

Popper came to these conclusions through his interest in, and knowledge
of, music. Indeed, the importance of music in Popper's thought has been overlooked by scholars, and it is not widely known that for a time Popper was a

13. Popper ignores the religious motivation behind modern Expressionism, but Schoenberg's writings indicate
that he never propounded a "theology without God."
14. *Style and Idea: Selected Writings,* ed. Leonard Stein and trans. Leo Black (London, 1975), 450 and 454.

student of music. First he studied musical composition with Erwin Stein, a pupil of Schoenberg; then he became a student of church music at the conservatory in Vienna; finally, he chose history of music as a second subject for his doctoral examination at the University of Vienna. According to Popper himself, these studies and the speculations they generated led him to three important insights:

> out of my interest in music there came at least three ideas which in-fluenced me for life. One was closely connected with my ideas on dog-matic and critical thinking, and with the significance of dogmas and traditions. The second was a distinction between two kinds of musical composition, which I then felt to be immensely important, and for which I appropriated for my own use the terms "objective" and "subjective." The third was a realization of the intellectual poverty and destructive power of historicist ideas in music and in the arts in general.[15]

With regard to the first idea, Popper, during his study of music, arrived at what he recognized as "perhaps untenable historical conjecture," namely, that musical and scientific creation seem to have this much in common:

> the use of dogma, or myth, as a man-made path along which we move into the unknown, exploring the world, both creating regularities or rules and probing for existing regularities. And once we have found or erected, some landmarks, we proceed by trying new ways of ordering the world, new coordinates, new modes of exploration and creation, new ways of building a new world, undreamt of in antiquity unless in the myth of the music of the spheres.
>
> Indeed, a great work of music (like a great scientific theory) is a cosmos imposed upon chaos—in its tension and harmonies, inexhaustible even for its creator. This was described with marvelous insight by Kepler in a passage devoted to the music of the heavens. . . .[16]

This historical conjecture was reinforced by Popper's reading of Immanuel Kant's *Critique of Pure Reason,* in which, for Popper, the central idea is that *"scientific theories are man-made, and that we try to impose them upon the world."*[17] Combining Kant's insight with some ideas of his own, Popper con-cluded:

> Our theories, beginning with primitive myths and evolving into the theories of science, are indeed man-made, as Kant said. We *do* try to im-pose them on the world, and we *can* always stick to them dogmatically if

15. Popper, *Unended Quest: An Intellectual Autobiography* (Glasgow, 1976), 55.
16. Ibid., 58–59.
17. Ibid., 59.

we so wish, even if they are false (as are not only most religious myths, it seems, but also Newton's theory, which is the one Kant had in mind). But although at first we have to stick to our theories—*without theories we cannot even begin,* for we have nothing else to go by—we can, in the course of time, adopt a more critical attitude towards them. We can try to replace them by something better if we have learned, with their help, where they let us down. Thus there may arise a scientific or critical phase of thinking, *which is necessarily preceded by an uncritical phase.*[18]

Of particular interest to Popper was the idea that dogmatic thinking, which he regarded as prescientific, was a necessary stage if critical thinking is to be possible. Critical thought must have before it something to criticize, and this something, according to Popper, must be the results of dogmatic thinking. When the growth of knowledge is viewed in this light, the problem becomes how to demarcate science from pseudo-science or myth. Popper's first attempts to solve this problem were directed toward music. According to his own account, he was early struck by what he thought was a difference between the compositions of Bach and those of Beethoven. This difference, he supposed, was the product of divergent attitudes, Bach's being objective and Beethoven's subjective.[19] The accuracy of Popper's characterizations is not germane here. What interests us is his distinction between an objective and a subjective approach or attitude, since this contrast became decisive in Popper's philosophy, influencing not only his theory of art but also his theory of knowledge.

Popper divides our knowledge of the universe into three "worlds": world 1, the physical world, consists of material things; world 2, the psychological world, consists of subjective thoughts in the minds of living creatures; and world 3, the creative world, consists of objective structures that are products of minds. Thus world 3 contains our cultural heritage, and its objects include such things as works of art and scientific theories. In Popper's words, world 3

> comprises not only the products of our intellect, together with the unintended consequences which emerge from them, but also the products of our mind in a much wider sense; for example, the products of our imagination. Even theories, products of our intellect, result from the criticism of myths, which are products of our imagination: they would not be possible without myths; nor would criticism be possible without the discovery of the distinction between fact and fiction, or truth and falsity. This is why myths and fictions should not be excluded from world 3. So we are led to include art and, in fact, all human products into which we have injected some of our ideas, and which incorporate the result of *criticism* (in a sense wider than merely intellectual criticism). We ourselves may be included,

18. Ibid., 59–60.
19. Ibid., 60–68.

since we absorb and criticize the ideas of our predecessors, and try to form ourselves, and so may our children and pupils, our traditions and institutions, or ways of life, our purposes, and our aims.[20]

World 3, then, does not comprise solely "embodied" objects such as a book or a painting. Indeed, the "unembodied" nature of much of world 3 becomes clear from Popper's treatment of the status of a musical composition. Although an object in world 3, a composition

has a very strange sort of existence. Certainly it at first exists encoded in the musician's head, but it will probably not even exist there as a totality, but, rather, as a sequence of efforts or attempts; and whether the composer does or does not retain a total score of the composition in his memory is in a sense not really essential to the question of the existence of the composition once it has been written down. But the written-down encoding is not identical with the composition—say, a symphony. For the symphony is something acoustic and the written-down encoding is obviously merely conventionally and arbitrarily related to the acoustic ideas which this written-down encoding tries to incorporate and to bring into a more stable and lasting form. So here there already arises a problem. Let us pose the problem in the following way. Clearly, Mozart's Jupiter Symphony is neither the score he wrote, which is only a kind of conventional and arbitrarily coded statement of the symphony; nor is it the sum total of the imagined acoustic experiences Mozart had while writing the symphony. Nor is it any of the performances. Nor is it all the performances together, nor the class of all possible performances. This is seen from the fact that performances may be good or less good, but that no performance can really be described as ideal. In a way, the symphony is the thing which can be interpreted in performances—it is something which has the possibility of being interpreted in a performance. One may even say that the whole depth of this World 3 object cannot be captured by any single performance, but only by hearing it again and again, in different interpretations. In that sense the World 3 object is a real ideal object which exists, but exists nowhere, and whose existence is somehow the potentiality of its being reinterpreted by human minds. So it is first the work of a human mind or of human minds, the product of human minds; and secondly it is endowed with the potentiality of being recaptured, perhaps only partly, by human minds again.[21]

From this conception of our created world—of the objective knowledge contained in world 3—Popper mounts his attack on subjectivist theories and, in

---

20. Ibid., 195.
21. Popper and Eccles, *The Self and Its Brain,* 449–50.

particular, on psychological theories of knowledge and learning by induction. Popper claims there is no such thing as unprejudiced observation, since all observation is an activity with an aim. He further claims that there is no such thing as passive experience, since experience is the result of active exploration by the organism in the course of its search for regularities or invariants. He claims also that there is no such thing as perception except in the context of interests and expectations and, hence, of regularities or "laws." As a consequence of these claims, Popper argues that knowledge and learning take place in a hypothetical-deductive manner:

> conjecture or hypotheses must come before observation or perception: we have inborn expectations; we have latent inborn knowledge, in the form of latent expectations, to be activated by stimuli to which we act as a rule while engaged in active exploration. All learning is modification (it may be refutation) of some prior knowledge and thus in the last analysis of inborn knowledge.[22]

Since Popper maintains there can be "knowledge without a knowing subject," he considers subjectivist approaches and theories of knowledge to be utterly misconceived because they overlook a vitally important aspect of knowledge in limiting knowledge to the knowing subject. Such theories, according to Popper, treat world-3 objects as if they were "mere utterances or expressions of the knowing subject." Popper attempts to replace this view of the relation of a man to his work by a very different view:

> Admitting that world 3 originates with us, I stress its considerable autonomy, and its immeasureable repercussions on us. Our minds, our selves, cannot exist without it; they are anchored in world 3. We owe to the interaction with world 3 our rationality, the practice of critical and self-critical thinking and acting. We owe to it our mental growth. And we owe to it our relation to our task, to our work, and its repercussions upon ourselves. . . . It is through the attempt to see objectively the work we have done—that is to see it critically—and to do it better, through the interaction between our actions and their objective results, that we can transcend our talents, and ourselves.[23]

Dialectic, then, is fundamental to Popper's thinking. He argues that the critical process alone contributes to the growth of knowledge, and he asserts, moreover, that only through the objective knowledge contained in world 3 is it possible for ideas to have histories. The latter point brings us to the third and last position adopted by Popper through his studies in music, namely, the pov-

22. Popper, *Unended Quest*, 52.
23. Ibid., 196.

erty of historicism.[24] By the term *historicism*, Popper denotes any argument from design—that is, any historical doctrine which holds that there are general laws of development rendering the course of history inevitable and predictable.[25] As opposed to arguments from design, Popper propounds an open-ended evolutionism in which the end or goal of history is not predictable and in which the course of events may be freely influenced by human creativity. For Popper,

> the universe, or its evolution, is creative, and . . . the evolution of sentient animals with conscious experiences has brought about something new. These experiences were first of a more rudimentary and later of a higher kind; and in the end that kind of consciousness of self and that kind of creativity emerged which, I suggest, we find in man. . . .
>
> What I describe by the word "creative" is described by Jacques Monod . . . when he speaks . . . of the unpredictability of the various species, and especially our own human species. . . .[26]

Popper argues that the critical process alone provides the impetus for the evolution of ideas, and the kind of critical process he advocates, namely, "falsification," constitutes the essence of his methodology of science. By *falsification* Popper designates a process of trial-and-error elimination or what he calls "conjecture and refutation."[27] Consisting generally "in the search for difficulties or contradictions and their tentative solutions,"[28] Popper's critical process commences with an act of the imagination, that is, with the proposal of bold hypotheses. We then expose these hypotheses to the severest criticism in order to detect where we have erred. In other words, we start our investigation with a problem, the solution to which, always tentative, entails an imaginative conjec-

---

24. Popper, *The Poverty of Historicism* (London, 1979). Popper's dedication—"In memory of the countless men and women of all creeds or nations or races who fell victims to the fascist and communist belief in Inexorable Laws of Historical Destiny"—reveals the fundamental thesis of his book, namely, "that the belief in historical destiny is sheer superstition, . . . that there can be no prediction of the course of human history by scientific or any other rational methods" (p. iv).

25. Popper singles out the panpsychism of Plato and Friedrich Hegel, the materialism of Karl Marx, and other historical methods modeled on theoretical, and especially, on classical physics (see also Popper, *The Open Society and Its Enemies* [London, 1945]).

26. Popper and Eccles, 15–16. Popper here refers to Jacques Monod's *Chance and Necessity* (Glasgow, 1977). On the subject of creative or "emergent" evolution, Popper has this to say:

> Against the acceptance of the view of emergent evolution there is a strong intuitive prejudice. It is the intuition that, if the universe consists of atoms or elementary particles, so that all things are structures of such particles, then every event in the universe ought to be explicable, and in principle predictable, in terms of *particle structure* and of *particle interaction*. (Popper and Eccles, 17)

Popper's creative evolutionism is based on the Darwinian principle of natural selection, but it is worth noting that other versions of creative evolutionism draw on arguments from design (see Kassler, "Heinrich Schenker's Epistemology and Philosophy of Music: an Essay on the Relations between Evolutionary Theory and Music Theory," *The Wider Domain of Evolutionary Thought*, ed. I. Langhan and D. Oldroyd (Dordrecht, 1983), 221–60.

27. *Conjectures and Refutations: The Growth of Scientific Knowledge* (London, 1978). See also Popper and Eccles, chap. P4, sec. 47 ("Conjectural versus Ultimate Explanation"), 171–76.

28. Popper, *Unended Quest*, 115.

ture, a hypothesis, or theory. Various competing theories are then compared and discussed critically so that we may detect their shortcomings. And the ever-changing, ever-inconclusive results of such critical debate constitute what Popper calls the "science of the day." For Popper, theories are our own inventions, but these theories "may be merely ill-reasoned guesses, bold conjectures, *hypotheses*. Out of these we create a world, not the real world, but our own nets in which we try to catch the real world."[29]

Popper's methodology of science has attracted wide attention among phi-losophers of science as well as among some scientists. Little notice, however, has been taken of its relation to art. Yet Popper not only attacks the long-lived theory of artistic inspiration but also consistently decries what he believes to be its concomitant historicist element. The latter, in Popper's view, is a conscious-ness of novelty, of having to produce something new.[30] Popper maintains that this stance has nothing to do with the fundamental aim of producing artworks that are the best of their kind. Moreover, he wonders why we ought not to pro-duce old-fashioned music in the style, say, of Bach, Haydn, or Mozart. The rage for novelty Popper detects in twentieth-century music is, in his words, "inspired by a mad religion, namely the religion of progress; the religion of hastening along as fast as possible and constantly looking back to see how far or how fast one goes."[31]

Popper admits he is conservative in his musical tastes. Even though he was involved for a short time in the Society for the Private Performance of Music, which was founded primarily for the purpose of presenting works by Arnold Schoenberg and his pupils, Popper tells us he "turned in disgust from [the] modernism of Schönberg, which involved constantly observing oneself, to see whether one was going sufficiently fast beyond what had just been reached."[32] Moreover, Popper had this to say about Anton Webern: "Nobody could doubt the purity of his heart. But there was not much music to be found in his modest compositions."[33] These comments appear to be the result of what Popper him-

---

29. Ibid., 60.
30. Nonetheless, Popper allows for novelty in his evolutionary scheme, as the following remarks make clear:
   The view that there is no new thing under the sun is, in a way, involved in the original meaning of the word "evolution": to evolve means to unroll; and evolution meant originally the unrolling of what is there al-ready: what is there, *preformed*, is to be made manifest. (To develop, similarly, means to unfold what is there.) This original meaning . . . still seems to play its role in the world-view of some materialists or physi-calists.

   Today some of us have learnt to use the term "evolution" differently. For we think that evolution —the evolution of the universe, and especially the evolution of life on earth—has produced new things: *real novelty*. . . . We should be more clearly aware of this real novelty. (Popper and Eccles, 14)
Popper's notion of novelty entails the unpredictable, and he decries the deterministic nature of the ideology of novelty in art.
31. Sir Peter Brian Medawar and Julian Henry Shelley, eds., *Structure in Science and Art: Proceedings of the Third C. H. Boehringer Sohn Symposium, Kronberg Taunus, 1979* (Amsterdam, 1980), 121.
32. Ibid., 122.
33. Popper, *Unended Quest*, 74.

self calls "dogmatic thinking"; that is, they are prescientific statements awaiting criticism.[34]

Popper's published writings, at least, support this observation, for there is no evidence in them that he has examined, for example, either the compositions or the writings of Schoenberg, who for all his emphasis on music as the expression of the inner life of the composer, shares with Popper a number of positions, including a commitment to the quest for knowledge,[35] an emphasis on human creativity,[36] the adoption of a realist philosophy of interaction,[37] and a belief in an open-ended evolutionism.[38] Yet Popper singles out Schoenberg's program of "expressionism," a program he dislikes for two principal reasons. First, according to the theory of inspiration, an artist is not responsible for his actions, since his mysterious "gifts," indeed his whole personality, determine what he does. The results of his actions may be good or bad according to whether an artist is

---

34. The critical retorts provided by György Ligeti and Charles Rosen during the Boehringer Sohn Symposium (see n. 31) do not constitute a systematic refutation of Popper's theory of art.

35. According to Schoenberg, *Theory of Harmony* (trans. of *Harmonielehre* [1911]), trans. Roy E. Carter (London, 1978), p. 1, what matters is "the search itself."

36. In Schoenberg's words:

The creative spirit strives for more, more and more; those who merely seek enjoyment are satisfied with fewer. Between this More and this Fewer the battles of art are fought. Here, truth, the search—there, aesthetics, that which has presumably been found, the reduction of what is worth striving for to what is within reach. What is worth striving for is to discover everything that lies within the natural tone, to attain thereby everything of which the human brain with its powers of association and its ability to systematize is capable. What is within reach has its temporary boundaries wherever our nature and the instruments we have invented have their temporary boundaries. What is attainable with the phenomenon outside ourselves, as far as the tone itself is concerned, theoretically speaking, has no boundaries. What has not yet been attained is what is worth striving for. (*Theory of Harmony*, 319)

It should be noted that Popper and Schoenberg differ on the source of creativity. For the latter, creativity is the province of artistic genius; for the former, it is the province of scientific genius.

37. Schoenberg argued that

order, . . . clarity . . . are there by chance, not by law, not by necessity; and what we claim to perceive as laws [defining order and clarity] may perhaps only be laws governing our perception, without therefore being the laws a work of art must obey. And that we think we see [laws, order] in the work of art can be analogous to our thinking we see ourselves in the mirror, although we are of course not there. The work of art is capable of mirroring what we project into it. The conditions our conceptual power imposes, a mirror image of our own nature . . . , may be observed in the work. This mirror image does not, however, reveal the plan upon which the work itself is oriented, but rather the way we orient ourselves to the work. Now if the work bears the same relation to its author, if it mirrors what he projects into it, then the laws *he* thinks he perceives may also be just such as were present in his imagination, but not such as are inherent in his work. And what he has to say about his formal purposes could be relatively inconsequential. It is perhaps subjectively, but not necessarily objectively, correct. One has only to look in the mirror from another point of view; then one can believe that mirror image, too, is actually projected by the observer, only this time the image is different. Now even if one can assume with certainty that the observer will not see in the work of art something entirely different from what is actually in it—since object and subject do indeed interact— even so the possibility of misapprehension is still too great to allow us to say with absolute confidence that the presumed order is not just that of the subject. All the same, the state of the observer can be ascertained from the order he sees. (*Theory of Harmony*, 30)

38. Schoenberg assumed there is only one "eternal law," namely, "evolution and change—this way has to be more fruitful than the other, where one assumes an end of evolution because one can thus round off the system." (*Theory of Harmony*, 31)

gifted or merely talented. Carried to its extreme, therefore, the theory of inspiration leads to voluntarism and ethical relativism. As Schoenberg himself wrote:

> The artist's creative activity is instinctive. Consciousness has little influence on it. He feels as if what he does were dictated to him. As if he did it only according to the will of some power or other within him, whose laws he does not know. He is merely the instrument of a will hidden from him, of instinct, of his unconscious. Whether it is new or old, good or bad, beautiful or ugly, he does not know. He feels only the instinctual compulsion, which he must obey. And in this instinct the old may find expression, and the new. Such as depends on the past, and such as points out paths to the future. Old truths or new errors. [It is] his musical nature, as he inherited it from a musical ancestor or acquired it through the literature, but [it is] perhaps also the outflow of an energy that is seeking new paths. Right or wrong, new or old, beautiful or ugly—how does one know who only senses the instinctual urge? Who would dare to differentiate right from wrong in the instinct, in the unconscious, to keep separate the knowledge inherited from predecessors and the intuitive power granted to the spirit?[39]

Second—Popper's other reason—the theory of inspiration is rooted in irrationalism. And here, perhaps, is the crux of the problem, for the concern of philosophers traditionally has been seen as a search for the intelligible and the universal—what Popper calls "invariants," "regularities," or "laws." This search, which is Apollinian, relies on conscious, sober, rational activity and on discursive notions of truth. In contrast, the concern of artists traditionally has been conceived as a search for the sensuous and particular—the expression of individual and personal emotions, especially the "feeling" for form. This search, which is Dionysian, relies on unconscious, irrational forces and on nondiscursive notions of truth. For philosophers, then, the artist's vision of truth is suspect, for this vision is thought to be apprehended in a nonsober and hence "mad" intuition. The classic statement of this kind of truth is found in two dialogues by Plato, *Ion* and *Phaedrus*,[40] in which truth denotes not factual correctness but rather divine truth. As Socrates puts it,

> the greatest blessings come by way of madness, indeed of madness that is heaven sent.
>
> . . . if any man comes to the gates of poetry without the madness of the Muses, persuaded that skill alone will make him a good poet, then shall he and his works of sanity with him be brought to nought by the poetry of

39. Ibid., 416.

40. Plato, *The Collected Dialogues,* ed. Edith Hamilton and Huntington Cairns (Princeton, 1973), 215–28 and 475–525. For Popper's discussion of *Ion*, see *Unended Quest,* 65–67. See also Morriss Henry Partee, "Inspiration in the Aesthetics of Plato," *Journal of Aesthetics and Art Criticism* 30 (1971): 87–95; Kenneth Dorter, "The Ion: Plato's Characterization of Art," *Journal of Aesthetics and Art Criticism* 32 (1973): 65–78.

madness, and behold, their place is nowhere to be found. (*Phaedrus,* 244a–b and 245a)[41]

For Plato, divine truth was none other than the ordering principle of all reality. Among the gods representing this divine truth, it is the Muses who infuse the artist with the ordering principle and, through him, infuse all who participate in the work he has created. It therefore follows that the artist has little or no conscious control over his art. As Socrates points out to the rhapsode Ion,

> this gift you have of speaking well on Homer is not an art; it is a power divine, impelling you like the power in the . . . magnet. . . . This stone does not simply attract the iron rings, just by themselves; it also imparts to the rings a force enabling them to do the same thing as the stone itself, that is, to attract another ring, so that sometimes a chain is formed, quite a long one, of iron rings, suspended one from another. For all of them, however, their power depends upon the loadstone. Just so the Muse. She first makes men inspired and then through these inspired ones others share in the enthusiasm, and a chain is formed, for epic poets, all the good ones, have their excellence, not from art, but are inspired, possessed, and thus they utter all these admirable poems. So is it also with the good lyric poets; as the worshipping Corybantes are not in their senses when they dance, so the lyric poets are not in their senses when they make these lovely lyric poems. No, when once they launch into harmony and rhythm, they are seized with the Bacchic transport, and are possessed—as the bacchants, when possessed, draw milk and honey from the rivers, but not when in their senses. So the spirit of the lyric poet works, according to their own report. (*Ion,* 533d–534a)[42]

Plato also recognizes that art is capable of revealing the intelligible and universal in the beauty of its structure, that is, through its "harmony" and "rhythm." For Plato these principles had cosmic significance, since he regarded them as reflections of divine truth. The imitation of divine truth furnishes art with its harmony and rhythm, and it is here that the distinctiveness of art lies and where we may seek its formal, Apollinian properties. But such an imitation is the result not of inspiration, the downward movement from the gods to the artist, but rather of aspiration, the upward movement from the artist to the gods. And Plato sees this upward motion as a tendency of the mind to ascend toward recollecting an awareness, however faint, of divine truth. Thus, as Ken-

---

41. Plato, 491–92.
42. Ibid., 219–20. In this passage, *art* denotes skill. According to Guthrie (p. 154), the Corybantes were servants of a cult of ecstatic or orgiastic ritual; and the Greek verb *korybantiaein* meant to be in a state of divine madness such that hallucinations occurred. This state was identified by Greek medical writers as a pathological condition.

neth Dorter has shown, "the function of the Muses, who provide man with the power of producing beauty, may be seen to be connected with philosophy."[43]

Plato's two kinds of movement, inspiration and aspiration, are also connected with two kinds of prophecy: the prophecy of the mystic, for whom intuition is decisive, and the prophecy of the augur, who has learned the art (*technē,* skill) of interpreting signs of the intelligible and universal. It is possible to view Schoenberg and Popper in the perspective of these two types of prophecy, inasmuch as both men believe in an objective and discernible truth. Yet for Schoenberg as for Popper, no man is ever in certain possession of that truth.[44] Despite these shared assumptions, Popper distrusts Schoenberg's artistic vision, chiefly because of what he conceives to be the irrational, relativistic nature of the composer's theory of art. Indeed Popper's ideal republic, like that of Plato, would seem to be one in which the philosophers are kings, for Popper believes that correctness of interpretation is achieved not through the prophecy of intuition but through the prophecy of dialectic.

Of course, Popper is concerned almost exclusively with the logic of discovery. He states that he early abandoned investigations into the psychology of discovery (and hence into the sources of inspiration), since these investigations, he holds, fall "into the traps of psychologism, idealism, positivism, phenomenalism, even solepsism."[45] But Popper seems to have forgotten that whatever the sources of inspiration, Schoenberg still faced, as do all artists, the task of presenting his discoveries not only as treatises on music but also as musical composi-

---

43. Dorter, 76.

44. In *Conjectures and Refutations* (p. 376), Popper states that one can appreciate "every step, every approach, . . . as valuable, indeed as invaluable," that "our traditions often help to encourage such steps" and that "without an intellectual tradition the individual could hardly take a single step towards the truth." In short, knowledge is always conjectural, never ultimate. In his *Theory of Harmony* (p. 8), Schoenberg writes:

I do not wish to quarrel with honest efforts to discover tentative laws of art. These efforts are necessary. They are necessary, above all, for the aspiring human mind. Our noblest impulse, the impulse to know and understand . . . , makes it our duty to search. And even a false theory, if only it was found through genuine searching, is for that reason superior to the complacent certainty of those who reject it because they presume to know. . . . Since we do definitely know the phenomena [as facts] we might be more justified in giving the name, "science". . . , to our [direct] knowledge . . . of the phenomena, rather than to those conjectures that are intended to explain them.

Yet these conjectures, too, have their justification: as experiments, as results of efforts to think, as mental gymnastics—perhaps sometimes even as preliminary steps to truth.

If art theory . . . could be satisfied with the rewards afforded by honest searching, then one could not object to it. But it is more ambitious. It is not content to be merely the attempt to find laws; it professes to have *the eternal* laws. It observes a number of phenomena, classifies them according to some common characteristics, and then derives laws from them. That is of course correct procedure, because unfortunately there is hardly any other way. But now begins the error. For it is falsely concluded that these laws, since apparently correct with regard to the phenomena previously observed must then surely hold for all future phenomena as well.

45. Popper, *Unended Quest,* 76. See also Popper, *The Logic of Scientific Discovery* (New York, 1959) and *Objective Knowledge: An Evolutionary Approach* (Oxford, 1972). To be sure, Popper does not believe that man is wholly rational. Nonetheless, he admits he is inclined "to protest against any exaggerations (arising largely from a vulgarization of psychoanalysis) of the irrationality of man and of human society." Even so, he is aware "not only of the power of emotions in human life, but also of their value" (*Conjectures and Refutations,* 357).

tions. Consequently, Schoenberg had to reconcile the antithetical domains of Dionysos and Apollo, as have many others before him.[46] In fact, this reconciliation took place in ancient Greece, for as William Guthrie has written, Dionysos

> had to be accorded a recognized and official position which would curb the wild irresponsibility that had marked his first entry into Greece and bring him as much as possible into line with the . . . ancestral tradition and conventions of the Greek people. And who was better qualified to do this than Apollo, the "national expositor" of these traditions? They did therefore the best that they could do: they gave Dionysos a place at Delphi.[47]

---

46. Schoenberg himself wrote that the Dionysian–Apollinian antithesis—"the one, in intoxication, smashes the glasses which the other has produced in an intoxication of the imagination"—is not so simple: "Things happen thus only . . . in the imagination of . . . a musicologist. Intoxication, whether Dionysian or Apollonian, of an artist's fantasy increases the clarity of his vision" (*Style and Idea*, 414).

47. Guthrie, 201.

OF ART MUSIC AND
CULTURAL CLASSES
WALTER WIORA

I

THE WORD *music* has been used since early times not only as an adjective that qualifies the term *art* (i.e., *mousikē technē* and *ars musica*) but also as a noun that can stand by itself. Apart from the type of music one creates through art, the nominative form could signify such music as is, factually or presumptively, a product of nature. By *naturalis* one meant the music of the cosmos as well as the music of man, *musica mundana* as well as folksong and children's song, so far as they agree in rhythm and intervallic structure with the fundamental principles of *musica artificialis*.

On the other hand, inasmuch as the musical high art of the Orient deviates from these principles it did not belong to true music as Antiquity and the Middle Ages understood it, and even today some researchers such as Hans Heinrich Eggebrecht want to limit the concept to European music and to what flows from it in other parts of the world.[1] Yet if one were to exclude from the notion 'music', for example, the Arabian art of music (notwithstanding the fact that it has embraced the principles of Greek music theory and even the word *music*), then why would those directions in the modern art of music and sound that consciously contradict the guiding idea of *musica,* namely, harmonic-rhythmic regulation, be included in the concept? Certainly we can permit narrower and broader ideas of music to coexist; the older ones from Antiquity on, together with the oldest, which involve dance and lyric poetry, can coexist with the

1. International Musicological Society, *Report of the Twelfth Congress, Berkeley, 1977* (Kassel, 1981), 776 and 800.

472

newer, which encompass the entire sphere of music ethnology as well as all the contemporary arts of tone and sound.

The other component of the expression *art music* is very complex. As art in the strict sense of the word one would understand *ars* as opposed to *usus,* autonomous music as opposed to functional music, meaningful music as opposed to empty entertainment, etc. Indeed, according to its context, the word has a different meaning and tone.

To the different ideas about music as art different cultural classes correspond. Here culture is understood in the broadest sense, which includes both schooling and knowledge. A two-part division of "cultural classes" into, say, the "educated" and the "uneducated" does not do justice to the concept. Even a ladder, with steps rising from the most primitive laymen to the connoisseurs of the subtlest style, would be too simple a scheme. For example, do critics who are very familiar with the works of their contemporaries stand on a higher rung than philosophers like Hegel who are less conversant with the particularities of composition and music theory?

II

THE GREEK word *technē,* which stems from an old Indo-European family of words, means the ability to fashion things, as do carpenters and other craftsmen.[2] In early times people likened the poet-singer to a wagon builder and characterized his creations as those of a carpenter. Linked to *mousikē, technē* later came to be distinguished as practice and teaching from *epistēmē* as reflection. This distinction lived on in the Middle Ages as *ars* and *scientia musica,* so that within the framework of the liberal arts music was a discipline of mathematical knowledge, a companion of arithmetic, geometry, and astronomy.

Accordingly, in the oft-emphasized opposition between *musicus* and *cantor*[3] those learned in numerical and acoustical matters who do not themselves practice music but only observe and judge could likewise be considered true *musici.* The person who is purely contemplative, purely intellectual and literate, stood many levels higher than the person with an interest in physical activity, that is, in the use of his own voice or instrument. Class perspectives as well as philosophical and religious predilections contributed to this evaluation.

Ars, in accordance with its meaning as something quite distinct from *scientia,* was the rational control and regulation of practice. Corresponding to *musica regulata,* a person considered to be a *musicus* was one who practices music correctly with knowledge of its rules. Also recognized in him was the special quality of mankind—the ability to think—while on principle the singer or

2. For supporting evidence, see my article "Zur Vor- und Frühgeschichte der musikalischen Grundbegriffe," *Acta Musicologica* 46 (1974): 148.

3. See Erich Reimer, "Musicus–cantor," *Handwörterbuch der musikalischen Terminologie,* ed. H. H. Eggebrecht, Lieferung 1978; also Reimer, "Musicus und Cantor: Zur Sozialgeschichte eines musikalischen Lehrstücks," *Archiv für Musikwissenschaft* 35 (1978): 1–32.

instrumentalist who is not schooled in art appeared to rise hardly above the level of the songbirds. In this dualism lay the cutting edge not between man and animal but between rational, conscious art and such activity as results merely from instinct, tradition, and habit.

In this sense *cantus* and *cantor* were conceived as necessary counterideas to *ars musica* and *musicus*. Yet many authors distinguished those who, for want of an artistically sound education in melody and polyphony, proceed without rules from others who, despite their lack of education, do not offend against the rules of *musica* but, on the contrary, sing or play correctly by virtue of innate musicality and good tradition. In contrast to strict rationalists who could only value the conscious carrying out of rules, more humanistic authors maintained that amateurs and untrained instrumentalists also frequently observed steady rhythms and adhered to the regular scales in their distribution of whole and half steps as well as in their finalis.[4]

But if the word *cantor* simply meant the singer, then one had to separate the *cantor per artem* from the *cantor per usum*.[5] On the other hand, the noun *musica* also admitted the antithetical adjectives *artificialis* and *vulgaris*. The later distinction between art music and folk music has its origin here. The concept 'folk music' was not entirely new when brought before the world by Montaigne or Herder.[6]

With the dissemination of notation through popular education and the organization of clubs and societies, the footing of the musically educated classes has shifted during the course of more recent times. Singing and playing from music or without music constituted a difference between two classes of laymen, of which the first extends into the realm of art music. In a folksong collection of 1876 we read:

> Though it may sound paradoxical, yet it is undeniable that true folk song is driven out by the existence of the choral society. Art song and folk song [*Naturgesang*] are opposites. The singer who is trained to read music looks down with a sympathetic smile on the "common sing-along" of the people.[7]

Yet today's higher evaluation of improvising and playing without actual music notation stands in opposition to the progressive struggle against musical "illiteracy" everywhere.

---

4. For supporting evidence, see my book *Europäische Volksmusik und abendländische Tonkunst* (Kassel, 1957), 90–93.
5. *Die Musik in Geschichte und Gegenwart* 9, col. 1110.
6. See my articles "Das Alter des Begriffes Volklied" and "*Cantus vulgi*," *Musikforschung* 23 (1970): 420ff., and 24 (1971): 299ff., respectively.
7. Hermann Dunger, *Rundâs und Reimsprüche aus dem Vogtlande* (Plauen, 1876), xxx.

III

APART from the theoretical foundation, notation and composition have been the basis of art music since the Middle Ages. Upon this basis now arises the idea of music as an art in an intensified sense. We can characterize it variously as (1) well wrought (learned), (2) artificial (subtle), and (3) expressive (meaningful).

Elaborate polyphony ought not to be interpreted as a national style or as that of a social stratum. Rather, it corresponds to an elevated level of musical understanding; in all countries it surpasses the mental capacities of most listeners. It may be indicative that in German the word *kunterbunt* ("in confusion, muddled") has arisen from the term *Kontrapunkt*. Glarean, who certainly knew how to prize intricate polyphony, pointed out the preeminence of good monophony, which everyone is capable of comprehending. For an artwork *(artificium)* of four or more voices is, in truth, understood by only a few among the very educated *(doctos)*, even though all praise the work when they hear it so as not to be considered less educated by finding fault with it.[8]

The expression *learned* was taken over from systematic study and applied to a concept of one style of composing. Only "connoisseurs" understood learned music, yet according to many authors it is accessible also to a higher level among music lovers generally.[9] Thus in 1771 Johann Georg Sulzer says,

> Since chamber music is for connoisseurs and amateurs, the pieces can be composed in a more learned and elaborate fashion than those works destined for public use, where everything must be simple and singable so that everyone understands it.[10]

Mozart in one of his letters recognizes a degree of difference between the two ideas and places them both at a distance from the philistine. About one person who heard *The Magic Flute* he says, "Although he is no connoisseur, at least he is a genuine amateur," and about another, "That one is a true nonentity; he would prefer a dinner."[11]

While polyphony, thematic development, and other artful modes of composing are primarily the concern of the experts, the so-called gallant style serves primarily the musical amateurs in the more comprehensive sense of this word. Following the same lines are other kinds of music to which amateurs and laymen are attracted and which are in large part also performed by them: the artless art

8. *Dodekachordon* (Basel, 1547), 2: 38.

9. The pair of concepts 'connoisseur' and 'music lover' developed in the first half of the eighteenth century. Erich Reimer has recorded different meanings and nuances of different authors in his contribution "Kenner–Liebhaber–Dilletant," *Handwörterbuch der musikalischen Terminologie*, Lieferung 1974.

10. *Allgemeine Theorie der schönen Kunst*, 2nd enl. ed. (Leipzig, 1792–99), 1: 441.

11. *Briefe und Aufzeichnungen/Gesamtausgabe*, ed. Wilhelm A. Bauer and Otto Erich Deutsch (Kassel, 1962–75), 4: 161.

song, folklike and popular (especially in the eighteenth century), salon music
and music for the home, etc. But in most types of public concerts since Beethoven's time practicing musical amateurs, whom one called (in a neutral or derogatory fashion) dilettantes, have had to yield for the most part to professional
musicians; the technical demands exceeded the potentialities of most of them.

Accessible to a significantly smaller class than well-wrought and learned
music in the sense of Glarean or Sulzer were, and are, more intense, artificial
styles like serial constructivism or the *ars subtilis* and *subtilior* of the late Middle
Ages. These styles are supported not, on the whole, by the connoisseurs or the
"higher classes" but by a faction of experts and intellectuals. In our century stern
opponents of the trivializing of music contributed to the high valuation of ex-
clusivity; historical development took place dialectically along both lines.

With the famous phrase "in the presence of the learned and those who
seek out the subtleties of the arts"[12] Johannes de Grocheo describes the audience
for the polytextual, secular motet in the Paris of the late thirteenth century. Yet
more ingenious than this was the isorhythmic motet of the Ars Nova, and a style
of French music of around 1400 was even more artful, especially in rhythm and
notation.[13] The expression *subtilis* in the passage by Johannes de Grocheo does
not signify simply higher art forms, but a much greater degree of ingenuity and
intricacy.

A third idea about music as art in the exalted sense embraces works of a
spiritual, expressive content that reaches out beyond the enchantment of sound
and the play of form. Music is empty and meaningless "when it lacks the principal feature of all art, namely, spiritual content and expression, and hence such
music ought not to be ranked a true art," emphasizes Hegel.

> It is only when the spiritual element is suitably expressed in the sensuous
> medium of tones and their diverse configurations that music rises up to a
> true art, whether this content receives a more precise definition by means
> of words or is necessarily experienced in a more indefinite manner by
> means of tones and their harmonic relations and melodic animation.[14]

Schumann and other Romantics called such music, including instrumental
music, "poetic" and fought on its behalf against prosaic-conventional music as
though against totally invalid art. Their guiding ideas encouraged in vocal music
and opera the turn to poetic texts of high quality and in instrumental music the
preference for the genre of the "symphonic poem," especially when connected to
literature of worldwide renown.

Corresponding to this idea of meaningful music were—as practitioner and

---

12. "Coram litteratis et illis, qui subtilitates artium sunt quaerentes." *Der Musiktraktat des Johannes de Grocheo,* ed. Ernst Rohloff (Leipzig, 1943), 56.
13. Ursula Günther has set forth good grounds for proposing the term *ars subtilior;* see esp. her article "Das
Ende der *ars nova,"* *Musikforschung* 16 (1963): 105ff.
14. *Ästhetik,* ed. Friedrich Bassenge (Berlin, 1955), 817.

listener, respectively—the "cultured musician" (such as Schumann and Mendelssohn, Wagner and Liszt) and the cultured music lover. Here the meaning of "culture" reaches out far beyond the narrow field of music. It extends the idea of humanistic culture and is connected with the cultivation of individuality.

IV

IF THE counterpoint of an elaborate polyphonic movement revolves around a simple, well-known tune, for example, *Vom Himmel hoch, da komm ich her,* the work, which in other respects is primarily the concern of the expert, is in an essential aspect accessible to the layman also. In most eras since the Middle Ages there have been works and genres that appealed to several cultural classes at the same time. In cyclic works like suites and symphonies movements that were difficult to understand alternated with those that were easy. Sonata form offered places for fugal and lyrical sections. Unlike serial music, in Franco-Flemish Masses artistically subtle procedures such as inversion and retrograde were joined with popular melodies like *L'Homme armé.*

In the period of Viennese Classicism dancelike rhythms and songlike melodies were fundamental. Many works were destined expressly or implicitly for both connoisseurs and amateurs in the more comprehensive sense of these words. That is true not for Haydn alone, whom despite his contrapuntal skill contemporaries praised for his ability to speak to the musical amateur. Indeed Mozart's own characterization in 1782 of his piano concertos applies equally well to many of his other works: "pleasant to the ears—Naturally, without descending into emptiness—here and there—only an expert can gain satisfaction—yet—so that the nonexpert must be satisfied without knowing why."[15]

So far as the audience attending public concerts and opera is composed of several cultural classes, it is quite appropriate that the works and programs be correspondingly multifaceted. In the century of Beethoven and Wagner and afterwards, this was striven for and achieved by Mahler, Strauss, Bartók, Shostakovich, and others.

Among the problems of modern music is the fact that in one main path of avant-garde composition after Schoenberg such diversity found it scarcely possible to manifest itself and was, moreover, despised as a commercial accommodation of supply to demand and, hence, inartistic. Since the decline of serial composition the situation has certainly changed; a more positive relationship to humanity has opened up. Theoretical and historical reflections on the relation of art music and cultural classes will be of use to further developments. Rich in perceptions and suggestions on this subject are the writings of Paul Henry Lang, to whom this essay—indeed the volume of which it forms a part—is respectfully dedicated.

(Translation by Barbara Turchin)

15. *Briefe und Aufzeichnungen,* 3: 245f.

THE WRITINGS OF
PAUL HENRY LANG:
A SELECTIVE
BIBLIOGRAPHY
DAVID OSSENKOP

Paul Henry Lang's published writings are extraordinarily extensive and varied. They include important scholarly books and articles as well as his almost numberless contributions to newspapers and popular periodicals such as the *New York Herald Tribune, High Fidelity,* and the *Saturday Review.* I remember his remarking in a graduate seminar during the late fifties that he wrote an average of forty pages a week, and indeed, a thorough examination of his output shows this must have been so.

Since considerations of space preclude the listing of all of Paul Lang's writings, it has been necessary to make a selected listing of his editorials, his contributions to magazine and newspaper columns, and his reviews. Among the omissions are some of the more topical of these pieces. Nevertheless, the selection presented here gives the reader an overview of the diversity of Paul Lang's interests.

There is another way in which this bibliography is incomplete. P. H. L. is still actively engaged in musicology and music criticism. His reviews and articles continue to appear in such sources as *Notes* and *High Fidelity,* and he is currently preparing a large monograph on performance practice to be published by Norton.

Books

BOOKS WRITTEN BY LANG

Music in Western Civilization. New York: Norton, 1941.
  Music in Western Civilization. London: Dent, 1942 British ed.
  Die Musik im Abendland. Trans. Rudolf von der Wehd and Maria von Schweinitz. 2 vols. Augsburg: Manu, 1947. German ed.

La música en la civilización occidental. Trans. José Clementi. Buenos Aires: Editorial Universitaria de Buenos Aires, 1963. Argentine ed.

Seiyôbunka to ongaku. Trans. Atsushi Sakai, Kô Tanimura, and Usaburô Mabuchi. 3 vols. Tokyo: Onkagu no tomo-sha, 1975–76. Japanese ed.

A Pictorial History of Music, with Otto Bettmann. New York: Norton, 1960. Text based on *Music in Western Civilization.*

A Pictorial History of Music, with Otto Bettmann. London: Hodder and Stoughton, 1960. British ed.

George Frideric Handel. New York: Norton, 1966; repr., 1977.

George Frideric Handel. London: Faber, 1967. British ed.

Georg Friedrich Haendel: sein Leben, sein Stil und seine Stellung im englischen Geistes- und Kulturleben. Trans. Eva Ultsch. Kassel: Bärenreiter, 1979. German ed.

Critic at the Opera. New York: Norton, 1971. Chapters drawn from reviews and Sunday articles on opera included in the *New York Herald Tribune* (1954–63); repr., with a change of title, 1973, as *The Experience of Opera.*

The Experience of Opera. London: Faber, 1973. British ed.

OTHER COLLECTIONS OF WRITINGS BY LANG

N.B. Contents of this series of four special issues of the *American Choral Review* were drawn from reviews and articles in the *New York Herald Tribune* (1954–63).

On Choral Music: Selected Essays and Reviews. American Choral Review, 17/2. New York: American Choral Foundation, 1975.

Bach and Handel. American Choral Review, 17/4. New York: American Choral Foundation, 1975.

The Symphonic Mass. American Choral Review, 18/2. New York: American Choral Foundation, 1976.

Choral Music in the Twentieth Century. American Choral Review, 19/2. New York: American Choral Foundation, 1977.

DISSERTATION

"The Literary Aspects of the History of Opera in France." Ph.D. diss., Cornell University, 1934.

PUBLISHED LECTURE

Music and History. Vassar College, Helen Kenyon Lectureship. Lecture 11 (1952). Poughkeepsie, N. Y.: Vassar College, 1953.

BOOKS EDITED BY LANG

N.B. All contain important prefatory essays by Lang.

Essays on Music, by Alfred Einstein. New York: Norton, 1956; repr., 1962.

One Hundred Years of Music in America. New York: G. Schirmer, 1961.

Problems of Modern Music: The Princeton Seminar in Advanced Musical Studies. New York: Norton, 1962. Repr. of articles in *The Musical Quarterly* 46 (1960): 145–259.

Contemporary Music in Europe: A Comprehensive Survey, with Nathan Broder. New York: G. Schirmer, 1965. Repr. from *The Musical Quarterly* 51 (1965): 1–297.

Contemporary Music in Europe: A Comprehensive Survey, with Nathan Broder. London: Dent, 1966. British ed.

The Creative World of Mozart. New York: Norton, 1963. Repr. of articles in *The Musical Quarterly* 27 (1941): 422–32, and 42 (1956): 145–235.

Mozart no sôsaku no sekai. Translated by Yô Kuniyasu and Taisuke Yoshida. Tokyo: Ongaku no tomo-sha, 1973. Japanese ed.

The Creative World of Beethoven. New York: Norton, 1971. Repr. of articles in *The Musical Quarterly* 56 (1970): 505–793.

(N.B. Both contain important prefatory essays by Lang.)

The Concerto, 1800–1900: A Norton Music Anthology. New York: Norton, 1969.
The Symphony, 1800–1900: A Norton Music Anthology: New York: Norton, 1969.

Essays in Periodicals, Collections,
and Encyclopedias

ARTICLES IN PERIODICALS

"Aggiornamento in Sacred Music." *Sacred Music* (Spring, 1965): 11–14. Repr. under title "Aggiornamento in Roman Catholic Church Music," in *Church Music* 1 (1966): 18–19.
"Amerikas Komponisten symphonischer Musik. Über die deutsche Tradition zum eigenen musikalischen Stil." *Musikhandel* 9 (1958): 405.
"Art of the Second Guess." *Saturday Review* (February 26, 1966): 50.
"The Bach Renascence." *High Fidelity* (August, 1961): 26.
"Background Music for 'Mein Kampf.' " *Saturday Review* (January 28, 1945): 5–9.
"Baroque Flourishes." *Opera News* (November 19, 1966): 16–17.
"Bartók at Columbia." *High Fidelity/Musical America* (March, 1981): 37–38.
"Béla Bartók." *Saturday Review* (January 26, 1946): 20. A tribute to the memory of Bartók (1881–1945).
"The Birth of Comedy." *Opera News* (February 16, 1963): 8–11.
"Carl Orff: Bungled Fireworks . . . or Skillful Effects," with R. D. Darrell. *High Fidelity/Musical America* (January, 1982): 52.
"A Debate on Language." *Saturday Review* (January 22, 1944): 24–25.
"Denis Diderot's *Le Neveu de Rameau.*" *Notes* 34 (1978): 581–84. Contribution to the series Classics of Musical Literature.
"The Department of Music and Its Function." *Proceedings of the Music Teachers National Association* 35 (1941): 259–64.
"Diderot as Musician." *Diderot Studies* 10 (1968): 95–107.
"Easter and Richard Wagner." *Saturday Review* (March 31, 1945): 12–13.
"Ecce Criticus." *American Scholar* 7 (1938): 478–95.
"The Enlightenment and Music." *Eighteenth-Century Studies* 1 (1967): 93–103.
"The Future of Opera." *Columbia University Quarterly* 30 (1938): 1.
"Harpsichord or Piano?" *Etude* (March, 1957): 16.
"Haydn and the Opera." *The Musical Quarterly* 18 (1932): 274–81; repr. in *Haydn Commemorative Issue of Musical Quarterly,* ed. Carl Engel. New York: Da Capo, 1982.
"Hoards of Music." *Harper's Magazine* (August, 1959): 57–59.
"In Remembrance Erich Hertzmann, 1902–1963." *Current Musicology* 1 (1965): 45–48.
"The Influence of Political Thought on the History of Music." *Papers of the American Musicological Society* (1940): 108–14.
"The Language of Music." *Saturday Review* (January 30, 1943): 13–14.
"Liebestraum." *Saturday Review* (January 25, 1947): 26.
"Liszt and the Romantic Movement," *The Musical Quarterly* 22 (1936): 314–25.
"LP and the Well-Appointed Library." *Library Journal* 88 (1963): 1809–12.
"Make Merry Music With Harp and Horn." *House and Garden* (December, 1962): 154–57.
"Manfred F. Bukofzer (1910–1958)." *Acta Musicologica* 28 (1956): 7–8.
"Mr. Bing and the 'Ring.' " *Reporter* (March 21, 1957): 40–41.
"Music and the Liberal Arts Colleges." *Proceedings of the Music Teachers National Association* 42 (1948): 32–44.
"The Music of the Hungarians Versus Hungarian Music." *Hungarian Quarterly* 7 (1941): 69–81.
"Musicology for Music." *Modern Music* 19 (1942): 92–95.
"Musicology in the 1980s: Points of Arrival and Goals: Introduction." *Journal of Musicology* 1 (1982): 1–4.

"New Thoughts on Old Music." *Saturday Review* (June 26, 1954): 46.
"Opera in America." *Theatre Arts* (January, 1961): 10.
"The Paradox of Opera." *Theatre Arts* (March, 1963): 10–12.
"The Patrimonium musicae sacrae and the Task of Sacred Music Today." *Sacred Music* (Winter, 1966–67): 119–31.
"The Place of Musicology in the College Curriculum." *Proceedings of the Music Teachers National Association* 29 (1934): 144–49.
"Rigor Antiquarii: The Great Performance-Practice Muddle." *High Fidelity/Musical America* (July, 1979): 121–26; to be reprinted in forthcoming book on performance practice.
"A Second Look at Manfredini." *High Fidelity* (April, 1963): 57–59. Comment on H. C. Robbins Landon's "A Pox on Manfredini," *High Fidelity* (June, 1961): 38.
"The So-Called Netherlands Schools." *The Musical Quarterly* 25 (1939), 48–59.
"Strictly Personal." *Saturday Review* (May 6, 1944): 13–14. Contribution to a regularly published column on personal viewpoints.
"The Style-Concerning Concepts of Eighteenth-Century Performance." *Musical America* (February 15, 1956): 10–11. Included in a special issue celebrating the two hundredth anniversary of W. A. Mozart's birth.
"Der Ursprung der Polyphonie." *Neue Musik-Zeitschrift* (April, 1949): 103–5.
"Verdi and the Hurdy-Gurdy Image." *Theatre Arts* (March, 1962): 14.
"William J. Mitchell (1906–1971)." *Journal of the American Musicological Society* 24 (1971): 503–4.

ESSAYS IN COLLECTIONS

"The Composer." In *Man Versus Society in Eighteenth-Century Britain: Six Points of View*, ed. James L. Clifford, 85–101. London: Cambridge University Press, 1968.
"The Equipment of the Musical Journalist." In *Music and Criticism: A Symposium*, ed. Richard F. French, 137–61. Cambridge, Mass.: Harvard University Press, 1948.
"The Formation of the Lyric Stage at the Confluence of Renaissance and Baroque." In *A Birthday Offering to Carl Engel*, comp. and ed. Gustave Reese, 143–54. New York: G. Schirmer, 1943.
"French Opera and the Spirit of the Revolution." In *Irrationalism in the Eighteenth Century*, ed. Harold E. Pagliaro, 97–112. Studies in Eighteenth-Century Culture, 2. Cleveland: Press of Case Western Reserve University, 1972.
"Handel—Churchman or Dramatist?" In *Festschrift Friedrich Blume zum 70. Geburtstag*, ed. Anna Amalie Abert and Wilhelm Pfannkuch, 214–20. Kassel: Bärenreiter, 1963.
"Mozart after Two Hundred Years." In *A Musicological Offering to Otto Kinkeldey upon the Occasion of His Eightieth Anniversary*, ed. Charles Seeger. *Journal of the American Musicological Society* 13 (1960): 197–205.
"Music and the Court in the Eighteenth Century." In *City and Society in the Eighteenth Century*, 149–63. Publications of the McMaster University Association for Eighteenth-Century Studies, 3. Toronto: Hakkert, 1973.
"Musicology and Musical Letters." In *Musik und Verlag: Karl Vötterle zum 65. Geburtstag*, ed. Richard Baum and Wolfgang Rehm, 403–9. Kassel: Bärenreiter, 1968.
"Musicology and Related Disciplines." In *Perspectives in Musicology: The Inaugural Lectures of the Ph.D. Program in Music at the City University of New York*, ed. Barry S. Brook, Edward O. D. Downes, and Sherman Van Solkema, 185–96. New York: Norton, 1972.
"Objectivity and Constructionism in the Vocal Music of the Fifteenth and Sixteenth Centuries." In *Natalicia musicologica Knud Jeppesen septuagenaria collegis oblata*. ed. Bjørn Hjelmborg and Søren Sørenson, 115–23. Copenhagen: Hansen, 1962.
"Palestrina across the Centuries." In *Festschrift Karl Gustav Fellerer zum sechzigsten Geburtstag am 7. Juli 1962 überreicht von Freunden und Schülern*, ed., Heinrich Hüschen, 294–302. Regensburg: Bosse, 1962.
"The Passing of the Middle Ages and the Coming of the Renaissance"; "Lassus and the Flemish School"; "The French Renaissance School"; "The German Renaissance School"; and "The Spanish Renaissance School." In *Music and Western Man; The Canadian Broadcasting Corporation Series*, ed. Peter Garvie, 74–107. New York: Philosophical Library, 1958.
"Portrait of a Publishing House." In *One Hundred Years of Music in America*, ed. Paul Henry Lang, 9–21. New York: G. Schirmer, 1961.

ENCYCLOPEDIA ARTICLES

"Byzantine Music." *International Cyclopedia of Music and Musicians*, ed. Oscar Thompson, 267–69. New York: Dodd, Mead, 1938.

"Epilogue" / "Epilog." *Die Musik in Geschichte und Gegenwart*, ed. Friedrich Blume, 16 (Kassel, 1979), English text x–xvii; German text, xviii–xxv. Repr. in *Notes* 36 (1980): 271–81.

INTRODUCTIONS TO WORKS BY OTHER AUTHORS

Foreword to *The Indebtedness of Handel to Works by Other Composers*, by Sedley Taylor. 1906; Repr. New York: Johnson Reprint Corp., 1971.

Introduction to *Musica divina* . . . [and] *Selectus novum missarum*, comp. and ed. Karl Proske. 10 vols., 1853–76; Repr. (10 vols. in 8) New York: Johnson Reprint Corp., 1973.

Preface to *Observations on the Florid Song*, by Pier Francesco Tosi, trans. J. E. Galliard. 2nd ed., 1743; Repr. New York: Johnson Reprint Corporation, 1968.

Foreword to *Protestant Church Music: A History*, by Friedrich Blume, in collaboration with Ludwig Finscher, *et al.* New York: Norton, 1974.

ABSTRACTS OF PAPERS

"Morphology of the Music of the Eighteenth Century." *Bulletin of the American Musicological Society* 1 (1936): 2–3. Paper delivered on February 3, 1935, before the Greater New York Chapter.

"Romantic Opera." *Bulletin of the American Musicological Society* 4 (1940): 3–4. Paper delivered on February 18, 1938, before the Greater New York Chapter.

"Spoken Drama and Music Drama." *Bulletin of the American Musicological Society* 9 (1947): 5. Paper delivered on March 1, 1943, before the Greater New York Chapter.

"Stylistic Elements in the Classic Era." In International Musicological Society, *Kongressbericht: 4. Kongress, Basel, 29 Juni–3 Juli 1949*, 22. Basel: Schweizerische Musikforschende Gesellschaft, 1949.

MISCELLANEOUS

"The International Inventory: American Secretariat," with Gustave Reese and Harold Spivacke. *Notes* 20 (1962–63): 45–46. Report on *RISM*.

"A Mixture of Instinct and Intellect,"with George Szell. *High Fidelity* (January, 1965): 42. An interview with the distinguished conductor.

"Musical Style Changes and General History," with Georg Knepler, *et al.* In International Musicological Society, *Report of the Tenth Congress, Ljubljana, 1967*, 251–70. Kassel: Bärenreiter; Ljubljana: University of Ljubljana, 1970. Transcription of round table held at the International Musicological Society Congress.

Report of the Fourth Congress of the International Musicological Society, Basel, June 29–July 3 [1949]. *Journal of the American Musicological Society* 2 (1949): 202–4.

"Why American Music?" In "American Music Abroad: A Symposium," ed. Charles Jones, *Juilliard Review* (Winter, 1955–56): 24–27.

Editorials from The Musical Quarterly *(Selective Listing)*

"Musical Scholarship at the Crossroads." 31 (1945): 371–80. A report on the state of musicological activity after World War II.

31 (1945): 517–35. An explanation of the reasons for the decline in the quality of church music.

32 (1946): 131–36. A memorial tribute to Béla Bartók (1881–1945), discussing his contributions as composer and ethnomusicologist.

32 (1946): 296–302. A discussion of stylistic differences in serious writing on music; Donald F. Tovey's *Beethoven* (New York, 1945) is contrasted with Adele Katz's *Challenge to Musical Tradition* (New York, 1945) and the writings of Katz's mentor, Heinrich Schenker.

32 (1946): 449–64. A review of Ernest Newman's *The Life of Richard Wagner*, Vol. 4 (New York, 1946).

32 (1946): 602–11. A discussion of Théophile Gautier's essays on music criticism.

33 (1947): 116–22. An assessment of the compositions of Dmitri Shostakovich.

33 (1947): 258–66. On the influence of the work of Wagner, Strauss, and Debussy on modern opera.

33 (1947): 557–64. On the growth of interest in musicological publications in the United States.

34 (1948): 246–48. On the establishment of the "Current Chronicle" column.

35 (1949): 437–47. A review of Alfred Einstein's *The Italian Madrigal*, 3 vols. (Princeton, 1949).

35 (1949): 602–8; 36 (1950): 83–91. On music teaching in institutions of higher learning.

36 (1950): 436–40. A review of Yvonne Rokseth's *Polyphonies du XIIIᵉ siècle: le Manuscrit H. 196 de la Faculté de Médécine de Montpellier*, Vol. 4 (Paris, 1939).

36 (1950): 574–78. On the J. S. Bach bicentennial.

37 (1951): 71–75. On the contributions of Otto Kinkeldey, Alfred Einstein, and Curt Sachs to American musicology.

38 (1951): 234–41. A discussion of problems encountered in writing about music, as illustrated in Adam Carse's *Eighteenth Century Symphonies* (London, 1951) and the critical commentary in Joseph Haydn, *The Complete Works:* 1st series, Vol. 9, *Symphonies No. 82–87* (Vienna and Boston: Haydn Society, 1950).

39 (1953): 232–40. An appraisal of the works of Spohr, Hummel, and Conradin Kreutzer, with reviews of recordings of Hummel's *Septet*, Op. 74 (Westminster WL 50–18), Kreutzer's *Septet*, Op. 62 (London LLP 420), and Spohr's *Nonet*, Op. 31 (Stradivari STR LP 609).

40 (1954): 384–90. On policies involving the reviewing of sound recordings in *The Musical Quarterly*.

41 (1955): 215–22. Review of *Grove's Dictionary of Music and Musicians*, 5th ed., ed. Eric Blom, 9 vols. (London, 1954).

44 (1958): 503–10. A discussion of the effects of the influence of Schoenberg's twelve-tone method on contemporary composition.

45 (1959): 185–87. An essay honoring Otto Kinkeldey on his eightieth birthday.

45 (1959): 223–29. The works of J. S. Bach and Handel compared.

45 (1959): 515–23. Discusses the commencement of the Haydn Institute of Cologne's new edition of Joseph Haydn's *Werke* (Munich and Duisburg, 1959–); 14th series, Vols. 3–4 (baryton trios), 23rd series, Vol. 2 (Masses 5–8), 30th series (part-songs), and 31st series (canons) reviewed.

47 (1961): 91–96. On the inception of *RISM*.

47 (1961): 224–32. Review of John Hollander's *The Untuning of the Sky* (Princeton, 1961).

48 (1962): 550–58. Review of sound recording series *Storia della musica italiana*, Vols. 1–2 (RCA Italiana LM 40000–40001).

49 (1963): 85–87. An essay honoring Friedrich Blume on his seventieth birthday.

49 (1963): 356–57. A memorial tribute to Erich Hertzmann (1902–63).

50 (1964): 77–90. Commentary on present-day orchestral performance, including a review of Herbert von Karajan's recording of Beethoven's *Symphonies* (Deutsche Grammophon SKL 101–8).

50 (1964): 215–26. On musicology in American higher education, including a review of Frank Ll. Harrison, Mantle Hood, and Claude V. Palisca's *Musicology* (Englewood Cliffs, N. J., 1963).

51 (1965): 674–79. On sacred music, including a review of Friedrich Blume's *Geschichte der evangelischen Kirchenmusik*, 2nd ed. (Kassel, 1965).

51 (1965): 387–95. Reviews of Oscar Thompson's *International Cyclopedia of Music and Musicians*, 9th ed., ed. Robert Sabin (New York, 1964), and *Musica Nova*, ed. H. Colin Slim, Monuments of Renaissance Music, 1 (Chicago, 1965).

53 (1967): 77–79. A tribute to the memory of Otto Kinkeldey (1878–1966).

53 (1967): 539–50. On Marxist theories involving art, and particularly on the influence of present-day Communist thought on music.

54 (1968): 249–51. A tribute to the memory of Nathan Broder (1905–67).

54 (1968): 361–75. A review of Leon Plantinga's *Schumann as Critic* (New Haven, 1967).

55 (1969): 545–58. A review of Christoph Wolff's *Der stile antico in der Musik Johann Sebastian Bachs* (Wiesbaden, 1968).

57 (1971): 506–18. A memorial tribute to Igor Stravinsky (1882–1971).

58 (1972): 117–27. A discussion of Baroque performance practice, including a review of J. S. Bach's *St. Matthew Passion*, conducted by Nikolaus Harnoncourt (Telefunken SAWT 9572/75 A).

59 (1973): 302–9. A discussion of the problems of providing precise musical terminology in different languages, including a review of the first installment of *Handwörterbuch der musikalischen Terminologie*, ed. by Hans Heinrich Eggebrecht (Wiesbaden, 1972–).

"Hearing Things," Saturday Review *(Selective Listing)*

"The Art of Performance." November 23, 1946: 44–45.
"Berlioz." December 14, 1946: 24–25.
"Charles Ives." May 1, 1946: 43.
"Church Music—What's Left of It." June 29, 1946: 30–31.
"Folk Song—Real and Faked." May 18, 1946: 32–33.
"Melody, Is It Dated?" January 11, 1947: 28–29.
"Music in American Life." March 2, 1946: 32.
"Music in Princeton." May 31, 1947: 30–31. A report on music performed on the occasion of the Princeton
    University bicentennial.
"Symposium at Harvard." July 5, 1947: 30–31. A report on the Symposium on Music Criticism held at
    Harvard University.

The New York Herald Tribune *(Selective Listing)*

(N.B. Collections of reviews and Sunday articles are listed above under the headings "Books . . ." and "Other Collections of Writings by Lang.")

FROM SUNDAY COLUMN ''MUSIC AND MUSICIANS''

"About Contemporary Music." June 25, 1956.
"All That Writing on All That Jazz." October 8, 1961.
"The American Conductor." January 5, 1958. Repr. in *News Letter,* American Symphony Orchestra League
    (January–March, 1958): 4.
"The American Folk Composer." March 4, 1956.
"American Music Abroad." January 29, 1956.
"And It All Passes for MUSIC." February 18, 1962.
"Another Anniversary." February 26, 1956. On the one hundredth anniversary of Robert Schumann's death.
"The Arranger Arraigned." October 21, 1962.
"The Big Orchestra." October 3, 1954.
"Bruckner, a Baroque Mystic Living in a Romantic World." March 6, 1960.
"California Diary." December 26, 1954, and January 2, 1955. Report on conductors' and music critics'
    forum cosponsored by the American Symphony Orchestra League and the Los Angeles Philharmonic
    Orchestra.
"Can Biographies Explain Greatness?" February 21, 1960.
"Classic Essence Lost in Bigness." April 23, 1961 (*see* "The Orchestras: Ways and Means").
" 'Definitive' Performance." December 5, 1954.
"Difficult Question of 'Light Music.' " July 17, 1960.
"A 'Don't Buy American' Art." September 25, 1955.
"Ecstatics and Alchemists." March 10, 1957. Repr. in *Bulletin of the American Composers Alliance,* 6/3
    (1957): 15.
"Electronic Game: Its Ground Rules." June 18, 1961.
"Esthetics, Si! Physics, No!" October 7, 1962.
"Exquisite Music Yet 'Poison.' " March 25, 1962.
"Fashionable Musicology." June 10, 1962.
"The Forgotten Toilers." October 7, 1956. A tribute to the International Musicological Society.
"Friends of Opera, Hold That Bravo!" February 4, 1962.
"God Save the Anthems." June 9, 1963.
"Government and the Arts." September 11, 1955.
"Handel's Dramatic Oratorios Seen in Fresh Perspective." May 31, 1959. Essentially a review of Winton
    Dean's *Handel's Dramatic Oratorios and Masques* (London and New York, 1959).
"He 'Bought Hyacinths.' " March 12, 1961. A tribute to the memory of Sir Thomas Beecham.

"How an Orchestra Works." January 12 and 19, 1958.

"Improvisation Has Its Limits." December 25, 1960.

"The Interpreter's Art." April 29, 1956.

"Is Orchestration Composition?" April 22, 1956.

"The Laws of Music." November 13, 1955.

"Mendelssohn as a Composer: Versatile, Engaging, Refined." May 24, 1959. Tribute on the 150th anniversary of Mendelssohn's birth.

"More on American Conductors." March 16, 1958. A continuation of the discussion initiated in "The American Conductor."

"Mozart, 1756–1956." January 8 and 15, 1956.

"Music by Hardware." May 20, 1956.

"Music Education." July 8, 1956.

"Music for Children." November 6, 1955.

"Music's Men of Letters." November 25, 1962.

"A Neglected Branch of Music." May 6, 1956. On concertos, *sinfonie concertanti,* and divertimentos for winds.

"No Possible Connection between Kitchen and Art." October 26, 1958.

"The Orchestras: Ways and Means"; "Classic Essence Lost in Bigness"; "Summing Up Eastern Big Three." April 16, 23, and 30, 1961. Series of three articles on American orchestras.

"P. T. Barnum's Legacy." January 1, 1956.

"Paying Overdue Debt of Gratitude." February 19, 1961. Tributes to the memory of Archibald T. Davison (1883–1961) and Richard S. Hill (1901–61).

"Professionals—Not Educators." July 8, 1962.

"Programs and What's behind Them." July 1, 1956.

"The Position of Igor Stravinsky." March 18, 1956.

"Rating Candidates Is Not a Science." May 8, 1960.

"The Realities of Criticism." November 4, 1962.

"The Role of Invention." October 9, 1955. Repr. in *Choral and Organ Guide* (February, 1958): 23–24.

"Russian Tragedy." October 23, 1955. On the effects of the "Decree of Music" of the Central Committee of the Communist Party.

"The Sad Waste of Conductors." January 15, 1961. On the infrequent concert appearances of assistant conductors.

"Sir Thomas Beecham, Musician and Warrior." February 19, 1956. Response to a letter of Sir Thomas Beecham, commenting on remarks made by Lang in his columns, "Mozart, 1756–1956." (Beecham's letter published in "Music and Musicians" on February 12, 1956.)

"Sonata Master Hardly Known." January 8, 1961. On the work of Muzio Clementi.

"The Strange Case of Gustav Mahler." January 10, 1960. Essay on the Mahler centennial.

"Summing Up Eastern Big Three." April 30, 1961 (*see* "The Orchestras: Ways and Means").

"Task of the Modern Performer." March 23, 1958.

"To Henry Purcell on His Anniversary." May 10, 1959. Tribute on the three hundredth anniversary of Purcell's birth.

"Tragic Genius of Hugo Wolf." November 20, 1960. Article on the one hundredth anniversary of Wolf's birth.

"The Ugly Price of Possession." March 26, 1961.

"Uncommon Man of Many Talents." June 26, 1960. On the achievements of Romain Rolland.

"Union Procedures through the Years." July 10, 1960.

"Verdi: Honest Man and Ruthless Artist." July 7, 1963 (*see* "Wagner: The Music Speaks Better Than the Man").

"The Violinist Has His Problems." September 27, 1955.

"Wagner: The Music Speaks Better Than the Man"; "Verdi: Honest Man and Ruthless Artist"; "Wagner and Verdi: The Old Rivals Co-Exist in Today's Opera Houses." June 30, July 7, and July 14, 1963. A three-part series of anniversary tributes to Wagner and Verdi.

"What Is Folksong?" February 13, 1955.

"What Is Music? Ideas Change." June 14, 1959.

"What Makes an Intelligent Musician?" November 25, 1962.

"What the Critics Miss." September 30, 1956. On problems with newspaper deadlines.

"White House Needs a Master of Music." September 27, 1959.

OTHER ARTICLES AND EDITORIALS

"Art Is Much More Than Entertainment."July 3, 1960.

"Civilization Can Destroy Culture." January 17, 1960.

"Death of a Conductor." February 18, 1962. A tribute to the memory of Bruno Walter (1876–1962).

"The Failure of Soviet Art." November 29, 1959.

"A Fifteen-Million-Dollar Debutante Graces the City's Arts." September 23, 1962. On the opening of Lincoln Center.

"The Genius of Kreisler, Dead at 86." January 30, 1962.

"Music's Battle of the Old and the New." August 12, 1962.

"What Is Good Music?" June 4, 1961. Part of a symposium, conducted by the *Herald Tribune,* on the meaning of good music.

"Who Shall Have Music?" April 10, 1960.

Selected Reviews

REVIEWS OF BOOKS

Review of Gerald Abraham, *The Concise Oxford History of Music* (London, 1979). *Notes* 37 (1980): 42–43.

Review of *Annales musicologiques,* Vol. 1 (1953). *The Musical Quarterly* 40 (1954): 266–74.

Review of Alfred Einstein, *Mozart: His Character, His Work* (New York, 1945). *The Musical Quarterly* 31 (1945): 261–63.

Review of *Festschrift für Walter Wiora zum 30. Dezember 1966,* ed. Ludwig Finscher and Christopher-Hellmut Mahling (Kassel, 1967). *Die Musikforschung* 22 (1969): 505–7.

Review of Ludwig Finscher. *Studien zur Geschichte des Streichquartetts,* Vol. 1 (Kassel, 1974). *The Musical Quarterly* 63 (1977): 133–43.

Review of Georg Kinsky, *Das Werk Beethovens,* completed and ed. by Hans Halm (Munich and Duisburg, 1955). *The Musical Quarterly* 44 (1958): 255–57.

Review of Ursula Kirkendale, *Antonio Caldara: sein Leben und seine venezianisch-römischen Oratorien* (Graz and Cologne, 1966). *The Musical Quarterly* 54 (1968): 118–27.

Review of H. C. Robbins Landon, *The Symphonies of Joseph Haydn* (London and New York, 1956). *The Musical Quarterly* 43 (1957): 411–15.

Reviews of *Die Musik in Geschichte und Gegenwart,* fascicle 1 and Vol. 1 (Kassel, 1949–51). *The Musical Quarterly* 36 (1950): 141–43; and 38 (1952): 477–79.

Review of Wolfgang Amadeus Mozart, *Briefs und Aufzeichnungen,* Vols. 1–2 (Kassel, 1962). *The Musical Quarterly* 49 (1963): 111–14.

Review of Marc Pincherle, *Antonio Vivaldi et la musique instrumentale,* 2 vols. (Paris, 1948). *The Musical Quarterly* 35 (1949): 156–59.

Review of Jean-Philippe Rameau, *Complete Theoretical Writings,* ed. Erwin R. Jacobi, 6 vols. (1967–72). *The Musical Quarterly* 57 (1971): 677–84.

Review of Leo Schrade, *Beethoven in France: The Growth of an Idea* (New Haven, 1942). *Romanic Review* 35 (1944): 73–82, and 36 (1945): 78–80.

Review of David Sices, *Music and the Musician in "Jean-Christophe"* (New Haven, 1968). *Romanic Review* 60 (1969): 312–17.

Review of Igor Stravinsky and Robert Craft, *Conversations with Igor Stravinsky* (Garden City, N.Y., 1959): "Fusillade from Stravinsky." *Saturday Review* (June 27, 1959): 50–51.

Review of Igor Stravinsky and Robert Craft, *Expositions and Developments* (Garden City, N.Y., 1962). *Notes* 20 (1963): 223–24.

Review of Virgil Thomson, *The Musical Scene* (NewYork, 1945). *New York Herald Tribune Weekly Book Review,* April 15, 1945.

Review of Walter Wiora, *Die vier Weltalter der Musik* (Stuttgart, 1961). *Die Musikforschung* 16 (1963): 80–81.

REVIEWS OF MUSIC

Review of *Anthologie de la chanson parisienne au XVI⁰ siècle*, ed. François Lesure, *et al.* (Monaco, 1953). *The Musical Quarterly* 39 (1953): 467–70.

Review of Béla Bartók, *Rumanian Folk Music*, ed. Benjamin Suchoff, 3 vols. (The Hague, 1967). *The Musical Quarterly* 54 (1968): 542–48.

Review of Elliott Carter, *String Quartet No. 2*, first performed by the Juilliard String Quartet, Juilliard Concert Hall, March 25, 1960. *New York Herald Tribune*, March 26, 1960.

Review of Aaron Copland, *Piano Fantasy*, first performed by William Masselos, Juilliard Concert Hall, October 25, 1957. "Current Chronicle," *The Musical Quarterly* 44 (1958): 89–92.

Review of Giuseppe Gazzaniga, *Don Giovanni, o sia Il convitato di pietra*, ed. Stefan Kunze (Kassel, 1974). *The Musical Quarterly* 62 (1976): 125–34.

Review of Johann Adolf Hasse, *Ruggiero*, ed. Klaus Hortschansky (Cologne, 1973). *The Musical Quarterly* 61 (1975): 490–95.

Review of Wolfgang Amadeus Mozart, *Idomeneo*, Neue Ausgabe sämtliche Werke: Serie 2, Werkgruppe 5, Band 11), ed. Daniel Heartz, 2 vols. (Kassel, 1972). *The Musical Quarterly* 60 (1974): 141–50.

Review of *Thomas Attwoods Theorie- und Kompositionsstudien bei Mozart* (Mozart, Neue Ausgabe sämtliche Werke: Serie 10, Werkgruppe 30, Band 11), ed. Erich Hertzmann and Cecil B. Oldman, and completed by Daniel Heartz and Alfred Mann (Kassel, 1966). *The Musical Quarterly* 52 (1966): 259–65.

Review of Antonio Salieri, *Tarare* (Die Oper, Vol. 2), ed. Rudolph Angermüller, 2 vols. (Munich, 1978) *Notes* 36 (1980): 972–73.

REVIEWS OF RECORDS

a. Discographies

"Beethoven on Records: Part VIII: The Symphonies." *High Fidelity/Musical America* (December, 1970): 49–68.

"In Defense of Antonio Vivaldi." *High Fidelity/Musical America* (March, 1978): 71–80.

b. Other Reviews

"Bach's *B Minor Mass*—Does the Concentus Musicus' Authenticity Make Musical Sense," with Clifford F. Gilmore. *High Fidelity/Musical America* (July, 1969): 76–78. This review of J. S. Bach's Mass in B minor (Telefunken SKH 20/1–3) elicited much correspondence, and some of the letters are printed in *High Fidelity/Musical America* (October, 1969): 6–10. Lang replies in "A Critic Answers His Critics," *High Fidelity/Musical America* (November, 1969): 22.

Review of Dietrich Buxtehude, Complete Organ Works, Vols. 1–7 (Westminster Records). *The Musical Quarterly* 45 (1959): 418–25.

Review of Muzio Clementi, Symphonies, WO 32–35 (Erato STU 71174): "Clementi's Mysterious Symphonies." *High Fidelity/Musical America* (May, 1979): 73–74.

Review of Karl Goldmark, *Die Königin von Saba* (Hungaroton SPLX 12179/82): "Goldmark's Exotic *Queen of Sheba* in a Splendid Revival." *High Fidelity/Musical America* (April, 1981): 70–72.

Review of George Frideric Handel, *Saul* (Vanguard BG 642–44). *The Musical Quarterly* 49 (1963): 545–48.

Review of George Frideric Handel, *Semele* (L'Oiseau-Lyre OL 50098–100). *The Musical Quarterly* 45 (1959): 275–85.

Review of Joseph Haydn, *Orlando paladino* (Philips 6707 029): "Haydn's *Orlando paladino*: A Heroic-Comic Delight." *High Fidelity/Musical America* (May, 1979): 73–74.

Review of *Italian Classical Symphonists* (Haydn Society HSL-C): "An Unworked Italian Lode." *Saturday Review* (January, 30, 1954): 48–49.

Review of Jean-Baptiste Lully, *Alceste* (Columbia M3 34580): "A Window on Lully's Operatic World." *High Fidelity/Musical America* (October, 1977): 95–97.

Review of *The Mannheim School* (Archiv 2723 068): "Music from Mannheim." *High Fidelity/Musical America* (June, 1981): 49–51.

Review of selected Archiv recordings. *The Musical Quarterly* 45 (1959): 124–35.

Review of *The Baroque Era*, Time-Life's Story of Great Music, Vol. 1: "Baroque on the Time-Life Plan." *Saturday Review* (April 30, 1966): 62–63; (July 30, 1966): 62–63. Includes correspondence with William J. Gold, editor of Time-Life Records.

Review of Antonio Vivaldi, Concertos and Chamber Music, Vol. I, nos. 1–12 (Library of Recorded Masterpieces). *The Musical Quarterly* 47 (1961): 565–75.

INDEX

489